READINGS FOR
SOCIOLOGY

FIFTH EDITION

FIFTH EDITION

READINGS FOR SOCIOLOGY

EDITED BY

Garth Massey

University of Wyoming

W. W. Norton & Company ■ New York ■ London

ISBN 0-393-92700-8 (pbk.)

W. W. Norton & Company, Inc., 500 Fifth Avenue, New York, N.Y. 10110
    www.wwnorton.com
W. W. Norton & Company Ltd., Castle House, 75/76 Wells Street, London W1T 3QT

1 2 3 4 5 6 7 8 9 0

CONTENTS

PART 2 THE INDIVIDUAL, CULTURE, AND SOCIETY

PART 4 SOCIAL INSTITUTIONS

PREFACE

When students open a sociology book for the first time, they have little idea what to expect. Sociology sounds like society, and they think they know what society is. They may have a sense that sociology is about families, poor people, crime, or work and leisure. They may have heard that their sociology teacher is "pretty liberal" though they may be unsure of what that means. They may be taking sociology because they want to help people, start a business, study abroad, be a lawyer, or figure out something about their life, their parents, their relationships, or those parts of the city where they never go. This is good.

Sociology **is** about society. The question is: What is society? How will I know it when I see it? Or can I see it? When the teacher begins talking about social structure as hidden dimensions of social control, as group processes revealed in statistics, as more apparent to minority-group members than to others, doubts begin to creep in. For the teacher, the challenge is to turn doubts into curiosity, uncertainty into intrigue, and to guide students into a new way of seeing. That is what makes sociology unique among the social sciences.

Sociology *is* about families and poor people and crime and work and leisure. But these subjects may not be presented in the way students expect. Sociology is as much about the police as the criminal, the employer as the employee, the wealthy as the working class, the busboy and receptionist as the customer and client. And it is about much more. Fortunately, families on television today are portrayed with more honesty and accuracy than they were two or three decades ago, and are more likely to reflect the actual families in American society. But what about families worldwide? And what about love, marriage and divorce, the intersection of work and family, the hidden work of mothers, disbanded and reconstructed families, and "alternative strategies of reproductive success"? Sociology invites the student to confront a welter of diversity, challenging the myths, pieties, and certainties that make for a complacent life. Most students will not be expecting this, but most will appreciate having had the experience.

Sociology is a critical discipline. Students often interpret this as reflecting the political views of their teacher. I recently asked my students to evaluate critically news they found on the Web. Several brought forward articles critical of George W. Bush. These are obviously biased, they told me, because they criticize the president. Perhaps the greatest challenge for the teacher of sociology is to disentangle critical from criticism, to help students embrace critique and feel comfortable looking beyond the surface appearance, the public pronouncements, the taken for granted, and yet avoid the stultifying cynicism of discovering that the emperor wears no clothes. The journey taken by sociology students—from Goffman's dissection of intimate relations through the historical demise of mass transit and the colonial reconfiguring of traditional societies—can help them acquire the sensibility for constructive doubt and a desire to know more. But as with any journey, students have to pack well, keep their eyes open, and be prepared for some mishaps.

I often think the world is a more difficult environment than when I was a youngster. It is harder to maneuver, more uncertain, and less forgiving. The instruments of social control are more finely honed. The commercially driven media are more widespread and sophisticated, more persuasive and alluring. Alternative images and contrary messages are both less available and systematically dismissed by the mainstream. Students know that the gap between rich and poor has grown wider, and to be in the middle class they must work harder, yet they will find less security there. I think students today must be better prepared than ever to confront the challenges facing them, not only to advance their personal well-being but to act as concerned citizens on behalf of a greater good. I believe the skills required for sociological thinking can help them to do this.

At the same time, students have more choices than when I grew up. And with more choices comes the necessity of making decisions based on good information. This is where sociology's value lies. Young women do have greater opportunity than ever, despite the prejudices and discrimination they continue to face. Worldwide, this situation is changing as well, but there is a long way to go. More and more students are taking time during their college careers to go abroad, spreading across the globe. And it is increasingly possible to imagine a life that is filled with experiences of cultural difference. In the global economy, few people can expect to sit still. New towns, new jobs, new careers, new friends—these are the reasonable expectations of young people, and they evoke both excitement and trepidation. Navigating all of this is not easy, but sociology can help.

Globalization is a stronger theme in this collection of *Readings for Sociology* than in the past. Built around the icon of the global economy— McDonald's—several readings explore the globalization debate. Inglehart and Baker's essay, subtitled "Who's Afraid of Ronald McDonald?" and James Watson's "McDonald's in Hong Kong," along with George Ritzer's "McDonald's System" and Benjamin R. Barber's "Jihad vs. McWorld," add depth and complexity to the question of globalization's power to transform societies. Robert Glennon's "Size Does Count, at Least in French Fries" illustrates the power of global corporations to affect not only what we eat but how we farm, our rivers and streams, and our environmental future. Richard Rodriguez's "Go North, Young Man" is as much about global culture as it is about migration. And not to be forgotten are the women in William M. Adler's "Job on the Line," who know intimately globalization's effect on working people.

Other themes this edition strengthens include race, identity, and the environment. Along with Heidi Ardizzone and Earl Lewis's, "Love and Race Caught in the Public Eye" from the fourth edition, new readings include Mary C. Waters's "Optional Ethnicities" and Anthony Walton's "My Secret Life as a Black Man." Russell Shorto's "Faith at Work" recognizes the growing visibility of religious identification and practices in American society, while Robert Glennon's essay and a new essay by Paul Wapner ("Greenpeace and Political Globalization") give this edition of *Readings for Sociology* a stronger focus on environmental issues.

It is important for students new to sociology to experience not only the excitement and range of topics captured by the sociological imagination. The wide range of approaches taken by sociologists and sociologically informed writers importantly reflects the scope of the discipline. Articles in this collection are based on personal experiences and accounts, participants' investigations of private and public settings, life histories, informal interviewing and astute observation, ethnographic and historical research of public records, social surveys, and the analysis of existing data. Readings range from the descriptive to the conceptual, analytic, and theoretical. And they display the long-running and ongoing dialogue over the role and potential impact of social research in the world, from Marx and Engels's *Communist Manifesto* to Peter L. Berger's *Invitation to Sociology* and Michael Burawoy's "Public Sociologies."

To my mind, a good sociology course shows students the tremendous value of structural analysis, so well displayed by Kelman and Hamilton in their account of the My Lai massacre, Shearing and Stenning's first-hand observations on Disney World, Wilson's explanation of unemployment in inner cities, and Messner's study of male socialization and sports. It never forgets, however, to recognize and illuminate the active agency of human beings, as revealed in several essays, including Pardo's study of the activism of East L.A. mothers, Paules's examination of waitressing, Romero's portrayal of household workers, and Friedan's response to the challenges of growing older.

As in the past, *Readings for Sociology* stresses the intersections of race, class, and gender as critical to sociological understanding. These are often set in the context of family, work, and community—Anderson's "Code of the Street," Hochschild's "Emotional Geography of Work and Family Life," Chambliss's "The Saints and the Roughnecks," Ehrenreich's *Nickel and Dimed*, Romero's *Maid in the U.S.A.*, Adler's "Job on the Line," Hunt's "Police Accounts of Normal Force," and several others. The context for these essays is spelled out in Reich's "What Happened to the American Social Compact?" Ritzer's "The McDonald's System," Thompson's "Hanging Tongues," Feagin and Parker's "Rise and Fall of Mass Rail Transit," and in other essays that have been retained in this edition.

My youngest sons, Elijah and Nathanael, are now in college, and I have thought often of them as I assembled this collection. What would I want them to read, discuss, think about, be challenged by, take away from the course, find interesting, and make connections to in their own lives? I have been doing sociology for a long time. Although it is difficult to communicate to anyone else one's passion for one's work, perhaps this is my way of telling my three sons—including my oldest, George: This is what I do for a living. I hope you will be as lucky.

TO THE INSTRUCTOR

If you are using this reader with Anthony Giddens, Mitchell Duneier, and Richard P. Appelbaum's *Introduction to Sociology*, Fifth Edition, you may consider assigning the readings corresponding to each text chapter below. If you are using this reader with another text, you can still follow this schema for most of the chapters.

Chapter	Readings
1. What is Sociology?	1, 2, 3, 4, 23, 25, 35
2. Asking and Answering Sociological Questions	1, 2, 3, 5, 6, 7, 12, 15, 24, 27, 28, 32, 37
3. Culture and Society	8, 9, 14, 17, 18, 36, 39, 45, 47
4. Socialization and the Life Cycle	5, 9, 10, 13, 18, 19
5. Social Interaction and Everyday Life	11, 12, 13, 18, 20, 24, 30, 31, 38, 44, 50
6. Groups, Networks, and Organizations	5, 16, 18, 23, 29, 30, 31, 33, 38, 41, 48, 49
7. Conformity, Deviance, and Crime	5, 18, 30, 32, 33, 45
8. Stratification, Class, and Inequality	12, 21, 22, 23, 24, 25, 26, 31, 44
9. Global Inequality	19, 34, 42, 46
10. Gender Inequality	12, 15, 17. 20, 27, 37, 38, 39, 42
11. Ethnicity and Race	7, 13, 14, 15, 18, 19, 26, 27, 32, 38
12. Aging	50
13. Government, Political Power and Social Movements	5, 22, 23 24, 34, 48, 49, 51
14. Work and Economic Life	20, 23, 24, 26, 27, 28, 35, 39, 40, 41, 42, 51
15. The Family and Intimate Relationships	9, 10, 15, 17, 36, 37, 38, 39, 45
16. Education and the Mass Media	15, 31
17. Religion in Modern Society	35, 43, 44, 46, 47
18. Sociology of the Body	10, 13, 36, 51
19. Urbanization, Population, and the Environment	16, 18, 19, 28, 29, 34, 49, 51
20. Globalization in a Changing World	9, 16, 19, 34, 39, 46, 47, 49, 51

PART ONE

THE STUDY OF SOCIOLOGY

1

Sociology as an Individual Pastime

FROM *Invitation to Sociology*

PETER L. BERGER

What does it mean to "think sociologically"? In this selection from his book Invitation to Sociology, *Peter Berger explains why sociologists are so annoying to the powers that be, the purveyors of conventional wisdom, advertisers, politicians, and others with a vested interest in your going along with their view of things. Sociologists have a reputation for stirring up the waters and occasionally making trouble. For Berger, this is just part of the way sociologists see the world.*

It is gratifying from certain value positions (including some of this writer's) that sociological insights have served in a number of instances to improve the lot of groups of human beings by uncovering morally shocking conditions or by clearing away collective illusions or by showing that socially desired results could be obtained in more humane fashion. One might point, for example, to some applications of sociological knowledge in the penological practice of Western countries. Or one might cite the use made of sociological studies in the Supreme Court decision of 1954 on racial segregation in the public schools. Or one could look at the applications of other sociological studies to the humane planning of urban redevelopment. Certainly the sociologist who is morally and politically sensitive will derive gratification from such instances. But, once more, it will be well to keep in mind that what is at issue here is not sociological understanding as such but certain applications of this understanding. It is not difficult to see how the same understanding could be applied with opposite intentions. Thus the sociological understanding of the dynamics of racial prejudice can be applied effectively by those promoting intragroup hatred as well as by those wanting to spread tolerance. And the sociological understanding of the nature of human solidarity can be employed in the service of both totalitarian and democratic regimes.

* * *

One [more recent] image [of the sociologist is that of] a gatherer of statistics about human behavior. The sociologist is here seen essentially as an aide-de-camp to an IBM machine. He* goes out with a questionnaire, interviews

---

*Berger wrote this in 1963, using gendered language (preferring *he* to the now-standard *he/she*). Today more than half of all sociology students are women (ed.).

people selected at random, then goes home, enters his tabulations onto innumerable punch cards, which are then fed into a machine. In all of this, of course, he is supported by a large staff and a very large budget. Included in this image is the implication that the results of all this effort are picayune, a pedantic re-statement of what everybody knows anyway. As one observer remarked pithily, a sociologist is a fellow who spends $100,000 to find his way to a house of ill repute.

This image of the sociologist has been strengthened in the public mind by the activities of many agencies that might well be called parasociological, mainly agencies concerned with public opinion and market trends. The pollster has become a well-known figure in American life, importuning people about their views from foreign policy to toilet paper. Since the methods used in the pollster business bear close resemblance to sociological research, the growth of this image of the sociologist is understandable. The Kinsey studies of American sexual behavior have probably greatly augmented the impact of this image. The fundamental sociological question, whether concerned with premarital petting or with Republican votes or with the incidence of gang knifings, is always presumed to be "how often?" or "how many?"

* * *

Now it must be admitted, albeit regretfully, that this image of the sociologist and his trade is not altogether a product of fantasy. Beginning shortly after World War I, American sociology turned rather resolutely away from theory to an intensive preoccupation with narrowly circumscribed empirical studies. In connection with this turn, sociologists increasingly refined their research techniques. Among these, very naturally, statistical techniques figured prominently. Since about the mid 1940s there has been a revival of interest in sociological theory, and there are good indications that this tendency away from a narrow empiricism is continuing to gather momentum. It remains true, however, that a goodly part of the sociological enterprise in this country continues to consist of little studies of obscure fragments of social life, irrelevant to any broader theoretical concern. One glance at the table of contents of the major sociological journals or at the list of papers read at sociological conventions will confirm this statement.

* * *

Statistical data by themselves do not make sociology. They become sociology only when they are sociologically interpreted, put within a theoretical frame of reference that is sociological. Simple counting, or even correlating different items that one counts, is not sociology. There is almost no sociology in the Kinsey reports. This does not mean that the data in these studies are not true or that they cannot be relevant to sociological understanding. They are, taken by themselves, raw materials that can be used in sociological interpretation. The interpretation, however, must be broader than the data themselves.

So the sociologist cannot arrest himself at the frequency tables of premarital petting or extramarital pederasty. These enumerations are meaningful to him only in terms of their much broader implications for an understanding of institutions and values in our society. To arrive at such understanding the sociologist will often have to apply statistical techniques, especially when he is dealing with the mass phenomena of modern social life. But sociology consists of statistics as little as philology consists of conjugating irregular verbs or chemistry of making nasty smells in test tubes.

Sociology has, from its beginnings, understood itself as a science. There has been much controversy about the precise meaning of this self-definition. * * * But the allegiance of sociologists to the scientific ethos has meant everywhere a willingness to be bound by certain scientific canons of procedure. If the sociologist remains faithful to his calling, his statements must be arrived at through the observation of certain rules of evidence that allow others to check on or to repeat or to develop his findings further. It is this scientific discipline that often supplies the motive for reading a sociological work as against, say, a novel on the same topic that might describe matters in much more impressive and convincing language. As sociologists tried to develop their scientific rules of evidence, they were compelled to reflect upon methodological problems. This is why methodology is a necessary and valid part of the sociological enterprise.

At the same time it is quite true that some sociologists, especially in America, have become so preoccupied with methodological questions that they have ceased to be interested in society at all. As a result, they have found out nothing of significance about any aspect of social life, since in science as in love a concentration on technique is quite likely to lead to impotence. Much of this fixation on methodology can be explained in terms of the urge of a relatively new discipline to find acceptance on the academic scene. Since science is an almost sacred entity among Americans in general and American academicians in particular, the desire to emulate the procedures of the older natural sciences is very strong among the newcomers in the marketplace of erudition.

* * *

As they become more secure in their academic status, it may be expected that this methodological inferiority complex will diminish even further.

The charge that many sociologists write in a barbaric dialect must also be admitted with similar reservations. Any scientific discipline must develop a terminology. This is self-evident for a discipline such as, say, nuclear physics that deals with matters unknown to most people and for which no words exist in common speech. However, terminology is possibly even more important for the social sciences, just because their subject matter *is* familiar and just because words *do* exist to denote it. Because we are well acquainted with the social institutions that surround us, our perception of them is imprecise and often erroneous. In very much the same way most of us will have considerable difficulty giving an accurate description of our parents, husbands or wives, children or close friends. Also, our language is often (and perhaps blessedly) vague and confusing in its references to social reality. Take for an example the concept of *class,* a very important one in sociology. There must be dozens of meanings that this term may have in common speech—income brackets, races, ethnic groups, power cliques, intelligence ratings, and many others. It is obvious that the sociologist must have a precise, unambiguous definition of the concept if his work is to proceed with any degree of scientific rigor. In view of these facts, one can understand that some sociologists have been tempted to invent altogether new words to avoid the semantic traps of the vernacular usage.

Finally, we would look at an image of the sociologist not so much in his professional role as in his being, supposedly, a certain kind of person. This is the image of the sociologist as a detached, sardonic observer, and a cold manipulator of men. Where this image prevails, it may represent an ironic triumph of the sociologist's own efforts to be accepted as a genuine scientist. The sociologist here becomes the self-appointed superior man, standing off from the warm vitality of common existence, finding his satisfactions not in living but in coolly appraising the lives of others, filing them away in little categories, and thus presumably missing the real significance of what he is observing. Further, there is the notion that, when he involves himself in social processes at all, the sociologist does so as an uncommitted technician, putting his manipulative skills at the disposal of the powers that be.

This last image is probably not very widely held. * * * As a general portrait of the contemporary sociologist it is certainly a gross distortion. It fits very few individuals that anyone is likely to meet in this country today. The problem of the political role of the social scientist is, nevertheless, a very genuine one. For instance, the employment of sociologists by certain branches of industry and government raises moral questions that ought to be faced more widely than they have been so far. These are, however, moral questions that concern all men in positions of responsibility in modern society. The image of the sociologist as an observer without compassion and a manipulator without conscience need not detain us further here. * * * As for contemporary sociologists, most of them would lack the emotional equipment for such a role, even if they should aspire to it in moments of feverish fantasy.

How then are we to conceive of the sociologist? In discussing the various images of him that abound in the popular mind we have already brought out certain elements that would have to go into our conception.

* * *

The sociologist, then, is someone concerned with understanding society in a disciplined way. The nature of this discipline is scientific. This means that what the sociologist finds and says about the social phenomena he studies occurs within a certain rather strictly defined frame of reference. One of the main characteristics of this scientific frame of reference is that operations are bound by certain rules of evidence. As a scientist, the sociologist tries to be objective, to control his personal preferences and prejudices, to perceive clearly rather than to judge normatively. This restraint, of course, does not embrace the totality of the sociologist's existence as a human being, but is limited to his operations *qua* sociologist. Nor does the sociologist claim that his frame of reference is the only one within which society can be looked at. For that matter, very few scientists in any field would claim today that one should look at the world only scientifically. The botanist looking at a daffodil has no reason to dispute the right of the poet to look at the same object in a very different manner. There are many ways of playing. The point is not that one denies other people's games but that one is clear about the rules of one's own. The game of the sociologist, then, uses scientific rules. As a result, the sociologist must be clear in his own mind as to the meaning of these rules. That is, he must concern himself with methodological questions. Methodology does not constitute his goal. The latter, let us recall once more, is the attempt to understand society. Methodology helps in reaching this goal. In order to understand society, or that segment of it that he is studying at the moment, the sociologist will use a variety of means. Among these are statistical techniques. Statistics can be very useful in answering certain sociological questions. But statistics does not constitute sociology. As a scientist, the sociologist will have to be concerned with the exact significance of the terms he is using. That is, he will have to be careful about terminology. This does not have to mean that he must invent a new language of his own, but it does mean that he cannot naively use the language of everyday discourse. Finally, the interest of the sociologist is primarily theoretical. That is, he is interested in understanding for its own sake. He may be aware of or even concerned with the practical applicability and consequences of his findings, but at that point he leaves the sociological frame of reference as such and moves into realms of values, beliefs and ideas that he shares with other men who are not sociologists.

* * *

[THE MOTIVATION TO DO SOCIOLOGY]

[W]e would like to go a little bit further here and ask a somewhat more personal (and therefore, no doubt, more controversial) question. We would like to ask not only what it is that the sociologist is doing but also what it is that drives him to it. Or, to use the phrase Max Weber used in a similar connection, we want to inquire a little into the nature of the sociologist's demon. In doing so, we shall evoke an image that is not so much ideal-typical in the above sense but more confessional in the sense of personal commitment. Again, we are not interested in excommunicating anyone. The game of sociology goes on in a spacious playground. We are just describing a little more closely those we would like to tempt to join our game.

We would say then that the sociologist (that is, the one we would really like to invite to our game) is a person intensively, endlessly, shamelessly interested in the doings of men. His natural habitat is all the human gathering places of the world, wherever men come together. The sociologist may be interested in many other things. But his consuming interest remains in the world of men, their institutions, their history, their passions. And since he is interested in men, nothing that men do can be altogether tedious for him. He will naturally be interested in the events that engage men's ultimate beliefs, their moments of tragedy and grandeur and ecstasy. But he will also be fascinated by the common place, the everyday. He will know reverence, but this reverence will not prevent him from wanting to see and to understand. He may sometimes feel revulsion or contempt. But this also will not deter him from wanting to have his questions answered. The sociologist, in his quest for understanding, moves through the world of men without respect for the usual lines of demarcation. Nobility and degradation, power and obscurity, intelligence and folly— these are equally *interesting* to him, however unequal they may be in his personal values or tastes. Thus his questions may lead him to all possible levels of society, the best and the least known places, the most respected and the most despised. And, if he is a good sociologist, he will find himself in all these places because his own questions have so taken possession of him that he has little choice but to seek for answers.

It would be possible to say the same things in a lower key. We could say that the sociologist, but for the grace of his academic title, is the man who must listen to gossip despite himself, who is tempted to look through keyholes, to read other people's mail, to open closed cabinets. Before some otherwise unoccupied psychologist sets out now to construct an aptitude test for sociologists on the basis of sublimated voyeurism, let us quickly say that we are speaking merely by way of analogy. Perhaps some little boys consumed with curiosity to watch their maiden aunts in the bathroom later become inveterate sociologists. This is quite uninteresting. What interests us is the curiosity that grips any sociologist in front of a closed door behind which there are human voices. If he is a good sociologist, he will want to open that door, to understand these voices. Behind each closed door he will anticipate some new facet of human life not yet perceived and understood.

The sociologist will occupy himself with matters that others regard as too sacred or as too distasteful for dispassionate investigation. He will find rewarding the company of priests or of prostitutes, depending not on his personal preferences but on the questions he happens to be asking at the moment. He will also concern himself with matters that others may find much too boring. He will be interested in the human interaction that goes with warfare or with great intellectual discoveries, but also in the relations between people employed in a restaurant or between a group of little girls playing with their dolls. His main focus of attention is not the ultimate significance of what men do, but the action in itself, as another example of the infinite richness of human conduct. So much for the image of our playmate.

In these journeys through the world of men the sociologist will inevitably encounter other professional Peeping Toms. Sometimes these will resent his presence, feeling that he is poaching on their preserves. In some places the sociologist will meet up with the economist, in others with the political scientist, in yet others with the psychologist or the ethnologist. Yet chances are that the questions that have brought him to these same places are different from the ones that propelled his fellow-trespassers. The sociologist's questions always remain essentially the same: "What are people doing with each other here?" "What are their relationships to each other?" "How are these relationships organized in institutions?" "What are the collective ideas that move men and institutions?" In trying to answer these questions in specific instances, the sociologist will, of course, have to deal with economic or political matters, but he will do so in a way rather different from that of the economist or the political scientist. The scene that he contemplates is the same human scene that these other scientists concern themselves with. But the sociologist's angle of vision is different. When this is understood, it becomes clear that it makes little sense to try to stake out a special enclave within which the sociologist will carry on business in his own right. * * * There is, however, one traveler whose path the sociologist will cross more often than anyone else's on his journeys. This is the historian. Indeed, as soon as the sociologist turns from the present to the past, his preoccupations are very hard indeed to distinguish from those of the historian. However, we shall leave this relationship to a later part of our considerations. Suffice it to say here that the sociological journey will be much impoverished unless it is punctuated frequently by conversation with that other particular traveler.

Any intellectual activity derives excitement from the moment it becomes a trail of discovery. In some fields of learning this is the discovery of worlds previously unthought and unthinkable. This is the excitement of the astronomer or of the nuclear physicist on the antipodal boundaries of the realities that man is capable of conceiving. But it can also be the excitement of bacteriology or geology. In a different way it can be the excitement of the linguist discovering new realms of human expression or of the anthropologist exploring human customs in faraway countries. In such discovery, when undertaken with passion, a widening of awareness, sometimes a veritable transformation of consciousness, occurs. The universe turns out to be much more wonderfull than one had ever dreamed. The excitement of sociology is usually of a different sort. Sometimes, it is true, the sociologist penetrates into worlds that had previously been quite unknown to him—for instance, the world of crime, or the world of some bizarre religious sect, or the world fashioned by the exclusive concerns of some group such as medical specialists or military leaders or advertising executives. However, much of the time the sociologist moves in sectors of experience that are familiar to him and to most people in his society. He investigates communities, institutions and activities that one can read about every day in the newspapers. Yet there is another excitement of discovery beckoning in his investigations. It is not the excitement of coming upon the totally unfamiliar, but rather the excitement of finding the familiar becoming transformed in its meaning. The fascination of sociology lies in the fact that its perspective makes us see in a new light the very world in which we have lived all our lives. This also constitutes a transformation of consciousness. Moreover, this transformation is more relevant existentially than that of many other intellectual disciplines, because it is more difficult to segregate in some special compartment of the mind. The astronomer does not live in the remote galaxies, and the nuclear physicist can, outside his laboratory, eat and laugh and marry and vote without thinking about the insides of the atom. The geologist looks at rocks only at appropriate times, and the linguist speaks English with his wife. The sociologist lives in society, on the job and off it. His own life, inevitably, is part of his subject matter. Men being what they are, sociologists too manage to segregate their professional insights from their everyday affairs. But it is a rather difficult feat to perform in good faith.

The sociologist moves in the common world of men, close to what most of them would call real. The categories he employs in his analyses are only refinements of the categories by which other men live—power, class, status, race, ethnicity. As a result, there is a deceptive simplicity and obviousness about some sociological investigations. One reads them, nods at the familiar scene, remarks that one has heard all this before and don't people have better things to do than to waste their time on truisms—until one is suddenly brought up against an insight that radically questions everything one had previously assumed about this familiar scene. This is the point at which one begins to sense the excitement of sociology.

Let us take a specific example. Imagine a sociology class in a Southern college where almost all the students are white Southerners. Imagine a lecture on the subject of the racial system of the South. The lecturer is talking here of matters that have been familiar to his students from the time of their infancy. Indeed, it may be that they are much more familiar with the minutiae of this system than he is. They are quite bored as a result. It seems to them that he is only using more pretentious words to describe what they already know. Thus he may use the term "caste," one commonly used now by American sociologists to describe the Southern racial system. But in explaining the term he shifts to traditional Hindu society, to make it clearer. He then goes on to analyze the magical beliefs inherent in caste tabus, the social dynamics of commensalism and connubium, the economic interests concealed within the system, the way in which religious beliefs relate to the tabus, the effects of the caste system upon the industrial development of the society and vice versa— all in India. But suddenly India is not very far away at all. The lecture then goes back to its Southern theme. The familiar now seems not quite so familiar any more. Questions are raised that are new, perhaps raised angrily, but raised all the same. And at least some of the students have begun to understand that there are functions involved in this business of race that they have not read about in the newspapers (at least not those in their hometowns) and that their parents have not told them—partly, at least, because neither the newspapers nor the parents knew about them.

It can be said that the first wisdom of sociology is this—things are not what they seem. This too is a deceptively simple statement. It ceases to be simple after a while. Social reality turns out to have many layers of meaning. The discovery of each new layer changes the perception of the whole.

Anthropologists use the term "culture shock" to describe the impact of a totally new culture upon a newcomer. In an extreme instance such shock will be experienced by the Western explorer who is told, halfway through dinner, that he is eating the nice old lady he had been chatting with the previous day—a shock with predictable physiological if not moral consequences. Most explorers no longer encounter cannibalism in their travels today. However, the first encounters with polygamy or with puberty rites or even with the way some nations drive their automobiles can be quite a shock to an American visitor. With the shock may go not only disapproval or disgust but a sense of excitement that things can *really* be that different from what they are at home. To some extent, at least, this is the excitement of any first travel abroad. The experience of sociological discovery could be described as "culture shock" minus geographical displacement. In other words, the sociologist travels at home—with shocking results. He is unlikely to find that he is eating a nice old lady for dinner. But the discovery, for instance, that his own church has considerable money invested in the missile industry or that a few blocks from his home there are people who engage in cultic orgies may not be drastically different in emotional impact. Yet we would not want to imply that sociological discoveries are always or even usually outrageous to moral sentiment. Not at all. What they have in common with exploration in distant lands, however, is the sudden illumination of new and unsuspected facets of human existence in society. This is the excitement and, as we shall try to show later, the humanistic justification of sociology.

People who like to avoid shocking discoveries, who prefer to believe that society is just what they were taught in Sunday School, who like the safety of the rules and the maxims of what Alfred Schuetz has called the "world-taken-for-granted," should stay away from sociology. People who feel no temptation before closed doors, who have no curiosity about human beings, who are content to admire scenery without wondering about the people who live in those houses on the other side of that river, should probably also stay away from sociology. They will find it unpleasant or, at any rate, unrewarding. People who are interested in human beings only if they can change, convert or reform them should also be warned, for they will find sociology much less useful than they hoped. And people whose interest is mainly in their own conceptual constructions will do just as well to turn to the study of little white mice. Sociology will do just as well to turn to the study of little white mice. Sociology will be satisfying, in the long run, only to those who can think of nothing more entrancing than to watch men and to understand things human.

* * *

To be sure, sociology is an individual pastime in the sense that it interests some men and bores others. Some like to observe human beings, others to experiment with mice. The world is big enough to hold all kinds and there is no logical priority for one interest as against another. But the word "pastime" is weak in describing what we mean. Sociology is more like a passion. The sociological perspective is more like a demon that possesses one, that drives one compellingly, again and again, to the questions that are its own. An introduction to sociology is, therefore, an invitation to a very special kind of passion.

2

FROM *The Sociological Imagination*

C. WRIGHT MILLS

C. Wright Mills wrote of his own work, "I have tried to be objective; I do not claim to be detached." He argues that sociologists' questions come from the same sources as the important questions everyone asks: their own experiences and the things that perplex, confuse, and inspire them. To be effective, sociology must make a connection between the individual and the social. It must allow the individual to see the larger social context in which his or her life is lived, and in this way give both understanding and meaning to personal experiences.

Nowadays men often feel that their private lives are a series of traps. They sense that within their everyday worlds, they cannot overcome their troubles, and in this feeling, they are often quite correct: What ordinary men are directly aware of and what they try to do are bounded by the private orbits in which they live; their visions and their powers are limited to the close-up scenes of job, family, neighborhood; in other milieux, they move vicariously and remain spectators. And the more aware they become, however vaguely, of ambitions and of threats which transcend their immediate locales, the more trapped they seem to feel.

Underlying this sense of being trapped are seemingly impersonal changes in the very structure of continent-wide societies. The facts of contemporary history are also facts about the success and the failure of individual men and women. When a society is industrialized, a peasant becomes a worker; a feudal lord is liquidated or becomes a businessman. When classes rise or fall, a man is employed or unemployed; when the rate of investment goes up or down, a man takes new heart or goes broke. When wars happen, an insurance salesman becomes a rocket launcher; a store clerk, a radar man; a wife lives alone; a child grows up without a father. Neither the life of an individual nor the history of a society can be understood without understanding both.

Yet men do not usually define the troubles they endure in terms of historical change and institutional contradiction. The well-being they enjoy, they do not usually impute to the big ups and downs of the societies in which they live. Seldom aware of the intricate connection between the patterns of their own lives and the course of world history, ordinary men do not usually know what this connection means for the kinds of men they are becoming and for the kinds of history-making in which they might take part. They do not possess the quality of mind essential to grasp the interplay of man and society, of biography and history, of self and world. They cannot cope with their personal troubles in such ways as to control the structural transformations that usually lie behind them.

Surely it is no wonder. In what period have so many men been so totally exposed at so fast a pace to such earthquakes of change? That Americans have not known such catastrophic changes as have the men and women of other societies is due to historical facts that are now quickly becoming 'merely history'. The history that now affects every man is world history. Within this scene and this period, in the course of a single generation, one sixth of mankind is transformed from all that is feudal and backward into all that is modern, advanced, and fearful. Political colonies are freed; new and less visible forms of imperialism installed. Revolutions occur; men feel the intimate grip of new kinds of authority. Totalitarian societies rise, and are smashed to bits—or succeed fabulously. After two centuries of ascendancy, capitalism is shown up as only one way to make society into an industrial apparatus. After two centuries of hope, even formal democracy is restricted to a quite small portion of mankind. Everywhere in the underdeveloped world, ancient ways of life are broken up and vague expectations become urgent demands. Everywhere in the overdeveloped world, the means of authority and of violence become total in scope and bureaucratic in form. Humanity itself now lies before us, the super-nation at either pole concentrating its most coordinated and massive efforts upon the preparation of World War Three.

The very shaping of history now outpaces the ability of men to orient themselves in accordance with cherished values. And which values? Even when they do not panic, men often sense that older ways of feeling and thinking have collapsed and that newer beginnings are ambiguous to the point of moral stasis. Is it any wonder that ordinary men feel they cannot cope with the larger worlds with which they are so suddenly confronted? That they cannot understand the meaning of their epoch for their own lives? That—in defense of selfhood—they become morally insensible, trying to remain altogether private men? Is it any wonder that they come to be possessed by a sense of the trap?

It is not only information that they need—in this Age of Fact, information often dominates their attention and overwhelms their capacities to assimilate it. It is not only the skills of reason that they need—although their struggles to acquire these often exhaust their limited moral energy.

What they need, and what they feel they need, is a quality of mind that will help them to use information and to develop reason in order to achieve lucid summations of what is going on in the world and of what may be happening within themselves. It is this quality, I am going to contend, that journalists and scholars, artists and publics, scientists and editors are coming to expect of what may be called the sociological imagination.

1

The sociological imagination enables its possessor to understand the larger historical scene in terms of its meaning for the inner life and the external career of a variety of individuals. It enables him to take into account how individuals, in the welter of their daily experience, often become falsely conscious of their social positions. Within that welter, the framework of modern society is sought, and within that framework the psychologies of a variety of men and women are formulated. By such means the personal uneasiness of individuals is focused upon explicit troubles and the indifference of publics is transformed into involvement with public issues.

The first fruit of this imagination—and the first lesson of the social science that embodies it—is the idea that the individual can understand his own experience and gauge his own fate only by locating himself within his period, that he can know his own chances in life only by becoming aware of those of all individuals in his circumstances. In many ways it is a terrible lesson; in many ways a magnificent one. We do not know the limits of man's capacities for supreme effort or willing degradation, for agony or glee, for pleasurable brutality or the sweetness of reason. But in our time we have come to know that the limits of 'human nature' are frighteningly broad. We have come to know that every individual lives, from one generation to the next, in some society; that he lives out a biography, and that he lives it out within some historical sequence. By the fact of his living he contributes, however minutely, to the shaping of this society and to the course of its history, even as he is made by society and by its historical push and shove.

The sociological imagination enables us to grasp history and biography and the relations between the two within society. That is its task and its promise. To recognize this task and this promise is the mark of the classic social analyst. And it is the signal of what is best in contemporary studies of man and society.

No social study that does not come back to the problems of biography, of history and of their intersections within a society has completed its intellectual journey. Whatever the specific problems of the classic social analysts, however limited or however broad the features of social reality they have examined, those who have been imaginatively aware of the promise of their work have consistently asked three sorts of questions:

1. What is the structure of this particular society as a whole? What are its essential components, and how are they related to one another? How does it differ from other varieties of social order? Within it, what is the meaning of any particular feature for its continuance and for its change?
2. Where does this society stand in human history? What are the mechanics by which it is changing? What is its place within and its meaning

for the development of humanity as a whole? How does any particular feature we are examining affect, and how is it affected by, the historical period in which it moves? And this period—what are its essential features? How does it differ from other periods? What are its characteristic ways of history-making?

3. What varieties of men and women now prevail in this society and in this period? And what varieties are coming to prevail? In what ways are they selected and formed, liberated and repressed, made sensitive and blunted? What kinds of 'human nature' are revealed in the conduct and character we observe in this society in this period? And what is the meaning for 'human nature' of each and every feature of the society we are examining?

Whether the point of interest is a great power state or a minor literary mood, a family, a prison, a creed—these are the kinds of questions the best social analysts have asked. They are the intellectual pivots of classic studies of man in society—and they are the questions inevitably raised by any mind possessing the sociological imagination. For that imagination is the capacity to shift from one perspective to another—from the political to the psychological; from examination of a single family to comparative assessment of the national budgets of the world; from the theological school to the military establishment; from considerations of an oil industry to studies of contemporary poetry. It is the capacity to range from the most impersonal and remote transformations to the most intimate features of the human self—and to see the relations between the two. Back of its use there is always the urge to know the social and historical meaning of the individual in the society and in the period in which he has his quality and his being.

That, in brief, is why it is by means of the sociological imagination that men now hope to grasp what is going on in the world, and to understand what is happening in themselves as minute points of the intersections of biography and history within society. In large part, contemporary man's self-conscious view of himself as at least an outsider, if not a permanent stranger, rests upon an absorbed realization of social relativity and of the transformative power of history. The sociological imagination is the most fruitful form of this self-consciousness. By its use men whose mentalities have swept only a series of limited orbits often come to feel as if suddenly awakened in a house with which they had only supposed themselves to be familiar. Correctly or incorrectly, they often come to feel that they can now provide themselves with adequate summations, cohesive assessments, comprehensive orientations. Older decisions that once appeared sound now seem to them products of a mind unaccountably dense. Their capacity for astonishment is made lively again. They acquire a new way of thinking, they experience a transvaluation of values: in a word, by their reflection and by their sensibility, they realize the cultural meaning of the social sciences.

2

Perhaps the most fruitful distinction with which the sociological imagination works is between 'the personal troubles of milieu' and 'the public issues of social structure.' This distinction is an essential tool of the sociological imagination and a feature of all classic work in social science.

Troubles occur within the character of the individual and within the range of his immediate relations with others; they have to do with his self and with those limited areas of social life of which he is directly and personally aware. Accordingly, the statement and the resolution of troubles properly lie within the individual as a biographical entity and within the scope of his immediate milieu—the social setting that is directly open to his personal experience and to some extent his willful activity. A trouble is a private matter: values cherished by an individual are felt by him to be threatened.

Issues have to do with matters that transcend these local environments of the individual and the range of his inner life. They have to do with the organization of many such milieux into the institutions of an historical society as a whole, with the ways in which various milieux overlap and interpenetrate to form the larger structure of social and historical life. An issue is a public matter: some value cherished by publics is felt to be threatened. Often there is a debate about what that value really is and about what it is that really threatens it. This debate is often without focus if only because it is the very nature of an issue, unlike even widespread trouble, that it cannot very well be defined in terms of the immediate and everyday environments of ordinary men. An issue, in fact, often involves a crisis in institutional arrangements, and often too it involves what Marxists call 'contradictions' or 'antagonisms.'

In these terms, consider unemployment. When, in a city of 100,000, only one man is unemployed, that is his personal trouble, and for its relief we properly look to the character of the man, his skills, and his immediate opportunities. But when in a nation of 50 million employees, 15 million men are unemployed, that is an issue, and we may not hope to find its solution within the range of opportunities open to any one individual. The very structure of opportunities has collapsed. Both the correct statement of the problem and the range of possible solutions require us to consider the economic and political institutions of the society, and not merely the personal situation and character of a scatter of individuals.

Consider war. The personal problem of war, when it occurs, may be how to survive it or how to die in it with honor; how to make money out of it; how to climb into the higher safety of the military apparatus; or how to contribute to the war's termination. In short, according to one's values, to find a set of milieux and within it to survive the war or make one's death in it meaningful. But the structural issues of war have to do with its causes; with what types of men it throws up into command; with its effects upon economic and political, family and religious institutions, with the unorganized irresponsibility of a world of nation-states.

Consider marriage. Inside a marriage a man and a woman may experience personal troubles, but when the divorce rate during the first four years of marriage is 250 out of every 1,000 attempts, this is an indication of a structural issue having to do with the institutions of marriage and the family and other institutions that bear upon them.

Or consider the metropolis—the horrible, beautiful, ugly, magnificent sprawl of the great city. For many upper-class people, the personal solution to 'the problem of the city' is to have an apartment with private garage under it in the heart of the city, and forty miles out, a house by Henry Hill, garden by Garrett Eckbo, on a hundred acres of private land. In these two controlled environments—with a small staff at each end and a private helicopter connection—most people could solve many of the problems of personal milieux caused by the facts of the city. But all this, however splendid, does not solve the public issues that the structural fact of the city poses. What should be done with this wonderful monstrosity? Break it all up into scattered units, combining residence and work? Refurbish it as it stands? Or, after evacuation, dynamite it and build new cities according to new plans in new places? What should those plans be? And who is to decide and to accomplish whatever choice is made? These are structural issues; to confront them and to solve them requires us to consider political and economic issues that affect innumerable milieux.

In so far as an economy is so arranged that slumps occur, the problem of unemployment becomes incapable of personal solution. In so far as war is inherent in the nation-state system and in the uneven industrialization of the world, the ordinary individual in his restricted milieu will be powerless—with or without psychiatric aid—to solve the troubles this system or lack of system imposes upon him. In so far as the family as an institution turns women into darling little slaves and men into their chief providers and unweaned dependents, the problem of a satisfactory marriage remains incapable of purely private solution. In so far as the overdeveloped megalopolis and the overdeveloped automobile are built-in features of the overdeveloped society, the issues of urban living will not be solved by personal ingenuity and private wealth.

What we experience in various and specific milieux, I have noted, is often caused by structural changes. Accordingly, to understand the changes of many personal milieux we are required to look beyond them. And the number and variety of such structural changes increase as the institutions within which we live become more embracing and more intricately connected with one another. To be aware of the idea of social structure and to use it with sensibility is to be capable of tracing such linkages among a great variety of milieux. To be able to do that is to possess the sociological imagination.

3

What Makes Sociology Different?

FROM *The Rules of Sociological Method*

ÉMILE DURKHEIM

Along with Karl Marx and Max Weber, Émile Durkheim (1858–1917) is considered a founder of modern sociology. In this essay he presents his most important contribution to the discipline: that social facts should be the subject matter for the study of social life and can provide explanations for human thinking and behavior. In more modern times, we describe social facts as "social structure" or the tangible features or characteristics of socially ordered human affairs. For many people, Durkheim provides a key to unlocking the mystery of why we do what we do.

Before beginning the search for the method appropriate to the study of social facts it is important to know what are the facts termed 'social.'

The question is all the more necessary because the term is used without much precision. It is commonly used to designate almost all the phenomena that occur within society, however little social interest of some generality they present. Yet under this heading there is, so to speak, no human occurrence that cannot be called social. Every individual drinks, sleeps, eats, or employs his reason, and society has every interest in seeing that these functions are regularly exercised. If therefore these facts were social ones, sociology would possess no subject matter peculiarly its own, and its domain would be confused with that of biology and psychology.

However, in reality there is in every society a clearly determined group of phenomena separable, because of their distinct characteristics, from those that form the subject matter of other sciences of nature.

When I perform my duties as a brother, a husband or a citizen and carry out the commitments I have entered into, I fulfill obligations which are defined in law and custom and which are external to myself and my actions. Even when they conform to my own sentiments and when I feel their reality within me, that reality does not cease to be objective, for it is not I who have prescribed these duties; I have received them through education. Moreover, how often does it happen that we are ignorant of the details of the obligations that we must assume, and that, to know them, we must consult the legal code and its authorized interpreters! Similarly the believer has discovered from birth, ready fashioned, the beliefs and practices of his religious life; if they existed before he did, it follows that they exist outside him. The system of signs that I employ to express my thoughts, the monetary system I use to pay my debts, the credit instruments I utilise in my commercial relationships, the practices I follow in my profession, etc., all function independently of the use I make of them. Considering in turn each member of society, the foregoing remarks can be repeated for each single one of them. Thus there are ways of acting, thinking and feeling which possess the remarkable property of existing outside the consciousness of the individual.

Not only are these types of behaviour and thinking external to the individual, but they are endowed with a compelling and coercive power by virtue of which, whether he wishes it or not, they impose themselves upon him. Undoubtedly when I conform to them of my own free will, this coercion is not felt or felt hardly at all, since it is unnecessary. None the less it is intrinsically a characteristic of these facts; the proof of this is that it asserts itself as soon as I try to resist. If I attempt to violate the rules of law they react against me so as to forestall my action, if there is still time. Alternatively, they annul it or make my action conform to the norm if it is already accomplished but capable of being reversed; or they cause me to pay the penalty for it if it is irreparable. If purely moral rules are at stake, the public conscience restricts any act which infringes them by the surveillance it exercises over the conduct of citizens and by the special punishments it has at its disposal. In other cases the constraint is less violent; nevertheless, it does not cease to exist. If I do not conform to ordinary conventions, if in my mode of dress I pay no heed to what is customary in my country and in my social class, the laughter I provoke, the social distance at which I am kept, produce, although in a more mitigated form, the same results as any real penalty. In other cases, although it may be indirect, constraint is no less effective. I am not forced to speak French with my compatriots, nor to use the legal currency, but it is impossible for me to do otherwise. If I tried to escape the necessity, my attempt would fail miserably. As an industrialist nothing prevents me from working with the processes and methods of the previous century, but if I do I will most certainly ruin myself. Even when in fact I can struggle free from these rules and successfully break them, it is never without being forced to fight against them. Even if in the end they are overcome, they make their constraining power sufficiently felt in the resistance that they afford. There is no innovator, even a fortunate one, whose ventures do not encounter opposition of this kind.

Here, then, is a category of facts which present very special characteristics: they consist of manners of acting, thinking and feeling external to the individual, which are invested with a coercive power by virtue of which they exercise control over him. Consequently, since they consist of representations and actions, they cannot be confused with organic phenomena, nor with psychical phenomena, which have no existence save in and through the individual consciousness. Thus they constitute a new species and to them must be exclusively assigned the term *social*. It is appropriate, since it is clear that, not having the individual as their substratum, they can have none other than society, either political society in its entirety or one of the partial groups that it includes-religious denominations, political and literary schools, occupational corporations, etc. Moreover, it is for such as these alone that the term is fitting, for the word 'social' has the sole meaning of designating those phenomena which fall into none of the categories of facts already constituted and labeled. They are consequently the proper field of sociology. It is true that this word 'constraint', in terms of which we define them, is in danger of infuriating those who zealously uphold out-and-out individualism. Since they maintain that the individual is completely autonomous, it seems to them that he is diminished every time he is made aware that he is not dependent on himself alone. Yet since it is indisputable today that most of our ideas and tendencies are not developed by ourselves, but come to us from outside, they can only penetrate us by imposing themselves upon us. This is all that our definition implies. Moreover, we know that all social constraints do not necessarily exclude the individual personality.

Yet since the examples just cited (legal and moral rules, religious dogmas, financial systems, etc.) consist wholly of beliefs and practices already well established, in view of what has been said it might be maintained that no social fact can exist except where there is a well defined social organization. But there are other facts which do not present themselves in this already crystallised form but which also possess the same objectivity and ascendancy over the individual. These are what are called social 'currents.' Thus in a public gathering the great waves of enthusiasm, indignation and pity that are produced have their seat in no one individual consciousness. They come to each one of us from outside and can sweep us along in spite of ourselves. If perhaps I abandon myself to them I may not be conscious of the pressure that they are exerting upon me, but that pressure makes its presence felt immediately I attempt to struggle against them. If an individual tries to pit himself against one of these collective manifestations, the sentiments that he is rejecting will be turned against him. Now if this external coercive power asserts itself so acutely in cases of resistance, it must be because it exists in the other instances cited above without our being conscious of it. Hence we are the victims of an illusion which leads us to believe we have ourselves produced what has been imposed upon us externally. But if the willingness with which we let ourselves be carried along disguises the pressure we have undergone, it does not eradicate it. Thus air does not cease to have weight, although we no longer feel that weight. Even when we have individually and spontaneously shared in the common emotion, the impression we have experienced is utterly different from what we would have felt if we had been alone. Once the assembly has broken up and these social influences have ceased to act upon us, and we are once more on our own, the emotions we have felt seem an alien phenomenon, one in which we no longer recognize ourselves. It is then we perceive that we have undergone the emotions much more than generated them. These emotions may even perhaps fill us with horror, so much do they go against the grain. Thus individuals who are normally perfectly harmless may, when gathered together in a crowd, let themselves be drawn into acts of atrocity. And what we assert about these transitory outbreaks likewise applies to those more lasting movements of opinion which relate to religious, political, literary and artistic matters, etc., and which are constantly being produced around us, whether throughout society or in a more limited sphere.

Moreover, this definition of a social fact can be verified by examining an experience that is characteristic. It is sufficient to observe how children are brought up. If one views the facts as they are and indeed as they have always been, it is patently obvious that all education consists of a continual effort to impose upon the child ways of seeing, thinking and acting which he himself would not have arrived at spontaneously. From his earliest years we oblige him to eat, drink and sleep at regular hours, and to observe cleanliness, calm and obedience; later we force him to learn how to be mindful of others, to respect customs and conventions, and to work, etc. If this constraint in time ceases to be felt it is because it gradually gives rise to habits, to inner tendencies which render it superfluous; but they supplant the constraint only because they are derived from it. It is true that, in [English social theorist Herbert] Spencer's view, a rational education should shun such means and allow the child complete freedom to do what he will. Yet as this educational theory has never been put into practice among any known people, it can only be the personal expression of a *desideratum* and not a fact which can be established in contradiction to the other facts given above. What renders these latter facts particularly illuminating is that education sets out precisely with the object of creating a social being. Thus there can be seen, as in an abbreviated form, how the social being has been fashioned historically. The pressure to which the child is subjected unremittingly is the same pressure of the social environment which seeks to shape him in its own image, and in which parents and teachers are only the representatives and intermediaries.

Thus it is not the fact that they are general which can serve to characterize sociological phenomena. Thoughts to be found in the consciousness of each individual and movements which are repeated by all individuals are not for this reason social facts. If some have been content with using this characteristic in order to define them it is because they have been confused, wrongly, with what might be termed their individual incarnations. What constitutes social facts are the beliefs, tendencies and practices of the group taken collectively. But the forms that these collective states may assume when they are 'refracted' through individuals are things of a different kind. What irrefutably demonstrates this duality of kind is that these two categories of facts frequently are manifested dissociated from each other. Indeed some of these ways of acting or thinking acquire, by dint of repetition, a sort of consistency which, so to speak, separates them out, isolating them from the particular events which reflect them. Thus they assume a shape, a tangible form peculiar to them and constitute a reality *sui generis* vastly distinct from the individual facts which manifest that reality. Collective custom does not exist only in a state of immanence in the successive actions which it determines, but, by a privilege without example in the biological kingdom, expresses itself once and for all in a formula repeated by word of mouth, transmitted by education and even enshrined in the written word. Such are the origins and nature of legal and moral rules, aphorisms and popular sayings, articles of faith in which religious or political sects epitomise their beliefs, and standards of taste drawn up by literary schools, etc. None of these modes of acting and thinking are to be found wholly in the application made of them by individuals, since they can even exist without being applied at the time.

Undoubtedly this state of dissociation does not always present itself with equal distinctiveness. It is sufficient for dissociation to exist unquestionably in the numerous important instances cited, for us to prove that the social fact exists separately from its individual effects. Moreover, even when the dissociation is not immediately observable, it can often be made so with the help of certain methodological devices. Indeed it is essential to embark on such procedures if one wishes to refine out the social fact from any amalgam and so observe it in its pure state. Thus certain currents of opinion, whose intensity varies according to the time and country in which they occur, impel us, for example, towards marriage or suicide, towards higher or lower birth-rates, etc. Such currents are plainly social facts. At first sight they seem inseparable from the forms they assume in individual cases. But statistics afford us a means of isolating them. They are indeed not inaccurately represented by rates of births, marriages and suicides, that is, by the result obtained after dividing the average annual total of marriages, births, and voluntary homicides by the number of persons of an age to marry, produce children, or commit suicide. Since each one of these statistics includes without distinction all individual cases, the individual circumstances which may have played some part in producing the phenomenon cancel each other out and consequently do not contribute to determining the nature of the phenomenon. What it expresses is a certain state of the collective mind.

That is what social phenomenon are when stripped of all extraneous elements. As regards their private manifestations, these do indeed having something social about them, since in part they reproduce the collective model. But to a large extent each one depends also upon the psychical and organic constitution of the individual, and on the particular circumstances in which he is placed. Therefore they are not phenomena which are in the strict sense sociological. They depend on both domains at the same time, and could be termed socio-psychical. They are of interest to the sociologist without constituting the immediate content of sociology. The same characteristic is to be found in the organisms of those mixed phenomena of nature studied in the combined sciences such as biochemistry.

It may be objected that a phenomenon can only be collective if it is common to all the members of society, or at the very least to a majority, and consequently, if it is general. This is doubtless the case, but if it is general it is because it is collective (that is, more or less obligatory); but it is very far from being collective because it is general. It is a condition of the group repeated in individuals because it imposes itself upon them. It is in each part because it is in the whole, but far from being in the whole because it is in the parts. This is supremely evident in those beliefs and practices which are handed down to us ready fashioned by previous generations. We accept and adopt them because, since they are the work of the collectivity and one that is centuries old, they are invested with a special authority that our education has taught us to recognize and respect. It is worthy of note that the vast majority of social phenomena come to us in this way. But even when the social fact is partly due to our direct co-operation, it is no different in nature. An outburst of collective emotion in a gathering does not merely express the sum total of what individual feelings share in common, but is something of a very different order, as we have demonstrated. It is a product of shared existence, of actions and reactions called into play between the consciousnesses of individuals. If it is echoed in each one of them it is precisely by virtue of the special energy derived from its collective origins. If all hearts beat in unison, this is not as a consequence of a spontaneous, preestablished harmony; it is because one and the same force is propelling them in the same direction. Each one is borne along by the rest.

We have therefore succeeded in delineating for ourselves the exact field of sociology. It embraces one single, well defined group of phenomena. A social fact is identifiable through the power of external coercion which it exerts or is capable of exerting upon individuals. The presence of this power is in turn recognizable because of the existence of some pre-determined sanction, or through the resistance that the fact opposes to any individual action that may threaten it. However, it can also be defined by ascertaining how widespread it is within the group, provided that, as noted above, one is careful to add a second essential characteristic; this is, that it exists independently of the particular forms that it may assume in the process of spreading itself within the group. In certain cases this latter criterion can even be more easily applied than the former one. The presence of constraint is easily ascertainable when it is manifested externally through some direct reaction of society, as in the case of law, morality, beliefs, customs and even fashions. But when constraint is merely indirect, as with that exerted by an economic organization, it is not always so clearly discernible. Generality combined with objectivity may then be easier to establish. Moreover, this second definition is simply another formulation of the first one: if a mode of behaviour existing outside the consciousnesses of individuals becomes general, it can only do so by exerting pressure upon them.

However, one may well ask whether this definition is complete. Indeed the facts which have provided us with its basis are all *ways of functioning*: they are 'physiological' in nature. But there are also collective *ways of being*, namely, social facts of an 'anatomical' or morphological nature. Sociology cannot dissociate itself from what concerns the substratum of collective life. Yet the number and nature of the elementary parts which constitute society, the way in which they are articulated, the degree of coalescence they have attained, the distribution of population over the earth's surface, the extent and nature of the network of communications, the design of dwellings, etc., do not at first sight seem relatable to ways of acting, feeling or thinking.

Yet, first and foremost, these various phenomena present the same characteristic which has served us in defining the others. These ways of being impose themselves upon the individual just as do the ways of acting we have dealt with. In fact, when we wish to learn how a society is divided up politically, in what its divisions consist and the degree of solidarity that exists between them, it is not through physical inspection and geographical observation that we may come to find this out: such divisions are social, although they may have some physical basis. It is only through public law that we can study such political organization, because this law is what determines its nature, just as it determines our domestic and civic relationships. The organization is no less a form of compulsion. If the population clusters together in our cities instead of being scattered over the rural areas, it is because there exists a trend of opinion, a collective drive which imposes this concentration upon individuals. We can no more choose the design of our houses than the cut of our clothes-at least, the one is as much obligatory as the other. The communication network forcibly prescribes the direction of internal migrations or commercial exchanges, etc., and even their intensity. Consequently, at the most there are grounds for adding one further category to the list of phenomena already enumerated as bearing the distinctive stamp of a social fact. But as that enumeration was in no wise strictly exhaustive, this addition would not be indispensable.

Moreover, it does not even serve a purpose, for these ways of being are only ways of acting that have been consolidated. A society's political structure is only the way in which its various component segments have become accustomed to living with each other. If relationships between them are traditionally close, the segments tend to merge together; if the contrary, they tend to remain distinct. The type of dwelling imposed upon us is merely the way in which everyone around us and, in part, previous generations, have customarily built their houses. The communication network is only the channel which has been cut by the regular current of commerce and migrations, etc., flowing in the same direction. Doubtless if phenomena of a morphological kind were the only ones that displayed this rigidity, it might be thought that they constituted a separate species. But a legal rule is no less permanent an arrangement than an architectural style, and yet it is a 'physiological' fact. A simple moral maxim is certainly more malleable, yet it is cast in forms much more rigid than a mere professional custom or fashion. Thus there exists a whole range of gradations which, without any break in continuity, join the most clearly delineated structural facts to those free currents of social life which are not yet caught in any definite mould. This therefore signifies that the differences between them concern only the degree to which they have become consolidated. Both are forms of life at varying stages of crystallisation. It would undoubtedly be advantageous to reserve the term 'morphological' for those social facts which relate to the social substratum, but only on condition that one is aware that they are of the same nature as the others. Our definition will therefore subsume all that has to be defined it if states:

> *A social fact is any way of acting, whether fixed or not, capable of exerting over the individual an external constraint;*

or:

> *which is general over the whole of a given society whilst having an existence of its own, independent of its individual manifestations.*

4

Public Sociologies:
Contradictions, Dilemmas, and Possibilities

MICHAEL BURAWOY

Since the middle of the nineteenth century, social scientists have been asking about the influence of their work on society. Should it contribute to social order and stability? Should it address problems and seek to devise solutions? Or should it promote social change that could lead to a new and more progressive form of society? One view of science is that the best research is guided by idle curiosity, while another argues that necessity and crisis spur the greatest discoveries. Some scholars embrace their work with personal passion, while others believe scientific objectivity is compromised by too much emotional investment. Sociology is not immune to these debates. This article, a version of the presidential address to the American Sociological Association, again raises the question the great sociologist Howard Becker asked years ago, "Whose side are you on?"

In 2003 the members of the American Sociological Association (ASA) were asked to vote on a member resolution opposing the war in Iraq. The resolution included the following justification: "[F]oreign interventions that do not have the support of the world community create more problems than solutions . . . Instead of lessening the risk of terrorist attacks, this invasion could serve as the spark for multiple attacks in years to come." It passed by a two-thirds majority (with 22% of voting members abstaining) and became the association's official position. In an opinion poll on the same ballot, 75% of the members who expressed an opinion were opposed to the war. To assess the ethos of sociologists today, it is worthwhile comparing these results with those of 1968 when a similar double item was presented to the membership with respect to the Vietnam war. Then two-thirds of the votes cast *opposed* the ASA adopting a resolution against the war and only 54% were individually opposed to the war (Rhoades 1981:60).

It is complicated to interpret this apparent shift in political orientation, given the different national and military contexts within which the voting took place, given the different wording of the questions. Still two hypotheses present themselves. First, the membership of the ASA, always leaning toward the liberal end of the political spectrum, has moved much further to the left. In 1968 the opinion of sociologists was close to the rest of the population (54% of sociologists opposed the war as compared to between 46% and 54% of the general public), whereas in 2003 the two distributions were the inverse of each other—75% of voting sociologists opposed the war at the end of April, 2003, while at the same time 75% of the public supported the war. One might conjecture that in 1968 a very different generation dominated the profession—a postwar generation celebratory of the U.S. and its "victory over fascism," among them pioneers of professional sociology. Today's post-Vietnam generations are more accustomed to criticizing the U.S. government and in particular its foreign policy. They are also less concerned about the purity of sociology as science and more likely to assume that our accumulated knowledge should be put to public use, whether in the form of member resolutions or policy interventions.

Second, the world itself is different. In 1968 the world seemed ripe for change for the better. The civil rights movements, the women's movement, student movements around the world, antiwar marches and sit-ins captured the imagination of a new generation of sociologists who saw conventional sociology as lagging behind the most progressive movements; whereas today the world is lagging behind sociology, unapologetic about its drift into political and economic fundamentalism. Sociologists shift their critical eye ever more away from sociology toward the world it describes, a shift reflected in the insurgent interest in public sociology. In short, over the last 35 years there has been a scissors movement. The political context and the sociological conscience have moved in opposite directions, so that the world we inhabit is increasingly in conflict with the ethos and principles that animate sociologists—an ethos opposed to inequality, to the erosion of civil liberties, to the destruction of public life, and to discrimination and exclusion.

This shift in sociological ethos is not uncontroversial. It has, indeed, generated its own opposition. Dissatisfied with the political winds, 102 ASA members signed a petition, sent to the association's Committee on Professional Ethics, charging that the anti-Iraq-war resolution violated the ASA's code of conduct. Why? Because it did not rely on "scientifically and professionally derived knowledge." The complaint did not get far because, unlike other professional associations, there are no clear rules that limit the types of resolutions the ASA can endorse. Nonetheless, the 102 (and presumably many others) did take a principled position: scientific sociologists have no business making moral or political pronouncements. Taking a moral or political position is incompatible with scientific objectivity. Opposition to the resolution also took a more pragmatic form, fears that such a visible and public stance against the war (and I have not found another association to have taken such a stance) would undermine what legitimacy we have as sociologists, conceivably threaten research funding, and even prompt political reprisals. Alas, this is not so far fetched. * * *

The "pure science" position that research must be completely insulated from politics is untenable since antipolitics is no less political than *public engagement*. The more usual "abstentionist" position limits politics to *professional self-defense*: that we should enter the political arena only to defend our immediate professional interests. Thus, we might mobilize resources to oppose the defunding of research into sexual behavior (as was attempted in Congress recently), or to protest the closure or dramatic cuts in a sociology department (as in Germany today), or to protect the human rights of an individual (e.g., Egyptian sociologist, Saad Eddin Ibrahim), or, most recently, to defend a journal's right to review and edit articles from "enemy" countries. In all these instances we enter the political arena, but solely to defend the integrity of our professional activities.

Between professional self-defense and public engagement there is a compromise position that moves from the defense of professional interests to *policy interventions*. Here the association takes a political position on the basis of an accumulated body of evidence whose validity is widely accepted and whose interpretation is unambiguous. One such example is the ASA's recent statement that summarized the sociological literature on race: race exists, it has social causes, and it has social consequences. An extension of this was the ASA's Amicus Curiae brief to the Supreme Court in the 2003 Michigan Law School affirmative action case, *Grutter* v. *Bollinger*. Again a body of sociological research was mobilized to show that racial discrimination exists and that efforts to diversify the student body would improve the educational experience of all.

So far, then, we have three possible political stances: "professional self-defense," "policy intervention" and "public engagement." There is, however, a fourth stance. The association is a political venue unto itself—a place to debate the stances we might adopt. We cannot advocate democracy for others if we are not internally democratic, if we do not attempt to arrive at public stances through maximal participation in collective deliberation. It is just such a critical debate that we are involved in today. The resolution against the Iraq War is but a dramatic instance of the broader issue we are discussing: what should be our involvement in the world beyond the academy? Recognizing we are part of the world we study, we must take some *stance* with respect to that world. To fail to do so is to take a stance by default.

We can problematize our place in society by asking two questions. The first was posed by Alfred McClung Lee in his 1976 Presidential Address to the American Sociological Association: "Knowledge for Whom?" As sociologists are we just talking to ourselves? Are we to remain locked up in the antechambers of society, never really entering its tumultuous currents, hiding behind the barricades of professional insularity? Or can we, ever cautious, ever vigilant, wade forth into society, armed with our sociological expertise? If we are going to talk to others, which others and how shall we do it? This leads directly to the second question, famously posed by Robert Lynd (1939): Knowledge for What? Do we take the values and goals of our research for granted, handed down to us by some external (funding or policy) agency? Should we only concentrate on providing solutions to predefined problems, focusing on the means to achieve predetermined ends, on what Weber called technical rationality and what I call *instrumental knowledge*? In other words, should we repress the question of ends and pretend that knowledge and laws spring spontaneously from the data, if only we can develop the right methods? Or should we be concerned explicitly with the goals for which our research may be mobilized, and with the values that underpin and guide our research? Going further afield, should sociologists be in the business of stimulating public discussions about the possible meanings of the "good society"? Like Weber, I believe that without value commitments there can be no sociology, no basis for the questions that guide our research programs. Without values social science is blind. * * * Thus, empirical science can only take us so far: it can help us understand the consequences of our value commitments and inform our value discussions, but it cannot determine those values. Determining values should take place through democratic and collective deliberation.

* * * Professional and policy sociology are forms of instrumental knowledge focusing respectively on academic and extra-academic audiences. Critical and public sociology are forms of reflexive knowledge focusing respectively on academic and extra-academic audiences. Let me consider each in turn.

Public sociology engages publics beyond the academy in dialogue about matters of political and moral concern. It has to be relevant to such publics without being faddish, that is subservient to publics. * * *

* * *

Public sociology should be distinguished from *policy sociology.* While public sociology generates conversation or debate between sociologist and public on a terrain of reciprocal engagement, policy sociology focuses on solutions to specific problems defined by clients. The relation between sociologist and client is often of a contractual character in which expertise is sold for a fee. The sociologist, thereby, cedes independence to the client. All manner of organizations may contract sociological expertise, from business to state, from multilateral organization to the small NGO [nongovernmental organization]. What makes the relation instrumental is that the research terrain is not defined by the sociologist. It is defined narrowly in the case of a "client" or broadly in the case of a "patron."

* * *

Public and policy sociologies could not exist without *professional sociology,* which provides legitimacy, expertise, distinctive problem definitions, relevant bodies of knowledge, and techniques for analyzing data. An effective public or policy sociology is not hostile to, but depends upon the professional sociology that lies at the core of our disciplinary field. Why do I call our disciplinary knowledge instrumental? As professional sociologists we are located in research traditions, sometimes going back to founding fathers (Weber, Durkheim, and Marx) and otherwise of a more recent pedigree (feminism, poststructuralism). These research traditions may be elaborated into self-conscious research programs—structural functionalism, stratification theory, sex-gender systems, experimental social psychology—with their grounding assumptions, distinctive questions, exemplary models and appropriate techniques of research. Research programs (Lakatos 1978) advance by resolving internal contradictions and absorbing anomalies (discrepancies between theoretical expectation and empirical observations). They require a community of scientists committed to working on the important (collectively defined) *puzzles* that the research program generates. Flourishing public and policy sociologies increase the stakes of our knowledge and thus makes the vigilant pursuit of coherent research programs all the more important.

In the world of normal science we cannot push forward the frontiers of knowledge and at the same time question its foundations. The latter task is the province of *critical sociology*. In much the same way that public sociology interrogates the value assumptions of policy sociology, so in a similar and more direct way critical sociology is the conscience of professional sociology. * * *

* * * As sociology grew, its institutional base differentiated, so that today sociologists work both inside and outside academia. Those outside tend to occupy positions in government agencies, such as the census bureau or the department of corrections; in consulting companies for human resource management; or in international NGOs. Then, there are sociologists who are employed in professional schools—business schools, public administration, educational schools, agricultural extension, and so forth—where they may engage non-academic audiences. Equally important is the complex hierarchy of the university system which ranges from elite private universities, to the different tiers of state university systems, liberal arts colleges, and two year community colleges. The configuration of the division of sociological labor will vary with a department's location in this system. Thus, in state colleges where teaching takes up so much of one's time, research has a public or policy dimension, often driven by local issues. Based on my attendance at the meetings of state associations, such as the North Carolina Sociological Association, I have found public sociology to be both more widely practiced and more highly valued in state colleges than in most elite departments. I have found projects ranging from research on displaced workers, toxic waste, housing inequalities, and educational reform, to advocacy for public health campaigns around HIV-AIDS or needle exchange to training community organizers to deal with the media. Sadly, all too often, this public (and policy) sociology, widespread though it may be, remains invisible and unrecognized because its practitioners lack the time or incentive to write it up.

History and hierarchy give one sense of the possible variation in the configuration of the disciplinary field, international comparisons give another. When one travels the world talking about public sociology, one quickly learns just how distinctively American the concept is, marking the unique strength of professional sociology in the U.S. In many countries it is taken for granted that sociology has a public face. Why else be a sociologist? The career of sociology in many Third World countries reflects the succession of different political regimes. One of the first acts of the Pinochet Regime in Chile was to abolish sociology. In South Africa sociology flourished in the late 1970s and 1980s as the anti-apartheid movement grew in strength, just as it has suffered amalgamation and budgetary cuts in the post-apartheid period. Soviet sociology, nonexistent under Stalinism, reappeared in the 1950s as an ideological and surveillance arm of the party state. Sociological opinion research was deployed as a weapon of critique, revealing public discontent in order to justify swings in policy. This instrumental use of sociology comes home to roost in the post-Soviet period where, increasingly, it has become a form of market research. If it is not co-opted or repressed by authoritarian regimes, sociology's reflexive side may sustain critical opposition, as was often the case in Eastern Europe. In the social democratic countries of Scandinavia, by contrast, it is the policy dimension that often stands out. Although when conservative parties assume power, the sociological winds shift direction from policy to public.

Here then are just a few hints at national variation, underlining once again just how peculiar is U.S. sociology. It is not just peculiar, it is also very powerful, dominating the world scene. Accordingly in the international division of sociological labor, professional sociology is concentrated in the resource rich United States, and to a lesser extent in Western Europe, while public sociology has relatively greater strength in the poorer countries—a distribution that mirrors the hierarchy within the U.S. * * *

* * *

Finally, we come to the critical question: what are the grounds for claiming sociology's affinity to the public? If political science's distinctive object of study is the state and its value the protection of political order, and if economics has as it distinctive object the economy and its value is the expansion of the market, then sociology's distinctive object is civil society and its value is the resilience and autonomy of the social. Sociology is born with civil society and dies with civil society. The classical sociology of Weber, Durkheim, Simmel, and Pareto arose with the expansion of trade unions, political parties, mass education, voluntary associations at the end of the nineteenth century, just as U.S. sociology was born amidst reform and religious organizations. Sociology disappears with the eclipse of civil society as in fascism, Stalinism or Pinochet's Chile, just as it quickly bubbles to the surface with the unfurling of perestroika in the Soviet Union or the civic and labor associations of South Africa's anti-apartheid movement.

* * *

The burgeoning interest in public sociology and the unanticipated vote against the war in Iraq suggest to me that the stakes are indeed becoming clearer. In a world tending toward market tyranny and state unilateralism, civil society is at once threatened with extinction and at the same time a major possible hold-out against deepening inequalities and multiplying threats to all manner of human rights. The interest of sociology in the very existence, let alone expansion, of civil society (even with all its warts) becomes the interest of humanity—locally, nationally and globally. If we can transcend our parochialism and recognize our distinctive relation to diverse publics within and across borders, sociologists could yet create the fulcrum around which a critical social science might evolve, one responsive to public issues while at the same time committed to professional excellence.

REFERENCES

Lakatos, Imre. 1978. *The Methodology of Scientific Research Programmes.* Cambridge University Press

Lee, Alfred McClung. 1976. "Sociology for Whom?" *American Sociological Review* 44:925–36

Lynd, Robert. 1939. *Knowledge for What? The Place of Social Sciences in American Culture.* Princeton University Press.

Rhoades, Lawrence. 1981. *A History of the American Sociological Association, 1905–1980.* American Sociological Association, Washington D.C.

5

The My Lai Massacre:
A Crime of Obedience?

FROM *Crimes of Obedience: Toward a Social Psychology*
of Authority and Responsibility

HERBERT C. KELMAN AND V. LEE HAMILTON

Understanding why people do what they do is never easy. It is especially difficult when behaviors are contrary to what anyone would expect or want people to do, as in the case of heinous crimes. In this account of the murder of hundreds of innocent people—perhaps the most painful episode of a long and unpopular war—Kelman and Hamilton depart from psychological explanations and focus on the sociology of men in war. They make a compelling case that the social conditions of these men dramatically weakened the moral inhibitions that otherwise would have prevented their doing the unthinkable.

March 16, 1968, was a busy day in U.S. history. Stateside, Robert F. Kennedy announced his presidential candidacy, challenging a sitting president from his own party—in part out of opposition to an undeclared and disastrous war. In Vietnam, the war continued. In many ways, March 16 may have been a typical day in that war. We will probably never know. But we do know that on that day a typical company went on a mission—which may or may not have been typical—to a village called Son (or Song) My. Most of what is remembered from that mission occurred in the subhamlet known to Americans as My Lai 4.

The My Lai massacre was investigated and charges were brought in 1969 and 1970. Trials and disciplinary actions lasted into 1971. Entire books have been written about the army's year-long cover-up of the massacre (for example, Hersh, 1972), and the cover-up was a major focus of the army's own investigation of the incident. Our central concern here is the massacre itself—a crime of obedience—and public reactions to such crimes, rather than the lengths to which many went to deny the event. Therefore this account concentrates on one day: March 16, 1968.[1]

Many verbal testimonials to the horrors that occurred at My Lai were available. More unusual was the fact that an army photographer, Ronald Haeberle, was assigned the task of documenting the anticipated military engagement at My Lai—and documented a massacre instead. Later, as the story of the

---

1. In reconstructing the events of that day, we consulted Hammer (1970), in addition to the sources cited in the text. Schell (1968) provided information on the region around My Lai. Concerning Vietnam and peasant rebellions, we consulted FitzGerald (1972), Paige (1975), Popkin (1979), and Wolf (1969).

massacre emerged, his photographs were widely distributed and seared the public conscience. What might have been dismissed as unreal or exaggerated was depicted in photographs of demonstrable authenticity. The dominant image appeared on the cover of *Life*: piles of bodies jumbled together in a ditch along a trail—the dead all apparently unarmed. All were Oriental, and all appeared to be children, women, or old men. Clearly there had been a mass execution, one whose image would not quickly fade.

So many bodies (over twenty in the cover photo alone) are hard to imagine as the handiwork of one killer. These were not. They were the product of what we call a crime of obedience. Crimes of obedience begin with orders. But orders are often vague and rarely survive with any clarity the transition from one authority down a chain of subordinates to the ultimate actors. The operation at Son My was no exception.

"Charlie" Company, Company C, under Lt. Col. Frank Barker's command, arrived in Vietnam in December of 1967. As the army's investigative unit, directed by Lt. Gen. William R. Peers, characterized the personnel, they "contained no significant deviation from the average" for the time. Seymour S. Hersh (1970) described the "average" more explicitly: "Most of the men in Charlie Company had volunteered for the draft; only a few had gone to college for even one year. Nearly half were black, with a few Mexican-Americans. Most were eighteen to twenty-two years old. The favorite reading matter of Charlie Company, like that of other line infantry units in Vietnam, was comic books" (p. 18). The action at My Lai, like that throughout Vietnam, was fought by a cross-section of those Americans who either believed in the war or lacked the social resources to avoid participating in it. Charlie Company was indeed average for that time, that place, and that war.

Two key figures in Charlie Company were more unusual. The company's commander, Capt. Ernest Medina, was an upwardly mobile Mexican-American who wanted to make the army his career, although he feared that he might never advance beyond captain because of his lack of formal education. His eagerness had earned him a nickname among his men: "Mad Dog Medina." One of his admirers was the platoon leader Second Lt. William L. Calley, Jr., an undistinguished, five-foot-three-inch junior-college dropout who had failed four of the seven courses in which he had enrolled his first year. Many viewed him as one of those "instant officers" made possible only by the army's then-desperate need for manpower. Whatever the cause, he was an insecure leader whose frequent claim was "I'm the boss." His nickname among some of the troops was "Surfside 5½," a reference to the swashbuckling heroes of a popular television show, "Surfside 6."

The Son My operation was planned by Lieutenant Colonel Barker and his staff as a search-and-destroy mission with the objective of rooting out the Forty-eighth Viet Cong Battalion from their base area of Son My village. Apparently no written orders were ever issued. Barker's superior, Col. Oran Henderson, arrived at the staging point the day before. Among the issues he reviewed with the assembled officers were some of the weaknesses of prior operations by their units, including their failure to be appropriately aggressive in pursuit of the enemy. Later briefings by Lieutenant Colonel Barker and his staff asserted that no one except Viet Cong was expected to be in the village after 7 A.M. on the following day. The "innocent" would all be at the market. Those present at the briefings gave conflicting accounts of Barker's exact orders, but he conveyed at least a strong suggestion that the Son My area was to be obliterated. As the army's inquiry reported: "While there is some conflict in the testimony as to whether LTC Barker ordered the destruction of houses, dwellings, livestock, and other foodstuffs in the Song My area, the preponderance of the evidence indicates that such destruction was implied, if not specifically directed, by his orders of 15 March" (Peers Report, in Goldstein et al., 1976, p. 94).

Evidence that Barker ordered the killing of civilians is even more murky. What does seem clear, however, is that—having asserted that civilians would be away at the market—he did not specify what was to be done with any who might nevertheless be found on the scene. The Peers Report therefore considered it "reasonable to conclude that LTC Barker's minimal or nonexistent instructions concerning the handling of noncombatants created the potential for grave misunderstandings as to his intentions and for interpretation of his orders as authority to fire, without restriction, on all persons found in target area" (Goldstein et al., 1976, p. 95). Since Barker was killed in action in June 1968, his own formal version of the truth was never available.

Charlie Company's Captain Medina was briefed for the operation by Barker and his staff. He then transmitted the already vague orders to his own men. Charlie Company was spoiling for a fight, having been totally frustrated during its months in Vietnam—first by waiting for battles that never came, then by incompetent forays led by inexperienced commanders, and finally by mines and booby traps. In fact, the emotion-laden funeral of a sergeant killed by a booby trap was held on March 15, the day before My Lai. Captain Medina gave the orders for the next day's action at the close of that funeral. Many were in a mood for revenge.

It is again unclear what was ordered. Although all participants were still alive by the time of the trials for the massacre, they were either on trial or probably felt under threat of trial. Memories are often flawed and self-serving at such times. It is apparent that Medina relayed to the men at least some of Barker's general message—to expect Viet Cong resistance, to burn, and to kill livestock. It is not clear that he ordered the slaughter of the inhabitants, but some of the men who heard him thought he had. One of those who claimed to have heard such orders was Lt. William Calley.

As March 16 dawned, much was expected of the operation by those who had set it into motion. Therefore a full complement of "brass" was present in helicopters overhead, including Barker, Colonel Henderson, and their superior, Major General Koster (who went on to become commandant of West

Point before the story of My Lai broke). On the ground, the troops were to carry with them one reporter and one photographer to immortalize the anticipated battle.

The action for Company C began at 7:30 as their first wave of helicopters touched down near the subhamlet of My Lai 4. By 7:47 all of Company C was present and set to fight. But instead of the Viet Cong Forty-eighth Battalion, My Lai was filled with the old men, women, and children who were supposed to have gone to market. By this time, in their version of the war, and with whatever orders they thought they had heard, the men from Company C were nevertheless ready to find Viet Cong everywhere. By nightfall, the official tally was 128 VC killed and three weapons captured, although later unofficial body counts ran as high as 500. The operation at Son My was over. And by nightfall, as Hersh reported: "the Viet Cong were back in My Lai 4, helping the survivors bury the dead. It took five days. Most of the funeral speeches were made by the Communist guerrillas. Nguyen Bat was not a Communist at the time of the massacre, but the incident changed his mind. 'After the shooting,' he said, 'all the villagers became Communists'" (1970, p. 74). To this day, the memory of the massacre is kept alive by markers and plaques designating the spots where groups of villagers were killed, by a large statue, and by the My Lai Museum, established in 1975 (Williams, 1985).

But what could have happened to leave American troops reporting a victory over Viet Cong when in fact they had killed hundreds of noncombatants? It is not hard to explain the report of victory; that is the essence of a cover-up. It is harder to understand how the killings came to be committed in the first place, making a cover-up necessary.

MASS EXECUTIONS AND THE DEFENSE OF SUPERIOR ORDERS

Some of the atrocities on March 16, 1968, were evidently unofficial, spontaneous acts: rapes, tortures, killings. For example, Hersh (1970) describes Charlie Company's Second Platoon as entering "My Lai 4 with guns blazing" (p. 50); more graphically, Lieutenant "Brooks and his men in the second platoon to the north had begun to systematically ransack the hamlet and slaughter the people, kill the livestock, and destroy the crops. Men poured rifle and machine-gun fire into huts without knowing—or seemingly caring—who was inside" (pp. 49–50).

Some atrocities toward the end of the action were part of an almost casual "mopping-up," much of which was the responsibility of Lieutenant LaCross's Third Platoon of Charlie Company. The Peers Report states: "The entire 3rd Platoon then began moving into the western edge of My Lai (4), for the mop-up operation. . . . The squad . . . began to burn the houses in the southwestern portion of the hamlet" (Goldstein et al., 1976, p. 133). They became mingled with other platoons during a series of rapes and killings of survivors for which it was impossible to fix responsibility. Certainly to a Vietnamese all GIs would by this point look alike: "Nineteen-year-old Nguyen Thi Ngoc Tuyet watched a baby trying to open her slain mother's blouse to nurse. A soldier shot the infant while it was struggling with the blouse, and then slashed it with his bayonet." Tuyet also said she saw another baby hacked to death by GIs wielding their bayonets. "Le Tong, a twenty-eight-year-old rice farmer, reported seeing one woman raped after GIs killed her children. Nguyen Khoa, a thirty-seven-year-old peasant, told of a thirteen-year-old girl who was raped before being killed. GIs then attacked Khoa's wife, tearing off her clothes. Before they could rape her, however, Khoa said, their six-year-old son, riddled with bullets, fell and saturated her with blood. The GIs left her alone" (Hersh, 1970, p. 72). All of Company C was implicated in a pattern of death and destruction throughout the hamlet, much of which seemingly lacked rhyme or reason.

But a substantial amount of the killing was *organized* and traceable to one authority: the First Platoon's Lt. William Calley. Calley was originally charged with 109 killings, almost all of them mass executions at the trail and other locations. He stood trial for 102 of these killings, was convicted of 22 in 1971, and at first received a life sentence. Though others—both superior and subordinate to Calley—were brought to trial, he was the only one convicted for the My Lai crimes. Thus, the only actions of My Lai for which *anyone* was ever convicted were mass executions, ordered and committed. We suspect that there are commonsense reasons why this one type of killing was singled out. In the midst of rapidly moving events with people running about, an execution of stationary targets is literally a still life that stands out and whose participants are clearly visible. It can be proven that specific people committed specific deeds. An execution, in contrast to the shooting of someone on the run, is also more likely to meet the legal definition of an act resulting from intent—with malice aforethought. Moreover, American military law specifically forbids the killing of unarmed civilians or military prisoners, as does the Geneva Convention between nations. Thus common sense, legal standards, and explicit doctrine all made such actions the likeliest target for prosecution.

When Lieutenant Calley was charged under military law it was for violation of the Uniform Code of Military Justice (UCMJ) Article 118 (murder). This article is similar to civilian codes in that it provides for conviction if an accused:

1. without justification or excuse, unlawfully kills a human being, when he—
2. has a premeditated design to kill;
3. intends to kill or inflict great bodily harm;
4. is engaged in an act which is inherently dangerous to others and evinces a wanton disregard of human life; or
5. is engaged in the perpetration or attempted perpetration of burglary, sodomy, rape, robbery, or aggravated arson. (Goldstein et al., 1976, p. 507)

For a soldier, one legal justification for killing is warfare; but warfare is subject to many legal limits and restrictions, including, of course, the inadmissibility of killing unarmed noncombatants or prisoners whom one has disarmed. The pictures of the trail victims at My Lai certainly portrayed one or the other of these. Such an action would be illegal under military law; ordering another to commit such an action would be illegal; and following such an order would be illegal.

But following an order may provide a second and pivotal justification for an act that would be murder when committed by a civilian. * * * American military law assumes that the subordinate is inclined to follow orders, as that is the normal obligation of the role. Hence, legally, obedient subordinates are protected from unreasonable expectations regarding their capacity to evaluate those orders:

> An order requiring the performance of a military duty may be inferred to be legal. An act performed manifestly beyond the scope of authority, or pursuant to an order that a man of ordinary sense and understanding would know to be illegal, or in a wanton manner in the discharge of a lawful duty, is not excusable. (Par. 216, Subpar. *d,* Manual for Courts Martial, United States, 1969 Rev.)

Thus what *may* be excusable is the good-faith carrying out of an order, as long as that order appears to the ordinary soldier to be a legal one. In military law, invoking superior orders moves the question from one of the action's consequences—the body count[2]—to one of evaluating the actor's motives and good sense.

In sum, if anyone is to be brought to justice for a massacre, common sense and legal codes decree that the most appropriate targets are those who make themselves executioners. This is the kind of target the government selected in prosecuting Lieutenant Calley with the greatest fervor. And in a military context, the most promising way in which one can redefine one's undeniable deeds into acceptability is to invoke superior orders. This is what Calley did in attempting to avoid conviction. Since the core legal issues involved points of mass execution—the ditches and trail where America's image of My Lai was formed—we review these events in greater detail.

The day's quiet beginning has already been noted. Troops landed and swept unopposed into the village. The three weapons eventually reported as the haul from the operation were picked up from three apparent Viet Cong who fled the village when the troops arrived and were pursued and killed by helicopter gunships. Obviously the Viet Cong did frequent the area. But it appears that by about 8:00 A.M. no one who met the troops was aggressive,

---

2. During the Vietnam War, the success of a military action was often measured by the number of "enemy" killed, relative to allied casualties (ed.).

and no one was armed. By the laws of war Charlie Company had no argument with such people.

As they moved into the village, the soldiers began to gather its inhabitants together. Shortly after 8:00 A.M. Lieutenant Calley told Pfc. Paul Meadlo that "you know what to do with" a group of villagers Meadlo was guarding. Estimates of the numbers in the group ranged as high as eighty women, children, and old men, and Meadlo's own estimate under oath was thirty to fifty people. As Meadlo later testified, Calley returned after ten or fifteen minutes: "He [Calley] said, 'How come they're not dead?' I said, 'I didn't know we were supposed to kill them.' He said, 'I want them dead.' He backed off twenty or thirty feet and started shooting into the people—the Viet Cong—shooting automatic. He was beside me. He burned four or five magazines. I burned off a few, about three. I helped shoot 'em" (Hammer, 1971, p. 155). Meadlo himself and others testified that Meadlo cried as he fired; others reported him later to be sobbing and "all broke up." It would appear that to Lieutenant Calley's subordinates something was unusual, and stressful, in these orders.

At the trial, the first specification in the murder charge against Calley was for this incident; he was accused of premeditated murder of "an unknown number, not less than 30, Oriental human beings, males and females of various ages, whose names are unknown, occupants of the village of My Lai 4, by means of shooting them with a rifle" (Goldstein et al., 1976, p. 497).

Among the helicopters flying reconnaissance above Son My was that of CWO Hugh Thompson. By 9:00 or soon after Thompson had noticed some horrifying events from his perch. As he spotted wounded civilians, he sent down smoke markers so that soldiers on the ground could treat them. They killed them instead. He reported to headquarters, trying to persuade someone to stop what was going on. Barker, hearing the message, called down to Captain Medina. Medina, in turn, later claimed to have told Calley that it was "enough for today." But it was not yet enough.

At Calley's orders, his men began gathering the remaining villagers—roughly seventy-five individuals, mostly women and children—and herding them toward a drainage ditch. Accompanied by three or four enlisted men, Lieutenant Calley executed several batches of civilians who had been gathered into ditches. Some of the details of the process were entered into testimony in such accounts as Pfc. Dennis Conti's: "A lot of them, the people, were trying to get up and mostly they was just screaming and pretty bad shot up. . . . I seen a woman tried to get up. I seen Lieutenant Calley fire. He hit the side of her head and blew it off" (Hammer, 1971, p. 125).

Testimony by other soldiers presented the shooting's aftermath. Specialist Four Charles Hall, asked by Prosecutor Aubrey Daniel how he knew the people in the ditch were dead, said: "There was blood coming from them. They were just scattered all over the ground in the ditch, some in piles and some scattered out 20, 25 meters perhaps up the ditch. . . . They were very old people, very young children, and mothers. . . . There was blood all over them"

(Goldstein et al., 1976, pp. 501–02). And Pfc. Gregory Olsen corroborated the general picture of the victims: "They were—the majority were women and children, some babies. I distinctly remember one middle-aged Vietnamese male dressed in white right at my feet as I crossed. None of the bodies were mangled in any way. There was blood. Some appeared to be dead, others followed me with their eyes as I walked across the ditch" (Goldstein et al., 1976, p. 502).

The second specification in the murder charge stated that Calley did "with premeditation, murder an unknown number of Oriental human beings, not less than seventy, males and females of various ages, whose names are unknown, occupants of the village of My Lai 4, by means of shooting them with a rifle" (Goldstein et al., 1976, p. 497). Calley was also charged with and tried for shootings of individuals (an old man and a child); these charges were clearly supplemental to the main issue at trial—the mass killings and how they came about.

It is noteworthy that during these executions more than one enlisted man avoided carrying out Calley's orders, and more than one, by sworn oath, directly refused to obey them. For example, Pfc. James Joseph Dursi testified, when asked if he fired when Lieutenant Calley ordered him to: "No. I just stood there. Meadlo turned to me after a couple of minutes and said 'Shoot! Why don't you shoot! Why don't you fire!' He was crying and yelling. I said, 'I can't! I won't!' And the people were screaming and crying and yelling. They kept firing for a couple of minutes, mostly automatic and semi-automatic" (Hammer, 1971, p. 143).

Specialist Four Ronald Grzesik reported an even more direct confrontation with Calley, although under oath he hedged about its subject:

GRZESIK: Well, Lieutenant Calley—I walked past the ditch. I was called back by someone, I don't recall who. I had a discussion with Lieutenant Calley. He said to take the fire team back into the village and help the second platoon search.
DANIEL: Did Lieutenant Calley say anything before he gave you that order?
GRZESIK: He said, "Finish them off." I refused.
DANIEL: What did you refuse to do?
GRZESIK: To finish them off.
DANIEL: What did he mean? Who did he mean to finish off?
GRZESIK: I don't know what he meant or who he meant by them. (Hammer, 1971, p. 150)

In preceding months, not under oath, Grzesik had indicated that he had a good idea what was meant but that he simply would not comply. It is likely that the jury at Calley's trial did not miss the point.

Disobedience of Lieutenant Calley's own orders to kill represented a serious legal and moral threat to a defense *based* on superior orders, such as Calley was attempting. This defense had to assert that the orders seemed reasonable enough to carry out, that they appeared to be legal orders. Even if the orders in question were not legal, the defense had to assert that an ordinary individual could not and should not be expected to see the distinction. In short, if what happened was "business as usual," even though it might be bad business, then the defendant stood a chance of acquittal. But under direct command from "Surfside 5½," some ordinary enlisted men managed to refuse, to avoid, or at least to stop doing what they were ordered to do. As "reasonable men" of "ordinary sense and understanding," they had apparently found something awry that morning; and it would have been hard for an officer to plead successfully that he was more ordinary than his men in his capacity to evaluate the reasonableness of orders.

Even those who obeyed Calley's orders showed great stress. For example, Meadlo eventually began to argue and cry directly in front of Calley. Pfc. Herbert Carter shot himself in the foot, possibly because he could no longer take what he was doing. We were not destined to hear a sworn version of the incident, since neither side at the Calley trial called him to testify.

The most unusual instance of resistance to authority came from the skies. CWO Hugh Thompson, who had protested the apparent carnage of civilians, was Calley's inferior in rank but was not in his line of command. He was also watching the ditch from his helicopter and noticed some people moving after the first round of slaughter—chiefly children who had been shielded by their mothers' bodies. Landing to rescue the wounded, he also found some villagers hiding in a nearby bunker. Protecting the Vietnamese with his own body, Thompson ordered his men to train their guns on the Americans and to open fire if the Americans fired on the Vietnamese. He then radioed for additional rescue helicopters and stood between the Vietnamese and the Americans under Calley's command until the Vietnamese could be evacuated. He later returned to the ditch to unearth a child buried, unharmed, beneath layers of bodies. In October 1969, Thompson was awarded the Distinguished Flying Cross for heroism at My Lai, specifically (albeit inaccurately) for the rescue of children hiding in a bunker "between Viet Cong forces and advancing friendly forces" and for the rescue of a wounded child "caught in the intense crossfire" (Hersh, 1970, p. 119). Four months earlier, at the Pentagon, Thompson had identified Calley as having been at the ditch.

By about 10:00 A.M., the massacre was winding down. The remaining actions consisted largely of isolated rapes and killings, "clean-up" shootings of the wounded, and the destruction of the village by fire. We have already seen some examples of these more indiscriminate and possibly less premeditated acts. By the 11:00 A.M. lunch break, when the exhausted men of Company C were relaxing, two young girls wandered back from a hiding place only to be invited to share lunch. This surrealist touch illustrates the extent to which the soldiers' action had become dissociated from its meaning. An hour earlier, some of these men were making sure that not even a child would escape the executioner's bullet. But now the job was done and it was time for lunch—and in this new context it seemed only natural to ask the children who had managed to escape execution to join them. The massacre had ended. It remained only for the Viet Cong to reap the political rewards among the survivors in hiding.

The army command in the area knew that something had gone wrong. Direct commanders, including Lieutenant Colonel Barker, had firsthand reports, such as Thompson's complaints. Others had such odd bits of evidence as the claim of 128 Viet Cong dead with a booty of only three weapons. But the cover-up of My Lai began at once. The operation was reported as a victory over a stronghold of the Viet Cong Forty-eighth.

My Lai might have remained a "victory" but for another odd twist. A soldier who had not even been at the massacre, Ronald Ridenhour, talked to several friends and acquaintances who had been. As he later wrote: "It was late in April, 1968 that I first heard of 'Pinkville' [a nickname reflecting the villagers' reputed Communist sympathies] and what allegedly happened there. I received that first report with some skepticism, but in the following months I was to hear similar stories from such a wide variety of people that it became impossible for me to disbelieve that something rather dark and bloody did indeed occur sometime in March, 1968 in a village called 'Pinkville' in the Republic of Viet Nam" (Goldstein et al., 1976, p. 34). Ridenhour's growing conviction that a massacre—or something close to it—had occurred was reinforced by his own travel over the area by helicopter soon after the event. My Lai was desolate. He gradually concluded that someone was covering up the incident within the army and that an independent investigation was needed.

At the end of March 1969, he finally wrote a letter detailing what he knew about "Pinkville." The letter, beginning with the paragraph quote above, was sent to thirty individuals—the president, Pentagon officials, and some members of the Senate and House. Ridenhour's congressman, fellow Arizonian Morris Udall, gave it particular heed. The slow unraveling of the cover-up began. During the following months, the army in fact initiated an investigation but carried it out in strict secrecy. Ridenhour, convinced that the cover-up was continuing, sought journalistic help and finally, by coincidence, connected with Seymour Hersh. Hersh followed up and broke the story, which eventually brought him a Pulitzer Prize and other awards for his investigative reporting. The cover-up collapsed, leaving only the question of the army's resolve to seek justice in the case: Against whom would it proceed, with how much speed and vigor, and with what end in mind?

William Calley was not the only man tried for the events at My Lai. The actions of over thirty soldiers and civilians were scrutinized by investigators; over half of these had to face charges or disciplinary action of some sort. Targets of investigation included Captain Medina, who was tried, and various higher-ups, including General Koster. But Lieutenant Calley was the only person convicted, the only person to serve time.

* * *

SANCTIONED MASSACRES

The slaughter at My Lai is an instance of a class of violent acts that can be described as sanctioned massacres (Kelman, 1973): acts of indiscriminate, ruthless, and often systematic mass violence, carried out by military or paramilitary personnel while engaged in officially sanctioned campaigns, the victims of which are defenseless and unresisting civilians, including old men, women, and children. Sanctioned massacres have occurred throughout history. Within American history, My Lai had its precursors in the Philippine war around the turn of the century (Schirmer, 1971) and in the massacres of American Indians. Elsewhere in the world, one recalls the Nazis' "final solution" for European Jews, the massacres and deportations of Armenians by Turks, the liquidation of the kulaks and the great purges in the Soviet Union, and more recently the massacres in Indonesia and Bangladesh, in Biafra and Burundi, in South Africa and Mozambique, in Cambodia and Afghanistan, in Syria and Lebanon. Sanctioned massacres may vary on a number of dimensions. For present purposes, however, we want to focus on features they share. Two of these are the *context* and the *target* of the violence.

Sanctioned massacres tend to occur in the context of an overall policy that is explicitly or implicitly genocidal: designed to destroy all or part of a category of people defined in ethnic, national, racial, religious, or other terms. Such a policy may be deliberately aimed at the systematic extermination of a population group as an end in itself, as was the case with the Holocaust during World War II. In the Nazis' "final solution" for European Jewry, a policy aimed at exterminating millions of people was consciously articulated and executed (see Levinson, 1973), and the extermination was accomplished on a mass-production basis through the literal establishment of a well-organized, efficient death industry. Alternatively, such a policy may be aimed at an objective other than extermination—such as the pacification of the rural population of South Vietnam, as was the case in U.S. policy for Indochina—but may include the deliberate decimation of large segments of a population as an acceptable means to that end.

We agree with Bedau's (1974) conclusion from his carefully reasoned argument that the charge of U.S. genocide in Vietnam has not been definitively proven, since such a charge requires evidence of a specific genocidal *intent*. Although the evidence suggests that the United States committed war crimes and crimes against humanity in Indochina (see Sheehan, 1971; Browning and Forman, 1972), it does not show that extermination was the conscious purpose of U.S. policy. The evidence reviewed by Bedau, however, suggests that the United States did commit genocidal acts in Vietnam as a means to other ends. Central to U.S. strategy in South Vietnam were such actions as unrestricted air and artillery bombardments of peasant hamlets, search-and-destroy missions by ground troops, crop destruction programs, and mass deportation of rural populations. These actions (and similar ones in Laos and Cambodia) were clearly and deliberately aimed at civilians and resulted in the death, injury, and/or uprooting of large numbers of that population and in the destruction of their countryside, their source of livelihood, and their social structure. These consequences were anticipated by policymakers and indeed were intended as part of their pacification effort; the actions were designed to clear the countryside and deprive guerrillas of their base of operations, even if this meant destroying the civilian population. Massacres of the kind that occurred at My Lai were not deliberately planned, but they took place in an atmosphere in which the rural Vietnamese population was viewed as expendable and actions that resulted in the killing of large numbers of that population as strategic necessities.

A second feature of sanctioned massacres is that their targets have not themselves threatened or engaged in hostile actions toward the perpetrators of the violence. The victims of this class of violence are often defenseless civilians, including old men, women, and children. By all accounts, at least after the first moments at My Lai, the victims there fit this description, although in guerrilla warfare there always remains some ambiguity about the distinction between armed soldiers and unarmed civilians. * * *

There are, of course, historical and situational reasons particular groups become victims of sanctioned massacres, but these do not include their own immediate harmfulness or violence toward the attackers. Rather, their selection as targets for massacre at a particular time can ultimately be traced to their relationship to the pursuit of larger policies. Their elimination may be seen as a useful tool[3] of their continued existence as an irritating obstacle in the execution of policy.

* * *

In searching for a psychological explanation for mass violence under these conditions, one's first inclination is to look for forces that might impel people toward such murderous acts. Can we identify, in massacre situations, psychological forces so powerful that they outweigh the moral restraints that would normally inhibit unjustifiable violence?

The most obvious approach—searching for psychological dispositions within those who perpetrate these acts—does not yield a satisfactory explanation of the phenomenon, although it may tell us something about the types of individuals most readily recruited for participation. For example, any explanation involving the attackers' strong sadistic impulses is inadequate. There is no evidence that the majority of those who participate in such killings are sadistically inclined. Indeed, speaking of the participants in the Nazi slaughters, Arendt (1964) points out that they "were not sadists or killers by nature; on the contrary, a systematic effort was made to weed out all those who derived physical pleasure from what they did" (p. 105). To be

---

3. Committing violence against innocents as a tool to achieve political goals is the hallmark of terrorism. (ed.)

sure, some of the commanders and guards of concentration camps could clearly be described as sadists, but what has to be explained is the existence of concentration camps in which these individuals could give play to their sadistic fantasies. These opportunities were provided with the participation of large numbers of individuals to whom the label of sadist could not be applied.

A more sophisticated type of dispositional approach seeks to identify certain characterological themes that are dominant within a given culture. An early example of such an approach is Fromm's (1941) analysis of the appeals of Nazism in terms of the prevalence of sadomasochistic strivings, particularly among the German lower middle class. It would be important to explore whether similar kinds of characterological dispositions can be identified in the very wide range of cultural contexts in which sanctioned massacres have occurred. However general such dispositions turn out to be, it seems most likely that they represent states of readiness to participate in sanctioned massacres when the opportunity arises rather than major motivating forces in their own right. Similarly, high levels of frustration within a population are probably facilitators rather than instigators of sanctioned massacres. * * *

Could participation in sanctioned massacres be traced to an inordinately intense hatred toward those against whom the violence is directed? The evidence does not seem to support such an interpretation. Indications are that many of the active participants in the extermination of European Jews, such as Adolf Eichmann (Arendt, 1964), did not feel any passionate hatred of Jews. There is certainly no reason to believe that those who planned and executed American policy in Vietnam felt a profound hatred of the Vietnamese population, although deeply rooted racist attitudes may conceivably have played a role.

To be sure, hatred and rage *play a part* in sanctioned massacres. Typically there is a long history of profound hatred against the groups targeted for violence—the Jews in Christian Europe, the Chinese in Southeast Asia, the Ibos in northern Nigeria—which helps establish them as suitable victims. Hostility also plays an important part at the point at which the killings are actually perpetrated, even if the official planning and the bureaucratic preparations that ultimately lead up to this point are carried out in a passionless and businesslike atmosphere. For example, Lifton's (1973) descriptions of My Lai, based on eyewitness reports, suggest that the killings were accompanied by generalized rage and by expressions of anger and revenge toward the victims. Hostility toward the target, however, does not seem to be the *instigator* of these violent actions. The expressions of anger in the situation itself can more properly be viewed as outcomes rather than causes of the violence. They serve to provide the perpetrators with an explanation and rationalization for their violent actions and appropriate labels for their emotional state. They also help reinforce, maintain, and intensify the violence, but the anger is not the primary source of the violence. Hostility toward the target, historically rooted or situationally induced, contributes heavily toward the violence, but it does so largely by dehumanizing the victims rather than by motivating violence against them in the first place.

In sum, the occurrence of sanctioned massacres cannot be adequately explained by the existence of psychological forces—whether these be characterological dispositions to engage in murderous violence or profound hostility against the target—so powerful that they must find expression in violent acts unhampered by moral restraints. Instead, the major instigators for this class of violence derive from the policy process. The question that really calls for psychological analysis is why so many people are willing to formulate, participate in, and condone policies that call for the mass killings of defenseless civilians. Thus it is more instructive to look not at the motives for violence but at the conditions under which the usual moral inhibitions against violence become weakened. Three social processes that tend to create such conditions can be identified: authorization, routinization, and dehumanization. Through authorization, the situation becomes so defined that the individual is absolved of the responsibility to make personal moral choices. Through routinization, the action becomes so organized that there is no opportunity for raising moral questions. Through dehumanization, the actors' attitudes toward the target and toward themselves become so structured that it is neither necessary nor possible for them to view the relationship in moral terms.

AUTHORIZATION

Sanctioned massacres by definition occur in the context of an authority situation, a situation in which, at least for many of the participants, the moral principles that generally govern human relationships do not apply. Thus, when acts of violence are explicitly ordered, implicitly encouraged, tacitly approved, or at least permitted by legitimate authorities, people's readiness to commit or condone them is enhanced. That such acts are authorized seems to carry automatic justification for them. Behaviorally, authorization obviates the necessity of making judgments or choices. Not only do normal moral principles become inoperative, but—particularly when the actions are explicitly ordered—a different kind of morality linked to the duty to obey superior orders, tends to take over.

In an authority situation, individuals characteristically feel obligated to obey the orders of the authorities, whether or not these correspond with their personal preferences. They see themselves as having no choice as long as they accept the legitimacy of the orders and of the authorities who give them. Individuals differ considerably in the degree to which—and the conditions under which—they are prepared to challenge the legitimacy of an order on the grounds that the order itself is illegal, or that those giving it have overstepped their authority, or that it stems from a policy that violates fundamental societal values. Regardless of subtle individual differences, however, the basic structure of a situation of legitimate authority requires subordinates to respond in terms of their role obligations rather than their personal preferences; they can openly disobey only by challenging the legitimacy of the authority. Often people obey without question even though the behavior they engage in may entail great personal sacrifice or great harm to others.

An important corollary of the basic structure of the authority situation is that actors often do not see themselves as personally responsible for the consequences of their actions. Again, there are individual differences, depending on actors' capacity and readiness to evaluate the legitimacy of orders received. Insofar as they see themselves as having had no choice in their actions, however, they do not feel personally responsible for them. They were not personal agents, but merely extensions of the authority. Thus, when their actions cause harm to others, they can feel relatively free of guilt. A similar mechanism operates when a person engages in antisocial behavior that was not ordered by the authorities but was tacitly encouraged and approved by them—even if only by making it clear that such behavior will not be punished. In this situation, behavior that was formerly illegitimate is legitimized by the authorities' acquiescence.

In the My Lai massacre, it is likely that the structure of the authority situation contributed to the massive violence in both ways—that is, by conveying the message that acts of violence against Vietnamese villagers were *required,* as well as the message that such acts, even if not ordered, were *permitted* by the authorities in charge. The actions at My Lai represented, at least in some respects, responses to explicit or implicit orders. Lieutenant Calley indicated, by orders and by example, that he wanted large numbers of villagers killed. Whether Calley himself had been ordered by his superiors to "waste" the whole area, as he claimed, remains a matter of controversy. Even if we assume, however, that he was not explicitly ordered to wipe out the village, he had reason to believe that such actions were expected by his superior officers. Indeed, the very nature of the war conveyed this expectation. The principal measure of military success was the "body count"—the number of enemy soldiers killed—and any Vietnamese killed by the U.S. military was commonly defined as a "Viet Cong." Thus, it was not totally bizarre for Calley to believe that what he was doing at My Lai was to increase his body count, as any good officer was expected to do.

Even to the extent that the actions at My Lai occurred spontaneously, without reference to superior orders, those committing them had reason to assume that such actions might be tacitly approved of by the military authorities. Not only had they failed to punish such acts in most cases, but the very strategies and tactics that the authorities consistently devised were based on the proposition that the civilian population of South Vietnam—whether "hostile" or "friendly"—was expendable. Such policies as search-and-destroy missions, the establishment of free-shooting zones, the use of antipersonnel weapons, the bombing of entire villages if they were suspected of harboring guerrillas, the forced migration of masses of the rural population, and the defoliation of vast forest areas helped legitimize acts of massive violence of the kind occurring at My Lai.

Some of the actions at My Lai suggest an orientation to authority based on unquestioning obedience to superior orders, no matter how destructive the actions these orders call for. Such obedience is specifically fostered in the course of military training and reinforced by the structure of the military authority situation. It also reflects, however, an ideological orientation that may be more widespread in the general population. * * *

ROUTINIZATION

Authorization processes create a situation in which people become involved in an action without considering its implications and without really making a decision. Once they have taken the initial step, they are in a new psychological and social situation in which the pressures to continue are powerful. As Lewin (1947) has pointed out, many forces that might originally have kept people out of a situation reverse direction once they have made a commitment (once they have gone through the "gate region") and now serve to keep them in the situation. For example, concern about the criminal nature of an action, which might originally have inhibited a person from becoming involved, may now lead to deeper involvement in efforts to justify the action and to avoid negative consequences.

Despite these forces, however, given the nature of the actions involved in sanctioned massacres, one might still expect moral scruples to intervene; but the likelihood of moral resistance is greatly reduced by transforming the action into routine, mechanical, highly programmed operations. Routinization fulfills two functions. First, it reduces the necessity of making decisions, thus minimizing the occasions in which moral questions may arise. Second, it makes it easier to avoid the implications of the action, since the actor focuses on the details of the job rather than on its meaning. The latter effect is more readily achieved among those who participate in sanctioned massacres from a distance—from their desks or even from the cockpits of their bombers.

Routinization operates both at the level of the individual actor and at the organizational level. Individual job performance is broken down into a series of discrete steps, most of them carried out in automatic, regularized fashion. It becomes easy to forget the nature of the product that emerges from this process. When Lieutenant Calley said of My Lai that it was "no great deal," he probably implied that it was all in a day's work. Organizationally, the task is divided among different offices, each of which has responsibility for a small portion of it. This arrangement diffuses responsibility and limits the amount and scope of decision making that is necessary. There is no expectation that the moral implications will be considered at any of these points, nor is there any opportunity to do so. The organizational processes also help further legitimize the actions of each participant. By proceeding in routine fashion—processing papers, exchanging memos, diligently carrying out their assigned tasks—the different units mutually reinforce each other in the view that what is going on must be perfectly normal, correct, and legitimate. The shared illusion that they are engaged in a legitimate enterprise helps the participants assimilate their activities to other purposes, such as the efficiency of their performance, the productivity of their unit, or the cohesiveness of their group (see Janis, 1972).

Normalization of atrocities is more difficult to the extent that there are constant reminders of the true meaning of the enterprise. Bureaucratic inventiveness in the use of language helps to cover up such meaning. For example, the SS had a set of *Sprachregelungen,* or "language rules," to govern descriptions of their extermination program. As Arendt (1964) points out, the term *language rule* in itself was "a code name; it meant what in ordinary language would be called a lie" (p. 85). The code names for killing and liquidation were "final solution," "evacuation," and "special treatment." The war in Indochina produced its own set of euphemisms, such as "protective reaction," "pacification," and "forced-draft urbanization and modernization." The use of euphemisms allows participants in sanctioned massacres to differentiate their actions from ordinary killing and destruction and thus to avoid confronting their true meaning.

DEHUMANIZATION

Authorization processes override standard moral considerations; routinization processes reduce the likelihood that such considerations will arise. Still, the inhibitions against murdering one's fellow human beings are generally so strong that the victims must also be stripped of their human status if they are to be subjected to systematic killing. Insofar as they are dehumanized, the usual principles of morality no longer apply to them.

Sanctioned massacres become possible to the extent that the victims are deprived in the perpetrators' eyes of the two qualities essential to being perceived as fully human and included in the moral compact that governs human relationships: *identity*—standing as independent, distinctive individuals, capable of making choices and entitled to live their own lives—and *community*—fellow membership in an interconnected network of individuals who care for each other and respect each other's individuality and rights (Kelman, 1973; see also Bakan, 1966, for a related distinction between "agency" and "communion"). Thus, when a group of people is defined entirely in terms of a category to which they belong, and when this category is excluded from the human family, moral restraints against killing them are more readily overcome.

Dehumanization of the enemy is a common phenomenon in any war situation. Sanctioned massacres, however, presuppose a more extreme degree of dehumanization, insofar as the killing is not in direct response to the target's threats or provocations. It is not what they have done that marks such victims for death but who they are—the category to which they happen to belong. They are the victims of policies that regard their systematic destruction as a desirable end or an acceptable means. Such extreme dehumanization becomes possible when the target group can readily be identified as a separate category of people who have historically been stigmatized and excluded by the victimizers; often the victims belong to a distinct racial, religious, ethnic, or political group regarded as inferior or sinister. The traditions, the habits, the images, and the vocabularies for dehumanizing such groups are already well established and can be drawn upon when the groups are selected for massacre. Labels help deprive the victims of identity and community, as in the epithet "gooks" that was commonly used to refer to Vietnamese and other Indochinese peoples.

The dynamics of the massacre process itself further increase the participants' tendency to dehumanize their victims. Those who participate as part of the bureaucratic apparatus increasingly come to see their victims as bodies to be counted and entered into their reports, as faceless figures that will determine their productivity rates and promotions. Those who participate in the massacre directly—in the field, as it were—are reinforced in their perception of the victims as less than human by observing their very victimization. The only way they can justify what is being done to these people—both by others and by themselves—and the only way they can extract some degree of meaning out of the absurd events in which they find themselves participating (see Lifton, 1971, 1973) is by coming to believe that the victims are subhuman and deserve to be rooted out. And thus the process of dehumanization feeds on itself.

* * *

REFERENCES

Arendt, H. (1964). *Eichmann in Jerusalem: A report on the banality of evil.* New York: Viking Press.

Bakan, D. (1966). *The duality of human existence.* Chicago: Rand McNally.

Browning, F., & Forman, D. (Eds.). (1972). *The wasted nations: Report of the International Commission of Enquiry into United States Crimes in Indochina, June 20–25, 1971.* New York: Harper & Row.

FitzGerald, F. (1972). *Fire in the lake: The Vietnamese and the Americans in Vietnam.* Boston: Atlantic–Little, Brown.

Fromm, E. (1941). *Escape from freedom.* New York: Rinehart.

Goldstein, J.; Marshall, B.; & Schwartz, J. (Eds.). (1976). *The My Lai massacre and its cover-up: Beyond the reach of law?* (The Peers report with a supplement and introductory essay on the limits of law.) New York: Free Press.

Hammer, R. (1970). *One morning in the war.* New York: Coward-McCann.

———. (1971). *The court-martial of Lt. Calley.* New York: Coward, McCann, & Geoghegan.

Hersh, S. (1970). *My Lai 4: A report on the massacre and its aftermath.* New York: Vintage Books.

Janis, I. L. (1972). *Victims of groupthink: A psychological study of foreign-policy decisions and fiascoes.* Boston: Houghton Mifflin.

Kelman, H. C. (1958). Compliance, identification, and internalization: Three processes of attitude change. *Journal of Conflict Resolution, 2,* 51–60.

———. (1972). The rights of the subject in social research: An analysis in terms of relative power and legitimacy. *American Psychologist, 27,* 989–1016.

———. (1973). Violence without moral restraint: Reflections on the dehumanization of victims and victimizers. *Journal of Social Issues, 29*(4), 25–61.

Levinson, S. (1973). Responsibility for crimes of war. *Philosophy and Public Affairs, 2,* 244–273.

Lifton, R. J. (1971). Existential evil. In N. Sanford, C. Comstock, & Associates, *Sanctions for evil: Sources of social destructiveness.* San Francisco: Jossey-Bass.

———. (1973). *Home from the war—Vietnam veterans: Neither victims nor executioners.* New York: Simon & Schuster.

Paige, J. (1975). *Agrarian revolution: Social movements and export agriculture in the underdeveloped world.* New York: Free Press.

Popkin, S. L. (1979). *The rational peasant: The political economy of rural society in Vietnam.* Berkeley: University of California Press.

Schell, J. (1968). *The military half.* New York: Vintage Books.

Schirmer, D. B. (1971, April 24). My Lai was not the first time. *New Republic,* pp. 18–21.

Sheehan, N. (1971, March 28). Should we have war crime trials? *The New York Times Book Review,* pp. 1–3, 30–34.

Williams, B. (1985, April 14–15). "I will never forgive," says My Lai survivor. *Jordan Times* (Amman), p. 4.

Wolf, E. (1969). *Peasant wars of the twentieth century.* New York: Harper & Row.

6

Telling the Truth about Damned Lies and Statistics

JOEL BEST

Many people feel they live in a world of information overload. Statistics are a big part of this feeling, continually thrown about to impress, sell, or convince. In many cases the statistics are not accurate, leading to distrust of all statistics. But as Joel Best explains, we need good statistics, and he shows why. Part of the "sociological imagination" is the capacity to think critically about information, including statistics, in order to answer questions and solve problems. As you read this essay, think of the last time you heard someone misuse a statistic. Better yet, think of the last time you did.

The dissertation prospectus began by quoting a statistic—a "grabber" meant to capture the reader's attention. The graduate student who wrote this prospectus undoubtedly wanted to seem scholarly to the professors who would read it; they would be supervising the proposed research. And what could be more scholarly than a nice, authoritative statistic, quoted from a professional journal in the student's field?

So the prospectus began with this (carefully footnoted) quotation: "Every year since 1950, the number of American children gunned down has doubled." I had been invited to serve on the student's dissertation committee. When I read the quotation, I assumed the student had made an error in copying it. I went to the library and looked up the article the student had cited. There, in the journal's 1995 volume, was exactly the same sentence: "Every year since 1950, the number of American children gunned down has doubled."

This quotation is my nomination for a dubious distinction: I think it may be the worst—that is, the most inaccurate—social statistic ever.

What makes this statistic so bad? Just for the sake of argument, let's assume that "the number of American children gunned down" in 1950 was one. If the number doubled each year, there must have been two children gunned down in 1951, four in 1952, eight in 1953, and so on. By 1960, the number would have been 1,024. By 1965, it would have been 32,768 (in 1965, the F.B.I. identified only 9,960 criminal homicides in the entire country, including adult as well as child victims). By 1970, the number would have passed one million; by 1980, one billion (more than four times the total U.S. population in that year). Only three years later, in 1983, the number of American children gunned down would have been 8.6 billion (nearly twice the earth's population at the time).

Another milestone would have been passed in 1987, when the number of gunned-down American children (137 billion) would have surpassed the best estimates for the total human population throughout history (110 billion). By 1995, when the article was published, the annual number of victims would have been over 35 trillion—a really big number, of a magnitude you rarely encounter outside economics or astronomy.

Thus my nomination: estimating the number of American child gunshot victims in 1995 at 35 trillion must be as far off—as hilariously, wildly wrong—as a social statistic can be. (If anyone spots a more inaccurate social statistic, I'd love to hear about it.)

Where did the article's author get this statistic? I wrote the author, who responded that the statistic came from the Children's Defense Fund, a well-known advocacy group for children. The C.D.F.'s *The State of America's Children Yearbook 1994* does state: "The number of American children killed each year by guns has doubled since 1950." Note the difference in the wording—the C.D.F. claimed there were twice as many deaths in 1994 as in 1950; the article's author reworded that claim and created a very different meaning.

It is worth examining the history of this statistic. It began with the C.D.F. noting that child gunshot deaths had doubled from 1950 to 1994. This is not quite as dramatic an increase as it might seem. Remember that the U.S. population also rose throughout this period; in fact, it grew about 73 percent—or nearly double. Therefore, we might expect all sorts of things—including the number of child gunshot deaths—to increase, to nearly double, just because the population grew. Before we can decide whether twice as many deaths indicates that things are getting worse, we'd have to know more. The C.D.F. statistic raises other issues as well: Where did the statistic come from? Who counts child gunshot deaths, and how? What is meant by a "child" (some C.D.F. statistics about violence include everyone under age 25)? What is meant by "killed by guns" (gunshot-death statistics often include suicides and accidents, as well as homicides)? But people rarely ask questions of this sort when they encounter statistics. Most of the time, most people simply accept statistics without question.

Certainly, the article's author didn't ask many probing, critical questions about the C.D.F.'s claim. Impressed by the statistic, the author repeated it—well, meant to repeat it. Instead, by rewording the C.D.F.'s claim, the author created a mutant statistic, one garbled almost beyond recognition.

But people treat mutant statistics just as they do other statistics—that is, they usually accept even the most implausible claims without question. For example, the journal editor who accepted the author's article for publication did not bother to consider the implications of child victims doubling each year. And people repeat bad statistics: The graduate student copied the garbled statistic and inserted it into the dissertation prospectus. Who knows whether still other readers were impressed by the author's statistic and remembered it or repeated it? The article remains on the shelf in hundreds of libraries, available to anyone who needs a dramatic quote. The lesson should be clear: Bad statistics live on; they take on lives of their own.

Some statistics are born bad—they aren't much good from the start, because they are based on nothing more than guesses or dubious data. Other statistics mutate; they become bad after being mangled (as in the case of the author's creative rewording). Either way, bad statistics are potentially important: They can be used to stir up public outrage or fear; they can distort our understanding of our world; and they can lead us to make poor policy choices.

The notion that we need to watch out for bad statistics isn't new. We've all heard people say, "You can prove anything with statistics." The title of my book, *Damned Lies and Statistics,* comes from a famous aphorism (usually attributed to Mark Twain or Benjamin Disraeli): "There are three kinds of lies: lies, damned lies, and statistics." There is even a useful little book, still in print after more than 40 years, called *How to Lie With Statistics.*

Statistics, then, have a bad reputation. We suspect that statistics may be wrong, that people who use statistics may be "lying"—trying to manipulate us by using numbers to somehow distort the truth. Yet, at the same time, we need statistics; we depend upon them to summarize and clarify the nature of our complex society. This is particularly true when we talk about social problems. Debates about social problems routinely raise questions that demand statistical answers: Is the problem widespread? How many people—and which people—does it affect? Is it getting worse? What does it cost society? What will it cost to deal with it? Convincing answers to such questions demand evidence, and that usually means numbers, measurements, statistics.

But can't you prove anything with statistics? It depends on what "prove" means. If we want to know, say, how many children are "gunned down" each year, we can't simply guess—pluck a number from thin air: 100, 1,000, 10,000, 35 trillion, whatever. Obviously, there's no reason to consider an arbitrary guess "proof" of anything. However, it might be possible for someone—using records kept by police departments or hospital emergency rooms or coroners—to keep track of children who have been shot; compiling careful, complete records might give us a fairly accurate idea of the number of gunned-down children. If that number seems accurate enough, we might consider it very strong evidence—or proof.

The solution to the problem of bad statistics is not to ignore all statistics, or to assume that every number is false. Some statistics are bad, but others are pretty good, and we need statistics—good statistics—to talk sensibly about social problems. The solution, then, is not to give up on statistics, but to become better judges of the numbers we encounter. We need to think critically about statistics—at least critically enough to suspect that the number of children gunned down hasn't been doubling each year since 1950.

A few years ago, the mathematician John Allen Paulos wrote *Innumeracy,* a short, readable book about "mathematical illiteracy." Too few people, he argued, are comfortable with basic mathematical principles, and this makes them poor judges of the numbers they encounter. No doubt this is one reason we have so many bad statistics. But there are other reasons, as well.

Social statistics describe society, but they are also products of our social arrangements. The people who bring social statistics to our attention have reasons for doing so; they inevitably want something, just as reporters and the other media figures who repeat and publicize statistics have their own goals. Statistics are tools, used for particular purposes. Thinking critically about statistics requires understanding their place in society.

While we may be more suspicious of statistics presented by people with whom we disagree—people who favor different political parties or have different beliefs—bad statistics are used to promote all sorts of causes. Bad statistics come from conservatives on the political right and liberals on the left, from wealthy corporations and powerful government agencies, and from advocates of the poor and the powerless.

In order to interpret statistics, we need more than a checklist of common errors. We need a general approach, an orientation, a mind-set that we can use to think about new statistics that we encounter. We ought to approach statistics thoughtfully. This can be hard to do, precisely because so many people in our society treat statistics as fetishes. We might call this the mind-set of the Awestruck—the people who don't think critically, who act as though statistics have magical powers. The awestruck know they don't always understand the statistics they hear, but this doesn't bother them. After all, who can expect to understand magical numbers? The reverential fatalism of the awestruck is not thoughtful—it is a way of avoiding thought. We need a different approach.

One choice is to approach statistics critically. Being critical does not mean being negative or hostile—it is not cynicism. The critical approach statistics thoughtfully; they avoid the extremes of both naive acceptance and cynical rejection of the numbers they encounter. Instead, the critical attempt to evaluate numbers, to distinguish between good statistics and bad statistics.

The critical understand that, while some social statistics may be pretty good, they are never perfect. Every statistic is a way of summarizing complex information into relatively simple numbers. Inevitably, some information, some of the complexity, is lost whenever we use statistics. The critical recognize that this is an inevitable limitation of statistics. Moreover, they realize that every statistic is the product of choices—the choice between defining a category broadly or narrowly, the choice of one measurement over another, the choice of a sample. People choose definitions, measurements, and samples for all sorts of reasons: Perhaps they want to emphasize some aspect of a problem; perhaps it is easier or cheaper to gather data in a particular way—many considerations can come into play. Every statistic is a compromise among choices. This means that every definition—and every measurement and every sample—probably has limitations and can be criticized.

Being critical means more than simply pointing to the flaws in a statistic. Again, every statistic has flaws. The issue is whether a particular statistic's flaws are severe enough to damage its usefulness. * * * Similarly, how do the choices of measurements and samples affect the statistic? What would happen if different measures or samples were chosen? And how is the statistic used? Is it being interpreted appropriately, or has its meaning been mangled to create a mutant statistic? Are the comparisons that are being made appropriate, or are apples being confused with oranges? How do different choices produce the conflicting numbers found in stat wars? These are the sorts of questions the critical ask.

As a practical matter, it is virtually impossible for citizens in contemporary society to avoid statistics about social problems. Statistics arise in all sorts of ways, and in almost every case the people promoting statistics want to persuade us. Activists use statistics to convince us that social problems are serious and deserve our attention and concern. Charities use statistics to encourage donations. Politicians use statistics to persuade us that they understand society's problems and that they deserve our support. The media use statistics to make their reporting more dramatic, more convincing, more compelling. Corporations use statistics to promote and improve their products. Researchers use statistics to document their findings and support their conclusions. Those with whom we agree use statistics to reassure us that we're on the right side, while our opponents use statistics to try and convince us that we are wrong. Statistics are one of the standard types of evidence used by people in our society.

It is not possible simply to ignore statistics, to pretend they don't exist. That sort of head-in-the-sand approach would be too costly. Without statistics, we limit our ability to think thoughtfully about our society; without statistics, we have no accurate ways of judging how big a problem may be, whether it is getting worse, or how well the policies designed to address that problem actually work. And awestruck or naive attitudes toward statistics are no better than ignoring statistics; statistics have no magical properties, and it is foolish to assume that all statistics are equally valid. Nor is a cynical approach the answer; statistics are too widespread and too useful to be automatically discounted.

It would be nice to have a checklist, a set of items we could consider in evaluating any statistic. The list might detail potential problems with definitions, measurements, sampling, mutation, and so on. These are, in fact, common sorts of flaws found in many statistics, but they should not be considered a formal, complete checklist. It is probably impossible to produce a complete list of statistical flaws—no matter how long the list, there will be other possible problems that could affect statistics.

The goal is not to memorize a list, but to develop thoughtful approach. Becoming critical about statistics requires being prepared to ask questions about numbers. When encountering a new statistic in, say, a news report, the critical try to assess it. What might be the sources for this number? How could one go about producing the figure? Who produced the number, and what interests might they have? What are the different ways key terms might have been defined, and which definitions have been chosen? How might the phenomena be measured, and which measurement choices have been made? What sort of sample was gathered, and how might that sample affect the result? Is the statistic being properly interpreted? Are comparisons being made, and if so, are the comparisons appropriate? Are there competing statistics? If so, what stakes do the opponents have in the issue, and how are those stakes likely to affect their use of statistics? And is it possible to figure out why the statistics seem to disagree, what the differences are in the ways the competing sides are using figures?

At first, this list of questions may seem overwhelming. How can an ordinary person—someone who reads a statistic in a magazine article or hears it on a news broadcast—determine the answers to such questions? Certainly news reports rarely give detailed information on the processes by which statistics are created. And few of us have time to drop everything and investigate the background of some new number we encounter. Being critical, it seems, involves an impossible amount of work.

In practice, however, the critical need not investigate the origin of every statistic. Rather, being critical means appreciating the inevitable limitations that affect all statistics, rather than being awestruck in the presence of numbers. It means not being too credulous, not accepting every statistic at face value. But it also means appreciating that statistics, while always imperfect, can be useful. Instead of automatically discounting every statistic, the critical reserve judgment. When confronted with an interesting number, they may try to learn more, to evaluate, to weigh the figure's strengths and weaknesses.

Of course, this critical approach need not—and should not—be limited to statistics. It ought to apply to all the evidence we encounter when we scan a news report, or listen to a speech—whenever we learn about social problems. Claims about social problems often feature dramatic, compelling examples; the critical might ask whether an example is likely to be a typical case or an extreme, exceptional instance. Claims about social problems often include quotations from different sources, and the critical might wonder why those sources have spoken and why they have been quoted: Do they have particular expertise? Do they stand to benefit if they influence others? Claims about social problems usually involve arguments about the problem's causes and potential solutions. The critical might ask whether these arguments are convincing. Are they logical? Does the proposed solution seem feasible and appropriate? And so on. Being critical—adopting a skeptical, analytical stance when confronted with claims—is an approach that goes far beyond simply dealing with statistics.

Statistics are not magical. Nor are they always true—or always false. Nor need they be incomprehensible. Adopting a critical approach offers an effective way of responding to the numbers we are sure to encounter. Being critical requires more thought, but failing to adopt a critical mindset makes us powerless to evaluate what others tell us. When we fail to think critically, the statistics we hear might just as well be magical.

7

Racism and Research:
The Case of the Tuskegee Syphilis Study

ALLAN M. BRANDT

Was it scientific zeal and the search for medical knowledge? Or was it a callous disregard for the lives and suffering of persons thought to be inferior in a racist society? Probably both, and the lessons remain important for everyone. This tragic study has become a classic example of how to do unethical research. Perhaps the lessons to be learned from it can somehow begin to make amends for the harm it did.

In 1932 the U.S. Public Health Service (USPHS) initiated an experiment in Macon County, Alabama, to determine the natural course of untreated, latent syphilis in black males. The test comprised 400 syphilitic men, as well as 200 uninfected men who served as controls. The first published report of the study appeared in 1936 with subsequent papers issued every four to six years, through the 1960s. When penicillin became widely available by the early 1950s as the preferred treatment for syphilis, the men did not receive therapy. In fact on several occasions, the USPHS actually sought to prevent treatment. Moreover, a committee at the federally operated Center for Disease Control decided in 1969 that the study should be continued. Only in 1972, when accounts of the study first appeared in the national press, did the Department of Health, Education, and Welfare halt the experiment. At that time seventy-four of the test subjects were still alive; at least twenty-eight, but perhaps more than 100 had died directly from advanced syphilitic lesions. In August 1972, HEW appointed an investigatory panel which issued a report the following year. The panel found the study to have been "ethically unjustified," and argued that penicillin should have been provided to the men.

This article attempts to place the Tuskegee Study in a historical context and to assess its ethical implications. Despite the media attention which the study received, the HEW *Final Report,* and the criticism expressed by several professional organizations, the experiment has been largely misunderstood. The most basic questions of *how* the study was undertaken in the first place and *why* it continued for forty years were never addressed by the HEW investigation. Moreover, the panel misconstrued the nature of the experiment, failing to consult important documents available at the National Archives which bear significantly on its ethical assessment. Only by examining the specific ways in which values are engaged in scientific research can the study be understood.

RACISM AND MEDICAL OPINION

A brief review of the prevailing scientific thought regarding race and heredity in the early twentieth century is fundamental for an understanding of the Tuskegee Study. By the turn of the century, Darwinism had provided a new rationale for American racism. Essentially primitive peoples, it was argued, could not be assimilated into a complex, white civilization. Scientists speculated that in the struggle for survival the Negro in America was doomed. Particularly prone to disease, vice, and crime, black Americans could not be helped by education or philanthropy. Social Darwinists analyzed census data to predict the virtual extinction of the Negro in the twentieth century, for they believed the Negro race in America was in the throes of a degenerative evolutionary process.

The medical profession supported these findings of late nineteenth- and early twentieth-century anthropologists, ethnologists, and biologists. Physicians studying the effects of emancipation on health concluded almost universally that freedom had caused the mental, moral, and physical deterioration of the black population. They substantiated this argument by citing examples in the comparative anatomy of the black and white races. As Dr. W. T. English wrote: "A careful inspection reveals the body of the negro a mass of minor defects and imperfections from the crown of the head to the soles of the feet. . . ." Cranial structures, wide nasal apertures, receding chins, projecting jaws, all typed the Negro as the lowest species in the Darwinian hierarchy.

Interest in racial differences centered on the sexual nature of blacks. The Negro, doctors explained, possessed an excessive sexual desire, which threatened the very foundations of white society. As one physician noted in the *Journal of the American Medical Association,* "The negro springs from a southern race, and as such his sexual appetite is strong; all of his environments stimulate this appetite, and as a general rule his emotional type of religion certainly does not decrease it." Doctors reported a complete lack of morality on the part of blacks:

> Virtue in the negro race is like angels' visits—few and far between. In a practice of sixteen years I have never examined a virgin negro over fourteen years of age.

A particularly ominous feature of this overzealous sexuality, doctors argued, was the black males' desire for white women. "A perversion from which most races are exempt," wrote Dr. English, "prompts the negro's inclination towards white women, whereas other races incline towards females of their own." Though English estimated the "gray matter of the negro brain" to be at least a thousand years behind that of the white races, his genital organs were overdeveloped. As Dr. William Lee Howard noted:

> The attacks on defenseless white women are evidences of racial instincts that are about as amenable to ethical culture as is the inherent odor of the race. . . .

When education will reduce the size of the negro's penis as well as bring about the sensitiveness of the terminal fibers which exist in the Caucasian, then will it also be able to prevent the African's birth-right to sexual madness and excess.

One southern medical journal proposed "Castration Instead of Lynching," as retribution for black sexual crimes. "An impressive trial by a ghost-like kuklux klan [sic] and a 'ghost' physician or surgeon to perform the operation would make it an event the 'patient' would never forget," noted the editorial.

According to these physicians, lust and immorality, unstable families, and reversion to barbaric tendencies made blacks especially prone to venereal diseases. One doctor estimated that over 50 percent of all Negroes over the age of twenty-five were syphilitic. Virtually free of disease as slaves, they were now overwhelmed by it, according to informed medical opinion. Moreover, doctors believed that treatment for venereal disease among blacks was impossible, particularly because in its latent stage the symptoms of syphilis become quiescent. As Dr. Thomas W. Murrell wrote:

> They come for treatment at the beginning and at the end. When there are visible manifestations or when harried by pain, they readily come, for as a race they are not averse to physic; but tell them not, though they look well and feel well, that they are still diseased. Here ignorance rates science a fool. . . .

Even the best educated black, according to Murrell, could not be convinced to seek treatment for syphilis. Venereal disease, according to some doctors, threatened the future of the race. The medical profession attributed the low birth rate among blacks to the high prevalence of venereal disease which caused stillbirths and miscarriages. Moreover, the high rates of syphilis were thought to lead to increased insanity and crime. One doctor writing at the turn of the century estimated that the number of insane Negroes had increased thirteen-fold since the end of the Civil War. Dr. Murrell's conclusion echoed the most informed anthropological and ethnological data:

> So the scourge sweeps among them. Those that are treated are only half cured, and the effort to assimilate a complex civilization driving their diseased minds until the results are criminal records. Perhaps here, in conjunction with tuberculosis, will be the end of the negro problem. Disease will accomplish what man cannot do.

This particular configuration of ideas formed the core of medical opinion concerning blacks, sex, and disease in the early twentieth century. Doctors generally discounted socioeconomic explanations of the state of black health, arguing that better medical care could not alter the evolutionary scheme. These assumptions provide the backdrop for examining the Tuskegee Syphilis Study.

THE ORIGINS OF THE EXPERIMENT

In 1929, under a grant from the Julius Rosenwald Fund, the USPHS conducted studies in the rural South to determine the prevalence of syphilis among blacks and explore possibilities for mass treatment. The USPHS found Macon County, Alabama, in which the town of Tuskegee is located to have the highest syphilis rate of the six counties surveyed. The Rosenwald Study concluded that mass treatment could be successfully implemented among rural blacks. Although it is doubtful that the necessary funds would have been allocated even in the best economic conditions, after the economy collapsed in 1929, the findings were ignored. It is, however, ironic that the Tuskegee Study came to be based on findings of the Rosenwald Study that demonstrated the possibilities of mass treatment.

Three years later, in 1932, Dr. Taliaferro Clark, Chief of the USPHS Venereal Disease Division and author of the Rosenwald Study report, decided that conditions in Macon County merited renewed attention. Clark believed the high prevalence of syphilis offered an "unusual opportunity" for observation. From its inception, the USPHS regarded the Tuskegee Study as a classic "study in nature,"[1] rather than an experiment. As long as syphilis was so prevalent in Macon and most of the blacks went untreated throughout life, it seemed only natural to Clark that it would be valuable to observe the consequences. He described it as a "ready-made situation." Surgeon General H. S. Cumming wrote to R. R. Moton, Director of the Tuskegee Institute:

> The recent syphilis control demonstration carried out in Macon County, with the financial assistance of the Julius Rosenwald Fund, revealed the presence of an unusually high rate in this county and, what is more remarkable, the fact that 99 per cent of this group was entirely without previous treatment. This combination, together with the expected cooperation of your hospital, offers an unparalleled opportunity for carrying on this piece of scientific research which probably cannot be duplicated anywhere else in the world.

Although no formal protocol appears to have been written, several letters of Clark and Cumming suggest what the USPHS hoped to find. Clark indicated that it would be important to see how disease affected the daily lives of the men:

> The results of these studies of case records suggest the desirability of making a further study of the effect of untreated syphilis on the human economy among people now living and engaged in their daily pursuits.

---

1. In 1865, Claude Bernard, the famous French physiologist, outlined the distinction between a "study in nature" and experimentation. A study in nature required simple observation, an essentially passive act, while experimentation demanded intervention which altered the original condition. The Tuskegee Study was thus clearly not a study in nature. The very act of diagnosis altered the original conditions. "It is on this very possibility of acting or not acting on a body," wrote Bernard, "that the distinction will exclusively rest between sciences called sciences of observation and sciences called experimental."

It also seems that the USPHS believed the experiment might demonstrate that antisyphilitic treatment was unnecessary. As Cumming noted: "It is expected the results of this study may have a marked bearing on the treatment, or conversely the non-necessity of treatment, of cases of latent syphilis. . . .

SELECTING THE SUBJECTS

Clark sent Dr. Raymond Vonderlehr to Tuskegee in September 1932 to assemble a sample of men with latent syphilis for the experiment. The basic design of the study called for the selection of syphilitic black males between the ages of twenty-five and sixty, a thorough physical examination including x-rays, and finally, a spinal tap to determine the incidence of neuro-syphilis. They had no intention of providing any treatment for the infected men. The USPHS originally scheduled the whole experiment to last six months; it seemed to be both a simple and inexpensive project.

The task of collecting the sample, however, proved to be more difficult than the USPHS had supposed. Vonderlehr canvassed the largely illiterate, poverty-stricken population of sharecroppers and tenant farmers in search of test subjects. If his circulars requested only men over twenty-five to attend his clinics, none would appear, suspecting he was conducting draft physicals. Therefore, he was forced to test large numbers of women and men who did not fit the experiment's specifications. This involved considerable expense since the USPHS had promised the Macon County Board of Health that it would treat those who were infected, but not included in the study. Clark wrote to Vonderlehr about the situation: "It never once occurred to me that we would be called upon to treat a large part of the county as return for the privilege of making this study. . . . I am anxious to keep the expenditures for treatment down to the lowest possible point because it is the one item of expenditure in connection with the study most difficult to defend despite our knowledge of the need therefor." Vonderlehr responded: "If we could find from 100 to 200 cases . . . we would not have to do another Wassermann on useless individuals. . . ."

Significantly, the attempt to develop the sample contradicted the prediction the USPHS had made initially regarding the prevalence of the disease in Macon County. Overall rates of syphilis fell well below expectations; as opposed to the USPHS projection of 35 percent, 20 percent of those tested were actually diseased. Moreover, those who had sought and received previous treatment far exceeded the expectations of the USPHS. Clark noted in a letter to Vonderlehr:

> I find your report of March 6th quite interesting but regret the necessity for Wassermanning [*sic*] . . . such a large number of individuals in order to uncover this relatively limited number of untreated cases.

Further difficulties arose in enlisting the subjects to participate in the experiment, to be "Wassermanned," and to return for a subsequent series of examinations. Vonderlehr found that only the offer of treatment elicited the cooperation of the men. They were told they were ill and were promised free care. Offered therapy, they became willing subjects. The USPHS did not tell the men that they were participants in an experiment; on the contrary, the subjects believed they were being treated for "bad blood"—the rural South's colloquialism for syphilis. They thought they were participating in a public health demonstration similar to the one that had been conducted by the Julius Rosenwald Fund in Tuskegee several years earlier. In the end, the men were so eager for medical care that the number of defaulters in the experiment proved to be insignificant.

To preserve the subjects' interest, Vonderlehr gave most of the men mercurial ointment, a noneffective drug, while some of the younger men apparently received inadequate dosages of neoarsphenamine. This required Vonderlehr to write frequently to Clark requesting supplies. He feared the experiment would fail if the men were not offered treatment.

* * *

The readiness of the test subjects to participate of course contradicted the notion that blacks would not seek or continue therapy.

The final procedure of the experiment was to be a spinal tap to test for evidence of neuro-syphilis. The USPHS presented this purely diagnostic exam, which often entails considerable pain and complications, to the men as a "special treatment." Clark explained to Moore:

> We have not yet commenced the spinal punctures. This operation will be deferred to the last in order not to unduly disturb our field work by any adverse reports by the patients subjected to spinal puncture because of some disagreeable sensations following this procedure. These negroes are very ignorant and easily influenced by things that would be of minor significance in a more intelligent group.

The letter to the subjects announcing the spinal tap read:

> Some time ago you were given a thorough examination and since that time we hope you have gotten a great deal of treatment for bad blood. You will now be given your last chance to get a second examination. This examination is a very special one and after it is finished you will be given a special treatment if it is believed you are in a condition to stand it. . . .
>
> REMEMBER THIS IS YOUR LAST CHANCE FOR SPECIAL FREE TREATMENT. BE SURE TO MEET THE NURSE.

The HEW investigation did not uncover this crucial fact: the men participated in the study under the guise of treatment.

Despite the fact that their assumption regarding prevalence and black attitudes toward treatment had proved wrong, the USPHS decided in the summer of 1933 to continue the study. Once again, it seemed only "natural" to pursue the research since the sample already existed, and with a depressed economy, the cost of treatment appeared prohibitive—although there is no indication it was ever considered. Vonderlehr first suggested extending the study in letters to Clark and Wenger:

> At the end of this project we shall have a considerable number of cases presenting various complications of syphilis, who have received only mercury and may still be considered untreated in the modern sense of therapy. Should these cases be followed over a period of from five to ten years many interesting facts could be learned regarding the course and complications of untreated syphilis.

"As I see it," responded Wenger, "we have no further interest in these patients *until they die.*" Apparently, the physicians engaged in the experiment believed that only autopsies could scientifically confirm the findings of the study.

Bringing the men to autopsy required the USPHS to devise a further series of deceptions and inducements. Wenger warned Vonderlehr that the men must not realize that they would be autopsied:

> There is one danger in the latter plan and that is if the colored population become aware that accepting free hospital care means a post-mortem, every darkey will leave Macon County and it will hurt [Dr. Eugene] Dibble's hospital.

The USPHS offered several inducements to maintain contact and to procure the continued cooperation of the men. Eunice Rivers, a black nurse, was hired to follow their health and to secure approval for autopsies. She gave the men non-effective medicines—"spring tonic" and aspirin—as well as transportation and hot meals on the days of their examinations. More important, Nurse Rivers provided continuity to the project over the entire forty-year period. By supplying "medicinals," the USPHS was able to continue to deceive the participants, who believed that they were receiving therapy from the government doctors. Deceit was integral to the study. When the test subjects complained about spinal taps one doctor wrote:

> They simply do not like spinal punctures. A few of those who were tapped are enthusiastic over the results but to most, the suggestion causes violent shaking of the head; others claim they were robbed of their procreative powers (regardless of the fact that I claim it stimulates them).

Letters to the subjects announcing an impending USPHS visit to Tuskegee explained: "[The doctor] wants to make a special examination to find out how you have been feeling and whether the treatment has improved your health." In fact, after the first six months of the study, the USPHS had furnished no treatment whatsoever.

Finally, because it proved difficult to persuade the men to come to the hospital when they became severely ill, the USPHS promised to cover their burial expenses. The Milbank Memorial Fund provided approximately $50 per man for this purpose beginning in 1935. This was a particularly strong inducement as funeral rites constituted an important component of the cultural life of rural blacks. One report of the study concluded. "Without this suasion it would, we believe, have been impossible to secure the cooperation of the group and their families."

Reports of the study's findings, which appeared regularly in the medical press beginning in 1936, consistently cited the ravages of untreated syphilis. The first paper, read at the 1936 American Medical Association annual meeting, found "that syphilis in this period [latency] tends to greatly increase the frequency of manifestations of cardiovascular disease." Only 16 percent of the subjects gave no sign of morbidity as opposed to 61 percent of the controls. Ten years later, a report noted coldly, "The fact that nearly twice as large a proportion of the syphilitic individuals as of the control group has died is a very striking one." Life expectancy, concluded the doctors, is reduced by about 20 percent.

A 1955 article found that slightly more than 30 percent of the test group autopsied had died *directly* from advanced syphilitic lesions of either the cardiovascular or the central nervous system. Another published account stated, "Review of those still living reveals that an appreciable number have late complications of syphilis which probably will result, for some at least, in contributing materially to the ultimate cause of death." In 1950, Dr. Wenger had concluded, "We now know, where we could only surmise before, that we have contributed to their ailments and shortened their lives." As black physician Vernal Cave, a member of the HEW panel, later wrote, "They proved a point, then proved a point, then proved a point."

During the forty years of the experiment the USPHS had sought on several occasions to ensure that the subjects did not receive treatment from other sources. To this end, Vonderlehr met with groups of local black doctors in 1934, to ask their cooperation in not treating the men. Lists of subjects were distributed to Macon County physicians along with letters requesting them to refer these men back to the USPHS if they sought care. The USPHS warned the Alabama Health Department not to treat the test subjects when they took a mobile VD unit into Tuskegee in the early 1940s. In 1941, the Army drafted several subjects and told them to begin antisyphilitic treatment immediately. The USPHS supplied the draft board with a list of 256 names they desired to have excluded from treatment, and the board complied.

In spite of these efforts, by the early 1950s many of the men had secured some treatment on their own. By 1952, almost 30 percent of the test subjects had received some penicillin, although only 7.5 percent had received what could be considered adequate doses. Vonderlehr wrote to one of the participating physicians, "I hope that the availability of antibiotics has not interfered too much with this project." A report published in 1955 considered whether the treatment that some of the men had obtained had "defeated" the study. The article attempted to explain the relatively low exposure to penicillin in an age of antibiotics, suggesting as a reason: "the stoicism of these men as a group; they still regard hospitals and medicines with suspicion and prefer an occasional dose of time-honored herbs or tonics to modern drugs." The authors failed to note that the men believed they already were under the care of the government doctors and thus saw no need to seek treatment elsewhere. Any treatment which the men might have received, concluded the report, had been insufficient to compromise the experiment.

When the USPHS evaluated the status of the study in the 1960s they continued to rationalize the racial aspects of the experiment. For example, the minutes of a 1965 meeting at the Center for Disease Control recorded:

> Racial issue was mentioned briefly. Will not affect the study. Any questions can be handled by saying these people were at the point that therapy would no longer help them. They are getting better medical care than they would under any other circumstances.

A group of physicians met again at the CDC in 1969 to decide whether or not to terminate the study. Although one doctor argued that the study should be stopped and the men treated, the consensus was to continue. Dr. J. Lawton Smith remarked, "You will never have another study like this; take advantage of it." A memo prepared by Dr. James B. Lucas, Assistant Chief of the Venereal Disease Branch, stated: "Nothing learned will prevent, find, or cure a single case of infectious syphilis or bring us closer to our basic mission of controlling venereal disease in the United States." He concluded, however, that the study should be continued "along its present lines." When the first accounts of the experiment appeared in the national press in July 1972, data were still being collected and autopsies performed.

THE HEW FINAL REPORT

HEW finally formed the Tuskegee Syphilis Study Ad Hoc Advisory Panel on August 28, 1972, in response to criticism that the press descriptions of the experiment had triggered. The panel, composed of nine members, five of them black, concentrated on two issues. First, was the study justified in 1932 and had the men given their informed consent? Second, should penicillin have been provided when it became available in the early 1950s? The panel was also charged with determining if the study should be terminated and assessing current policies regarding experimentation with human subjects. The group issued their report in June 1973.

By focusing on the issues of penicillin therapy and informed consent, the *Final Report* and the investigation betrayed a basic misunderstanding of the experiment's purposes and design. The HEW report implied that the failure to provide penicillin constituted the study's major ethical misjudgment; implicit was the assumption that no adequate therapy existed prior to penicillin. Nonetheless medical authorities firmly believed in the efficacy of arsenotherapy for treating syphilis at the time of the experiment's inception in 1932. The panel further failed to recognize that the entire study had been predicated on nontreatment. Provision of effective medication would have violated the rationale of the experiment—to study the natural course of the disease until death. On several occasions, in fact, the USPHS had prevented the men from receiving proper treatment. Indeed, there is no evidence that the USPHS ever considered providing penicillin.

The other focus of the *Final Report*—informed consent—also served to obscure the historical facts of the experiment. In light of the deceptions and exploitations which the experiment perpetrated, it is an understatement to declare, as the *Report* did, that the experiment was "ethically unjustified," because it failed to obtain informed consent from the subjects. The *Final Report's* statement, "Submitting voluntarily is not informed consent," indicated that the panel believed that the men had volunteered *for the experiment.* The records in the National Archives make clear that the men did not submit voluntarily to an experiment; they were told and they believed that they were getting free treatment from expert government doctors for a serious disease. The failure of the HEW *Final Report* to expose this critical fact—that the USPHS lied to the subjects—calls into question the thoroughness and credibility of their investigation.

Failure to place the study in a historical context also made it impossible for the investigation to deal with the essentially racist nature of the experiment. The panel treated the study as an aberration, well-intentioned but misguided. Moreover, concern that the *Final Report* might be viewed as a critique of human experimentation in general seems to have severely limited the scope of the inquiry. The *Final Report* is quick to remind the reader on two occasions: "The position of the Panel must not be construed to be a general repudiation of scientific research with human subjects." The *Report* assures as that a better designed experiment could have been justified:

> It is possible that a scientific study in 1932 of untreated syphilis, properly conceived with a clear protocol and conducted with suitable subjects who fully understood the implications of their involvement, might have been justified in the pre-penicillin era. This is especially true when one considers the uncertain nature of the results of treatment of late latent syphilis and the highly toxic nature of therapeutic agents then available.

This statement is questionable in view of the proven dangers of untreated syphilis known in 1932.

Since the publication of the HEW *Final Report,* a defense of the Tuskegee Study has emerged. These arguments, most clearly articulated by Dr. R. H. Kampmeier in the *Southern Medical Journal,* center on the limited knowledge of effective therapy for latent syphilis when the experiment began. Kampmeier argues that by 1950, penicillin would have been of no value for these men. Others have suggested that the men were fortunate to have been spared the highly toxic treatments of the earlier period. Moreover, even these contemporary defenses assume that the men never would have been treated anyway. As Dr. Charles Barnett of Stanford University wrote in 1974, "The lack of treatment was not contrived by the USPHS but was an established fact of which they proposed to take advantage." Several doctors who participated in the study continued to justify the experiment. Dr. J. R. Heller, who on one occasion had referred to the test subjects as the "Ethiopian population," told reporters in 1972:

> I don't see why they should be shocked or horrified. There was no racial side to this. It just happened to be in a black community. I feel this was a perfectly straightforward study, perfectly ethical, with controls. Part of our mission as physicians is to find out what happens to individuals with disease and without disease.

These apologies, as well as the HEW *Final Report,* ignore many of the essential ethical issues which the study poses, The Tuskegee Study reveals the persistence of beliefs within the medical profession about the nature of blacks, sex, and disease—beliefs that had tragic repercussions long after their alleged "scientific" bases were known to be incorrect. Most strikingly, the entire health of a community was jeopardized by leaving a communicable disease untreated. There can be little doubt that the Tuskegee researchers regarded their subjects as less than human. As a result, the ethical canons of experimenting on human subjects were completely disregarded.

The study also raises significant questions about professional self-regulation and scientific bureaucracy. Once the USPHS decided to extend the experiment in the summer of 1933, it was unlikely that the test would be halted short of the men's deaths. The experiment was widely reported for forty years without evoking any significant protest within the medical community. Nor did any bureaucratic mechanism exist within the government for the periodic reassessment of the Tuskegee experiment's ethics and scientific value. The USPHS sent physicians to Tuskegee every several years to check on the study's progress, but never subjected the morality or usefulness of the experiment to serious scrutiny. Only the press accounts of 1972 finally punctured the continued rationalizations of the USPHS and brought the study to an end. Even the HEW investigation was compromised by fear that it would be considered a threat to future human experimentation.

In retrospect the Tuskegee Study revealed more about the pathology of racism than it did about the pathology of syphilis; more about the nature of scientific inquiry than the nature of the disease process. The injustice committed by the experiment went well beyond the facts outlined in the press and the HEW *Final Report.* The degree of deception and damages have been seriously underestimated. As this history of the study suggests, the notion that science is a value-free discipline must be rejected. The need for greater vigilance in assessing the specific ways in which social values and attitudes affect professional behavior is clearly indicated.

PART TWO

THE INDIVIDUAL, CULTURE, AND SOCIETY

8

Queer Customs

FROM *Mirror for Man*

CLYDE KLUCKHOLM

Culture provides "a storehouse of the pooled learning" of a group of people, accord-ing to the author. It provides meaning to the physical world and to our thoughts and emotions. Culture is a human construction and thus flexible and diverse. Yet to those who possess a particular culture, it is deadly serious. Culture is like a map—with it you can navigate a society; without it you will be barely human.

Why do the Chinese dislike milk and milk products? Why would the Japanese die willingly in a Banzai charge that seemed senseless to Americans? Why do some nations trace descent through the father, others through the mother, still others through both parents? Not because they were destined by God or Fate to different habits, not because the weather is differ-ent in China and Japan and the United States. Sometimes shrewd common sense has an answer that is close to that of the anthropologist: "because they were brought up that way." By "culture" anthropology means the total life way of a people, the social legacy the individual acquires from his group. Or culture can be regarded as that part of the environment that is the creation of man.

This technical term has a wider meaning than the "culture" of history and lit-erature. A humble cooking pot is as much a cultural product as is a Beethoven sonata. In ordinary speech a man of culture is a man who can speak languages other than his own, who is familiar with history, literature, philosophy, or the fine arts. In some cliques that definition is still narrower. The cultured person is one who can talk about James Joyce, Scarlatti, and Picasso. To the anthro-pologist, however, to be human is to be cultured. There is culture in general, and then there are the specific cultures such as Russian, American, British, Hottentot, Inca. The general abstract notion serves to remind us that we can-not explain acts solely in terms of the biological properties of the people con-cerned, their individual past experience, and the immediate situation. The past experience of other men in the form of culture enters into almost every event. Each specific culture constitutes a kind of blueprint for all of life's activities.

One of the interesting things about human beings is that they try to under-stand themselves and their own behavior. While this has been particularly true of Europeans in recent times, there is no group which has not developed a scheme or schemes to explain man's actions. To the insistent human query "why?" the most exciting illumination anthropology has to offer is that of the concept of culture. Its explanatory importance is comparable to categories such as evolution in biology, gravity in physics, disease in medicine. A good deal of human behavior can be understood, and indeed predicted, if we know a people's design for living. Many acts are neither accidental nor due to personal peculiarities nor caused by supernatural forces nor simply mysterious. Even those of us who pride ourselves on our individualism follow most of the time a pattern not of our own making. We brush our teeth on arising. We put on pants—not a loincloth or a grass skirt. We eat three meals a day—not four or five or two. We sleep in a bed—not in a hammock or on a sheep pelt. I do not have to know the individual and his life history to be able to predict these and countless other regularities, including many in the thinking process, of all Americans who are not incarcerated in jails or hospitals for the insane.

To the American woman a system of plural wives seems "instinctively" abhorrent. She cannot understand how any woman can fail to be jealous and uncomfortable if she must share her husband with other women. She feels it "unnatural" to accept such a situation. On the other hand, a Koryak woman of Siberia, for example, would find it hard to understand how a woman could be so selfish and so undesirous of feminine companionship in the home as to wish to restrict her husband to one mate.

Some years ago I met in New York City a young man who did not speak a word of English and was obviously bewildered by American ways. By "blood" he was an American as you or I, for his parents had gone from Indiana to China as missionaries. Orphaned in infancy, he was reared by a Chinese family in a remote village. All who met him found him more Chinese than American. The facts of his blue eyes and light hair were less impressive than a Chinese style of gait, Chinese arm and hand movements, Chinese facial expression, and Chinese modes of thought. The biological heritage was American, but the cultural training had been Chinese. He returned to China.

Another example of another kind: I once knew a trader's wife in Arizona who took a somewhat devilish interest in producing a cultural reaction. Guests who came her way were often served delicious sandwiches filled with a meat that seemed to be neither chicken nor tuna fish yet was reminiscent of both. To queries she gave no reply until each had eaten his fill. She then explained that what they had eaten was not chicken, not tuna fish, but the rich, white flesh of freshly killed rattlesnakes. The response was instantaneous—vomiting, often violent vomiting. A biological process is caught in a cultural web.

A highly intelligent teacher with long and successful experience in the public schools of Chicago was finishing her first year in an Indian school. When asked how her Navaho pupils compared in intelligence with Chicago youngsters, she replied, "Well, I just don't know. Sometimes the Indians seem just as bright. At other times they just act like dumb animals. The other night we had a dance in the high school. I saw a boy who is one of the best students in my English class standing off by himself. So I took him over to a pretty girl and told them to dance. But they just stood there with their heads down. They wouldn't even say anything." I inquired if she knew whether or not they were members of the same clan. "What difference would that make?"

"How would you feel about getting into bed with your brother?" The teacher walked off in a huff, but, actually, the two cases were quite comparable in principle. To the Indian the type of bodily contact involved in our social dancing has a directly sexual connotation. The incest taboos between members of the same clan are as severe as between true brothers and sisters. The shame of the Indians at the suggestion that a clan brother and sister should dance and the indignation of the white teacher at the idea that she should share a bed with an adult brother represent equally nonrational responses, culturally standardized unreason.

All this does not mean that there is no such thing as raw human nature. The very fact that certain of the same institutions are found in all known societies indicates that at bottom all human beings are very much alike. The files of the Cross-Cultural Survey at Yale University are organized according to categories such as "marriage ceremonies," "life crisis rites," "incest taboos." At least seventy-five of these categories are represented in every single one of the hundreds of cultures analyzed. This is hardly surprising. The members of all human groups have about the same biological equipment. All men undergo the same poignant life experiences such as birth, helplessness, illness, old age, and death. The biological potentialities of the species are the blocks with which cultures are built. Some patterns of every culture crystallize around focuses provided by the inevitables of biology: the difference between the sexes, the presence of persons of different ages, the varying physical strength and skill of individuals. The facts of nature also limit culture forms. No culture provides patterns for jumping over trees or for eating iron ore.

There is thus no "either-or" between nature and that special form of nurture called culture. Culture determinism is as one-sided as biological determinism. The two factors are interdependent. Culture arises out of human nature, and its forms are restricted both by man's biology and by natural laws. It is equally true that culture channels biological processes—vomiting, weeping, fainting, sneezing, the daily habits of food intake and waste elimination. When a man eats, he is reacting to an internal "drive," namely, hunger contractions consequent upon the lowering of blood sugar, but his precise reaction to these internal stimuli cannot be predicted by physiological knowledge alone. Whether a healthy adult feels hungry twice, three times, or four times a day and the hours at which this feeling recurs is a question of culture. *What* he eats is of course limited by availability, but is also partly regulated by culture. It is a biological fact that some types of berries are poisonous; it is a cultural fact that, a few generations ago, most Americans considered tomatoes to be poisonous and refused to eat them. Such selective, discriminative use of the environment is characteristically cultural. In a still more general sense, too, the process of eating is channeled by culture. Whether a man eats to live, lives to eat, or merely eats and lives is only in part an individual matter, for there are also cultural trends. Emotions are physiological events. Certain situations will evoke fear in people from any culture. But sensations of pleasure, anger, and lust may be stimulated by cultural cues that would leave unmoved someone who has been reared in a different social tradition.

Except in the case of newborn babies and of individuals born with clearcut structural or functional abnormalities we can observe innate endowments only as modified by cultural training. In a hospital in New Mexico where Zuñi Indian, Navaho Indian, and white American babies are born, it is possible to classify the newly arrived infants as unusually active, average, and quiet. Some babies from each "racial" group will fall into each category, though a higher proportion of the white babies will fall into the unusually active class. But if a Navaho baby, a Zuñi baby, and a white baby—all classified as unusually active at birth—are again observed at the age of two years, the Zuñi baby will no longer seem given to quick and restless activity—*as compared with the white child*—though he may seem so as compared with the other Zuñis of the same age. The Navaho child is likely to fall in between as contrasted with the Zuñi and the white, though he will probably still seem more active than the average Navaho youngster.

It was remarked by many observers in the Japanese relocation centers that Japanese who were born and brought up in this country, especially those who were reared apart from any large colony of Japanese, resemble in behavior their white neighbors much more closely than they do their own parents who were educated in Japan.

I have said "culture channels biological processes." It is more accurate to say "the biological functioning of individuals is modified if they have been trained in certain ways and not in others." Culture is not a disembodied force. It is created and transmitted by people. However, culture, like well-known concepts of the physical sciences, is a convenient abstraction. One never sees gravity. One sees bodies falling in regular ways. One never sees an electromagnetic field. Yet certain happenings that can be seen may be given a neat abstract formulation by assuming that the electromagnetic field exists. Similarly, one never sees culture as such. What is seen are regularities in the behavior or artifacts of a group that has adhered to a common tradition. The regularities in style and technique of ancient Inca tapestries or stone axes from Melanesian islands are due to the existence of mental blueprints for the group.

Culture is a *way* of thinking, feeling, believing. It is the group's knowledge stored up (in memories of men; in books and objects) for future use. We study the products of this "mental" activity: the overt behavior, the speech and gestures and activities of people, and the tangible results of these things such as tools, houses, cornfields, and what not. It has been customary in lists of "culture traits" to include such things as watches or lawbooks. This is a convenient way of thinking about them, but in the solution of any important problem we must remember that they, in themselves, are nothing but metals, paper, and ink. What is important is that some men know how to make them, others set a value on them, are unhappy without them, direct their activities in relation to them, or disregard them.

It is only a helpful shorthand when we say "The cultural patterns of the Zulu were resistant to Christianization." In the directly observable world of course, it was individual Zulus who resisted. Nevertheless, if we do not forget that we are speaking at a high level of abstraction, it is justifiable to speak of culture as a cause. One may compare the practice of saying "syphilis caused the extinction of the native population of the island." Was it "syphilis" or "syphilis germs" or "human beings who were carriers of syphilis"?

"Culture," then, is "a theory." But if a theory is not contradicted by any relevant fact and if it helps us to understand a mass of otherwise chaotic facts, it is useful. Darwin's contribution was much less the accumulation of new knowledge than the creation of a theory which put in order data already known. An accumulation of facts, however large, is no more a science than a pile of bricks is a house. Anthropology's demonstration that the most weird set of customs has a consistency and an order is comparable to modern psychiatry's showing that there is meaning and purpose in the apparently incoherent talk of the insane. In fact, the inability of the older psychologies and philosophies to account for the strange behavior of madmen and heathens was the principal factor that forced psychiatry and anthropology to develop theories of the unconscious and of culture.

Since culture is an abstraction, it is important not to confuse culture with society. A "society" refers to a group of people who interact more with each other than they do with other individuals—who cooperate with each other for the attainment of certain ends. You can see and indeed count the individuals who make up a society. A "culture" refers to the distinctive ways of life of such a group of people. Not all social events are culturally patterned. New types of circumstances arise frequently.

A culture constitutes a storehouse of the pooled learning of the group. A rabbit starts life with some innate responses. He can learn from his own experience and perhaps from observing other rabbits. A human infant is born with fewer instincts and greater plasticity. His main task is to learn the answers that persons he will never see, persons long dead, have worked out. Once he has learned the formulas supplied by the culture of his group, most of his behavior becomes almost as automatic and unthinking as if it were instinctive. There is a tremendous amount of intelligence behind the making of a radio, but not much is required to learn to turn it on.

The members of all human societies face some of the same unavoidable dilemmas, posed by biology and other facts of the human situation. This is why the basic categories of all cultures are so similar. Human culture without language is unthinkable. No culture fails to provide for aesthetic expression and aesthetic delight. Every culture supplies standardized orientations toward the deeper problems, such as death. Every culture is designed to perpetuate the group and its solidarity, to meet the demands of individuals for an orderly way of life and for satisfaction of biological needs.

However, the variations on these basic themes are numberless. Some languages are built up out of twenty basic sounds, others out of forty. Nose plugs were considered beautiful by the predynastic Egyptians but are not by the modern French. Puberty is a biological fact. But one culture ignores it, another prescribes informal instructions about sex but no ceremony, a third has impressive rites for girls only, a fourth for boys and girls. In this culture, the first menstruation is welcomed as a happy, natural event; in that culture the atmosphere is full of dread and supernatural threat. Each culture dissects nature according to its own system of categories. The Navaho Indians apply the same word to the color of a robin's egg and to that of grass. A psychologist once assumed that this meant a difference in the sense organs, that Navahos didn't have the physiological equipment to distinguish "green" from "blue." However, when he showed them objects of the two colors and asked them if they were exactly the same colors, they looked at him with astonishment. His dream of discovering a new type of color blindness was shattered.

Every culture must deal with the sexual instinct. Some, however, seek to deny all sexual expression before marriage, whereas a Polynesian adolescent who was not promiscuous would be distinctly abnormal. Some cultures enforce lifelong monogamy, others, like our own, tolerate serial monogamy; in still other cultures, two or more women may be joined to one man or several men to a single woman. Homosexuality has been a permitted pattern in the Greco-Roman world, in parts of Islam, and in various primitive tribes. Large portions of the population of Tibet, and of Christendom at some places and periods, have practiced complete celibacy. To us marriage is first and foremost an arrangement between two individuals. In many more societies marriage is merely one facet of a complicated set of reciprocities, economic and otherwise, between two families or two clans.

The essence of the cultural process is selectivity. The selection is only exceptionally conscious and rational. Cultures are like Topsy.* They just grew. Once, however, a way of handling a situation becomes institutionalized, there is ordinarily great resistance to change or deviation. When we speak of "our sacred beliefs," we mean of course that they are beyond criticism and that the person who suggests modification or abandonment must be punished. No person is emotionally indifferent to his culture. Certain cultural premises may become totally out of accord with a new factual situation. Leaders may recognize this and reject the old ways in theory. Yet their emotional loyalty continues in the face of reason because of the intimate conditionings of early childhood.

---

*[Topsy is a young slave girl in Harriet Beecher Stowe's *Uncle Tom's Cabin* who explained to her new mistress, when asked if she know about God and her creator, "I spect I grow'd. Don't think nobody never made me."]

A culture is learned by individuals as the result of belonging to some particular group, and it constitutes that part of learned behavior which is shared with others. It is our social legacy, as contrasted with our organic heredity. It is one of the important factors which permits us to live together in an organized society, giving us ready-made solutions to our problems, helping us to predict the behavior of others, and permitting others to know what to expect of us.

Culture regulates our lives at every turn. From the moment we are born until we die there is, whether we are conscious of it or not, constant pressure upon us to follow certain types of behavior that other men have created for us. Some paths we follow willingly, others we follow because we know no other way, still others we deviate from or go back to most unwillingly. Mothers of small children know how unnaturally most of this comes to us—how little regard we have, until we are "culturalized," for the "proper" place, time, and manner for certain acts such as eating, excreting, sleeping, getting dirty, and making loud noises. But by more or less adhering to a system of related designs for carrying out all the acts of living, a group of men and women feel themselves linked together by a powerful chain of sentiments. Ruth Benedict gave an almost complete definition of the concept when she said, "Culture is that which binds men together."

It is true any culture is a set of techniques for adjusting both to the external environment and to other men. However, cultures create problems as well as solve them. If the lore of a people states that frogs are dangerous creatures, or that it is not safe to go about at night because of witches or ghosts, threats are posed which do not arise out of the inexorable facts of the external world. Cultures produce needs as well as provide a means of fulfilling them. There exists for every group culturally defined, acquired drives that may be more powerful in ordinary daily life than the biologically inborn drives. Many Americans, for example, will work harder for "success" than they will for sexual satisfaction.

Most groups elaborate certain aspects of their culture far beyond maximum utility or survival value. In other words, not all culture promotes physical survival. At times, indeed, it does exactly the opposite. Aspects of culture which once were adaptive may persist long after they have ceased to be useful. An analysis of any culture will disclose many features which cannot possibly be construed as adaptations to the total environment in which the group now finds itself. However, it is altogether likely that these apparently useless features represent survivals, with modifications through time, of cultural forms once useful.

Any cultural practice must be functional or it will disappear before long. That is, it must somehow contribute to the survival of the society or to the adjustment of the individual. However, many cultural functions are not manifest but latent. A cowboy will walk three miles to catch a horse which he then rides one mile to the store. From the point of view of manifest function this is positively irrational. But the act has the latent function of maintaining the cowboy's prestige in the terms of his own subculture. One can instance the buttons on the sleeve of a man's coat, our absurd English spelling, the use of capital letters, and a host of other apparently nonfunctional customs. They serve mainly the latent function of assisting individuals to maintain their security by preserving continuity with the past and by making certain sectors of life familiar and predictable.

Every culture is a precipitate of history. In more than one sense history is a sieve. Each culture embraces those aspects of the past which, usually in altered form and with altered meanings, live on in the present. Discoveries and inventions, both material and ideological, are constantly being made available to a group through its historical contacts with other peoples or being created by its own members. However, only those that fit the total immediate situation in meeting the group's needs for survival or in promoting the psychological adjustment of individuals will become part of the culture. The process of culture building may be regarded as an addition to man's innate biological capacities, an addition providing instruments which enlarge, or may even substitute for, biological functions, and to a degree compensating for biological limitations—as in ensuring that death does not always result in the loss to humanity of what the deceased has learned.

Culture is like a map. Just as a map isn't the territory but an abstract representation of a particular area, so also a culture is an abstract description of trends toward uniformity in the words, deeds, and artifacts of a human group. If a map is accurate and you can read it, you won't get lost; if you know a culture you will know your way around in the life of a society.

9

Growing Up as a Fore Is to Be "In Touch" and Free

E. RICHARD SORENSON

The author greatly admires the way these people of New Guinea traditionally imparted trust, independence, and the knowledge of Fore culture to their children. Sorenson shows how, in time, the extremely open-minded Fore, because they were vulnerable to new cultural influences, experienced a radical change to their society. The transformation of their society raises questions about human nature and cultural influences. Also, with the passing of the Fore way of life, the cultural diversity of the world was diminished. A reduction in the world's cultural diversity may have the same effect on our future needs as the extinction of species of plant and animal.

Untouched by the outside world, they had lived for thousands of years in isolated mountains and valleys deep in the interior of Papua New Guinea. They had no cloth, no metal, no money, no idea that their homeland was an island—or that what surrounded it was salt water. Yet the Fore (*for'-ay*) people had developed remarkable and sophisticated approaches to human relations, and their child-rearing practices gave their young unusual freedom to explore. Successful as hunter-gatherers and as subsistence gardeners, they also had great adaptability, which brought rapid accommodation with the outside world after their lands were opened up.

It was alone that I first visited the Fore in 1963—a day's walk from a recently built airstrip. I stayed six months. Perplexed and fascinated, I returned six times in the next ten years, eventually spending a year and a half living with them in their hamlets.

Theirs was a way of life different from anything I had seen or heard about before. There were no chiefs, patriarchs, priests, medicine men or the like. A striking personal freedom was enjoyed even by the very young, who could move about at will and be where or with whom they liked. Infants rarely cried, and they played confidently with knives, axes and fire. Conflict between old and young did not arise; there was no "generation gap."

Older children enjoyed deferring to the interests and desires of the younger, and sibling rivalry was virtually undetectable. A responsive sixth sense seemed to attune the Fore hamlet mates to each other's interests and needs. They did not have to directly ask, inveigle, bargain or speak out for what they needed or wanted. Subtle, even fleeting expressions of interest, desire and discomfort were quickly read and helpfully acted on by one's associates. This spontaneous urge to share food, affection, work, trust, tools and pleasure was the social cement that held the Fore hamlets together. It was a pleasant way of life, for one could always be with those with whom one got along well.

Ranging and planting, sharing and living, the Fore diverged and expanded through high virgin lands in a pioneer region. They hunted out their gardens, tilled them while they lasted, then hunted again. Moving ever away from lands peopled and used, they had a self-contained life with its own special ways.

The underlying ecological conditions were like those that must have encompassed the world before agriculture set its imprint so broadly. Abutting the Fore was virtually unlimited virgin land, and they had food plants they could introduce into it. Like hunter-gatherers they sought their sources of sustenance first in one locale and then another, across an extended range, following opportunities provided by a providential nature. But like agriculturalists they concentrated their effort and attention more narrowly on selected sites of production, on their gardens. They were both seekers and producers. A pioneer people in a pioneer land, they ranged freely into a vast territory, but they planted to live.

Cooperative groups formed hamlets and gardened together. When the fertility of a garden declined, they abandoned it. Grass sprang up to cover these abandoned sites of earlier cultivation, and, as the Fore moved on to other parts of the forest, they left uninhabited grasslands to mark their passage.

The traditional hamlets were small, with a rather fluid system of social relations. A single large men's house provided shelter for 10 to 20 men and boys and their visiting friends. The several smaller women's houses each normally sheltered two married women, their unmarried daughters and their sons up to about six years of age. Formal kinship bonds were less important than friendship was. Fraternal "gangs" of youths formed the hamlets; their "clubhouses" were the men's houses.

During the day the gardens became the center of life. Hamlets were virtually deserted as friends, relatives and children went to one or more garden plots to mingle their social, economic and erotic pursuits in a pleasant and emotionally filled Gestalt of garden life. The boys and unmarried youths preferred to explore and hunt in the outlying lands, but they also passed through and tarried in the gardens.

Daily activities were not scheduled. No one made demands, and the land was bountiful. Not surprisingly the line between work and play was never clear.

The transmission of the Fore behavioral patterns to the young began in early infancy during a period of unceasing human physical contact. The effect of being constantly "in touch" with hamlet mates and their daily life seemed to start a process which proceeded by degrees: close rapport, involvement in regular activity, ability to handle seemingly dangerous implements safely, and responsible freedom to pursue individual interests at will without danger.

While very young, infants remained in almost continuous bodily contact with their mother, her house mates or her gardening associates. At first, mothers' laps were the center of activity, and infants occupied themselves there by nursing, sleeping and playing with their own bodies or those of their caretakers. They were not put aside for the sake of other activities, as when food was being prepared or heavy loads were being carried. Remaining in close, uninterrupted physical contact with those around them, their basic needs such as rest, nourishment, stimulation and security were continuously satisfied without obstacle.

By being physically in touch from their earliest days, Fore youngsters learned to communicate needs, desires and feelings through a body language of touch and response that developed before speech. This opened the door to a much closer rapport with those around them than otherwise would have been possible, and led ultimately to the Fore brand of social cement and the sixth sense that bound groups together through spontaneous, responsive sharing.

As the infant's awareness increased, his interests broadened to the things his mother and other caretakers did and to the objects and materials they used. Then these youngsters began crawling out to explore things that attracted their attention. By the time they were toddling, their interests continually took them on short sorties to nearby objects and persons. As soon as they could walk well, the excursions extended to the entire hamlet and its gardens, and then beyond with other children. Developing without interference or supervision, this personal exploratory learning quest freely touched on whatever was around, even axes, knives, machetes, fire, and the like. When I first went to the Fore, I was aghast.

Eventually I discovered that this capability emerged naturally from the Fore infant-handling practices in their milieu of close human physical proximity and tactile interaction. Because touch and bodily contact lend themselves naturally to satisfying the basic needs of young children, an early kind of communicative experience fostered cooperative interaction between infants and their caretakers, also kinesthetic contact with the activities at hand. This made it easy for them to learn the appropriate handling of the tools of life.

The early pattern of exploratory activity included frequent return to one of the "mothers." Serving as home base, the bastion of security, a woman might occasionally give the youngster a nod of encouragement, if he glanced in her direction with uncertainty. Yet rarely did the women attempt to control or direct, nor did they participate in the child's quests or jaunts.

As a result Fore children did not have to adjust to rule and schedule in order to find their place in life. They could pursue their interests and whims wherever they might lead and still be part of a richly responsive world of human touch which constantly provided sustenance, comfort, diversion and security.

Learning proceeded during the course of pursuing interests and exploring. Constantly "in touch" with people who were busy with daily activities, the Fore young quickly learned the skills of life from example. Muscle tone, movement and mood were components of this learning process; formal lessons and commands were not. Kinesthetic skills developed so quickly that infants were able to casually handle knives and similar objects before they could walk.

Even after several visits I continued to be surprised that the unsupervised Fore toddlers did not recklessly thrust themselves into unappreciated dangers, the way our own children tend to do. But then, why should they? From their earliest days, they enjoyed a benevolent sanctuary from which the world could be confidently viewed, tested and appreciated. This sanctuary remained ever available, but did not demand, restrain or impose. One could go and come at will.

In close harmony with their source of life, the Fore young were able confidently, not furtively, to extend their inquiry. They could widen their understanding as they chose. There was no need to play tricks or deceive in order to pursue life.

Emerging from this early childhood was a freely ranging young child rather in tune with his older and younger hamlet mates, disinclined to act out impulsively, and with a capable appreciation of the properties of potentially dangerous objects. Such children could be permitted to move out on their own, unsupervised and unrestricted. They were safe.

Such a pattern could persist indefinitely, re-creating itself in each new generation. However, hidden within the receptive character it produced was an Achilles heel: it also permitted adoption of new practices, including child-handling practices, which did *not* act to perpetuate the pattern. In only one generation after Western contact, the cycle of Fore life was broken.

Attuned as they were to individual pursuit of economic and social good, it did not take the Fore long to recognize the value of the new materials, practices and ideas that began to flow in. Indeed, change began almost immediately with efforts to obtain steel axes, salt, medicine and cloth. The Fore were quick to shed indigenous practices in favor of the Western example. They rapidly altered their ways to adapt to Western law, government, religion, materials and trade.

Sometimes change was so rapid that many people seemed to be afflicted by a kind of cultural shock. An anomie, even cultural amnesia, seemed to pervade some hamlets for a time. There were individuals who appeared temporarily to have lost memory of recent past events. Some Fore even forgot what type and style of traditional garments they had worn only a few years earlier, or that they had used stone axes and had eaten their dead close relatives.

Remarkably open-minded, the Fore so readily accepted reformulation of identity and practice that suggestion or example by the new government officers, missionaries and scientists could alter tribal affiliation, place names, conduct and hamlet style. When the first Australian patrol officer began to map the region in 1957, an error in communication led him to refer to these people as the "Fore." Actually they had had no name for themselves and the word, Fore, was their name for a quite different group, the Awa, who spoke another language and lived in another valley. They did not correct the patrol officer but adopted his usage. They all now refer to themselves as the Fore. Regional and even personal names changed just as readily.

More than anything else, it was the completion of a steep, rough, always muddy Jeep road into the Fore lands that undermined the traditional life. Almost overnight their isolated region was opened. Hamlets began to move down from their ridgetop sites in order to be nearer the road, consolidating with others.

The power of the road is hard to overestimate. It was a great artery where only restricted capillaries had existed before. And down this artery came a flood of new goods, new ideas and new people. This new road, often impassable even with four-wheel-drive vehicles, was perhaps the single most dramatic stroke wrought by the government. It was to the Fore an opening to a new world. As they began to use the road, they started to shed traditions evolved in the protective insularity of their mountain fastness, to adopt in their stead an emerging market culture.

THE COMING OF THE COFFEE ECONOMY

"Walkabout," nonexistent as an institution before contact, quickly became an accepted way of life. Fore boys began to roam hundreds of miles from their homeland in the quest for new experience, trade goods, jobs and money. Like the classic practice of the Australian aborigine, this "walkabout" took one away from his home for periods of varying length. But unlike the Australian practice, it usually took the boys to jobs and schools rather than to a solitary life in traditional lands. Obviously it sprang from the earlier pattern of individual freedom to pursue personal interests and opportunity wherever it might lead. It was a new expression of the old Fore exploratory pattern.

Some boys did not roam far, whereas others found ways to go to distant cities. The roaming boys often sought places where they might be welcomed as visitors, workers or students for a while. Mission stations and schools, plantation work camps, and the servants' quarters of the European population became way stations in the lives of the modernizing Fore boys.

Some took jobs on coffee plantations. Impressed by the care and attention lavished on coffee by European planters and by the money they saw paid to coffee growers, these young Fore workers returned home with coffee beans to plant.

Coffee grew well on the Fore hillsides, and in the mid-1960s, when the first sizable crop matured. Fore who previously had felt lucky to earn a few dollars found themselves able to earn a few hundred dollars. A rush to coffee ensued, and when the new gardens became productive a few years later, the

Fore income from coffee jumped to a quarter of a million dollars a year. The coffee revolution was established.

At first the coffee was carried on the backs of its growers (sometimes for several days) over steep, rough mountain trails to a place where it could be sold to a buyer with a Jeep. However, as more and more coffee was produced, the villagers began to turn their efforts to planning and constructing roads in association with neighboring villages. The newly built roads, in turn, stimulated further economic development and the opening of new trade stores throughout the region.

Following European example, the segregated collective men's and women's houses were abandoned. Family houses were adopted. This changed the social and territorial arena for all the young children, who hitherto had been accustomed to living equally with many members of their hamlet. It gave them a narrower place to belong, and it made them more distinctly someone's children. Uncomfortable in the family houses, boys who had grown up in a freer territory began to gather in "boys' houses," away from the adult men who were now beginning to live in family houses with their wives. Mothers began to wear blouses, altering the early freer access to the breast. Episodes of infant and child frustration, not seen in traditional Fore hamlets, began to take place along with repeated incidents of anger, withdrawal, aggressiveness and stinginess.

So Western technology worked its magic on the Fore, its powerful materials and practices quickly shattering their isolated autonomy and life-style. It took only a few years from the time Western intruders built their first grass-thatched patrol station before the Fore way of life they found was gone.

Fortunately, enough of the Fore traditional ways were systematically documented on film to reveal how unique a flower of human creation they were. Like nothing else, film made it possible to see the behavioral patterns of this way of life. The visual record once made, captured data which was unnoticed and unanticipated at the time of filming and which was simply impossible to study without such records. Difficult-to-spot subtle patterns and fleeting nuances of manner, mood and human relations emerged by use of repeated reexamination of related incidents, some times by slow motion and stopped frame. Eventually the characteristic behavioral patterns of Fore life became clear, and an important aspect of human adaptive creation was revealed.

The Fore way of life was only one of the many natural experiments in living that have come into being through thousands of years of independent development in the world. The Fore way is now gone—those which remain are threatened. Under the impact of modern technology and commerce, the entire world is now rapidly becoming one system. By the year 2000 all the independent natural experiments that have come into being during the world's history will be merging into a single world system.

One of the great tragedies of our modern time may be that most of these independent experiments in living are disappearing before we can discover the implications of their special expressions of human possibility. Ironically, the same technology responsible for the worldwide cultural convergence has also provided the means by which we may capture detailed visual records of the yet remaining independent cultures. The question is whether we will be able to seize this never-to-be repeated opportunity. Soon it will be too late. Yet, obviously, increasing our understanding of the behavioral repertoire of humankind would strengthen our ability to improve life in the world.

10

Boyhood, Organized Sports,
and the Construction of Masculinities

MICHAEL A. MESSNER

Though young women are now participating in sports in unprecedented numbers, the influence of sports activity on boys' identity and socialization experience remains a major interest in gender studies. Michael Messner, one of the pioneers and most prominent researchers of this topic, examines the way sports focus and define what it is to be masculine, the variations in sports' influence across social classes, and some unsuspected lessons sports participation imparts for relationships beyond the gym, pool, and fields of play. In reading this article, you might want to ask yourself: What would this article be saying if the subject was young women?

In this study I explore and interpret the meanings that males themselves attribute to their boyhood participation in organized sport. In what ways do males construct masculine identities within the institution of organized sports? In what ways do class and racial differences mediate this relationship and perhaps lead to the construction of different meanings, and perhaps different masculinities? And what are some of the problems and contradictions within these constructions of masculinity?

DESCRIPTION OF RESEARCH

Between 1983 and 1985, I conducted interviews with 30 male former athletes. Most of the men I interviewed had played the (U.S.) "major sports"—football, basketball, baseball, track. At the time of the interview, each had been retired from playing organized sports for at least five years. Their ages ranged from 21 to 48, with the median, 33; 14 were black, 14 were white, and two were Hispanic; 15 of the 16 black and Hispanic men had come from poor or working-class families, while the majority (9 of 14) of the white men had come from middle-class or professional families. All had at some time in their lives based their identities largely on their roles as athletes and could therefore be said to have had "athletic careers." Twelve had played organized sports through high school, 11 through college, and seven had been professional athletes. Though the sample was not randomly selected, an effort was made to see that the sample had a range of difference in terms of race and social class backgrounds, and that there was some variety in terms of age, types of sports played, and levels of success in athletic careers. Without exception, each man contacted agreed to be interviewed.

The tape-recorded interviews were semi-structured and took from one and one-half to six hours, with most taking about three hours. I asked each man to talk about four broad eras in his life: (1) his earliest experiences with sports in boyhood, (2) his athletic career, (3) retirement or disengagement from the athletic career, and (4) life after the athletic career. In each era, I focused the interview on the meanings of "success and failure," and on the boy's/man's relationships with family, with other males, with women, and with his own body.

In collecting what amounted to life histories of these men, my overarching purpose was to use feminist theories of masculine gender identity to explore how masculinity develops and changes as boys and men interact within the socially constructed world of organized sports. In addition to using the data to move toward some generalizations about the relationship between "masculinity and sport," I was also concerned with sorting out some of the variations among boys, based on class and racial inequalities, that led them to relate differently to athletic careers. I divided my sample into two comparison groups. The first group was made up of 10 men from higher-status backgrounds, primarily white, middle-class, and professional families. The second group was made up of 20 men from lower-status backgrounds, primarily minority, poor, and working-class families.

BOYHOOD AND THE PROMISE OF SPORTS

Zane Grey once said, "All boys love baseball. If they don't they're not real boys" (as cited in Kimmel 1990). This is, of course, an ideological statement; in fact, some boys do *not* love baseball, or any other sports, for that matter. There are millions of males who at an early age are rejected by, become alienated from, or lose interest in organized sports. Yet all boys are, to a greater or lesser extent, judged according to their ability, or lack of ability, in competitive sports (Eitzen, 1975; Sabo, 1985). In this study I focus on those males who did become athletes—males who eventually poured thousands of hours into the development of specific physical skills. It is in boyhood that we can discover the roots of their commitment to athletic careers.

How did organized sports come to play such a central role in these boy's lives? When asked to recall how and why they initially got into playing sports, many of the men interviewed for this study seemed a bit puzzled: after all, playing sports was "just the thing to do." A 42-year-old black man who had played college basketball put it this way:

It was just what you did. It's kind of like, you went to school, you played athletics, and if you didn't, there was something wrong with you. It was just like brushing your teeth: it's just what you did. It's part of your existence.

Spending one's time playing sports with other boys seemed as natural as the cycle of the seasons: baseball in the spring and summer, football in the fall, basketball in the winter—and then it was time to get out the old baseball glove and begin again. As a black 35-year-old former professional football star said:

> I'd say when I wasn't in school, 95% of the time was spent in the park playing. It was the only thing to do. It just came as natural.

And a black, 34-year-old professional basketball player explained his early experiences in sports:

> My principal and teacher said, "Now if you work at this you might be pretty damned good." So it was more or less a community thing—everybody in the community said, "Boy, if you work hard and keep your nose clean, you gonna be good." Cause it was natural instinct.

"It was natural instinct." "I was a natural." Several athletes used words such as these to explain their early attraction to sports. But certainly there is nothing "natural" about throwing a ball through a hoop, hitting a ball with a bat, or jumping over hurdles. A boy, for instance, may have amazingly dexterous inborn hand-eye coordination, but this does not predispose him to a career of hitting baseballs any more than it predisposes him to a life as a brain surgeon. When one listens closely to what these men said about their early experiences in sports, it becomes clear that their adoption of the self-definition of "natural athlete" was the result of what Connell (1990) has called "a collective practice" that constructs masculinities. The boyhood development of masculine identity and status—truly problematic in a society that offers no official rite of passage into adulthood— results from a process of interaction with people and social institutions. Thus, in discussing early motivations in sports, men commonly talk of the importance of relationships with family members, peers, and the broader community.

FAMILY INFLUENCES

Though most of the men in this study spoke of their mothers with love, respect, even reverence, their descriptions of their earliest experiences in sports are stories of an exclusively male world. The existence of older brothers or uncles who served as teachers and athletic role models—as well as sources of competition for attention and status within the family—was very common. An older brother, uncle, or even close friend of the family who was a successful athlete appears to have acted as a sort of standard of achievement against whom to measure oneself. A 34-year-old black man who had been a three-sport star in high school said:

> My uncles—my Uncle Harold went to the Detroit Tigers, played pro ball—all of 'em, everybody played sports, so I wanted to be better than anybody else. I knew that everybody in this town knew them—their names were something. I wanted my name to be just like theirs.

Similarly, a black 41-year-old former professional football player recalled:

> I was the younger of three brothers and everybody played sports, so consequently I was more or less forced into it. 'Cause one brother was always better than the next brother and then I came along and had to show them that I was just as good as them. My oldest brother was an all-city ballplayer, then my other brother comes along he's all-city and all-state, and then I have to come along.

For some, attempting to emulate or surpass the athletic accomplishments of older male family members created pressures that were difficult to deal with. A 33-year-old white man explained that he was a good athlete during boyhood, but the constant awareness that his two older brothers had been better made it difficult for him to feel good about himself, or to have fun in sports:

> I had this sort of reputation that I followed from the playgrounds through grade school, and through high school. I followed these guys who were all-conference and all-state.

Most of these men, however, saw their relationships with their athletic older brothers and uncles in a positive light; it was within these relationships that they gained experience and developed motivations that gave them a competitive "edge" within their same-aged peer group. As a 33-year-old black man describes his earliest athletic experiences:

> My brothers were role models. I wanted to prove—especially to my brothers—that I had heart, you know, that I was a man.

When asked, "What did it mean to you to be 'a man' at that age?" he replied:

> Well, it meant that I didn't want to be a so-called scaredy-cat. You want to hit a guy even though he's bigger than you to show that, you know, you've got this macho image. I remember that at that young an age, that feeling was exciting to me. And that carried over, and as I got older, I got better and I began to look around me and see, well hey! I'm competitive with these guys, even though I'm younger, you know? And then of course all the compliments come—and I began

to notice a change, even in my parents—especially in my father—he was proud of that, and that was very important to me. He was extremely important . . . he showed me more affection, now that I think of it.

As this man's words suggest, if men talk of their older brothers and uncles mostly as role models, teachers, and "names" to emulate, their talk of their relationships with their fathers is more deeply layered and complex. Athletic skills and competition for status may often be learned from older brothers, but it is in boys' relationships with fathers that we find many of the keys to the emotional salience of sports in the development of masculine identity.

RELATIONSHIPS WITH FATHERS

The fact that boys' introductions to organized sports are often made by fathers who might otherwise be absent or emotionally distant adds a powerful emotional charge to these early experiences (Osherson 1986). Although playing organized sports eventually came to feel "natural" for all of the men interviewed in this study, many needed to be "exposed" to sports, or even gently "pushed" by their fathers to become involved in activities like Little League baseball. A white, 33-year-old-man explained:

> I still remember it like it was yesterday—Dad and I driving up in his truck, and I had my glove and my hat and all that—and I said, "Dad, I don't want to do it." He says, "What?" I says, "I don't want to do it." I was nervous. That I might fail. And he says, "Don't be silly. Lookit: There's Joey and Petey and all your friends out there." And so Dad says, "You're gonna do it, come on." And in my memory he's never said that about anything else; he just knew I needed a little kick in the pants and I'd do it. And once you're out there and you see all the other kids making errors and stuff, and you know you're better than those guys, you know: Maybe I *do* belong here. As it turned out, Little League was a good experience.

Some who were similarly "pushed" by their fathers were not so successful as the aforementioned man had been in Little League baseball, and thus the experience was not altogether a joyous affair. One 34-year-old white man, for instance, said he "inherited" his interest in sports from his father, who started playing catch with him at the age of four. Once he got into Little League, he felt pressured by his father, one of the coaches, who expected him to be the star of the team:

> I'd go 0-for-four sometimes, strike out three times in a Little League game, and I'd dread the ride home. I'd come home and he'd say, "Go in the bathroom and swing the bat in the mirror for an hour," to get my swing level . . . It didn't help much, though, I'd go out and strike out three or four times again the next game too [laughs ironically].

When asked if he had been concerned with having his father's approval, he responded:

Failure in his eyes? Yeah, I always thought that he wanted me to get some kind of [athletic] scholarship. I guess I was afraid of him when I was a kid. He didn't hit that much, but he had a rage about him—he'd rage, and that voice would just rattle you.

Similarly, a 24-year-old black man described his awe of his father's physical power and presence, and his sense of inadequacy in attempting to emulate him:

My father had a voice that sounded like rolling thunder. Whether it was intentional on his part or not, I don't know, but my father gave me a sense, an image of him being the most powerful being on earth, and that no matter what I ever did I would never come close to him . . . There were definite feelings of physical inadequacy that I couldn't work around.

It is interesting to note how these feelings of physical inadequacy relative to the father lived on as part of this young man's permanent internalized image. He eventually became a "feared" high school football player and broke school records in weight-lifting, yet,

As I grew older, my mother and friends told me that I had actually grown to be a larger man than my father. Even though in time I required larger clothes than he, which should have been a very concrete indication, neither my brother nor I could ever bring ourselves to say that I was bigger. We simply couldn't conceive of it.

Using sports activities as a means of identifying with and "living up to" the power and status of one's father was not always such a painful and difficult task for the men I interviewed. Most did not describe fathers who "pushed" them to become sports stars. The relationship between their athletic strivings and their identification with their fathers was more subtle. A 48-year-old black man, for instance, explained that he was not pushed into sports by his father, but was aware from an early age of the community status his father had gained through sports. He saw his own athletic accomplishments as a way to connect with and emulate his father:

I wanted to play baseball because my father had been quite a good baseball player in the Negro leagues before baseball was integrated, and so he was kind of a model for me. I remember, quite young, going to a baseball game he was in— this was before the war and all—I remember being in the stands with my mother and seeing him on first base, and being aware of the crowd . . . I was aware of people's confidence in him as a serious baseball player. I don't think my father ever said anything to me like "play sports" . . . [But] I knew he would like it if I did well. His admiration was important . . . he mattered.

Similarly, a 24-year-old white man described his father as a somewhat distant "role model" whose approval mattered:

> My father was more of an example . . . he definitely was very much in touch with and still had very fond memories of being an athlete and talked about it, bragged about it. . . . But he really didn't do that much to teach me skills, and he didn't always go to every game I played like some parents. But he approved and that was important, you know. That was important to get his approval. I always knew that playing sports was important to him, so I knew implicitly that it was good and there was definitely a value on it.

First experiences in sports might often come through relationships with brothers or older male relatives, and the early emotional salience of sports was often directly related to a boy's relationship with his father. The sense of commitment that these young boys eventually made to the development of athletic careers is best explained as a process of development of masculine gender identity and status in relation to same-sex peers.

MASCULINE IDENTITY AND EARLY COMMITMENT TO SPORTS

When many of the men in this study said that during childhood they played sports because "it's just what everybody did," they of course meant that it was just what *boys* did. They were introduced to organized sports by older brothers and fathers, and once involved, found themselves playing within an exclusively male world. Though the separate (and unequal) gendered worlds of boys and girls came to appear as "natural," they were in fact socially constructed. Thorne's observations of children's activities in schools indicated that rather than "naturally" constituting "separate gendered cultures," there is considerable interaction between boys and girls in classrooms and on playgrounds. When adults set up legitimate contact between boys and girls, Thorne observed, this usually results in "relaxed interactions." But when activities in the classroom or on the playground are presented to children as sex-segregated activities and gender is marked by teachers and other adults ("boys line up here, girls over there"), "gender boundaries are heightened, and mixed-sex interaction becomes an explicit arena of risk" (Thorne 1986; 70). Thus sex-segregated activities such as organized sports as structured by adults, provide the context in which gendered identities and separate "gendered cultures" develop and come to appear natural. For the boys in this study, it became "natural" to equate masculinity with competition, physical strength, and skills. Girls simply did not (could not, it was believed) participate in these activities.

Yet it is not simply the separation of children, by adults, into separate activities that explains why many boys came to feel such a strong connection with sports activities, while so few girls did. As I listened to men recall their earliest experiences in organized sports, I heard them talk of insecurity, loneliness, and especially a need to connect with other people as a primary motivation in their early sports strivings. As a 42-year-old white man stated, "The most important thing was just being out there with the rest of the guys—being friends." Another 32-year-old interviewee was born in Mexico and moved to the United States at a fairly young age. He never knew his father, and his mother died when he was only nine years old. Suddenly he felt rootless, and threw himself into sports. His initial motivations, however, do not appear to be based on a need to compete and win:

> Actually, what I think sports did for me is it brought me into kind of an instant family. By being on a Little League team, or even just playing with all kinds of different kids in the neighborhood, it brought what I really wanted, which was some kind of closeness. It was just being there, and being friends.

Clearly, what these boys needed and craved was that which was most problematic for them: connection and unity with other people. But why do these young males find *organized sports* such an attractive context in which to establish "a kind of closeness" with others? Comparative observations of young boys' and girls' game-playing behaviors yield important insights into this question. Piaget (1965) and Lever (1976) both observed that girls tend to have more "pragmatic" and "flexible" orientations to the rules of games; they are more prone to make exceptions and innovations in the middle of a game in order to make the game more "fair." Boys, on the other hand, tend to have a more firm, even inflexible orientation to the rules of a game; to them, the rules are what protects any fairness. This difference, according to Gilligan (1982), is based on the fact that early developmental experiences have yielded deeply rooted differences between males' and females' developmental tasks, needs, and moral reasoning. Girls, who tend to define themselves primarily through connection with others, experience highly competitive situations (whether in organized sports or in other hierarchical institutions) as threats to relationships, and thus to their identities. For boys, the development of gender identity involves the construction of positional identities, where a sense of self is solidified through separation from others (Chodorow 1978). Yet feminist psychoanalytic theory has tended to oversimplify the internal lives of men (Lichterman 1986). Males do appear to develop positional identities, yet despite their fears of intimacy, they also retain a human need for closeness and unity with others. This ambivalence toward intimate relationships is a major thread running through masculine development throughout the life course. Here we can conceptualize what Craib (1987) calls the "elective affinity" between personality and social structure: For the boy who both seeks and fears attachment with others, the rule-bound structure of organized sports can promise to be a safe place in which to seek nonintimate attachment with others within a context that maintains clear boundaries, distance, and separation.

COMPETITIVE STRUCTURES AND CONDITIONAL SELF-WORTH

Young boys may initially find that sports gives them the opportunity to experience "some kind of closeness" with others, but the structure of sports and athletic careers often undermines the possibility of boys learning to transcend their fears of intimacy, thus becoming able to develop truly close and intimate relationships with others (Kidd 1990; Messner 1987). The sports world is extremely hierarchical, and an incredible amount of importance is placed on winning, on "being number one." For instance, a few years ago I observed a basketball camp put on for boys by a professional basketball coach and his staff. The youngest boys, about eight years old (who could barely reach the basket with their shots) played a brief scrimmage. Afterwards, the coaches lined them up in a row in front of the older boys who were sitting in the grandstands. One by one, the coach would stand behind each boy, put his hand on the boy's head (much in the manner of a priestly benediction), and the older boys in the stands would applaud and cheer, louder or softer, depending on how well or poorly the young boy was judged to have performed. The two or three boys who were clearly the exceptional players looked confident that they would receive the praise they were due. Most of the boys, though, had expressions ranging from puzzlement to thinly disguised terror on their faces as they awaited the judgments of the older boys.

This kind of experience teaches boys that it is not "just being out there with the guys—being friends," that ensures the kind of attention and connection that they crave; it is being *better* than the other guys—*beating* them—that is the key to acceptance. Most of the boys in this study did have some early successes in sports, and thus their ambivalent need for connection with others was met, at least for a time. But the institution of sport tends to encourage the development of what Schafer (1975) has called "conditional self-worth" in boys. As boys become aware that acceptance by others is contingent upon being good—a "winner"—narrow definitions of success, based upon performance and winning become increasingly important to them. A 33-year-old black man said that by the time he was in his early teens:

> It was expected of me to do well in all my contests—I mean by my coaches, my peers, and my family. So I in turn expected to do well, and if I didn't do well, then I'd be very disappointed.

The man from Mexico, discussed above, who said that he had sought "some kind of closeness" in his early sports experiences began to notice in his early teens that if he played well, was a *winner,* he would get attention from others:

> It got to the point where I started realizing, noticing that people were always there for me, backing me all the time—sports got to be really fun because I always had some people there backing me. Finally my oldest brother started going to all my games, even though I had never really seen who he was [laughs]—after the game, you know, we never really saw each other, but he was at all my baseball games, and it seemed like we shared a kind of closeness there, but only in those situations. Off the field, when I wasn't in uniform, he was never around.

By high school, he said, he felt "up against the wall." Sports hadn't delivered what he had hoped it would, but he thought if he just tried harder, won one more championship trophy, he would get the attention he truly craved. Despite his efforts, this attention was not forthcoming. And, sadly, the pressures he had put on himself to excel in sports had taken most of the fun out of playing.

For many of the men in this study, throughout boyhood and into adolescence, this conscious striving for successful achievement became the primary means through which they sought connection with other people (Messner 1987). But it is important to recognize that young males' internalized ambivalences about intimacy do not fully determine the contours and directions of their lives. Masculinity continues to develop through interaction with the social world—and because boys from different backgrounds are interacting with substantially different familial, educational, and other institutions, these differences will lead them to make different choices and define situations in different ways. Next, I examine the differences in the ways that boys from higher- and lower-status families and communities related to organized sports.

STATUS DIFFERENCES AND COMMITMENTS TO SPORTS

In discussing early attractions to sports, the experiences of boys from higher- and lower-status backgrounds are quite similar. Both groups indicate the importance of fathers and older brothers in introducing them to sports. Both groups speak of the joys of receiving attention and acceptance among family and peers for early successes in sports. Note the similarities, for instance, in the following descriptions of boyhood athletic experiences of two men. First, a man born in a white, middle-class family:

> I loved playing sports so much from a very early age because of early exposure. A lot of the sports came easy at an early age, and because they did, and because you were successful at something, I think that you're inclined to strive for that

gratification. It's like, if you're good, you like it, because it's instant gratification. I'm doing something that I'm good at and I'm gonna keep doing it.

Second, a black man from a poor family:

Fortunately I had some athletic ability, and, quite naturally, once you start doing good in whatever it is—I don't care if it's jacks—you show off what you do. That's your ability, that's your blessing, so you show it off as much as you can.

For boys from both groups, early exposure to sports, the discovery that they had some "ability," shortly followed by some sort of family, peer, and community recognition, all eventually led to the commitment of hundreds and thousands of hours of playing, practicing, and dreaming of future stardom. Despite these similarities, there are also some identifiable differences that begin to explain the tendency of males from lower-status backgrounds to develop higher levels of commitment to sports careers. The most clear-cut difference was that while men from higher-status backgrounds are likely to describe their earliest athletic experiences and motivations almost exclusively in terms of immediate family, men from lower-status backgrounds more commonly describe the importance of a broader community context. For instance, a 46-year-old man who grew up in a "poor working class" black family in a small town in Arkansas explained:

In that community, at the age of third or fourth grade, if you're a male, they expect you to show some kind of inclination, some kind of skill in football or basketball. It was an expected thing, you know? My mom and my dad, they didn't push at all. It was the general environment.

A 48-year-old man describes sports activities as a survival strategy in his poor black community:

Sports protected me from having to compete in gang stuff, or having to be good with my fists. If you were an athlete and got into the fist world, that was your business, and that was okay—but you didn't have to if you didn't want to. People would generally defer to you, give you your space away from trouble.

A 35-year-old man who grew up in "a poor black ghetto" described his boyhood relationship to sports similarly:

Where I came from, either you were one of two things: you were in sports or you were out on the streets being a drug addict, or breaking into places. The guys who were in sports, we had it a little easier, because we were accepted by both groups. . . . So it worked out to my advantage, cause I didn't get into a lot of trouble—some trouble, but not a lot.

The fact that boys in lower-status communities faced these kinds of realities gave salience to their developing athletic identities. In contrast, sports were important to boys from higher-status backgrounds, yet the middle-class environment seemed more secure, less threatening, and offered far more options. By the time most of these boys got into junior high or high school, many had made conscious decisions to shift their attentions away from athletic careers to educational and (nonathletic) career goals. A 32-year-old white college athletic director told me that he had seen his chance to pursue a pro baseball career as "pissing in the wind," and instead, focused on education. Similarly, a 33-year-old white dentist who was a three-sport star in high school, decided not to play sports in college, so he could focus on getting into dental school. As he put it,

> I think I kind of downgraded the stardom thing. I thought it was small potatoes. And sure, that's nice in high school and all that, but on a broad scale, I didn't think it amounted to all that much.

This statement offers an important key to understanding the construction of masculine identity within a middle-class context. The status that this boy got through sports had been *very* important to him, yet he could see that "on a broad scale," this sort of status was "small potatoes." This sort of early recognition is more than a result of the oft-noted middle-class tendency to raise "future-oriented" children (Rubin 1976; Sennett and Cobb 1973). Perhaps more important, it is that the *kinds* of future orientations developed by boys from higher-status backgrounds are consistent with the middle-class context. These men's descriptions of their boyhoods reveal that they grew up immersed in a wide range of institutional frameworks, of which organized sports was just one. And—importantly—they could see that the status of adult males around them was clearly linked to their positions within various professions, public institutions, and bureaucratic organizations. It was clear that access to this sort of institutional status came through educational achievement, not athletic prowess. A 32-year-old black man who grew up in a professional-class family recalled that he had idolized Wilt Chamberlain and dreamed of being a pro basketball player, yet his father discouraged his athletic strivings:

> He knew I liked the game. I *loved* the game. But basketball was not recommended; my dad would say, "That's a stereotyped image for black youth. . . . When your basketball is gone and finished, what are you gonna do? One day, you might get injured. What are you gonna look forward to?" He stressed education.

Similarly, a 32-year-old man who was raised in a white, middle-class family, had found in sports a key means of gaining acceptance and connection in his peer group. Yet he was simultaneously developing an image of himself as a "smart student," and becoming aware of a wide range of nonsports life options:

> My mother was constantly telling me how smart I was, how good I was, what a nice person I was, and giving me all sorts of positive strokes, and those positive strokes became a self-motivating kind of thing. I had this image of myself as smart, and I lived up to that image.

It is not that parents of boys in lower-status families did not also encourage their boys to work hard in school. Several reported that their parents "stressed books first, sports second." It's just that the broader social context—education, economy, and community—was more likely to *narrow* lower-status boys' perceptions of real-life options, while boys from higher-status backgrounds faced an expanding world of options. For instance, with a different socioeconomic background, one 35-year-old black man might have become a great musician instead of a star professional football running back. But he did not. When he was a child, he said, he was most interested in music:

> I wanted to be a drummer. But we couldn't afford drums. My dad couldn't go out and buy me a drum set or a guitar even—it was just one of those things; he was just trying to make ends meet.

But he *could* afford, as could so many in his socioeconomic condition, to spend countless hours at the local park, where he was told by the park supervisor

> that I was a natural—not only in gymnastics or baseball—whatever I did, I was a natural. He told me I shouldn't waste this talent, and so I immediately started watching the big guys then.

In retrospect, this man had potential to be a musician or any number of things, but his environment limited his options to sports, and he made the best of it. Even within sports, he, like most boys in the ghetto, was limited:

> We didn't have any tennis courts in the ghetto—we used to have a lot of tennis balls, but no racquets. I wonder today how good I might be in tennis if I had gotten a racquet in my hands at an early age.

It is within this limited structure of opportunity that many lower-status young boys found sports to be *the* place, rather than *a* place, within which to construct masculine identity, status, the relationships. A 36-year-old white man explained that his father left the family when he was very young and his mother faced a very difficult struggle to make ends meet. As his words suggest, the more limited a boy's options, and the more insecure his family situation, the more likely he is to make an early commitment to an athletic career.

> I used to ride my bicycle to Little League practice—if I'd waited for someone to pick me up and take me to the ball park I'd have never played. I'd get to the ball park and all the other kids would have their dad bring them to practice or games. But I'd park my bike to the side and when it was over I'd get on it and go home. Sports was the way for me to move everything to the side—family problems, just all the embarrassments—and think about one thing, and that was sports . . . In the third grade, when the teacher went around the classroom and asked everybody, "What do you want to be when you grow up?," I said, "I want to be a major league baseball player," and everybody laughed their heads off.

This man eventually did enjoy a major league baseball career. Most boys from lower-status backgrounds who make similar early commitments to athletic careers are not so successful. As stated earlier, the career structure of organized sports is highly competitive and hierarchical. In fact, the chances of attaining professional status in sports are approximately 4:100,000 for a white man, 2:100,000 for a black man, and 3:1 million for a Hispanic man in the United States (Leonard and Reyman 1988). Nevertheless, the immediate rewards (fun, status, attention), along with the constricted (nonsports) structure of opportunity, attract disproportionately large numbers of boys from lower-status backgrounds to athletic careers as their major means of constructing a masculine identity. These are the boys who later, as young men, had to struggle with "conditional self-worth," and, more often than not, occupational dead ends. Boys from higher-status backgrounds, on the other hand, bolstered their boyhood, adolescent, and early adult status through their athletic accomplishments. Their wider range of experiences and life chances led to an early shift away from sports careers as the major basis of identity (Messner 1989).

CONCLUSION

The conception of the masculinity-sports relationship developed here begins to illustrate the idea of an "elective affinity" between social structure and personality. Organized sports is a "gendered institution"—an institution constructed by gender relations. As such, its structure and values (rules, formal organization, sex composition, etc.), reflect dominant conceptions of masculinity and femininity. Organized sports is also a "gendering institution"—an institution that helps to construct the current gender order. Part of this construction of gender is accomplished through the "masculinizing" of male bodies and minds.

Yet boys do not come to their first experiences in organized sports as "blank slates," but arrive with already "gendering" identities due to early developmental experiences and previous socialization. I have suggested here that an important thread running through the development of masculine identity is males' ambivalence toward intimate unity with others. Those boys who experience early athletic successes find in the structure of organized sport an affinity with this masculine ambivalence toward intimacy: The rule-bound, competitive, hierarchical world of sport offers boys an attractive means of establishing an emotionally distant (and thus "safe") connection with others. Yet as boys begin to define themselves as "athletes," they learn that in order to be accepted (to have connection) through sports, they must be winners. And in order to be winners, they must construct relationships with others (and with themselves) that are consistent with the competitive and hierarchical values and structure of the sports world. As a result, they often develop a "conditional self-worth" that leads them to construct more instrumental relationships with themselves and others. This ultimately exacerbates their difficulties in constructing intimate relationships with others. In effect, the interaction between the young male's preexisting internalized ambivalence toward intimacy with the competitive hierarchical institution of sport has resulted in the construction of a masculine personality that is characterized by instrumental rationality, goal-orientation, and difficulties with intimate connection and expression (Messner 1987).

This theoretical line of inquiry invites us not simply to examine how social institutions "socialize" boys, but also to explore the ways that boys' already-gendering identities interact with social institutions (which, like organized sport, are themselves the product of gender relations). This study has also suggested that it is not some singular "masculinity" that is being constructed through athletic careers. It may be correct, from a psychoanalytic perspective, to suggest that all males bring ambivalences toward intimacy to their interactions with the world, but "the world" is a very different place for males from different racial and socioeconomic backgrounds. Because males have substantially different interactions with the world, based on class, race, and other differences and inequalities, we might expect the construction of masculinity to take on different meanings for boys and men from differing backgrounds (Messner 1989). Indeed, this study has suggested that boys from higher-status backgrounds face a much broader range of options than do their lower-status counterparts. As a result, athletic careers take on different meanings for these boys. Lower-status boys are likely to see athletic careers as *the* institutional context for the construction of their masculine status and identities, while higher-status males make an early shift away from athletic careers toward other institutions (usually education and nonsports careers). A key line of inquiry for future studies might begin by exploring this irony of sports careers: Despite the fact that "the athlete" is currently an example of an exemplary form of masculinity in public ideology, the vast majority of boys who become most committed to athletic careers are never well-rewarded for their efforts. The fact that class and racial dynamics lead boys from higher-status backgrounds, unlike their lower-status counterparts, to move into nonsports careers illustrates how the construction of different kinds of masculinities is a key component of the overall construction of the gender order.

REFERENCES

Chodorow, N. (1978). *The Reproduction of Mothering.* Berkeley: Univ. of California Press.

Connell, R. W. (1987). *Gender and Power.* Stanford, CA: Stanford Univ. Press.

Connell, R. W. (1990). "An iron man: the body and some contradictions of hegemonic masculinity." In M. A. Messner and D. F. Sabo (eds.) *Sport, Men and the Gender Order: Critical Feminist Perspectives.* Champaign. IL: Human Kinetics.

Craib, I. (1987). "Masculinity and male dominance." *Soc. Rev.* 38: 721–743.

Eitzen, D. S. (1975). "Athletics in the status system of male adolescents: a replication of Coleman's *The Adolescent Society." Adolescence* 10: 268–276.

Gilligan, C. (1982). *In a Different Voice: Psychological Theory and Women's Development.* Cambridge, MA: Harvard Univ. Press.

Kidd, B. (1990). "The men's cultural center: sports and the dynamic of women's oppression/men's repression," In M. A. Messner and D. F. Sabo (eds.) *Sport, Men and the Gender Order: Critical Feminist Perspectives.* Champaign, IL: Human Kinetics.

Kimmel, M. S. (1990). "Baseball and the reconstitution of American masculinity: 1880–1920." In M. A. Messner and D. F. Sabo (eds.) *Sport, Men and the Gender Order: Critical Feminist Perspectives.* Champaign, IL: Human Kinetics.

Leonard, W. M. II and J. M. Reyman (1988). "The odds of attaining professional athlete status: refining the computations." *Sociology of Sport J.* 5: 162–169.

Lever, J. (1976). "Sex differences in the games children play." *Social Problems* 23: 478–487.

Lichterman, P. (1986). "Chodorow's psychoanalytic sociology: a project half-completed." *California Sociologist* 9: 147–166.

Messner, M. (1987). "The meaning of success: the athletic experience and the development of male identity," pp. 193–210 in H. Brod (ed.) *The Making of Masculinities: The New Men's Studies.* Boston: Allen and Unwin.

Messner, M. (1989). "Masculinities and athletic careers." *Gender and Society* 3: 71–88.

Osherson, S. (1986). *Finding Our Fathers: How a Man's Life Is Shaped by His Relationship with His Father.* New York: Fawcett Columbine.

Piaget, J. H. (1965). *The Moral Judgment of the Child.* New York: Free Press.

Rubin, L. B. (1976). *Worlds of Pain: Life in the Working Class Family.* New York: Basic Books.

Sabo, D. (1985). "Sport, patriarchy and male identity: new questions about men and sport." *Arena Rev.* 9: 2.

Schafer, W. E. (1975). "Sport and male sex role socialization." *Sport Sociology Bull.* 4: 47–54.

Sennett, R. and J. Cobb (1973). *The Hidden Injuries of Class.* New York: Random House.

Thorne, B. (1986). "Girls and boys together . . . but mostly apart: gender arrangements in elementary schools," pp. 167–184 in W. W. Hartup and Z. Rubin (eds.) *Relationships and Development.* Hillsdale, NJ: Lawrence Erlbaum.

11

On Face-Work

ERVING GOFFMAN

Many students find the idea of a "self presentation" to be manipulative, insincere and inauthentic. What Goffman's work shows is that we cannot avoid the work of presenting a "face" or identity in social interaction. We can deny that this activity goes on and we can be unaware of what we are doing, but all of us must do this work in order to carry on social interaction. Goffman takes sociology into the deepest realm of social life: our most intimate relations and our most private ideas about who we are.

Every person lives in a world of social encounters, involving him either in face-to-face or mediated contact with other participants. In each of these contacts, he tends to act out what is sometimes called a *line*—that is, a pattern of verbal and nonverbal acts by which he expresses his view of the situation and through this his evaluation of the participants, especially himself. Regardless of whether a person intends to take a line, he will find that he has done so in effect. The other participants will assume that he has more or less willfully taken a stand, so that if he is to deal with their response to him he must take into consideration the impression they have possibly formed of him.

The term *face* may be defined as the positive social value a person effectively claims for himself by the line others assume he has taken during a particular contact. Face is an image of self delineated in terms of approved social attributes—albeit an image that others may share, as when a person makes a good showing for his profession or religion by making a good showing for himself.

A person tends to experience an immediate emotional response to the face which a contact with others allows him; he cathects his face; his "feelings" become attached to it. If the encounter sustains an image of him that he has long taken for granted, he probably will have few feelings about the matter. If events establish a face for him that is better than he might have expected, he is likely to "feel good"; if his ordinary expectations are not fulfilled, one expects that he will "feel bad" or "feel hurt." In general, a person's attachment to a particular face, coupled with the ease with which disconfirming information can be conveyed by himself and others, provides one reason why he finds that participation in any contact with others is a commitment. A person will also have feelings about the face sustained for the other participants, and while these feelings may differ in quantity and direction from those he has for his own face, they constitute an involvement in the face of others that is as immediate and spontaneous as the involvement he has in his own face. One's own face and the face of others are constructs of the same order; it is the rules of the group and the definition of the situation which determine how much feeling one is to have for face and how this feeling is to be distributed among the faces involved.

A person may be said to *have*, or *be in*, or *maintain* face when the line he effectively takes presents an image of him that is internally consistent, that is supported by judgments and evidence conveyed by other participants, and that is confirmed by evidence conveyed through impersonal agencies in the situation. At such times the person's face clearly is something that is not lodged in or on his body, but rather something that is diffusely located in the flow of events in the encounter and becomes manifest only when these events are read and interpreted for the appraisals expressed in them.

The line maintained by and for a person during contact with others tends to be of a legitimate institutionalized kind. During a contact of a particular type, an interactant of known or visible attributes can expect to be sustained in a particular face and can feel that it is morally proper that this should be so. Given his attributes and the conventionalized nature of the encounter, he will find a small choice of lines will be open to him and a small choice of faces will be waiting for him. Further, on the basis of a few known attributes, he is given the responsibility of possessing a vast number of others. His coparticipants are not likely to be conscious of the character of many of these attributes until he acts perceptibly in such a way as to discredit his possession of them; then everyone becomes conscious of these attributes and assumes that he willfully gave a false impression of possessing them.

* * *

A person may be said to *be in wrong face* when information is brought forth in some way about his social worth which cannot be integrated, even with effort, into the line that is being sustained for him. A person may be said to *be out of face* when he participates in a contact with others without having ready a line of the kind participants in such situations are expected to take. The intent of many pranks is to lead a person into showing a wrong face or no face, but there will also be serious occasions, of course, when he will find himself expressively out of touch with the situation.

When a person senses that he is in face, he typically responds with feelings of confidence and assurance. Firm in the line he is taking, he feels that he can hold his head up and openly present himself to others. He feels some security and some relief—as he also can when the others feel he is in wrong face but successfully hide these feelings from him.

When a person is in wrong face or out of face, expressive events are being contributed to the encounter which cannot be readily woven into the expressive fabric of the occasion. Should he sense that he is in wrong face or out of face, he is likely to feel ashamed and inferior because of what has happened to the activity on his account and because of what may happen to his reputation as a participant. Further, he may feel bad because he had relied upon the encounter to support an image of self to which he has become emotionally attached and which he now finds threatened. Felt lack of judgmental support from the encounter may take him aback, confuse him, and momentarily incapacitate him as an interactant. His manner and bearing may falter, collapse, and crumble. He may become embarassed and chagrined; he may become shamefaced. The feeling, whether warranted or not, that he is perceived in a flustered state by others, and that he is presenting no usable line, may add further injuries to his feelings, just as his change from being in wrong face or out of face to being shamefaced can add further disorder to the expressive organization of the situation. Following common usage, I shall employ the term *poise* to refer to the capacity to suppress and conceal any tendency to become shamefaced during encounters with others.

In our Anglo-American society, as in some others, the phrase "to lose face" seems to mean to be in wrong face, to be out of face, or to be shame faced. The phrase "to save one's face" appears to refer to the process by which the person sustains an impression for others that he has not lost face. Following Chinese usage, one can say that "to give face" is to arrange for another to take a better line than he might otherwise have been able to take, the other thereby gets face given him, this being one way in which he can gain face.

* * *

Just as the member of any group is expected to have self-respect, so also he is expected to sustain a standard of considerateness; he is expected to go to certain lengths to save the feelings and the face of others present, and he is expected to do this willingly and spontaneously because of emotional identification with the others and with their feelings. In consequence, he is disinclined to witness the defacement of others. The person who can witness another's humiliation and unfeelingly retain a cool countenance himself is said in our society to be "heartless," just as he who can unfeelingly participate in his own defacement is thought to be "shameless."

The combined effect of the rule of self-respect and the rule of considerateness is that the person tends to conduct himself during an encounter so as to maintain both his own face and the face of the other participants. This means that the line taken by each participant is usually allowed to prevail, and each participant is allowed to carry off the role he appears to have chosen for himself. A state where everyone temporarily accepts everyone else's line is established. This kind of mutual acceptance seems to be a basic structural feature of interaction, especially the interaction of face-to-face talk. It is typically a "working" acceptance, not a "real" one, since it tends to be based not on agreement of candidly expressed heart-felt evaluations, but upon a willingness to give temporary lip service to judgments with which the participants do not really agree.

The mutual acceptance of lines has an important conservative effect upon encounters. Once the person initially presents a line, he and the others tend to build their later responses upon it, and in a sense become stuck with it. Should the person radically alter his line, or should it become discredited, then confusion results, for the participants will have prepared and committed themselves for actions that are now unsuitable.

Ordinarily, maintenance of face is a condition of interaction, not its objective. Usual objectives, such as gaining face for oneself, giving free expression to one's true beliefs, introducing depreciating information about the others, or solving problems and performing tasks, are typically pursued in such a way as to be consistent with the maintenance of face. To study face-saving is to study the traffic rules of social interaction; one learns about the code the person adheres to in his movement across the paths and designs of others, but not where he is going, or why he wants to get there. One does not even learn why he is ready to follow the code, for a large number of different motives can equally lead him to do so. He may want to save his own face because of his emotional attachment to the image of self which it expresses, because of his pride or honor, because of the power his presumed status allows him to exert over the other participants, and so on. He may want to save the others' face because of his emotional attachment to an image of them, or because he feels that his coparticipants have a moral right to this protection, or because he wants to avoid the hostility that may be directed toward him if they lose their face. He may feel that an assumption has been made that he is the sort of person who shows compassion and sympathy toward others, so that to retain his own face, he may feel obliged to be considerate of the line taken by the other participants.

* * *

THE BASIC KINDS OF FACE-WORK

The Avoidance Process. The surest way for a person to prevent threats to his face is to avoid contacts in which these threats are likely to occur. In all societies one can observe this in the avoidance relationship and in the tendency for certain delicate transactions to be conducted by go-betweens. Similarly, in many societies, members know the value of voluntarily making a gracious withdrawal before an anticipated threat to face has had a chance to occur.

Once the person does chance an encounter, other kinds of avoidance practices come into play. As defensive measures, he keeps off topics and away from activities that would lead to the expression of information that is inconsistent with the line he is maintaining. At opportune moments he will change the topic of conversation or the direction of activity. He will often present initially a front of diffidence and composure, suppressing any show of feeling until he has found out what kind of line the others will be ready to support for him. Any claims regarding self may be made with belittling modesty, with strong qualifications, or with a note of unseriousness; by hedging in these ways he will have prepared a self for himself that will not be discredited by exposure, personal failure, or the unanticipated acts of others. And if he does not hedge his claims about self, he will at least attempt to be realistic about them, knowing that otherwise events may discredit him and make him lose face.

Certain protective maneuvers are as common as these defensive ones. The person shows respect and politeness, making sure to extend to others any ceremonial treatment that might be their due. He employs discretion; he leaves unstated facts that might implicitly or explicitly contradict and embarrass the positive claims made by others. He employs circumlocutions and deceptions, phrasing his replies with careful ambiguity so that the others' face is preserved even if their welfare is not. He employs courtesies, making slight modifications of his demands on or appraisals of the others so that they will be able to define the situation as one in which their self-respect is not threatened. In making a belittling demand upon the others, or in imputing uncomplimentary attributes to them, he may employ a joking manner, allowing them to take the line that they are good sports, able to relax from their ordinary standards of pride and honor. And before engaging in a potentially offensive act, he may provide explanations as to why the others ought not to be affronted by it. For example, if he knows that it will be necessary to withdraw from the encounter before it has terminated, he may tell the others in advance that it is necessary for him to leave, so that they will have faces that are prepared for it. But neutralizing the potentially offensive act need not be done verbally; he may wait for a propitious moment or natural break—for example, in conversation, a momentary lull when no one speaker can be affronted—and then leave, in this way using the context instead of his words as a guarantee of inoffensiveness.

When a person fails to prevent an incident, he can still attempt to maintain the fiction that no threat to face has occurred. The most blatant example of this is found where the person acts as if an event that contains a threatening expression has not occurred at all. He may apply this studied nonobservance to his own acts—as when he does not by any outward sign admit that his stomach is rumbling—or to the acts of others, as when he does not "see" that another has stumbled. Social life in mental hospitals owes much to this process; patients employ it in regard to their own peculiarities, and visitors employ it, often with tenuous desperation, in regard to patients. In general, tactful blindness of this kind is applied only to events that, if perceived at all, could be perceived and interpreted only as threats to face.

* * *

Another kind of avoidance occurs when a person loses control of his expressions during an encounter. At such times he may try not so much to overlook the incident as to hide or conceal his activity in some way, thus making it possible for the others to avoid some of the difficulties created by a participant who has not maintained face. Correspondingly, when a person is caught out of face because he had not expected to be thrust into interaction, or because strong feelings have disrupted his expressive mask, the others may protectively turn away from him or his activity for a moment, to give him time to assemble himself.

The Corrective Process. When the participants in an undertaking or encounter fail to prevent the occurrence of an event that is expressively incompatible with the judgments of social worth that are being maintained, and when the event is of the kind that is difficult to overlook, then the participants are likely to give it accredited status as an incident—to ratify it as a threat that deserves direct official attention—and to proceed to try to correct for its effects. At this point one or more participants find themselves in an established state of ritual disequilibrium or disgrace, and an attempt must be made to re-establish a satisfactory ritual state for them. I use the term *ritual* because I am dealing with acts through whose symbolic component the actor shows how worthy he is of respect or how worthy he feels others are of it. The imagery of equilibrium is apt here because the length and intensity of the corrective effort is nicely adapted to the persistence and intensity of the threat. One's face, then, is a sacred thing, and the expressive order required to sustain it is therefore a ritual one.

The sequence of acts set in motion by an acknowledged threat to face, and terminating in the re-establishment of ritual equilibrium, I shall call an *interchange.* Defining a message or move as everything conveyed by an actor during a turn at taking action, one can say that an interchange will involve two or more moves and two or more participants. Obvious examples in our society may be found in the sequence of "Excuse me" and "Certainly," and in the exchange of presents or visits. The interchange seems to be a basic concrete unit of social activity and provides one natural empirical way to study interaction of all kinds. Face-saving practices can be usefully classified according to their position in the natural sequence of moves that comprise this unit. Aside from the event which introduces the need for a corrective interchange, four classic moves seem to be involved.

There is, first, the challenge, by which participants take on the responsibility of calling attention to the misconduct; by implication they suggest that the threatened claims are to stand firm and that the threatening event itself will have to be brought back into line.

The second move consists of the offering, whereby a participant, typically the offender, is given a chance to correct for the offense and reestablish the expressive order. Some classic ways of making this move are available. On the one hand, an attempt can be made to show that what admittedly appeared to be a threatening expression is really a meaningless event, or an unintentional act, or a joke not meant to be taken seriously, or an unavoidable, "understandable" product of extenuating circumstances. On the other hand, the meaning of the event may be granted and effort concentrated on the creator of it. Information may be provided to show that the creator was under the influence of something and not himself, or that he was under the command of somebody else and not acting for himself. When a person claims that an act was meant in jest, he may go on and claim that the self that seemed to lie behind the act was also projected as a joke. When a person suddenly finds that he has demonstrably failed in capacities that the others assumed him to have and to claim for himself—such as the capacity to spell, to perform minor tasks, to talk without malapropisms, and so on—he may quickly add, in a serious or unserious way, that he claims these incapacities as part of his self. The meaning of the threatening incident thus stands, but it can now be incorporated smoothly into the flow of expressive events.

As a supplement to or substitute for the strategy of redefining the offensive act or himself, the offender can follow two other procedures: he can provide compensations to the injured—when it is not his own face that he has threatened; or he can provide punishment, penance, and expiation for himself. These are important moves or phases in the ritual interchange. Even though the offender may fail to prove his innocence, he can suggest through these means that he *is* now a renewed person, a person who has paid for his sin against the expressive order and is once more to be trusted in the judgmental scene. Further, he can show that he does not treat the feelings of the others lightly, and that if their feelings have been injured by him, however innocently, he is prepared to pay a price for his action. Thus he assures the others that they can accept his explanations without this acceptance constituting a sign of weakness and a lack of pride on their part. Also, by his treatment of himself, by his self-castigation, he shows that he is clearly aware of the kind of crime he would have committed had the incident been what it first appeared to be, and that he knows the kind of punishment that ought to be accorded to one who would commit such a crime. The suspected person thus shows that he is thoroughly capable of taking the role of the others toward his own activity, that he can still be used as a responsible participant in the ritual process, and that the rules of conduct which he appears to have broken are still sacred, real, and unweakened. An offensive act may arouse anxiety about the ritual code; the offender allays this anxiety by showing that both the code and he as an upholder of it are still in working order.

After the challenge and the offering have been made, the third move can occur: the persons to whom the offering is made can accept it as a satisfactory means of re-establishing the expressive order and the faces supported by this order. Only then can the offender cease the major part of his ritual offering.

In the terminal move of the interchange, the forgiven person conveys a sign of gratitude to those who have given him the indulgence of forgiveness.

The phases of the corrective process—challenge, offering, acceptance, and thanks—provide a model for interpersonal ritual behavior, but a model that may be departed from in significant ways. For example, the offended parties may give the offender a chance to initiate the offering on his own before a challenge is made and before they ratify the offense as an incident. This is a common courtesy, extended on the assumption that the recipient will introduce a self-challenge. Further, when the offended persons accept the corrective offering, the offender may suspect that this has been grudgingly done from tact, and so he may volunteer additional corrective offerings, not allowing the matter to rest until he has received a second or third acceptance of his repeated apology. Or the offended persons may tactfully take over the role of the offender and volunteer excuses for him that will, perforce, be acceptable to the offended persons.

An important departure from the standard corrective cycle occurs when a challenged offender patently refuses to heed the warning and continues with his offending behavior, instead of setting the activity to rights. This move shifts the play back to the challengers. If they countenance the refusal to meet their demands, then it will be plain that their challenge was a bluff and that the bluff has been called. This is an untenable position; a face for themselves cannot be derived from it, and they are left to bluster. To avoid this fate, some classic moves are open to them. For instance, they can resort to tactless, violent retaliation, destroying either themselves or the person who had refused to heed their warning. Or they can withdraw from the undertaking in a visible huff—righteously indignant, outraged, but confident of ultimate vindication. Both tacks provide a way of denying the offender his status as an interactant, and hence denying the reality of the offensive judgment he has made. Both strategies are ways of salvaging face, but for all concerned the costs are usually high. It is partly to forestall such scenes that an offender is usually quick to offer apologies; he does not want the affronted persons to trap themselves into the obligation to resort to desperate measures.

It is plain that emotions play a part in these cycles of response, as when anguish is expressed because of what one has done to another's face, or anger because of what has been done to one's own. I want to stress that these emotions function as moves, and fit so precisely into the logic of the ritual game that it would seem difficult to understand them without it.[1] In fact, spontaneously expressed feelings are likely to fit into the formal pattern of the ritual interchange more elegantly than consciously designed ones.

COOPERATION IN FACE-WORK

When a face has been threatened, face-work must be done, but whether this is initiated and primarily carried through by the person whose face is threatened, or by the offender, or by a mere witness, is often of secondary importance. Lack of effort on the part of one person induces compensatory effort

---

1. Even when a child demands something and is refused, he is likely to cry and sulk not as an irrational expression of frustration but as a ritual move, conveying that he already has a face to lose and that its loss is not to be permitted lightly. Sympathetic parents may even allow for such display, seeing in these crude strategies the beginnings of a social self.

from others; a contribution by one person relieves the others of the task. In fact, there are many minor incidents in which the offender and the offended simultaneously attempt to initiate an apology. Resolution of the situation to everyone's apparent satisfaction is the first requirement; correct apportionment of blame is typically a secondary consideration.

Since each participant in an undertaking is concerned, albeit for differing reasons, with saving his own face and the face of the others, then tacit cooperation will naturally arise so that the participants together can attain their shared but differently motivated objectives.

One common type of tacit cooperation in face-saving is the tact exerted in regard to face-work itself. The person not only defends his own face and protects the face of the others, but also acts so as to make it possible and even easy for the others to employ face-work for themselves and him. He helps them to help themselves and him. Social etiquette, for example, warns men against asking for New Year's Eve dates too early in the season, lest the girl find it difficult to provide a gentle excuse for refusing. This second-order tact can be further illustrated by the wide-spread practice of negative-attribute etiquette. The person who has an unapparent negatively valued attribute often finds it expedient to begin an encounter with an unobtrusive admission of his failing, especially with persons who are uninformed about him. The others are thus warned in advance against making disparaging remarks about his kind of person and are saved from the contradiction of acting in a friendly fashion to a person toward whom they are unwittingly being hostile. This strategy also prevents the others from automatically making assumptions about him which place him in a false position and saves him from painful forbearance or embarrassing remonstrances.

* * *

Another form of tacit cooperation, and one that seems to be much used in many societies, is reciprocal self-denial. Often the person does not have a clear idea of what would be a just or acceptable apportionment of judgments during the occasion, and so he voluntarily deprives or depreciates himself while indulging and complimenting the others, in both cases carrying the judgments safely past what is likely to be just. The favorable judgments about himself he allows to come from the others; the unfavorable judgments of himself are his own contributions. This "after you, Alphonse" technique works, of course, because in depriving himself he can reliably anticipate that the others will compliment or indulge him. Whatever allocation of favors is eventually established, all participants are first given a chance to show that they are not bound or constrained by their own desires and expectations, that they have a properly modest view of themselves, and that they can be counted upon to support the ritual code. Negative bargaining, through which each participant tries to make the terms of trade more favorable to the other side, is another instance; as a form of exchange perhaps it is more widespread than the economist's kind.

A person's performance of face-work, extended by his tacit agreement to help others perform theirs, represents his willingness to abide by the ground rules of social interaction. Here is the hallmark of his socialization as an interactant. If he and the others were not socialized in this way, interaction in most societies and most situations would be a much more hazardous thing for feelings and faces. The person would find it impractical to be oriented to symbolically conveyed appraisals of social worth, or to be possessed of feelings—that is, it would be impractical for him to be a ritually delicate object. And as I shall suggest, if the person were not a ritually delicate object, occasions of talk could not be organized in the way they usually are. It is no wonder that trouble is caused by a person who cannot be relied upon to play the face-saving game.

THE RITUAL ROLES OF THE SELF

So far I have implicitly been using a double definition of self: the self as an image pieced together from the expressive implications of the full flow of events in an undertaking; and the self as a kind of player in a ritual game who copes honorably or dishonorably, diplomatically or undiplomatically, with the judgmental contingencies of the situation. A double mandate is involved. As sacred objects, men are subject to slights and profanation; hence as players of the ritual game they have had to lead themselves into duels, and wait for a round of shots to go wide of the mark before embracing their opponents.

* * *

Further, within limits the person has a right to forgive other participants for affronts to his sacred image. He can forbearantly overlook minor slurs upon his face, and in regard to somewhat greater injuries he is the one person who is in a position to accept apologies on behalf of his sacred self. This is a relatively safe prerogative for the person to have in regard to himself, for it is one that is exercised in the interests of the others or of the undertaking. Interestingly enough, when the person commits a *gaffe* against himself, it is not he who has the license to forgive the event; only the others have that prerogative, and it is a safe prerogative for them to have because they can exercise it only in his interests or in the interests of the undertaking. One finds, then, a system of checks and balances by which each participant tends to be given the right to handle only those matters which he will have little motivation for mishandling. In short, the rights and obligations of an interactant are designed to prevent him from abusing his role as an object of sacred value.

When a person begins a mediated or immediate encounter, he already stands in some kind of social relationship to the others concerned, and expects to stand in a given relationship to them after the particular encounter ends. This, of course, is one of the ways in which social contacts are geared into the wider society. Much of the activity occurring during an encounter can be understood as an effort on everyone's part to get through the occasion and all the unanticipated and unintentional events that can cast participants in an undesirable light, without disrupting the relationships of the participants. And if relationships are in the process of change, the object will be to bring the encounter to a satisfactory close without altering the expected course of development. This perspective nicely accounts, for example, for the little ceremonies of greeting and farewell which occur when people begin a conversational encounter or depart from one. Greetings provide a way of showing that a relationship is still what it was at the termination of the previous coparticipation, and, typically, that this relationship involves sufficient suppression of hostility for the participants temporarily to drop their guards and talk. Farewells sum up the effect of the encounter upon the relationship and show what the participants may expect of one another when they next meet. The enthusiasm of greetings compensates for the weakening of the relationship caused by the absence just terminated, while the enthusiasm of farewells compensates the relationship for the harm that is about to be done to it by separation.

12

The Dynamics of Welfare Stigma

ROBIN ROGERS-DILLON

Ethnographic studies present the rich texture of peoples' lives in a way that survey research often misses. It also allows us to understand the meanings that people give to their actions, their social environment, and to themselves. In this essay, the author listens to women who use food stamps to help support their families. In so doing they put themselves in a position to be stigmatized by others. How they cope with it is a lesson in the difficult battle over social status.

INTRODUCTION

I give you an example, when you're in the grocery store and I do the shopping for one month. I budget. I can go with my coupons. I save like almost $50 a month for coupons. I have one cart behind me and one in front of me, and I'm coming through and people are being nice, you know. People are waiting. I say, "I'm sorry it's taking so long. I go once a month. I'm sorry. Thanks for your patience." . . . Soon as they see you come out with that food stamp pack, it, their whole demeanor changes. You can almost . . . Maybe I'm looking from within. Maybe I . . . Maybe it's me. Maybe it's my own feelings, but I really think their whole attitude changes.

—Diane,[1] welfare recipient

In the above quotation, Diane, a white woman in her early thirties, describes pulling out food stamps in the grocery store. In her mind, other people's attitudes toward her change dramatically when they see that she is on welfare. Yet she is not completely certain that it is their attitudes and not her own feelings of embarrassment that she is sensing. She says: "Maybe I'm looking from within. Maybe I . . . Maybe it's me, Maybe it's my own feelings (. . .)," Diane describes this moment of feeling stigmatized in very relational terms. She does not feel strongly stigmatized about being on welfare until the other people in the store see her using food stamps. It is her being on food stamps *in relation* to other people that creates Diane's feelings of stigmatization in the grocery store. In this paper I present the results of an exploratory study on the nature of welfare stigma based on an empirical application of the symbolic interactionist

---

1. All names have been changed to protect confidentiality.

115

tradition. * * * The study is based on in-depth interviews with ten women who received means-tested public assistance, including Aid to Families with Dependent Children (AFDC), food stamps, and Women, Infants and Children (WIC). I have considered all forms of noncontributory, means-tested public assistance as publicly understood to be "welfare," although there are important differences among them that I will discuss in the conclusion.

* * *

[P]rior research does not investigate the ways in which social interactions create welfare stigma, the nature of welfare stigma, or how recipients' prior social position influences their perceptions of stigma. * * * The aim of this pilot study is to begin an investigation into the nature of welfare stigma and the mechanisms that create it. The complex and often contradictory feelings of stigma reported by the respondents in this study suggest that welfare stigma may vary depending on the social audience, situation, and recipient's life history. This calls into question the assumption underlying most research on welfare stigma that welfare stigma is a coherent and relatively constant entity. These findings suggest that the symbolic interactionist tradition may enrich our understanding of welfare stigma by highlighting the relational and situational aspects of welfare stigma, which other approaches have over-looked.

THE SOCIAL POSITION OF WELFARE RECIPIENTS

Assistance, to which the community is committed in its own interest, but which the poor person has no right to claim, makes the poor person into an object of the activity of the group and places him at a distance from the whole, which at times makes him live as a *corpus vile* by the mercy of the whole and at times, because of this, makes him into a bitter enemy.

(Simmel 1971 [1908]: 172)

Simmel observed that when a community provides an individual with financial assistance out of concern for the community's interests rather than out of the individual's right to receive assistance, the recipient of that assistance becomes an outsider, an object of the community's actions rather than a member of that community. Being an outsider, Simmel argues, the recipient of assistance is at the mercy of the group and can be perceived as an enemy of the group. This observation about the nature of the relationship between a recipient of public assistance and the state still has validity today. The term "welfare mother" is often contrasted with "tax-paying citizens," suggesting that women who receive welfare have a distinct and degraded social position within American society that is defined by their receiving welfare.

For example, in the current public debate on welfare, Lawrence Mead argues that welfare recipients need to engage in waged labor in order to fulfill the obligations of citizenship and, on this basis, proposes that compulsory work requirements be attached to welfare benefits. The popularity and influence of Mead's ideas suggest that within the American culture there is a perceived need for welfare recipients to earn back their citizenship through work. But what is it about receiving welfare that seems to alter a welfare recipient's social position, and even imputed right to citizenship? A brief discussion of the historical development of Aid to Families with Dependent Children* will help us to understand the social position of contemporary welfare recipients.

The mothers' pension programs of the early 1900's, precursors to AFDC, explicitly categorized recipients as being objects of social reform. These programs, fought for by middle class reformers, were premised on the idea that women (often immigrants) who were widowed or abandoned should be provided with cash assistance and moral guidance that would help them to raise their children according to middle class standards. In essence, the state would take over the role of the absent husband. This would, it was argued, create a stronger nation by improving the quality of poor women's offspring. Assistance was given only to women who were thought to be capable of raising good children. Many southern states explicitly denied black women help; other states did so in practice though not in policy[.]

* * *

Erving Goffman (1986) defines stigma as a disjunction between one's virtual social identity and one's actual social identity. According to Goffman, virtual social identity is the social identity that others impute on the basis of surface appearances, relying primarily on stereotypes of what is considered normal for a person of a particular age, race, class, sex, occupation, et cetera. Actual social identity, in contrast, is composed of the attributes that a person can be shown to possess. If one's actual social identity contains an attribute that is considered undesirable and incompatible with one's virtual social identity, that attribute becomes a stigma. As Goffman writes, "The term stigma, then, will be used to refer to an attribute that is deeply discrediting, but it should be seen that a language of relationships, not attributes, is really needed" (1986: 3) In fact, it is the language of welfare stigmatizing relationships, as they are framed and defined in situations, that will be explored in the remainder of this paper.

The virtual identity of all adult Americans includes full social citizenship. The possession of full social citizenship, however, is contested for American welfare recipients. This creates a disjunction between the virtual and actual social identities of all American welfare recipients and makes receiving welfare stigmatizing. Americans who go on welfare may also experience disruptions in their personal identities that are akin to stigma. For example, if a formerly middle class suburban housewife is forced on to welfare after a divorce, she

---

* This program was eliminated in 1996.

may have trouble incorporating her degraded social status into her personal identity. She therefore may experience a disturbance in both her social and personal identities, because her virtual identity and self-concept have been those of a middle class person.

Goffman noted that stigmatized people fall into the categories of discredited or discreditable. For the discreditable, those whose stigmas are not known to others, managing information about themselves and their stigma is extremely important. Women who receive welfare are primarily discreditable, as receiving welfare is not generally a visible attribute. But there are situations that force a welfare recipient publicly to claim her discredited identity. Food stamps, for example, label the user as a welfare recipient and constitute what Goffman (1986) termed "stigma symbols." Managing the use of food stamps emerged as a central concern for the women in this study and is a focal point of this paper.

METHODOLOGY AND DATA

My sample for this study consisted of ten divorced or separated[2] women on welfare. I chose to look at divorced or separated women to avoid confounding the stigma of unwed motherhood with welfare stigma. By doing this, however, I have excluded welfare recipients who were never married, a group that is central to the welfare debate and who may very well experience welfare stigma differently than their previously married counterparts.

Respondents were recruited through displaced homemaker programs, the Philadelphia County Assistance Program, suburban Domestic Relations offices, ads in two Philadelphia area free newspapers for parents (*Parents Express* and *Metro Kids*) and personal referrals. All of the respondents had children, although this was not a requirement for participation in the study, and children were often present during the interviews. Most of the interviews took place in respondents' homes, a few in restaurants, and one at a local community college. Seven of the women lived in urban areas and three in the suburbs. No one lived in a public housing project, but several respondents lived in subsidized Section 8 housing. The women ranged in age from their early twenties to mid forties.

The sample was selected for diversity, and it is not random. The respondents were racially diverse; two women were Latina, five were African Amer-

---

2. Initially, I intended to interview only divorced women on welfare because this would allow me to look at women from a range of social backgrounds who had come to welfare through the common and relatively un-stigmatized means of divorce. In the course of my study, however, I expanded the target population to include women who had gone on welfare after a separation. Many women go on welfare after separating because, despite having a legal marriage, they and their children lose all support from their husbands. Although I still aimed to find divorced women, I did not hold legal divorce as a strict criterion for accepting respondents.

ican, and three were white. Some of the women came from impoverished families, while others came from families that made $40,000 a year or more. Given the exploratory nature of this study, its small non-random sample, and the exclusion of never-married respondents, the empirical findings presented in this paper should not be generalized to other welfare recipients.

The interviews, which on average took two hours to complete, focused on four main areas: 1) Family history, particularly in regard to receiving public assistance and attitudes toward public assistance; 2) Respondents' attitudes about welfare; 3) Whom respondents told that they were receiving public assistance, what they told them and why; and 4) The ways in which receiving welfare affected (or did not affect) daily activities such as grocery shopping.

Race and class differences between myself and the respondents shaped some of the information that I received. In one of the interviews an African American woman began to talk about seeing white women with food stamps but then looked at me, a white woman, and redirected her comments away from racial issues. There was probably more censoring of racial issues that I did not see. Class differences were also important. Respondents, particularly those from lower socio-economic backgrounds, were keenly aware that I was middle class and often tested me to see what my attitudes about welfare were. After concluding one interview, a woman asked me if I needed her (welfare) case number. When I told her that not only did I not need it, but also that I did not want it because I did not want anything to compromise her confidentiality, she sat me back down and began to tell me things that she had left out of our initial conversation. Though I gained some level of trust from this woman, my resemblance to a caseworker influenced the responses that I received.

THE EXPERIENCE OF WELFARE STIGMA

The women in this study described going on to welfare in terms of necessity. The stigma of receiving welfare was almost meaningless in the face of pressing needs for food, shelter, and other goods. Most of the respondents reported that going on to welfare was not a difficult decision to make, with no job or child support, they had no other options.

> It is instinctive. You don't have to think about there is a crumb and I'm hungry, go get it. It's survival. You do what you have to do. It is demeaning. I hate it.
>
> (Diane, white, poor during marriage)

> No other options. No more money could I get, (. . .) no more things could I sell. I didn't have anything left to sell, so it is either welfare or no fare, you know?
>
> (Erica, African American, middle class during marriage)

Though the stigma of welfare was not a deterrent to applying for assistance, respondents were very aware of the stereotypes of welfare recipients. They saw the public's image of most welfare recipients as one of lazy, baby-making women living off of other people's labor.

> Well [people think] that's another welfare case, you know. She's lazy. Basically that's what I hear. I hear a lot that you know, they're lazy, they don't wanna do nothing and all this kind of stuff, (...) A lot of men have like a stigma about women being on DPA. And a lot of them think that, you know, you lazy and you not trying to do better, all that kind of stuff. Then [I] feel a lot of times I wouldn't even let them know.
>
> (Jenny, African American, working class during marriage)

> I mean when you're on welfare you really supposed to be looking for a man, you know? It's like come and take me. (...) Well, [people think] you're staying home all day making more babies.
>
> (Erica, African American, middle class during marriage)

Kim, the 18-year-old daughter of a respondent, spoke about her own feelings towards public assistance recipients, before her mother became one:

> I think if someone had said they were on welfare to me, my immediate reaction would have been to the people, they are lazy and they are unmotivated and they are not as smart and they didn't get a good education and they are bleeding the government and they are bleeding us.
>
> (Kim, white, formerly middle class)

Kim's description illustrates how powerfully negative the image of welfare recipients can be.

Many of the respondents felt the need to defend themselves against unflattering assumptions that they felt others made about them based on their status as welfare recipients. For example, Erica, who only has one child, feels that by virtue of being on welfare she must defend herself against accusations that women on welfare have many children. She feels that she must distance herself from this image of the "welfare mother" even though it does not accurately reflect her situation.

> To be honest, I'm going to tell you, frankly as far as men feel about it, men feel women on welfare have a lot of children. They are promiscuous. As far as being in the African American community, it's like if you have a lot of children, forget it. Because it's like everybody is looking for a dad. And I'm not looking for a damn daddy.
>
> (Erica, African American, middle class during marriage)

The stereotype of the "welfare mother" exists apart from the actual situations of the women in this study and each of the women had to face this stereotype, but they did so in different contexts. The meaning of welfare was different for each woman, and it was shaped by her life history. For example, for Lynn, a young woman who had only a brief marriage and knew a number of other women on public assistance, welfare held little symbolic meaning, and it gave her the opportunity to go back to school.

> You know, I was like I was supposed to get this degree. . . . Not that I don't wanna get off [welfare] and be independent.
>
> (Lynn, African American, poor during marriage)

In contrast, for Lisa, a middle-aged woman who had never been poor before her divorce, food stamps symbolized her fall from the middle class and were imbued with the pain of having lost her marriage, middle class standing and the future for which she had worked for twenty years. Lisa describes trying to make sense of her unexpected entrance into the welfare system in the following way:

> I think it's [her feelings of humiliation over receiving welfare] probably a reaction to where I am now, which is not at all where I expected to be. It's interesting, like the first time I went in there, I was talking to the first in-take person, I just broke down and sobbed. I said I can't believe I'm here. I can't believe it. And she said to me. . . . She was actually very nice about it. She said to me, "Lisa, you don't understand." She said, "More and more over the last five years we've had more women who were wives or ex-wives of doctors and lawyers and very successful businessmen come in and say those exact words." You just cannot believe that, I guess, that your life has taken such a major turn.
>
> (Lisa, white, middle class during marriage)

Being on welfare simply does not make sense to Lisa. Similarly, Erica, an African American woman who had surpassed her parents' economic position during her marriage, now bitterly compares her position to theirs:

> . . . and it was like my parents are so successful and not having any damn problems and that was a big thing, that it was just me. It was a total admission of failure, you know?
>
> (Erica, African American, middle class during marriage)

Another formerly middle class woman, Amy, who recently separated from her husband, explained to me how welfare benefits should be used. In the course of her explanation, it became evident that Amy was struggling to come to terms with her new economic position. Amy sounded confident and assertive as she discussed what welfare recipients should do in the abstract, but toward the end of her statement Amy's focus shifted to her own situation and her voice trailed off until it was almost inaudible:

> I think that anyone who is eligible [for welfare benefits] should be able to receive it if they chose to, but I don't think they—that you should look at that [welfare] as something that you are always going to get. You should always look to the future and see that you've got to get off it. This is just, for me this is just kind of a stopgap thing to get me through where I can afford . . . something. . . . I don't know what . . . just to manage.
>
> (Amy, white, middle class during marriage)

The fall from the middle class created tremendous confusion and anxiety for Linda, Erica and Amy. Respondents who came from families that had received public assistance at some time, on the other hand, did not experience the same kind of confusion. This is not to say that being on welfare was necessarily any easier, or even more acceptable, for them. For example, Diane, who had a very difficult relationship with her mother, a welfare recipient herself, saw receiving welfare as being a part of a painful legacy:

> She [her mother] probably expected me to continue the legacy of raising children on welfare and doing nothing with my life. If I did anything other than that she would probably be very disappointed with herself.
>
> (Diane, white, poor during marriage)

In contrast, Sally, whose mother had also been on welfare, was able to use her mother's experiences, and those of other family members who had received welfare, to legitimate her own use of welfare:

> Public assistance is not a taboo. I mean my mother was on it when she needed to be, when she was separated from my father and she had lost her two businesses she went on public assistance. She went to college when she was on public assistance and once she got a job she got off of it. So, that's the way I saw it. You use it until, you know, you have an income.
>
> (Sally, Latina, poor during marriage)

As the last two examples illustrate, former class status, while important, did not define how respondents experienced being on welfare. Rather, a combination of the respondent's social locations and personal histories seem to have shaped their feelings about being on welfare. The specific ways in which class, race and personal histories influenced the respondents' construction of personal identity is beyond the scope of this paper. The findings in this study, however, do suggest that the effects of personal background on welfare recipients' experiences of stigma and construction of personal identities may be fertile ground for further research.[3]

FOOD STAMPS AND STIGMA MANAGEMENT

Food stamps are highly visible stigma symbols, they instantly, and very publicly, reveal the user's economic position and status as a welfare recipient. Even respondents who stated that receiving welfare was nothing to be ashamed of bristled over having their status as public assistance recipients revealed in the course of their daily activities and without their consent. The women often talked about having lost their privacy and about being frustrated that other people "know their business." For example, Diane explained why she dislikes the objects that mark her as a welfare recipient:

> Food stamps and that little stupid blue health pass card they give you is just another way of labeling you. Your status is reduced now. You're not who you walked in as because now they see that you're less than in their mind, you're a welfare recipient.
>
> (Diane, white, poor during marriage)

Being labeled as a welfare recipients is extremely painful for Diane, and she generally tries to keep her status as a welfare recipient a secret. But this is not always possible, as the following story illustrates.

> When I moved here, I figured a new neighborhood, nobody knows my business. . . . The building I moved up out [of] in West Philly, everybody was on welfare. . . . [I]t was that kind of building. Everybody had food stamps and money problems and the whole bit. When I moved here I thought, oh good, this. . . . I mean there's a lot of poor people but they don't know my business. They don't know me and I can come in with some anonymity and it didn't work, because my landlord told everybody, oh the girl that's moving in she's on Section 8. He lives six houses down. So everybody knew my business and I felt so like. . . . With my mask and I couldn't even put it on, you know?
>
> (Diane, white, poor during marriage)

It is particularly hard for Diane to avoid being revealed as a welfare recipient when she uses food stamps:

> One day I was in the store and the lady needed change. You have to pay five. . . . There's five, tens and ones. And she said, I need change. I need some ones. And

---

3. See David Snow and Leon Anderson's *Down on Their Luck* (1993); especially chapter 7, for a discussion of the some of the ways homeless street people construct and negotiate their personal identities in light of their stigmatized social identities.

the girl several registers down said, I just gave you ones. And she said, For *food stamps!* I couldn't crawl small enough and close enough to the ground I felt so bad.

(Diane, white, poor during marriage)

Many of the respondents described feeling awkward using food stamps in front of particular people or groups of people. For example, Gina, who was raised in a working class family, talked about how she feels more hesitant to use food stamps in white neighborhoods. In her description, the social audience and situation in grocery stores outside of the inner city create a stigma that she does not feel when she shops in inner city neighborhoods:

Sometime I go and I don't shop in, say the inner city neighborhoods, my girlfriend and I we'll get in her car and we'll drive out to say a white neighborhood to go shopping—Super Fresh, or you know things like that and sometimes you are afraid, you don't want other people to see you pulling out food stamps.

(Gina, African American, poor during marriage)

Another respondent, Lisa, avoids being seen by people who know her by shopping in a grocery store outside of her neighborhood:

When I know I have to go shopping now I go to another store altogether . . . [N]ormally I would go to the Acme here. I've been going there for 16 years. Most of the people, the checkers, know me. Most of them have seen my kids grow up. Whereas if I go to the other one they don't know me and I am just kind of a face in the crowd. I don't know how to put this equation together. If you know what I mean. And I don't know whether it's something I perceive or if it's wished that when I pay with food stamps it's almost like I'm a nonentity. But I don't know if they're really reacting to me that way or if I choose to. . . . They sit there looking at me that way.

(Lisa, white, middle class during marriage)

Several of the women in this study were also concerned with how their children managed their use of food stamps. Pam, a young woman who had been raised in a working class family and was homeless for a time after escaping an extremely violent marriage, explains that she tries to teach her son to be discreet when he uses food stamps:

My oldest son, with the food stamps, he thinks it's like hey! And I told him, this is nothing you wanna, he wants to get food stamps and go to the corner store and buy some chips, a bag of chips and a soda. And I tell him no, it's not a thing like that. . . . It is like our family secret. . . . They can remember when we was in the shelter and so I tell them this is just like that. We just have to go through, but it's not something we want to make flyers and put out and make everybody know.

(Pam, African American, poor during marriage)

In contrast, Jenny, who is also from a working class background, has tried to teach her daughter not to feel awkward about using food stamps:

> So I learned in fact she [her daughter] felt funny about it especially when I would send her to the store with food stamps or whatever. You know, I didn't know it but she told me she was ashamed to use them. I thought the kid was just being lazy about going to the store. . . . But when she found out some kind of way that some of her friends were on DPA—so like now she is starting to understand that we're not the only ones in this boat, you know.
>
> (Jenny, African American, working class during marriage)

Though Pam and Jenny view food stamps differently, they have both had to teach their children how to manage food stamps and the information that food stamps convey.

Food stamps convey a degraded social status, and yet they also provide essential goods. Respondents disliked the social meaning of food stamps, but most also found food stamps helpful for budgeting and getting through the month. When I asked the women if they thought that food stamps should be replaced with cash, almost all said no. For the respondents, balancing the practical advantages of food stamps with potentially negative social consequences was a central task.

The Avoidance Strategy

Because of their power to discredit, almost all of the women in this study could think of times when they had chosen not to use food stamps. Using cash rather than food stamps was a common strategy used by respondents to avoid being labeled as welfare recipients. For example, Pam reported:

> One time I was with a friend, it was a guy, not my boyfriend but it was a friend and we was in the Acme and I felt so bad afterward because I only had a couple of dollars, you know green dollars, but I felt the way that I didn't want him to know that I was receiving public assistance.
>
> (Pam, African American, poor during marriage)

Similarly, Sally, a young woman whose mother had also received welfare, reported that she had chosen not to use food stamps when she recognized a person in the grocery store:

> I think someone was in line that was a parent of my son's [friend] . . . something like that, and I don't like them knowing my business.
>
> (Sally, Latina, poor during marriage)

Diane chose not to use food stamps to preserve an image of herself in front of two men that she did not even know:

> And then one time I was shopping and there were two good looking, really good looking guys—a couple of years ago when I was really thin. And they were making little comments about me. And I was going on a picnic with my then best friend Judy, who was the one on welfare, single parent and section 8 too. And I wouldn't pay with my food stamps. I paid in cash because I didn't want them to get a different idea of me. And she got on my case all the way to the car, all the way to the park. She said, that was so stupid. Why would you do that? I said, Judy, everybody was looking at me. They noticed me and I didn't want them to think any less of me, so, you know, I paid cash instead of stamps. Now, I know I'm going to suffer at the end of the month for doing that, but I did it.
>
> (Diane, white, poor during marriage)

Terri, who lives in an area where food stamps are common, often avoids being publicly discredited altogether by sending her boyfriend to the grocery store with her food stamps rather than going herself:

> I don't go to the store. I send my boyfriend. I call him up and he says "I don't care [about using food stamps], I'll go." Then he goes to the store.
>
> (Terri, Latina, poor during marriage)

Using food stamps in the grocery store brought the women's status as welfare recipients into sharp focus. In front of specific social audiences, such as boyfriends, neighbors, et cetera, being labeled as a welfare recipient was particularly troublesome to the respondents. In order to avoid being discredited in these situations, respondents employed several strategies: using cash rather than food stamps, shopping in different neighborhoods, and sending someone else to the grocery store. These strategies, especially using cash rather than food stamps, are difficult to sustain. The respondents had to choose carefully in which situations being discredited outweighed the relative hardships of an avoidance strategy. The calculations made by respondents highlights the dynamic nature of welfare stigma; if welfare stigma were static, then there would be no need to employ strategies that can only be used sporadically.

The Recasting Strategy

Recasting welfare in a more positive light was another strategy used by respondents to manage welfare stigma. Though they could not eliminate the negative public images of welfare recipients, respondents could, and did, recast welfare in a more positive light for themselves. Knowing that other people used or accepted food stamps helped some of the respondents to view their own use of food stamps more positively. In a striking example of recasting welfare, Lynn "discovered" (incorrectly) that food stamps were legal tender outside of the United States:

> And as I found out from my sister, she is really intelligent. She's been around and everything. She told me she's taken her food stamps outside the United States and used them because you can. . . . She said they are legal tender just like money. I was shocked, you know. She was like with somebody important. And she went into the store and pulled out food stamps. I was like, oh my god. I was like, you go girl. I didn't know that. . . . It's just to know that . . . to know that they're legal tender elsewhere.
>
> (Lynn, African American, poor during marriage)

Hearing that her sister was able to use food stamps outside of the United States helped Lynn to view food stamps as being legitimate, "just like money" in every way. Similarly, seeing her sister use food stamps in front of "someone important" helped Lynn to be less ashamed about using food stamps herself. In a similar story, Jenny, an African American respondent, explained that seeing white people use food stamps helped her to view food stamps as being legitimate and nothing to be embarrassed about:

> I was pretty much embarrassed. . . . Then I seen some of the white people around here with them, I said, "oh well that's it." So now it didn't bother me.
>
> (Jenny, African American, working class during marriage)

Sally, a young Latina woman, was able to construct a positive image of welfare recipients based on her own experiences:

> The only images [of welfare recipients] I had were of my mother or my family members and I knew that they were on the system because they needed to be on the system.
>
> (Sally, Latina, poor during marriage)

The positive image of welfare recipients that Sally gained from her family helped her to legitimate being on welfare herself.

Lisa and Erica, two formerly middle class respondents, framed their being on welfare as a consequence of larger social forces. Lisa was able to depersonalize and manage the stigma of welfare by seeing her economic decline as being, in part, a result of an economic recession.

> There's so many people in unemployment and then on the welfare when unemployment runs out. Many of them have no alternative but to go on welfare whether it's food stamps or, you know, total assistance. And again that's not through any fault of their own. And I don't know what the proportions are, but

my guess is there's probably a whole lot bigger numbers of people on some form
of public assistance now as a direct result. I mean, I call it a depression.

(Lisa, white, middle class during marriage)

Lisa also viewed being on welfare as the result of her divorce and of unjust
divorce laws:

I think with the divorce rate coming up, a lot of women . . . the divorce laws
totally inadequate, totally inadequate. Leaves a lot of women who otherwise
would still be in whatever marriage. Leaves them out on a limb because the laws
aren't there to protect their interests and their children's interest.

(Lisa, white, middle class during marriage)

Erica viewed her entrance onto welfare as the combined result of her
divorce, economic hard times and racism. During her marriage Erica had
achieved a middle class household income of around $40,000. After her hus-
band left, Erica struggled financially but survived. She supported herself and
her son for several years before she lost her job when the hospital at which she
worked was sold:

I'm going to be honest and tell you. Being African American, there's a lot of us
who are out of work and there is a lot of us who are. . . . If we're getting the assistance ourselves [or] we know somebody who say getting assistance and it is not
the big embarrassment that it might be, other people, you know. And you're the
last hired, first fired. You tend to have to find stopgap measures.

(Erica, African American, middle class during marriage)

One interesting aspect of the recasting strategy is that there seemed to be
a class pattern to it. Formerly working and lower class respondents, such as
Lynn, Sally, and Jenny, tended to recast welfare itself in a positive light, seeing
it as a legitimate form of income. In contrast, formerly middle class respondents, such as Lynn and Erica, emphasized the larger social forces, such as
economic hard times combined with racial and gender inequality, that made
their receipt of welfare inevitable. Seeing their being on welfare as the
inevitable outcome of social inequality, the middle class women were able to
deflect some of the stigma of welfare. In both of these strategies, the respondents redefined the meaning of their being on welfare in a more positive light.

CONCLUSION

The preceding accounts illustrate some of the ways in which welfare stigma
is constructed and managed in the daily lives of the women in this study. This
study suggests that welfare stigma is produced in the interaction of situation,
social audience, and the recipient's life history. This conceptualization of

welfare stigma fits with Goffman's identification of stigma as situated and produced within specific relationships. As each individual has numerous relationships, the meaning of welfare stigma may vary depending on the situation and the people involved. These findings suggest that further exploration of the ways in which receiving welfare is incorporated into the construction of identity would be worthwhile.

* * *

The theoretical frame of this study suggests that the stigma of welfare is inherent to the current American welfare system and that the perception that welfare recipients are "cheating tax-paying citizens" is, at least in part, a result of the history and design of the American welfare system. Yet the ways in which welfare stigma is constructed and managed in recipients' daily lives remains largely unexplored. Older approaches to studying welfare stigma, such as stigma indices, do not account for possible situational and relational aspects of stigma and therefore do not, by themselves, provide a sufficiently thorough understanding of the nature of welfare stigma. By applying symbolic interactionism to the study of welfare stigma, this paper begins to illuminate the situational and relational aspects of welfare stigma, particularly in terms of the management of food stamps as stigma symbols.

Further research on the daily interactions of welfare recipients is essential for a deeper understanding of the nature of welfare stigma and the ways in which it is created and managed in daily life. The current * * * welfare system focuses on bringing welfare recipients back into the American mainstream by demanding that recipients work and by limiting welfare benefits. But it is not clear that non-work or dependency on government assistance in themselves place welfare recipients outside of the mainstream. Homemakers do not engage in waged labor, and many elderly are dependent on social security, yet there is no sense that these people are outsiders in America. Why welfare recipients have a degraded social status, how this status is constructed, and what the effects of this status are on recipients' lives remain unanswered questions. Given the centrality of welfare reform as a political issue and the rising poverty rates in America, these questions are crucial. Exploring the construction and management of welfare stigma at a daily level may prove to be a particularly important path for research to take in approaching these questions.

REFERENCES

Goffman, E. 1986. *Stigma,* New York: Simon and Schuster.

Simmel, Georg. 1971[1908]. *Georg Simmel on Individuality and Social Forms: Selected Writings,* Chicago: University of Chicago Press.

Skocpol, T. 1992. *Protecting Soldiers and Mothers,* Cambridge: Harvard University Press.

Snow, D., and Anderson, L. 1993. *Down on Their Luck,* Berkeley: University of California Press.

13

My Secret Life as a Black Man

ANTHONY WALTON

Willingly or not, we all provide clues, signs and bits of information that others use to identify and interact with us. Sometimes this information is to our advantage; sometimes it is not. In all cases, we find it difficult to convince others that they have read a "cultural marker" wrongly or that they are attaching exaggerated importance to it. In this essay, the author takes us into the thinking of a man who, while proud to be African American, finds others' expectations a barrier to the kind of life he would like to lead.

I have often thought of myself as having two lives: my life as a black man and my other, real life. Since grammar school I've felt a tension at play in my inner life, a pull between what was expected of me as a young black boy, adolescent, and man, and what I wanted as myself, Anthony. I've been at war, and the stakes of the battle are who I am and who I can become. When I was younger, I thought this struggle would end at some point. Now, at thirty-six, I realize it won't end; that its roots are as deep as the most fundamental problem of philosophy—the uneasy coexistence of body and soul. As William James writes in *The Principles of Psychology,* "Our bodies themselves, are they simply ours, or are they *us?*"

One night last November I walked along the pier at the southern tip of Miami Beach with an old friend from school, a white woman. The evening was unseasonably warm, and moonlit. We hadn't seen each other in eight or nine months, and we were chatting amiably, taking our time. My friend was excited about a book of poems by David Malouf and was exhorting me to read it.

About a third of the way out we passed a middle-aged black woman who remarked on my friend's considerable beauty and the color of her blond hair. I thought to myself, "How nice!," but when I entered the woman's frame of vision, she launched into a tirade. "Oh, I see," she hissed, "one of them who done married a white wife. Think you too good!" She followed us most of the way down the pier for what felt like an excruciating length of time, berating my friend for being with me, excoriating me for treason to the race—then she suddenly turned back and disappeared as abruptly as she had pounced.

I don't know if the woman was deranged or just angry, but the incident—this is what troubles me most—wasn't really anything new. That night in

Miami was merely one more instance in which I'd offended another person, in this case a black person, by doing nothing more than living my own life.

I can remember conflicts years before with certain black kids in Aurora, Illinois, the town where I grew up, over my bookishness, my flagrant love of school and the library, and my tendency to make friends outside of the race and to join groups like Little League and Boy Scouts, activities considered insufficiently "black." One girl was so outraged by my failure to follow her tightly circumscribed ideas of how the black kids in our neighborhood should act that for two years she and the boys in her clique threw my books in the mud, picked fights with me after school, and threatened a white friend of mine in an attempt to stop us from sharing a locker. In the end, I withdrew from public school and enrolled in a Catholic school.

All along there were conflicts with white kids as well—over the appropriateness of my aspirations and the threat these aspirations posed to them. I wasn't in their group, and many seemed to think there was only so much achievement to go around. Along the way I also butted heads with black and white teachers, both groups declaring me too big for my britches, though for different reasons—some whites thinking I was uppity and arrogant, some blacks thinking I was more brazenly self-confident than was healthy for a young black.

Most troubling were the struggles with my parents, who for a long time disapproved of my "over-involvement" with the arts. *I* wanted to be Martin Scorsese or Sting; in *their* scenario, I was to be a doctor or a pastor, the crown jewel of our family's long struggle up from slavery. At times my parents seemed heartbroken over our lack of common ground. To their thinking, I was courting disaster by turning my back on the way that black people had done things for ages.

Finally, there were the momentary, or ongoing, scrapes with white strangers—the wider world—those people too busy, fearful, or thoughtless to perceive others in any fashion other than as stereotypes. When these people gazed upon me, they saw only what their culture and society had constructed and coded as a "black man." And a six-foot, two-hundred-fifty pound one at that—a threat to doormen, security guards, and cabdrivers; someone suspicious, dangerous, but irrelevant.

Black strangers, like the woman in Miami, were often just as troubling, expecting me to conform completely to their ideological and cosmological positions, even though we knew nothing about each other.

The problem of defining the self, of authenticity, is a problem for every human. But, for better and worse, it is more sharply and starkly dramatized for blacks. Walking down the street, I can't simply be lost in my thoughts, in my soul—in what I'll have for dinner, a movie I saw the night before, an essay I read about Flaubert—because I'm constantly jolted and reminded, by the looks in strangers' eyes, of my *body,* and of the assumptions and expectations that go along with it. What I think of as myself, my soul, is under crippling siege.

A black man * * * is still constantly being told—by society, by the media, by white behavior and stricture, by other blacks—what he should think, what his soul's affinities should be, whom he should love and be in love with, what his ultimate loyalties are.

I have tried to imagine what the black woman in Miami thought she saw that evening and why she reacted the way she did. I can forgive her the rage, if not the bad manners. It was almost as if two different zones of reality and history—with their varied expectations of behavior and duty—had collided. To the woman, perhaps my white friend was the symbol of everything that had oppressed her and her people down through time. To me, she was someone I'd sat next to in class. I suppose the black woman and I each had to live up to, and live with, our respective interpretations of the scene, but as blacks we have historically been expected to agree with each other—which in this case was impossible.

The desires and intentions others have for me, however profound or super-fluous, usually conflict with my own. And so of necessity I devised a way of navigating these treacherous shoals of expectation, a mode of being that allows me to maneuver through society, black, white, rich, poor—and one that I sus-pect has cost me something. I learned, quite unconsciously, how to be a "black man," how to slide through the surface of any situation. I developed, in fact, a great many ways of being, a sense of the self as a shape-shifter, a kind of post-modern extrapolation of DuBois's "double-consciousness."

In Harlem, talk crap and slap palms; in Scarsdale, be the soul of probity; in Mississippi, agree with whoever is talking; with my parents, steer the conver-sation away from anything remotely "controversial." I became like Ralph Elli-son's Rinehart, the chameleon of *Invisible Man*—all things to all people, who-ever they wanted him to be.

A black man, if he chooses to enter mainstream society, must manipulate many contexts, must alter his appearance often and change his diction and demeanor as circumstances require. Classically, this was known as "bowing and scraping," but today, with a wider range of possibilities in a society that is itself fragmenting, the reality is far more complex.

A black man's "identity" in the boardroom of a bank is different from his "identity" as an anonymous black motorist stopped by the police, and both of those are different from his "identity" as a husband and father, or with his friends, be they black, white, or black and white. A day in Los Angeles that might start in South Central could finish in Orange County. How much skill and energy and psychic strength is required to "pass" in these wildly differ-ent places? These (and many more) fragments of identity are shifting and overlapping and contradicting one another daily.

Other questions of identity underlie and plague this fluid, protean self. Am I a human first? A male? A Christian? A black? A black male? Or am I a South-erner? A Midwesterner? A college graduate? A bourgeois? A writer?

I think it's safe to say that being black is not necessarily the irreducible fact of black people's lives. My parents, and millions of other blacks like them, think of themselves as African-Americans. They could be fairly described as militantly proud of that fact. But if you said to them, or many other blacks, that they had to choose between their Christianity or blackness, they would happily choose Christianity even if it meant they would be martyred.

My various modes of moving through and effacing a society, black and white, * * * were conceived as techniques for surviving the resulting fragmentation of self. I now see, as I get older, that the techniques *themselves* are something I must survive, as they pose a danger of leading me away from being true to myself (and thus true to others).

The problem, put simply, is one of authenticity—of preserving the capacity for being whole in a specific moment and honest with one's self, and with others.

I had been forced to consider if somehow I owed it to the woman on the pier to be strolling that night with a black woman. This brings me to the question, *Is* there a me that is not defined by others, and not defined solely in opposition to them?

The philosopher Charles Taylor has written, "Being true to myself means being true to my own originality, which is something that only I can articulate and discover. In articulating it, I am also defining myself."

Each of us is an original, and has an original way of existing as a human, though we may not ever fully realize it. Emerson emphasized that the soul was a unique and private thing, to be guarded from the world, to be mined, probed, and created in secret. But what does this notion of defining one's self mean to a black man?

Throughout my life what I've been hearing in various forms is, "Be true to your kind." But I wonder who, exactly, are my kind: the black kids who tried to stop me from going to the library, or the old white lady librarian who, without my asking, set aside special books for me on subjects I liked? People who share my epidermal melanin content, and perhaps little else, or those who share my obsessive interests in Glenn Gould, Thelonious Monk, and string quartets? Am I my skin color, my gender, my family's social position? Or instead, am I my loyalties, my pleasures, those people and things I love? How do I choose who I am? How much is society choosing for me, and how much am I choosing for myself? Can I be, irreducibly, anything that I do not choose to be?

There are, classically, three constituents of identity—biology, culture, and belief—and the problem in our society is that we are always turning the categorical (abstractions humans invent in order to assign meaning and hierarchy) into the biological (descriptive facts that cannot be modified and that can have an irrevocable impact on one's fate). To describe someone as "black" or "Irish" or "Cuban" is to say something very different about that person than to describe him as male or as left-handed or as having heart disease, but we often invest the two kinds of description with equal authority. As Ellison wrote in *Invisible Man,* however, blackness is "not exactly a matter of a biochemical accident [of] my epidermis. . . . [it] occurs because of a peculiar disposition of the eyes of those with whom I come in contact." This "peculiar disposition," I might add, occurs in the eyes of blacks as well as whites.

It becomes tempting, taking into account the dangers of imprecise descriptors, to say that there is no such thing as a "black man," or any of the other socially constructed categories we have become used to declaiming. But we know that this is not quite true, or I wouldn't be writing this essay.

* * *

When, late at night, I get on the elevator in the library of the college where I teach, the female student who reacts uncomfortably to my presence as we ride down alone is not necessarily interested in the fact that I'm carrying books by Emerson, Gordimer, and Rorty. On my good days, I shrug and say to myself, it's not me—not a black man—that she finds so alarming, but the general category of "male."

When I think of my lonely hours in the library, or in contemplation and in prayer, I don't see why my most personal affinities should be of interest, or meaning, to anyone but me and those few with whom I choose to open my self. Why must the people I love, the things and places I treasure, my lifetime's accumulation of an interior life, become subject to other people's politics, shallow rhetoric, and public scrutiny?

We live in a society that forces sincere and law-abiding people to break themselves into little pieces in order to survive it, to inhabit the margins of the culture rather than to embrace it whole. Democracy, in its pure, and even its corrupted form, should allow us to choose a self freely. Instead, in its modern-day American version, it leads, in the end, to a more fragmented self. The tragic legacy of our democracy, as described by Ralph Ellison, is that as we are freed from sweeping social categories, from fixed, generational identities— and in order to flee the anguish of choice and responsibility, we simply create our own smaller categories and defend them viciously. We are "Asian," "black," "gay," "suburban," "Latino," "white," "feminist," "conservative"— a legacy of soundbites, the commodified self, the "self" bought and sold for its utility.

It is almost structurally impossible for an American—and I stress that I'm speaking for more than black males here—simultaneously and openly to embrace and enjoy all of the aspects of the culture for which he or she might feel an affinity.

Are we becoming a nation of Rineharts, with different personas at work, at home, at play, at church? Is this the new human condition * * * ? Race, religion, gender, sexual preference, social class, economic power, age—definitions of some aspect of identity are always going to be at odds with others and preclude simple choices.

I am a black man, however, and I suspect that the question, finally, is not "What does it mean to be a black man?" but rather, "What is living as a black man in this society doing to me, to my soul?" *Is* there a me aside from the black man? Am I finally, and only, my body, or are the soul and body of a black man two different things?

There is a Zen koan that says, "Show me your original face; show me the face you had before you were born." The question is, Can an American black man in the late twentieth century find that original face under the noise and expectations that surround and overwhelm him once he is in the world? Dare he show it? Can others see it?

14

Optional Ethnicities: For Whites Only?

MARY C. WATERS

Social status—both positive and negative—is often a matter of choice or accomplishment, what sociologists call achieved status. In other cases status is ascribed, based on features associated with the group with which we are identified or associated, like it or not. Sex, age, visible disabilities, and skin color are important ascribed characteristics in American society. Less visible are national origin and ethnicity. Some people choose to be ethnically identified, usually to benefit from a positive personal identity or the celebration of a proud tradition. Others do not choose an ethnic identity, nor does it always confer benefits. For them, ethnicity is not optional. This essay by Mary Waters may help some students understand a little better what others are saying about the meaning of being Black or Chicano or Asian or American Indian or another nonoptional ethnicity.

ETHNIC IDENTITY FOR WHITES IN THE 1990s

What does it mean to talk about ethnicity as an option for an individual? To argue that an individual has some degree of choice in their ethnic identity flies in the face of the common sense notion of ethnicity many of us believe in—that one's ethnic identity is a fixed characteristic, reflective of blood ties and given at birth. However, social scientists who study ethnicity have long concluded that while ethnicity is based in a *belief* in a common ancestry, ethnicity is primarily a *social* phenomenon, not a biological one. The belief that members of an ethnic group have that they share a common ancestry may not be a fact. There is a great deal of change in ethnic identities across generations through intermarriage, changing allegiances, and changing social categories. There is also a much larger amount of change in the identities of individuals over their life than is commonly believed. While most people are aware of the phenomena known as "passing"—people raised as one race who change at some point and claim a different race as their identity, there are similar life course changes in ethnicity that happen all the time and are not given the same degree of attention as "racial passing."

White Americans of European ancestry can be described as having a great deal of choice in terms of their ethnic identities. The two major types of options White Americans can exercise are (1) the option of whether to claim any specific ancestry, or to just be "White" or American, and (2) the choice of which of their European ancestries to choose to include in their description of their own identities. In both cases, the option of choosing how to present yourself on surveys and in everyday social interactions exists for Whites because of social changes and societal conditions that have created a great deal of social mobility, immigrant assimilation, and political and economic power for Whites in the United States. Specifically, the option of being able to not claim any ethnic identity exists for Whites of European background in the United States because they are the majority group—in terms of holding political and social power, as well as being a numerical majority. The option of choosing among different ethnicities in their family backgrounds exists because the degree of discrimination and social distance attached to specific European backgrounds has diminished over time.

The Ethnic Miracle

When European immigration to the United States was sharply curtailed in the late 1920s, a process was set in motion whereby the European ethnic groups already in the United States were for all intents and purposes cut off from any new arrivals. As a result, the composition of the ethnic groups began to age generationally. The proportion of each ethnic group made up of immigrants or the first generation began to gradually decline, and the proportion made up of the children, grandchildren, and eventually great-grandchildren began to increase. Consequently, by 1990 most European-origin ethnic groups in the United States were composed of a very small number of immigrants, and a very large proportion of people whose link to their ethnic origins in Europe was increasingly remote.

This generational change was accompanied by unprecedented social and economic changes. The very success of the assimilation process these groups experienced makes it difficult to imagine how much the question of the immigrants' eventual assimilation was an open one at the turn of the century. At the peak of immigration from southern and central Europe there was widespread discrimination and hostility against the newcomers by established Americans. Italians, Poles, Greeks, and Jews were called derogatory names, attacked by nativist mobs, and derided in the press. Intermarriage across ethnic lines was very uncommon—castelike in the words of some sociologists (Pagnini and Morgan 1990). The immigrants and their children were residentially segregated, occupationally specialized, and generally poor.

After several generations in the United States, the situation has changed a great deal. The success and social mobility of the grandchildren and great-grandchildren of that massive wave of immigrants from Europe has been called "The Ethnic Miracle" (Greeley 1976). These Whites have moved away from the inner-city ethnic ghettos to White middle-class suburban homes. They are doctors, lawyers, entertainers, academics, governors, and Supreme Court justices. But contrary to what some social science theorists and some politicians predicted or hoped for, these middle-class Americans have not completely given up ethnic identity. Instead, they have maintained some connection with their immigrant ancestors' identities—becoming Irish American doctors, Italian American Supreme Court justices, and Greek American presidential candidates. In the tradition of cultural pluralism, successful middle-class Americans in the late twentieth century maintain some degree of identity with their ethnic backgrounds. They have remained "hyphenated Americans." So while social mobility and declining discrimination have created the option of not identifying with any European ancestry, most White Americans continue to report some ethnic background.

* * *

Symbolic Ethnicities for White Americans

What do these ethnic identities mean to people and why do they cling to them rather than just abandoning the tie and calling themselves American? My own field research with suburban Whites in California and Pennsylvania found that later-generation descendants of European origin maintain what are called "symbolic ethnicities." Symbolic ethnicity is a term coined by Herbert Gans (1979) to refer to ethnicity that is individualistic in nature and without real social cost for the individual. These symbolic identifications are essentially leisure time activities, rooted in nuclear family traditions and reinforced by the voluntary enjoyable aspects of being ethnic (Waters 1990). Richard Alba (1990) also found later-generation Whites in Albany, New York, who chose to keep a tie with an ethnic identity because of the enjoyable and voluntary aspects to those identities, along with the feelings of specialness they entailed. An example of symbolic ethnicity is individuals who identify as Irish, for example, on occasions such as Saint Patrick's Day, on family holidays, or for vacations. They do not usually belong to Irish American organizations, live in Irish neighborhoods, work in Irish jobs, or marry other Irish people. The symbolic meaning of being Irish American can be constructed by individuals from mass media images, family traditions, or other intermittent social activities. In other words, for later-generation White ethnics, ethnicity is not something that influences their lives unless they want it to. In the world of work and school and neighborhood, individuals do not have to admit to being ethnic unless they choose to. And for an increasing number of European-origin individuals whose parents and grandparents have intermarried, the ethnicity they claim is largely a matter of personal choice as they sort through all of the possible combinations of groups in their genealogies.

* * *

In responding to the ancestry question, the comparative latitude that White respondents have does not mean that Whites pick and choose ethnicities out of thin air. For the most part people choose an identity that corresponds with some element of their family tree. However, there are many anecdotal instances of people adopting ethnicities when they marry or move to a strongly identified neighborhood or community. For instance Micaela di Leonardo (1984) reported instances of non-Italian women who married into Italian American families and "became Italian." Karen Leonard (1992) describes a community of Mexican American women who married Punjabi immigrants in California. Some of the Punjabi immigrants and their descendants were said to have "become Mexican" when they joined their wives kin group and social worlds. Alternatively she describes the community acknowledging that Mexican women made the best curry, as they adapted to life with Indian-origin men.

But what do these identities mean to individuals? Surely an identity that is optional in a number of ways—not legally defined on a passport or birth certificate, not socially consequential in terms of societal discrimination in terms of housing or job access, and not economically limiting in terms of blocking opportunities for social mobility—cannot be the same as an identity that results from and is nurtured by societal exclusion and rejection. The choice to have a symbolic ethnicity is an attractive and widespread one despite its lack of demonstrable content, because having a symbolic ethnicity combines individuality with feelings of community. People reported to me that they liked having an ethnic identity because it gave them a uniqueness and a feeling of being special. They often contrasted their own specialness by virtue of their ethnic identities with "bland" American-ness. Being ethnic makes people feel unique and special and not just "vanilla" as one of my respondents put it. * * *

* * *

Symbolic ethnicity is the best of all worlds for these respondents. These White ethnics can claim to be unique and special, while simultaneously finding the community and conformity with others that they also crave. But that "community" is of a type that will not interfere with a person's individuality. It is not as if these people belong to ethnic voluntary organizations or gather as a group in churches or neighborhoods or union halls. They work and reside within the mainstream of American middle-class life, yet they retain the interesting benefits—the "specialness"—of ethnic allegiance, without any of its drawbacks.

* * *

RACE RELATIONS AND SYMBOLIC ETHNICITY

However much symbolic ethnicity is without cost for the individual, there is a cost associated with symbolic ethnicity for the society. That is because symbolic ethnicities of the type described here are confined to White Americans of European origin. Black Americans, Hispanic Americans, Asian Americans, and American Indians do not have the option of a symbolic ethnicity at present in the United States. For all of the ways in which ethnicity does not matter for White Americans, it does matter for non-Whites. Who your ancestors are does affect your choice of spouse, where you live, what job you have, who your friends are, and what your chances are for success in American society, if those ancestors happen not to be from Europe. The reality is that White ethnics have a lot more choice and room for maneuver than they themselves think they do. The situation is very different for members of racial minorities, whose lives are strongly influenced by their race or national origin regardless of how much they may choose not to identify themselves in terms of their ancestries.

When White Americans learn the stories of how their grandparents and great-grandparents triumphed in the United States over adversity, they are usually told in terms of their individual efforts and triumphs. The important role of labor unions and other organized political and economic actors in their social and economic successes are left out of the story in favor of a generational story of individual Americans rising up against communitarian, Old World intolerance and New World resistance. As a result, the "individualized" voluntary, cultural view of ethnicity for Whites is what is remembered.

One important implication of these identities is that they tend to be very individualistic. There is a tendency to view valuing diversity in a pluralist environment as equating all groups. The symbolic ethnic tends to think that all groups are equal; everyone has a background that is their right to celebrate and pass on to their children. This leads to the conclusion that all identities are equal and all identities in some sense are interchangeable—"I'm Italian American, you're Polish American. I'm Irish American, you're African American." The important thing is to treat people as individuals and all equally. However, this assumption ignores the very big difference between an individualistic symbolic ethnic identity and a socially enforced and imposed racial identity.

* * *

* * * When White Americans equate their own symbolic ethnicities with the socially enforced identities of non-White Americans, they obscure the fact that the experiences of Whites and non-Whites have been qualitatively different in the United States and that the current identities of individuals partly reflect that unequal history.

In the next section I describe how relations between Black and White students on college campuses reflect some of these asymmetries in the understanding of what a racial or ethnic identity means. While I focus on Black and White students in the following discussion, you should be aware that the myriad other groups in the United States—Mexican Americans, American Indians, Japanese Americans—all have some degree of social and individual influences on their identities, which reflect the group's social and economic history and present circumstance.

Relations on College Campuses

Both Black and White students face the task of developing their race and ethnic identities. Sociologists and psychologists note that at the time people leave home and begin to live independently from their parents, often ages eighteen to twenty-two, they report a heightened sense of racial and ethnic identity as they sort through how much of their beliefs and behaviors are idiosyncratic to their families and how much are shared with other people. It is not until one comes in close contact with many people who are different from oneself that individuals realize the ways in which their backgrounds may influence their individual personality. This involves coming into contact with people who are different in terms of their ethnicity, class, religion, region, and race. For White students, the ethnicity they claim is more often than not a symbolic one—with all of the voluntary, enjoyable, and intermittent characteristics I have described above.

Black students at the university are also developing identities through interactions with others who are different from them. Their identity development is more complicated than that of Whites because of the added element of racial discrimination and racism, along with the "ethnic" developments of finding others who share their background. Thus Black students have the positive attraction of being around other Black students who share some cultural elements, as well as the need to band together with other students in a reactive and oppositional way in the face of racist incidents on campus.

Colleges and universities across the country have been increasing diversity among their student bodies in the last few decades. This has led in many cases to strained relations among students from different racial and ethnic backgrounds. The 1980s and 1990s produced a great number of racial incidents and high racial tensions on campuses. While there were a number of racial incidents that were due to bigotry, unlawful behavior, and violent or vicious attacks, much of what happens among students on campuses involves a low level of tension and awkwardness in social interactions.

Many Black students experience racism personally for the first time on campus. The upper-middle-class students from White suburbs were often isolated enough that their presence was not threatening to racists in their high schools. Also, their class background was known by their residence and this may have prevented attacks being directed at them. Often Black students at the university who begin talking with other students and recognizing racial slights will remember incidents that happened to them earlier that they might not have thought were related to race.

* * *

* * * Black students do experience a tension and a feeling of being singled out. It is unfair that this is part of their college experience and not that of White students. Dealing with incidents like this, or the ever-present threat of such incidents, is an ongoing developmental task for Black students that takes

energy, attention, and strength of character. It should be clearly understood that this is an asymmetry in the "college experience" for Black and White students. It is one of the unfair aspects of life that results from living in a society with ongoing racial prejudice and discrimination. It is also very understandable that it makes some students angry at the unfairness of it all, even if there is no one to blame specifically. * * *

In some sense then, as Blauner (1992) has argued, you can see Black students coming together on campus as both an "ethnic" pull of wanting to be together to share common experiences and community, and a "racial" push of banding together defensively because of perceived rejection and tension from Whites. In this way the ethnic identities of Black students are in some sense similar to, say, Korean students wanting to be together to share experiences. And it is an ethnicity that is generally much stronger than, say, Italian Americans. But for Koreans who come together there is generally a definition of themselves as "different from" Whites. For Blacks reacting to exclusion, there is a tendency for the coming together to involve both being "different from" but also "opposed to" Whites.

The anthropologist John Ogbu (1990) has documented the tendency of minorities in a variety of societies around the world, who have experienced severe blocked mobility for long periods of time, to develop such oppositional identities. An important component of having such an identity is to describe others of your group who do not join in the group solidarity as devaluing and denying their very core identity. This is why it is not common for successful Asians to be accused by others of "acting White" in the United States, but it is quite common for such a term to be used by Blacks and Latinos. The oppositional component of a Black identity also explains how Black people can question whether others are acting "Black enough." On campus, it explains some of the intense pressures felt by Black students who do not make their racial identity central and who choose to hang out primarily with non-Blacks. This pressure from the group, which is partly defining itself by not being White, is exacerbated by the fact that race is a physical marker in American society. No one immediately notices the Jewish students sitting together in the dining hall, or the one Jewish student sitting surrounded by non-Jews, or the Texan sitting with the Californians, but everyone notices the Black student who is or is not at the "Black table" in the cafeteria.

An example of the kinds of misunderstandings that can arise because of different understandings of the meanings and implications of symbolic versus oppositional identities concerns questions students ask one another in the dorms about personal appearances and customs. A very common type of interaction in the dorm concerns questions Whites ask Blacks about their hair. Because Whites tend to know little about Blacks, and Blacks know a lot about Whites, there is a general asymmetry in the level of curiosity people have about one another. Whites, as the numerical majority, have had little contact with Black culture; Blacks, especially those who are in college, have had to develop bicultural skills—knowledge about the social worlds of both Whites and Blacks. Miscommunication and hurt feelings about White students' questions about Black students' hair illustrate this point. One of the things that happens freshman year is that White students are around Black students as they fix their hair. White students are generally quite curious about Black students' hair—they have basic questions such as how often Blacks wash their hair, how they get it straightened or curled, what products they use on their hair, how they comb it, etc. Whites often wonder to themselves whether they should ask these questions. One thought experiment Whites perform is to ask themselves whether a particular question would upset them. Adopting the "do unto others" rule, they ask themselves, "If a Black person was curious about my hair would I get upset?" The answer usually is "No, I would be happy to tell them." Another example is an Italian American student wondering to herself, "Would I be upset if someone asked me about calamari?" The answer is no, so she asks her Black roommate about collard greens, and the roommate explodes with an angry response such as, "Do you think all Black people eat watermelon too?" Note that if this Italian American knew her friend was Trinidadian American and asked about peas and rice the situation would be more similar and would not necessarily ignite underlying tensions.

* * * Because Blacks tend to have more knowledge about Whites than vice versa, there is not an even exchange going on, the Black freshman is likely to have fewer basic questions about his White roommate than his White roommate has about him. Because of the differences historically in the group experiences of Blacks and Whites there are some connotations to Black hair that don't exist about White hair. (For instance, is straightening your hair a form of assimilation, do some people distinguish between women having "good hair" and "bad hair" in terms of beauty and how is that related to looking "White"?). Finally, even a Black freshman who cheerfully disregards or is unaware that there are these asymmetries will soon slam into another asymmetry if she willingly answers every innocent question asked of her. In a situation where Blacks make up only 10 percent of the student body, if every non-Black needs to be educated about hair, she will have to explain it to nine other students. As one Black student explained to me, after you've been asked a couple of times about something so personal you begin to feel like you are an attraction in a zoo, that you are at the university for the education of the White students.

Institutional Responses

Our society asks a lot of young people. We ask young people to do something that no one else does as successfully on such a wide scale—that is to live together with people from very different backgrounds, to respect one another, to appreciate one another, and to enjoy and learn from one another. The successes that occur every day in this endeavor are many, and they are too often overlooked. However, the problems and tensions are also real, and they will not vanish on their own. We tend to see pluralism working in the United States in much the same way some people expect capitalism to work. If you put together people with various interests and abilities and resources, the "invisible hand" of capitalism is supposed to make all the parts work together in an economy for the common good.

There is much to be said for such a model—the invisible hand of the market can solve complicated problems of production and distribution better than any "visible hand" of a state plan. However, we have learned that unequal power relations among the actors in the capitalist marketplace, as well as "externalities" that the market cannot account for, such as long-term pollution, or collusion between corporations, or the exploitation of child labor, means that state regulation is often needed. Pluralism and the relations between groups are very similar. There is a lot to be said for the idea that bringing people who belong to different ethnic or racial groups together in institutions with no interference will have good consequences. Students from different backgrounds will make friends if they share a dorm room or corridor, and there is no need for the institution to do any more than provide the locale. But like capitalism, the invisible hand of pluralism does not do well when power relations and externalities are ignored. When you bring together individuals from groups that are differentially valued in the wider society and provide no guidance, there will be problems. In these cases the "invisible hand" of pluralist relations does not work, and tensions and disagreements can arise without any particular individual or group of individuals being "to blame." On college campuses in the 1990s some of the tensions between students are of this sort. They arise from honest misunderstandings, lack of a common background, and very different experiences of what race and ethnicity mean to the individual.

The implications of symbolic ethnicities for thinking about race relations are subtle but consequential. If your understanding of your own ethnicity and its relationship to society and politics is one of individual choice, it becomes harder to understand the need for programs like affirmative action, which recognize the ongoing need for group struggle and group recognition, in order to bring about social change.* It also is hard for a White college student to understand the need that minority students feel to band together against discrimination. It also is easy, on the individual level, to expect everyone else to be able to turn their ethnicity on and off at will, the way you are able to, without understanding that ongoing discrimination and societal attention to minority status makes that impossible for individuals from minority groups to do. The paradox of symbolic ethnicity is that it depends upon the ultimate goal of a pluralist society, and at the same time makes it more difficult to achieve that ultimate goal. It is dependent upon the concept that all ethnicities mean the same thing, that enjoying the traditions of one's heritage is an option available to a group or an individual, but that such a heritage should not have any social costs associated with it.

---

*[See Massey 2004.]

* * * [T]here are many societal issues and involuntary ascriptions associated with non-White identities. The developments necessary for this to change are not individual but societal in nature. Social mobility and declining racial and ethnic sensitivity are closely associated. The legacy and the present reality of discrimination on the basis of race or ethnicity must be overcome before the ideal of a pluralist society, where all heritages are treated equally and are equally available for individuals to choose or discard at will, is realized.

REFERENCES

Alba, Richard D. (1990). *Ethnic Identity: The Transformation of White America.* New Haven: Yale University Press.

Blauner, Robert (1992). "Talking Past Each Other: Black and White Languages of Race." *American Prospect* (summer): 55–64.

di Leonardo, Micaela (1984). *The Varieties of Ethnic Experience: Kinship, Class and Gender Among Italian Americans.* Ithaca, NY: Cornell University Press.

Gans, Herbert (1979). "Symbolic Ethnicity: The Future of Ethnic Groups and Cultures in America." *Ethnic and Racial Studies* 2: 1–20.

Greeley, Andrew H. (1976). "The Ethnic Miracle." *Public Interest* 45 (fall): 20–36.

Leonard, Karen (1992). *Making Ethnic Choices: California's Punjabi Mexican Americans.* Philadelphia: Temple University Press.

Massey, Garth (2004). "Thinking about Affirmative Action: Arguments Supporting Preferential Policies." *Review of Policy Research,* 21 (6): 783–797.

Ogbu, John (1990). "Minority Status and Literacy in Comparative Perspective." *Daedalus* 119: 141–169.

Pagnini, Deanna L., and S. Philip Morgan (1990). "Intermarriage and Social Distance among U.S. Immigrants at the Turn of the Century." *American Journal of Sociology* 96 (2): 405–432.

Waters, Mary C. (1990). *Ethnic Options: Choosing Identities in America.* Berkeley and Los Angeles: University of California Press.

15

Love and Race Caught in the Public Eye

HEIDI ARDIZZONE AND EARL LEWIS

The tragic consequences of racial prejudice are nowhere more appalling than in love and marriage. This essay chronicles a love story caught up in racism as well as class prejudice and gender discrimination. It challenges the reader to ask, What is the meaning of race? We continue to ask this question, even when we believe it has or should have no meaning in our relationships. This essay also describes a research approach often found in sociology—the use of existing records. Ardizzone and Lewis reminds us that social inquiry is an ongoing process that seldom provides final answers or solid conclusions.

Lovers seek to create a place that they can inhabit together against the obstacles of the world. Marriage promises that they will live in that place forever. What happens, though, when love cannot keep out the world's strictures? What happens when the bond severs, and the nation serves as a witness to marital separation? And what happens when a culture's notions about love and romance come into conflict with the lines dividing races and classes?

In 1925 Alice Beatrice Jones and Leonard "Kip" Rhinelander found themselves painfully trapped in this conflict between love and family, desire and social standing. Their marriage had the trappings of a fairy tale—wealthy New York scion marries humble girl from New Rochelle—yet the events that led to their estrangement provide an unusual window into the nation's attitudes about race, class, and sexuality. Their sensational annulment trial scandalized 1920's America and opened their private life to public scrutiny, amid cultural conflicts over racial definitions, class propriety, proper courtship and sexual behavior, and racial mixing.

As a Rhinelander, Leonard was descended from several of New York's oldest and wealthiest families. Had he followed in the family tradition, Leonard might have attended Columbia University, joined the Rhinelander Real Estate Company, and made his mark on New York society through philanthropy and support of the arts.

By contrast, Alice's parents immigrated in 1891 to the United States from England, where they had both worked as servants. George Jones had had some success in his adopted country; he eventually owned a fleet of taxicabs and several small properties. Alice, her sisters, and their husbands worked primarily as domestics and servants—solid members of the working class.

Despite this pronounced class difference, Alice and Leonard met and began dating in 1921. Their love deepened over the next three years, tested by months and years of separation as Leonard's father tried to keep them apart. Philip Rhinelander's efforts were in vain, however. From 1921 to 1924 the lovers exchanged hundreds of letters and visited when possible. As soon as Leonard turned 21 and received money from a trust fund, he left school and returned to Alice. In the fall of 1924, they quietly married in a civil ceremony at the New Rochelle City Hall.

Had reporters from the *New Rochelle Standard Star* ignored the entry in the City Hall records, the couple might have lived their lives away from the public spotlight. They did not. Someone eventually realized that a Rhinelander had married a local woman, and it was news. And once they discovered who Alice Jones was, it was big news. The first story appeared one month after their wedding, announcing to the world that the son of a Rhinelander had married the daughter of a colored man.

Or had he? Well, at least he had married the daughter of a working-class man, and that was enough to start a tremor of gossip throughout New York. Reporters rushed to sift through the legal documents and contradictory accounts of and by the Joneses and the newlyweds. Despite the confidence of the first announcement, there was confusion for quite some time as to George Jones's—and therefore Alice's—precise racial identity.

Leonard initially stood by his wife during the tumult of national coverage of their cross-class, possibly cross-racial, marriage. But after two weeks, he left her and signed an annulment complaint that his father's lawyers had prepared. The suit charged Alice with misrepresenting her racial identity to her would-be husband. She was black, the document asserted, but had tried to pass as white. She was not the woman Leonard thought she was when he married her.

Our interest in the Rhinelander case began more than 18 years ago, when Earl came across newspaper accounts of the trial in the *Norfolk Journal and Guide.* The story pulsed with the complexities of race and identity in Jim Crow-era America, and he couldn't pull himself away from it. A dozen years later he mentioned the story to Heidi, who began tracking down more information but eventually decided not to incorporate it into her dissertation. Instead, we decided to try a collaborative effort, and Heidi began a series of trips to Westchester County and New York City, tracking trial records, legal documents, and New York newspaper coverage and looking for surviving members of the families involved. We produced an article and quickly turned to writing a book.

Every researcher knows that of the many paths of inquiry planned, some will inevitably lead nowhere. We were, nonetheless, quite surprised to find that, despite repeated inquiries, our research failed to produce an extant copy of the court transcript in the Westchester County courthouses or their archives, or in the appellate courts, newspaper archives, or lawyers' offices.

Tantalizing hints of its existence materialized, including an index of testimony and documents from subsequent legal challenges. Unfortunately, none of the courts could produce the transcript.

Without a transcript, we turned to newspaper coverage of the case. We culled pertinent coverage from several dozen national newspapers—black- and white-published—including dailies and tabloids from New York City and neighboring communities. From these sources we recreated the trial, some- times overlaying numerous accounts of the same event to reconcile discrep- ancies or omissions. Our ability to do so was aided immensely by several daily newspapers' habit of reproducing each day's court record alongside their sum- maries, editorials, photographs, and cartoon coverage.

The regional and racial diversity of the sources gave us a more highly tex- tured story than we first imagined, one that enabled us to gauge how the nation responded to its unfolding. Depending on newspapers made us aware not only of the immense popularity of the case but also of how the story reached differ- ent audiences with different messages and, to some extent, how the reader- ship responded. Our book became a study of the cultural response to the trial and the issues it raised as much as it was an analysis of the trial itself.

Another path we hoped to pursue lay in finding Alice or Leonard or family members who might have more information about their relationship and lives after the trial. We quickly learned that Leonard had died in 1936, but we had no idea if Alice had remarried, had had children, or still lived. *The New York Times* had no obituary for her, nor did the *New Rochelle Standard Star*. While Alice was listed in city directories until the 1960's, apparently still living in her childhood home, thereafter she either moved or maintained an unlisted address. Local people remembered the case, but no one knew where she was.

One day in New Rochelle, after pursuing several unfruitful leads, Heidi stopped by the local cemetery, where she knew Alice's parents were buried. The office had no record of Alice being buried with her family, but Heidi decided to visit the family plot anyway. As she walked around reading the graves, she literally tripped over a small flat stone lying almost flush with the grass. There was Alice's grave. She had died in 1989.

More so than the absence of a transcript, the inability to interview partici- pants and observers of the events left several still-unanswered questions. (Though more distant Rhinelanders did reply to our inquiries, most family members could not be found or declined to respond.) Most importantly, how did George and Alice define themselves racially? At the beginning of the trial, Alice's lawyers said that Alice "had some colored blood in her veins." Although the lawyers said they had only made the admission "for the purposes of the trial" and were careful never to call her black most Americans understood that having colored ancestry meant she was black, albeit of mixed ancestry.

Her sisters both acknowledged on the witness stand that they were colored, and that they had never denied it. Their mother, Elizabeth, who was white, made a sharp distinction between having colored blood and being black. She was surprised that her husband was considered a Negro in the United States. She believed he was a mulatto but not black. This distinction, of course, contradicted white America's system of popular and legal racial classification, which held that just one drop of black blood made one black. As a rule, Americans made few distinctions between colored and Negro by the 1920's; gradations in mixed blood had given way to absolutes.

The illogic of such definitions did not go unnoticed by many blacks and some whites. Still, George Jones's skin was dark enough that all who saw him agreed that in the American racial lexicon he could not be called white. He claimed only to know that his mother was white and his father had been a subject of the British colonies. But his daughters' appearances were more ambiguous. Interviews with family members, neighbors, and friends did not clarify matters much. They offered conflicting stories of what people thought they were, how they presented themselves, and whether they defined themselves as black, white, colored, or something else entirely.

Whether or not George and Elizabeth thought he was black, the family was clearly considered mixed by most people in their community, and their union threatened settled assumptions in Jim Crow—era America. By the 1920's, prohibitions against interracial marriage existed in more than half of the states. Most of these statutes also tried to define who was black and who was white—most using the one-drop rule, some offering a specific blood quantum (such as anyone with at least one-eighth black ancestry was black).

Although the U.S. Supreme Court had refused in *Plessy* v. *Ferguson* to provide a definition of black and white, it did offer an opinion in 1924 on whether Asian Indians were white. The case in question involved an Indian immigrant, Bhagat Thind, who argued that he was Caucasian and therefore white and therefore eligible for U.S. citizenship, from which Asian immigrants were excluded. The court agreed with him on one count: He was Caucasian. The majority concluded he was not white, however, since the perceptions and beliefs of the average man defined whiteness by pale skin and European ancestry. The *Thind* case made clear that American legal racial categories were socially constructed, not based in scientific racialism. It also highlighted the racial fissure many immigrants like George Jones experienced as they found themselves placed in a different classification in the United States than they had previously occupied.

At the conclusion of our research it had become quite obvious that "passing" did not adequately explain Alice's life. She and her family seemed to live in between the worlds of black and white, a difficult but not unknown act in the age of social and legal segregation. In admitting colored blood but avoiding identification as black, the Jones family raised serious challenges to the meaning of race—social, cultural, and biological.

Alice's admission of colored blood did not solve the ambiguity of her racial identity. In a state that had never made interracial marriages illegal, the primary issue turned on whether Leonard had known she wasn't white when he married her. The question became not was she black or white, but how could he and other white Americans know? Thus, the case continued to expose many of the nation's contradictory definitions of race.

Throughout the trial, reporters carefully scrutinized Alice's deportment, clothing, and appearance. They searched for any detail that might explain who she was and give a fuller hint of her race. They also looked to see if she betrayed any lingering affection for Leonard. The reporters characterized her as "fair" or "slightly tanned" or "dusky" or even "ebony," her skin tone waxing and waning with the tides of evidence and scandal. At perhaps the most memorable point of the trial, Alice, at the request of her lawyer, partially disrobed before the court, baring her breasts, back, and legs. Although no reporters were actually in the judge's chambers when she exposed her body, all were sure she had proven her attorney's point: that Leonard must have known from viewing her body prior to marriage that she was not white.

While she gave a few interviews to the press, Alice never actually testified, never told her story for the court record. She won her case, however. The annulment was denied, and the marriage was upheld. Editors generally agreed that the weight of evidence had been on her side, although some were surprised that Leonard's race and class standing didn't sway the jury. After another round of appeals Leonard disappeared, amidst continued speculation that the two had reunited. In 1930 Leonard resurfaced alone in Nevada, where he won a divorce that was recognized only in that state; they later signed a separation agreement in New York.

According to the terms, Leonard paid Alice a $32,500 lump sum and $3,600 per year for life. In return, Alice forfeited all claims to the Rhinelander estate and agreed not to use the Rhinelander name, nor to lecture or write publicly about her story, pledges she honored the rest of her life. Her parents and Leonard all died during the 1930's, events that recalled the trial for local and New York City newspapers. So did a series of trials between Alice and the Rhinelander heirs over her annuity, which Alice again won. By the time she died, the print media and their readers had forgotten the case and her past notoriety. No one noticed that upon dying, and without speaking, she would get the last word. Her gravestone reads "Alice J. Rhinelander"—a reclamation of her identity as Leonard's wife.

* * *

While Alice got the last word in her own story, we do not expect to do so with our book [Love on Trial: An American Scandal in Black and White]. Even now, a previously abandoned research path has reopened. This latest twist came just a few months ago, long after we had turned in the manuscript. We heard from the literary scholar Werner Sollors that one of his former students had obtained a copy of the trial transcript from the New York Bar Association.

In March, after an initial report that it did not exist there either, we received a copy of the transcript.

Did finding it change anything? Yes and no. We now have the full texts of Leonard's two letters that no newspaper was willing to print in full due to their explicit sexual nature. We can also answer a few other questions of detail, which we plan to do on a Web site (www.Love.On. Trial.umich.edu). So far we have found nothing that would alter either our narrative or our overall analysis of the Rhinelander/Jones case. In fact, we are convinced that the route we took, while more difficult, made for a richer story.

And what about the other paths we could not follow? Will publication of this book prompt Alice's heirs or other Rhinelander family members to tell their story? That would be a fascinating development, indeed. What might we learn about Alice and Leonard's relationship? The Jones family's thoughts about race and their own identity?

Alice's family must have played a role in placing her married name on her gravestone. Perhaps Alice would get the last word once again.

16

McDonald's in Hong Kong: Consumerism, Dietary Change, and the Rise of a Children's Culture

FROM *Golden Arches East*

JAMES L. WATSON

McDonald's has not only become the symbol of globalization. It is emblematic of the influence of the West, and particularly the United States, on the rest of the world. Many people question the value of this bequest, seeing fast food as a corrosive and crude intrusion on traditional practices, to say nothing of its questionable nutritional value. James Watson takes exception, not because he necessarily loves fast food and wants to speed up the erosion of local practices, but because he finds in those who are encouraged to take up Western practices—in this case the McDonald's "experience"—more selectivity and creativity than is usually supposed. Although South Koreans openly oppose and reject McDonald's, many in Hong King have redefined McDonald's in ways that reveal the human capacity to shape culture and find compatibility between the old and the new.

TRANSNATIONALISM AND THE FAST FOOD INDUSTRY

Does the roaring success of McDonald's and its rivals in the fast food industry mean that Hong Kong's local culture is under siege? Are food chains helping to create a homogenous, "global" culture better suited to the demands of a capitalist world order? Hong Kong would seem to be an excellent place to test the globalization hypothesis, given the central role that cuisine plays in the production and maintenance of a distinctive local identity. Man Tso-chuen's great-grandchildren are today avid consumers of Big Macs, pizza, and Coca-Cola; does this somehow make them less "Chinese" than their grandfather?

It is my contention that the cultural arena in places like Hong Kong is changing with such breathtaking speed that the fundamental assumptions underlining such questions are themselves questionable. Economic and social realities make it necessary to construct an entirely new approach to global issues, one that takes the consumers' own views into account. Analyses based on neomarxian and dependency (center/periphery) models that were popular in the 1960s and 1970s do not begin to capture the complexity of emerging transnational systems.

This chapter represents a conscious attempt to bring the discussion of globalism down to earth, focusing on one local culture. The people of Hong Kong have embraced American-style fast foods, and by so doing they might appear to be in the vanguard of a worldwide culinary revolution. But they have not been stripped of their cultural traditions, nor have they become "American-ized" in any but the most superficial of ways. Hong Kong in the late 1990s constitutes one of the world's most heterogeneous cultural environments. Younger people, in particular, are fully conversant in transnational idioms, which include language, music, sports, clothing, satellite television, cyber-communications, global travel, and—of course—cuisine. It is no longer possible to distinguish what is local and what is not. In Hong Kong, as I hope to show in this chapter, the transnational *is* the local.

EATING OUT: A SOCIAL HISTORY OF CONSUMPTION

By the time McDonald's opened its first Hong Kong restaurant in 1975, the idea of fast food was already well established among local consumers. Office workers, shop assistants, teachers, and transport workers had enjoyed various forms of take-out cuisine for well over a century; an entire industry had emerged to deliver mid-day meals direct to workplaces. In the 1960s and 1970s thousands of street vendors produced snacks and simple meals on demand, day or night. Time has always been money in Hong Kong; hence, the dual keys to success in the catering trade were speed and convenience. Another essential characteristic was that the food, based primarily on rice or noodles, had to be hot. Even the most cosmopolitan of local consumers did not (and many still do not) consider cold foods, such as sandwiches and salads, to be acceptable meals. Older people in South China associate cold food with offerings to the dead and are understandably hesitant to eat it.

The fast food industry in Hong Kong had to deliver hot items that could compete with traditional purveyors of convenience foods (noodle shops, dumpling stalls, soup carts, portable grills). The first modern chain to enter the fray was Café de Coral, a local corporation that began operation in 1969 and is still a dominant player in the Hong Kong fast food market (with 109 outlets and a 25 percent market share, compared to McDonald's 20 percent market share in 1994).* Café de Coral's strategy was simple: It moved Hong Kong's street foods indoors, to a clean, well-lighted cafeteria that offered instant service and moderate prices; popular Cantonese items were then combined with (sinicized) "Western" foods that had been popular in Hong Kong for decades. Café de Coral's menu reads like the *locus classicus* of Pacific Rim cuisine: deep-fried chicken wings, curry on rice, hot dogs, roast pork in soup noodles, spaghetti with meat balls, barbecued ribs, red bean sundaes, Ovaltine, Chinese tea, and Coca-Cola (with lemon, hot or cold). The formula was so successful it spawned dozens of imitators, including three full-scale chains.

---

*Seven of the world's ten busiest McDonald's restaurants are located in Hong Kong. When McDonald's first opened in 1975, few thought it would survive more than a few months. By January 1, 1997, Hong Kong had 125 outlets, which means that there was one McDonald's for every 51,200 residents, compared to one for every 30,000 people in the United States.

* * *

McDonald's mid-1970s entry also corresponded to an economic boom associated with Hong Kong's conversion from a low-wage, light-industrial outpost to a regional center for financial services and high-technology industries. McDonald's takeoff thus paralleled the rise of a new class of highly educated, affluent consumers who thrive in Hong Kong's ever-changing urban environment—one of the most stressful in the world. These new consumers eat out more often than their parents and have created a huge demand for fast, convenient foods of all types. In order to compete in this market, McDonald's had to offer something different. That critical difference, at least during the company's first decade of operation, was American culture packaged as all-American, middle-class food.

* * *

MENTAL CATEGORIES: SNACK VERSUS MEAL

As in other parts of East Asia, McDonald's faced a serious problem when it began operation in Hong Kong: Hamburgers, fries, and sandwiches were perceived as snacks (Cantonese *siu sihk,* literally "small eats"); in the local view these items did not constitute the elements of a proper meal. This perception is still prevalent among older, more conservative consumers who believe that hamburgers, hot dogs, and pizza can never be "filling." Many students stop at fast food outlets on their way home from school; they may share hamburgers and fries with their classmates and then eat a full meal with their families at home. This is not considered a problem by parents, who themselves are likely to have stopped for tea and snacks after work. Snacking with friends and colleagues provides a major opportunity for socializing (and transacting business) among southern Chinese. Teahouses, coffee shops, bakeries, and ice cream parlors are popular precisely because they provide a structured yet informal setting for social encounters. Furthermore, unlike Chinese restaurants and banquet halls, snack centers do not command a great deal of time or money from customers.

Contrary to corporate goals, therefore, McDonald's entered the Hong Kong market as a purveyor of snacks. Only since the late 1980s has its fare been treated as the foundation of "meals" by a generation of younger consumers who regularly eat non-Chinese food. Thanks largely to McDonald's, hamburgers and fries are now a recognized feature of Hong Kong's lunch scene. The evening hours remain, however, the weak link in McDonald's marketing plan; the real surprise was breakfast, which became a peak traffic period.

The mental universe of Hong Kong consumers is partially revealed in the everyday use of language. Hamburgers are referred to, in colloquial Cantonese, as *han bou bao—han* being a homophone for "ham" and *bao* the common term for stuffed buns or bread rolls. *Bao* are quintessential snacks, and however excellent or nutritious they might be, they do not constitute the basis of a satisfying (i.e., filling) meal. In South China that honor is reserved for culinary arrangements that rest, literally, on a bed of rice (*fan*). Foods that accompany rice are referred to as *sung*, probably best translated as "toppings" (including meat, fish, and vegetables). It is significant that hamburgers are rarely categorized as meat (*yuk*); Hong Kong consumers tend to perceive anything that is served between slices of bread (Big Macs, fish sandwiches, hot dogs) as *bao*. In American culture the hamburger is categorized first and foremost as a meat item (with all the attendant worries about fat and cholesterol content), whereas in Hong Kong the same item is thought of primarily as bread.

FROM EXOTIC TO ORDINARY: MCDONALD'S BECOMES LOCAL

Following precedents in other international markets, the Hong Kong franchise promoted McDonald's basic menu and did not introduce items that would be more recognizable to Chinese consumers (such as rice dishes, tropical fruit, soup noodles). Until recently the food has been indistinguishable from that served in Mobile, Alabama, or Moline, Illinois. There are, however, local preferences: the best-selling items in many outlets are fish sandwiches and plain hamburgers; Big Macs tend to be the favorites of children and teenagers. Hot tea and hot chocolate outsell coffee, but Coca-Cola remains the most popular drink.

McDonald's conservative approach also applied to the breakfast menu. When morning service was introduced in the 1980s, American-style items such as eggs, muffins, pancakes, and hash brown potatoes were not featured. Instead, the local outlets served the standard fare of hamburgers and fries for breakfast. McDonald's initial venture into the early morning food market was so successful that Mr. Ng hesitated to introduce American-style breakfast items, fearing that an abrupt shift in menu might alienate consumers who were beginning to accept hamburgers and fries as a regular feature of their diet. The transition to eggs, muffins, and hash browns was a gradual one, and today most Hong Kong customers order breakfasts that are similar to those offered in American outlets. But once established, dietary preferences change slowly: McDonald's continues to feature plain hamburgers (but not the Big Mac) on its breakfast menu in most Hong Kong outlets.

Management decisions of the type outlined above helped establish McDonald's as an icon of popular culture in Hong Kong. From 1975 to approximately 1985, McDonald's became the "in" place for young people wishing to associate themselves with the laid-back, nonhierarchical dynamism they perceived American society to embody. The first generation of consumers patronized McDonald's precisely because it was *not* Chinese and was *not* associated with Hong Kong's past as a backward-looking colonial outpost where (in their view) nothing of consequence ever happened. Hong Kong was changing and, as noted earlier, a new consumer culture was beginning to take shape. McDonald's caught the wave of this cultural movement and has been riding it ever since.

* * *

* * * Today, McDonald's restaurants in Hong Kong are packed—wall-to-wall—with people of all ages, few of whom are seeking an American cultural experience. Twenty years after Mr. Ng opened his first restaurant, eating at McDonald's has become an ordinary, everyday experience for hundreds of thousands of Hong Kong residents. The chain has become a local institution in the sense that it has blended into the urban landscape; McDonald's outlets now serve as rendezvous points for young and old alike.

* * *

WHAT'S IN A SMILE? FRIENDLINESS AND PUBLIC SERVICE

American consumers expect to be served "with a smile" when they order fast food, but this is not true in all societies. In Hong Kong people are suspicious of anyone who displays what is perceived to be an excess of congeniality, solicitude, or familiarity. The human smile is not, therefore, a universal symbol of openness and honesty. "If you buy an apple from a hawker and he smiles at you," my Cantonese tutor once told me, "you know you're being cheated."

Given these cultural expectations, it was difficult for Hong Kong management to import a key element of the McDonald's formula—service with a smile—and make it work. Crew members were trained to treat customers in a manner that approximates the American notion of "friendliness." Prior to the 1970s, there was not even an indigenous Cantonese term to describe this form of behavior. The traditional notion of friendship is based on loyalty to close associates, which by definition cannot be extended to strangers. Today the concept of *public* friendliness is recognized—and verbalized—by younger people in Hong Kong, but the term many of them use to express this quality is "friendly," borrowed directly from English. McDonald's, through its television advertising, may be partly responsible for this innovation, but to date it has had little effect on workers in the catering industry.

During my interviews it became clear that the majority of Hong Kong consumers were uninterested in public displays of congeniality from service personnel. When shopping for fast food most people cited convenience, cleanliness, and table space as primary considerations; few even mentioned service except to note that the food should be delivered promptly. Counter staff in Hong Kong's fast food outlets (including McDonald's) rarely make great efforts to smile or to behave in a manner Americans would interpret as friendly. Instead, they project qualities that are admired in the local culture:

competence, directness, and unflappability. In a North American setting the facial expression that Hong Kong employees use to convey these qualities would likely be interpreted as a deliberate attempt to be rude or indifferent. Workers who smile on the job are assumed to be enjoying themselves at the consumer's (and management's) expense: In the words of one diner I overheard while standing in a queue, "They must be playing around back there. What are they laughing about?"

CONSUMER DISCIPLINE?

[A] hallmark of the American fast food business is the displacement of labor costs from the corporation to the consumers. For the system to work, consumers must be educated—or "disciplined"—so that they voluntarily fulfill their side of an implicit bargain: We (the corporation) will provide cheap, fast service, if you (the customer) carry your own tray, seat yourself, and help clean up afterward. Time and space are also critical factors in the equation: Fast service is offered in exchange for speedy consumption and a prompt departure, thereby making room for others. This system has revolutionized the American food industry and has helped to shape consumer expectations in other sectors of the economy. How has it fared in Hong Kong? Are Chinese customers conforming to disciplinary models devised in Oak Brook, Illinois?

The answer is both yes and no. In general Hong Kong consumers have accepted the basic elements of the fast food formula, but with "localizing" adaptations. For instance, customers generally do not bus their own trays, nor do they depart immediately upon finishing. Clearing one's own table has never been an accepted part of local culinary culture, owing in part to the low esteem attaching to this type of labor. During McDonald's first decade in Hong Kong, the cost of hiring extra cleaners was offset by low wages. A pattern was thus established, and customers grew accustomed to leaving without attending to their own rubbish. Later, as wages escalated in the late 1980s and early 1990s, McDonald's tried to introduce self-busing by posting announcements in restaurants and featuring the practice in its television advertisements. As of February 1997, however, little had changed. Hong Kong consumers * * * have ignored this aspect of consumer discipline.

What about the critical issues of time and space? Local managers with whom I spoke estimated that the average eating time for most Hong Kong customers was between 20 and 25 minutes, compared to 11 minutes in the United States fast food industry. This estimate confirms my own observations of McDonald's consumers in Hong Kong's central business districts (Victoria and Tsimshatsui). A survey conducted in the New Territories city of Yuen Long—an old market town that has grown into a modern urban center—revealed that local McDonald's consumers took just under 26 minutes to eat.

Perhaps the most striking feature of the American-inspired model of consumer discipline is the queue. Researchers in many parts of the world have reported that customers refuse, despite "education" campaigns by the chains involved, to form neat lines in front of cashiers. Instead, customers pack themselves into disorderly scrums and jostle for a chance to place their orders. Scrums of this nature were common in Hong Kong when McDonald's opened in 1975. Local managers discouraged this practice by stationing queue monitors near the registers during busy hours and, by the 1980s, orderly lines were the norm at McDonald's. The disappearance of the scrum corresponds to a general change in Hong Kong's public culture as a new generation of residents, the children of refugees, began to treat the territory as their home. Courtesy toward strangers was largely unknown in the 1960s: Boarding a bus during rush hour could be a nightmare and transacting business at a bank teller's window required brute strength. Many people credit McDonald's with being the first public institution in Hong Kong to enforce queuing, and thereby helping to create a more "civilized" social order. McDonald's did not, in fact, introduce the queue to Hong Kong, but this belief is firmly lodged in the public imagination.

HOVERING AND THE NAPKIN WARS

Purchasing one's food is no longer a physical challenge in Hong Kong's McDonald's but finding a place to sit is quite another matter. The traditional practice of "hovering" is one solution: Choose a group of diners who appear to be on the verge of leaving and stake a claim to their table by hovering nearby, sometimes only inches away. Seated customers routinely ignore the intrusion; it would, in fact, entail a loss of face to notice. Hovering was the norm in Hong Kong's lower- to middle-range restaurants during the 1960s and 1970s, but the practice has disappeared in recent years. Restaurants now take names or hand out tickets at the entrance; warning signs, in Chinese and English, are posted: "Please wait to be seated." Customers are no longer allowed into the dining area until a table is ready.

Fast food outlets are the only dining establishments in Hong Kong where hovering is still tolerated, largely because it would be nearly impossible to regulate. Customer traffic in McDonald's is so heavy that the standard restaurant design has failed to reproduce American-style dining routines: Rather than ordering first and finding a place to sit afterward, Hong Kong consumers usually arrive in groups and delegate one or two people to claim a table while someone else joins the counter queues. Children make ideal hoverers and learn to scoot through packed restaurants, zeroing in on diners who are about to finish. It is one of the wonders of comparative ethnography to witness the speed with which Hong Kong children perform this reconnaissance duty. Foreign visitors are sometimes unnerved by hovering, but residents accept it as part of everyday life in one of the world's most densely populated cities. It is not surprising, therefore, that Hong Kong's fast food chains have made few efforts to curtail the practice.

Management is less tolerant of behavior that affects profit margins. In the United States fast food companies save money by allowing (or requiring) customers to collect their own napkins, straws, plastic flatware, and condiments. Self-provisioning is an essential feature of consumer discipline, but it only works if the system is not abused. In Hong Kong napkins are dispensed, one at a time, by McDonald's crew members who work behind the counter; customers who do not ask for napkins do not receive any. This is a deviation from the corporation's standard operating procedure and adds a few seconds to each transaction, which in turn slows down the queues. Why alter a well-tested routine? The reason is simple: napkins placed in public dispensers disappear faster than they can be replaced.

* * *

Buffets, like fast food outlets, depend upon consumers to perform much of their own labor in return for reduced prices. Abuse of the system—wasting food or taking it home—is taken for granted and is factored into the price of buffet meals. Fast food chains, by contrast, operate at lower price thresholds where consumer abuse can seriously affect profits.

Many university students of my acquaintance reported that they had frequently observed older people pocketing wads of paper napkins, three to four inches thick, in restaurants that permit self-provisioning. Management efforts to stop this behavior are referred to, in the Cantonese-English slang of Hong Kong youth, as the "Napkin Wars." Younger people were appalled by what they saw as the waste of natural resources by a handful of customers. As they talked about the issue, however, it became obvious that the Napkin Wars represented more—in their eyes—than a campaign to conserve paper. The sight of diners abusing public facilities reminded these young people of the bad old days of their parents and grandparents, when Hong Kong's social life was dominated by refugees who had little stake in the local community. During the 1960s and 1970s, economic insecurities were heightened by the very real prospect that Red Guards might take over the colony at any moment. The game plan was simple during those decades: Make money as quickly as possible and move on. In the 1980s a new generation of local-born youth began treating Hong Kong as home and proceeded to build a public culture better suited to their vision of life in a cosmopolitan city. In this new Hong Kong, consumers are expected to be sophisticated and financially secure, which means that it would be beneath their dignity to abuse public facilities. Still, McDonald's retains control of its napkins.

* * *

CHILDREN AS CONSUMERS

During the summer of 1994, while attending a business lunch in one of Hong Kong's fanciest hotels, I watched a waiter lean down to consult with a customer at an adjoining table. The object of his attention was a six-year-old child who studied the menu with practiced skill. His parents beamed as their prodigy performed; meanwhile, sitting across the table, a pair of grandparents sat bolt upright, scowling in obvious disapproval. Twenty years ago the sight of a child commanding such attention would have shocked the entire restaurant into silence. No one, save the immediate party (and this observer), even noticed in 1994.

Hong Kong children rarely ate outside their home until the late 1970s, and when they did, they were expected to eat what was put in front of them. The idea that children might actually order their own food or speak to a waiter would have outraged most adults; only foreign youngsters (notably the off-spring of British and American expatriates) were permitted to make their preferences known in public. Today, Hong Kong children as young as two or three participate in the local economy as full-fledged consumers, with their own tastes and brand loyalties. Children now have money in their pockets and they spend it on personal consumption, which usually means snacks. In response, new industries and a specialized service sector has emerged to "feed" these discerning consumers. McDonald's was one of the first corporations to recognize the potential of the children's market; in effect, the company started a revolution by making it possible for even the youngest consumers to *choose* their own food.

* * *

Many Hong Kong children of my acquaintance are so fond of McDonald's that they refuse to eat with their parents or grandparents in Chinese-style restaurants or *dim sam* teahouses. This has caused intergenerational distress in some of Hong Kong's more conservative communities. In 1994, a nine-year-old boy, the descendant of illustrious ancestors who settled in the New Territories eight centuries ago, talked about his concerns as we consumed Big Macs, fries, and shakes at McDonald's: "A-bak [uncle], I like it here better than any place in the world. I want to come here every day." His father takes him to McDonald's at least twice a week, but his grandfather, who accompanied them a few times in the late 1980s, will no longer do so. "I prefer to eat *dim sam*," the older man told me later. "That place [McDonald's] is for kids." Many grandparents have resigned themselves to the new consumer trends and take their preschool grandchildren to McDonald's for mid-morning snacks—precisely the time of day that local teahouses were once packed with retired people. Cantonese grandparents have always played a prominent role in child minding, but until recently the children had to accommodate to the proclivities of their elders. By the 1990s grandchildren were more assertive and the mid-morning *dim sam* snack was giving way to hamburgers and Cokes.

* * *

RONALD MCDONALD AND THE INVENTION OF BIRTHDAY PARTIES

Until recently most people in Hong Kong did not even know, let alone celebrate, their birthdates in the Western calendrical sense; dates of birth according to the lunar calendar were recorded for divinatory purposes but were not noted in annual rites. By the late 1980s, however, birthday parties, complete with cakes and candles, were the rage in Hong Kong. Any child who was anyone had to have a party, and the most popular venue was a fast food restaurant, with McDonald's ranked above all competitors. The majority of Hong Kong people live in overcrowded flats, which means that parties are rarely held in private homes.

Except for the outlets in central business districts, McDonald's restaurants are packed every Saturday and Sunday with birthday parties, cycled through at the rate of one every hour. A party hostess, provided by the restaurant, leads the children in games while the parents sit on the sidelines, talking quietly among themselves. For a small fee celebrants receive printed invitation cards, photographs, a gift box containing toys and a discount coupon for future trips to McDonald's. Parties are held in a special enclosure, called the Ronald Room, which is equipped with low tables and tiny stools—suitable only for children. Television commercials portray Ronald McDonald leading birthday celebrants on exciting safaris and expeditions. The clown's Cantonese name, Mak Dong Lou Suk-Suk ("Uncle McDonald"), plays on the intimacy of kinship and has helped transform him into one of Hong Kong's most familiar cartoon figures.

* * *

MCDONALD'S AS A YOUTH CENTER

Weekends may be devoted to family dining and birthday parties for younger children, but on weekday afternoons, from 3:00 to 6:00 P.M., McDonald's restaurants are packed with teenagers stopping for a snack on their way home from school. In many outlets 80 percent of the late afternoon clientele appear in school uniforms, turning the restaurants into a sea of white frocks, light blue shirts, and dark trousers. The students, aged between 10 and 17, stake out tables and buy snacks that are shared in groups. The noise level at this time of day is deafening; students shout to friends and dart from table to table. Few adults, other than restaurant staff, are in evidence. It is obvious that

McDonald's is treated as an informal youth center, a recreational extension of school where students can unwind after long hours of study.

* * *

In contrast to their counterparts in the United States, where fast food chains have devised ways to discourage lingering, McDonald's in Hong Kong does not set a limit on table time. When I asked the managers of several Hong Kong outlets how they coped with so many young people chatting at tables that might otherwise be occupied by paying customers, they all replied that the students were "welcome." The obvious strategy is to turn a potential liability into an asset: "Students create a good atmosphere which is good for our business," said one manager as he watched an army of teenagers—dressed in identical school uniforms—surge into his restaurant. Large numbers of students also use McDonald's as a place to do homework and prepare for exams, often in groups. Study space of any kind, public or private, is hard to find in overcrowded Hong Kong. * * *

CONCLUSIONS: WHOSE CULTURE IS IT?

In concluding this chapter, I would like to return to the questions raised in my opening remarks: In what sense, if any, is McDonald's involved in these cultural transformations (the creation of a child-centered consumer culture, for instance)? Has the company helped to create these trends, or merely followed the market? Is this an example of American-inspired, transnational culture crowding out indigenous cultures? * * *

* * * The deeper I dig into the lives of consumers themselves, in Hong Kong and elsewhere, the more complex the picture becomes. Having watched the processes of culture change unfold for nearly thirty years, it is apparent to me that the ordinary people of Hong Kong have most assuredly *not* been stripped of their cultural heritage, nor have they become the uncomprehending dupes of transnational corporations. Younger people—including many of the grandchildren of my former neighbors in the New Territories—are avid consumers of transnational culture in all of its most obvious manifestations: music, fashion, television, and cuisine. At the same time, however, Hong Kong has itself become a major center for the *production* of transnational culture, not just a sinkhole for its *consumption*. Witness, for example, the expansion of Hong Kong popular culture into China, Southeast Asia, and beyond: "Cantopop" music is heard on radio stations in North China, Vietnam, and Japan; the Hong Kong fashion industry influences clothing styles in Los Angeles, Bangkok, and Kuala Lumpur; and, perhaps most significant of all, Hong Kong is emerging as a center for the production and dissemination of satellite television programs throughout East, Southeast, and South Asia.

A lifestyle is emerging in Hong Kong that can best be described as postmodern, postnationalist, and flamboyantly transnational. The wholesale acceptance and appropriation of Big Macs, Ronald McDonald, and birthday parties are small, but significant aspects of this redefinition of Chinese cultural identity. In closing, therefore, it seems appropriate to pose an entirely new set of questions: Where does the transnational end and the local begin? Whose culture is it, anyway? In places like Hong Kong the postcolonial periphery is fast becoming the metropolitan center, where local people are consuming and simultaneously producing new cultural systems.

* * *

17

A Look Behind the Veil

ELIZABETH W. FERNEA AND ROBERT A. FERNEA

In many societies where people practice the religion of Islam, the social structure both dictates and is reflected in the wearing of the veil. Gender relations, especially, are expressed in the veiling of women. To people who live in other societies—where women seem to be able to wear whatever they want—the veil seems confining. But not all women who wear the veil feel this way. That is why, despite changes going on in their societies, it is an open question whether or not the veil will be lifted.

What objects do we notice in societies other than our own? Ishi, the last of a "lost" tribe of North American Indians who stumbled into 20th Century California in 1911, is reported to have said that the truly interesting objects in the white man's culture were pockets and matches. Rifa'ah Tahtawi, one of the first young Egyptians to be sent to Europe to study in 1826, wrote an account of French society in which he noted that Parisians used many unusual articles of dress, among them something called a belt. Women wore belts, he said, apparently to keep their bosoms erect, and to show off the slimness of their waists and the fullness of their hips. Europeans are still fascinated by the Stetson hats worn by American cowboys; an elderly Dutch lady of our acquaintance recently carried six enormous Stetsons back to The Hague as presents for the male members of her family.

Many objects signify values in society and become charged with meaning, a meaning that may be different for members of the society and for observers of that society. The veil is one object used in Middle Eastern societies that stirs strong emotions in the West. "The feminine veil has become a symbol: that of the slavery of one portion of humanity," wrote French ethnologist Germaine Tillion in 1966. A hundred years earlier, Sir Richard Burton, British traveler, explorer, and translator of the *Arabian Nights*, recorded a different view. "Europeans inveigh against this article [the face veil] . . . for its hideousness and jealous concealment of charms made to be admired," he wrote in 1855. "It is, on the contrary, the most coquettish article of woman's attire . . . it conceals coarse skins, fleshy noses, wide mouths and vanishing chins, whilst it sets off to best advantage what in these lands is most lustrous and liquid— the eye. Who has not remarked this at a masquerade ball?"

In the present generation, the veil and purdah, or seclusion, have become a focus of attention for Western writers, both popular and academic, who take a measure of Burton's irony and Tillion's anger to equate modernization of the Middle East with the discarding of the veil. "Iranian women return to veil in a resurgence of spirituality," headlines one newspaper; another writes, "Iran's 16 million women have come a long way since their floor-length cotton veil officially was abolished in 1935." The thousands of words written about the appearance and disappearance of the veil and of purdah do little to help us understand the Middle East or the cultures that grew out of the same Judeo-Christian roots as our own. The veil and the all-enveloping garments that inevitably accompany it (the *milayah* in Egypt, the *abbayah* in Iraq, the *chadoor* in Iran, the *yashmak* in Turkey, the *burga'* in Afghanistan, and the *djellabah* and the *haik* in North Africa) are only the outward manifestations of a cultural pattern and idea that is rooted deep in Mediterranean society.

"Purdah" is a Persian word meaning curtain or barrier. The Arabic word for veiling and secluding comes from the root *hajaba*. A *hijab* is an amulet worn to keep away the evil eye; it also means a diaphragm used to prevent conception. The gatekeeper or doorkeeper who guards the entrance to a government minister's office is a *hajib,* and in casual conversation a person might say, "I want to be more informal with my friend so-and-so, but she always puts a *hijab* (barrier) between us."

In Islam, the Koranic verse that sanctions the barrier between men and women is called the Sura of the *hijab* (curtain): "Prophet, enjoin your wives, your daughters and the wives of true believers to draw their veils close round them. That is more proper, so that they may be recognized and not molested. Allah is forgiving and merciful."

Certainly seclusion and some forms of veiling had been practiced before the time of Muhammad, at least among the upper classes, but it was his followers who apparently felt that his women should be placed in a special category. According to history, the *hijab* was established after a number of occasions on which Muhammad's wives were insulted by people who were coming to the mosque in search of the prophet. When chided for their behavior, they said they had mistaken Muhammad's wives for slaves. The *hijab* was established, and in the words of the historian Nabia Abbott, "Muhammad's women found themselves, on the one hand, deprived of personal liberty, and on the other hand, raised to a position of honor and dignity."

The veil bears many messages and tells us many things about men and women in Middle Eastern society, but as an object in and of itself it is far less important to members of the society than the values it represents. Nouha al Hejailan, wife of the Saudi Arabian ambassador to London, told Sally Quinn of *The Washington Post,* "If I wanted to take it all off (her *abbayah* and veil), I would have long ago. It wouldn't mean as much to me as it does to you." Early Middle Eastern feminists felt differently. Huda Sh'arawi, an early Egyptian activist who formed the first Women's Union, made a dramatic gesture of removing her veil in public to demonstrate her dislike of society's attitudes toward women and her defiance of the system. But Basima Bezirgan, a contemporary

Iraqi feminist, says, "Compared to the real issues that are involved between men and women in the Middle East today, the veil is unimportant." A Moroccan linguist who buys her clothes in Paris laughs when asked about the veil. "My mother wears a *djellabah* and a veil. I have never worn them. But so what? I still cannot get divorced as easily as a man, and I am still a member of my family group and responsible to them for everything I do. What is the veil? A piece of cloth."

"The seclusion of women has many purposes," states Egyptian anthropologist Nadia Abu Zahra. "It expresses men's status, power, wealth, and manliness. It also helps preserve men's image of virility and masculinity, but men do not admit this; on the contrary they claim that one of the purposes of the veil is to guard women's honor." The veil and purdah are symbols of restriction, to men as well as to women. A respectable woman wearing a veil on a public street is signaling, "Hands off. Don't touch me or you'll be sorry." Cowboy Jim Sayre of Deadwood, South Dakota, says, "If you deform a cowboy's hat, he'll likely deform you." In the same way, a man who approaches a veiled woman is asking for trouble; not only the woman but also her family is shamed, and serious problems may result. "It is clear," says Egyptian anthropologist Ahmed Abou Zeid, "that honor and shame which are usually attributed to a certain individual or a certain kinship group have in fact a bearing on the total social structure, since most acts involving honor or shame are likely to affect the existing social equilibrium."

Veiling and seclusion almost always can be related to the maintenance of social status. Historically, only the very rich could afford to seclude their women, and the extreme example of this practice was found among the sultans of prerevolutionary Turkey. Stories of these secluded women, kept in harems and guarded by eunuchs, formed the basis for much of the Western folklore concerning the nature of male-female relationships in Middle Eastern society. The stereotype is of course contradictory; Western writers have never found it necessary to reconcile the erotic fantasies of the seraglio with the sexual puritanism attributed to the same society.

Poor men could not always afford to seclude or veil their women, because the women were needed as productive members of the family economic unit, to work in the fields and in cottage industries. Delta village women in Egypt have never been veiled, nor have the Berber women of North Africa. But this lack of veiling placed poor women in ambiguous situations in relation to strange men.

"In the village, no one veils, because everyone is considered a member of the same large family," explained Aisha bint Mohammed, a working-class wife of Marrakech. "But in the city, veiling is *sunnah,* required by our religion." Veiling is generally found in towns and cities, among all classes, where families feel that it is necessary to distinguish themselves from other strangers in the city.

Veiling and purdah not only indicate status and wealth, they also have some religious sanction and protect women from the world outside the home. Purdah delineates private space, distinguishes between the public and private sectors of society, as does the traditional architecture of the area. Older Middle Eastern houses do not have picture windows facing on the street, nor walks leading invitingly to front doors. Family life is hidden from strangers; behind blank walls may lie courtyards and gardens, refuges from the heat, the cold, the bustle of the outside world, the world of non-kin that is not to be trusted. Outsiders are pointedly excluded.

Even within the household, among her close relatives, a traditional Muslim woman veils before those kinsmen whom she could legally marry. If her maternal or paternal male cousins, her brothers-in-law, or sons-in-law come to call, she covers her head, or perhaps her whole face. To do otherwise would be shameless.

The veil does more than protect its wearers from known and unknown intruders; it can also be used to conceal identity. Behind the anonymity of the veil, women can go about a city unrecognized and uncriticized. Nadia Abu Zahra reports anecdotes of men donning women's veils in order to visit their lovers undetected; women may do the same. The veil is such an effective disguise that Nouri Al-Said, the late prime minister of Iraq, attempted to escape death by wearing the *abbayah* and veil of a woman; only his shoes gave him away.

Political dissidents in many countries have used the veil for their own ends. The women who marched, veiled, through Cairo during the Nationalist demonstrations against the British after World War I were counting on the strength of Western respect for the veil to protect them against British gunfire. At first they were right. Algerian women also used the protection of the veil to carry bombs through French army checkpoints during the Algerian revolution. But when the French discovered the ruse, Algerian women discarded the veil and dressed like Europeans to move about freely.

The multiple meanings and uses of purdah and the veil do not explain how the pattern came to be so deeply embedded in Mediterranean society. Its origins lie somewhere in the basic Muslim attitudes about men's roles and women's roles. Women, according to Fatima Mernissi, a Moroccan sociologist, are seen by men in Islamic societies as in need of protection because they are unable to control their sexuality, are tempting to men, and hence are a danger to the social order. In other words, they need to be restrained and controlled so that society may function in an orderly way.

The notion that women present a danger to the social order is scarcely limited to Muslim society. Anthropologist Julian Pitt-Rivers has pointed out that the supervision and seclusion of women is also to be found in Christian Europe, even though veiling was not usually practiced there. "The idea that women not subjected to male authority are a danger is a fundamental one in the writings of the moralists from the Archpriest of Talavera to Padre Haro, and it is echoed in the modern Andalusian *pueblo*. It is bound up with the fear of ungoverned female sexuality which had been an integral element of European folklore ever since prudent Odysseus lashed himself to the mast to escape the sirens."

Pitt-Rivers is writing about Mediterranean society, which, like all Middle Eastern societies, is greatly concerned with honor and shame rather than with individual guilt. The honor of the Middle Eastern extended family, its ancestors and its descendants, is the highest social value. The misdeeds of the grandparents are indeed visited on the children. Men and women always remain members of their natal families. Marriage is a legal contract but a fragile one that is often broken; the ties between brother and sister, mother and child, father and child are lifelong and enduring. The larger family is the group to which the individual belongs and to which the individual owes responsibility in exchange for the social and economic security that the family group provides. It is the group, not the individual, that is socially shamed or socially honored.

Male honor and female honor are both involved in the honor of the family, but each is expressed differently. The honor of a man, *sharaf,* is a public matter, involving bravery, hospitality, piety. It may be lost, but it may also be regained. The honor of a woman, *'ard,* is a private matter involving only one thing, her sexual chastity. Once lost, it cannot be regained. If the loss of female honor remains only privately known, a rebuke—and perhaps a reveiling—may be all that takes place. But if the loss of female honor becomes public knowledge, the other members of the family may feel bound to cleanse the family name. In extreme cases, the cleansing may require the death of the offending female member. Although such killings are now criminal offenses in the Middle East, suspended sentences are often given, and the newspapers in Cairo and Baghdad frequently carry sad stories of runaway sisters "gone bad" in the city and revenge taken upon them in the name of family honor by their brothers or cousins.

This emphasis on female chastity, many say, originated in the patrilineal society's concern with the paternity of the child and the inheritance that follows the male line. How does a man know that the child in his wife's womb is his own, and not that of another man? Obviously he cannot know unless his wife is a virgin at marriage. From this consideration may have developed the protective institutions called variously purdah, seclusion, or veiling.

Middle Eastern women also look upon seclusion as practical protection. In the Iraqi village where we lived from 1956 to 1958, one of us (Elizabeth) wore the *abbayah* and found that it provided a great sense of protection from prying eyes, dust, heat, flies. Parisian ladies visiting Istanbul in the 16th Century were so impressed by the ability of the all-enveloping garment to keep dresses clean of mud and manure and to keep women from being attacked by importuning men that they tried to introduce it into French fashion.

Perhaps of greater importance for many women reared in traditional cultures is the degree to which their sense of personal identity is tied to the use of the veil. Many women have told us that they felt self-conscious, vulnerable, and even naked when they first walked on a public street without the veil and *abbayah*—as if they were making a display of themselves.

The resurgence of the veil in countries like Morocco, Libya, and Algeria, which have recently established their independence from colonial dominance, is seen by some Middle Eastern and Western scholars as an attempt by men to reassert their Muslim identity and to reestablish their roles as heads of families. The presence of the veil is a sign that the males of the household are once more able to assume the responsibilities that were disturbed or usurped by foreign colonial powers.

But a veiled woman is seldom seen in Egypt or in many parts of Lebanon, Syria, Iran, Tunisia, Turkey, or the Sudan. And as respectable housewives have abandoned the veil, in some of these Middle Eastern countries prostitutes have put it on. They indicate their availability by manipulating the veil in flirtatious ways, but as Burton pointed out more than a century ago, prostitutes are not the first to discover the veil's seductiveness. Like women's garments in the West, the veil can be sturdy, utilitarian, and forbidding—or it can be filmy and decorative, hinting at the charms beneath it.

The veil is the outward sign of a complex reality. Observers are often deceived by the absence of that sign, and fail to see that in most Middle Eastern societies (and in many parts of Europe) basic attitudes are unchanged. Women who have taken off the veil continue to play the old roles within the family, and their chastity remains crucial. A woman's behavior is still the key to the honor and the reputation of her family.

In Middle Eastern societies, feminine and masculine continue to be strong polarities of identification. This is in marked contrast to Western society, where for more than a generation social critics have been striving to blur distinctions in dress, in status, and in type of labor. Almost all Middle Eastern reformers (most of whom are middle and upper class) are still arguing from the assumption of a fundamental difference between men and women. They do not demand an end to the veil (which is passing out of use anyway) but an end to the old principles, which the veil symbolizes, that govern patrilineal society. Middle Eastern reformers are calling for equal access to divorce, child custody, and inheritance; equal opportunities for education and employment; abolition of female circumcision and "crimes of honor"; and a law regulating the age of marriage.

An English woman film director, after several months in Morocco, said in an interview, "This business about the veil is nonsense. We all have our veils, between ourselves and other people. That's not what the Middle East is about. The question is what veils are used for, and by whom." The veil triggers Western reactions simply because it is the dramatic, visible sign of vexing questions, questions that are still being debated, problems that have still not been solved, in the Middle East or in Western societies.

Given the biological differences between men and women, how are the sexes to be treated equitably? Men and women are supposed to share the labor of society and yet provide for the reproduction and nurture of the next generation. If male fear and awe of woman's sexuality provokes them to control and seclude women, can they be assuaged? Rebecca West said long ago that "the difference between men and women is the rock on which civilization will split before it can reach any goal that could justify its expenditure of effort." Until human beings come to terms with this basic issue, purdah and the veil, in some form, will continue to exist in both the East and the West.

18

The Code of the Street

ELIJAH ANDERSON

The capacity of sociology to look beyond the headlines is captured in this ethno-graphic account of a culture of respect, violence, and control on urban streets. Anderson describes this as "a cultural adaptation" to poverty, discrimination in public services, and social marginality. The presentation of self examined in this essay is a fascinating social construction and one with deadly serious consequences for everyone, not only for those who embrace the code of the street. The rich com-plexity of social life is revealed in Anderson's account, as is the difficulty in altering cultural practices without changing the circumstances of those who live the culture.

Of all the problems besetting the poor inner-city black community, none is more pressing than that of interpersonal violence and aggression. It wreaks havoc daily with the lives of community residents and increasingly spills over into downtown and residential middle-class areas. Muggings, bur-glaries, carjackings, and drug-related shootings, all of which may leave their victims or innocent bystanders dead, are now common enough to concern all urban and many suburban residents. The inclination to violence springs from the circumstances of life among the ghetto poor—the lack of jobs that pay a living wage, the stigma of race, the fallout from rampant drug use and drug trafficking, and the resulting alienation and lack of hope for the future.

Simply living in such an environment places young people at special risk of falling victim to aggressive behavior. Although there are often forces in the community which can counteract the negative influences, by far the most pow-erful being a strong, loving, "decent" (as inner-city residents put it) family com-mitted to middle-class values, the despair is pervasive enough to have spawned an oppositional culture, that of "the streets," whose norms are often consciously opposed to those of mainstream society. These two orientations—decent and street—socially organize the community, and their coexistence has important consequences for residents, particularly children growing up in the inner city. Above all, this environment means that even youngsters whose home lives reflect mainstream values—and the majority of homes in the community do—must be able to handle themselves in a street-oriented environment.

This is because the street culture has evolved what may be called a code of the streets, which amounts to a set of informal rules governing interper-sonal public behavior, including violence. The rules prescribe both a proper comportment and a proper way to respond if challenged. They regulate the use of violence and so allow those who are inclined to aggression to precipitate violent encounters in an approved way. The rules have been established and are enforced mainly by the street-oriented, but on the streets the distinction between street and decent is often irrelevant; everybody knows that if the rules are violated, there are penalties. Knowledge of the code is thus largely defensive; it is literally necessary for operating in public. Therefore, even though families with a decency orientation are usually opposed to the values of the code, they often reluctantly encourage their children's familiarity with it to enable them to negotiate the inner-city environment.

At the heart of the code is the issue of respect—loosely defined as being treated "right," or granted the deference one deserves. However, in the troublesome public environment of the inner city, as people increasingly feel buffeted by forces beyond their control, what one deserves in the way of respect becomes more and more problematic and uncertain. This in turn further opens the issue of respect to sometimes intense interpersonal negotiation. In the street culture, especially among young people, respect is viewed as almost an external entity that is hard-won but easily lost, and so must constantly be guarded. The rules of the code in fact provide a framework for negotiating respect. The person whose very appearance—including his clothing, demeanor, and way of moving—deters transgressions feels that he possesses, and may be considered by others to possess, a measure of respect. With the right amount of respect, for instance, he can avoid "being bothered" in public. If he is bothered, not only may he be in physical danger but he has been disgraced or "dissed" (disrespected). Many of the forms that dissing can take might seem petty to middle-class people (maintaining eye contact for too long, for example), but to those invested in the street code, these actions become serious indications of the other person's intentions. Consequently, such people become very sensitive to advances and slights, which could well serve as warnings of imminent physical confrontation.

This hard reality can be traced to the profound sense of alienation from mainstream society and its institutions felt by many poor inner-city black people, particularly the young. The code of the streets is actually a cultural adaptation to a profound lack of faith in the police and the judicial system. The police are most often seen as representing the dominant white society and not caring to protect inner-city residents. When called, they may not respond, which is one reason many residents feel they must be prepared to take extraordinary measures to defend themselves and their loved ones against those who are inclined to aggression. Lack of police accountability has in fact been incorporated into the status system: the person who is believed capable of "taking care of himself" is accorded a certain deference, which translates into a sense of physical and psychological control. Thus the street code emerges where the influence of the police ends and personal responsibility for one's safety is felt to begin. Exacerbated by the proliferation of drugs and easy access to guns, this volatile situation results in the ability of the street-oriented minority (or those who effectively "go for bad") to dominate the public spaces.

DECENT AND STREET FAMILIES

Although almost everyone in poor inner-city neighborhoods is struggling financially and therefore feels a certain distance from the rest of America, the decent and the street family in a real sense represent two poles of value orientation, two contrasting conceptual categories. The labels "decent" and "street," which the residents themselves use, amount to evaluative judgments that confer status on local residents. The labeling is often the result of a social contest among individuals and families of the neighborhood. Individuals of the two orientations often coexist in the same extended family. Decent residents judge themselves to be so while judging others to be of the street, and street individuals often present themselves as decent, drawing distinctions between themselves and other people. In addition, there is quite a bit of circumstantial behavior—that is, one person may at different times exhibit both decent and street orientations, depending on the circumstances. Although these designations result from so much social jockeying, there do exist concrete features that define each conceptual category.

Generally, so-called decent families tend to accept mainstream values more fully and attempt to instill them in their children. Whether married couples with children or single-parent (usually female) households, they are generally "working poor" and so tend to be better off financially than their street-oriented neighbors. They value hard work and self-reliance and are willing to sacrifice for their children. Because they have a certain amount of faith in mainstream society, they harbor hopes for a better future for their children, if not for themselves. Many of them go to church and take a strong interest in their children's schooling. Rather than dwelling on the real hardships and inequities facing them, many such decent people, particularly the increasing number of grandmothers raising grandchildren, see their difficult situation as a test from God and derive great support from their faith and from the church community.

Extremely aware of the problematic and often dangerous environment in which they reside, decent parents tend to be strict in their child-rearing practices, encouraging children to respect authority and walk a straight moral line. They have an almost obsessive concern about trouble of any kind and remind their children to be on the lookout for people and situations that might lead to it. At the same time, they are themselves polite and considerate of others, and teach their children to be the same way. At home, at work, and in church, they strive hard to maintain a positive mental attitude and a spirit of cooperation.

So-called street parents, in contrast, often show a lack of consideration for other people and have a rather superficial sense of family and community. Though they may love their children, many of them are unable to cope with the physical and emotional demands of parenthood, and find it difficult to reconcile their needs with those of their children. These families, who are more fully invested in the code of the streets than the decent people are, may aggressively socialize their children into it in a normative way. They believe in the code and judge themselves and others according to its values.

In fact the overwhelming majority of families in the inner-city community try to approximate the decent-family model, but there are many others who clearly represent the worst fears of the decent family. Not only are their financial resources extremely limited, but what little they have may easily be misused. The lives of the street-oriented are often marked by disorganization. In the most desperate circumstances people frequently have a limited understanding of priorities and consequences, and so frustrations mount over bills, food, and, at times, drink, cigarettes, and drugs. Some tend toward self-destructive behavior; many street-oriented women are crack-addicted ("on the pipe"), alcoholic, or involved in complicated relationships with men who abuse them. In addition, the seeming intractability of their situation, caused in large part by the lack of well-paying jobs and the persistence of racial discrimination, has engendered deep-seated bitterness and anger in many of the most desperate and poorest blacks, especially young people. The need both to exercise a measure of control and to lash out at somebody is often reflected in the adults' relations with their children. At the least, the frustrations of persistent poverty shorten the fuse in such people—contributing to a lack of patience with anyone, child or adult, who irritates them.

In these circumstances a woman—or a man, although men are less consistently present in children's lives—can be quite aggressive with children, yelling at and striking them for the least little infraction of the rules she has set down. Often little if any serious explanation follows the verbal and physical punishment. This response teaches children a particular lesson. They learn that to solve any kind of interpersonal problem one must quickly resort to hitting or other violent behavior. Actual peace and quiet, and also the appearance of calm, respectful children conveyed to her neighbors and friends, are often what the young mother most desires, but at times she will be very aggressive in trying to get them. Thus she may be quick to beat her children, especially if they defy her law, not because she hates them but because this is the way she knows to control them. In fact, many street-oriented women love their children dearly. Many mothers in the community subscribe to the notion that there is a "devil in the boy" that must be beaten out of him or that socially "fast girls need to be whupped." Thus much of what borders on child abuse in the view of social authorities is acceptable parental punishment in the view of these mothers.

Many street-oriented women are sporadic mothers whose children learn to fend for themselves when necessary, foraging for food and money any way they can get it. The children are sometimes employed by drug dealers or become addicted themselves. These children of the street, growing up with little supervision, are said to "come up hard." They often learn to fight at an early age, sometimes using short-tempered adults around them as role models. The street-oriented home may be fraught with anger, verbal disputes, physical aggression, and even mayhem. The children observe these goings-on, learning the lesson that might makes right. They quickly learn to hit those who cross them, and the dog-eat-dog mentality prevails. In order to survive, to protect oneself, it is necessary to marshal inner resources and be ready to deal with adversity in a hands-on way. In these circumstances physical prowess takes on great significance. * * *

CAMPAIGNING FOR RESPECT

These realities of inner-city life are largely absorbed on the streets. At an early age, often even before they start school, children from street-oriented homes gravitate to the streets, where they "hang"—socialize with their peers. Children from these generally permissive homes have a great deal of latitude and are allowed to "rip and run" up and down the street. They often come home from school, put their books down, and go right back out the door. On school nights eight- and nine-year-olds remain out until nine or ten o'clock (and teenagers typically come in whenever they want to). On the streets they play in groups that often become the source of their primary social bonds. Children from decent homes tend to be more carefully supervised and are thus likely to have curfews and to be taught how to stay out of trouble.

When decent and street kids come together, a kind of social shuffle occurs in which children have a chance to go either way. Tension builds as a child comes to realize that he must choose an orientation. The kind of home he comes from influences but does not determine the way he will ultimately turn out—although it is unlikely that a child from a thoroughly street-oriented family will easily absorb decent values on the streets. Youths who emerge from street-oriented families but develop a decency orientation almost always learn those values in another setting—in school, in a youth group, in church. Often it is the result of their involvement with a caring "old head" (adult role model).

In the street, through their play, children pour their individual life experiences into a common knowledge pool, affirming, confirming, and elaborating on what they have observed in the home and matching their skills against those of others. And they learn to fight. Even small children test one another, pushing and shoving, and are ready to hit other children over circumstances not to their liking. In turn, they are readily hit by other children, and the child who is toughest prevails. Thus the violent resolution of disputes, the hitting and cursing, gains social reinforcement. The child in effect is initiated into a system that is really a way of campaining for respect.

In addition, younger children witness the disputes of older children, which are often resolved through cursing and abusive talk, if not aggression or outright violence. They see that one child succumbs to the greater physical and mental abilities of the other. They are also alert and attentive witnesses to the verbal and physical fights of adults, after which they compare notes and share their interpretations of the event. In almost every case the victor is the person who physically won the altercation, and this person often enjoys the esteem and respect of onlookers. These experiences reinforce the lessons the children have learned at home: might makes right, and toughness is a virtue, while humility is not. In effect they learn the social meaning of fighting. When it is left virtually unchallenged, this understanding becomes an ever more important part of the child's working conception of the world. Over time the code of the streets becomes refined.

Those street-oriented adults with whom children come in contact—including mothers, fathers, brothers, sisters, boyfriends, cousins, neighbors, and friends—help them along in forming this understanding by verbalizing the messages they are getting through experience: "Watch your back." "Protect yourself." "Don't punk out." "If somebody messes with you, you got to pay them back." "If someone disses you, you got to straighten them out." Many parents actually impose sanctions if a child is not sufficiently aggressive. For example, if a child loses a fight and comes home upset, the parent might respond, "Don't you come in here crying that somebody beat you up; you better get back out there and whup his ass. I didn't raise no punks! Get back out there and whup his ass. If you don't whup his ass, I'll whup your ass when you come home." Thus the child obtains reinforcement for being tough and showing nerve.

* * *

SELF-IMAGE BASED ON "JUICE"

By the time they are teenagers, most youths have either internalized the code of the streets or at least learned the need to comport themselves in accordance with its rules, which chiefly have to do with interpersonal communication. The code revolves around the presentation of self. Its basic requirement is the display of a certain predisposition to violence. Accordingly, one's bearing must send the unmistakable if sometimes subtle message to "the next person" in public that one is capable of violence and mayhem when the situation requires it, that one can take care of oneself. The nature of this communication is largely determined by the demands of the circumstances but can include facial expressions, gait, and verbal expressions—all of which are geared mainly to deterring aggression. Physical appearance, including clothes, jewelry, and grooming, also plays an important part in how a person is viewed; to be respected, it is important to have the right look.

Even so, there are no guarantees against challenges, because there are always people around looking for a fight to increase their share of respect—or "juice," as it is sometimes called on the street. Moreover, if a person is assaulted, it is important, not only in the eyes of his opponent but also in the eyes of his "running buddies," for him to avenge himself. Otherwise he risks being "tried" (challenged) or "moved on" by any number of others. To maintain his honor he must show he is not someone to be "messed with" or "dissed." In general, the person must "keep himself straight" by managing his position of respect among others; this involves in part his self-image, which is shaped by what he thinks others are thinking of him in relation to his peers.

Objects play an important and complicated role in establishing self-image. Jackets, sneakers, gold jewelry, reflect not just a person's taste, which tends to be tightly regulated among adolescents of all social classes, but also a willingness to possess things that may require defending. A boy wearing a fashionable, expensive jacket, for example, is vulnerable to attack by another who covets the jacket and either cannot afford to buy one or wants the added satisfaction of depriving someone else of his. However, if the boy forgoes the desirable jacket and wears one that isn't "hip," he runs the risk of being teased and possibly even assaulted as an unworthy person. To be allowed to hang with certain prestigious crowds, a boy must wear a different set of expensive clothes—sneakers and athletic suit—every day. Not to be able to do so might make him appear socially deficient. The youth comes to covet such items—especially when he sees easy prey wearing them.

In acquiring valued things, therefore, a person shores up his identity—but since it is an identity based on having things, it is highly precarious. This very precariousness gives a heightened sense of urgency to staying even with peers, with whom the person is actually competing. Young men and women who are able to command respect through their presentation of self—by allowing their possessions and their body language to speak for them—may not have to campaign for regard but may, rather, gain it by the force of their manner. Those who are unable to command respect in this way must actively campaign for it—and are thus particularly alive to slights.

One way of campaigning for status is by taking the possessions of others. In this context, seemingly ordinary objects can become trophies imbued with symbolic value that far exceeds their monetary worth. Possession of the trophy can symbolize the ability to violate somebody—to "get in his face," to take something of value from him, to "dis" him, and thus to enhance one's own worth by stealing someone else's. The trophy does not have to be something material. It can be another person's sense of honor, snatched away with a derogatory remark. It can be the outcome of a fight. It can be the imposition of a certain standard, such as a girl's getting herself recognized as the most beautiful. Material things, however, fit easily into the pattern. Sneakers, a pistol, even somebody else's girlfriend, can become a trophy. When a person can take something from another and then flaunt it, he gains a certain regard by being the owner, or the controller, of that thing. But this display of ownership can then provoke other people to challenge him. This game of who controls what is thus constantly being played out on inner-city streets, and the trophy—extrinsic or intrinsic, tangible or intangible—identifies the current winner.

An important aspect of this often violent give-and-take is its zero-sum quality. That is, the extent to which one person can raise himself up depends on his ability to put another person down. This underscores the alienation that permeates the inner-city ghetto community. There is a generalized sense that very little respect is to be had, and therefore everyone competes to get what affirmation he can of the little that is available. The craving for respect that results gives people thin skins. Shows of deference by others can be highly soothing, contributing to a sense of security, comfort, self-confidence, and self-respect. Transgressions by others which go unanswered diminish these feelings and are believed to encourage further transgressions. Hence one must be ever vigilant against the transgressions of others or even *appearing* as if transgressions will be tolerated. Among young people, whose sense of self-esteem is particularly vulnerable, there is an especially heightened concern with being disrespected. Many inner-city young men in particular crave respect to such a degree that they will risk their lives to attain and maintain it.

The issue of respect is thus closely tied to whether a person has an inclination to be violent, even as a victim. In the wider society people may not feel required to retaliate physically after an attack, even though they are aware that they have been degraded or taken advantage of. They may feel a great need to defend themselves *during* an attack, or to behave in such a way as to deter aggression (middle-class people certainly can and do become victims of street-oriented youths), but they are much more likely than street-oriented people to feel that they can walk away from a possible altercation with their self-esteem intact. Some people may even have the strength of character to flee, without any thought that their self-respect or esteem will be diminished.

In impoverished inner-city black communities, however, particularly among young males and perhaps increasingly among females, such flight would be extremely difficult. To run away would likely leave one's self-esteem in tatters. Hence people often feel constrained not only to stand up and at least attempt to resist during an assault but also to "pay back"—to seek revenge—after a successful assault on their person. This may include going to get a weapon or even getting relatives involved. Their very identity and self-respect, their honor, is often intricately tied up with the way they perform on the streets during and after such encounters. This outlook reflects the circumscribed opportunities of the inner-city poor. Generally people outside the ghetto have other ways of gaining status and regard, and thus do not feel so dependent on such physical displays.

BY TRIAL OF MANHOOD

On the street, among males these concerns about things and identity have come to be expressed in the concept of "manhood." Manhood in the inner city means taking the prerogatives of men with respect to strangers, other men, and women—being distinguished as a man. It implies physicality and a certain ruthlessness. Regard and respect are associated with this concept in large part because of its practical application: if others have little or no regard for a person's manhood, his very life and those of his loved ones could be in jeopardy. But there is a chicken-and-egg aspect to this situation: one's physical safety is more likely to be jeopardized in public *because* manhood is associated with respect. In other words, an existential link has been created between the idea of manhood and one's self-esteem, so that it has become hard to say which is primary. For many inner-city youths, manhood and respect are flip sides of the same coin; physical and psychological well-being are inseparable, and both require a sense of control, of being in charge.

The operating assumption is that a man, especially a real man, knows what other men know—the code of the streets. And if one is not a real man, one is somehow diminished as a person, and there are certain valued things one simply does not deserve. There is thus believed to be a certain justice to the code, since it is considered that everyone has the opportunity to know it. Implicit in this is that everybody is held responsible for being familiar with the code. If the victim of a mugging, for example, does not know the code and so responds "wrong," the perpetrator may feel justified even in killing him and may feel no remorse. He may think, "Too bad, but it's his fault. He should have known better."

So when a person ventures outside, he must adopt the code—a kind of shield, really—to prevent others from "messing with" him. In these circumstances it is easy for people to think they are being tried or tested by others even when this is not the case. For it is sensed that something extremely valuable is at stake in every interaction, and people are encouraged to rise to the occasion, particularly with strangers. For people who are unfamiliar with the code—generally people who live outside the inner city—the concern with respect in the most ordinary interactions can be frightening and incomprehensible. But for those who are invested in the code, the clear object of their demeanor is to discourage strangers from even thinking about testing their manhood. And the sense of power that attends the ability to deter others can be alluring even to those who know the code without being heavily invested in it—the decent inner-city youths. Thus a boy who has been leading a basically decent life can, in trying circumstances, suddenly resort to deadly force.

Central to the issue of manhood is the widespread belief that one of the most effective ways of gaining respect is to manifest "nerve." Nerve is shown when one takes another person's possessions (the more valuable the better), "messes with" someone's woman, throws the first punch, "gets in someone's face," or pulls a trigger. Its proper display helps on the spot to check others who would violate one's person and also helps to build a reputation that works to prevent future challenges. But since such a show of nerve is a forceful expression of disrespect toward the person on the receiving end, the victim may be greatly offended and seek to retaliate with equal or greater force. A display of nerve, therefore, can easily provoke a life-threatening response, and the background knowledge of that possibility has often been incorporated into the concept of nerve.

True nerve exposes a lack of fear of dying. Many feel that it is acceptable to risk dying over the principle of respect. In fact, among the hard-core street-oriented, the clear risk of violent death may be preferable to being "dissed" by another. The youths who have internalized this attitude and convincingly display it in their public bearing are among the most threatening people of all, for it is commonly assumed that they fear no man. As the people of the community say, "They are the baddest dudes on the street." They often lead an existential life that may acquire meaning only when they are faced with the possibility of imminent death. Not to be afraid to die is by implication to have few compunctions about taking another's life. Not to be afraid to die is the quid pro quo of being able to take somebody else's life—for the right reasons, if the situation demands it. When others believe this is one's position, it gives one a real sense of power on the streets. Such credibility is what many inner-city youths strive to achieve, whether they are decent or street-oriented, both because of its practical defensive value and because of the positive way it makes them feel about themselves. The difference between the decent and the street-oriented youth is often that the decent youth makes a conscious decision to appear tough and manly; in another setting—with teachers, say, or at his part-time job—he can be polite and deferential. The street-oriented youth, on the other hand, has made the concept of manhood a part of his very identity; he has difficulty manipulating it—it often controls him.

GIRLS AND BOYS

Increasingly, teenage girls are mimicking the boys and trying to have their own version of "manhood." Their goal is the same—to get respect, to be recognized as capable of setting or maintaining a certain standard. They try to achieve this end in the ways that have been established by the boys, including posturing, abusive language, and the use of violence to resolve disputes, but the issues for the girls are different. Although conflicts over turf and status exist among the girls, the majority of disputes seem rooted in assessments of beauty (which girl in a group is "the cutest"), competition over boyfriends, and attempts to regulate other people's knowledge of and opinions about a girl's behavior or that of someone close to her, especially her mother.

A major cause of conflicts among girls is "he say, she say." This practice begins in the early school years and continues through high school. It occurs when "people," particularly girls, talk about others, thus putting their "business in the streets." Usually one girl will say something negative about another in the group, most often behind the person's back. The remark will then get back to the person talked about. She may retaliate or her friends may feel required to "take up for" her. In essence this is a form of group gossiping in which individuals are negatively assessed and evaluated. As with much gossip, the things said may or may not be true, but the point is that such imputations can cast aspersions on a person's good name. The accused is required to defend herself against the slander, which can result in arguments and fights, often over little of real substance. Here again is the problem of low self-esteem, which encourages youngsters to be highly sensitive to slights and to be vulnerable to feeling easily "dissed." To avenge the dissing, a fight is usually necessary.

Because boys are believed to control violence, girls tend to defer to them in situations of conflict. Often if a girl is attacked or feels slighted, she will get a brother, uncle, or cousin to do her fighting for her. Increasingly, however, girls are doing their own fighting and are even asking their male relatives to teach them how to fight. Some girls form groups that attack other girls or take things from them. A hard-core segment of inner-city girls inclined toward violence seems to be developing. As one thirteen-year-old girl in a detention center for youths who have committed violent acts told me, "To get people to leave you alone, you gotta fight. Talking don't always get you out of stuff." One major difference between girls and boys: girls rarely use guns. Their fights are therefore not life-or-death struggles. Girls are not often willing to put their lives on the line for "manhood." The ultimate form of respect on the male-dominated inner-city street is thus reserved for men.

"GOING FOR BAD"

In the most fearsome youths such a cavalier attitude toward death grows out of a very limited view of life. Many are uncertain about how long they are going to live and believe they could die violently at any time. They accept this fate; they live on the edge. Their manner conveys the message that nothing intimidates them; whatever turn the encounter takes, they maintain their attack—rather like a pit bull, whose spirit many such boys admire. The demonstration of such tenacity "shows heart" and earns their respect.

This fearlessness has implications for law enforcement. Many street-oriented boys are much more concerned about the threat of "justice" at the hands of a peer than at the hands of the police. Moreover, many feel not only that they have little to lose by going to prison but that they have something to gain. The toughening-up one experiences in prison can actually enhance one's reputation on the streets. Hence the system loses influence over the hard core who are without jobs, with little perceptible stake in the system. If mainstream society has done nothing *for* them, they counter by making sure it can do nothing *to* them.

At the same time, however, a competing view maintains that true nerve consists in backing down, walking away from a fight, and going on with one's business. One fights only in self-defense. This view emerges from the decent philosophy that life is precious, and it is an important part of the socialization process common in decent homes. It discourages violence as the primary means of resolving disputes and encourages youngsters to accept nonviolence and talk as confrontational strategies. But "if the deal goes down," self-defense is greatly encouraged. When there is enough positive support for this orientation, either in the home or among one's peers, then nonviolence has a chance to prevail. But it prevails at the cost of relinquishing a claim to being bad and tough, and therefore sets a young person up as at the very least alienated from street-oriented peers and quite possibly a target of derision or even violence.

Although the nonviolent orientation rarely overcomes the impulse to strike back in an encounter, it does introduce a certain confusion and so can prompt a measure of soul-searching, or even profound ambivalence. Did the person back down with his respect intact or did he back down only to be judged a "punk"—a person lacking manhood? Should he or she have acted? Should he or she have hit the other person in the mouth? These questions beset many young men and women during public confrontations. What is the "right" thing to do? In the quest for honor, respect, and local status—which few young people are uninterested in—common sense most often prevails, which leads many to opt for the tough approach, enacting their own particular versions of the display of nerve. The presentation of oneself as rough and tough is very often quite acceptable until one is tested. And then that presentation may help the person pass the test, because it will cause fewer questions to be asked about what he did and why. It is hard for a person to explain why he lost the fight or why he backed down. Hence many will strive to appear to "go for bad," while hoping they will never be tested. But when they are tested, the outcome of the situation may quickly be out of their hands, as they become wrapped up in the circumstances of the moment.

AN OPPOSITIONAL CULTURE

The attitudes of the wider society are deeply implicated in the code of the streets. Most people in inner-city communities are not totally invested in the code, but the significant minority of hard-core street youths who are have to maintain the code in order to establish reputations, because they have—or feel they have—few other ways to assert themselves. For these young people the standards of the street code are the only game in town. The extent to which some children—particularly those who through upbringing have become most alienated and those lacking in strong and conventional social support—experience, feel, and internalize racist rejection and contempt from mainstream society may strongly encourage them to express contempt for the more conventional society in turn. In dealing with this contempt and rejection, some youngsters will consciously invest themselves and their considerable mental resources in what amounts to an oppositional culture to preserve themselves and their self-respect. Once they do, any respect they might be able to garner in the wider system pales in comparison with the respect available in the local system; thus they often lose interest in even attempting to negotiate the mainstream system.

At the same time, many less alienated young blacks have assumed a street-oriented demeanor as a way of expressing their blackness while really embracing a much more moderate way of life; they, too, want a nonviolent setting in which to live and raise a family. These decent people are trying hard to be part of the mainstream culture, but the racism, real and perceived, that they encounter helps to legitimate the oppositional culture. And so on occasion they adopt street behavior. In fact, depending on the demands of the situation, many people in the community slip back and forth between decent and street behavior.

A vicious cycle has thus been formed. The hopelessness and alienation many young inner-city black men and women feel, largely as a result of endemic joblessness and persistent racism, fuels the violence they engage in. This violence serves to confirm the negative feelings many whites and some middle-class blacks harbor toward the ghetto poor, further legitimating the oppositional culture and the code of the streets in the eyes of many poor young blacks. Unless this cycle is broken, attitudes on both sides will become increasingly entrenched, and the violence, which claims victims black and white, poor and affluent, will only escalate.

19

Go North, Young Man

RICHARD RODRIGUEZ

Written autobiographically, this reflection on family, ethnicity, place and change draws a picture relevant to the global community. The assumption that cultural diversity—in the United States and elsewhere—would succumb to the pressures of assimilation, that a "melting pot" of modern technology and popular culture would blend all differences into a palatable stew, has not occurred, especially where millions of immigrants have made their homes. Richard Rodriguez raises questions, provides observations, and muses about what it means to be a North American. Though looking to his past, the author suggests what may lie in all of our futures.

Traditionally, America has been an east-west country. We have read our history, right to left across the page. We were oblivious of Canada. We barely noticed Mexico, except when Mexico got in the way of our westward migration, which we interpreted as the will of God, "manifest destiny."

In a Protestant country that believed in rebirth (the Easter promise), land became our metaphor for possibility. As long as there was land ahead of us—Ohio, Illinois, Nebraska—we could believe in change; we could abandon our in-laws, leave disappointments behind, to start anew further west. California symbolized ultimate possibility, future-time, the end of the line, where loonies and prophets lived, where America's fads necessarily began.

Nineteenth-century real estate developers and 20th-century Hollywood moguls may have advertised the futuristic myth of California to the rest of America. But the myth was one Americans were predisposed to believe. The idea of California was invented by Americans many miles away. Only a few early voices from California ever warned against optimism. Two decades after California became American territory, the conservationist John Muir stood at the edge of California and realized that America is a finite idea: We need to preserve the land, if the dream of America is to survive. Word of Muir's discovery slowly traveled backward in time, from the barely populated West (the future) to the crowded brick cities of the East Coast (the past).

I grew up in California of the 1950s, when the state was filling with people from New York and Oklahoma. Everyone was busy losing weight and changing hair color and becoming someone new. There was, then, still plenty of cheap land for tract houses, under the cloudless sky.

The 1950s, the 1960s—those years were our golden age. Edmund G. "Pat" Brown was governor of optimism. He created the University of California system, a decade before the children of the suburbs rebelled, portraying themselves as the "counterculture." Brown constructed freeways that permitted Californians to move farther and farther away from anything resembling an urban center. He even made the water run up the side of a mountain.

By the 1970s, optimism was running out of space. Los Angeles needed to reinvent itself as Orange County. Then Orange County got too crowded and had to reinvent itself as North County San Diego. Then Californians started moving into the foothills or out to the desert, complaining all the while of the traffic and of the soiled air. And the immigrants!

Suddenly, foreign immigrants were everywhere—Iranians were buying into Beverly Hills; the Vietnamese were moving into San Jose; the Chinese were taking all the spaces in the biochemistry courses at UCLA. And Mexicans, poor Mexicans, were making hotel beds, picking peaches in the Central Valley, changing diapers, even impersonating Italian chefs at Santa Monica restaurants.

The Mexicans and the Chinese had long inhabited California. But they never resided within the golden myth of the state. Nineteenth-century California restricted the Chinese to Chinatowns or to a city's outskirts. Mexicans were neither here nor there. They were imported by California to perform cheap labor, then deported in bad economic times.

The East Coast had incorporated Ellis Island in its myth. The West Coast regarded the non-European immigrant as doubly foreign. Though Spaniards may have colonized the place and though Mexico briefly claimed it, California took its meaning from "internal immigrants"—Americans from Minnesota or Brooklyn who came West to remake their parents' version of America.

But sometime in the 1970s, it became clear to many Californians that the famous blond myth of the state was in jeopardy. ("We are sorry to intrude, señor, we are only looking for work.") Was L.A. "becoming" Mexican?

Latin Americans arrived, describing California as "el norte." The "West Coast" was a finite idea; el norte in the Latin American lexicon means wide-open. Whose compass was right?

Meanwhile, with the lifting of anti-Asian immigration restrictions, jumbo jets were arriving at LAX from Bangkok and Seoul. People getting off the planes said about California, "This is where the United States begins." Californians objected, "No, no. California is where the United States comes to an end—we don't have enough room for you." Whose compass was truer?

It has taken two more decades for the East Coast to get the point. Magazines and television stories from New York today describe the golden state as "tarnished." The more interesting possibility is that California has become the intersection between comedy and tragedy. Foreign immigrants are replanting optimism on California soil; the native-born know the wisdom of finitude. Each side has a knowledge to give the other.

Already, everywhere in California, there is evidence of miscegenation—Keanu Reeves, sushi tacos, blond Buddhists, Salvadoran Pentecostals. But the forces that could lead to marriage also create gridlock on the Santa Monica freeway. The native-born Californian sits disgruntled in traffic going nowhere. The flatbed truck in front of him is filled with Mexicans; in the Mercedes next to him is a Japanese businessman using a car phone.

There are signs of backlash. Pete Wilson has become the last east-west governor of California. In a state founded by people seeking a softer winter and famous internationally for being "laid back," Californians vote for Proposition 187, hoping that illegal immigrants will stay away if there are no welfare dollars.

But immigrants are most disconcerting to California because they are everywhere working, transforming the ethos of the state from leisure to labor. Los Angeles is becoming a vast working city, on the order of Hong Kong or Mexico City. Chinese kids are raising the admission standards to the University of California. Mexican immigrant kids are undercutting union wages, raising rents in once-black neighborhoods.

Californians used to resist any metaphor drawn from their state's perennial earthquakes and floods and fires. Now Californians take their meaning from natural calamity. People turn away from the sea, imagine the future as existing backward in time.

"I'm leaving California, I'm going to Colorado."

"I'm headed for Arizona."

After hitting the coastline like flies against glass, we look in new directions. Did Southern California's urban sprawl invent NAFTA? For the first time, Californians now talk of the North and the South—new points on our national compass.

"I've just bought a condo in Baja."

"I'm leaving California for Seattle."

"I'm moving to Vancouver. I want someplace cleaner."

"Go North, young man."

Puerto Ricans, Mexicans: Early in this century we were immigrants. Or not immigrants exactly. Puerto Ricans had awakened one day to discover that they suddenly lived on U.S. territory. Mexicans had seen Mexico's northern territory annexed and renamed the southwestern United States.

We were people from the South in an east-west country. We were people of mixed blood in a black and white nation. We were Catholics in a Protestant land. Many millions of us were Indians in an east-west country that imagined the Indian to be dead.

Today, Los Angeles is the largest Indian city in the United States, though Hollywood filmmakers persist in making movies about the dead Indian. (For seven bucks, you can see cowboys slaughter Indians in the Kevin Costner movie—and regret it from your comfortable chair.) On any day along Sunset Boulevard you can see Toltecs and Aztecs and Mayans.

Puerto Ricans, Mexicans—we are the earliest Latin American immigrants to the United States. We have turned into fools. We argue among ourselves, criticize one another for becoming too much the gringo or maybe not gringo enough. We criticize each other for speaking too much Spanish or not enough Spanish. We demand that politicians provide us with bilingual voting ballots, but we do not trouble to vote.

Octavio Paz, the Mexican writer, has observed that the Mexican-American is caught between cultures, thus a victim of history—unwilling to become a Mexican again, unable to belong to the United States. Michael Novak, the United States writer, has observed that what unites people throughout the Americas is that we all have said goodbye to our motherland. To Europe. To Africa. To Asia. *Farewell!*

The only trouble is: Adios was never part of the Mexican-American or Puerto Rican vocabulary. There was no need to turn one's back on the past. Many have traveled back and forth, between rivals, between past and future, commuters between the Third World and First. After a few months in New York or Los Angeles, it would be time to head "home." After a few months back in Mexico or Puerto Rico, it would be time to head "home" to the United States.

We were nothing like the famous Ellis Island immigrants who arrived in America with no expectation of return to the "old country." In a nation that believed in the future, we were a puzzle.

We were also a scandal to Puerto Rico and Mexico. Our Spanish turned bad. Our values were changing—though no one could say why or how exactly. "Abuelita" (grandmother) complained that we were growing more guarded. Alone.

There is a name that Mexico uses for children who have forgotten their true address: "pocho." The pocho is the child who wanders away, ends up in the United States, among the gringos, where he forgets his true home.

The Americas began with a confusion about maps and a joke about our father's mistake. Columbus imagined himself in a part of the world where there were Indians.

We smile because our 15th-century "papi" thought he was in India. I'm not certain, however, that even today we know where in the world we live. We are only beginning to look at the map. We are only beginning to wonder what the map of the hemisphere might mean.

Latin Americans have long complained that the gringo, with characteristic arrogance, hijacked the word "American" and gave it all to himself—"the way he stole the land." I remember, years ago, my aunt in Mexico City scolding me when I told her I came from "America." Pocho! Didn't I realize that the entire hemisphere is America? "Listen," my Mexican aunt told me, "people who live in the United States are norteamericanos."

Well, I think to myself—my aunt is now dead, God rest her soul—I wonder what she would have thought a couple of years ago when the great leaders—

the president of Mexico, the president of the United States, the Canadian prime minister—gathered to sign the North American Free Trade Agreement. Mexico signed a document acknowledging that she is a North American.

I predict that Mexico will suffer a nervous breakdown in the next 10 years. She will have to check into the Betty Ford Clinic for a long rest. She will need to determine just what exactly it means that she is, with the dread gringo, a norteamericana.

Canada, meanwhile, worries about the impact of the Nashville music channel on its cable TV; Pat Buchanan imagines a vast wall along our southern flank; and Mexican nationalists fear a Clinton bailout of the lowly peso.

We all speak of North America. But has anyone ever actually met a North American? Oh, there are Mexicans. And there are Canadians. And there are so-called Americans. But a North American?

I know one.

Let me tell you about him—this North American. He is a Mixteco Indian who comes from the Mexican state of Oaxaca. He is trilingual. His primary language is the language of his tribe. His second language is Spanish, the language of Cortés. Also, he has a working knowledge of U.S. English, because, for several months of the year, he works near Stockton, Calif.

He commutes over thousands of miles of dirt roads and freeways, knows several centuries, two currencies, two sets of hypocrisy. He is a criminal in one country and an embarrassment to the other. He is pursued as an "illegal" by the U.S. border patrol. He is preyed upon by Mexican officers who want to shake him down because he has hidden U.S. dollars in his shoes.

In Oaxaca, he lives in a 16th-century village, where his wife watches blond Venezuelan soap operas. A picture of la Virgen de Guadalupe rests over his bed. In Stockton, there is no Virgin Mary, only the other Madonna—the material girl.

He is the first North American.

A journalist once asked Chou En-lai, the Chinese premier under Mao Zedong, what he thought of the French Revolution. Chou En-lai gave a wonderful Chinese reply: "It's too early to tell."

I think it may even be too early to tell what the story of Columbus means. The latest chapter of the Columbus saga may be taking place right now, as Latin American teenagers with Indian faces violate the U.S. border. The Mexican kids standing on the line tonight between Tijuana and San Diego—if you ask them why they are coming to the United States of America, they will not say anything about Thomas Jefferson or *The Federalist Papers*. They have only heard that there is a job in a Glendale dry cleaner's or that some farmer is hiring near Fresno.

They insist: They will be returning to Mexico in a few months. They are only going to the United States for the dollars. They certainly don't intend to become gringos. They don't want anything to do with the United States, except the dollars.

But the months will pass, and the teenagers will be changed in the United States. When they go back to their Mexican village, they will no longer be easy. They will expect an independence and an authority that the village cannot give them. Much to their surprise, they will have been Americanized by the job in Glendale.

For work in the United States is our primary source of identity. There is no more telling question we Americans ask one another than "What do you do?" We do not ask about family or village or religion. We ask about work.

The Mexican teenagers will return to Glendale.

Mexicans, Puerto Ricans—most of us end up in the United States, living in the city. Peasants end up in the middle of a vast modern metropolis, having known only the village, with its three blocks of familiar facades.

The arriving generation is always the bravest. New immigrants often change religion with their move to the city. They need to make their peace with isolation, so far from relatives. They learn subway and bus routes that take them far from home every day. Long before they can read English, they learn how to recognize danger and opportunity. Their lives are defined by change.

Their children or their grandchildren become, often, very different. The best and the brightest, perhaps, will go off to college—become the first in their family—but they talk about "keeping" their culture. They start speaking Spanish, as a way of not changing; they eat in the cafeteria only with others who look like themselves. They talk incessantly about "culture" as though it were some little thing that can be preserved and kept in a box.

The unluckiest children of immigrants drop out of high school. They speak neither good English nor Spanish. Some end up in gangs—family, man— "blood." They shoot other kids who look exactly like themselves. If they try to leave their gang, the gang will come after them for their act of betrayal. If they venture to some other part of the city, they might get shot or they might merely be unable to decipher the freeway exits that speed by.

They retreat to their "turf"—three blocks, just like in their grandmother's village, where the journey began.

One of the things that Mexico had never acknowledged about my father— I insist that you at least entertain this idea—is the possibility that my father and others like him were the great revolutionaries of Mexico. Pocho pioneers. They, not Pancho Villa, not Zapata, were heralds of the modern age in Mexico. They left for the United States and then they came back to Mexico. And they changed Mexico forever.

A childhood friend of my father's—he worked in Chicago in the 1920s, then returned one night to his village in Michoacan with appliances for mamasita and crisp dollars. The village gathered round him—this is a true story—and asked, "What is it like up there in Chicago?"

The man said, "It's OK."

That rumor of "OK" spread across Michoacán, down to Jalisco, all the way down to Oaxaca, from village to village to village.

Futurists and diplomats talk about a "new moment in the Americas." The Latin American elite have condos in Miami and send their children to Ivy League schools. U.S. and Canadian businessmen project the future on a north-south graph. But for many decades before any of this, Latin American peasants have been traveling back and forth, north and south.

Today, there are remote villages in Latin America that are among the most international places on earth. Tiny Peruvian villages know when farmers are picking pears in the Yakima valley in Washington state.

I am the son of a prophet. I am a fool. I am a victim of history. I am confused. I do not know whether I am coming or going. I speak bad Spanish. And yet I tell Latin America this: Because I grew up Hispanic in California, I know more Guatemalans than I would if I had grown up in Mexico, more Brazilians than if I lived in Peru. Because I live in California, it is routine for me to know Nicaraguans and Salvadorans and Cubans. As routine as knowing Chinese or Vietnamese.

My fellow Californians complain loudly about the uncouth southern invasion. I say this to California: Immigration is always illegal. It is a rude act, the leaving of home. Immigration begins as a violation of custom, a youthful act of defiance, an insult to the village. I know a man from El Salvador who has not spoken to his father since the day he left his father's village. Immigrants horrify the grandmothers they leave behind.

Illegal immigrants trouble U.S. environmentalists and Mexican nationalists. Illegal immigrants must trouble anyone, on either side of the line, who imagines that the poor are under control.

But they have also been our civilization's prophets. They, long before the rest of us, saw the hemisphere whole.

PART THREE

STRUCTURES OF POWER

20

"Getting" and "Making" a Tip

FROM *Dishing It Out: Power and Resistance among
Waitresses in a New Jersey Restaurant*

GRETA FOFF PAULES

*Waitresses, like many people who provide a service, are highly vulnerable to the whim
of the customers who, by their tips, decide their daily earnings. Waitresses structure
their encounters with more care than most of us realize. The reason for this is the need
to have some power over their work and their livelihood. For those of you who have
never been a waiter or waitress, this participant observation study may change forever the way you think about being served and treat those who serve you.*

> The waitress can't help feeling a sense of personal failure and public censure
> when she is "stiffed."
>
> —*William F. Whyte*, "When Workers and Customers Meet"

> They're rude, they're ignorant, they're obnoxious, they're inconsiderate. . . . Half
> these people don't deserve to come out and eat, let alone try and tip a waitress.
>
> —*Route [Restaurant] waitress*

The financial and emotional hazards inherent in the tipping system have
drawn attention from sociologists, and more recently anthropologists,
concerned with the study of work. In general these researchers have concluded that workers who receive gratuities exercise little control over the
material outcome of tipping and less over its symbolic implications.

* * *

MAKING A TIP AT ROUTE [RESTAURANT]

A common feature of past research is that the worker's control over the
tipping system is evaluated in terms of her efforts to con, coerce, compel, or
otherwise manipulate a customer into relinquishing a bigger tip. Because
these efforts have for the most part proven futile, the worker has been seen
as having little defense against the financial vicissitudes of the tipping system. What these studies have overlooked is that an employee can increase her
tip income by controlling the number as well as the size of tips she receives.
This oversight has arisen from the tendency of researchers to concentrate
narrowly on the relationship between server and served, while failing to take

193

into account the broader organizational context in which this relationship takes place.

Like service workers observed in earlier studies, waitresses at Route strive to boost the amount of individual gratuities by rendering special services and being especially friendly. As one waitress put it, "I'll sell you the world if you're in my station." In general though, waitresses at Route Restaurant seek to boost their tip income, not by increasing the amount of individual gratuities, but by increasing the number of customers they serve. They accomplish this (a) by securing the largest or busiest stations and working the most lucrative shifts; (b) by "turning" their tables quickly; and (c) by controlling the flow of customers within the restaurant.

Technically, stations at Route are assigned on a rotating basis so that all waitresses, including rookies, work fast and slow stations equally. Station assignments are listed on the work schedule that is posted in the office window where it can be examined by all workers on all shifts, precluding the possibility of blatant favoritism or discrimination. Yet a number of methods exist whereby experienced waitresses are able to circumvent the formal rotation system and secure the more lucrative stations for themselves. A waitress can trade assignments with a rookie who is uncertain of her ability to handle a fast station; she can volunteer to take over a large station when a *call-out* necessitates reorganization of station assignments; or she can establish herself as the only waitress capable of handling a particularly large or chaotic station. Changes in station assignments tend not to be formally recorded, so inconsistencies in the rotation system often do not show up on the schedule. Waitresses on the same shift may notice of course that a co-worker has managed to avoid an especially slow station for many days, or has somehow ended up in the busiest station two weekends in a row, but the waitresses' code of noninterference * * * inhibits them from openly objecting to such irregularities.

A waitress can also increase her tip income by working the more lucrative shifts. Because day is the busiest and therefore most profitable shift at Route, it attracts experienced, professional waitresses who are most concerned and best able to maximize their tip earnings. There are exceptions: some competent, senior-ranking waitresses are unable to work during the day due to time constraints of family or second jobs. Others choose not to work during the day despite the potential monetary rewards, because they are unwilling to endure the intensely competitive atmosphere for which day shift is infamous.

The acutely competitive environment that characterizes day shift arises from the aggregate striving of each waitress to maximize her tip income by serving the greatest possible number of customers. Two strategies are enlisted to this end. First, each waitress attempts to *turn* her tables as quickly as possible. Briefly stated, this means she takes the order, delivers the food, clears and resets a table, and begins serving the next party as rapidly as customer lingering and the speed of the kitchen allow. A seven-year veteran of Route describes the strategy and its rewards:

> What I do is I prebus my tables. When the people get up and go all I got is glasses and cups, pull off, wipe, set, and I do the table turnover. But see that's from day shift. See the girls on graveyard . . . don't understand the more times you turn that table the more money you make. You could have three tables and still make a hundred dollars. If you turn them tables.

As the waitress indicates, a large part of turning tables involves getting the table cleared and set for the next customer. During a rush, swing and grave waitresses tend to leave dirty tables standing, partly because they are less experienced and therefore less efficient, partly to avoid being given parties, or *sat,* when they are already behind. In contrast, day waitresses assign high priority to keeping their tables cleared and ready for customers. The difference in method reflects increased skill and growing awareness of and concern with money-making strategies.

A waitress can further increase her customer count by controlling the flow of customers within the restaurant. Ideally the hostess or manager running the front house rotates customers among stations, just as stations are rotated among waitresses. Each waitress is given, or *sat,* one party at a time in turn so that all waitresses have comparable customer counts at the close of a shift. When no hostess is on duty, or both she and the manager are detained and customers are waiting to be seated, waitresses will typically seat incoming parties.

Whether or not a formal hostess is on duty, day waitresses are notorious for bypassing the rotation system by racing to the door and directing incoming customers to their own tables. A sense of the urgency with which this strategy is pursued is conveyed in the comment of one five-year veteran, "They'll run you down to get that person at the door, to seat them in their station." The competition for customers is so intense during the day that some waitresses claim they cannot afford to leave the floor (even to use the restroom) lest they return to find a co-worker's station filled at their expense. "In the daytime, honey," remarks an eight-year Route waitress, "in the daytime it's like pulling teeth. You got to stay on the floor to survive. To survive." It is in part because they do not want to lose customers and tips to their co-workers that waitresses do not take formal breaks. Instead, they rest and eat between waiting tables or during lulls in business, returning to the floor intermittently to check on parties in progress and seat customers in their stations.

The fast pace and chaotic nature of restaurant work provide a cover for the waitress's aggressive pursuit of customers, since it is difficult for other servers to monitor closely the allocation of parties in the bustle and confusion of a rush. Still, it is not uncommon for waitresses to grumble to management and co-workers if they notice an obvious imbalance in customer distribution. Here again, the waitress refrains from directly criticizing her fellow servers, voicing her displeasure by commenting on the paucity of customers in her own station, rather than the overabundance of customers in the stations of certain co-waitresses. In response to these grumblings, other waitresses may moderate somewhat their efforts to appropriate new parties, and management may make a special effort to seat the disgruntled server favorably.

A waitress can also exert pressure on the manager or hostess to keep her station filled. She may, for instance, threaten to leave if she is not seated enough customers.

> I said, "Innes [a manager], I'm in [station] one and two. If one and two is not filled at all times from now until three, I'm getting my coat, my pocketbook, and I'm leaving." And one and two was filled, and I made ninety-five dollars.

Alternatively, she can make it more convenient for the manager or hostess to seat her rather than her co-workers, either by keeping her tables open (as described), or by taking extra tables. If customers are waiting to be seated, a waitress may offer to pick up parties in a station that is closed or, occasionally, to pick up parties in another waitress's station. In attempting either strategy, but especially the latter, the waitress must be adept not only at waiting tables, but in interpersonal restaurant politics. Autonomy and possession are of central concern to waitresses, and a waitress who offers to pick up tables outside her station must select her words carefully if she is to avoid being accused of invading her co-workers' territory. Accordingly, she may choose to present her bid for extra parties as an offer to help—the manager, another waitress, the restaurant, customers—rather than as a request.

The waitress who seeks to increase her tip income by maximizing the number of customers she serves may endeavor to cut her losses by refusing to serve parties that have stiffed her in the past. If she is a low-ranking waitress, her refusal is likely to be overturned by the manager. If she is an experienced and valuable waitress, the manager may ask someone else to take the party, assure the waitress he will take care of her (that is, pad the bill and give her the difference), or even pick up the party himself. Though the practice is far from common, a waitress may go so far as to demand a tip from a customer who has been known to stiff in the past.

> This party of two guys come in and they order thirty to forty dollars worth of food . . . and they stiff us. Every time. So Kaddie told them, "If you don't tip us, we're not going to wait on you." They said, "We'll tip you." So Kaddie waited on them, and they tipped her. The next night they came in, I waited on them and they didn't tip me. The third time they came in [the manager] put them in my station and I told [the manager] straight up, "I'm not waiting on them. . . ." So he made Hailey pick them up. And they stiffed Hailey. So when they came in the next night . . . [they] said, "Are you going to give us a table?" I said, "You going to tip me? I'm not going to wait on you. You got all that money, you sell all that

crack on the streets and you come here and you can't even leave me a couple bucks?" . . . So they left me a dollar. So when they come in Tuesday night, I'm telling them a dollar ain't enough.

The tactics employed by waitresses, and particularly day-shift waitresses, to increase their customer count and thereby boost their tip earnings have earned them a resounding notoriety among their less competitive co-workers. Day (and some swing) waitresses are described as "money hungry," "sneaky little bitches," "self-centered," "aggressive," "backstabbing bitches," and "cut-throats over tables." The following remarks of two Route waitresses, however, indicate that those who employ these tactics see them as defensive, not aggressive measures. A sense of the waitress's preoccupation with autonomy and with protecting what is hers also emerges from these comments.

> You have to be like that. Because if you don't be like that, people step on you. You know, like as far as getting customers. I mean, you know, I'm sorry everybody says I'm greedy. I guess that's why I've survived this long at Route. Cause I am greedy. . . . *I want what's mine,* and if it comes down to me cleaning your table or my table, I'm going to clean my table. Because see I went through all that stage where I would do your table. To be fair. And you would walk home with seventy dollars, and I'd have twenty-five, cause I was being fair all night. (emphasis added)
>
> If the customer comes in the door and I'm there getting that door, don't expect me to cover your backside while you in the back smoking a cigarette and I'm here working for myself. You not out there working for me. . . . When I go to the door and get the customers, when I keep my tables clean and your tables are dirty, and you wonder why you only got one person . . . then that's just tough shit. . . . You're damn right my station is filled. *I'm not here for you.* (emphasis added)

Whether the waitress who keeps her station filled with customers is acting aggressively or defensively, her tactics are effective. It is commonly accepted that determined day waitresses make better money than less competitive co-workers even when working swing or grave. Moreover Nera, the waitress most infamous for her relentless use of "money-hungry" tactics, is at the same time most famous for her consistently high daily takes. While other waitresses jingle change in their aprons, Nera is forced to store wads of bills in her shoes and in paper bags to prevent tips from overflowing her pockets. She claims to make a minimum of five hundred dollars a week in tip earnings; her record for one day's work exceeds two hundred dollars and is undoubtedly the record for the restaurant.

INVERTING THE SYMBOLISM OF TIPPING

It may already be apparent that the waitress views the customer—not as a master to pamper and appease—but as substance to be processed as quickly and in as large a quantity as possible. The difference in perspective is expressed in the objectifying terminology of waitresses: a customer or party is referred to as a *table,* or by table number, as *table five* or simply *five;* serving successive parties at a table is referred to as *turning the table;* taking an order is also known as *picking up a table;* and to serve water, coffee, or other beverages is to *water, coffee,* or *beverage* a table, number, or customer. Even personal acquaintances assume the status of inanimate matter, or tip-bearing plants, in the language of the server:

> I got my fifth-grade teacher [as a customer] one time. . . . I kept her coffeed. I kept her boyfriend coked all night. Sodaed. . . . And I kept them filled up.

If the customer is perceived as material that is processed, the goal of this processing is the production or extraction of a finished product: the tip. This image too is conveyed in the language of the floor. A waitress may comment that she "got a good tip" or "gets good tips," but she is more likely to say that she "made" or "makes good tips." She may also say that she "got five bucks out of" a customer, or complain that some customers "don't want to give up on" their money. She may accuse a waitress who stays over into her shift of "tapping on" her money, or warn an aspiring waitress against family restaurants on the grounds that "there's no money in there." In all these comments (and all are actual), the waitress might as easily be talking about mining for coal or drilling for oil as serving customers.

Predictably, the waitress's view of the customer as substance to be processed influences her perception of the meaning of tips, and especially substandard tips. At Route, low tips and stiffs are not interpreted as a negative reflection on the waitress's personal qualities or social status. Rather, they are felt to reveal the refractory nature or poor quality of the raw material from which the tip is extracted, produced, or fashioned. In less metaphorical terms, a low tip or stiff is thought to reflect the negative qualities and low status of the customer who is too cheap, too poor, too ignorant, or too coarse to leave an appropriate gratuity. In this context, it is interesting to note that *stiff,* the term used in restaurants to refer to incidents of nontipping or to someone who does not tip, has also been used to refer to a wastrel or penniless man, * * * a hobo, tramp, vagabond, deadbeat, and a moocher.

* * *

Evidence that waitresses assign blame for poor tips to the tipper is found in their reaction to being undertipped or stiffed. Rather than breaking down in tears and lamenting her "personal failure," the Route waitress responds to a stiff by announcing the event to her co-workers and managers in a tone of angry disbelief. Co-workers and managers echo the waitress's indignation and typically ask her to identify the party (by table number and physical description), or if she has already done so, to be more specific. This identification is crucial for it allows sympathizers to join the waitress in analyzing the cause of the stiff, which is assumed a priori to arise from some shortcoming of the party, not the waitress. The waitress and her co-workers may conclude that the customers in question were rude, troublemakers, or bums, or they may explain their behavior by identifying them as members of a particular category of customers. It might be revealed for instance, that the offending party was a church group: church groups are invariably tightfisted. It might be resolved that the offenders were senior citizens, Southerners, or business people: all well-known cheapskates. If the customers were European, the stiff will be attributed to ignorance of the American tipping system; if they were young, to immaturity; if they had children, to lack of funds.

These classifications and their attendant explanations are neither fixed nor trustworthy. New categories are invented to explain otherwise puzzling incidents, and all categories are subject to exception. Though undependable as predictive devices, customer typologies serve a crucial function: they divert blame for stiffs and low tips from the waitress to the characteristics of the customer. It is for this reason that it is "important" for workers to distinguish between different categories of customers, despite the fact that such distinctions are based on "unreliable verbal and appearance clues." In fact, it is precisely the unreliability, or more appropriately the flexibility, or customer typologies that makes them valuable to waitresses. When categories can be constructed and dissolved on demand, there is no danger that an incident will fall outside the existing system of classification and hence be inexplicable.

While waitresses view the customer as something to be processed and the tip as the product of this processing, they are aware that the public does not share their understanding of the waitress-diner-tip relationship. Waitresses at Route recognize that many customers perceive them as needy creatures willing to commit great feats of service and absorb high doses of abuse in their anxiety to secure a favorable gratuity or protect their jobs. They are also aware that some customers leave small tips with the intent to insult the server and that others undertip on the assumption that for a Route waitress even fifty cents will be appreciated. One waitress indicated that prior to being employed in a restaurant, she herself subscribed to the stereotype of the down-and-out waitress "because you see stuff on television, you see these wives or single ladies who waitress and they live in slummy apartments or slummy houses and they dress in rags." It is these images of neediness and desperation, which run so strongly against the waitress's perception of herself and her position, that she attacks when strained relations erupt into open conflict.

Five rowdy black guys walked in the door and they went to seat themselves at table seven. I said, "Excuse me. You all got to wait to be seated." "We ain't got to do *shit*. We here to eat. . . ." So they went and sat down. And I turned around and just looked at them. And they said, "Well, I hope you ain't our waitress, cause you blew your tip. Cause you ain't getting nothing from us." And I turned around and I said, "You need it more than I do, baby."

This waitress's desire to confront the customer's assumption of her destitution is widely shared among service workers whose status as tipped employees marks them as needy in the eyes of their customers. [One study] reports that among cabdrivers "a forever repeated story is of the annoyed driver, who, after a grueling trip with a Lady Shopper, hands the coin back, telling her, 'Lady, keep your lousy dime. You need it more than I do.'" [Another study reports] a hotel waitress's claim that "if she had served a large family with children for one or two weeks, and then was given a 10p[ence] piece, she would give the money back, saying, 'It's all right, thank you, I've got enough change for my bus fare home.'" In an incident I observed (not at Route), a waitress followed two male customers out of a restaurant calling, "Excuse me! You forgot this!" and holding up the coins they had left as a tip. The customers appeared embarrassed, motioned for her to keep the money, and continued down the sidewalk. The waitress, now standing in the outdoor seating area of the restaurant and observed by curious diners, threw the money after the retreating men and returned to her work. Episodes such as these allow the worker to repudiate openly the evaluation of her financial status that is implied in an offensively small gratuity, and permit her to articulate her own understanding of what a small tip says and about whom. If customers can only afford to leave a dime, or feel a 10p piece is adequate compensation for two weeks' service, they must be very hard up or very ignorant indeed.

In the following incident the waitress interjects a denial of her neediness into an altercation that is not related to tipping, demonstrating that the customer's perception of her financial status is a prominent and persistent concern for her.

She [a customer] wanted a California Burger with mayonnaise. And when I got the mayonnaise, the mayonnaise had a little brown on it. . . . So this girl said to me, she said, "What the fuck is this you giving me?" And I turned around, I thought, "Maybe she's talking to somebody else in the booth with her." And I turned around and I said, "Excuse me?" She said, "You hear what I said. I said, 'What the fuck are you giving me?'" And I turned around, I said, "I don't know if you're referring your information to *me*," I said, "but if you're referring your information to *me*," I said, "I don't *need* your bullshit." I said, "I'm not going to even take it. . . . Furthermore, I could care less if you eat or *don't* eat. . . . And you see this?" And I took her check and I ripped it apart. . . . And I took the California Burger and I says, "You don't have a problem anymore now, right?" She went up to the manager. And she says, "That black waitress"—I says, "Oh. By the way, what is my name? I don't have a name, [using the words] 'that black waitress.' . . . My name happens to be Nera. . . . That's N-E-R-A. . . . And I don't need your bullshit, sweetheart. . . . People like you I can walk on, because you don't know how to talk to human beings." And I said, "I don't need you. I don't need your quarters. I don't need your nickels. I don't need your dimes. So if you want service, be my guest. Don't you *ever* sit in my station, cause I won't wait on you." The manager said, "Nera, please. Would you wait in the back?" I said, "No. I don't take back seats no more for nobody."

In each of these cases, the waitress challenges the customer's definition of the relationship in which tipping occurs. By speaking out, by confronting the customer, she demonstrates that she is not subservient or in fear of losing her job; that she is not compelled by financial need or a sense of social hierarchy to accept abuse from customers; that she does not, in Nera's words, "take back seats no more for nobody." At the same time, she reverses the symbolic force of the low tip, converting a statement on her social status or work skills into a statement on the tipper's cheapness or lack of savoir faire.

21

Upward Mobility Through Sport?

D. STANLEY EITZEN

You can trace the history of twentieth-century immigration in the United States by reading the list of boxers who held the title of Champion of the World. The names of Irish, Jewish, Italian, African-American, and Latino boxers record the stirrings of upward mobility for those who shared the boxers' ethnicity or nationality. But the lives of the boxers themselves were often far less successful than a championship title would indicate. And what of sports more generally? In true sociological fashion, Stanley Eitzen shows us that sports may do far less in advancing the life chances of young people than is often assumed.

Typically, Americans believe that sport is a path to upward social mobility. This belief is based on the obvious examples we see as poor boys and men (rarely girls and women) from rural and urban areas, whether white or black, sometimes skyrocket to fame and fortune through success in sports. Sometimes the financial reward has been astounding, such as the high pay that some African American athletes received in recent years. In 1997 Tracy McGrady, an NBA-bound high school star, bypassed college, signed a $12 million deal over 6 years with Adidas. Golfer Tiger Woods in his first year as a professional made $6.82 million in winnings (U.S. and worldwide) and appearance fees plus signed a series of five-year deals with Nike, Titleist, American Express, and Rolex worth $95.2 million. In 1998 Woods's earnings from endorsements totaled $28 million. Boxer Mike Tyson made $75 million in 1996. It is estimated that Michael Jordan made over $100 million in 1998, including salary, endorsements, and income from merchandise and videos. The recent deals for baseball stars, some exceeding $15 million a year for multiyear contracts, further underscores the incredible money given to some individuals for their athletic talents.

But while the possibility of staggering wealth and status through sport is possible, the reality is that dramatic upward mobility through sport is highly improbable. A number of myths, however, combine to lead us to believe that sport is a social mobility escalator.

MYTH: SPORT PROVIDES A FREE EDUCATION

Good high school athletes get college scholarships. These athletic scholarships are especially helpful to poor youth who otherwise would not be able to attend college because of the high costs. The problem with this assumption is that while true for some, very few high school athletes actually receive full scholarships. Football provides the easiest route to a college scholarship because Division I-A colleges have 85 football scholarships, but even this avenue is exceedingly narrow. In Colorado there were 3,481 male high school seniors who played football during the 1994 season. Of these, 31 received full scholarships at Division I-A schools (0.0089 percent).

Second, of all the male varsity athletes at all college levels only about 15 percent to 20 percent have full scholarships. Another 15 percent to 25 percent have partial scholarships, leaving 55 percent to 70 percent of all intercollegiate athletes without any sport related financial assistance. Third, as low as the chances are for men, women athletes have even less chance to receive an athletic scholarship. While women comprise about 52 percent of all college students, they make up only 35 percent of intercollegiate athletes with a similar disproportionate distribution of scholarships. Another reality is that if you are a male athlete in a so-called minor sport (swimming, tennis, golf, gymnastics, cross-country, wrestling), the chances of a full scholarship are virtually nil. The best hope is a partial scholarship, if that, since these sports are underfunded and in danger of elimination at many schools.

MYTH: SPORT LEADS TO A COLLEGE DEGREE

College graduates exceed high school graduates by hundreds of thousands of dollars in lifetime earnings. Since most high school and college athletes will never play at the professional level, the attainment of a college degree is a crucial determinant of upward mobility through sport. The problem is that relatively few male athletes in the big time revenue producing sports, compared to their non-athletic peers, actually receive college degrees. This is especially the case for African American men who are over represented in the revenue producing sports. In 1996, for example, looking at the athletes who entered Division I schools in 1990, only 45 percent of African American football players and 39 percent of African American basketball players had graduated (compared to 56 percent of the general student body).

There are a number of barriers to graduation for male athletes. The demands on their time and energy are enormous even in the off-season. Many athletes, because of these pressures, take easy courses to maintain eligibility but do not lead to graduation. The result is either to delay graduation or to make graduation an unrealistic goal.

Another barrier is that they are recruited for athletic prowess rather than academic ability. Recent data show that football players in big time programs are, on average, more than 200 points behind their non-athletic classmates on SAT test scores. Poorly prepared students are the most likely to take easy courses, cheat on exams, hire surrogate test takers, and otherwise do the minimum.

A third barrier to graduation for male college athletes is themselves, as they may not take advantage of their scholarships to obtain a quality education. This is especially the case for those who perceive their college experience only as preparation for their professional careers in sport. Study for them is necessary only to maintain their eligibility. The goal of a professional career is unrealistic for all but the superstars. The superstars who do make it at the professional level, more likely than not, will have not graduated from college; nor will they go back to finish their degrees when their professional careers are over. This is also because even a successful professional athletic career is limited to a few years, and not many professional athletes are able to translate their success in the pros to success in their post-athletic careers. Such a problem is especially true for African Americans, who often face employment discrimination in the wider society.

MYTH: A SPORTS CAREER IS PROBABLE

A recent survey by the Center for the Study of Sport in Society found that two-thirds of African American males between the ages of 13 and 18 believe that they can earn a living playing professional sports (more than double the proportion of young white males who hold such beliefs). Moreover, African American parents were four times more likely than white parents to believe that their sons are destined for careers as professional athletes.

If these young athletes could play as professionals, the economic rewards are excellent, especially in basketball and baseball. In 1998 the average annual salary for professional basketball was $2.24 million. In baseball the average salary was $1.37 million with 280 of the 774 players on opening day rosters making $1 million or more (of them, 197 exceeded $2 million or more, while 32 of them made $6 million or more). The average salaries for the National Hockey League and National Football League were $892,000 and $795,000, respectively. In football, for example, 19 percent of the players (333 of 1,765) exceeded $1 million in salary. These numbers are inflated by the use of averages, which are skewed by the salaries of the superstars. Use of the median (in which half the players make more and half make less), reveals that the median salary in basketball was $1.4 million; baseball—$500,000; football—$400,000; and hockey—$500,000. Regardless of the measure, the financial allure of a professional sports career is great.

A career in professional sports is nearly impossible to attain because of the fierce competition for so few openings. In an average year there are approximately 1,900,000 American boys playing high school football, basketball, and baseball. Another 68,000 men are playing those sports in college, and 2,490 are participating at the major professional level. In short, one in 27 high school players in these sports will play at the college level, and only one in 736 high school players will play at the major professional level (0.14 percent). In baseball, each year about 120,000 players are eligible for the draft (high school seniors, college seniors, collegians over 21, junior college players, and foreign players). Only about 1,200 (1 percent) are actually drafted, and most of them will never make it to the major leagues. Indeed, only one in ten of those players who sign a professional baseball contract ever play in the major leagues for at least one day.

The same rigorous condensation process occurs in football. About 15,000 players are eligible for the NFL draft each year. Three hundred thirty-six are drafted and about 160 actually make the final roster. Similarly, in basketball and hockey, only about 40 new players are added to the rosters in the NBA and 60 rookies make the NHL each year. In tennis only about 100 men and 100 women make enough money to cover expenses. In golf, of the 165 men eligible for the PGA tour in 1997, their official winnings ranged from $2,066,833 (Tiger Woods) to $10,653 (Chip Beck). The competition among these golfers is fierce. On average, the top 100 golfers on the tour play within 2 strokes of each other for every 18 holes, yet Tiger Woods, the tops in winnings won over $2 million, and the 100th finisher won only $250,000. Below the PGA tour is the Nike Tour where the next best 125 golfers compete. Their winnings were a top of $225,201 to a low of $9,944.

MYTH: SPORT IS A WAY OUT OF POVERTY

Sport appears to be a major way for African Americans to escape the ghetto. African Americans dominate the major professional sports numerically. While only 12 percent of the population, African Americans comprise about 80 percent of the players in professional basketball, about 67 percent of professional football players, and 18 percent of professional baseball players (Latinos also comprise about 17 percent of professional baseball players). Moreover, African Americans dominate the list of the highest moneymakers in sport (salaries, commercial sponsorships). These facts, while true, are illusory.

While African Americans dominate professional basketball, football, and to a lesser extent baseball, they are rarely found in certain sports such as hockey, automobile racing, tennis, golf, bowling, and skiing. Moreover, African Americans are severely under-represented in positions of authority in sport—as head coaches, referees, athletic directors, scouts, general managers, and owners. In the NFL in 1997, for example, where more than two-thirds of the players were African American, only three head coaches and five offensive or defensive coordinators were African American. In that year there were 11 head coaching vacancies filled, none by African Americans. The reason for this racial imbalance in hiring, according to white sports columnist for the *Rocky Mountain News* Bob Kravitz is that: "something here stinks, and it stinks a lot like racism."

Second, while the odds of African American males making it as professional athletes are more favorable than is the case for whites (about 1 in 3,500 African American male high school athletes, compared to 1 in 10,000 white male high school athletes) these odds remain slim. Of the 40,000 or so African Americans boys who play high school basketball, only 35 will make the NBA and only 7 will be starters. Referring to the low odds for young African Americans, Harry Edwards, an African American sociologist specializing in the sociology of sport, said with a bit of hyperbole: "Statistically, you have a better chance of getting hit by a meteorite in the next ten years than getting work as an athlete."

Despite these discouraging facts, the myth is alive for poor youth. As noted earlier, two-thirds of African American boys believe they can be professional athletes. Their parents, too, accept this belief (African American parents are four times more likely than white parents to believe that their children will be professional athletes). The film *Hoop Dreams* and Darcey Frey's book *The Last Shot: City Street, Basketball Dreams* document the emphasis that young African American men place on sports as a way up and their ultimate disappointments from sport. For many of them, sport represents their only hope of escape from a life of crime, poverty, and despair. They latch on to the dream of athletic success partly because of the few opportunities for middle-class success. They spend many hours per day developing their speed, strength, jumping height, or "moves" to the virtual exclusion of those abilities that have a greater likelihood of paying off in upward mobility such as reading comprehension, mathematical reasoning, communication skills, and computer literacy.

Sociologist Jay Coakley puts it this way: "My best guess is that less than 3,500 African Americans . . . are making their livings as professional athletes. At the same time (in 1996), there are about 30,015 black physicians and about 30,800 black lawyers currently employed in the U.S. Therefore, there are 20 times more blacks working in these two professions than playing top level professional sports. And physicians and lawyers usually have lifetime earnings far in excess of the earnings of professional athletes, whose playing careers, on average, last less than five years."

Harry Edwards posits that by spending their energies and talents on athletic skills, young African Americans are not pursuing occupations that would help them meet their political and material needs. Thus, because of belief in the "sports as a way up" myth, they remain dependent on whites and white institutions. Salim Muwakkil, an African American political analyst, argues that "If African Americans are to exploit the socio-economic options opened by varied civil rights struggles more fully, blacks must reduce the disproportionate allure of sports in their communities. Black leadership must contextualize athletic success by promoting other avenues to social status, intensifying the struggle for access to those avenues and better educating youth about those pot-holes on the road to the stadium."

John Hoberman in his book *Darwin's Athletes* also challenges the assumption that sport has progressive consequences. The success of African Americans in the highly visible sports gives white Americans a false sense of black progress and interracial harmony. But the social progress of African Americans in general has little relationship to the apparent integration that they have achieved on the playing fields.

Hoberman also contends that the numerical superiority of African Americans in sport, coupled with their disproportionate under-representation in other professions reinforces the racist ideology that African Americans, while physically superior to whites are inferior to them intellectually.

I do not mean to say that African Americans should not seek a career in professional sport. What is harmful is that the odds of success are so slim, making the extraordinary efforts over many years futile and misguided for the vast majority.

MYTH: WOMEN HAVE SPORT AS A VEHICLE

Since the passage of Title IX in 1972 that required schools receiving federal funds to provide equal opportunities for women and men, sports participation by women in high school and college has increased dramatically. In 1973, for example, when 50,000 men received some form of college scholarship for their athletic abilities, women received only 50. Now, women receive about 35 percent of the money allotted for college athletic scholarships (while a dramatic improvement, this should not be equated with gender equality as many would have us believe). This allows many women athletes to attend college who otherwise could not afford it, thus receiving an indirect upward mobility boost.

Upward mobility as a result of being a professional athlete is another matter for women. Women have fewer opportunities than men in professional team sports. Beach volley-ball is a possibility for a few but the rewards are minimal. Two professional women's basketball leagues began in 1997, but the pay was very low compared to men and the leagues were on shaky financial ground (the average salary in the American Basketball League was $80,000). The other option for women is to play in professional leagues in Europe, Australia, and Asia but the pay is relatively low.

Women have more opportunities as professionals in individual sports such as tennis, golf, ice-skating, skiing, bowling, cycling, and track. Ironically, the sports with the greatest monetary rewards for women are those of the middle and upper classes (tennis, golf, and ice skating). These sports are expensive and require considerable individual coaching and access to private facilities.

Ironically, with the passage of Title IX, which increased the participation rates of women so dramatically, there has been a decline in the number and proportion of women as coaches and athletic administrators. In addition to the glaring pay gap between what the coaches of men's teams receive compared to the coaches of women's teams, men who coach women's teams tend to have higher salaries than women coaching women's teams. Women also have fewer opportunities than men as athletic trainers, officials, sports journalists, and other adjunct positions.

MYTH: SPORTS PROVIDES LIFELONG SECURITY

Even when a professional sport career is attained, the probabilities of fame and fortune are limited. Of course, some athletes make incomes from salaries and endorsements that if invested wisely, provide financial security for life. Many professional athletes make relatively low salaries. During the 1996 season, for example, 17 percent of major league baseball players made the minimum salary of $247,500 for veterans and $220,000 for rookies. This is a lot of money, but for these marginal players their careers may not last very long. Indeed, the average length of a professional career in a team sport is about five years. A marginal athlete in individual sports such as golf, tennis, boxing, and bowling, struggle financially. They must cover their travel expenses, health insurance, equipment, and the like with no guaranteed paycheck. The brief career diverts them during their youth from developing other career skills and experiences that would benefit them.

Ex-professional athletes leave sport, on average, when they are in their late 20s or early 30s, at a time when their non-athletic peers have begun to establish themselves in occupations leading toward retirement in 40 years or so. What are the ex-professional athletes to do with their remaining productive years?

Exiting a sports career can be relatively smooth or difficult. Some athletes have planned ahead, preparing for other careers either in sport (coaching, scouting, administering) or some non-sport occupation. Others have not prepared for this abrupt change. They did not graduate from college. They did not spend the off seasons apprenticing non-sport jobs. Exiting the athlete role is difficult for many because they lose: (1) What has been the focus of their being for most of their lives; (2) the primary source of their identities; (3) their physical prowess; (4) the adulation bordering on worship from others; (5) the money and the perquisites of fame; (6) the camaraderie with teammates; (7) the intense "highs" of competition; and (8) for most ex-athletes retirement means a loss of status. As a result of these "losses," many ex-professional athletes have trouble adjusting to life after sport. A study by the NFL Players Association found, that emotional difficulties, divorce, and financial strain were common problems for ex-professional football players. A majority had "permanent injuries" from football.

The allure of sport, however, remains strong and this has at least two negative consequences. First, ghetto youngsters who devote their lives to the pursuit of athletic stardom are, except for the fortunate few, doomed to failure in sport and in the real world where sports skills are essentially irrelevant to occupational placement and advancement. The second negative consequence is more subtle but very important. Sport contributes to the ideology that legitimizes social inequalities and promotes the myth that all it takes is extraordinary effort to succeed. Sport sociologist George H. Sage makes this point forcefully: "Because sport is by nature meritocratic—that is, superior performance brings status and rewards—it provides convincing symbolic support for hegemonic [the dominant] ideology—that ambitious, dedicated, hard working individuals, regardless of social origin, can achieve success and ascend in the social hierarchy, obtaining high status and material rewards, while those who don't move upward simply didn't work hard enough. Because the rags-to-riches athletes are so visible, the social mobility theme is maintained. This reflects the opportunity structure of society in general—the success of a few reproduces the belief in social mobility among the many."

22

What Happened to the American Social Compact?

ROBERT B. REICH

The idea of the United States as a "two-tiered society" would not surprise the poor or minorities who have known discrimination, but it runs counter to the perception of opportunity and equality held by most Americans. Not only federal tax and spending policies but larger structural changes involving globalization and new technologies have widened the gap between the rich and the poor, including the working poor. Perhaps there is a "common peril" that Reich believes can motivate a nation to action and address what he sees as a crisis in American society.

Six years of economic recovery have failed to reverse the trends that began in the late 1970s toward declining wages and shrinking health and pension benefits for the bottom half of the American workforce, and toward widening inequality in earnings and wealth. The real weekly earnings of the median full-time worker are still below its level in 1989. Even in the robust twelve months from the middle of 1996 to the middle of 1997, the real median weekly earnings of full-time workers increased just three-tenths of one percent. But employer-provided health and pension benefits continue to drop, so at least half the workforce is getting nowhere. Meanwhile, all the rungs on the economic ladder are now further apart than they were a generation ago, and the space between them continues to spread.

Many families have made up for the steady decline by working longer hours, which the current tight labor market has facilitated. But for most mortals who do not relish what they do for pay, more hours at work does not translate into a higher standard of living. At the same time, the upper reaches of America—mostly college educated, mostly professional or managerial—have never had it so good. Their pay and benefits have continued to rise, and their shares of stock have exploded in value. Nearly 40% of the nation's financial wealth is held by the richest 1% of the population. Even taking into account pension wealth held on behalf of workers, the top 1% still owns 22% of all financial assets.

This tenacious trend toward a two-tiered society is deeply troubling. Yet, America is strangely immobilized. Rather than giving us the confidence we need to move forward, the good economic news on growth and jobs * * * seems rather to have anaesthetized us. Future generations looking back on this era will ask why—when today's Americans had * * * no depression or recession to cope with, no great drain on our resources or our spirits—we did so little.

Little, that is, relative to what the situation demanded. Little, relative to what we could have done. Did we simply assume that the economic expansion would last forever, and that the disparities would automatically shrink? Did we deny the problem to begin with? Or had we simply resigned ourselves to the inevitability of a sharply two-tiered society?

The budget deficit, which has so obsessed the nation, began to vanish this year [1998] even before the White House and Congress reached agreement, with much fanfare, to make it do so officially. The economic expansion boosted earnings so much, particularly for those at the upper rungs of the economic ladder, that tax revenues poured into the Treasury to a far greater extent than had been foreseen. But rather than dedicate this unexpected largesse to what has been most neglected and is most needed—universal health care, child care, better schools, jobs for the poor who will lose welfare, public transportation, and other means of helping the bottom half of our population move upward—most of this windfall is going to the wealthiest members of our society in the form of the largest federal tax cut on upper incomes since 1981.

* * *

The most important thing the United States could achieve now is to get back on the track we were on during the first three decades after World War II, toward a more inclusive, more equitable society. We got off that track in the late 1970s and have veered even further off it since. A large part of the reason why earnings began diverging then, as we all know, was the combined effects of two revolutions—one in computer technology, the other in global economic integration—the combined effect of which has been to shift demand in favor of workers with the appropriate education and skills to take advantage of these changes, and against workers without them. Two minor forces are also at work—the shrinkage of the unionized segment of the workforce (also related, in part, to technological advances and to globalization), and the decline in the real value of the minimum wage; the first force has disproportionately affected lower-wage men, while the second has largely affected lower-wage women. But even all of this combined together would not reveal the whole story.

The real paradox is why, at this juncture in history, the social compact that America fashioned during most of this century—to help ensure that prosperity was widely shared and that no one should disproportionately suffer the risks and burdens of economic change—should now be coming undone. In the world's preeminent democratic-capitalist society, one might have expected just the reverse: As the economy grew through technological progress and global integration, the "winners" from this process would compensate the "losers" and still come out far ahead. Rather than being weakened, the social compact would be strengthened.

Nations are not passive victims of economic forces. Citizens can, if they so choose, assert that their mutual obligations extend beyond their economic usefulness to one another, and act accordingly. Throughout our history, the

United States has periodically asserted the public's interest when market outcomes threatened social peace—curbing the power of the great trusts, establishing pure food and drug laws, implementing a progressive federal tax, imposing a forty-hour workweek, barring child labor, creating a system of social security, expanding public schooling and access to higher education, extending health care to the elderly, and so forth. We effected part of this reform explicitly through laws, regulations, and court rulings, and part through social norms and expectations about how we wanted our people to live and work productively together. In short, this nation developed and refined a strong social compact which gave force to the simple proposition that prosperity could include almost everyone. The puzzle is why we seem to have stopped.

Every society and culture possesses a social compact—sometimes implicit, sometimes spelled out in detail, but usually a mix of both. The compact sets out the obligations of members of that society toward one another. Indeed, a society or culture is *defined* by its social compact. It is found within the pronouns "we," "our," and "us." *We* hold these truths to be self-evident; *our* peace and freedom are at stake; the problem affects all of *us*. A quarter century ago, when the essential provisions of the American social compact were taken for granted by American society, there was hardly any reason to state them. Today, as these provisions wither, they deserve closer scrutiny.

The first provision pertained to the private sector. As companies did better, their workers should have as well. Wages should have risen, as should have employer-provided health and pension benefits, and jobs should have been reasonably secure. This provision of the compact was reinforced by labor unions, to which, by the mid-1950s, about thirty-five percent of the private-sector workforce belonged. But it was enforced in the first instance by public expectations. We were all in it together, and as a result grew together. It would be unseemly for a company, whose profits were increasing, to fail to share its prosperity with its employees and the communities in which they lived. The job of management, proclaimed Frank Abrams, chairman of Standard Oil of New Jersey in a 1951 address that was typical of the era, is to maintain

> an *equitable and working balance* among the claims of the various directly interested groups . . . stockholders, employees, customers, and the public at large. . . .
> Business managers are gaining in professional status partly because they see in their work the basic responsibilities [to the public] that other professional men have long recognized in theirs.[1]

The second provision of the social compact was social insurance through which Americans pooled their resources against the risk that any one of us— through illness or bad luck—might become impoverished. Hence, unemploy-

---

1. Gilbert Burck, *The Jersey Company,* Fortune, Oct. 1951, at 99.

ment insurance, Social Security for the elderly and disabled, aid to widows which became Aid to Families with Dependent Children, and Medicare and Medicaid. "Cradle to grave," Franklin D. Roosevelt told my predecessor, Frances Perkins, "from the cradle to the grave they ought to be in a social insurance system." And, for the next half century or so, most Americans agreed.

The third provision was the promise of a good education. The national role began in the nineteenth century with the Morrill Act, establishing land grant colleges. In the early decades of this century, a national movement to create free high school educations through the twelfth grade for every young person swept across America. After the Second World War, the GI Bill made college a reality for millions of returning veterans. Other young people gained access to advanced education through a vast expansion of state-subsidized public universities and community colleges. In the 1950s, our collective conscience, embodied in the Supreme Court, finally led us to resolve that all children, regardless of race, must have the same—not separate—educational opportunities.

It is important to understand what this social compact was and what it was not. It defined our sense of fair play, but it was not primarily about redistributing wealth. There would still be the rich and the poor in America. The compact merely proclaimed that at some fundamental level we were all in it together, and that as a society we depended on one another. The economy could not prosper unless vast numbers of employees had more money in their pockets. None of us could be economically secure unless we shared the risks of economic life. A better educated workforce was in all our interests.

The unraveling of the first provision, pertaining to the private sector, began in the late 1970s and early 1980s, and it continues today. Profitable companies now routinely downsize their workforces, or they resort to what might be called "down-waging" and down-benefitting." Layoffs in the current expansion are occuring at an even higher rate than in the expansion of the 1980s. Companies are replacing full-time workers with independent contractors, temporary workers, and part-timers; they are bringing in new full-time workers at lower wage scales than current workers; or, they are sub-contracting the work to smaller firms offering lower wages and benefits. Employer-provided health benefits are declining across the board, and health costs are being shifted to employees in the form of higher co-payments, deductibles, and premiums. * * * Meanwhile, beginning in the early 1980s, American companies battled against unionization with more ferocity than at any other time in the last half century. The incidence of companies illegally firing their employees for trying to organize unions (adjusted for the number of certification elections and union voters) increased from 8% in the early 1970s to 14% in the late 1970s, and then leaped to 32% in the early 1980s, where it has more or less remained. The unionized portion of the private-sector workforce, which had been 35% in 1955, continues to shrink. It is now 10%.

The relentless drive among American companies to reduce their labor costs is perhaps understandable given that payrolls typically constitute 70% of the costs of doing business, and that pressures on companies to cut costs and show profits have intensified. Competition is more treacherous in this new economy, where large size and low unit costs no longer guarantee competitive advantage, and where institutional investors demand instant performance. Yet, it is also the case that the compensation of senior management, professional, and highly-skilled technical workers has escalated in recent years. In large companies, top executive compensation has been increasing for over a decade at the rate of over ten percent per year, after inflation. Top executives and their families receive ever more generous health benefits, and their pension benefits are soaring in the form of compensation deferred until retirement. Although they have no greater job security than others, when they lose their jobs it is not uncommon for them to receive "golden parachutes" studded with diamonds.

The second provision—that of social insurance—is also breaking down. We see evidence of this in who has been asked to bear the largest burden in balancing the budget—disproportionately the poor and near poor, whose programs have borne the largest cuts. Unemployment insurance now covers a smaller proportion of workers than it did twenty years ago—now, only thirty-five percent of the unemployed. Even before welfare "reform," welfare payments were shrinking in many states. In fact, the entire idea of a common risk pool is now under assault. Proposals are being floated for the wealthier and healthier to opt out. Whether in the form of private "medical savings accounts" to replace Medicare, or "personal security accounts" to replace Social Security, the effect would be much the same; the wealthier and healthier would no longer share the risk with those who have a much higher probability of being sicker or poorer.

The third part of the social compact, access to a good education, is also under severe strain. * * * As Americans increasingly segregate by level of income into different townships, local tax bases in poorer areas cannot support the quality of schooling available to the wealthier. Public expenditures per pupil are significantly lower in school districts in which the median household income is less than $20,000 than they are in districts where the median household income is $35,000 or more—even though the challenge of educating poorer children, many of whom are immigrants with poor English language skills or who have other social or behavioral problems, is surely greater than the challenge of educating children from relatively more affluent households. De facto racial segregation has become the norm in several large metropolitan areas.

Across the United States, state-subsidized higher education is waning under severe budget constraints, and its cost has risen three times faster than median family income. Elite colleges and universities are abandoning "need-blind" admissions policies, by which they guaranteed that any qualified student could afford to attend. Young people from families with incomes in the top 25% are three times more likely to go to college than are young people from the bottom quarter, and the percentage is rising.

Why is the social compact coming undone—especially at a time when it is most needed? The reasons relate to the same basic forces that have divided the workforce. Technological advances—primarily in information and communication—and global trade and investment have rendered a substantial portion of the tax base footloose. Capital can move at the speed of an electronic impulse. Well-educated professionals are also relatively mobile. As a result, governments are forced to impose taxes disproportionately on labor—typically lower-wage labor, which is the most rooted. As technology continues to advance and global markets continue to integrate, this "mobility gap" will continue to widen, resulting in wider disparities in tax burdens.

* * *

Yet, even this analysis does not entirely explain the paradox. Today's wealthy investors and skilled professionals are not merely winners in a growing economy; they are also citizens in a splitting society. Wealthier and more fortunate members of society have long engaged in efforts to improve their community or nation—spearheading not just charitable activities but also progressive reforms. Why would they now allow the social compact to unravel? Are other forces weakening the bonds of affiliation and empathy on which a social compact is premised?

I do not have a clear answer, but I do have several hypotheses. The first is that Americans no longer face the common perils of Depression, hot war, or cold war that were defining experiences for the generations that reached adulthood between the 1930s and the 1960s. Each of these events posed a threat to American society and culture. Each was experienced directly or indirectly by virtually all Americans. Under those circumstances, it was not difficult to sense mutual dependence and to conceive of a set of responsibilities shared by all members, which exacted certain sacrifices for the common good. Today, fewer Americans remember these events or the "social bonding" that accompanied them. Peace and prosperity are delightful, but they do not necessarily pull citizens together.

Second, in the new global economy, those who are more skilled, more talented, or simply wealthier are not as economically dependent on the local or regional economy surrounding them as they once were, and thus have less selfish interest in ensuring that their fellow inhabitants are as productive as possible. Alexis de Tocqueville noted that the better-off Americans he met in his travels of the 1830s invested in their communities because they knew they would reap some of the gains from the resulting economic growth—in contrast to Europe's traditions of honor, duty, and *noblesse oblige*:

> The Americans . . . are fond of explaining almost all the actions of their lives by the principle of interest rightly understood; they show with complacency how an

enlightened regard for themselves constantly prompts them to assist each other and inclines them willingly to sacrifice a portion of their time and property to the welfare of the State.[2]

Today, increasingly, the geographic community within which an individual may live is of less consequence to his or her economic well being. It is now possible to be linked directly, by modem and fax, to the great financial or commercial centers of the world.

Third, any social compact is premised on "it could happen to me"—type thinking. Social insurance assumes that certain risks are commonly shared. Today's wealthy and poor, however, are likely to have markedly different life experiences. Disparities have grown so large that even though some of the rich (or their children) may become poor and some of the poor (or their children) will become rich, the chances of either occurring are less than they were several decades ago. The wealthy are no longer under a "veil of ignorance" about their futures, to borrow philosopher John Rawls's felicitous phrase, and they know that any social compact is likely to be one-sided—they will be required to subsidize the poor.

Perhaps all of these hypotheses are at work to some degree. But there should be no doubt that, unchecked, the disintegration of the social compact threatens the stability and moral authority of this nation. It also threatens continued economic growth. Those who believe that they bear a disproportionate share of the burdens and risks of growth but enjoy few, if any, of the benefits will not passively accept their fates. Unless they feel some stake in economic growth, they are likely to withdraw their tacit support for free trade, capital mobility, relatively open immigration, deregulation, and similar aspects of open economies that generate growth, but which simultaneously impose losses and insecurities on them. Some aspects of this backlash can already be observed in the resistance shown by the public to renewal of "fast track" authority enabling the President to move trade treaties quickly through Congress. Public opinion polls over the past decade have shown a distinct decline in support of immigration as well, as evidenced in the anti-immigrant aspects of recent welfare legislation. Note, too, the "communitarian" movement's increasing resistance to capital mobility. Social conservatives have recently decried the openings of K-Marts and Wal-Marts in various communities, charging that they undermine "community values."

The current situation—widening inequality coupled, paradoxically, with a weakening social compact—is not sustainable. Those who are losing ground will not allow it to continue unabated. One of two things will occur. Either a new, more virulent form of statism will emerge, which achieves stability at the cost of economic growth. Or, the better-off members of society will participate

---

2. Alexis De Tocqueville, *Democracy in America* 146–47 (Henry Reeve, trans., Longman, Green, Longman, and Roberts, new ed. 1862).

in the creation of a new social compact that permits economic dynamism and growth, but also compensates economic "losers" and gives them a full opportunity to become "winners." At this moment in time, when the economy is expanding briskly and even those in the bottom half have high hopes of doing better for themselves in the future, such warnings may seem far-fetched. But history counsels wariness. The social compact is a promise we made with one another, and we are not keeping that promise when we can most afford to do so.

23

Manifesto of the Communist Party

KARL MARX AND FRIEDRICH ENGELS

Europe in the eighteenth and nineteenth centuries changed dramatically with the onset of industrialization and the phenomenal growth of cities. While some writers saw great promise of abundance and freedom in these changes, the reality for millions of people was increased labor and grinding poverty. Karl Marx (1818–1883) was one of the nineteenth century's most articulate critics of the disparity between possibility and reality. Here he and his collaborator, Friedrich Engels, explain the reasons for this in this pamphlet written for Belgian workers.

I. BOURGEOIS AND PROLETARIANS[1]

The history of all hitherto existing society[2] is the history of class struggles.

Freeman and slave, patrician and plebeian, lord and serf, guild-master[3] and journeyman, in a word, oppressor and oppressed, stood in constant opposition to one another, carried on an uninterrupted, now hidden, now open fight, a fight that each time ended, either in a revolutionary re-constitution of society at large, or in the common ruin of the contending classes.

---

1. By bourgeoisie is meant the class of modern Capitalists, owners of the means of social production and employers of wage-labour. By proletariat, the class of modern wage-labourers who, having no means of production of their own, are reduced to selling their labour-power in order to live. [*Engels, English edition of 1888*]

2. That is, all *written* history. In 1847, the pre-history of society, the social organisation existing previous to recorded history, was all but unknown. Since then, Haxthausen discovered common ownership of land in Russia, Maurer proved it to be the social foundation from which all Teutonic races started in history, and by and by village communities were found to be, or to have been the primitive form of society everywhere from India to Ireland. The inner organisation of this primitive Communistic society was laid bare, in its typical form, by Morgan's crowning discovery of the true nature of the *gens* and its relation to the *tribe*. With the dissolution of these primaeval communities society begins to be differentiated into separate and finally antagonistic classes. I have attempted to retrace this process of dissolution in: "Der Ursprung der Familie, des Privateigenthums und des Staats" [*The Origin of the Family, Private Property and the State*], 2nd edition, Stuttgart 1886. [*Engels, English edition of 1888*]

3. Guild-master, that is, a full member of a guild, a master within, not a head of a guild. [*Engels, English edition of 1888*]

In the earlier epochs of history, we find almost everywhere a complicated arrangement of society into various orders, a manifold gradation of social rank. In ancient Rome we have patricians, knights, plebeians, slaves; in the Middle Ages, feudal lords, vassals, guild-masters, journey-men, apprentices, serfs; in almost all of these classes, again, subordinate gradations.

The modern bourgeois society that has sprouted from the ruins of feudal society has not done away with class antagonisms. It has but established new classes, new conditions of oppression, new forms of struggle in place of the old ones.

Our epoch, the epoch of the bourgeoisie, possesses, however, this distinctive feature: it has simplified the class antagonisms: Society as a whole is more and more splitting up into two great hostile camps, into two great classes directly facing each other: Bourgeoisie and Proletariat.

From the serfs of the Middle Ages sprang the chartered burghers of the earliest towns. From these burgesses the first elements of the bourgeoisie were developed.

The discovery of America, the rounding of the Cape, opened up fresh ground for the rising bourgeoisie. The East-Indian and Chinese markets, the colonisation of America, trade with the colonies, the increase in the means of exchange and in commodities generally, gave to commerce, to navigation, to industry, an impulse never before known, and thereby, to the revolutionary element in the tottering feudal society, a rapid development.

The feudal system of industry, under which industrial production was monopolised by closed guilds, now no longer sufficed for the growing wants of the new markets. The manufacturing system took its place. The guild-masters were pushed on one side by the manufacturing middle class; division of labour between the different corporate guilds vanished in the face of division of labour in each single workshop.

Meantime the markets kept ever growing, the demand ever rising. Even manufacture no longer sufficed. Thereupon, steam and machinery revolutionised industrial production. The place of manufacture was taken by the giant, Modern Industry, the place of the industrial middle class, by industrial millionaires, the leaders of whole industrial armies, the modern bourgeois.

Modern industry has established the world-market, for which the discovery of America paved the way. This market has given an immense development to commerce, to navigation, to communication by land. This development has, in its turn, reacted on the extension of industry; and in proportion as industry, commerce, navigation, railways extended, in the same proportion the bourgeoisie developed, increased its capital, and pushed into the background every class handed down from the Middle Ages.

We see, therefore, how the modern bourgeoisie is itself the product of a long course of development, of a series of revolutions in the modes of production and of exchange.

Each step in the development of the bourgeoisie was accompanied by a corresponding political advance of that class. An oppressed class under the sway of the feudal nobility, an armed and self-governing association in the mediaeval commune;[4] here independent urban republic (as in Italy and Germany), there taxable "third estate" of the monarchy (as in France), afterwards, in the period of manufacture proper, serving either the semi-feudal or the absolute monarchy as a counterpoise against the nobility, and, in fact, corner-stone of the great monarchies in general, the bourgeoisie has at last, since the establishment of Modern Industry and of the world-market, conquered for itself, in the modern representative State, exclusive political sway. The executive of the modern State is but a committee for managing the common affairs of the whole bourgeoisie.

The bourgeoisie, historically, has played a most revolutionary part.

The bourgeoisie, wherever it has got the upper hand, has put an end to all feudal, patriarchal, idyllic relations. It has pitilessly torn asunder the motley feudal ties that bound man to his "natural superiors," and has left remaining no other nexus between man and man than naked self-interest, than callous "cash payment." It has drowned the most heavenly ecstasies of religious fervour, of chivalrous enthusiasm, of philistine sentimentalism, in the icy water of egotistical calculation. It has resolved personal worth into exchange value, and in place of the numberless indefeasible chartered freedoms, has set up that single, unconscionable freedom—Free Trade. In one word, for exploitation, veiled by religious and political illusions, it has substituted naked, shameless, direct, brutal exploitation.

The bourgeoisie has stripped of its halo every occupation hitherto honoured and looked up to with reverent awe. It has converted the physician, the lawyer, the priest, the poet, the man of science, into its paid wage-labourers.

The bourgeoisie has torn away from the family its sentimental veil, and has reduced the family relation to a mere money relation.

The bourgeoisie has disclosed how it came to pass that the brutal display of vigour in the Middle Ages, which Reactionists so much admire, found its fitting complement in the most slothful indolence. It has been the first to show what man's activity can bring about. It has accomplished wonders far surpassing Egyptian pyramids, Roman aqueducts, and Gothic cathedrals; it has conducted expeditions that put in the shade all former Exoduses of nations and crusades.

---

4. "Commune" was the name taken, in France, by the nascent towns even before they had conquered from their feudal lords and masters local self-government and political rights as the "Third Estate." Generally speaking, for the economical development of the bourgeoisie, England is here taken as the typical country; for its political development, France. [*Engels, English edition of 1888*]

   This was the name given their urban communities by the townsmen of Italy and France, after they had purchased or wrested their initial rights of self-government from their feudal lords. [*Engels, German edition of 1890*]

The bourgeoisie cannot exist without constantly revolutionising the instruments of production, and thereby the relations of production, and with them the whole relations of society. Conservation of the old modes of production in unaltered form, was, on the contrary, the first condition of existence for all earlier industrial classes. Constant revolutionising of production, uninterrupted disturbance of all social conditions, everlasting uncertainty and agitation distinguish the bourgeois epoch from all earlier ones. All fixed, fast-frozen relations, with their train of ancient and venerable prejudices and opinions, are swept away, all new-formed ones become antiquated before they can ossify. All that is solid melts into air, all that is holy is profaned, and man is at last compelled to face with sober senses, his real conditions of life, and his relations with his kind.

The need of a constantly expanding market for its products chases the bourgeoisie over the whole surface of the globe. It must nestle everywhere, settle everywhere, establish connexions everywhere.

The bourgeoisie has through its exploitation of the world-market given a cosmopolitan character to production and consumption in every country. To the great chagrin of Reactionists, it has drawn from under the feet of industry the national ground on which it stood. All old-established national industries have been destroyed or are daily being destroyed. They are dislodged by new industries, whose introduction becomes a life and death question for all civilised nations, by industries that no longer work up indigenous raw material, but raw material drawn from the remotest zones; industries whose products are consumed, not only at home, but in every quarter of the globe. In place of the old wants, satisfied by the productions of the country, we find new wants, requiring for their satisfaction the products of distant lands and climes. In place of the old local and national seclusion and self-sufficiency, we have intercourse in every direction, universal inter-dependence of nations. And as in material, so also in intellectual production. The intellectual creations of individual nations become common property. National one-sidedness and narrow-mindedness become more and more impossible, and from the numerous national and local literatures, there arises a world literature.

The bourgeoisie, by the rapid improvement of all instruments of production, by the immensely facilitated means of communication, draws all, even the most barbarian, nations into civilisation. The cheap prices of its commodities are the heavy artillery with which it batters down all Chinese walls, with which it forces the barbarians' intensely obstinate hatred of foreigners to capitulate. It compels all nations, on pain of extinction, to adopt the bourgeois mode of production; it compels them to introduce what it calls civilisation into their midst, *i.e.,* to become bourgeois themselves. In one word, it creates a world after its own image.

The bourgeoisie has subjected the country to the rule of the towns. It has created enormous cities, has greatly increased the urban population as compared with the rural, and has thus rescued a considerable part of the population from the idiocy of rural life. Just as it has made the country dependent on the towns, so it has made barbarian and semi-barbarian countries dependent on the civilised ones, nations of peasants on nations of bourgeois, the East on the West.

The bourgeoisie keeps more and more doing away with the scattered state of the population, of the means of production, and of property. It has agglomerated population, centralised means of production, and has concentrated property in a few hands. The necessary consequence of this was political centralisation. Independent, or but loosely connected provinces, with separate interests, laws, governments and systems of taxation, became lumped together into one nation, with one government, one code of laws, one national class-interest, one frontier and one customs-tariff.

The bourgeoisie, during its rule of scarce one hundred years, has created more massive and more colossal productive forces than have all preceding generations together. Subjection of Nature's forces to man, machinery, application of chemistry to industry and agriculture, steam-navigation, railways, electric telegraphs, clearing of whole continents for cultivation, canalisation of rivers, whole populations conjured out of the ground—what earlier century had even a presentiment that such productive forces slumbered in the lap of social labour?

We see then: the means of production and of exchange, on whose foundation the bourgeoisie built itself up, were generated in feudal society. At a certain stage in the development of these means of production and of exchange, the conditions under which feudal society produced and exchanged, the feudal organisation of agriculture and manufacturing industry, in one word, the feudal relations of property became no longer compatible with the already developed productive forces; they became so many fetters. They had to be burst asunder; they were burst asunder.

Into their place stepped free competition, accompanied by a social and political constitution adapted to it, and by the economical and political sway of the bourgeois class.

A similar movement is going on before our own eyes. Modern bourgeois society with its relations of production, of exchange and of property, a society that has conjured up such gigantic means of production and of exchange, is like the sorcerer, who is no longer able to control the powers of the nether world whom he has called up by his spells. For many a decade past the history of industry and commerce is but the history of the revolt of modern productive forces against modern conditions of production, against the property relations that are the conditions for the existence of the bourgeoisie and of its rule. It is enough to mention the commercial crises that by their periodical return put on its trial, each time more threateningly, the existence of the entire bourgeois society. In these crises a great part not only of the existing products, but also of the previously created productive forces, are periodically destroyed. In these crises there breaks out an epidemic that, in all earlier epochs, would have seemed an absurdity—the epidemic of over-production. Society suddenly finds itself put back into a state of momentary barbarism; it appears as if a famine, a universal war of devastation had cut off the supply of every means of subsistence; industry and commerce seem to be destroyed; and why? Because there is too much civilisation, too much means of subsistence, too much industry, too much commerce. The productive forces at the disposal of society no longer tend to further the development of the conditions of bourgeois property; on the contrary, they have become too powerful for these conditions, by which they are fettered, and so soon as they overcome these fetters, they bring disorder into the whole of bourgeois society, endanger the existence of bourgeois property. The conditions of bourgeois society are too narrow to comprise the wealth created by them. And how does the bourgeoisie get over these crises? On the one hand by enforced destruction of a mass of productive forces; on the other, by the conquest of new markets, and by the more thorough exploitation of the old ones. That is to say, by paving the way for more extensive and more destructive crises, and by diminishing the means whereby crises are prevented.

The weapons with which the bourgeoisie felled feudalism to the ground are now turned against the bourgeoisie itself.

But not only has the bourgeoisie forged the weapons that bring death to itself; it has also called into existence the men who are to wield those weapons—the modern working class—the proletarians.

In proportion as the bourgeoisie, *i.e.,* capital, is developed, in the same proportion is the proletariat, the modern working class, developed—a class of labourers, who live only so long as they find work, and who find work only so long as their labour increases capital. These labourers, who must sell themselves piece-meal, are a commodity, like every other article of commerce, and are consequently exposed to all the vicissitudes of competition, to all the fluctuations of the market.

Owing to the extensive use of machinery and to division of labour, the work of the proletarians has lost all individual character, and consequently, all charm for the workman. He becomes an appendage of the machine, and it is only the most simple, most monotonous, and most easily acquired knack, that is required of him. Hence, the cost of production of a workman is restricted, almost entirely, to the means of subsistence that he requires for his maintenance, and for the propagation of his race. But the price of a commodity, and therefore also of labour,[5] is equal to its cost of production. In proportion, therefore, as the repulsiveness of the work increases, the wage decreases. Nay more, in proportion as the use of machinery and division of labour increases, in the same proportion the burden of toil also increases, whether by prolongation of the working hours, by increase of the work exacted in a given time or by increased speed of the machinery, etc.

---

5. Subsequently Marx pointed out that the worker sells not his labour but his labour power.

Modern industry has converted the little workshop of the patriarchal master into the great factory of the industrial capitalist. Masses of labourers, crowded into the factory, are organised like soldiers. As privates of the industrial army they are placed under the command of a perfect hierarchy of officers and sergeants. Not only are they slaves of the bourgeois class, and of the bourgeois State; they are daily and hourly enslaved by the machine, by the over-looker, and, above all, by the individual bourgeois manufacturer himself. The more openly this despotism proclaims gain to be its end and aim, the more petty, the more hateful and the more embittering it is.

The less the skill and exertion of strength implied in manual labour, in other words, the more modern industry becomes developed, the more is the labour of men superseded by that of women. Differences of age and sex have no longer any distinctive social validity for the working class. All are instruments of labour, more or less expensive to use, according to their age and sex.

No sooner is the exploitation of the labourer by the manufacturer, so far, at an end, that he receives his wages in cash, than he is set upon by the other portions of the bourgeoisie, the landlord, the shopkeeper, the pawnbroker, etc.

The lower strata of the middle class—the small tradespeople, shopkeepers, and retired tradesmen generally, the handicraftsmen and peasants—all these sink gradually into the proletariat, partly because their diminutive capital does not suffice for the scale on which Modern Industry is carried on, and is swamped in the competition with the large capitalists, partly because their specialised skill is rendered worthless by new methods of production. Thus the proletariat is recruited from all classes of the population.

The proletariat goes through various stages of development. With its birth begins its struggle with the bourgeoisie. At first the contest is carried on by individual labourers, then by the workpeople of a factory, then by the operatives of one trade, in one locality, against the individual bourgeois who directly exploits them. They direct their attacks not against the bourgeois conditions of production, but against the instruments of production themselves; they destroy imported wares that compete with their labour, they smash to pieces machinery, they set factories ablaze, they seek to restore by force the vanished status of the workman of the Middle Ages.

At this stage the labourers still form an incoherent mass scattered over the whole country, and broken up by their mutual competition. If anywhere they unite to form more compact bodies, this is not yet the consequence of their own active union, but of the union of the bourgeoisie, which class, in order to attain its own political ends, is compelled to set the whole proletariat in motion, and is moreover yet, for a time, able to do so. At this stage, therefore, the proletarians do not fight their enemies, but the enemies of their enemies, the remnants of absolute monarchy, the landowners, the non-industrial bourgeois, the petty bourgeoisie. Thus the whole historical movement is concentrated in the hands of the bourgeoisie; every victory so obtained is a victory for the bourgeoisie.

But with the development of industry the proletariat not only increases in number; it becomes concentrated in greater masses, its strength grows, and it feels that strength more. The various interests and conditions of life within the ranks of the proletariat are more and more equalised, in proportion as machinery obliterates all distinctions of labour, and nearly everywhere reduces wages to the same low level. The growing competition among the bourgeois, and the resulting commercial crises, make the wages of the workers ever more fluctuating. The unceasing improvement of machinery, ever more rapidly developing, makes their livelihood more and more precarious; the collisions between individual workmen and individual bourgeois take more and more the character of collisions between two classes. Thereupon the workers begin to form combinations (Trades Unions) against the bourgeois; they club together in order to keep up the rate of wages; they found permanent associations in order to make provision beforehand for these occasional revolts. Here and there the contest breaks out into riots.

Now and then the workers are victorious, but only for a time. The real fruit of their battles lies, not in the immediate result, but in the ever-expanding union of the workers. This union is helped on by the improved means of communication that are created by modern industry and that place the workers of different localities in contact with one another. It was just this contact that was needed to centralise the numerous local struggles, all of the same character, into one national struggle between classes. But every class struggle is a political struggle. And that union, to attain which the burghers of the Middle Ages, with their miserable highways, required centuries, the modern proletarians, thanks to railways, achieve in a few years.

This organisation of the proletarians into a class, and consequently into a political party, is continually being upset again by the competition between the workers themselves. But it ever rises up again, stronger, firmer, mightier. It compels legislative recognition of particular interests of the workers, by taking advantage of the divisions among the bourgeoisie itself. Thus the ten-hours' bill in England was carried.

Altogether collisions between the classes of the old society further, in many ways, the course of development of the proletariat. The bourgeoisie finds itself involved in a constant battle. At first with the aristocracy; later on, with those portions of the bourgeoisie itself, whose interests have become antagonistic to the progress of industry; at all times, with the bourgeoisie of foreign countries. In all these battles it sees itself compelled to appeal to the proletariat, to ask for its help, and thus, to drag it into the political arena. The bourgeoisie itself, therefore, supplies the proletariat with its own elements of political and general education, in other words, it furnishes the proletariat with weapons for fighting the bourgeoisie.

Further, as we have already seen, entire sections of the ruling classes are, by the advance of industry, precipitated into the proletariat, or are at least threatened in their conditions of existence. These also supply the proletariat with fresh elements of enlightenment and progress.

Finally, in times when the class struggle nears the decisive hour, the process of dissolution going on within the ruling class, in fact within the whole range of society, assumes such a violent, glaring character, that a small section of the ruling class cuts itself adrift, and joins the revolutionary class, the class that holds the future in its hands. Just as, therefore, at an earlier period, a section of the nobility went over to the bourgeoisie, so now a portion of the bourgeoisie goes over to the proletariat, and in particular, a portion of the bourgeois ideologists, who have raised themselves to the level of comprehending theoretically the historical movement as a whole.

Of all the classes that stand face to face with the bourgeoisie today, the proletariat alone is a really revolutionary class. The other classes decay and finally disappear in the face of Modern Industry; the proletariat is its special and essential product.

The lower middle class, the small manufacturer, the shopkeeper, the artisan, the peasant, all these fight against the bourgeoisie, to save from extinction their existence as fractions of the middle class. They are therefore not revolutionary, but conservative. Nay more, they are reactionary, for they try to roll back the wheel of history. If by chance they are revolutionary, they are so only in view of their impending transfer into the proletariat, they thus defend not their present, but their future interests, they desert their own standpoint to place themselves at that of the proletariat.

The "dangerous class," the social scum, that passively rotting mass thrown off by the lowest layers of old society, may, here and there, be swept into the movement by a proletarian revolution; its conditions of life, however, prepare it far more for the part of a bribed tool of reactionary intrigue.

In the conditions of the proletariat, those of old society at large are already virtually swamped. The proletarian is without property; his relation to his wife and children has no longer anything in common with the bourgeois family-relations; modern industrial labour, modern subjection to capital, the same in England as in France, in America as in Germany, has stripped him of every trace of national character. Law, morality, religion, are to him so many bourgeois prejudices, behind which lurk in ambush just as many bourgeois interests.

All the preceding classes that got the upper hand, sought to fortify their already acquired status by subjecting society at large to their conditions of appropriation. The proletarians cannot become masters of the productive forces of society, except by abolishing their own previous mode of appropriation, and thereby also every other previous mode of appropriation. They have nothing of their own to secure and to fortify; their mission is to destroy all previous securities for, and insurances of, individual property.

All previous historical movements were movements of minorities, or in the interests of minorities. The proletarian movement is the self-conscious, independent movement of the immense majority, in the interests of the immense majority. The proletariat, the lowest stratum of our present society, cannot stir, cannot raise itself up, without the whole superincumbent strata of official society being sprung into the air.

Though not in substance, yet in form, the struggle of the proletariat with the bourgeoisie is at first a national struggle. The proletariat of each country must, of course, first of all settle matters with its own bourgeoisie.

In depicting the most general phases of the development of the proletariat, we traced the more or less veiled civil war, raging within existing society, up to the point where that war breaks out into open revolution, and where the violent overthrow of the bourgeoisie lays the foundation for the sway of the proletariat.

Hitherto, every form of society has been based, as we have already seen, on the antagonism of oppressing and oppressed classes. But in order to oppress a class, certain conditions must be assured to it under which it can, at least, continue its slavish existence. The serf, in the period of serfdom, raised himself to membership in the commune, just as the petty bourgeois, under the yoke of feudal absolutism, managed to develop into a bourgeois. The modern labourer, on the contrary, instead of rising with the progress of industry, sinks deeper and deeper below the conditions of existence of his own class. He becomes a pauper, and pauperism develops more rapidly than population and wealth. And here it becomes evident, that the bourgeoisie is unfit any longer to be the ruling class in society, and to impose its conditions of existence upon society as an over-riding law. It is unfit to rule because it is incompetent to assure an existence to its slave within his slavery, because it cannot help letting him sink into such a state, that it has to feed him, instead of being fed by him. Society can no longer live under this bourgeoisie, in other words, its existence is no longer compatible with society.

The essential condition for the existence, and for the sway of the bourgeois class, is the formation and augmentation of capital; the condition for capital is wage-labour. Wage-labour rests exclusively on competition between the labourers. The advance of industry, whose involuntary promoter is the bourgeoisie, replaces the isolation of the labourers, due to competition, by their revolutionary combination, due to association. The development of Modern Industry, therefore, cuts from under its feet the very foundation on which the bourgeoisie produces and appropriates products. What the bourgeoisie, therefore, produces, above all, is its own grave-diggers. Its fall and the victory of the proletariat are equally inevitable.

24

Nickel and Dimed:
On (Not) Getting By in America

BARBARA EHRENREICH

Major changes in welfare legislation in 1996 eliminated cash payments to millions of America's poor, requiring them to find employment in order to support themselves and their families. This change in the law, though popular, raised questions for many people, including Barbara Ehrenreich, who had doubts about the "uplifting benefits" of working in the low-wage economy. One of America's most popular sociological writers, Ehrenreich traveled to the heart of the low-wage economy to see firsthand what it has to offer.

At the beginning of June 1998 I leave behind everything that normally soothes the ego and sustains the body—home, career, companion, reputation, ATM card—for a plunge into the low-wage workforce. There, I become another, occupationally much diminished "Barbara Ehrenreich"—depicted on job-application forms as a divorced homemaker whose sole work experience consists of housekeeping in a few private homes. I am terrified, at the beginning, of being unmasked for what I am: a middle-class journalist setting out to explore the world that welfare mothers are entering, at the rate of approximately 50,000 a month, as welfare reform* kicks in. Happily, though, my fears turn out to be entirely unwarranted: during a month of poverty and toil, my name goes unnoticed and for the most part unuttered. In this parallel universe where my father never got out of the mines and I never got through college, I am "baby," "honey," "blondie," and, most commonly, "girl."

My first task is to find a place to live. I figure that if I can earn $7 an hour—which, from the want ads, seems doable—I can afford to spend $500 on rent, or maybe, with severe economies, $600. In the Key West area, where I live, this pretty much confines me to flophouses and trailer homes—like the one, a pleasing fifteen-minute drive from town, that has no air-conditioning, no screens, no fans, no television, and, by way of diversion, only the challenge of evading the landlord's Doberman pinscher. The big problem with this place, though, is the

---

*[On the basis of 1996 federal legislation, states were required to adopt new guidelines for providing social assistance. The most important program providing cash assistance, Aid to Families with Dependent Children (AFDC), was eliminated and replaced by requirements that poor adults work or participate in job training in order to qualify for cash assistance.]

rent, which at $675 a month is well beyond my reach. All right, Key West is expensive. But so is New York City, or the Bay Area, or Jackson Hole, or Telluride, or Boston, or any other place where tourists and the wealthy compete for living space with the people who clean their toilets and fry their hash browns.[1] Still, it is a shock to realize that "trailer trash" has become, for me, a demographic category to aspire to.

So I decide to make the common trade-off between affordability and convenience, and go for a $500-a-month efficiency thirty miles up a two-lane highway from the employment opportunities of Key West, meaning forty-five minutes if there's no road construction and I don't get caught behind some sun-dazed Canadian tourists. I hate the drive, along a road-side studded with white crosses commemorating the more effective head-on collisions, but it's a sweet little place—a cabin, more or less, set in the swampy back yard of the converted mobile home where my landlord, an affable TV repairman, lives with his bartender girlfriend. Anthropologically speaking, a bustling trailer park would be preferable, but here I have a gleaming white floor and a firm mattress, and the few resident bugs are easily vanquished.

Besides, I am not doing this for the anthropology. My aim is nothing so mistily subjective as to "experience poverty" or find out how it "really feels" to be a long-term low-wage worker. I've had enough unchosen encounters with poverty and the world of low-wage work to know it's not a place you want to visit for touristic purposes; it just smells too much like fear. And with all my real-life assets—bank account, IRA, health insurance, multiroom home—waiting indulgently in the background, I am, of course, thoroughly insulated from the terrors that afflict the genuinely poor.

No, this is a purely objective, scientific sort of mission. The humanitarian rationale for welfare reform—as opposed to the more punitive and stingy impulses that may actually have motivated it—is that work will lift poor women out of poverty while simultaneously inflating their self-esteem and hence their future value in the labor market. Thus, whatever the hassles involved in finding child care, transportation, etc., the transition from welfare to work will end happily, in greater prosperity for all. Now there are many problems with this comforting prediction, such as the fact that the economy will inevitably undergo a downturn, eliminating many jobs. Even without a downturn, the influx of a million former welfare recipients into the low-wage labor market could depress wages by as much as 11.9 percent, according to the Economic Policy Institute (EPI) in Washington, D.C.

---

1. According to the Department of Housing and Urban Development, the "fair-market rent" for an efficiency is $551 here in Monroe County, Florida. A comparable rent in the five boroughs of New York City is $704; in San Francisco, $713; and in the heart of Silicon Valley, $808. The fair-market rent for an area is defined as the amount that would be needed to pay rent plus utilities for "privately owned, decent, safe, and sanitary rental housing of a modest (non-luxury) nature with suitable amenities."

But is it really possible to make a living on the kinds of jobs currently avail-able to unskilled people? Mathematically, the answer is no, as can be shown by taking $6 to $7 an hour, perhaps subtracting a dollar or two an hour for child care, multiplying by 160 hours a month, and comparing the result to the pre-vailing rents. According to the National Coalition for the Homeless, for ex-ample, in 1998 it took, on average nationwide, an hourly wage of $8.89 to afford a one-bedroom apartment, and the Preamble Center for Public Policy esti-mates that the odds against a typical welfare recipient's landing a job at such a "living wage" are about 97 to 1. If these numbers are right, low-wage work is not a solution to poverty and possibly not even to homelessness.

It may seem excessive to put this proposition to an experimental test. As certain family members keep unhelpfully reminding me, the viability of low-wage work could be tested, after a fashion, without ever leaving my study. I could just pay myself $7 an hour for eight hours a day, charge myself for room and board, and total up the numbers after a month. Why leave the people and work that I love? But I am an experimental scientist by training. In that busi-ness, you don't just sit at a desk and theorize; you plunge into the everyday chaos of nature, where surprises lurk in the most mundane measurements. Maybe, when I got into it, I would discover some hidden economies in the world of the low-wage worker. After all, if 30 percent of the workforce toils for less than $8 an hour, according to the EPI, they may have found some tricks as yet unknown to me. Maybe—who knows?—I would even be able to detect in myself the bracing psychological effects of getting out of the house, as promised by the welfare wonks at places like the Heritage Foundation. Or, on the other hand, maybe there would be unexpected costs—physical, mental, or financial—to throw off all my calculations. Ideally, I should do this with two small children in tow, that being the welfare average, but mine are grown and no one is willing to lend me theirs for a month-long vacation in penury. So this is not the perfect experiment, just a test of the best possible case: an unencumbered woman, smart and even strong, attempting to live more or less off the land.

On the morning of my first full day of job searching, I take a red pen to the want ads, which are suspiciously numerous. Everyone in Key West's boom-ing "hospitality industry" seems to be looking for someone like me—train-able, flexible, and with suitably humble expectations as to pay. I know I pos-sess certain traits that might be advantageous—I'm white and, I like to think, well-spoken and poised—but I decide on two rules: One, I cannot use any skills derived from my education or usual work—not that there are a lot of want ads for satirical essayists anyway. Two, I have to take the best-paid job that is offered me and of course do my best to hold it[.] * * * In addition, I rule out various occupations for one reason or another: Hotel front-desk clerk, for example, which to my surprise is regarded as unskilled and pays around $7 an hour, gets eliminated because it involves standing in one spot for eight hours a day. Waitressing is similarly something I'd like to avoid, because I remember it leaving me bone tired when I was eighteen, and I'm decades of varicosities and back pain beyond that now. Telemarketing, one of the first refuges of the suddenly indigent, can be dismissed on grounds of personality. This leaves certain supermarket jobs, such as deli clerk, or housekeeping in Key West's thousands of hotel and guest rooms. Housekeeping is especially appealing, for reasons both atavistic and practical: it's what my mother did before I came along, and it can't be too different from what I've been doing part-time, in my own home, all my life.

So I put on what I take to be a respectful-looking outfit of ironed Bermuda shorts and scooped-neck T-shirt and set out for a tour of the local hotels and supermarkets. Best Western, Econo Lodge, and HoJo's all let me fill out application forms, and these are, to my relief, interested in little more than whether I am a legal resident of the United States and have committed any felonies. My next stop is Winn-Dixie, the supermarket, which turns out to have a particularly onerous application process, featuring a fifteen-minute "interview" by computer since, apparently, no human on the premises is deemed capable of representing the corporate point of view. I am conducted to a large room decorated with posters illustrating how to look "professional" (it helps to be white and, if female, permed) and warning of the slick promises that union organizers might try to tempt me with. The interview is multiple choice: Do I have anything, such as child-care problems, that might make it hard for me to get to work on time? Do I think safety on the job is the responsibility of management? Then, popping up cunningly out of the blue: How many dollars' worth of stolen goods have I purchased in the last year? Would I turn in a fellow employee if I caught him stealing? Finally, "Are you an honest person?"

Apparently, I ace the interview, because I am told that all I have to do is show up in some doctor's office tomorrow for a urine test. This seems to be a fairly general rule: if you want to stack Cheerio boxes or vacuum hotel rooms * * * you have to be willing to squat down and pee in front of some health worker (who has no doubt had to do the same thing herself). The wages Winn-Dixie is offering—$6 and a couple of dimes to start with—are not enough, I decide, to compensate for this indignity.[2]

I lunch at Wendy's, where $4.99 gets you unlimited refills at the Mexican part of the Superbar, a comforting surfeit of refried beans and "cheese sauce." A teenage employee, seeing me studying the want ads, kindly offers me an application form, which I fill out, though here, too, the pay is just $6 and change an hour. Then it's off for a round of the locally owned inns and guesthouses. At

---

2. According to the *Monthly Labor Review* (November 1996), 28 percent of work sites surveyed in the service industry conduct drug tests (corporate workplaces have much higher rates), and the incidence of testing has risen markedly since the Eighties. The rate of testing is highest in the South (56 percent of work sites polled), with the Midwest in second place (50 percent). The drug most likely to be detected—marijuana, which can be detected in urine for weeks—is also the most innocuous, while heroin and cocaine are generally undetectable three days after use.

"The Palms," let's call it, a bouncy manager actually takes me around to see the rooms and meet the existing housekeepers, who, I note with satisfaction, look pretty much like me—faded ex-hippie types in shorts with long hair pulled back in braids. Mostly, though, no one speaks to me or even looks at me except to proffer an application form. At my last stop, a palatial B&B, I wait twenty minutes to meet "Max," only to be told that there are no jobs now but there should be one soon, since "nobody lasts more than a couple weeks." (Because none of the people I talked to knew I was a reporter, I have changed their names to protect their privacy and, in some cases perhaps, their jobs.)

Three days go by like this, and, to my chagrin, no one out of the approximately twenty places I've applied calls me for an interview. I had been vain enough to worry about coming across as too educated for the jobs I sought, but no one even seems interested in finding out how overqualified I am. Only later will I realize that the want ads are not a reliable measure of the actual jobs available at any particular time. They are, as I should have guessed from Max's comment, the employers' insurance policy against the relentless turnover of the low-wage work force. Most of the big hotels run ads almost continually, just to build a supply of applicants to replace the current workers as they drift away or are fired, so finding a job is just a matter of being at the right place at the right time and flexible enough to take whatever is being offered that day. This finally happens to me at one of the big discount hotel chains, where I go, as usual, for housekeeping and am sent, instead, to try out as a waitress at the attached "family restaurant," a dismal spot with a counter and about thirty tables that looks out on a parking garage and features such tempting fare as "Pollish [sic] sausage and BBQ sauce" on 95-degree days. Phillip, the dapper young West Indian who introduces himself as the manager, interviews me with about as much enthusiasm as if he were a clerk processing me for Medicare, the principal questions being what shifts can I work and when can I start. I mutter something about being woefully out of practice as a waitress, but he's already on to the uniform: I'm to show up tomorrow wearing black slacks and black shoes; he'll provide the rust-colored polo shirt with HEARTHSIDE embroidered on it, though I might want to wear my own shirt to get to work, ha ha. At the word "tomorrow," something between fear and indignation rises in my chest. I want to say, "Thank you for your time, sir, but this is just an experiment, you know, not my actual life."

So begins my career at the Hearthside, I shall call it, one small profit center within a global discount hotel chain, where for two weeks I work from 2:00 till 10:00 P.M. for $2.43 an hour plus tips.[3] In some futile bid for gentility, the man-

---

3. According to the Fair Labor Standards Act, employers are not required to pay "tipped employees," such as restaurant servers, more than $2.13 an hour in direct wages. However, if the sum of tips plus $2.13 an hour falls below the minimum wage, or $5.15 an hour, the employer is required to make up the difference. This fact was not mentioned by managers or otherwise publicized at either of the restaurants where I worked.

agement has barred employees from using the front door, so my first day I enter through the kitchen, where a red-faced man with shoulder-length blond hair is throwing frozen steaks against the wall and yelling, "Fuck this shit!" "That's just Jack," explains Gail, the wiry middle-aged waitress who is assigned to train me. "He's on the rag again"—a condition occasioned, in this instance, by the fact that the cook on the morning shift had forgotten to thaw out the steaks. For the next eight hours, I run after the agile Gail, absorbing bits of instruction along with fragments of personal tragedy. All food must be trayed, and the reason she's so tired today is that she woke up in a cold sweat thinking of her boyfriend, who killed himself recently in an upstate prison. No refills on lemonade. And the reason he was in prison is that a few DUIs caught up with him, that's all, could have happened to anyone. Carry the creamers to the table in a monkey bowl, never in your hand. And after he was gone she spent several months living in her truck, peeing in a plastic pee bottle and reading by candlelight at night, but you can't live in a truck in the summer, since you need to have the windows down, which means anything can get in, from mosquitoes on up.

At least Gail puts to rest any fears I had of appearing overqualified. From the first day on, I find that of all the things I have left behind, such as home and identity, what I miss the most is competence. Not that I have ever felt utterly competent in the writing business, in which one day's success augurs nothing at all for the next. But in my writing life, I at least have some notion of procedure: do the research, make the outline, rough out a draft, etc. As a server, though, I am beset by requests like bees: more iced tea here, ketchup over there, a to-go box for table fourteen, and where are the high chairs, anyway? Of the twenty-seven tables, up to six are usually mine at any time, though on slow afternoons or if Gail is off, I sometimes have the whole place to myself. There is the touch-screen computer-ordering system to master, which is, I suppose, meant to minimize server-cook contact, but in practice requires constant verbal fine-tuning: "That's gravy on the mashed, okay? None on the meatloaf," and so forth—while the cook scowls as if I were inventing these refinements just to torment him. Plus, something I had forgotten in the years since I was eighteen: about a third of a server's job is "side work" that's invisible to customers—sweeping, scrubbing, slicing, refilling, and restocking. If it isn't all done, every little bit of it, you're going to face the 6:00 P.M. dinner rush defenseless and probably go down in flames. I screw up dozens of times at the beginning, sustained in my shame entirely by Gail's support—"It's okay, baby, everyone does that sometime"—because, to my total surprise and despite the scientific detachment I am doing my best to maintain, I care.

The whole thing would be a lot easier if I could just skate through it as Lily Tomlin in one of her waitress skits, but I was raised by the absurd Booker T. Washingtonian precept that says: If you're going to do something, do it well. In fact, "well" isn't good enough by half. Do it better than anyone has ever done it before. Or so said my father, who must have known what he was talking about because he managed to pull himself, and us with him, up from the mile-deep copper mines of Butte to the leafy suburbs of the Northeast, ascending from boilermakers to martinis before booze beat out ambition. As in most endeavors I have encountered in my life, doing it "better than anyone" is not a reasonable goal. Still, when I wake up at 4:00 A.M. in my own cold sweat, I am not thinking about the writing deadlines I'm neglecting; I'm thinking about the table whose order I screwed up so that one of the boys didn't get his kiddie meal until the rest of the family had moved on to their Key Lime pies. That's the other powerful motivation I hadn't expected—the customers, or "patients," as I can't help thinking of them on account of the mysterious vulnerability that seems to have left them temporarily unable to feed themselves. After a few days at the Hearthside, I feel the service ethic kick in like a shot of oxytocin, the nurturance hormone. The plurality of my customers are hard-working locals—truck drivers, construction workers, even housekeepers from the attached hotel—and I want them to have the closest to a "fine dining" experience that the grubby circumstances will allow. No "you guys" for me; everyone over twelve is "sir" or "ma'am." I ply them with iced tea and coffee refills; I return, mid-meal, to inquire how everything is; I doll up their salads with chopped raw mushrooms, summer squash slices, or whatever bits of produce I can find that have survived their sojourn in the cold-storage room mold-free.

* * *

Ten days into it, this is beginning to look like a livable lifestyle. I like Gail, who is "looking at fifty" but moves so fast she can alight in one place and then another without apparently being anywhere between them. I clown around with Lionel, the teenage Haitian busboy, and catch a few fragments of conversation with Joan, the svelte fortyish hostess and militant feminist who is the only one of us who dares to tell Jack to shut the fuck up. I even warm up to Jack when, on a slow night and to make up for a particularly unwarranted attack on my abilities, or so I imagine, he tells me about his glory days as a young man at "coronary school"—or do you say "culinary"?—in Brooklyn, where he dated a knock-out Puerto Rican chick and learned everything there is to know about food. I finish up at 10:00 or 10:30, depending on how much side work I've been able to get done during the shift, and cruise home[.] * * * To bed by 1:30 or 2:00, up at 9:00 or 10:00, read for an hour while my uniform whirls around in the landlord's washing machine, and then it's another eight hours spent following Mao's central instruction, as laid out in the Little Red Book, which was: Serve the people.

I could drift along like this, in some dreamy proletarian idyll, except for two things. One is management. If I have kept this subject on the margins thus far it is because I still flinch to think that I spent all those weeks under the surveillance of men (and later women) whose job it was to monitor my behavior for signs of sloth, theft, drug abuse, or worse. Not that managers and especially "assistant managers" in low-wage settings like this are exactly the class enemy. In the restaurant business, they are mostly former cooks or servers, still capable of pinch-hitting in the kitchen or on the floor, just as in hotels they are likely to be former clerks, and paid a salary of only about $400 a week. But everyone knows they have crossed over to the other side, which is, crudely put, corporate as opposed to human. Cooks want to prepare tasty meals; servers want to serve them graciously; but managers are there for only one reason—to make sure that money is made for some theoretical entity that exists far away in Chicago or New York, if a corporation can be said to have a physical existence at all. Reflecting on her career, Gail tells me ruefully that she had sworn, years ago, never to work for a corporation again. "They don't cut you no slack. You give and you give, and they take."

Managers can sit—for hours at a time if they want—but it's their job to see that no one else ever does, even when there's nothing to do, and this is why, for servers, slow times can be as exhausting as rushes. You start dragging out each little chore, because if the manager on duty catches you in an idle moment, he will give you something far nastier to do. So I wipe, I clean, I consolidate ketchup bottles and recheck the cheesecake supply, even tour the tables to make sure the customer evaluation forms are all standing perkily in their places—wondering all the time how many calories I burn in these strictly theatrical exercises. When, on a particularly dead afternoon, Stu finds me glancing at a *USA Today* a customer has left behind, he assigns me to vacuum the entire floor with the broken vacuum cleaner that has a handle only two feet long, and the only way to do that without incurring orthopedic damage is to proceed from spot to spot on your knees.

On my first Friday at the Hearthside there is a "mandatory meeting for all restaurant employees," which I attend, eager for insight into our overall marketing strategy and the niche (your basic Ohio cuisine with a tropical twist?) we aim to inhabit. But there is no "we" at this meeting. Phillip, our top manager except for an occasional "consultant" sent out by corporate headquarters, opens it with a sneer: "The break room—it's disgusting. Butts in the ashtrays, newspapers lying around, crumbs." This windowless little room, which also houses the time clock for the entire hotel, is where we stash our bags and civilian clothes and take our half-hour meal breaks. But a break room is not a right, he tells us. It can be taken away. We should also know that the lockers in the break room and whatever is in them can be searched at any time. Then comes gossip; there has been gossip; gossip (which seems to mean employees talking among themselves) must stop. Off-duty employees are henceforth barred from eating at the restaurant, because "other servers gather around them and gossip." When Phillip has exhausted his agenda of rebukes, Joan complains about the condition of the ladies' room and I throw in my two bits about the vacuum cleaner. But I don't see any backup coming from my fellow servers, each of whom has subsided into her own personal funk; Gail, my role model, stares sorrowfully at a point six inches from her nose. The meeting ends when

Andy, one of the cooks, gets up, muttering about breaking up his day off for this almighty bullshit.

Just four days later we are suddenly summoned into the kitchen at 3:30 P.M., even though there are live tables on the floor. We all—about ten of us—stand around Phillip, who announces grimly that there has been a report of some "drug activity" on the night shift and that, as a result, we are now to be a "drug-free" workplace, meaning that all new hires will be tested, as will possibly current employees on a random basis. I am glad that this part of the kitchen is so dark, because I find myself blushing as hard as if I had been caught toking up in the ladies' room myself: I haven't been treated this way—lined up in the corridor, threatened with locker searches, peppered with carelessly aimed accusations—since junior high school.

* * *

The other problem, in addition to the less-than-nurturing management style, is that this job shows no sign of being financially viable. You might imagine, from a comfortable distance, that people who live, year in and year out, on $6 to $10 an hour have discovered some survival stratagems unknown to the middle class. But no. It's not hard to get my co-workers to talk about their living situations, because housing, in almost every case, is the principal source of disruption in their lives, the first thing they fill you in on when they arrive for their shifts. After a week, I have compiled the following survey:

- Gail is sharing a room in a well-known downtown flophouse for which she and a roommate pay about $250 a week. Her roommate, a male friend, has begun hitting on her, driving her nuts, but the rent would be impossible alone.
- Claude, the Haitian cook, is desperate to get out of the two-room apartment he shares with his girlfriend and two other, unrelated, people. As far as I can determine, the other Haitian men (most of whom only speak Creole) live in similarly crowded situations.
- Annette, a twenty-year-old server who is six months pregnant and has been abandoned by her boyfriend, lives with her mother, a postal clerk.
- Marianne and her boyfriend are paying $170 a week for a one-person trailer.
- Jack, who is, at $10 an hour, the wealthiest of us, lives in the trailer he owns, paying only the $400-a-month lot fee.
- The other white cook, Andy, lives on his dry-docked boat, which, as far as I can tell from his loving descriptions, can't be more than twenty feet long. He offers to take me out on it, once it's repaired, but the offer comes with inquiries as to my marital status, so I do not follow up on it.
- Tina and her husband are paying $60 a night for a double room in a Days Inn. This is because they have no car and the Days Inn is within

walking distance of the Heartside. When Marianne, one of the break-fast servers, is tossed out of her trailer for subletting (which is against the trailer-park rules), she leaves her boyfriend and moves in with Tina and her husband.

- Joan, who had fooled me with her numerous and tasteful outfits (host-esses wear their own clothes), lives in a van she parks behind a shop-ping center at night and showers in Tina's motel room. The clothes are from thrift shops.[4]

It strikes me, in my middle-class solipsism, that there is gross improvidence in some of these arrangements. When Gail and I are wrapping silverware in napkins—the only task for which we are permitted to sit—she tells me she is thinking of escaping from her roommate by moving into the Days Inn herself. I am astounded: How can she even think of paying between $40 and $60 a day? But if I was afraid of sounding like a social worker, I come out just sounding like a fool. She squints at me in disbelief, "And where am I supposed to get a month's rent and a month's deposit for an apartment?" I'd been feeling pretty smug about my $500 efficiency, but of course it was made possible only by the $1,300 I had allotted myself for start-up costs when I began my low-wage life: $1,000 for the first month's rent and deposit, $100 for initial groceries and cash in my pocket, $200 stuffed away for emergencies. In poverty, as in certain propositions in physics, starting conditions are everything.

There are no secret economies that nourish the poor; on the contrary, there are a host of special costs. If you can't put up the two months' rent you need to secure an apartment, you end up paying through the nose for a room by the week. If you have only a room, with a hot plate at best, you can't save by cook-ing up huge lentil stews that can be frozen for the week ahead. You eat fast food, or the hot dogs and styrofoam cups of soup that can be microwaved in a convenience store. If you have no money for health insurance—and the Hearth-side's niggardly plan kicks in only after three months—you go without routine care or prescription drugs and end up paying the price.

* * *

My own situation, when I sit down to assess it after two weeks of work, would not be much better if this were my actual life. The seductive thing about waitressing is that you don't have to wait for payday to feel a few bills in your pocket, and my tips usually cover meals and gas, plus something left over to stuff into the kitchen drawer I use as a bank. But as the tourist business slows in the summer heat, I sometimes leave work with only $20 in tips (the gross

---

4. I could find no statistics on the number of employed people living in cars or vans, but according to the National Coalition for the Homeless's 1997 report "Myths and Facts About Homelessness," nearly one in five homeless people (in twenty-nine cities across the nation) is employed in a full- or part-time job.

is higher, but servers share about 15 percent of their tips with the bus-boys and bartenders). With wages included, this amounts to about the minimum wage of $5.15 an hour. Although the sum in the drawer is piling up, at the present rate of accumulation it will be more than a hundred dollars short of my rent when the end of the month comes around. Nor can I see any expenses to cut. True, I haven't gone the lentil-stew route yet, but that's because I don't have a large cooking pot, pot holders, or a ladle to stir with (which cost about $30 at Kmart, less at thrift stores), not to mention onions, carrots, and the indispensable bay leaf. I do make my lunch almost every day—usually some slow-burning, high-protein combo like frozen chicken patties with melted cheese on top and canned pinto beans on the side. Dinner is at the Hearthside, which offers its employees a choice of BLT, fish sandwich, or hamburger for only $2. The burger lasts longest, especially if it's heaped with gut-puckering jalapeños, but by midnight my stomach is growling again.

So unless I want to start using my car as a residence, I have to find a second, or alternative, job. I call all the hotels where I filled out housekeeping applications weeks ago—the Hyatt, Holiday Inn, Econo Lodge, HoJo's, Best Western, plus a half dozen or so locally run guesthouses. Nothing. Then I start making the rounds again, wasting whole mornings waiting for some assistant manager to show up, even dipping into places so creepy that the front-desk clerk greets you from behind bulletproof glass and sells pints of liquor over the counter. But either someone has exposed my real-life housekeeping habits—which are, shall we say, mellow—or I am at the wrong end of some infallible ethnic equation: most, but by no means all, of the working housekeepers I see on my job searches are African Americans, Spanish-speaking, or immigrants from the Central European post-Communist world, whereas servers are almost invariably white and monolingually English-speaking. When I finally get a positive response, I have been identified once again as server material. Jerry's, which is part of a well-known national family restaurant chain and physically attached here to another budget hotel chain, is ready to use me at once. The prospect is both exciting and terrifying, because, with about the same number of tables and counter seats, Jerry's attracts three or four times the volume of customers as the gloomy old Hearthside.

Picture a fat person's hell, and I don't mean a place with no food. Instead there is everything you might eat if eating had no bodily consequences—cheese fries, chicken-fried steaks, fudge-laden desserts—only here every bite must be paid for, one way or another, in human discomfort. The kitchen is a cavern, a stomach leading to the lower intestine that is the garbage and dishwashing area, from which issue bizarre smells combining the edible and the offal: creamy carrion, pizza barf, and that unique and enigmatic Jerry's scent—citrus fart. The floor is slick with spills, forcing us to walk through the kitchen with tiny steps[.] * * * Sinks everywhere are clogged with scraps of lettuce, decomposing lemon wedges, waterlogged toast crusts. Put your hand down on any counter and you risk being stuck to it by the film of ancient syrup spills, and this is unfortunate, because hands are utensils here, used for scooping up lettuce onto salad plates, lifting out pie slices, and even moving hash browns from one plate to another. The regulation poster in the single unisex restroom admonishes us to wash our hands thoroughly and even offers instructions for doing so, but there is always some vital substance missing—soap, paper towels, toilet paper—and I never find all three at once. You learn to stuff your pockets with napkins before going in there, and too bad about the customers, who must eat, though they don't realize this, almost literally out of our hands.

The break room typifies the whole situation: there is none, because there are no breaks at Jerry's. For six to eight hours in a row, you never sit except to pee. Actually, there are three folding chairs at a table immediately adjacent to the bathroom, but hardly anyone ever sits here, in the very rectum of the gastro-architectural system. Rather, the function of the peritoilet area is to house the ashtrays in which servers and dishwashers leave their cigarettes burning at all times, like votive candles, so that they don't have to waste time lighting up again when they dash back for a puff. Almost everyone smokes as if his or her pulmonary well-being depended on it—the multinational mélange of cooks, the Czech dishwashers, the servers, who are all American natives— creating an atmosphere in which oxygen is only an occasional pollutant. My first morning at Jerry's, when the hypoglycemic shakes set in, I complain to one of my fellow servers that I don't understand how she can go so long without food. "Well, I don't understand how you can go so long without a cigarette," she responds in a tone of reproach—because work is what you do for others; smoking is what you do for yourself. I don't know why the antismoking crusaders have never grasped the element of defiant self-nurturance that makes the habit so endearing to its victims—as if, in the American workplace, the only thing people have to call their own is the tumors they are nourishing and the spare moments they devote to feeding them.

Now, the Industrial Revolution is not an easy transition, especially when you have to zip through it in just a couple of days. I have gone from craft work straight into the factory, from the air-conditioned morgue of the Hearthside directly into the flames. Customers arrive in human waves, sometimes disgorged fifty at a time from their tour buses, peckish and whiny. Instead of two "girls" on the floor at once, there can be as many as six of us running around in our brilliant pink-and-orange Hawaiian shirts.

* * *

I start out with the beautiful, heroic idea of handling the two jobs at once, and for two days I almost do it: the breakfast/lunch shift at Jerry's, which goes till 2:00, arriving at the Hearthside at 2:10, and attempting to hold out until 10:00. In the ten minutes between jobs, I pick up a spicy chicken sandwich at the Wendy's drive-through window, gobble it down in the car, and change from khaki slacks to black, from Hawaiian to rust polo. There is a problem, though. When during the 3:00 to 4:00 P.M. dead time I finally sit down to wrap silver, my flesh seems to bond to the seat. I try to refuel with a purloined cup of soup, as I've seen Gail and Joan do dozens of times, but a manager catches me and hisses "No eating!" though there's not a customer around to be offended by the sight of food making contact with a server's lips. So I tell Gail I'm going to quit, and she hugs me and says she might just follow me to Jerry's herself.

But the chances of this are minuscule. She has left the flophouse and her annoying roommate and is back to living in her beat-up old truck. But guess what? she reports to me excitedly later that evening: Phillip has given her permission to park overnight in the hotel parking lot, as long as she keeps out of sight, and the parking lot should be totally safe, since it's patrolled by a hotel security guard! With the Hearthside offering benefits like that, how could anyone think of leaving?

Gail would have triumphed at Jerry's, I'm sure, but for me it's a crash course in exhaustion management. Years ago, the kindly fry cook who trained me to waitress at a Los Angeles truck stop used to say: Never make an unnecessary trip; if you don't have to walk fast, walk slow; if you don't have to walk, stand. But at Jerry's the effort of distinguishing necessary from unnecessary and urgent from whenever would itself be too much of an energy drain. The only thing to do is to treat each shift as a one-time-only emergency: you've got fifty starving people out there, lying scattered on the battlefield, so get out there and feed them! Forget that you will have to do this again tomorrow, forget that you will have to be alert enough to dodge the drunks on the drive home tonight—just burn, burn, burn! Ideally, at some point you enter what servers call "a rhythm" and psychologists term a "flow state," in which signals pass from the sense organs directly to the muscles, bypassing the cerebral cortex, and a Zen-like emptiness sets in. * * *

But there's another capacity of the neuromuscular system, which is pain. I start tossing back drugstore-brand ibuprofen pills as if they were vitamin C, four before each shift, because an old mouse-related repetitive-stress injury in my upper back has come back to full-spasm strength, thanks to the tray carrying. In my ordinary life, this level of disability might justify a day of ice packs and stretching.

* * *

I make friends, over time, with the other "girls" who work my shift: Nita, the tattooed twenty-something who taunts us by going around saying brightly, "Have we started making money yet?" Ellen, whose teenage son cooks on the graveyard shift and who once managed a restaurant in Massachusetts but won't try out for management here because she prefers being a "common worker" and not "ordering people around." Easy-going fiftyish Lucy, with the raucous laugh, who limps toward the end of the shift because of something that has gone wrong with her leg, the exact nature of which cannot be determined without health insurance. We talk about the usual girl things—men, children, and the sinister allure of Jerry's chocolate peanut-butter cream pie—

though no one, I notice, ever brings up anything potentially expensive, like shopping or movies. As at the Hearthside, the only recreation ever referred to is partying, which requires little more than some beer, a joint, and a few close friends. Still, no one here is homeless, or cops to it anyway, thanks usually to a working husband or boyfriend. All in all, we form a reliable mutual-support group: If one of us is feeling sick or overwhelmed, another one will "bev" a table or even carry trays for her. If one of us is off sneaking a cigarette or a pee,[5] the others will do their best to conceal her absence from the enforcers of corporate rationality.

But my saving human connection—my oxytocin receptor, as it were—is George, the nineteen-year-old, fresh-off-the-boat Czech dishwasher. We get to talking when he asks me, tortuously, how much cigarettes cost at Jerry's. I do my best to explain that they cost over a dollar more here than at a regular store and suggest that he just take one from the half-filled packs that are always lying around on the break table. But that would be unthinkable. Except for the one tiny earring signaling his allegiance to some vaguely alternative point of view, George is a perfect straight arrow—crew-cut, hardworking, and hungry for eye contact. "Czech Republic," I ask, "or Slovakia?" and he seems delighted that I know the difference. "Václav Havel," I try. "Velvet Revolution, Frank Zappa!" "Yes, yes, 1989," he says, and I realize we are talking about history.

* * *

I make the decision to move closer to Key West. First, because of the drive. Second and third, also because of the drive: gas is eating up $4 to $5 a day, and although Jerry's is as high-volume as you can get, the tips average only 10 percent, and not just for a newbie like me. Between the base pay of $2.15 an hour and the obligation to share tips with the busboys and dishwashers, we're averaging only about $7.50 an hour. Then there is the $30 I had to spend on the regulation tan slacks worn by Jerry's servers—a setback it could take weeks to absorb. (I had combed the town's two downscale department stores hoping for something cheaper but decided in the end that these marked-down Dockers, originally $49, were more likely to survive a daily washing.) Of my

---

5. Until April 1998, there was no federally mandated right to bathroom breaks. According to Marc Linder and Ingrid Nygaard, authors of *Void Where Prohibited: Rest Breaks and the Right to Urinate on Company Time* (Cornell University Press, 1997). "The right to rest and void at work is not high on the list of social or political causes supported by professional or executive employees, who enjoy personal workplace liberties that millions of factory workers can only daydream about. . . . While we were dismayed to discover that workers lacked an acknowledged legal right to void at work, [the workers] were amazed by outsiders' naive belief that their employers would permit them to perform this basic bodily function when necessary. . . . A factory worker, not allowed a break for six-hour stretches, voided into pads worn inside her uniform; and a kindergarten teacher in a school without aides had to take all twenty children with her to the bathroom and line them up outside the stall door when she voided."

fellow servers, everyone who lacks a working husband or boyfriend seems to have a second job: Nita does something at a computer eight hours a day; another welds. Without the forty-five-minute commute, I can picture myself working two jobs and having the time to shower between them.

So I take the $500 deposit I have coming from my landlord, the $400 I have earned toward the next month's rent, plus the $200 reserved for emergencies, and use the $1,100 to pay the rent and deposit on trailer number 46 in the Overseas Trailer Park, a mile from the cluster of budget hotels that constitute Key West's version of an industrial park. Number 46 is about eight feet in width and shaped like a barbell inside, with a narrow region—because of the sink and the stove—separating the bedroom from what might optimistically be called the "living" area, with its two-person table and half-sized couch. The bathroom is so small my knees rub against the shower stall when I sit on the toilet, and you can't just leap out of the bed, you have to climb down to the foot of it in order to find a patch of floor space to stand on. Outside, I am within a few yards of a liquor store, a bar that advertises "free beer tomorrow," a convenience store, and a Burger King—but no supermarket or, alas, laundromat. By reputation, the Overseas park is a nest of crime and crack, and I am hoping at least for some vibrant, multicultural street life. But desolation rules night and day, except for a thin stream of pedestrian traffic heading for their jobs at the Sheraton or 7-Eleven. There are not exactly people here but what amounts to canned labor, being preserved from the heat between shifts.

In line with my reduced living conditions, a new form of ugliness arises at Jerry's. First we are confronted—via an announcement on the computers through which we input orders—with the new rule that the hotel bar is henceforth off-limits to restaurant employees. The culprit, I learn through the grapevine, is the ultra-efficient gal who trained me—another trailer-home dweller and a mother of three. Something had set her off one morning, so she slipped out for a nip and returned to the floor impaired. This mostly hurts Ellen, whose habit it is to free her hair from its rubber band and drop by the bar for a couple of Zins before heading home at the end of the shift, but all of us feel the chill. Then the next day, when I go for straws, for the first time I find the dry-storage room locked. Ted, the portly assistant manager who opens it for me, explains that he caught one of the dishwashers attempting to steal something, and, unfortunately, the miscreant will be with us until a replacement can be found—hence the locked door. I neglect to ask what he had been trying to steal, but Ted tells me who he is—the kid with the buzz cut and the earring [: George].

* * *

When my month-long plunge into poverty is almost over, I finally land my dream job—housekeeping. I do this by walking into the personnel office of the only place I figure I might have some credibility, the hotel attached to Jerry's, and confiding urgently that I have to have a second job if I am to pay my rent and, no, it couldn't be front-desk clerk. "All right," the personnel lady fairly spits, "So it's housekeeping," and she marches me back to meet Maria, the housekeeping manager, a tiny, frenetic Hispanic woman who greets me as "babe" and hands me a pamphlet emphasizing the need for a positive attitude. The hours are nine in the morning till whenever, the pay is $6.10 an hour, and there's one week of vacation a year. I don't have to ask about health insurance once I meet Carlotta, the middle-aged African-American woman who will be training me. Carla, as she tells me to call her, is missing all of her top front teeth.

On that first day of housekeeping and last day of my entire project—although I don't yet know it's the last—Carla is in a foul mood. We have been given nineteen rooms to clean, most of them "checkouts," as opposed to "stay-overs," that require the whole enchilada of bed-stripping, vacuuming, and bathroom-scrubbing. When one of the rooms that had been listed as a stay-over turns out to be a checkout, Carla calls Maria to complain, but of course to no avail. "So make up the motherfucker," Carla orders me, and I do the beds while she sloshes around the bathroom. For four hours without a break I strip and remake beds, taking about four and a half minutes per queen-sized bed, which I could get down to three if there were any reason to. We try to avoid vacuuming by picking up the larger specks by hand, but often there is nothing to do but drag the monstrous vacuum cleaner—it weighs about thirty pounds—off our cart and try to wrestle it around the floor. Sometimes Carla hands me the squirt bottle of "BAM" (an acronym for something that begins, ominously, with "butyric"; the rest has been worn off the label) and lets me do the bathrooms. No service ethic challenges me here to new heights of performance. I just concentrate on removing the pubic hairs from the bathtubs, or at least the dark ones that I can see.

I had looked forward to the breaking-and-entering aspect of cleaning the stay-overs, the chance to examine the secret, physical existence of strangers. But the contents of the rooms are always banal and surprisingly neat—zipped up shaving kits, shoes lined up against the wall (there are no closets), flyers for snorkeling trips, maybe an empty wine bottle or two. It is the TV that keeps us going, from *Jerry* to *Sally* to *Hawaii Five-O* and then on to the soaps. If there's something especially arresting, like "Won't Take No for an Answer" on *Jerry,* we sit down on the edge of a bed and giggle for a moment as if this were a pajama party instead of a terminally dead-end job. The soaps are the best, and Carla turns the volume up full blast so that she won't miss anything from the bathroom or while the vacuum is on. In room 503, Marcia confronts Jeff about Lauren. In 505, Lauren taunts poor cuckolded Marcia. In 511, Helen offers Amanda $10,000 to stop seeing Eric, prompting Carla to emerge from the bathroom to study Amanda's troubled face. "You take it, girl," she advises. "I would for sure."

The tourists' rooms that we clean and, beyond them, the far more expensively appointed interiors in the soaps, begin after a while to merge. We have entered a better world—a world of comfort where every day is a day off, waiting to be filled up with sexual intrigue. We, however, are only gate-crashers in this fantasy, forced to pay for our presence with backaches and perpetual thirst. The mirrors, and there are far too many of them in hotel rooms, contain the kind of person you would normally find pushing a shopping cart down a city street—bedraggled, dressed in a damp hotel polo shirt two sizes too large, and with sweat dribbling down her chin like drool. I am enormously relieved when Carla announces a half-hour meal break, but my appetite fades when I see that the bag of hot-dog rolls she has been carrying around on our cart is not trash salvaged from a checkout but what she has brought for her lunch.

When I request permission to leave at about 3:30, another housekeeper warns me that no one has so far succeeded in combining housekeeping at the hotel with serving at Jerry's: "Some kid did it once for five days, and you're no kid." With that helpful information in mind, I rush back to number 46, down four Advils (the name brand this time), shower, stooping to fit into the stall, and attempt to compose myself for the on coming shift. So much for what Marx termed the "reproduction of labor power," meaning the things a worker has to do just so she'll be ready to work again. The only unforeseen obstacle to the smooth transition from job to job is that my tan Jerry's slacks, which had looked reasonably clean by 40-watt bulb last night when I handwashed my Hawaiian shirt, prove by daylight to be mottled with ketchup and ranch-dressing stains. I spend most of my hour-long break between jobs attempting to remove the edible portions with a sponge and then drying the slacks over the hood of my car in the sun.

I can do this two-job thing, is my theory, if I can drink enough caffeine and avoid getting distracted by George's ever more obvious suffering.[6]

* * *

I resolve to give him all my tips that night and to hell with the experiment in low-wage money management. At eight, Ellen and I grab a snack together standing at the mephitic end of the kitchen counter, but I can only manage two or three mozzarella sticks and lunch had been a mere handful of McNuggets. I am not tired at all, I assure myself, though it may be that there is simply no more "I" left to do the tiredness monitoring. What I would see, if I were more alert to the situation, is that the forces of destruction are already massing against me. There is only one cook on duty, a young man named Jesus ("Hay-Sue," that is) and he is new to the job. And there is Joy, who shows up to take

---

6. In 1996, the number of persons holding two or more jobs averaged 7.8 million, or 6.2 percent of the workforce. It was about the same rate for men and for women (6.1 versus 6.2), though the kinds of jobs differ by gender. About two thirds of multiple jobholders work one job full-time and the other part-time. Only a heroic minority—4 percent of men and 2 percent of women—work two full-time jobs simultaneously. (From John F. Stinson Jr., "New Data on Multiple Jobholding Available from the CPS," in the *Monthly Labor Review*, March 1997.)

over in the middle of the shift, wearing high heels and a long, clingy white dress and fuming as if she'd just been stood up in some cocktail bar.

Then it comes, the perfect storm. Four of my tables fill up at once. Four tables is nothing for me now, but only so long as they are obligingly staggered. As I bev table 27, tables 25, 28, and 24 are watching enviously. As I bev 25, 24 glowers because their bevs haven't even been ordered. Twenty-eight is four yuppyish types, meaning everything on the side and agonizing instructions as to the chicken Caesars. Twenty-five is a middle-aged black couple, who complain, with some justice, that the iced tea isn't fresh and the tabletop is sticky. But table 24 is the meteorological event of the century: ten British tourists who seem to have made the decision to absorb the American experience entirely by mouth. Here everyone has at least two drinks—iced tea and milk shake, Michelob and water (with lemon slice, please)—and a huge promiscuous orgy of breakfast specials, mozz sticks, chicken strips, quesadillas, burgers with cheese and without, sides of hash browns with cheddar, with onions, with gravy, seasoned fries, plain fries, banana splits. Poor Jesus! Poor me! Because when I arrive with their first tray of food—after three prior trips just to refill bevs—Princess Di refuses to eat her chicken strips with her pancake-and-sausage special, since, as she now reveals, the strips were meant to be an appetizer. Maybe the others would have accepted their meals, but Di, who is deep into her third Michelob, insists that everything else go back while they work on their "starters." Meanwhile, the yuppies are waving me down for more decaf and the black couple looks ready to summon the NAACP.

Much of what happened next is lost in the fog of war. Jesus starts going under. The little printer on the counter in front of him is spewing out orders faster than he can rip them off, much less produce the meals. Even the invincible Ellen is ashen from stress. I bring table 24 their reheated main courses, which they immediately reject as either too cold or fossilized by the microwave. When I return to the kitchen with their trays (three trays in three trips), Joy confronts me with arms akimbo: "What is this?" She means the food—the plates of rejected pancakes, hash browns in assorted flavors, toasts, burgers, sausages, eggs. "Uh, scrambled with cheddar," I try, "and that's ..." "NO," she screams in my face. "Is it a traditional, a super-scramble, an eye-opener?" I pretend to study my check for a clue, but entropy has been up to its tricks, not only on the plates but in my head, and I have to admit that the original order is beyond reconstruction. "You don't know an eye-opener from a traditional?" she demands in outrage. All I know, in fact, is that my legs have lost interest in the current venture and have announced their intention to fold. I am saved by a yuppie (mercifully not one of mine) who chooses this moment to charge into the kitchen to bellow that his food is twenty-five minutes late. Joy screams at him to get the hell out of her kitchen, please, and then turns on Jesus in a fury, hurling an empty tray across the room for emphasis.

I leave. I don't walk out, I just leave. I don't finish my side work or pick up my credit-card tips, if any, at the cash register or, of course, ask Joy's permission to go. And the surprising thing is that you can walk out without permission, that the door opens, that the thick tropical night air parts to let me pass, that my car is still parked where I left it. There is no vindication in this exit, no fuck-you surge of relief, just an overwhelming, dank sense of failure pressing down on me and the entire parking lot. I had gone into this venture in the spirit of science, to test a mathematical proposition, but somewhere along the line, in the tunnel vision imposed by long shifts and relentless concentration, it became a test of myself, and clearly I have failed. Not only had I flamed out as a house-keeper/server, I had even forgotten to give George my tips, and, for reasons perhaps best known to hardworking, generous people like Gail and Ellen, this hurts. I don't cry, but I am in a position to realize, for the first time in many years, that the tear ducts are still there, and still capable of doing their job.

When I moved out of the trailer park, I gave the key to number 46 to Gail and arranged for my deposit to be transferred to her. She told me that Joan is still living in her van and that Stu had been fired from the Hearthside. I never found out what happened to George.

In one month, I had earned approximately $1,040 and spent $517 on food, gas, toiletries, laundry, phone, and utilities. If I had remained in my $500 efficiency, I would have been able to pay the rent and have $22 left over (which is $78 less than the cash I had in my pocket at the start of the month). During this time I bought no clothing except for the required slacks and no prescription drugs or medical care (I did finally buy some vitamin B to compensate for the lack of vegetables in my diet). Perhaps I could have saved a little on food if I had gotten to a supermarket more often, instead of convenience stores, but it should be noted that I lost almost four pounds in four weeks, on a diet weighted heavily toward burgers and fries.

How former welfare recipients and single mothers will (and do) survive in the low-wage workforce, I cannot imagine. Maybe they will figure out how to condense their lives—including child-raising, laundry, romance, and meals—into the couple of hours between full-time jobs. Maybe they will take up residence in their vehicles, if they have one. All I know is that I couldn't hold two jobs and I couldn't make enough money to live on with one. And I had advantages unthinkable to many of the long-term poor—health, stamina, a working car, and no children to care for and support. Certainly nothing in my experience contradicts the conclusion of Kathryn Edin and Laura Lein, in their recent book *Making Ends Meet: How Single Mothers Survive Welfare and Low-Wage Work*, that low-wage work actually involves more hardship and deprivation than life at the mercy of the welfare state. In the coming months and years, economic conditions for the working poor are bound to worsen, even without the almost inevitable recession. As mentioned earlier, the influx of former welfare recipients into the low-skilled workforce will have a depressing effect on both wages and the number of jobs available. A general economic downturn will only enhance these effects, and the working poor will of course be facing it without the slight, but nonetheless often saving, protection of welfare as a backup.

The thinking behind welfare reform was that even the humblest jobs are morally uplifting and psychologically buoying. In reality they are likely to be fraught with insult and stress. But I did discover one redeeming feature of the most abject low-wage work—the camaraderie of people who are, in almost all cases, far too smart and funny and caring for the work they do and the wages they're paid. The hope, of course, is that someday these people will come to know what they're worth, and take appropriate action.

25

Uses of the Underclass in America

HERBERT J. GANS

This essay is vintage sociology, taking what everyone thinks they know and turning it on its head. Gans shows how the lives and work of the so called "undeserving poor" benefit the non-poor in ways most Americans seldom recognize. "Poverty is good for you," is another way to express Gans's message, "as long as you are not among the poor." This essay also shows how functional analysis, often accused of being conservative, can be a critical perspective.

I. INTRODUCTION

Poverty, like any other social phenomenon, can be analyzed in terms of the *causes* which initiate and perpetuate it, but once it exists, it can also be studied in terms of the consequences or *functions* which follow. These functions can be both *positive* and *negative*, adaptive and destructive, depending on their nature and the people and interests affected.

Poverty has many negative functions (or dysfunctions), most for the poor themselves, but also for the nonpoor. Among those of most concern to both populations, perhaps the major one is that a small but visible proportion of poor people is involved in activities which threaten their physical safety, for example street crime, or which deviate from important norms claimed to be "mainstream," such as failing to work, bearing children in adolescence and out of wedlock, and being "dependent" on welfare. In times of high unemployment, illegal and even legal immigrants are added to this list for endangering the job opportunities of native-born Americans.

Furthermore, many better-off Americans believe that the number of poor people who behave in these ways is far larger than it actually is. More important, many think that poor people act as they do because of moral shortcomings that express themselves in lawlessness or in the rejection of mainstream norms. Like many other sociologists, however, I argue that the behavior patterns which concern the more fortunate classes are *poverty-related*, because they are, and have historically been, associated with poverty. * * * They are in fact caused by poverty, although a variety of other causes must also be at work since most poor people are not involved in any of these activities.

* * *

Because their criminal or disapproved behavior is ascribed to moral short-comings, the poor people who resort to it are often classified as unworthy or *undeserving.* For example, even though the failure of poor young men (or women) to work may be the effect of a lack of jobs, they are frequently accused of laziness, and then judged undeserving. Likewise, even though poor young mothers may decide not to marry the fathers of their children, because they, being jobless, cannot support them, the women are still accused of violating conventional familial norms, and also judged undeserving. Moreover, once judged to be undeserving, poor people are then no longer thought to be deserving of public aid that is financially sufficient and secure enough to help them escape poverty.

Judgments of the poor as undeserving are not based on evidence, but derive from a stereotype, even if, like most others, it is a stereotype with a "kernel of truth" (e.g., the monopolization of street crime by the poor). Furthermore, it is a very old stereotype; Cicero already described the needy of Rome as criminals. By the middle of the sixteenth century, complicated laws to distinguish between the deserving and undeserving were in existence. However, the term undeserving poor was first used regularly in England in the 1830s, at the time of the institution of the Poor Law.[1]

In America, a series of other, more specific, terms were borrowed or invented, with new ones replacing old ones as conditions and fashions changed. Such terms have included *beggar, pauper,* the *dangerous class, rabble, vagabond* and *vagrant,* and so on, which the United States borrowed from Europe. America also invented its own terms, including *shiftless, tramp,* and *feeble-minded,* and in the late twentieth century, terms like *hard-core, drifter, culturally deprived*—and most recently, *underclass.*[2] Nonetheless, in terms of its popular uses and the people to whom it is applied, the term underclass differs little from its predecessors.[3]

---

1. However, the *Oxford English Dictionary,* compiled by J. A. Simpson and E. S. Weiner (New York: Oxford University Press, 1989), 19: 996, already has a 1647 reference to beggars as undeserving, and the adjective itself was earlier used to refer to nonpoor people, for example, by Shakespeare.

2. These terms were often, but not exclusively, applied to the poor "races" who arrived in the nineteenth and early twentieth century from Ireland, Germany and later, Eastern and Southern Europe. They have also been applied, during and after slavery, to Blacks. Nonetheless, the functions to be discussed in this article are consequences of poverty, not of race, even though a disproportionate rate of those "selected" to be poor have always been darker-skinned than the more fortunate classes.

3. The popular definition of underclass must be distinguished from Gunnar Myrdal's initial scholarly one, which viewed the underclass as a stratum driven to the margins or out of the labor force by what are today called the postindustrial and global economies. Gunnar Myrdal, *Challenge to Affluence* (New York: Pantheon Books, 1963), 10 and passim. Myrdal's definition viewed the underclass as victims of economic change, and said nothing about its moral state.

It is not difficult to understand why people, poor and more fortunate, are fearful of street crime committed by poor people, and even why the jobless poor and welfare recipients, like paupers before them, may be perceived as economic threats for not working and drawing on public funds, at least in bad economic times. Also, one can understand why other forms of poverty-related behavior, such as the early sexual activity of poor youngsters and the dramatic number of poor single-parent families are viewed as moral threats, since they violate norms thought to uphold the two-parent nuclear family and related normative bases of the social order. However, there would seem to be no inherent reason for exaggerating these threats, for example, in the case of welfare recipients who obtain only a tiny proportion of governmental expenditures, or more generally, by stereotyping poor people as undeserving without evidence of what they have and have not done, and why.

One reason, if not the only one, for the exaggeration and the stereotyping, and for the continued attractiveness of the concept of the undeserving poor itself, is that undeservingness has a number of *positive* functions for the better-off population. Some of these functions, or uses, are positive for everyone who is not poor, but most are positive only for some people, interest groups, and institutions, ranging from moderate income to wealthy ones. Needless to say, that undeservingness has uses for some people does not justify it; the existence of functions just helps to explain why it persists.

My notion of function, or empirically observable adaptive consequence, is adapted from the classic conceptual scheme of Robert K. Merton. My analysis will concentrate on those positive functions which Merton conceptualized as *latent,* which are unrecognized and/or unintended, but with the proviso that the functions which are identified as latent would probably not be abolished once they were widely recognized. Positive functions are, after all, also benefits, and people are not necessarily ready to give up benefits, including unintended ones, even if they become aware of them.

* * *

II. FUNCTIONS OF THE UNDESERVING POOR[4]

I will discuss five sets of positive functions: microsocial, economic, normative-cultural, political, and macrosocial, which I divide into 13 specific functions, although the sets are arbitrarily chosen and interrelated, and I could add many more functions. The functions are not listed in order of importance, for such a listing is not possible without empirical research on the various beneficiaries of undeservingness.

---

4. For brevity's sake, I will hereafter refer to the undeserving poor instead of the poor-labeled undeserving, but I always mean the latter.

Two Microsocial Functions

1. *Risk reduction.* Perhaps the primary use of the idea of the undeserving poor, primary because it takes place at the microsocial scale of everyday life, is that it distances the labeled from those who label them. By stigmatizing people as undeserving, labelers protect themselves from the responsibility of having to associate with them, or even to treat them like moral equals, which reduces the risk of being hurt or angered by them. Risk reduction is a way of dealing with actual or imagined threats to physical safety, for example from people who might be muggers, or cultural threats attributed to poor youngsters or normative ones imagined to come from welfare recipients. All pejorative labels and stereotypes serve this function, which may help to explain why there are so many such labels.

2. *Scapegoating and displacement.* By being thought undeserving, the stigmatized poor can be blamed for virtually any shortcoming of everyday life which can be credibly ascribed to them—violations of the laws of logic or social causation notwithstanding. Faulting the undeserving poor can also support the desire for revenge and punishment. In a society in which punishment is reserved for legislative, judicial, and penal institutions, *feelings* of revenge and punitiveness toward the undeserving poor supply at least some emotional satisfaction.

Since labeling poor people undeserving opens the door for nearly unlimited scapegoating, the labeled are also available to serve what I call the displacement function. Being too weak to object, the stigmatized poor can be accused of having caused social problems which they did not actually cause and can serve as cathartic objects on which better-off people can unload their own problems, as well as those of the economy, the polity, or of any other institutions, for the shortcomings of which the poor can be blamed.

Whether societywide changes in the work ethic are displaced on to "shiftlessness," or economic stagnation on to "welfare dependency," the poor can be declared undeserving for what ails the more affluent. This may also help to explain why the national concern with poor Black unmarried mothers, although usually ascribed to the data presented in the 1965 Moynihan Report, did not gather steam until the beginning of the decline of the economy in the mid-1970s. Similarly, the furor about poor "babies having babies" waited for the awareness of rising adolescent sexual activity among the better-off classes in the 1980s— at which point rates of adolescent pregnancy among the poor had already declined. But when the country became ambivalent about the desirability of abortions, the issue was displaced on the poor by making it almost impossible for them to obtain abortions.

Many years ago, James Baldwin, writing in *The Fire Next Time,* illustrated the displacement function in racial terms, arguing that, as Andrew Hacker put it, Whites "need the 'nigger' because it is the 'nigger' within themselves that they cannot tolerate. Whatever it is that Whites feel 'nigger' signifies about Blacks—lust and laziness, stupidity or squalor, in fact exists within themselves.

* * * By creating such a creature, Whites are able to say that because only members of the Black race can carry that taint, it follows that none of its attributes will be found in White people.[5]

Three Economic Functions

3. *Economic banishment and the reserve army of labor.* People who have successfully been labeled as undeserving can be banished from the formal labor market. If young people are designated "school dropouts," for example; they can also be thought to lack the needed work habits, such as proper adherence to the work ethic, and may not be offered jobs to begin with. Often, they are effectively banished from the labor market before entering it because employers imagine them to be poor workers simply because they are young, male, and Black. Many ex-convicts are declared unemployable in similar fashion, and some become recidivists because they have no other choice but to go back to their criminal occupations.

Banishing the undeserving also makes room for immigrant workers, who may work for lower wages, are more deferential, and are more easily exploitable by being threatened with deportation. In addition, banishment helps to reduce the official jobless rate, a sometimes useful political function, especially if the banished drop so completely out of the labor force that they are not even available to be counted as "discouraged workers."

The economic banishment function is in many ways a replacement for the old reserve army of labor function, which played itself out when the undeserving poor could be hired as strikebreakers, as defense workers in the case of sudden wartime economic mobilization, as "hypothetical workers," who by their very presence could be used to depress the wages of other workers, or to put pressure on the unions not to make wage and other demands. Today, however, with a plentiful supply of immigrants, as well as of a constantly growing number of banished workers who are becoming surplus labor, a reserve army is less rarely needed—and when needed, can be recruited from sources other than the undeserving poor.

* * *

4. *Supplying illegal goods.* The undeserving poor who are banished from other jobs remain eligible for work in the manufacture and sale of illegal goods, including drugs. Although it is estimated that 80 percent of all illegal drugs are sold to Whites who are not poor, the sellers are often people banished from the formal labor market. Other suppliers of illegal goods include the illegal immigrants, considered undeserving in many American communities, who work for garment industry sweatshops manufacturing clothing under illegal conditions.

---

5. Hacker is paraphrasing Baldwin. Andrew Hacker, *Two Nations: Black and White, Separate, Hostile, Unequal* (New York: Scribner, 1992), 61.

5. *Job creation.* Perhaps the most important economic function of the undeserving poor today is that their mere presence creates jobs for the better-off population, including professional ones. Since the undeserving poor are thought to be dangerous or improperly socialized, their behavior either has to be modified so that they act in socially approved ways, or they have to be isolated from the deserving sectors of society. The larger the number of people who are declared undeserving, the larger also the number of people needed to modify and isolate as well as control, guard, and care for them. Among these are the social workers, teachers, trainers, mentors, psychiatrists, doctors and their support staffs in juvenile training centers, "special" schools, drug treatment centers, and penal behavior modification institutions, as well as the police, prosecutors, defense attorneys, judges, court officers, probation personnel and others who constitute the criminal courts, and the guards and others who run the prisons.

Jobs created by the presence of undeserving poor also include the massive bureaucracy of professionals, investigators, and clerks who administer welfare. Other jobs go to the officials who seek out poor fathers for child support monies they may or may not have, as well as the welfare office personnel needed to take recipients in violation of welfare rules off the rolls, and those needed to put them back on the rolls when they reapply. In fact, one can argue that some of the rules for supervising, controlling, and punishing the undeserving poor are more effective at performing the latent function of creating clerical and professional jobs for the better-off population than the manifest function of achieving their official goals.

More jobs are created in the social sciences and in journalism for conducting research about the undeserving poor and producing popular books, articles, and TV documentaries for the more fortunate who want to learn about them. The "job chain" should also be extended to the teachers and others who train those who serve, control, and study the undeserving poor.

In addition, the undeserving poor make jobs for what I call the salvation industries, religious, civil, or medical, which also try to modify the behavior of those stigmatized as undeserving. Not all such jobs are paid, for the undeserving poor also provide occasional targets for charity and thus offer volunteer jobs for those providing it—and paid jobs for the professional fundraisers who obtain most of the charitable funds these days. Among the most visible volunteers are the members of "café" and "high" society who organize and contribute to these benefits.

Three Normative Functions

6. *Moral legitimation.* Undeservingness justifies the category of deservingness and thus supplies moral and political legitimacy, almost by definition, to the institutions and social structures that include the deserving and exclude the undeserving. Of these structures, the most important is undoubtedly the class hierarchy, for the existence of an undeserving class or stratum legitimates the

deserving classes, if not necessarily all of their class-related behavior. The alleged immorality of the undeserving also gives a moral flavor to, and justification for, the class hierarchy, which may help to explain why upward mobility itself is so praiseworthy.

7. *Norm reinforcement*. By violating, or being imagined as violating, a number of mainstream behavioral patterns and values, the undeserving poor help to reaffirm and reinforce the virtues of these patterns—and to do so visibly, since the violations by the undeserving are highly publicized. As Emile Durkheim pointed out nearly a century ago, norm violations and their punishments also provide an opportunity for preserving and reaffirming the norms. This is not insignificant, for norms sometimes disparaged as "motherhood" values gain new moral power when they are violated, and their violators are stigmatized.

If the undeserving poor can be imagined to be lazy, they help to reaffirm the Protestant work ethic; if poor single-parent families are publicly condemned, the two-parent family is once more legitimated as ideal. In the 1960s, middle-class morality was sometimes criticized as culturally parochial and therefore inappropriate for the poor, but since the 1980s, mainstream values have once more been regarded as vital sources of behavioral guidance for them.

Enforcing the norms also contributes further to preserving them in another way, for one of the standard punishments of the undeserving poor for misbehaving—as well as standard obligation in exchange for help—is practicing the mainstream norms, including those that the members of the mainstream may only be preaching, and that might die out if the poor were not required to incorporate them in their behavior. Old work rules that can no longer be enforced in the rest of the economy can be maintained in the regulations for workfare; old-fashioned austerity and thrift are built into the consumption patterns expected of welfare recipients. Economists like to argue that if the poor want to be deserving, they should take any kind of job, regardless of its low pay or demeaning character, reflecting a work ethic which economists themselves have never practiced.

Similarly, welfare recipients may be removed from the rolls if they are found to be living with a man—but the social worker who removes them has every right to cohabit and not lose his or her job. In most states, welfare recipients must observe rules of housecleaning and child care that middle-class people are free to ignore without being punished. While there are many norms and laws governing child care, only the poor are monitored to see if they obey these. Should they use more physical punishment on their children than social workers consider desirable, they can be charged with child neglect or abuse and can lose their children to foster care.[6]

---

6. Poor immigrants who still practice old-country discipline norms are particularly vulnerable to being accused of child abuse.

The fact is that the defenders of such widely preached norms as hard work, thrift, monogamy, and moderation need people who can be accused, accurately or not, of being lazy, spendthrift, promiscuous, and immoderate. One reason that welfare recipients are a ready target for punitive legislation is that politicians, and most likely some of their constituents, imagine them to be enjoying leisure and an active sex life at public expense. Whether or not very many poor people actually behave in the ways that are judged undeserving is irrelevant if they can be imagined as doing so. Once imagining and stereotyping are allowed to take over, then judgments of undeservingness can be made without much concern for empirical accuracy. For example, in the 1990s, the idea that young men from poor single-parent families were highly likely to commit street crimes became so universal that the news media no longer needed to quote experts to affirm the accuracy of the charge.

Actually, most of the time most of the poor are as law abiding and observant of mainstream norms as are other Americans. Sometimes they are even more observant; thus the proportion of welfare recipients who cheat is always far below the percentage of taxpayers who do so. Moreover, survey after survey has shown that the poor, including many street criminals and drug sellers, want to hold respectable jobs like everyone else, hope someday to live in the suburbs, and generally aspire to the same American dream as most moderate and middle-income Americans.[7]

8. *Supplying popular culture villains.* The undeserving poor have played a long-term role in supplying American popular culture with villains, allowing the producers of the culture both to reinforce further mainstream norms and to satisfy audience demands for revenge, notably by showing that crime and other norm violations do not pay. Street criminals are shown dead or alive in the hands of the police on local television news virtually every day, and more dramatically so in the crime and action movies and television series.

For many years before and after World War II, the criminal characters in Hollywood movies were often poor immigrants, frequently of Sicilian origin. Then they were complemented for some decades by communist spies and other Cold War enemies who were not poor, but even before the end of the Cold War, they were being replaced by Black and Hispanic drug dealers and gang leaders.

At the same time, however, the popular culture industry has also supplied music and other materials offering marketable cultural and political protest which does not reinforce mainstream norms, or at least not directly. Some of the creators and performers come from poor neighborhoods, however, and it may be that some rap music becomes commercially successful by displacing on ghetto musicians the cultural and political protest of record buyers from more affluent classes.

---

7. See Mark R. Rank, *Living on the Edge: The Realities of Welfare in America* (New York: Columbia University Press, 1994), 93.

Three Political Functions

9. *Institutional scapegoating.* The scapegoating of the undeserving poor mentioned in Function 2 above also extends to institutions which mistreat them. As a result, some of the responsibility for the existence of poverty, slums, unemployment, poor schools, and the like is taken off the shoulders of elected and appointed officials who are supposed to deal with these problems. For example, to the extent that educational experts decide that the children of the poor are learning disabled or that they are culturally or genetically inferior in intelligence, attempts to improve the schools can be put off or watered down.

To put it another way, the availability of institutional scapegoats both personalizes and exonerates social systems. The alleged laziness of the jobless and the anger aimed at beggars take the heat off the failure of the economy, and the imagined derelictions of slum dwellers and the homeless, off the housing industry. In effect, the undeserving poor are blamed both for their poverty and also for the absence of "political will" among the citizenry to do anything about it.

10. *Conservative power shifting.* Once poor people are declared undeserving, they also lose their political legitimacy and whatever little political influence they had before they were stigmatized. Some cannot vote, and many do not choose to vote or mobilize because they know politicians do not listen to their demands. Elected officials might ignore them even if they voted or mobilized, because these officials and the larger polity cannot easily satisfy their demands for economic and other kinds of justice.[8] As a result, the political system is able to pay additional attention to the demands of more affluent constituents. It can therefore shift to the "right."

The same shift to the right also takes place ideologically. Although injustices of poverty help justify the existence of liberals and the more radical left, the undeserving poor themselves provide justification and opportunities for conservatives to attack their ideological enemies on their left. When liberals can be accused of favoring criminals over victims, their accusers can launch and legitimate incursions on the civil liberties and rights of the undeserving poor, and concurrently on the liberties and rights of defenders of the poor. Moreover, the undeservingness of the poor can be used to justify attacks on the welfare state. Charles Murray understood the essence of this ideological function when he argued that welfare and other welfare state legislation for the poor only increased the number of poor people.[9]

---

8. In addition, the undeserving poor make a dangerous constituency. Politicians who say kind words about them or who act to represent their interests are likely to be attacked for their words and actions. Jesse Jackson was hardly the first national politician to be criticized for being too favorable to the poor.

9. Charles Murray, *Losing Ground: American Social Policy, 1950–1980* (New York: Basic Books, 1984).

11. *Spatial purification.* Stigmatized populations are often used, deliberately or not, to stigmatize the areas in which they live, making such areas eligible for various kinds of purification. As a result, "underclass areas" can be torn down and their inhabitants moved to make room for more affluent residents or higher taxpayers.

However, such areas can also be used to isolate stigmatized poor people and facilities by selecting them as locations for homeless shelters, halfway houses for the mentally ill or for ex-convicts, drug treatment facilities, and even garbage dumps, which have been forced out of middle- and working-class areas following NIMBY (not in my backyard) protests. Drug dealers and other sellers of illegal goods also find a haven in areas stigmatized as underclass areas, partly because these supply some customers, but also because police protection in such areas is usually minimal enough to allow illegal activities without significant interference from the law. In fact, municipalities would face major economic and political obstacles to their operations without stigmatized areas in which stigmatized people and activities can be located.

Two Macrosocial Functions

12. *Reproduction of stigma and the stigmatized.* For centuries now, undeservingness has given rise to policies and agencies which are manifestly set up to help the poor economically and otherwise to become deserving, but which actually prevent the undeserving poor from being freed of their stigma, and which also manage, unwittingly, to see to it that their children face the same obstacles. In some instances, this process works so speedily that the children of the stigmatized face "anticipatory stigmatization," among them the children of welfare recipients who are frequently predicted to be unable to learn, to work, and to remain on the right side of the law even before they have been weaned.

If this outcome were planned deliberately, one could argue that politically and culturally dominant groups are reluctant to give up an easily accessible and always available scapegoat. In actuality, however, the reproduction function results unwittingly from other intended and seemingly popular practices. For example, the so-called War on Drugs, which has unsuccessfully sought to keep hard drugs out of the United States, but has meanwhile done little to provide drug treatment to addicts who want it, thereby aids the continuation of addiction, street crime, and a guaranteed prison population, not to mention the various disasters that visit the families of addicts and help to keep them poor.

The other major source of reproducing stigma and the stigmatized is the routine activities of the organizations which service welfare recipients, the homeless, and other stigmatized poor, and end up mistreating them. For one thing, such agencies, whether they exist to supply employment to the poor or to help the homeless, are almost certain to be underfunded because of the powerlessness of their clientele. No organization has ever had the funds or power to buy, build, or rehabilitate housing for the homeless in sufficient number. Typically, they have been able to fund or carry out small demonstration projects.

In addition, organizations which serve stigmatized people often attract less well-trained and qualified staff than those with high-status clients, and if the clients are deemed undeserving, competence may become even less important in choosing staff. Then too, helping organizations generally reflect the societal stratification hierarchy, which means that organizations with poor, low-status clients frequently treat them as undeserving. If they also fear some of their clients, they may not only withhold help, but attack the clients on a preemptive strike basis. Last but not least, the agencies that serve the undeserving poor are bureaucracies which operate by rules and regulations that routinize the work, encourage the stability and growth of the organizations, and serve the needs of their staffs before those of their clients.

When these factors are combined, as they often are, and become cumulative, as they often do, it should not be surprising that the organizations cut off escape routes from poverty not only for the clients, but in doing so, also make sure that some of their children remain poor as well.

13. *Extermination of the surplus.* In earlier times, when the living standards of all poor people were at or below subsistence, many died at an earlier age than the better off, thus performing the set of functions for the latter forever associated with Thomas Malthus. Standards of living, even for the very poor, have risen considerably in the last century, but even today, morbidity and mortality rates remain much higher among the poor than among moderate-income people. To put it another way, various social forces combine to do away with some of the people who have become surplus labor and are no longer needed by the economy.

Several of the killing illnesses and pathologies of the poor change over time; currently, they include AIDS, tuberculosis, hypertension, heart attacks, and cancer, as well as psychosis, substance abuse, street crime, injury and death during participation in the drug trade and other underworld activities, and intraclass homicide resulting from neighborhood conflicts over turf and "respect." Whether the poor people whose only problem is being unfairly stereotyped and stigmatized as undeserving die earlier than other poor people is not known.

Moreover, these rates can be expected to remain high or even to rise as rates of unemployment—and of banishment from the labor force—rise, especially for the least skilled. Even the better-off jobless created by the downsizing of the 1990s blame themselves for their unemployment if they cannot eventually find new jobs, become depressed, and in some instances begin the same process of being extruded permanently from the labor market experienced by the least skilled of the jobless.

* * *

The early departure of poor people from an economy and society which do not need them is useful for those who remain. Since the more fortunate classes have already developed a purposive blindness to the structural causes of unemployment and to the poverty-related causes of pathology and crime that follow, those who benefit from the current job erosion and the possible extermination of the surplus labor may not admit it consciously either. Nonetheless, those left over to compete for scarce jobs and other resources will have a somewhat easier time in the competition, thus assigning undeservingness a final positive function for the more fortunate members of society.

III. CONCLUSION

I have described thirteen of the more important functions of the undeserving poor, enough to support my argument that both the idea of the undeserving poor and the stigmas with which some poor people are thus labeled may persist in part because they are useful in a variety of ways to the people who are not poor.

This analysis does not imply that undeservingness will or should persist. Whether it *will* persist is going to be determined by what happens to poverty in America. If it declines, poverty-related crime should also decline, and then fewer poor people will probably be described as undeserving. If poverty worsens, so will poverty-related crime, as well as the stereotyping and stigmatization of the poor, and any worsening of the country's economy is likely to add to the kinds and numbers of undeserving poor, if only because they make convenient and powerless scapegoats.

The functions that the undeserving poor play cannot, by themselves, perpetuate either poverty or undeservingness, for as I noted earlier, functions are not causes. For example, if huge numbers of additional unskilled workers should be needed, as they were for the World War II war effort, the undeserving poor will be welcomed back into the labor force, at least temporarily. Of course, institutions often try to survive once they have lost both their reasons for existence and their functions. Since the end of the Cold War, parts of the military-industrial establishment both in the United States and Russia have been campaigning for the maintenance of some Cold War forces and weapons to guarantee their own futures, but these establishments also supply jobs to their national economies, and in the United States, for the constituents of elected officials. Likewise, some of the institutions and interest groups that benefit from the existence of undeservingness, or from controlling the undeserving poor, may try to maintain undeservingness and its stigma. They may not even need to, for if Emile Durkheim was right, the decline of undeservingness would lead to the criminalization, or at least stigmatization, of new behavior patterns.

Whether applying the label of undeservingness to the poor *should* persist is a normative question which ought to be answered in the negative. Although people have a right to judge each other, that right does not extend to judging large numbers of people as a single group, with one common moral fault, or to stereotyping them without evidence either about their behavior or their values. Even if a case could be made for judging large cohorts of people as undeserving, these judgments should be distributed up and down the socio-economic hierarchy, requiring Americans also to consider whether and how people in the working, middle, and upper classes are undeserving.

The same equality should extend to the punishment of crimes. Today, many Americans and courts still treat white-collar and upper-class criminals more leniently than poor ones. The public excuse given is that the street crime of the undeserving poor involves violence and thus injury or death, but as many students of white-collar and corporate crime have pointed out, these also hurt and kill people, and often in larger numbers, even if they do so less directly and perhaps less violently.

Changes also need to be made in the American conception of deviance, which like that of other countries, conflates people whose behavior is *different* with those whose behavior is socially *harmful.* Bearing children without marriage is a long-standing tradition among the poor. Born of necessity rather than preference, it is a poverty-related practice, but it is not, by itself, harmful, or at least not until it can be shown that either the children—or the moral sensibilities of the people who oppose illegitimacy—are significantly hurt. Poor single-parent families are hardly desirable, but as the lack of condemnation of more affluent single-parent families should suggest, the major problem of such families is not the number of parents, actual or surrogate, in the family, but its poverty.

Finally, because many of the poor are stereotyped unjustly as undeserving, scholars, writers, journalists, and others should launch a systematic and public effort to deconstruct and delegitimate the notion of the undeserving poor. This effort, which is necessary to help make effective antipoverty programs politically acceptable again, should place the following five ideas on the public agenda and encourage discussion as well as dissemination of available research.

The five ideas, all discussed earlier in this article, are that (1) the criminal and deviant behavior among the poor is largely poverty related rather than the product of free choice based on distinctive values; (2) the undeservingness of the poor is an ancient stereotype, and like all stereotypes, it vastly exaggerates the actual dangers that stem from the poor; (3) poverty-related deviance is not necessarily harmful just because it does not accord with mainstream norms; (4) the notion of undeservingness survives in part because of the positive functions it has for the better-off population; and (5) the only certain way to eliminate both this notion and the functions is to eliminate poverty.[10]

---

10. A fuller discussion of policy proposals * * * appear[s] in my * * * book, *Ending the War against the Poor.*

26

FROM *When Work Disappears:*
The World of the New Urban Poor

WILLIAM JULIUS WILSON

For individuals who want and need to work for a living, being unemployed is a devastating experience. In modern society nearly all valuable things come through work: income, social status, friendships, and a sense of identity and importance. But millions are unemployed, and many of the places where people live—especially the chronically poor—are (dis)organized in ways that make steady, gainful employment extremely difficult or, for some, impossible. In this section of his book, the author explores the historical emergence of urban ghettos as sites that structure chronic urban unemployment and its attendant social problems.

Since the early twentieth century, Chicago has been a laboratory for the scientific investigation of the social, economic, and historical forces that create and perpetuate economically depressed and isolated urban communities. The most distinctive phase of this research, referred to as the Chicago School of urban sociology, was completed before 1950 and was conducted by social scientists at the University of Chicago. Immediately following World War I, the Chicago School produced several classic studies, many of which were conducted under the guidance of Robert E. Park and Ernest W. Burgess over the next three decades. These studies often combined statistical and observational analyses in making distinctive empirical and theoretical contributions to our understanding of urban processes, social problems and urban growth, and, commencing in the late 1930s, the nature of race and class subjugation in urban areas.

The Chicago social scientists recognized and legitimized the neighborhood—including the ghetto neighborhood—as a subject for scientific analysis. Chicago, a community of neighborhoods, was considered a laboratory from which generalizations about broader urban conditions could be made.

The perspectives on urban processes that guided the Chicago School's approach to the study of race and class have undergone subtle changes through the years. In the 1920s, Park and Burgess argued that the immigrant slums, and the social problems that characterized them, were temporary conditions on the pathway toward inevitable progress. They further maintained that blacks represented the latest group of migrants involved in the "interaction cycle" that "led from conflict to accommodation to assimilation."

The view that blacks fit the pattern of immigrant assimilation appeared in subsequent studies by E. Franklin Frazier in the 1930s. But Frazier, an African-American sociologist trained at the University of Chicago, also recognized and emphasized a problem ignored in the earlier work of Park and Burgess—the important link between the black family structure and the industrial economy. Frazier believed that the availability of employment opportunities in the industrial sector would largely determine the upward mobility of African-Americans and their eventual assimilation into American life.

In 1945, a fundamental revision in the Chicago framework came with the publication of St. Clair Drake and Horace Cayton's classic study, *Black Metropolis*. Drake and Cayton first examined black progress in employment, housing, and social integration using census, survey, and archival data. Their analysis clearly revealed the existence of a color line that effectively blocked black occupational, residential, and social mobility. They demonstrated that any assumption about urban blacks duplicating the immigrant experience had to confront the issue of race. Moreover, as the historian Alice O'Connor puts it, "Drake and Cayton recognized that the racial configuration of Chicago was not the expression of an organic process of city growth, but the product of human behavior, institutional practices and political decisions."

Black Metropolis also deviated from the earlier Chicago School studies in its inclusion of an ethnographic study. Using W. Lloyd Warner's anthropological techniques, Drake and Cayton studied patterns of daily life in three of Chicago's South Side community areas (Washington Park, Grand Boulevard, and Douglas). They labeled these three areas "Bronzeville," a term that was used by the local residents themselves to describe their community. Combining data based on the Chicago School-style research and anthropological methods, *Black Metropolis* presented a much less encouraging view of the prospects for black progress.

In the revised and enlarged edition of *Black Metropolis* published in 1962, Drake and Cayton examined the changes that had occurred in Bronzeville since the publication of the first edition with a sense of optimism. They felt that America in the 1960s was "experiencing a period of prosperity" and that African-Americans were "living in the era of integration." Of course, they had no way of anticipating the rapid social and economic deterioration of communities like Bronzeville that would begin in the next decade.

The most fundamental difference between today's inner-city neighborhoods and those studied by Drake and Cayton is the much higher levels of joblessness. Indeed, there is a new poverty in our nation's metropolises that has consequences for a range of issues relating to the quality of life in urban areas, including race relations.

* * *

Upon the publication of the first edition of *Black Metropolis* in 1945, there was much greater class integration within the black community. As Drake and Cayton pointed out, Bronzeville residents had limited success in "sorting them-selves out into broad community areas designated as 'lower class' and 'middle class.'. . . Instead of middle-class *areas,* Bronzeville tends to have middle-class *buildings* in all areas, or a few middle-class blocks here and there." Though they may have lived on different streets, blacks of all classes in inner-city areas such as Bronzeville lived in the same community and shopped at the same stores. Their children went to the same schools and played in the same parks. Although there was some class antagonism, their neighborhoods were more stable than the inner-city neighborhoods of today; in short, they featured higher levels of what social scientists call "social organization."

When I speak of social organization I am referring to the extent to which the residents of a neighborhood are able to maintain effective social control and realize their common goals. There are three major dimensions of neighborhood social organization: (1) the prevalence, strength, and interdependence of social networks; (2) the extent of collective supervision that the residents exercise and the degree of personal responsibility they assume in addressing neighbor-hood problems; and (3) the rate of resident participation in voluntary and formal organizations. Formal institutions (e.g., churches and political party organiza-tions), voluntary associations (e.g., block clubs and parent-teacher organiza-tions), and informal networks (e.g., neighborhood friends and acquaintances, coworkers, marital and parental ties) all reflect social organization.

Neighborhood social organization depends on the extent of local friend-ship ties, the degree of social cohesion, the level of resident participation in for-mal and informal voluntary associations, the density and stability of formal organizations, and the nature of informal social controls. Neighborhoods in which adults are able to interact in terms of obligations, expectations, and relationships are in a better position to supervise and control the activities and behavior of children. In neighborhoods with high levels of social organization, adults are empowered to act to improve the quality of neighborhood life—for example, by breaking up congregations of youths on street corners and by supervising the leisure activities of youngsters.

Neighborhoods plagued by high levels of joblessness are more likely to experience low levels of social organization: the two go hand in hand. High rates of joblessness trigger other neighborhood problems that undermine social organization, ranging from crime, gang violence, and drug trafficking to family breakups and problems in the organization of family life.

* * *

The rise of new poverty neighborhoods represents a movement away from what the historian Allan Spear has called an institutional ghetto—whose structure and activities parallel those of the larger society, as portrayed in Drake and Cayton's description of Bronzeville—toward a jobless ghetto, which features a severe lack of basic opportunities and resources, and inadequate social controls.

What can account for the growing proportion of jobless adults and the corresponding increase in problems of social organization in inner-city communities such as Bronzeville? An easy answer is racial segregation. However, a race-specific argument is not sufficient to explain recent changes in neighborhoods like Bronzeville. After all, Bronzeville was *just as segregated by skin color in 1950* as it is today, yet the level of employment was much higher then.

Nonetheless, racial segregation does matter. If large segments of the African-American population had not been historically segregated in inner-city ghettos, we would not be talking about the new urban poverty. The segregated ghetto is not the result of voluntary or positive decisions on the part of the residents who live there. As Massey and Denton have carefully documented, the segregated ghetto is the product of systematic racial practices such as restrictive covenants, redlining by banks and insurance companies, zoning, panic peddling by real estate agents, and the creation of massive public housing projects in low-income areas.

Segregated ghettos are less conducive to employment and employment preparation than are other areas of the city. Segregation in ghettos exacerbates employment problems because it leads to weak informal employment networks and contributes to the social isolation of individuals and families, thereby reducing their chances of acquiring the human capital skills, including adequate educational training, that facilitate mobility in a society. Since no other group in society experiences the degree of segregation, isolation, and poverty concentration as do African-Americans, they are far more likely to be disadvantaged when they have to compete with other groups in society, including other despised groups, for resources and privileges.

To understand the new urban poverty, one has to account for the ways in which segregation interacts with other changes in society to produce the recent escalating rates of joblessness and problems of social organization in inner-city ghetto neighborhoods.

* * *

Although changes in the economy (industrial restructuring and reorganization) and changes in the class, racial, and demographic composition of inner-city ghetto neighborhoods are important factors in the shift from institutional to jobless ghettos since 1970, we ought not to lose sight of the fact that this process actually began immediately following World War II.

The federal government contributed to the early decay of inner-city neighborhoods by withholding mortgage capital and by making it difficult for urban areas to retain or attract families able to purchase their own homes. Spurred on by massive mortgage foreclosures during the Great Depression, the federal government in the 1940s began underwriting mortgages in an effort to enable citizens to become homeowners. But the mortgage program was selectively administered by the Federal Housing Administration (FHA), and urban neighborhoods considered poor risks were redlined—an action that excluded virtually all the black neighborhoods and many neighborhoods with a considerable number of European immigrants. It was not until the 1960s that the FHA discontinued its racial restrictions on mortgages.

By manipulating market incentives, the federal government drew middle-class whites to the suburbs and, in effect, trapped blacks in the inner cities. Beginning in the 1950s, the suburbanization of the middle-class was also facilitated by a federal transportation and highway policy, including the building of freeway networks through the hearts of many cities, mortgages for veterans, mortgage-interest tax exemptions, and the quick, cheap production of massive amounts of tract housing.

In the nineteenth and early twentieth centuries, with the offer of municipal services as an inducement, cities tended to annex their suburbs. But the relations between cities and suburbs in the United States began to change following a century-long influx of poor migrants who required expensive services and paid relatively little in taxes. Annexation largely ended in the mid-twentieth century as suburbs began to resist incorporation successfully. Suburban communities also drew tighter boundaries through the manipulation of zoning laws and discriminatory land-use controls and site-selection practices, making it difficult for inner-city racial minorities to penetrate.

As separate political jurisdictions, suburbs exercised a great deal of autonomy in their use of zoning, land-use policies, covenants, and deed restrictions. In the face of mounting pressures calling for integration in the 1960s, "suburbs chose to diversify by race rather than class. They retained zoning and other restrictions that allowed only affluent blacks (and in some instances Jews) to enter, thereby intensifying the concentration and isolation of the urban poor."*

* * *

The disappearance of work in many inner-city neighborhoods is partly related to the nationwide decline in the fortunes of low-skilled workers. Although the growing wage inequality has hurt both low-skilled men and women, the problem of declining employment has been concentrated among low-skilled men. In 1987–89, a low-skilled male worker was jobless eight and a half weeks longer than he would have been in 1967–69. Moreover, the proportion of men who "permanently" dropped out of the labor force was more than twice as high in the late 1980s than it had been in the late 1960s. A precipitous drop in real wages—that is, wages adjusted for inflation—has accompanied the increases in joblessness among low-income workers. If you arrange all wages into five groups according to wage percentile (from highest to lowest), you see that men in the bottom fifth of this income distribution experienced more than a 30 percent drop in real wages between 1970 and 1989.

---

*Center for Budget and Policy Priorities (1995). "Is the EITC Growing at a Rate That Is 'Out of Control'?" Washington, DC. May 9: 1.

Even the low-skilled workers who are consistently employed face problems of economic advancement. Job ladders—opportunities for promotion within firms—have eroded, and many less-skilled workers stagnate in dead-end, low-paying positions. This suggests that the chances of improving one's earnings by changing jobs have declined: if jobs inside a firm have become less available to the experienced workers in that firm, they are probably even more difficult for outsiders to obtain.

* * *

Finally, policymakers indirectly contributed to the emergence of jobless ghettos by making decisions that have decreased the attractiveness of low-paying jobs and accelerated the relative decline in wages for low-income workers. In particular, in the absence of an effective labor-market policy, they have tolerated industry practices that undermine worker security, such as the reduction in benefits and the rise of involuntary part-time employment, and they have "allowed the minimum wage to erode to its second-lowest level in purchasing power in 40 years." After adjusting for inflation, "the minimum wage is 26 percent below its average level in the 1970s."[†] Moreover, they virtually eliminated AFDC benefits for families in which a mother is employed at least half-time. In the early 1970s, a working mother with two children whose wages equaled 75 percent of the amount designated as the poverty line could receive AFDC benefits as a wage supplement in forty-nine states; in 1995 only those in three states could. [E]ven with the expansion of the earned income tax credit (a wage subsidy for the working poor) such policies make it difficult for poor workers to support their families and protect their children.

[†]Center for Budget and Policy Priorities (1995). "The Earned Income Tax Credit Reductions in the Senate Budget Resolution." Washington, DC. June 5: 3.

27

FROM *Maid in the USA*

MARY ROMERO

The opposite of "celebrity" is probably the invisible worker, the person who labors in a space others have left (e.g., in another's home during the day) or at night, or alone. This person's work holds no glamour. It also describes housework, whether done for a wage or within one's own household. Mary Romero examines the gender, class, and ethnic divides that exist in the invisible work of domestics. Her essay explores the "dual shift" performed by most women who work outside the home yet are responsible for the lion's share of housework. Like Greta Foff Paule (Reading 20), Romero recognizes the way people acquire a measure of control in their lives despite working in a situation where they appear utterly powerless.

A PERSONAL NARRATIVE ON THE DEVELOPMENT OF THE RESEARCH PROBLEM

When I was growing up many of the women whom I knew worked cleaning other people's houses. Domestic service was part of my taken-for-granted reality. Later, when I had my own place, I considered housework something you did before company came over. My first thought that domestic service and housework might be a serious research interest came as a result of a chance encounter with live-in domestics along the U.S.-Mexican border. Before beginning a teaching position at the University of Texas in El Paso, I stayed with a colleague while apartment hunting. My colleague had a live-in domestic to assist with housecleaning and cooking. Asking around, I learned that live-in maids were common in El Paso, even among apartment and condominium dwellers. The hiring of maids from Mexico was so common that locals referred to Monday as the border patrol's day off because the agents ignored the women crossing the border to return to their employers' homes after their weekend off. The practice of hiring undocumented Mexican women as domestics, many of whom were no older than fifteen, seemed strange to me. It was this strangeness that raised the topic of domestic service as a question and made problematic what had previously been taken for granted.

I must admit that I was shocked at my colleague's treatment of the sixteen-year-old domestic whom I will call Juanita. Only recently hired, Juanita was still adjusting to her new environment. She was extremely shy, and her timidity was made even worse by constant flirting from her employer. As far as I could see, every attempt Juanita made to converse was met with teasing so that the conversation could never evolve into a serious discussion. Her employer's sexist, paternalistic banter effectively silenced the domestic, kept her constantly on guard, and made it impossible for her to feel comfortable at work. For instance, when she informed the employer of a leaky faucet, he shot her a look of disdain, making it clear that she was overstepping her boundaries. I observed other encounters that clearly served to remind Juanita of her subservient place in her employer's home.

Although Juanita was of the same age as my colleague's oldest daughter and but a few years older than his two sons, she was treated differently from the other teenagers in the house. She was expected to share her bedroom with the ironing board, sewing machine, and other spare-room types of objects. More importantly, she was assumed to have different wants and needs. I witnessed the following revealing exchange. Juanita was poor. She had not brought toiletries with her from Mexico. Since she had not yet been paid, she had to depend on her employer for necessities. Yet instead of offering her a small advance in her pay so she could purchase the items herself and giving her a ride to the nearby supermarket to select her own toiletries, the employer handled Juanita's request for toothbrush, toothpaste, shampoo, soap, and the like in the following manner. In the presence of all the family and the house guest, he made a list of the things she needed. Much teasing and joking accompanied the encounter. The employer shopped for her and purchased only generic brand items, which were a far cry from the brand-name products that filled the bathroom of his sixteen-year-old daughter. Juanita looked at the toothpaste, shampoo, and soap with confusion; she may never have seen generic products before, but she obviously knew that a distinction had been made.

One evening I walked into the kitchen as the employer's young sons were shouting orders at Juanita. They pointed to the dirty dishes on the table and pans in the sink and yelled "WASH!" "CLEAN!" Juanita stood frozen next to the kitchen door, angry and humiliated. Aware of possible repercussions for Juanita if I reprimanded my colleague's sons, I responded awkwardly by reallocating chores to everyone present. I announced that I would wash the dishes and the boys would clear the table. Juanita washed and dried dishes alongside me, and together we finished cleaning the kitchen. My colleague returned from his meeting to find us in the kitchen washing the last pan. The look on his face was more than enough to tell me that he was shocked to find his houseguest—and future colleague—washing dishes with the maid. His embarrassment at my behavior confirmed my suspicion that I had violated the normative expectations of class behavior within the home. He attempted to break the tension with a flirtatious and sexist remark to Juanita which served to excuse her from the kitchen and from any further discussion.

The conversation that followed revealed how my colleague chose to interpret my behavior. Immediately after Juanita's departure from the kitchen, he initiated a discussion about "Chicano radicals" and the Chicano movement.

Although he was a foreign-born Latino, he expressed sympathy for *la causa*. Recalling the one Chicano graduate student he had known to obtain a Ph.D. in sociology, he gave several accounts of how the student's political behavior had disrupted the normal flow of university activity. Lowering his voice to a confidential whisper, he confessed to understanding why Marxist theory has become so popular among Chicano students. The tone of his comments and the examples that he chose made me realize that my "outrageous" behavior was explained, and thus excused, on the basis of my being one of those "Chicano radicals." He interpreted my washing dishes with his maid as a symbolic act; that is, I was affiliated with *los de abajo*.

My behavior had been comfortably defined without addressing the specific issue of maids. My colleague then further subsumed the topic under the rubric of "the servant problem" along the border. (His reaction was not unlike the attitude employers have displayed toward domestic service in the United States for the last hundred years.) He began by providing me with chapter and verse about how he had aided Mexican women from Juarez by helping them cross the border and employing them in his home. He took further credit for introducing them to the appliances found in an American middle class home. He shared several funny accounts about teaching country women from Mexico to use the vacuum cleaner, electric mixer, and microwave (remember the maid scene in the movie *El Norte*?) and implicitly blamed them for their inability to work comfortably around modern conveniences. For this "on-the-job training" and introduction to American culture, he complained, his generosity and goodwill had been rewarded by a high turnover rate. As his account continued, he assured me that most maids were simply working until they found a husband. In his experience they worked for a few months or less and then did not return to work on Monday morning after their first weekend off. Of course it never dawned on him that they may simply have found a job with better working conditions.

The following day, Juanita and I were alone in the house. As I mustered up my best Spanish, we shared information about our homes and families. After a few minutes of laughter about my simple sentence structure, Juanita lowered her head and in a sad, quiet voice told me how isolated and lonely she felt in this middle-class suburb literally within sight of Juarez. Her feelings were not the consequence of the work or of frustrations with modern appliances, nor did she complain about the absence of Mexican people in the neighborhood; her isolation and loneliness were in response to the norms and values surrounding domestic service. She described the situation quite clearly in expressing puzzlement over the social interactions she had with her employer's family: why didn't her employer's children talk to her or include her in any of their activities when she wasn't working? Her reaction was not unlike that of Lillian Pettengill, who wrote about her two-year experience as a domestic in Philadelphia households at the turn of the century: "I feel my isolation alone in a big house full of people."

Earlier in the day, Juanita had unsuccessfully tried to initiate a conversation with the sixteen-year-old daughter while she cleaned her room. She was of the same age as the daughter (who at that moment was in bed reading and watching TV because of menstrual cramps—a luxury the maid was not able to claim). She was rebuffed and ignored and felt that she became visible only when an order was given. Unable to live with this social isolation, she had already made up her mind not to return after her day off in Juarez. I observed the total impossibility of communication. The employer would never know why she left, and Juanita would not know that she would be considered simply another ungrateful Mexican whom he had tried to help.

After I returned to Denver, I thought a lot about the situations of Juanita and the other young undocumented Mexican women living in country club areas along the border. They worked long days in the intimacy of American middle class homes but were starved for respect and positive social interaction. Curiously, the employers did not treat the domestics as "one of the family," nor did they consider themselves employers. Hiring a domestic was likely to be presented within the context of charity and good works; it was considered a matter of helping "these Mexican women" rather than recognized as a work issue.

I was bothered by my encounter along the border, not simply for the obvious humanitarian reasons, but because I too had once worked as a domestic, just as my mother, sister, relatives, and neighbors had. As a teenager, I cleaned houses with my mother on weekends and vacations. My own working experience as a domestic was limited because I had always been accompanied by my mother or sister instead of working alone. Since I was a day worker, my time in the employer's home was limited and I was able to return to my family and community each day. In Juanita's situation as a live-in domestic, there was no distinction between the time on and off work. I wondered whether domestic service had similarly affected my mother, sister, and neighbors. Had they too worked beyond the agreed upon time? Did they have difficulty managing relationships with employers? I never worked alone and was spared the direct negotiations with employers. Instead, I cooperated with my mother or sister in completing the housecleaning as efficiently and quickly as possible.

I could not recall being yelled at by employers or their children, but I did remember anger, resentment, and the humiliation I had felt at kneeling to scrub other people's toilets while they gave step-by-step cleaning instructions. I remember feeling uncomfortable around employers' children who never acknowledged my presence except to question where I had placed their belongings after I had picked them up off the floor to vacuum. After all, my experience was foreign to them; at the age of fourteen I worked as a domestic while they ran off to swimming, tennis, and piano lessons. Unlike Juanita, I preferred to remain invisible as I moved around the employer's house cleaning. Much later, I learned that the invisibility of workers in domestic service is a common characteristic of the occupation. Ruth Schwartz Cowan has commented on the historical aspect of invisibility:

> The history of domestic service in the United States is a vast, unresolved puzzle, because the social role "servant" so frequently carries with it the unspoken adjective *invisible*. In diaries and letters, the "invisible" servant becomes visible only when she departs employment ("Mary left today"). In statistical series, she appears only when she is employed full-time, on a live-in basis; or when she is willing to confess the nature of her employment to a census taker, and (especially since the Second World War) there have frequently been good reasons for such confessions to go unmade.

Although I remained invisible to most of the employers' family members, the mothers, curiously enough, seldom let me move around the house invisibly, dusting the woodwork and vacuuming carpets. Instead, I was subjected to constant supervision and condescending observations about "what a good little girl I was, helping my mother clean house." After I had moved and cleaned behind a hide-a-bed and lazy-boy chair, vacuumed three floors including two sets of stairs, and carried the vacuum cleaner up and downstairs twice because "little Johnny" was napping when I was cleaning the bedrooms—I certainly didn't feel like a "little girl helping mother." I felt like a domestic worker!

There were employers who attempted to draw parallels between my adolescent experience and their teenagers' behavior: they'd point to the messy bedrooms and claim, "Well, you're a teenager, you understand clothes, books, papers, and records on the floor." Even at fourteen, I knew that being sloppy and not picking up after yourself was a privilege. I had two brothers and three sisters. I didn't have my own bedroom but shared a room with my sisters. Not one of us would think of leaving our panties on the floor for the others to pick up. I didn't bother to set such employers straight but continued to clean in silence, knowing that at the end of day I would get cash and confident that I would soon be old enough to work elsewhere.

Many years later, while attending graduate school, I returned to domestic service as an "off-the-record" means to supplement my income. Graduate fellowships and teaching assistantships locked me into a fixed income that frequently was not enough to cover my expenses. So once again I worked alongside my mother for seven hours as we cleaned two houses. I earned about fifty dollars for the day. Housecleaning is strenuous work, and I returned home exhausted from climbing up and down stairs, bending over, rubbing, and scrubbing.

* * *

I came to El Paso with all of these experiences unquestioned in my memory. My presuppositions about domestic service were called into question only after observing the more obviously exploitative situation in the border town. I saw how vulnerable undocumented women employed as live-in domestics are and what little recourse they have to improve their situation, short of finding another job. Experiencing Juanita's shame and disgust at my colleague's sons' behavior brought back a flood of memories that eventually influenced me to study the paid housework that I had once taken-for-granted. I began to wonder professionally about the Chicanas employed as domestics that I had known throughout my own life: how vulnerable were they to exploitation, racism, and sexism? Did their day work status and U.S. citizenship provide protection against degradation and humiliation? How did Chicanas go about establishing a labor arrangement within a society that marked them as racial and cultural inferiors? How did they deal with racial slurs and sexist remarks within their employers' homes? How did Chicanas attempt to negotiate social interactions and informal labor arrangements with employers and their families?

* * *

CHICANA PRIVATE HOUSEHOLD WORKERS AS WORKING MOTHERS

* * *

The appropriate metaphor for housework is Hercules mucking out the [Augean] stables. Women in their own homes experience it as the work they can neither stop nor finish. Chicana domestics like Mrs. Lucero know the frustration well:

> You can work all day at your house and by the time your kids come home from school—it doesn't look like you did anything. By four o'clock it looks the same as it did when you started.

It does not seem possible, but, for women employed as private household workers, even more of their lives is taken up by household chores and child care. Inquiries about daily and weekly routines revealed schedules organized around homemaking and housework. As I asked them about their own housework, it was obvious that the separate spheres of work and family, so frequently employed as analytical categories in both social science and popular literature, had little relevance to these Chicanas' lives. Unlike characterizations in the literature that portray working mothers in conflict between worlds of work and family, these Chicana working mothers described their employment as an extension of their homemaking activities. That is, they cleaned other women's houses to support their own household.

Not only was their day dominated by housework, their work histories reflected life cycles organized around the demands of housework and child care. Like most women, they used events such as children's births or entrances into grade school to recall their own work histories. It became clear in their accounts that leaving and returning to the labor market were regulated by the family cycle. For example, the three women who worked as domestics prior to marriage left their occupations upon marriage and later returned as day workers when their children entered school. The following description of Chicanas' experience as housewives and working mothers illustrate how employment as a household worker functioned as an extension of and strategy for fulfilling their homemaking responsibilities.

For Chicana private household workers, having a job meant doing paid housework during the day and returning to do unpaid housework in their own homes. At home or on the job, there was no respite from housework. Notice the language that Mrs. Castro, mother of five, used to describe her double day. The word "and" connects her thoughts on housework in a never ending series:

> And then I go to clean houses and I come home and it's a drag when you come home and your house is a mess, cause you just came from a clean house. It really upsets me.

Mrs. Lucero expressed a similar attitude but found relief in the fact that "at least I'm not there [at the employer's home] to see things get messy again." Differences from the paid housework done for employers were further distinguished by the structure of their unpaid housework in their own homes.

> It's [housework] so different in your own home because in your own home you don't only clean. You're doing laundry. You're keeping up with the kids. My phone is constantly ringing. . . . It takes me all day to do my house.

These women understood all too well the plight of working women. Homemaking activities ranged from the usual housecleaning, cooking, laundry, and shopping to endless errands, nursing, and child care. Although tasks and the amount of work differed among families, mothers with younger children were faced with additional tasks related to child care, including extra laundry, cooking, and housecleaning. Child care duties were frequently socialized to other family members by women who lived near their families of orientation; babysitting nephews, nieces, and grandchildren was not unusual.

* * *

Like most working-class families living from paycheck to paycheck, Chicana housewives were constantly seeking ways to reduce expenses. Many of the "modern conveniences" were eschewed "to make ends meet." Thus, in order to keep food costs down, Chicanas engaged in time-consuming food production to avoid the higher costs of ready-made, premixed, or frozen foods. One woman even passed up the ready-made *masa* for tortillas because flour and lard were cheaper. A few women canned fruits and vegetables, not as a hobby but because it saved on food expenses. Almost all the women roasted and froze green chiles Most women assisted in the family garden. Other types of money-saving practices included hanging the laundry outside to dry rather than using the clothes dryer, darning socks, and patching clothes. Middle class people generally use the phrase "time is money" to justify buying convenience food and labor-saving devices. In the lives of these women, whose time was not highly valued in the marketplace, it meant the opposite—saving money by spending time.

In many cases the women arranged the job so that they were always at home when their families were there. Husbands' and children's schedules were rarely inconvenienced or altered. Consequently, husbands were not faced with the need to change the division of household labor. Like so many other mothers and wives, Chicanas were expected to cook, wash, iron, vacuum, dust, and care for children. For the most part, they did not escape the sexual division of labor that dominates household work today. About half of the women described a rigid sexual division of labor in household duties. One of the most extreme cases was described by thirty-two-year-old Mrs. Ortega, mother of two.

> I don't pick up anything in the yard. I don't take care of any of the vehicles or nothing. I don't even have to worry about gas in the cars. He knows the inside of the house is my job and the outside around the house and the vehicle is his job.

All of the women approved of their husbands helping with housework, child care, cooking, and other household chores; yet this did not mean that they voiced dissatisfaction with the division of labor between wife and husband. To some degree, the issue of equity was related to the husbands' perceived position as breadwinners. The women tended to discount the importance of their economic contributions to the family, characterizing their wages as "pin money." They described their wages as providing "extras" not afforded by their husbands' incomes. Objectively, however, the items included food, clothes, tuition, and bills. Clearly, the "extras" purchased by these wage-earning mothers are necessities rather than extras. They may not indeed be necessary for survival, but these items, which husbands' paychecks cannot cover, would be considered necessary by most middle-class families.

Despite their traditional orientation, these women did not define their husbands' contributions to the family and home as limited to bringing home a paycheck. In discussing the allocation of household chores, the women were quick to cite a long list of their husbands' activities. Husbands' tasks included gardening and yardwork, chopping wood, hunting and fishing, and house repairs. Two-thirds of the husbands maintained and repaired the family vehicles, thus saving on labor costs and limiting transportation expenses to gas and the purchase of parts. One-fourth of the homes used wood burning stoves to curtail heating bills, and husbands were responsible for chopping wood and keeping the fire going. House repairs mentioned by the women were not limited to minor do-it-yourself projects; they included building a garage, a deck, and remodeling the kitchen.

Although hunting and fishing were considered recreational activities, one-fifth of the husbands packed their freezers with meat and fish that supplemented the family's diet and reduced the yearly food bill. Husbands took responsibility for the work related to hunting and fishing, including butchering deer and elk, cleaning fish, and smoking or freezing their catch. Some made *carne seca* (jerky). Similarly, gardening was approached as serious productive activity. Husbands usually did the initial heavy work of tilling and planting, but both husbands and wives shared in the ongoing weeding and watering. Although these husbands' activities were not different in kind from the hobbies and Saturday chores of middle class men, the former approached the tasks with a seriousness rooted in economic necessity. * * * Nonetheless, regardless of the chores that husbands performed, their work rarely equaled the never ending labor their wives faced every day.

Most of the women whom I interviewed actively pushed for a more equitable distribution of family labor. The only ones to accept the division of labor as unchangeable were married to husbands who disapproved of their employment. Despite cultural stereotypes about male roles in the Chicano community, most husbands approved of their wives' employment. Of the four husbands who wanted their wives to quit, three wanted their wives to be full-time homemakers; the fourth disapproved not of his wife's working per se but of her employment in domestic service. These four husbands expressed their dissatisfaction and pressured their wives by refusing to help with household chores. All four women accepted the unequal division of labor as the price they paid to work outside the home. Mrs. Lovato described her husband's tactic:

He'll pick up his clothes and take it down to the hamper but he won't help me clean. He won't pick up a dish. He won't fry himself an egg—nothing.

* * *

As "shadow work," domestic service was relegated to the peculiar nonwork status commonly given to housework. Even when husbands and other family members did not discourage the women from entering or continuing domestic service, their behavior indicates that they did not value housework as "work." Not only was work done by wives in their own homes not considered "real work" by their families, five of the women said that their employment as household workers was not treated as a "real job" by their families. This attitude was particularly common in families in which mothers worked part-time.

* * *

My inquiries about husbands helping with housework were usually interpreted as having to do with child care. Descriptions of the ways in which husbands "helped out" were almost uniformly the same: when wives were not home, husbands were responsible for the children. They watched the children and sometimes fed them if the wife had prepared food before she left. However, "watching the kids" did not necessarily involve the broad range of tasks such as bathing or cleaning up after the children. Husbands were more likely to supervise older children and make sure that their chores were done. In fact, most of the married women with school age children mentioned that their husbands helped with the housework by telling the children to do their chores. * * *

A few husbands were noted for cooking at barbecues or occasionally preparing a favorite recipe, however, only four women said that their husbands "started dinner" if they came home from work first. The difference between "starting dinner" and "making dinner" typified most husbands' activities in the home. That is, they were more likely to be described as "helping out" with a particular task rather than undertaking the entire job. They were more likely to reheat leftovers than to cook, and they helped with the laundry by removing the clothes from the washer and placing them into the dryer. Taking responsibility for doing the entire activity of cooking or laundry tended to occur only under unusual circumstances. Mrs. Chavez gave an example of such an event:

> The only time he cooks is when I've been in the hospital [laughs]—when he knows I'm not going to come home for the rest of the evening and figures I might as well get busy and do some cooking. . . . then he'll cook. But not just because I'm working, no he doesn't cook.

Husbands were more likely to do the grocery shopping, vacuuming, and picking up if they were retired, unemployed, or worked different shifts. Mrs. Gallegos said that she had argued with her husband for years over the household chores. As a construction worker, he experienced long periods of unemployment during the winter. After fifteen years, he finally assumed most of the housework during his layoffs, including cooking and laundry.

The sexual division of labor found among husbands and wives did not necessarily extend to sons and daughters. Not one of these Chicanas voiced a belief in "men's" or "women's" work in reference to their children. Both sons and daughters were expected to help with housework, particularly washing dishes, feeding pets, and picking up after themselves. These mothers expressed the importance for both male and female children to learn homemaking skills.

* * *

Although not as sex stereotyped as adult roles, the division of labor among children was influenced by the age of the child and the number of children. Older children were expected to babysit younger brothers and sisters and were responsible for more household chores. Women with female children usually acknowledged that their daughters did more housework than their sons, but they did not exempt boys from household chores. The general situation seems to be: if the daughter(s) was the oldest child at home, she frequently did more than her brothers.

* * *

It is critical to understand, however, that despite the allocation of various household chores to both sons and daughters, mothers retained full responsibility for the work and did more than other family members. The only exceptions were found in homes with unemployed or underemployed older daughters. For instance, Mrs. Quintana was a single head of household with two daughters. Her older daughter worked full-time and contributed financially to the household. The younger daughter was unemployed and was therefore responsible for all the cooking, laundry, and housecleaning. In return, she received financial support from her mother and sister. Mrs. Quintana and her daughters were each responsible for ironing their own clothes, making their own beds and picking up after themselves. They shared equally in many other homemaking activities, such as grocery shopping and washing dishes.

In sum, the division of household labor left all these women with the double day. Like many other working mothers, Chicanas did not have enough help with housework, child care, laundry, and cooking. Mrs. Chacon voiced a wish to be able to afford to hire someone to help her with the spring-cleaning in her own home.

> I would appreciate someone—to be able to afford someone to come in and help me instead of taking one or two weeks to do the job. Instead you'd be able to pay someone to come in and have it done the way you want it done too.

Unlike higher-paid workers, they were unable to gain relief from the double day by replacing their labor with the labor of another. As workers in a poorly-paid occupation, Chicana household workers had limited resources and certainly could not afford the same solutions as middle-class women. Rarely could they afford to take the family to restaurants, order take-out, or fill the refrigerator with expensive frozen or precooked food. Nor could they afford to pay for child care. The cost of day care can be a burden for middle class women; it is especially onerous for low-paid workers.

* * *

The Chicanas that I interviewed represented their choice of employment as a conscious strategy. When I asked, "Why did you start doing housework?" their response was not, "I couldn't find any other job." Rather, they began by comparing housework with previously held unskilled jobs. Jobs as line workers, nurse's aides, waitresses, or dishwashers had fixed schedules. Taking days off from fast-food restaurants, car washes or turkey farms jeopardized their employment. Explanations about the way in which domestic service was compatible with taking care of their families followed.

They emphasized that domestic service allowed them to arrange their own hours, and they could easily add or drop employers to lengthen or shorten the workweek. As private household workers, they were able to arrange hours and the workweek to care for sick children, to attend PTA meetings, or to take children to the dentist. The flexible schedule also permitted women to participate in school functions or be active in church and community activities. Having control over their own schedules permitted the women to get their children off to school in the morning and be back home when school was over. Domestic service did not demand rigid commitments of time, nor did the occupation force women to make the job their first priority. Mrs. Garcia explained:

> You can change the dates if you can't go a certain day and if you have an appointment, you can go later, and work later, just as long as you get the work done. . . . I try to be there at the same time, but if I don't get there for some reason or another, I don't have to think I'm going to lose my job or something.

Two-thirds of the interviewees said that they selected domestic service over other low-paying jobs because the occupation offered the flexibility to fulfill family obligations. As Mrs. Lopez related:

> That's one thing with doing daywork—the children are sick or something, you just stayed home because that was my responsibility to get them to the doctor.

Mothers with preschool children preferred domestic service over other low-paying jobs that they had held in the past. Unable to afford a sitter or day-care, domestic service offered an alternative. Mrs. Rodriguez, a thirty-three-year-old mother of two, took her preschool children to work with her:

> I could take my kids with me. There were never any restrictions to taking the children. Most of the people I've worked for like kids, so I just take the kids with me. It's silly to have to work and pay a sitter. It won't work.

Mrs. Cordova also mentioned this aspect of domestic service as grounds for selecting the occupation:

> So that's what I enjoyed about housework is that I could take the kids along and not worry about not having a reliable baby-sitter. So that's mainly the reason I did it [domestic service], because I knew the kids were going to be all right and they were with me and they were fed and taken care of.

Flexibility was not an inherent characteristic of domestic service. Neither was taking children to the job. Provisions for both had to be negotiated in informal contracts and labor arrangements with employers. Employers who requested workers to stay longer—for instance, to do extra household work, babysit, or wait for repairmen—complicated arrangements made for child care. They were often dropped in favor of employers who were agreeable to working conditions compatible with their care needs. If the women had young children, they were not likely to continue working for employers who did not allow children to accompany them. If they had to be home at the end of the school day, they did not keep employers who were unwilling to let them leave work at the specified time.

* * *

Although cultural values regarding traditional sex roles appear to be a major factor in selecting domestic service, a closer look reveals other operative factors, including social and economic conditions that circumscribe and limit Chicanas' choices. The two oldest women interviewed (sixty-eight and sixty-four years old), attributed to discrimination and racism the limited job choices they had experienced throughout their lives. Mrs. Portillo did day work for thirty years. She stated:

> There was a lot of discrimination and Spanish people got just regular housework or laundry work. . . . There was so much discrimination that Spanish people couldn't get jobs outside of washing dishes, things like that.

Younger interviewees tended to blame themselves, citing lack of experience and education before opportunity as obstacles they had encountered in the labor market. After nine years of working in domestic service, Mrs. Fernandez identified lack of skills and other experience as limiting her employment options. With four children, this thirty-five-year-old woman with an eleventh-grade education pondered her future if she were to become head of household:

> I'm not qualified to do much you know. I've often thought about going back to school and getting some kind of training. I don't know what I would do if I really have to quit housework because that wouldn't be a job to raise a family on if I had to. So I would have to go back and get some training in something.

CONCLUSION

The literature on domestic service universally reports that women find the stigma attached to the role painful. Chicanas' descriptions of domestic service as a strategy for fulfilling both economic and homemaking activities, while true, masks the fact that their accounts also serves as mechanisms to cope with the stigma attached to the occupation. * * *

Emphasizing aspects of domestic service compatible with traditional roles of mother and wife was another way in which they coped with the personal pain of being domestics. Highlighting benefits to her family shifted the woman's social identity from work roles to family. Instead of viewing employment as a second career, they treated paid housework as an extension of their family obligations. Working was not considered the path to fulfillment or even upward mobility. They worked to contribute financially to the family. Unlike the common image that working mothers feel guilty about not being full-time homemakers, most Chicanas defined their paid labor as raising the family's living standard and, thus, as an extension of their obligations as mothers and wives. Since the status of motherhood is much higher than that of a domestic worker, identification with the traditional family role minimizes the stigma attached to the work role.

Analyzing the situation of the "wageless housewife" as well as private household workers directs our attention again to centripetal factors and social practices that assign women to housework and unite women over the housework issue. There are also centrifugal factors which fragment the consciousness of sisterhood into ethnic, racial, and class antagonisms. Domestic workers and their employers are caught up in a complex dialectic in which they construct and reconstruct the organization of housework.

Housewives and domestics encounter each other over housework, which is culturally defined not as work but as a "labor of love." As women, both employer and employee are responsible for housework in their own homes. In a sense both could be considered powerless victims. Although the burden of housework unites women, however, the completion of its tasks defines women's class differences. Poor working-class women are unlikely to have the financial resources to hire other people to do the work. Consequently, they can gain relief from the burden of housework only by reallocating tasks to other members of their families, frequently other females in their households. Hiring a woman from a different class and ethnic background to do the household labor provides white middle-class women with an escape from both the stigma and the drudgery of the work. White middle-class women not only benefit from racial and class discrimination which provides them cheap labor but actively contribute to the maintenance and reproduction of an oppressive system by continuing to pay low wages and by not providing health insurance, social security, sick pay, and vacation.

Relationships between white women employers and minority women are strained by the nature of the work domestics are expected to do. Women of color are hired to perform not only physical labor but emotional labor* as well, and they are used to fulfill psychological needs. Housewives, whose work is defined as an expression of love, expect a domestic to possess similar emotional attachment to the work and to demonstrate loyalty to her employer. It

---

*"Emotional labor" is a concept first used by Arlie Hochschild in her book, *The Managed Heart,* to describe a public display of positive feeling that is part of the job for which one is paid.

follows that the more personal service is included in the domestic's daily work, the more emotional labor is extracted and the more likely the employer will insist that the domestic is "one of the family." Conflict arising from the extraction of emotional labor may be related to the employer's refusal to pay for fulfilling psychological needs. To understand the way in which emotional labor is tied to the structure of housework, we need to consider the employer-employee relationship in domestic service within the broader labor process. The structural approach turns our attention away from narrow psychological views of "personalism and asymmetry" as unique features arising from interactions among women toward more comprehensive and universal questions of how employers extract emotional labor from workers. * * * Recognizing the opposing class positions of the women involved transforms sisterhood either into another means for employers to extract emotional and physical labor, or, conversely, into the means for employees to improve working conditions and increase pay and benefits.

* * *

A consensus that gender accounts for many of the oppressive aspects of the structure of housework is emerging among researchers. As Oakley claimed, "Some of housework's low status is due to the low status of the people who do it—women." Similarly, Rollins attributed some of the experience of oppression to gender issues: "the origins of household work are with women." Certainly gender accounts for some of the low status of housework—but not all.

It is important for the development of feminism to transcend simplistic notions that housework is "naturally" dirty work resulting in stigma. I agree with Ellen Malos that the structure of housework is determined by a variety of social factors, and housework in itself is "not necessarily menial and uninteresting. . . . but that it is the context in which [the tasks] are carried out that makes them oppressive." By expanding the discussion of domestic work to include both paid and unpaid labor, the structure of housework becomes visible. We can begin to describe the historical processes that transformed the work into "women's work" and, in the case of domestic service, into "black" or "Mexican women's work." We can also glimpse the form in which capitalist relations transformed housework, submitting domestic workers to scientific management and other forms of manipulation and subjugation. * * *

Household work remains socially devalued. As Julie Matthaei stated so succinctly: "The impact of work on the social position of the worker has never been determined by the importance of that work to the economy; rather, work's social meaning is determined by the constellation of social relationships within which the work takes place."

28

Size Does Count, at Least for French Fries: Minnesota's Straight River

FROM *Water Follies: Groundwater Pumping and the Fate of America's Fresh Waters*

ROBERT GLENNON

When most of us make a decision, we usually think about how the decision will affect us. But the sociological perspective urges us to look beyond ourselves to what are called the manifest and latent functions and the dysfunctions of social actions. That is, as sociologists we seek to anticipate and recognize unintended consequences. With growing awareness of human threats to the natural environment, one branch of sociology traces the chain of human activities to realms normally examined by the physical and biological sciences, and in so doing has expanded the sociological perspective to include global ecology. In this chapter from the author's book Water Follies, *a seemingly benign decision by McDonald's to make its French fries "consumer friendly" sets off a chain reaction of social and environmental change far beyond whatever discussions might have been held in the boardroom of the corporation.*

I wish to make it clear to you, there is not sufficient water to irrigate all the lands which could be irrigated. . . .

—John Wesley Powell (1893)

Ray Kroc, the founder of McDonald's, revolutionized the french fry in the 1950s. It was not mere marketing prowess that allowed him to do so. It was science. He discovered that potatoes vary widely in their water content. A potato that contains too much water will become soggy when fried. Kroc actually sent employees armed with hydrometers into the potato fields of his suppliers to ensure that the potatoes contained the optimum percentage of water. A freshly harvested potato typically consists of 80 percent water. The french frying process essentially removes most of that water and replaces it with fat. The high fat content makes french fries unhealthy, but it also makes them delicious. The typical American consumes thirty pounds of french fries a year, a 700 percent increase since the 1950s, when Ray Kroc began to mass-produce french fries. According to Eric Schlosser, author of *Fast Food Nation,* "French fries have become the most widely sold foodservice item in the United States." Frozen french fries have also nudged aside fresh potatoes, called "table stock" by the food industry, in the at-home diets of many Americans. Potato manufacturers have thoughtfully nurtured our enjoyment of convenience foods by packaging french fries to suit our every whim for a fry of a certain size, shape, or flavoring. The freezer section of a Safeway supermarket is likely to carry some twelve different types of Ore-Ida french fries: shoestring, crinkles, twirls, crispers, fajita-seasoned, zesties, country style, tater tots, hash browns (country and southern style), potatoes O'Brien, and, of course, plain old french fries.

Any baking potato will suffice to make french fries, though the fast-food industry prefers Burbank russet potatoes, a variety that is mealy or starchy, not waxy. When ready for processing, the potatoes are washed, steam-peeled, sliced, and blanched, all of which ensures that the inside will have a fluffy texture. After quick drying, the potatoes are deep-fried for thirty seconds to produce a crisp shell. These steps usually occur at a processing plant located close to the potato fields to save on transportation costs. The fries are then frozen and shipped to a warehouse, which delivers them to retail outlets as needed. The fries remain frozen until the moment of service. At this point, they are deep-fried again for approximately three minutes.

Some potato species that we cultivate today were gathered and cultivated in the Peruvian and Bolivian Andes of South America for thousands of years before the first European explorations. Potatoes first reached North America from England in the early 1600s. The Irish potato blight in the 1840s taught the lesson that cross-fertilization and new cultivars ward off insects and fungi that attack potatoes. In the United States, the intense cultivation of Burbank russets has required growers to use large quantities of insecticides, pesticides, and herbicides to protect the single cultivar. One recent study found that babies in the Red River Valley in North Dakota, a major potato farming region, had low birth weights and a high incidence of birth defects, conditions blamed on the local use of herbicides and other agricultural chemicals.

The potato industry has recently fallen on hard times. To break even, a potato farmer must receive about $5 per hundred pounds. In 1996–97, potato prices fell to $1.50 per hundredweight. By 2001, the prices had declined to $1 per hundred pounds. Most small producers have left the business, and the process of consolidation has resulted in a small number of corporate farms, each growing thousands of acres of potatoes. As large as these farms are, the farmers are still beholden to the processors, who, in turn, must answer to the fast-food chains. In the business of potato farming, a very small number of buyers wield extraordinary power over a large number of sellers.

The advent of the fast-food industry and the converging technologies that made it possible have created American consumers who expect the same uniformity in their food products that they find in their vehicles, shoes, or notebook paper. In the past, fast-food french fries came in small waxed paper bags. The small bags would not stand up, so they often tipped over and spilled the fries, making a bit of a mess. For marketing reasons, in 1988, McDonald's began to offer consumers "super-sized" meals with larger portions of fries now served in rectangular boxes with flat bottoms. They were a huge hit.

French fries are a tremendously competitive component of the fast-food industry. The hook that keeps customers coming back to a particular franchise is not only the taste of the french fries but also their appearance. According to Dean John Gardner of the University of Missouri Agricultural Extension program, the fast-food industry decided that the french fry, to appeal aesthetically to consumers, had to be a certain length. It needed to jut out of the super-size box by just the right amount, so that the consumer can grasp the potato between index finger and thumb and dip it in ketchup.

Ron Offutt grew up on his family's 240-acre farm in Moorhead, Minnesota. After graduation from college in 1964, he began to expand his family's potato growing operation. He recognized that the sandy soil of central Minnesota would provide an ideal medium for growing potatoes if the lands were irrigated. The R. D. Offutt Company now farms 200,000 acres of land in eleven states, with 66,000 acres in potatoes, making Ron the country's largest potato grower. His farms annually produce 2.9 billion pounds of potatoes.

As Ron's farming operation expanded, he needed a lot of tractors, so he acquired a John Deere franchise. Soon, RDO Equipment Co. became the nation's largest John Deere agricultural retailer *and* its largest construction equipment dealer, with forty-six stores in ten states. Ron also realized, in the 1970s, that it would be useful to own a french fry processing plant. So he bought one. In 1980, he completed construction of another processing plant in Park Rapids, Minnesota. He has since added two more processing facilities. Today, R.D. Offutt Company serves as the umbrella for a vast, vertically integrated agribusiness enterprise. Dean Gardner describes R. D. Offutt Company as "a classic, commercial success story for the production of an industrial potato for french fries." Industrial, he suggests, because the length and size of the potato is a critical part of the marketing. A uniform-length fry requires a uniform potato, which requires irrigation.

Until rather recently, many farms in the United States were "dryland farmed," meaning that the farmers had no system of irrigation. Their fortunes varied with the precipitation that Mother Nature provided, from flood to drought, in any given growing season. Many farmers, especially in the Midwest and the East, have come to realize that an occasional supplemental irrigation produces greater yields per acre and larger crops. Irrigation also enables farmers to apply fertilizers or pesticides to their fields through water-soluble solutions.

Americans' love affair with processed foods caused potato farmers to shift from dryland to irrigation farming. The problem with dryland potatoes is that their size, shape, and texture depend heavily on seasonal weather patterns. During the growing season, potatoes need constant moisture or they will have knobs and odd shapes. A misshapen or knobby potato is perfectly edible, but it is not an acceptable potato for the fast-food industry, at least in the United States. According to a potato processing executive, "American consumers were spoiled by the McDonald's of the world. They haven't made that mistake in Japan, where the specifications for potatoes are more reasonable. More of the potato gets used there than here." In Minnesota, potato farmers irrigate their fields because the two big suppliers for fast-food restaurants—Frito-Lay and Simplot—will contract only with potato growers who irrigate their fields in order to obtain potatoes with a uniform length, appearance, and color.

The R. D. Offutt Company farm near Park Rapids, Minnesota, in the Straight River basin, grows about 7,500 acres of Burbank russet potatoes, mostly for french fries, though also for tater tots, hash browns, and potato wedges. During the four-week harvesting season, potatoes are sent to the Lamb Weston/RDO Frozen processing plant in Park Rapids, which is a joint venture between Lamb-Weston Foods Corp. (a major supplier to McDonald's) and R. D. Offutt Company. The plant immediately processes some potatoes but stores the rest for up to eleven months. Storing potatoes creates two problems for processors. Most American consumers understand the first problem: they occasionally purchase a bag of potatoes, which they store under the sink and promptly forget. When finally discovered, the potatoes have become soft and flabby through dehydration and are suitable only for a child's science project. Once harvested, a potato begins to lose moisture to the air. To combat this problem, growers and processors store potatoes in a 95 percent humidity environment to prevent the loss of weight, which can be as much as 30 percent, or nearly one-third of the cash value.

Minnesota potato growers and processors face an additional problem. Most of us have enjoyed a summertime glass of iced tea with moisture on the outside of the glass. As we may remember from our own science classes, the cold glass chills the air immediately around it, and because the chilled air cannot hold the same amount of moisture as warmer air elsewhere in the room, water vapor condenses on the outside of the glass. The differential in temperature that produces condensation poses a problem for potato storage. The moisture in the high-humidity storage facility eventually condenses, which usually occurs on the facility's inside walls in a place with winters as cold as Minnesota. As moisture forms on the walls and ceiling of the plant, it begins to drip onto the potatoes, which, if wet, will eventually rot.

The humidity and temperature of stored potatoes are not important to the typical consumer who buys a large bag of potatoes, stores them in the garage or attic during the wintertime, and eats them over a six- or eight-month period. But humidity and temperature *are* critical for the fast-food industry. When a potato is stored at a cool temperature, its carbohydrates naturally turn to sugars. When baked, the potato will be somewhat sweeter from the sugars that caramelize during baking. If this potato is used for french fries, the caramelized sugar produces a brown color that is aesthetically unacceptable. As Larry Monico, director of operations for the R.D. Offutt farm in Park Rapids has explained, "We as Americans, or somebody, has decided that french fries should be white in color and not brown. If you made french fries out of potatoes that have been stored at a cold temperature, they would be brown in color like shoe leather. Not that they would taste bad, or anything else, but they are undesirable to us as consumers." Consequently, processors must use water to store potatoes at a precise temperature and humidity.

The Lamb Weston/RDO Frozen storage facility in Park Rapids, Minnesota, has a capacity of 26.5 million pounds of potatoes. They must store the entire crop so that there is not more than a one degree Fahrenheit difference between any two potatoes in the entire building. Otherwise, when fried, they might be slightly different colors. According to Larry Monico, "McDonald's won't accept french fries that aren't all white, and so, therefore, we have to keep the temperature constant so that they will all fry to the same color." To achieve the required uniform humidity and temperature, the inside walls are entirely separated from the exterior walls by an air space or cavity that creates an envelope separating the potato storage area from the exterior walls. A separate furnace heats the cavity to a certain temperature and prevents the outside air from affecting the temperature and the humidity at which the potatoes are stored. A computer-controlled system regulates the temperature and humidity in the storage area.

The Straight River in north-central Minnesota, about 180 miles northwest of the Twin Cities, is quite deep and meanders, contrary to its name, in a series of S turns. Typical of rivers and streams in the upper Midwest, the Straight River flows through glacial outwash. As a consequence of the sandy soil, the surface and groundwater are very closely connected hydrologically. At the end of Minnesota's legendary winters, snowmelt rapidly recharges substantial quantities of water to shallow aquifers that, in turn, quickly transmit the water to the river.

In the past, local farmers eked out a living by dryland farming corn and small grains such as wheat, barley, and oats. The sandy soil made farming a marginal economic enterprise. The genius of Ron Offutt was to realize the region's potential for growing potatoes, if the lands were irrigated. The uniform texture of the sandy soils, aided by the application of water, provided an ideal medium for producing the uniform potatoes demanded by the fast-food industry. The threat to the Straight River comes from this shift from dryland to irrigated farming and from changes in the technology of irrigation.

Airplane passengers regularly query flight attendants about conspicuous green circles that dot the landscape of the Great Plains from North Dakota to Texas and that contrast dramatically with the arid land surrounding them. The circles are produced by center-pivot irrigation systems. In a center-pivot system, a well drilled in the center of a quarter-section (160 acres) attaches by a swivel to aluminum pipes suspended six or eight feet off the ground, which are supported by A-frame towers with tandem wheels on the base. A hydraulic drive or a diesel or electric motor supplies power that slowly pivots the pipes and towers in a circle around the well. The resulting irrigation-water pattern produces a perfect circle easily seen from 35,000 feet. Unlike older forms of row irrigation, center-pivot systems allow farmers to tailor precisely the frequency and amount of water applied in order to achieve better yields. Modern center-point systems reduce evaporation loss by using low pressure with specially designed nozzles that produce larger droplets aimed toward the ground and that can achieve an efficiency of 90 percent. Older systems relied on high pressure to spray fine mists of water into the air. Much of the water evaporated before it ever reached the ground.

Center-pivot irrigation has transformed the Straight River basin; in the 1940s, there were only five irrigation wells in the area. By 1998, farmers had drilled seventy center-pivot irrigation systems within two miles of the river, and they now pump almost 3 billion gallons of groundwater each growing season. Groundwater adjacent to the Straight River irrigates the potatoes and provides water for processing.

Beneath and immediately adjacent to the Straight River, the glacial outwash constitutes a shallow, quite permeable aquifer. Below this aquifer lies a confining layer of glacial till, a mixture of clay and other relatively impermeable sediments, and below that lies a deeper aquifer from deposits during earlier glacial periods. The confining layer retards but does not completely block water moving between the shallow and deep aquifers. Pumping from the deep aquifer will increase recharge from the shallow aquifer to the deep aquifer and, depending on the location of the well, may also reduce discharge from the shallow aquifer to the Straight River. One thing is certain: groundwater pumping from the *shallow* aquifer reduces discharge from the aquifer to the Straight River.

Hydrologists are confident about this conclusion for a quite surprising reason. All water bodies contain radioactive isotopes, the product of either natural geologic processes or atomic fallout from nuclear bomb tests that stopped in the 1950s. Because isotopes have differing half-lives, the law of radioactive decay allows hydrologists to calculate the length of time that it takes for precipitation to infiltrate the ground and to discharge to a stream. It turns out that 95 percent of the water in the Straight River comes from discharge from the shallow aquifer. As of 1988, about half the irrigation wells pumped water from the shallow aquifer and the other half from the deeper aquifer.

One of Minnesota's most productive trout fishing streams, the Straight River contains brown trout that can weigh up to nine pounds. Although brown trout are not as sensitive to water temperatures as other trout species, they still require cold, clear water. Reduced flow in the Straight River produces higher ambient water temperatures that threaten the brown trout. A 1994 U.S. Geological Survey (USGS) report identified three factors that degrade the Straight River's trout habitat: (1) a decrease in stream flow from groundwater withdrawals for irrigation that reduces discharge from the aquifer to the stream; (2) higher-temperature irrigation water that percolates into the groundwater system and then discharges to the river; and (3) the introduction of agricultural chemicals to the river when irrigation water percolates into the ground and then discharges into the river. According to the USGS, the river's flow typically decreased during the summer, "possibly as a result of ground-water withdrawal for irrigation." Compared to farms in the West, Minnesota farmers use only a small amount of groundwater—approximately twelve inches per acre per year. Even this modest amount of pumping has the potential, according to the USGS, to reduce the Straight River's flow by as much as 34 percent during the irrigation season. This reduction in flow would increase the water temperature and might adversely affect the brown trout.

The USGS also found an increase in nitrate concentrations in the shallow aquifer along the Straight River. Farmers typically apply 235 pounds per acre of nitrogen fertilizer to grow Burbank russets. Biochemical processes convert organic nitrogen into inorganic nitrate that dissolves in water and leaches into the aquifer. Although the number of documented cases of human illness caused by nitrate-contaminated groundwater is small, the potential health hazards pose a significant environmental concern. A 1994 USGS study found that 6 percent of 600 groundwater samples from shallow wells in the Midwest had nitrate levels that exceeded the U.S. Environmental Protection Agency drinking water limit.

In the mid-1990s, Lamb Weston/RDO Frozen proposed a $60 million expansion of the potato processing plant at Park Rapids. The Minnesota chapter of Trout Unlimited, the Minnesota Center for Environmental Advocacy, and the Headwaters Chapter of the Audubon Society filed a lawsuit to prevent the state of Minnesota from issuing the necessary permits for the plant. The environmental groups feared that the plant's increased groundwater pumping would reduce Straight River flows and that the plant's effluent would adversely affect water quality. The lawsuit ultimately was settled when Lamb Weston/RDO Frozen agreed to change its operations in significant ways. First, it funded monitoring and other data collection efforts. Lamb Weston/RDO Frozen donated in excess of $300,000 to the Minnesota Department of Natural Resources (DNR) to help fund a comprehensive watershed study and a hydrologic model that could predict changes in river flow from groundwater pumping. Between 1996 and 1998, DNR placed a moratorium on issuing new water appropriation permits in order to conduct its study, but the resulting model was not precise enough to provide sufficiently accurate data to predict the impact of specific wells on the river. Lamb Weston/RDO Frozen also capped wells located at the processing plant and drilled two new ones, at a cost of $100,000, about a mile north of the plant in an area that hydrologists determined would not affect the Straight River. The company made these changes solely for the possible benefit of the Straight River. To get the water from the new wells to the processing plant, it built an $80,000 pipeline. Lamb Weston/RDO Frozen also upgraded the wastewater treatment facilities, at a cost of $14 million, and uses the effluent from the treatment plant to irrigate nearby crops.

After DNR lifted its moratorium, Lamb Weston/RDO Frozen ultimately obtained the necessary permits and expanded the plant, which is an enormous operation. Each day, seventy-five semitrailer truckloads of potatoes arrive for processing. Each year, the plant receives almost one billion pounds of potatoes and produces approximately 540 million pounds of french fries. It takes two pounds of potatoes to make one pound of french fries that are acceptable to the plant's largest customer—McDonald's. The plant uses 600 million gallons per year of groundwater in its washing, peeling, and storing operations. It's a lot of water, but R. D. Offutt Company's potato farming and processing businesses employ approximately 600 people and generate $11 million in annual payroll, which has a huge impact in rural Minnesota.

For the moment, the Straight River trout population is in no danger. However, a tall stack of groundwater permit applications waits to be processed by DNR. A large increase in irrigation for potatoes, with new wells being drilled in the deeper aquifer, would change the equilibrium. A 1999 Minnesota DNR study concluded: "Potential expansion in potato farming and irrigation could put the Straight River trout population at further risk of thermal impact and eventually raise water temperatures beyond their threshold of survival." Increased pumping from the deeper aquifer would increase recharge from the shallow aquifer, thus reducing discharge from the shallow aquifer to the river. Lower flows would mean higher ambient water temperatures and less dilution of nitrates that contaminate the river. One long-term answer, of course, is for us, as American consumers, to accept french fries that have slightly different colors, or minor discolorations, or even ones that are not long enough to stick out from a super-size carton.

29

The Rise and Fall of Mass Rail Transit

FROM *Building American Cities: The Urban Real Estate Game*

JOE R. FEAGIN AND ROBERT PARKER

There are more automobiles than people in Los Angeles. Is this a reflection of the preferences and choices of individual consumers, a reflection of the so-called American love affair with the automobile, or is it a consequence of structured choices? The authors show that far-sighted corporations found common cause in organizing transportation to suit their interests, and the romance of Americans and their cars began a new chapter.

[M]ost U.S. cities have become *multinucleated,* with major commercial, industrial, and residential areas no longer closely linked to or dependent upon the downtown center. Decentralization has become characteristic of our cities from coast to coast. Essential to decentralization has been the development and regular extension of an automobile-dominated transportation system serving businesses and the general citizenry, but mostly paid for by rank-and-file taxpayers. With and without citizen consent, corporate capitalists, industrialists and developers, and allied political officials have made key decisions fundamentally shaping the type of transportation system upon which all Americans now depend.

THE AUTO-OIL-RUBBER INDUSTRIAL COMPLEX

The auto-oil-rubber industrial complex has long been central to both the general economy and the urban transportation system in the United States. Automobile and auto-related industries provide a large proportion, sometimes estimated at one-sixth, of all jobs, although this proportion may be decreasing with the decline and stagnation in the auto industry over the last two decades. An estimated one-quarter to one-half of the land in central cities is used for the movement, storage, selling, and parking of automobiles, trucks, and buses. The expanding production of automobiles and trucks has been coordinated with the expansion of highways and freeways and has facilitated the bulging suburbanization around today's cities.

Because of the dominance of autos and trucks in the U.S. transportation system, the traditional social scientists * * * have typically viewed that transportation system as preordained by the American "love" for the automobile. For example, in a recent book on Los Angeles, historian Scott Bottles argues that "America's present urban transportation system largely reflects choices made by the public itself"; the public freely chose the automobile as a "liberating and democratic technology." Conventional explanations for auto-centered patterns focus on the response of a market system to these consumers. Auto-linked technologies are discussed as though they force human decisions: Thus "the city dweller, especially in recent times, has been a victim of the technological changes that have been wrought in transportation systems." * * * [T]raditional ecologists and other social scientists view the complexity and shape of cities as largely determined by technological developments in transportation—a reasonable view—but these technologies are not carefully examined in terms of their economic contexts, histories, and possible technological alternatives. For example, unlike the United States, numerous capitalist countries in Europe, including prosperous West Germany, have a mixed rail transit/automobile transport system. There interurban and intraurban rail transit remains very important. For this reason, the U.S. system cannot be assumed to be simply the result of "free" consumer choices in a market context. The capitalistic history and decision-making contexts that resulted in the positioning of automobiles at the heart of the U.S. transportation system must be examined.

EARLY MASS RAIL TRANSIT

Rural and urban Americans have not always been so dependent on automobiles for interurban and intraurban transport. In the years between the 1880s and the 1940s many cities had significant mass transit systems. By 1890 electric trolleys were in general use. Indeed, electric trolley routes, elevated railroads, and subways facilitated the first urban expansion and decentralization. Some investor-owned rail transit companies extended their trolley lines beyond existing urbanized areas out into the countryside in an attempt to profit from the land speculation along the rail lines. Glenn Yago has documented how transit owners and real estate speculators worked together to ensure the spatial and economic development of cities by private enterprise. Transit companies were a significant force in urban sprawl. The suburban spread of Los Angeles, for example, got its initial push from the expansion of trolley rail lines. Not initially laid out as an automobile city, this sprawling metropolis developed along streetcar tracks; only later was the streetcar network displaced by automobiles.

The reorganization and disruption of mass rail transit that took place in the early 1900s did not result just from the challenge of improved automobile technology. Rather, capitalist entrepreneurs and private corporations seeking profits reorganized and consolidated existing rail transit systems. Electrification of horse-drawn streetcars increased investment costs and stimulated concentration of ownership in larger "transit trusts" of landowning, finance, and utility entrepreneurs. Mergers of old transit firms and the assembly of new companies were commonplace, and there was much speculation in transit company stock. Yago has provided evidence on the corrupt accounting practices, over-extension of lines for real estate speculation, and overcapitalization which led to the bankruptcy of more than one-third of the private urban transit companies during the period 1916–1923. Sometimes the capitalists involved in the transit companies were too eager for profits. "These actions in turn," Charles Cheape notes, "drained funds, discouraged additional investment, and contributed significantly to the collapse and reorganization of many transit systems shortly after World War I and again in the 1930s."

Ironically, one consequence of the so-called "progressive" political reform movement in cities in the first decades of the twentieth century was that supervision of rail transit systems was often placed in the hands of business-dominated regulatory commissions, many of whose members were committed to the interests of corporate America (for example, transit stock manipulation for profit), rather than to the welfare of the general public. In numerous cases the extraordinary profits made by rail transit entrepreneurs, together with their ties to corrupt politicians, created a negative public image—which in turn made the public less enthusiastic about new tax-supported subsidies and fare hikes for the troubled rail transit systems. Moreover, as the profits of many of the private transit firms declined, public authorities in some cities, including Boston and New York, were forced to take over the transit lines from the poorly managed private companies in response to citizen pressure for mass transportation. This fact suggests that there has long been popular *demand* for publicly owned rail transit that is reliable, convenient, and inexpensive. Indeed, during the period 1910–1930 a *majority* of Americans either could not afford, because of modest incomes, or could not use, because of age or handicap, an automobile.

A CORPORATE PLAN TO KILL MASS TRANSIT?

By the late 1910s and 1920s the ascension of the U.S. auto-oil-rubber industrial complex brought new corporate strategies to expand automobile markets and secure government subsidies for road infrastructure. Mass rail transit hindered the profit-oriented interests of this car-centered industrial complex, whose executives became involved not only in pressuring governments to subsidize roads but also in the buying up of mass transit lines. For example, in the early 1920s, Los Angeles had the largest and most effective trolley car system in the United States. Utilizing more than a thousand miles of track, the system transported millions of people yearly. During World War II, the streetcars ran 2,800 scheduled runs a day. But by the end of that war, the trolleys were disappearing. And their demise had little to do with consumer choice. As news analyst Harry Reasoner has observed, it "was largely a result of a criminal conspiracy":

> The way it worked was that General Motors, Firestone Tire and Standard Oil of California and some other companies, depending on the location of the tar-

get, would arrange financing for an outfit called National City Lines, which cozied up to city councils and county commissioners and bought up transit systems like L.A.'s. Then they would junk or sell the electric cars and pry up the rails for scrap and beautiful, modern buses would be substituted, buses made by General Motors and running on Firestone Tires and burning Standard's gas.

Within a month after the trolley system in Los Angeles was purchased, 237 new buses arrived. It is important to realize that, for all the financial and management problems created by the private owners of the rail transit firms, the old transit systems were still popular. In the year prior to the takeover, the Los Angeles electric lines made $1.5 million in profits and carried more than 200 million passengers. The logic behind the corporate takeover plan was clear. The auto-related firms acted because a trolley car can carry the passengers of several dozen automobiles.

During the 1930s GM created a holding company through which it and other auto-related companies channeled money to buy up electric transit systems in 45 cities from New York to Los Angeles. As researcher Bradford Snell has outlined it, the process had three stages. First, General Motors (GM) helped the Greyhound corporation displace long-distance passenger transportation from railroads to buses. Then GM and other auto-related companies bought up and dismantled numerous local electric transit systems, replacing them with the GM-built buses. Moreover, in the late 1940s, GM was convicted in a Chicago federal court of having conspired to destroy electric transit and to convert trolley systems to diesel buses, whose production GM monopolized. William Dixon, the man who put together the criminal conspiracy case for the federal government, argued that individual corporate executives should be sent to jail. Instead, each received a trivial $1 fine. The corporations were assessed a modest $5,000 penalty, the maximum under the law. In spite of this conviction, GM continued to play a role in converting electric transit systems to diesel buses. And these diesel buses provided more expensive mass transit: "The diesel bus, as engineered by GM, has a shorter life expectancy, higher operating costs, and lower overall productivity than electric buses. GM has thus made the bus economically noncompetitive with the car also." One source of public discontent with mass transit was this inferiority of the new diesel buses compared to the rail transit cars that had been displaced without any consultation with consumers. Not surprisingly, between 1936 and 1955 the number of operating trolley cars in the United States dropped from about 40,000 to 5,000.

In a lengthy report GM officials have argued that electric transit systems were already in trouble when GM began intervening. As noted above, some poorly managed transit systems were declining already, and some had begun to convert partially to buses before GM's vigorous action. So from GM's viewpoint, the corporation's direct intervention only accelerated the process. This point has been accented by Bottles, who shows that GM did not single-handedly destroy the streetcar systems in Los Angeles. These privately controlled systems were providing a lesser quality of service before GM became involved. The profit milking and corruption of the private streetcar firms in Los Angeles were not idiosyncratic but were common for privately owned mass transport in numerous cities.

Also important in destroying mass transit was the new and aggressive multimillion-dollar marketing of automobiles and trucks by General Motors and other automobile companies across the United States. And the automobile companies and their advertisers were not the only powerful actors involved in killing off numerous mass transit systems. Bankers and public officials also played a role. Yago notes that "after World War II, banks sold bankrupt and obsolete transit systems throughout the country at prices that bore no relation to the systems' real values." Often favoring the auto interests, local banks and other financial institutions tried to limit government bond issues that could be used to finance new equipment and refurbish the remaining rail transit systems.

Because of successful lobbying by executives from the auto-oil-rubber complex, and their own acceptance of a motorization perspective, most government officials increasingly backed street and highway construction. They cooperated with the auto industry in eliminating many mass transit systems. Increased governmental support for auto and truck transportation systems has meant systematic disinvestment in mass transit systems. Over the several decades since World War II, governmental mass transit subsidies have been small compared with highway subsidies. This decline has hurt low- and moderate-income people the most. Less public transit since World War II has meant increased commuting time in large cities where people are dependent on the automobile, which is especially troublesome for moderate-income workers who may not be able to afford a reliable car; less mass transit has also meant increased consumer expenditures for automobiles and gasoline. Auto expansion has frustrated the development of much mass transit because growing street congestion slows down buses and trolleys, further reducing their ridership. As a result, governmental funding for public rail transit has been cut, again chasing away riders who dislike poorly maintained equipment. And fares have been increased. Riders who can use automobiles do so. And the downward spiral has continued to the point of extinction of most public rail transit systems.

Mass transit was allowed to decline by the business-oriented government officials in most cities. Consumer desires were only partly responsible for this. Consumers did discover the freedom of movement of autos, and even in cities with excellent rail transit systems many prefer the auto for at least some types of travel. But consumers make their choices *from the alternatives available*. With no real rail transportation alternative to the automobile in most urban areas, consumers turned to it as a necessity. Ironically, as the auto and truck congestion of the cities has mounted between the 1950s and the 1980s, more and more citizens, and not a few business leaders, have called for new mass transit systems for their cities.

* * *

MASS TRANSIT IN OTHER CAPITALISTIC COUNTRIES

Comparative research on U.S. and German transportation systems by Yago has demonstrated the importance of looking at corporate power and economic structure. Mass rail transport developed in Germany before 1900. In the 1870s and 1880s the German national and local governments became interested in mass transit; at that time the coal, steel, iron, chemical, and electrical manufacturing companies were dominant in German capitalism. Interestingly, corporate executives in these industries supported the development of rail transportation; by 1900 the national and local governments had subsidized and institutionalized intraurban and interurban rail transport systems, which served the transport needs not only of the citizenry but also of the dominant coal, steel, chemical, and electrical industries. These industries also supplied equipment and supplies for the rail networks. In contrast, in the United States early transport companies were involved in manipulation and land speculation; transit service was rarely the central goal of the early rail transit firms. In contrast to Germany, dominance of U.S. industry by a major economic concentration did not come to the United States until after 1900, and when it did come, the auto-oil-rubber industrial complex was dominant. There was no other integrated industrial complex to contest this dominance of the auto-related firms, and governmental intervention was directed at support of motorization and the automobile. In Germany governmental intervention for mass rail transit had preceded this dominance of the motorization lobby. This suggests that the *timing* of the implementation of technological innovations in relation to corporate development is critical to their dominance, or lack of dominance, in cities and societies.

Interestingly, it was the Nazi interest in motorization and militarization in the 1930s that sharply increased the role of auto and truck transport in Germany. Adolf Hitler worked hard to motorize the military and the society. After World War II, the German auto lobby increased in power, and an auto transport system was placed alongside the rail transport system. However, the West German government and people have maintained a strong commitment to both systems; and the OPEC-generated oil crises of the 1970s brought an unparalleled revival of mass transit in Germany, whereas in the United States there was a more modest revival. The reason for the dramatic contrast between the two countries was that Germany had retained a rail passenger transport system, one that is still viable and energy conserving to the present day.

30

From the Panopticon* to Disney World

CLIFFORD D. SHEARING AND PHILLIP C. STENNING

To live in a modern society is to know and live within a vast array of invisible struc-
tures designed to ensure orderly behavior. Other structures are quite visible but not
recognized: actual physical barriers, corridors, and messages directing us to come,
go, turn, stop, be silent, not smoke, wear a shirt and shoes, and so forth. We con-
form to control systems with our own consent or what Shearing and Stenning call
"structured compliance." Disney World is not the only place where this occurs, but it
offers a good illustration for your own investigations.

One of the most distinctive features of that quintessentially American
playground known as Disney World is the way it seeks to combine a
sense of comfortable—even nostalgic—familiarity with an air of innovative
technological advance. Mingled with the fantasies of one's childhood are the
dreams of a better future. Next to the Magic Kingdom is the Epcot Center.
As well as providing for a great escape, Disney World claims also to be a
design for better living. And what impresses most about this place is that it
seems to run like clockwork.

Yet the Disney order is no accidental by-product. Rather, it is a designed-in
feature that provides—to the eye that is looking for it, but not to the casual
visitor—an exemplar of modern private corporate policing. Along with the rest
of the scenery of which it forms a discreet part, it too is recognizable as a design
for the future.

We invite you to come with us on a guided tour of this modern police facility
in which discipline and control are, like many of the characters one sees about,
in costume.

The fun begins the moment the visitor enters Disney World. As one arrives
by car one is greeted by a series of smiling young people who, with the aid of
clearly visible road markings, direct one to one's parking spot, remind one to
lock one's car and to remember its location and then direct one to await the
rubber-wheeled train that will convey visitors away from the parking lot. At
the boarding location one is directed to stand safely behind guard rails and to
board the train in an orderly fashion. While climbing on board one is reminded

---

*Jeremy Bentham (1748–1832) coined this term to describe a futuristic prison where noth-
ing could be done outside the view of the custodial staff.

to remember the name of the parking area and the row number in which one is parked (for instance, "Donald Duck, 1"). Once on the train one is encouraged to protect oneself from injury by keeping one's body within the bounds of the carriage and to do the same for children in one's care. Before disembarking one is told how to get from the train back to the monorail platform and where to wait for the train to the parking lot on one's return. At each transition from one stage of one's journey to the next, one is wished a happy day and a "good time" at Disney World (this begins as one drives in and is directed by road signs to tune one's car radio to the Disney radio network).

As one moves towards the monorail platform the directions one has just received are reinforced by physical barriers (that make it difficult to take a wrong turn), pavement markings, signs and more cheerful Disney employees who, like their counterparts in other locations, convey the message that Disney World is a "fun place" designed for one's comfort and pleasure. On approaching the monorail platform one is met by enthusiastic attendants who quickly and efficiently organize the mass of people moving onto it into corrals designed to accommodate enough people to fill one compartment on the monorail. In assigning people to these corrals the attendants ensure that groups visiting Disney World together remain together. Access to the edge of the platform is prevented by a gate which is opened once the monorail has arrived and disembarked the arriving passengers on the other side of the platform. If there is a delay of more than a minute or two in waiting for the next monorail one is kept informed of the reason for the delay and the progress the expected train is making towards the station.

Once aboard and the automatic doors of the monorail have closed, one is welcomed aboard, told to remain seated and "for one's own safety" to say away from open windows. The monorail takes a circuitous route to one of the two Disney locations (the Epcot Center or the Magic Kingdom) during which time a friendly disembodied voice introduces one briefly to the pleasures of the world one is about to enter and the methods of transport available between its various locations. As the monorail slows towards its destination one is told how to disembark once the automatic doors open and how to move from the station to the entrance gates, and reminded to take one's possessions with one and to take care of oneself, and children in one's care, on disembarking. Once again these instructions are reinforced, in a variety of ways, as one moves towards the gates.

It will be apparent from the above that Disney Productions is able to handle large crowds of visitors in a most orderly fashion. Potential trouble is anticipated and prevented. Opportunities for disorder are minimized by constant instruction, by physical barriers which severely limit the choice of action available and by the surveillance of omnipresent employees who detect and rectify the slightest deviation.

The vehicles that carry people between locations are an important component of the system of physical barriers. Throughout Disney World vehicles are used as barriers. This is particularly apparent in the Epcot Center, . . . where many exhibits are accessible only via special vehicles which automatically secure one once they begin moving.

Control strategies are embedded in both environmental features and structural relations. In both cases control structures and activities have other functions which are highlighted so that the control function is over-shadowed. Nonetheless, control is pervasive. For example, virtually every pool, fountain, and flower garden serves both as an aesthetic object and to direct visitors away from, or towards, particular locations. Similarly, every Disney Productions employee, while visibly and primarily engaged in other functions, is also engaged in the maintenance of order. This integration of functions is real and not simply an appearance: beauty *is* created, safety *is* protected, employees *are* helpful. The effect is, however, to embed the control function into the "woodwork" where its presence is unnoticed but its effects are ever present.

A critical consequence of this process of embedding control in other structures is that control becomes consensual. It is effected with the willing cooperation of those being controlled so that the controlled become, as Foucault (1977) has observed, the source of their own control. Thus, for example, the batching that keeps families together provides for family unity while at the same time ensuring that parents will be available to control their children. By seeking a definition of order within Disney World that can convincingly be presented as being in the interest of visitors, order maintenance is established as a voluntary activity which allows coercion to be reduced to a minimum. Thus, adult visitors willingly submit to a variety of devices that increase the flow of consumers through Disney World, such as being corralled on the monorail platform, so as to ensure the safety of their children. Furthermore, while doing so they gratefully acknowledge the concern Disney Productions has for their family, thereby legitimating its authority, not only in the particular situation in question, but in others as well. Thus, while profit ultimately underlies the order Disney Productions seeks to maintain, it is pursued in conjunction with other objectives that will encourage the willing compliance of visitors in maintaining Disney profits. This approach to profit making, which seeks a coincidence of corporate and individual interests (employee and consumer alike), extends beyond the control function and reflects a business philosophy to be applied to all corporate operations (Peters and Waterman, 1982).

The coercive edge of Disney's control system is seldom far from the surface, however, and becomes visible the moment the Disney-visitor consensus breaks down, that is, when a visitor attempts to exercise a choice that is incompatible with the Disney order. It is apparent in the physical barriers that forcefully prevent certain activities as well as in the action of employees who detect breaches of order. This can be illustrated by an incident that occurred during a visit to Disney World by Shearing and his daughter, during the course of which she developed a blister on her heel. To avoid further irritation she removed her shoes and proceeded to walk barefooted. They had not progressed ten yards before they were approached by a very personable security guard dressed as a Bahamian police officer, with white pith helmet and white gloves that perfectly suited the theme of the area they were moving through (so that he, at first, appeared more like a scenic prop than a security person), who informed them that walking barefoot was, "for the safety of visitors," not permitted. When informed that, given the blister, the safety of this visitor was likely to be better secured by remaining barefooted, at least on the walkways, they were informed that their safety and how best to protect it was a matter for Disney Productions to determine while they were on Disney property and that unless they complied he would be compelled to escort them out of Disney World. Shearing's daughter, on learning that failure to comply with the security guard's instruction would deprive her of the pleasures of Disney World, quickly decided that she would prefer to further injure her heel and remain on Disney property. As this example illustrates, the source of Disney Productions' power rests both in the physical coercion it can bring to bear and in its capacity to induce co-operation by depriving visitors of a resource that they value.

The effectiveness of the power that control of a "fun place" has is vividly illustrated by the incredible queues of visitors who patiently wait, sometimes for hours, for admission to exhibits. These queues not only call into question the common knowledge that queueing is a quintessentially English pastime (if Disney World is any indications Americans are at least as good, if not better, at it), but provide evidence of the considerable inconvenience that people can be persuaded to tolerate so long as they believe that their best interests require it. While the source of this perception is the image of disney World that the visitor brings to it, it is, interestingly, reinforced through the queueing process itself. In many exhibits queues are structured so that one is brought close to the entrance at several points, thus periodically giving one a glimpse of the fun to come while at the same time encouraging one that the wait will soon be over.

Visitor participation in the production of order within Disney World goes beyond the more obvious control examples we have noted so far. An important aspect of the order Disney Productions attempts to maintain is a particular image of Disney World and the American industrialists who sponsor its exhibits (General Electric, Kodak, Kraft Foods, etc.). Considerable care is taken to ensure that every feature of Disney World reflects a positive view of the American Way, especially its use of, and reliance on, technology. Visitors are, for example, exposed to an almost constant stream of directions by employees, robots in human form and disembodied recorded voices (the use of recorded messages and robots permits precise control over the content and tone of the directions given) that convey the desired message. Disney World acts as a giant magnet attracting millions of Americans and visitors from other lands who pay to learn of the wonders of American capitalism.

Visitors are encouraged to participate in the production of the Disney image while they are in Disney World and to take it home with them so that they can reproduce it for their families and friends. One way this is done is through the "Picture Spots," marked with signposts, to be found throughout Disney World, that provide direction with respect to the images to capture on film (with cameras that one can borrow free of charge) for the slide shows and photo albums to be prepared "back home." Each spot provides views which exclude anything unsightly (such as garbage containers) so as to ensure that the visual images visitors take away of Disney World will properly capture Disney's order. A related technique is the Disney characters who wander through the complex to provide "photo opportunities" for young children. These characters apparently never talk to visitors, and the reason for this is presumably so that their mediabased images will not be spoiled.

As we have hinted throughout this discussion, training is a pervasive feature of the control system of Disney Productions. It is not, however, the redemptive soul-training of the carceral project but an ever-present flow of directions for, and definitions of, order directed at every visitor. Unlike carceral training, these messages do not require detailed knowledge of the individual. They are, on the contrary, for anyone and everyone. Messages are, nonetheless, often conveyed to single individuals or small groups of friends and relatives. For example, in some of the newer exhibits, the vehicles that take one through swivel and turn so that one's gaze can be precisely directed. Similarly, each seat is fitted with individual sets of speakers that talk directly to one, thus permitting a seductive sense of intimacy while simultaneously imparting a uniform message.

In summary, within Disney World control is embedded, preventative, subtle, co-operative and apparently non-coercive and consensual. It focuses on categories, requires no knowledge of the individual and employs pervasive surveillance. Thus, although disciplinary, it is distinctively non-carceral. Its order is instrumental and determined by the interests of Disney Productions rather than moral and absolute. As anyone who has visited Disney World knows, it is extraordinarily effective.

While this new instrumental discipline is rapidly becoming a dominant force in social control it is as different from the Orwellian totalitarian nightmare as it is from the carceral regime. Surveillance is pervasive but it is the antithesis of the blatant control of the Orwellian State: its source is not government and its vehicle is not Big Brother. The order of instrumental discipline is not the unitary order of a central State but diffuse and separate orders defined by private authorities responsible for the feudal-like domains of Disney World, condominium estates, commercial complexes and the like. Within contemporary discipline, control is as fine-grained as Orwell imagined but its features are very different. It is thus, paradoxically, not to Orwell's socialist-inspired Utopia that we must look for a picture of contemporary control but to the capitalist-inspired disciplinary model conceived of by Huxley, who, in his *Brave New World,* painted a picture of consensually based control that bears a striking resemblance to the disciplinary control of Disney World and other corporate control systems. Within Huxley's imaginary world people are seduced into conformity by the pleasures offered by the drug "soma" rather than coerced into compliance by threat of Big Brother, just as people are today seduced to conform by the pleasures of consuming the goods that corporate power has to offer.

The contrasts between morally based justice and instrumental control, carceral punishment and corporate control, the Panopticon and Disney World and Orwell's and Huxley's visions is succinctly captured by the novelist Beryl Bainbridge's (1984) observations about a recent journey she made retracing J.B. Priestley's (1933) celebrated trip around Britain. She notes how during his travels in 1933 the center of the cities and towns he visited were defined by either a church or a center of government (depicting the coalition between Church and State in the production of order that characterizes morally based regimes).

During her more recent trip one of the changes that struck her most forcibly was the transformation that had taken place in the center of cities and towns. These were now identified not by churches or town halls, but by shopping centers; often vaulted glass-roofed structures that she found reminiscent of the cathedrals they had replaced both in their awe-inspiring architecture and in the hush that she found they sometimes created. What was worshipped in these contemporary cathedrals, she noted, was not an absolute moral order but something much more mundane: people were "worshipping shopping" and through it, we would add, the private authorities, the order and corporate power their worship makes possible.

REFERENCES

Bainbridge, B. (1984). Television interview with Robert Fulford on "Realities" Global Television, Toronto, October.

Foucault, M. (1977). *Discipline and Punish: The Birth of the Prison.* New York: Vintage.

Peters, T. J. and Waterman, R. H. (1982). *In Search of Excellence.* New York: Warner Books.

Priestly, J. B. (1934). *English Journey: Being a Rambling but Truthful Account of What One Man Saw and Heard and Felt and Thought during a Journey through England Autumn of the Year 1933.* London: Heinemann and Gollancz.

31

The Saints and the Roughnecks

WILLIAM J. CHAMBLISS

Almost every student can identify the "Saints" and "Roughnecks" in their high school, but it requires an astute observer like William Chambliss to show us the hidden implications of this dichotomy in a class-structured society. Social class matters, just as high school social hierarchies matter, because people are treated according to their position, and not necessarily in terms of who they are or what they actually do.

Eight promising young men—children of good, stable, white upper-middle-class families, active in school affairs, good pre-college students—were some of the most delinquent boys at Hanibal High School. While community residents knew that these boys occasionally sowed a few wild oats, they were totally unaware that sowing wild oats completely occupied the daily routine of these young men. The Saints were constantly occupied with truancy, drinking, wild driving, petty theft, and vandalism. Yet no one was officially arrested for any misdeed during the two years I observed them.

This record was particularly surprising in light of my observations during the same two years of another gang of Hanibal High School students, six lower-class white boys known as the Roughnecks. The Roughnecks were constantly in trouble with police and community even though their rate of delinquency was about equal with that of the Saints. What was the cause of this disparity? the result? The following consideration of the activities, social class, and community perceptions of both gangs may provide some answers.

THE SAINTS FROM MONDAY TO FRIDAY

The Saints' principal daily concern was with getting out of school as early as possible. The boys managed to get out of school with minimum danger that they would be accused of playing hookey through an elaborate procedure for obtaining "legitimate" release from class. The most common procedure was for one boy to obtain the release of another by fabricating a meeting of some committee, program, or recognized club. Charles might raise his hand in his 9:00 chemistry class and ask to be excused—a euphemism for going to the bathroom. Charles would go to Ed's math class and inform the teacher that Ed was needed for a 9:30 rehearsal of the drama club play. The math teacher would recognize Ed and Charles as "good students" involved in numerous school activities and would permit Ed to leave at 9:30. Charles would return to his class, and Ed would go to Tom's English class to obtain his release. Tom would engineer Charles's escape. The strategy would continue until as many of the Saints as possible were freed. After a stealthy trip to the car (which had been parked in a strategic spot), the boys were off for a day of fun.

Over the two years I observed the Saints, this pattern was repeated nearly every day. There were variations on the theme, but in one form or another, the boys used this procedure for getting out of class and then off the school grounds. Rarely did all eight of the Saints manage to leave school at the same time. The average number avoiding school on the days I observed them was five.

Having escaped from the concrete corridors the boys usually went either to a pool hall on the other (lower-class) side of town or to a café in the suburbs. Both places were out of the way of people the boys were likely to know (family or school officials), and both provided a source of entertainment. The pool hall entertainment was the generally rough atmosphere, the occasional hustler, the sometimes drunk proprietor and, of course, the game of pool. The café's entertainment was provided by the owner. The boys would "accidentally" knock a glass on the floor or spill cola on the counter—not all the time, but enough to be sporting. They would also bend spoons, put salt in sugar bowls and generally tease whoever was working in the café. The owner had opened the café recently and was dependent on the boys' business which was, in fact, substantial since between the horsing around and the teasing they bought food and drinks.

THE SAINTS ON WEEKENDS

On weekends the automobile was even more critical than during the week, for on weekends the Saints went to Big Town—a large city with a population of over a million 25 miles from Hanibal. Every Friday and Saturday night most of the Saints would meet between 8:00 and 8:30 and would go into Big Town. Big Town activities included drinking heavily in taverns or nightclubs, driving drunkenly through the streets, and committing acts of vandalism and playing pranks.

By midnight on Fridays and Saturdays the Saints were usually thoroughly high, and one or two of them were often so drunk they had to be carried to the cars. Then the boys drove around town, calling obscenities to women and girls; occasionally trying (unsuccessfully so far as I could tell) to pick girls up; and driving recklessly through red lights and at high speeds with their lights out. Occasionally they played "chicken." One boy would climb out the back window of the car and across the roof to the driver's side of the car while the car was moving at high speed (between 40 and 50 miles an hour); then the driver would move over and the boy who had just crawled across the car roof would take the driver's seat.

Searching for "fair game" for a prank was the boys' principal activity after they left the tavern. The boys would drive alongside a foot patrol-man and ask directions to some street. If the policeman leaned on the car in the course of answering the question, the driver would speed away, causing him to lose his balance. The Saints were careful to play this prank only in an area where they were not going to spend much time and where they could quickly disappear around a corner to avoid having their license plate number taken.

Construction sites and road repair areas were the special province of the Saints' mischief. A soon-to-be-repaired hole in the road inevitably invited the Saints to remove lanterns and wooden barricades and put them in the car, leaving the hole unprotected. The boys would find a safe vantage point and wait for an unsuspecting motorist to drive into the hole. Often, though not always, the boys would go up to the motorist and commiserate with him about the dreadful way the city protected its citizenry.

Leaving the scene of the open hole and the motorist, the boys would then go searching for an appropriate place to erect the stolen barricade. An "appropriate place" was often a spot on a highway near a curve in the road where the barricade would not be seen by an oncoming motorist. The boys would wait to watch an unsuspecting motorist attempt to stop and (usually) crash into the wooden barricade. With saintly bearing the boys might offer help and understanding.

A stolen lantern might well find its way onto the back of a police car or hang from a street lamp. Once a lantern served as a prop for a reenactment of the "midnight ride of Paul Revere" until the "play," which was taking place at 2:00 A.M. in the center of a main street of Big Town, was interrupted by a police car several blocks away. The boys ran, leaving the lanterns on the street, and managed to avoid being apprehended.

Abandoned houses, especially if they were located in out-of-the-way places, were fair game for destruction and spontaneous vandalism. The boys would break windows, remove furniture to the yard and tear it apart, urinate on the walls, and scrawl obscenities inside.

Through all the pranks, drinking, and reckless driving the boys managed miraculously to avoid being stopped by police. Only twice in two years was I aware that they had been stopped by a Big Town policeman. Once was for speeding (which they did every time they drove whether they were drunk or sober), and the driver managed to convince the policeman that it was simply an error. The second time they were stopped they had just left a nightclub and were walking through an alley. Aaron stopped to urinate and the boys began making obscene remarks. A foot patrolman came into the alley, lectured the boys and sent them home. Before the boys got to the car one began talking in a loud voice again. The policeman, who had followed them down the alley, arrested this boy for disturbing the peace and took him to the police station where the other Saints gathered. After paying a $5.00 fine, and with the assurance that there would be no permanent record of the arrest, the boy was released.

The boys had a spirit of frivolity and fun about their escapades. They did not view what they were engaged in as "delinquency," though it surely was by any reasonable definition of that word. They simply viewed themselves as having a little fun and who, they would ask, was really hurt by it? The answer had to be no one, although this fact remains one of the most difficult things to explain about the gang's behavior. Unlikely though it seems, in two years of drinking, driving, carousing, and vandalism no one was seriously injured as a result of the Saints' activities.

THE SAINTS IN SCHOOL

The Saints were highly successful in school. The average grade for the group was "B," with two of the boys having close to a straight "A" average. Almost all of the boys were popular and many of them held offices in the school. One of the boys was vice president of the student body one year. Six of the boys played on athletic teams.

At the end of their senior year, the student body selected ten seniors for special recognition as the "school wheels"; four of the ten were Saints. Teachers and school officials saw no problem with any of these boys and anticipated that they would all "make something of themselves."

How the boys managed to maintain this impression is surprising in view of their actual behavior in school. Their technique for covering truancy was so successful that teachers did not even realize that the boys were absent from school much of the time. Occasionally, of course, the system would backfire and then the boy was on his own. A boy who was caught would be most contrite, would plead guilty and ask for mercy. He inevitably got the mercy he sought.

Cheating on examinations was rampant, even to the point of orally communicating answers to exams as well as looking at one another's papers. Since none of the group studied, and since they were primarily dependent on one another for help, it is surprising that grades were so high. Teachers contributed to the deception in their admitted inclination to give these boys (and presumably others like them) the benefit of the doubt. When asked how the boys did in school, and when pressed on specific examinations, teachers might admit that they were disappointed in John's performance, but would quickly add that they "knew that he was capable of doing better," so John was given a higher grade than he had actually earned. How often this happened is impossible to know. During the time that I observed the group, I never saw any of the boys take homework home. Teachers may have been "understanding" very regularly.

One exception to the gang's generally good performance was Jerry, who had a "C" average in his junior year, experienced disaster the next year, and failed to graduate. Jerry had always been a little more nonchalant than the others about the liberties he took in school. Rather than wait for someone to come get him from class, he would offer his own excuse and leave. Although he probably did not miss any more class than most of the others in the group, he did not take the requisite pains to cover his absences. Jerry was the only Saint whom I ever heard talk back to a teacher. Although teachers often called him a "cut up" or a "smart kid," they never referred to him as a troublemaker or as a kid headed for trouble. It seems likely, then, that Jerry's failure his senior year and his mediocre performance his junior year were consequences of his not playing the game the proper way (possibly because he was disturbed by his parents' divorce). His teachers regarded him as "immature" and not quite ready to get out of high school.

THE POLICE AND THE SAINTS

The local police saw the Saints as good boys who were among the leaders of the youth in the community. Rarely, the boys might be stopped in town for speeding or for running a stop sign. When this happened the boys were always polite, contrite and pled for mercy. As in school, they received the mercy they asked for. None ever received a ticket or was taken into the precinct by the local police.

The situation in Big Town, where the boys engaged in most of their delinquency, was only slightly different. The police there did not know the boys at all, although occasionally the boys were stopped by a patrolman. Once they were caught taking a lantern from a construction site. Another time they were stopped for running a stop sign, and on several occasions they were stopped for speeding. Their behavior was as before: contrite, polite and penitent. The urban police, like the local police, accepted their demeanor as sincere. More important, the urban police were convinced that these were good boys just out for a lark.

THE ROUGHNECKS

Hanibal townspeople never perceived the Saints' high level of delinquency. The Saints were good boys who just went in for an occasional prank. After all, they were well dressed, well mannered and had nice cars. The Roughnecks were a different story. Although the two gangs of boys were the same age, and both groups engaged in an equal amount of wild-oat sowing, everyone agreed that the not-so-well-dressed, not-so-well-mannered, not-so-rich boys were heading for trouble. Townspeople would say, "You can see the gang members at the drugstore, night after night, leaning against the storefront (sometimes drunk) or slouching around inside buying cokes, reading magazines, and probably stealing old Mr. Wall blind. When they are outside and girls walk by, even respectable girls, these boys make suggestive remarks. Sometimes their remarks are downright lewd."

From the community's viewpoint, the real indication that these kids were in trouble was that they were constantly involved with the police. Some of them had been picked up for stealing, mostly small stuff, of course, "but still it's stealing small stuff that leads to big time crimes." "Too bad," people said. "Too bad that these boys couldn't behave like the other kids in town; stay out of trouble, be polite to adults, and look to their future."

The community's impression of the degrees to which this group of six boys (ranging in age from 16 to 19) engaged in delinquency was somewhat distorted. In some ways the gang was more delinquent than the community thought; in other ways they were less.

The fighting activities of the group were fairly readily and accurately perceived by almost everyone. At least once a month, the boys would get into some sort of fight, although most fights were scraps between members of the group or involved only one member of the group and some peripheral hanger-on. Only three times in the period of observation did the group fight together: once against a gang from across town, once against two blacks, and once against a group of boys from another school. For the first two fights the group went out "looking for trouble"—and they found it both times. The third fight followed a football game and began spontaneously with an argument on the football field between one of the Roughnecks and a member of the opposition's football team.

Jack has a particular propensity for fighting and was involved in most of the brawls. He was a prime mover of the escalation of arguments into fights.

More serious than fighting, had the community been aware of it, was theft. Although almost everyone was aware that the boys occasionally stole things, they did not realize the extent of the activity. Petty stealing was a frequent event for the Roughnecks. Sometimes they stole as a group and coordinated their efforts; other things they stole in pairs. Rarely did they steal alone.

The thefts ranged from very small things like paperback books, comics, and ballpoint pens to expensive items like watches. The nature of the thefts varied from time to time. The gang would go through a period of systematically lifting items from automobiles or school lockers. Types of thievery varied with the whim of the gang. Some forms of thievery were more profitable than others, but all thefts were for profit, not just thrills.

Roughnecks siphoned gasoline from cars as often as they had access to an automobile, which was not very often. Unlike the Saints, who owned their own cars, the Roughnecks would have to borrow their parents' cars, an event which occurred only eight or nine times a year. The boys claimed to have stolen cars for joy rides from time to time.

Ron committed the most serious of the group's offenses. With an unidentified associate the boy attempted to burglarize a gasoline station. Although this station had been robbed twice previously in the same month, Ron denied any involvement in either of the other thefts. When Ron and his accomplice approached the station, the owner was hiding in the bushes beside the station. He fired both barrels of a double-barreled shotgun at the boys. Ron was severely injured; the other boy ran away and was never caught. Though he remained in critical condition for several months, Ron finally recovered and served six months of the following year in reform school. Upon release from reform school, Ron was put back a grade in school, and began running around with a different gang of boys. The Roughnecks considered the new gang less delinquent than themselves, and during the following year Ron had no more trouble with the police.

The Roughnecks, then, engaged mainly in three types of delinquency: theft, drinking, and fighting. Although community members perceived that this gang of kids was delinquent, they mistakenly believed that their illegal activities were primarily drinking, fighting, and being a nuisance to passersby. Drinking was limited among the gang members, although it did occur, and theft was much more prevalent than anyone realized.

Drinking would doubtless have been more prevalent had the boys had ready access to liquor. Since they rarely had automobiles at their disposal, they could not travel very far, and the bars in town would not serve them. Most of the boys had little money, and this, too, inhibited their purchase of alcohol. Their major source of liquor was a local drunk who would buy them a fifth if they would give him enough extra to buy himself a pint of whiskey or a bottle of wine.

The community's perception of drinking as prevalent stemmed from the fact that it was the most obvious delinquency the boys engaged in. When one of the boys had been drinking, even a casual observer seeing him on the corner would suspect that he was high.

There was a high level of mutual distrust and dislike between the Roughnecks and the police. The boys felt very strongly that the police were unfair and corrupt. Some evidence existed that the boys were correct in their perception.

The main source of the boys' dislike for the police undoubtedly stemmed from the fact that the police would sporadically harass the group. From the standpoint of the boys, these acts of occasional enforcement of the law were whimsical and uncalled for. It made no sense to them, for example, that the police would come to the corner occasionally and threaten them with arrest for loitering when the night before the boys had been out siphoning gasoline from cars and the police had been nowhere in sight. To the boys, the police were stupid on the one hand, for not being where they should have been and catching the boys in a serious offense, and unfair on the other hand, for trumping up "loitering" charges against them.

From the viewpoint of the police, the situation was quite different. They knew, with all the confidence necessary to be a policeman, that these boys were engaged in criminal activities. They knew this partly from occasionally catching them, mostly from circumstantial evidence ("the boys were around when those tires were slashed"), and partly because the police shared the view of the community in general that this was a bad bunch of boys. The best the police could hope to do was to be sensitive to the fact that these boys were engaged in illegal acts and arrest them whenever there was some evidence that they had been involved. Whether or not the boys had in fact committed a particular act in a particular way was not especially important. The police had a broader view: their job was to stamp out these kids' crimes; the tactics were not as important as the end result.

Over the period that the group was under observation, each member was arrested at least once. Several of the boys were arrested a number of times and spent at least one night in jail. While most were never taken to court, two of the boys were sentenced to six months' incarceration in boys' schools.

THE ROUGHNECKS IN SCHOOL

The Roughnecks' behavior in school was not particularly disruptive. During school hours they did not all hang around together, but tended instead to spend most of their time with one or two other members of the gang who were their special buddies. Although every member of the gang attempted to avoid school as much as possible, they were not particularly successful and most of them attended school with surprising regularity. They considered school a burden—something to be gotten through with a minimum of conflict. If they were "bugged" by a particular teacher, it could lead to trouble. One of the boys, Al, once threatened to beat up a teacher and, according to the other boys, the teacher hid under a desk to escape him.

Teachers saw the boys the way the general community did, as heading for trouble, as being uninterested in making something of themselves. Some were also seen as being incapable of meeting the academic standards of the school. Most of the teachers expressed concern for this group of boys and were willing to pass them despite poor performance, in the belief that failing them would only aggravate the problem.

The group of boys had a grade point average just slightly above "C." No one in the group failed either grade, and no one had better than a "C" average. They were very consistent in their achievement or, at least, the teachers were consistent in their perception of the boys' achievement.

Two of the boys were good football players. Herb was acknowledged to be the best player in the school and Jack was almost as good. Both boys were criticized for their failure to abide by training rules, for refusing to come to practice as often as they should, and for not playing their best during practice. What they lacked in sportsmanship they made up for in skill, apparently, and played every game no matter how poorly they had performed in practice or how many practice sessions they had missed.

TWO QUESTIONS

Why did the community, the school, and the police react to the Saints as though they were good, upstanding, nondelinquent youths with bright futures but to the Roughnecks as though they were tough, young criminals who were headed for trouble? Why did the Roughnecks and the Saints in fact have quite different careers after high school—careers which, by and large, lived up to the expectations of the community?

The most obvious explanation for the differences in the community's and law enforcement agencies' reactions to the two gangs is that one group of boys was "more delinquent" than the other. Which group was more delinquent? The answer to this question will determine in part how we explain the differential responses to these groups by the members of the community and, particularly, by law enforcement and school officials.

In sheer number of illegal acts, the Saints were the more delinquent. They were truant from school for at least part of the day almost every day of the week. In addition, their drinking and vandalism occurred with surprising regularity. The Roughnecks, in contrast, engaged sporadically in delinquent episodes. While these episodes were frequent, they certainly did not occur on a daily or even a weekly basis.

The difference in frequency of offenses was probably caused by the Roughnecks' inability to obtain liquor and to manipulate legitimate excuses from school. Since the Roughnecks had less money than the Saints, and teachers carefully supervised their school activities, the Roughnecks' hearts may have been as black as the Saints', but their misdeeds were not nearly as frequent.

There are really no clear-cut criteria by which to measure qualitative differences in antisocial behavior. The most important dimension is generally referred to as the "seriousness" of the offenses.

If seriousness encompasses the relative economic costs of delinquent acts, then some assessment can be made. The Roughnecks probably stole an average of about $5.00 worth of goods a week. Some weeks the figure was considerably higher, but these times must be balanced against long periods when almost nothing was stolen.

The Saints were more continuously engaged in delinquency but their acts were not for the most part costly to property. Only their vandalism and occasional theft of gasoline would so qualify. Perhaps once or twice a month they would siphon a tankful of gas. The other costly items were street signs, construction lanterns, and the like. All of these acts combined probably did not quite average $5.00 a week, partly because much of the stolen equipment was abandoned and presumably could be recovered. The difference in cost of stolen property between the two groups was trivial, but the Roughnecks probably had a slightly more expensive set of activities than did the Saints.

Another meaning of seriousness is the potential threat of physical harm to members of the community and to the boys themselves. The Roughnecks were more prone to physical violence; they not only welcomed an opportunity to fight; they went seeking it. In addition, they fought among themselves frequently. Although the fighting never included deadly weapons, it was still a menace, however minor, to the physical safety of those involved.

The Saints never fought. They avoided physical conflict both inside and outside the group. At the same time, though, the Saints frequently endangered their own and other people's lives. They did so almost every time they drove a car, especially if they had been drinking. Sober, their driving was risky;

under the influence of alcohol it was horrendous. In addition, the Saints endangered the lives of others with their pranks. Street excavations left unmarked were a very serious hazard.

Evaluating the relative seriousness of the two gangs' activities is difficult. The community reacted as though the behavior of the Roughnecks was a problem, and they reacted as though the behavior of the Saints was not. But the members of the community were ignorant of the array of delinquent acts that characterized the Saints' behavior. Although concerned citizens were unaware of much of the Roughnecks' behavior as well, they were much better informed about the Roughnecks' involvement in delinquency than they were about the Saints'.

VISIBILITY

Differential treatment of the two gangs resulted in part because one gang was infinitely more visible than the other. This differential visibility was a direct function of the economic standing of the families. The Saints had access to automobiles and were able to remove themselves from the sight of the community. In as routine a decision as to where to go to have a milkshake after school, the Saints stayed away from the mainstream of community life. Lacking transportation, the Roughnecks could not make it to the edge of town. The center of town was the only practical place for them to meet since their homes were scattered throughout the town and any noncentral meeting place put an undue hardship on some members. Through necessity the Roughnecks congregated in a crowded area where everyone in the community passed frequently, including teachers and law enforcement officers. They could easily see the Roughnecks hanging around the drugstore.

The Roughnecks, of course, made themselves even more visible by making remarks to passersby and by occasionally getting into fights on the corner. Meanwhile, just as regularly, the Saints were either at the café on one edge of town or in the pool hall at the other edge of town. Without any particular realization that they were making themselves inconspicuous, the Saints were able to hide their time-wasting. Not only were they removed from the mainstream of traffic, but they were almost always inside a building.

On their escapades the Saints were also relatively invisible, since they left Hanibal and traveled to Big Town. Here, too, they were mobile, roaming the city, rarely going to the same area twice.

DEMEANOR

To the notion of visibility must be added the difference in the responses of group members to outside intervention with their activities. If one of the Saints was confronted with an accusing policeman, even if he felt he was truly innocent of a wrongdoing, his demeanor was apologetic and penitent. A

Roughneck's attitude was almost the polar opposite. When confronted with a threatening adult authority, even one who tried to be pleasant, the Roughneck's hostility and disdain were clearly observable. Sometimes he might attempt to put up a veneer of respect, but it was thin and was not accepted as sincere by the authority.

School was no different from the community at large. The Saints could manipulate the system by feigning compliance with the school norms. The availability of cars at school meant that once free from the immediate sight of the teacher, the boys could disappear rapidly. And this escape was well enough planned that no administrator or teacher was nearby when the boys left. A Roughneck who wished to escape for a few hours was in a bind. If it were possible to get free from class, downtown was still a mile away, and even if he arrived there, he was still very visible. Truancy for the Roughnecks meant almost certain detection, while the Saints enjoyed almost complete immunity from sanctions.

BIAS

Community members were not aware of the transgressions of the Saints. Even if the Saints had been less discreet, their favorite delinquencies would have been perceived as less serious than those of the Roughnecks.

In the eyes of the police and school officials, a boy who drinks in an alley and stands intoxicated on the street corner is committing a more serious offense than is a boy who drinks to inebriation in a nightclub or a tavern and drives around afterwards in a car. Similarly, a boy who steals a wallet from a store will be viewed as having committed a more serious offense than a boy who steals a lantern from a construction site.

Perceptual bias also operates with respect to the demeanor of the boys in the two groups when they are confronted by adults. It is not simply that adults dislike the posture affected by boys of the Roughneck ilk; more important is the conviction that the posture adopted by the Roughnecks is an indication of their devotion and commitment to deviance as a way of life. The posture becomes a cue, just as the type of the offense is a cue, to the degree to which the known transgressions are indicators of the youths' potential for other problems.

Visibility, demeanor, and bias are surface variables which explain the day-to-day operations of the police. Why do these surface variables operate as they do? Why did the police choose to disregard the Saints' delinquencies while breathing down the backs of the Roughnecks?

The answer lies in the class structure of American society and the control of legal institutions by those at the top of the class structure. Obviously, no representative of the upper class drew up the operational chart for the police which led them to look in the ghettos and on streetcorners—which led them to see the demeanor of lower-class youth as troublesome and that of upper-middle-class youth as tolerable. Rather, the procedures simply developed from experience—experience with irate and influential upper-middle-class parents insisting that their son's vandalism was simply a prank and his drunkenness only a momentary "sowing of wild oats"—experience with cooperative or indifferent, powerless, lower-class parents who acquiesced to the law's definition of their son's behavior.

ADULT CAREERS OF THE SAINTS AND THE ROUGHNECKS

The community's confidence in the potential of the Saints and the Roughnecks apparently was justified. If anything, the community members underestimated the degree to which these youngsters would turn out "good" or "bad."

Seven of the eight members of the Saints went on to college immediately after high school. Five of the boys graduated from college in four years. The sixth one finished college after two years in the army, and the seventh spent four years in the air force before returning to college and receiving a B.A. degree. Of these seven college graduates, three went on for advanced degrees. One finished law school and is now active in state politics, one finished medical school and is practicing near Hanibal, and one boy is now working for a Ph.D. The other four college graduates entered submanagerial, managerial, or executive training positions with larger firms.

The only Saint who did not complete college was Jerry. Jerry had failed to graduate from high school with the other Saints. During his second senior year, after the other Saints had gone on to college, Jerry began to hang around with what several teachers described as a "rough crowd"—the gang that was heir apparent to the Roughnecks. At the end of his second senior year, when he did graduate from high school, Jerry took a job as a used-car salesman, got married, and quickly had a child. Although he made several abortive attempts to go to college by attending night school, when I last saw him (ten years after high school) Jerry was unemployed and had been living on unemployment for almost a year. His wife worked as a waitress.

Some of the Roughnecks have lived up to community expectations. A number of them were headed for trouble. A few were not.

Jack and Herb were the athletes among the Roughnecks and their athletic prowess paid off handsomely. Both boys received unsolicited athletic scholarships to college. After Herb received his scholarship (near the end of his senior year), he apparently did an about-face. His demeanor became very similar to that of the Saints. Although he remained a member in good standing of the Roughnecks, he stopped participating in most activities and did not hang on the corner as often.

Jack did not change. If anything, he became more prone to fighting. He even made excuses for accepting the scholarship. He told the other gang members that the school had guaranteed him a "C" average if he would come to play football—an idea that seems far-fetched, even in this day of highly competitive recruiting.

During the summer after graduation from high school, Jack attempted suicide by jumping from a tall building. The jump would certainly have killed most people trying it, but Jack survived. He entered college in the fall and played four years of football. He and Herb graduated in four years, and both are teaching and coaching in high schools. They are married and have stable families. If anything, Jack appears to have a more prestigious position in the community than does Herb, though both are well respected and secure in their positions.

Two of the boys never finished high school. Tommy left at the end of his junior year and went to another state. That summer he was arrested and placed on probation on a manslaughter charge. Three years later he was arrested for murder; he pleaded guilty to second degree murder and is serving a 30-year sentence in the state penitentiary.

Al, the other boy who did not finish high school, also left the state in his senior year. He is serving a life sentence in a state penitentiary for first degree murder.

Wes is a small-time gambler. He finished high school and "bummed around." After several years he made contact with a bookmaker who employed him as a runner. Later he acquired his own area and has been working it ever since. His position among the bookmakers is almost identical to the position he had in the gang; he is always around but no one is really aware of him. He makes no trouble and he does not get into any. Steady, reliable, capable of keeping his mouth closed, he plays the game by the rules, even though the game is an illegal one.

That leaves only Ron. Some of his former friends reported that they had heard he was "driving a truck up north," but no one could provide any concrete information.

REINFORCEMENT

The community responded to the Roughnecks as boys in trouble, and the boys agreed with that perception. Their pattern of deviancy was reinforced, and breaking away from it became increasingly unlikely. Once the boys acquired an image of themselves as deviants, they selected new friends who affirmed that self-image. As that self-conception became more firmly entrenched, they also became willing to try new and more extreme deviances. With their growing alienation came freer expression of disrespect and hostility for representatives of the legitimate society. This disrespect increased the community's negativism, perpetuating the entire process of commitment to deviance. Lack of a commitment to deviance works the same way. In either case, the process will perpetuate itself unless some event (like a scholarship to college or a sudden failure) external to the established relationship intervenes. For two of the Roughnecks (Herb and Jack), receiving college athletic scholarships created new relations and culminated in a break with the established pattern of deviance. In the case of one of the Saints (Jerry), his parents' divorce and his failing to graduate from high school changed some of his other relations. Being held back in school for a year and losing his place among the Saints had sufficient impact on Jerry to alter his self-image and virtually to assure that he would not go on to college as his peers did. Although the experiments of life can rarely be reversed, it seems likely in view of the behavior of the other boys who did not enjoy this special treatment by the school that Jerry, too, would have "become something" had he graduated as anticipated. For Herb and Jack outside intervention worked to their advantage; for Jerry it was his undoing.

Selective perception and labeling—finding, processing, and punishing some kinds of criminality and not others—means that visible, poor, non-mobile, outspoken, undiplomatic "tough" kids will be noticed, whether their actions are seriously delinquent or not. Other kids, who have established a reputation for being bright (even though underachieving), disciplined, and involved in respectable activities, who are mobile and monied, will be invisible when they deviate from sanctioned activities. They'll sow their wild oats—perhaps even wider and thicker than their lower-class cohorts—but they won't be noticed. When it's time to leave adolescence most will follow the expected path, settling into the ways of the middle class, remembering fondly the delinquent but unnoticed fling of their youth. The Roughnecks and others like them may turn around, too. It is more likely that their noticeable deviance will have been so reinforced by police and community that their lives will be effectively channeled into careers consistent with their adolescent background.

32

The Border Patrol State

LESLIE MARMON SILKO

A routine encounter with the police may reassure some people that the servants of the people are doing their job. For others, authority figures can take on a hostile and alien quality. It depends on your perspective. In this essay, you are invited to adopt the perspective of the less powerful, those low in status, the distrusted people for whom suspicion is common and fair treatment is not always forthcoming.

I used to travel the highways of New Mexico and Arizona with a wonderful sensation of absolute freedom as I cruised down the open road and across the vast desert plateaus. On the Laguna Pueblo reservation, where I was raised, the people were patriotic despite the way the U.S. government had treated Native Americans. As proud citizens, we grew up believing the freedom to travel was our inalienable right, a right that some Native Americans had been denied in the early twentieth century. Our cousin, old Bill Pratt, used to ride his horse 300 miles overland from Laguna, New Mexico, to Prescott, Arizona, every summer to work as a fire lookout.

In school in the 1950s, we were taught that our right to travel from state to state without special papers or threat of detainment was a right that citizens under communist and totalitarian governments did not possess. That wide open highway told us we were U.S. citizens; we were free. . . .

Not so long ago, my companion Gus and I were driving south from Albuquerque, returning to Tucson after a book promotion for the paperback edition of my novel *Almanac of the Dead*. I had settled back and gone to sleep while Gus drove, but I was awakened when I felt the car slowing to a stop. It was nearly midnight on New Mexico State Road 26, a dark, lonely stretch of two-lane highway between Hatch and Deming. When I sat up, I saw the headlights and emergency flashers of six vehicles—Border Patrol cars and a van were blocking both lanes of the highway. Gus stopped the car and rolled down the window to ask what was wrong. But the closest Border Patrolman and his companion did not reply; instead, the first agent ordered us to "step out of the car." Gus asked why, but his question seemed to set them off. Two more Border Patrol agents immediately approached our car, and one of them snapped, "Are you looking for trouble?" as if he would relish it.

I will never forget that night beside the highway. There was an awful feeling of menace and violence straining to break loose. It was clear that the uniformed men would be only too happy to drag us out of the car if we did not speedily comply with their request (asking a question is tantamount to resistance, it seems). So we stepped out of the car and they motioned for us to stand on the shoulder of the road. The night was very dark, and no other traffic had come down the road since we had been stopped. All I could think about was a book I had read—*Nunca Més*—the official report of a human rights commission that investigated and certified more than 12,000 "disappearances" during Argentina's "dirty war" in the late 1970s.

The weird anger of these Border Patrolmen made me think about descriptions in the report of Argentine police and military officers who became addicted to interrogation, torture and the murder that followed. When the military and police ran out of political suspects to torture and kill, they resorted to the random abduction of citizens off the streets. I thought how easy it would be for the Border Patrol to shoot us and leave our bodies and car beside the highway, like so many bodies found in these parts and ascribed to "drug runners."

Two other Border Patrolmen stood by the white van. The one who had asked if we were looking for trouble ordered his partner to "get the dog," and from the back of the van another patrolman brought a small female German shepherd on a leash. The dog apparently did not heel well enough to suit him, and the handler jerked the leash. They opened the doors of our car and pulled the dog's head into it, but I saw immediately from the expression in her eyes that the dog hated them, and that she would not serve them. When she showed no interest in the inside of our car, they brought her around back to the trunk, near where we were standing. They half-dragged her up into the trunk, but still she did not indicate any stowed-away human beings or illegal drugs.

Their mood got uglier; the officers seemed outraged that the dog could not find any contraband, and they dragged her over to us and commanded her to sniff our legs and feet. To my relief, the strange violence the Border Patrol agents had focused on us now seemed shifted to the dog. I no longer felt so strongly that we would be murdered. We exchanged looks—the dog and I. She was afraid of what they might do, just as I was. The dog's handler jerked the leash sharply as she sniffed us, as if to make her perform better, but the dog refused to accuse us: She had an innate dignity that did not permit her to serve the murderous impulses of those men. I can't forget the expression in the dog's eyes; it was as if she were embarrassed to be associated with them. I had a small amount of medicinal marijuana in my purse that night, but she refused to expose me. I am not partial to dogs, but I will always remember the small German shepherd that night.

Unfortunately, what happened to me is an everyday occurrence here now. Since the 1980s, on top of greatly expanding border checkpoints, the Immigration and Naturalization Service and the Border Patrol have implemented policies that interfere with the rights of U.S. citizens to travel freely within our borders. I.N.S. agents now patrol all interstate highways and roads that lead to or from the U.S.-Mexico border in Texas, New Mexico, Arizona and California. Now, when you drive east from Tucson on Interstate 10 toward El Paso, you encounter an I.N.S. check station outside Las Cruces, New Mexico. When you drive north from Las Cruces up Interstate 25, two miles north of the town of Truth or Consequences, the highway is blocked with orange emergency barriers, and all traffic is diverted into a two-lane Border Patrol checkpoint—ninety-five miles north of the U.S.-Mexico border.

I was detained once at Truth or Consequences, despite my and my companion's Arizona driver's licenses. Two men, both Chicanos, were detained at the same time, despite the fact that they too presented ID and spoke English without the thick Texas accents of the Border Patrol agents. While we were stopped, we watched as other vehicles—whose occupants were white—were waved through the checkpoint. White people traveling with brown people, however, can expect to be stopped on suspicion they work with the sanctuary movement, which shelters refugees. White people who appear to be clergy, those who wear ethnic clothing or jewelry and women with very long hair or very short hair (they could be nuns) are also frequently detained; white men with beards or men with long hair are likely to be detained, too, because Border Patrol agents have "profiles" of "those sorts" of white people who may help political refugees. (Most of the political refugees from Guatemala and El Salvador are Native American or mestizo because the indigenous people of the Americas have continued to resist efforts by invaders to displace them from their ancestral lands.) Alleged increases in illegal immigration by people of Asian ancestry means that the Border Patrol now routinely detains anyone who appears to be Asian or part Asian, as well.

Once your car is diverted from the Interstate Highway into the checkpoint area, you are under the control of the Border Patrol, which in practical terms exercises a power that no highway patrol or city patrolman possesses: They are willing to detain anyone, for no apparent reason. Other law-enforcement officers need a shred of probable cause in order to detain someone. On the books, so does the Border Patrol; but on the road, it's another matter. They'll order you to stop your car and step out; then they'll ask you to open the trunk. If you ask why or request a search warrant, you'll be told that they'll have to have a dog sniff the car before they can request a search warrant, and the dog might not get there for two or three hours. The search warrant might require an hour or two past that. They make it clear that if you force them to obtain a search warrant for the car, they will make you submit to a strip search as well.

Traveling in the open, though, the sense of violation can be even worse. Never mind high-profile cases like that of former Border Patrol agent Michael Elmer, acquitted of murder by claiming self-defense, despite admitting that as an officer he shot an "illegal" immigrant in the back and then hid the body, which remained undiscovered until another Border Patrolman reported the event. (Last month [1994], Elmer was convicted of reckless endangerment in a separate incident, for shooting at least ten rounds from his M-16 too close to a group of immigrants as they were crossing illegally into Nogales in March 1992.) Or that in El Paso, a high school football coach driving a vanload of his players in full uniform was pulled over on the freeway and a Border Patrol agent put a cocked revolver to his head. (The football coach was Mexican-American, as were most of the players in his van; the incident eventually caused a federal judge to issue a restraining order against the Border Patrol.) We've a mountain of personal experiences like that which never make the newspapers. A history professor at U.C.L.A. told me she had been traveling by train from Los Angeles to Albuquerque twice a month doing research. On each of her trips, she had noticed that the Border Patrol agents were at the station in Albuquerque scrutinizing the passengers. Since she is six feet tall and of Irish and German ancestry, she was not particularly concerned. Then one day when she stepped off the train in Albuquerque, two Border Patrolmen accosted her, wanting to know what she was doing, and why she was traveling between Los Angeles and Albuquerque twice a month. She presented identification and an explanation deemed "suitable" by the agents, and was allowed to go about her business.

Just the other day, I mentioned to a friend that I was writing this article and he told me about his 73-year-old father, who is half Chinese and had set out alone by car from Tucson to Albuquerque the week before. His father had become confused by road construction and missed a turnoff from Interstate 10 to Interstate 25; when he turned around and circled back, he missed the turnoff a second time. But when he looped back for yet another try, Border Patrol agents stopped him and forced him to open his trunk. After they satisfied themselves that he was not smuggling Chinese immigrants, they sent him on his way. He was so rattled by the event that he had to be driven home by his daughter.

This is the police state that has developed in the southwestern United States since the 1980s. No person, no citizen, is free to travel without the scrutiny of the Border Patrol. In the city of South Tucson, where 80 percent of the respondents were Chicano or Mexicano, a joint research project by the University of Wisconsin and the University of Arizona recently concluded that one out of every five people there had been detained, mistreated verbally or nonverbally, or questioned by I.N.S. agents in the past two years.

Manifest Destiny may lack its old grandeur of theft and blood—"lock the door" is what it means now, with racism a trump card to be played again and again, shamelessly, by both major political parties. "Immigration," like "street crime" and "welfare fraud," is a political euphemism that refers to people of color. Politicians and media people talk about "illegal aliens" to dehumanize and demonize undocumented immigrants, who are for the most part people of color. Even in the days of Spanish and Mexican rule, no attempts were made to interfere with the flow of people and goods from south to north and north to south. It is the U.S. government that has continually attempted to sever contact between the tribal people north of the border and those to the south.[1]

Now that the "Iron Curtain" is gone, it is ironic that the U.S. government and its Border Patrol are constructing a steel wall ten feet high to span sections of the border with Mexico. While politicians and multinational corporations extol the virtues of NAFTA and "free trade" (in goods, not flesh), the ominous curtain is already up in a six-mile section at the border crossing at Mexicali; two miles are being erected but are not yet finished at Naco; and at Nogales, sixty miles south of Tucson, the steel wall has been all rubber-stamped and awaits construction likely to begin in March. Like the pathetic multimillion-dollar "antidrug" border surveillance balloons that were continually deflated by high winds and made only a couple of meager interceptions before they blew away, the fence along the border is a theatrical prop, a bit of pork for contractors. Border entrepreneurs have already used blowtorches to cut passageways through the fence to collect "tolls," and are doing a brisk business. Back in Washington, the I.N.S. announces a $300 million computer contract to modernize its record-keeping and Congress passes a crime bill that shunts $255 million to the I.N.S. for 1995, $181 million earmarked for border control, which is to include 700 new partners for the men who stopped Gus and me in our travels, and the history professor, and my friend's father, and as many as they could from South Tucson.

It is no use; borders haven't worked, and they won't work, not now, as the indigenous people of the Americas reassert their kinship and solidarity with one another. A mass migration is already under way; its roots are not simply economic. The Uto-Aztecan languages are spoken as far north as Taos Pueblo near the Colorado border, all the way south to Mexico City. Before the arrival of the Europeans, the indigenous communities throughout this region not only conducted commerce, the people shared cosmologies, and oral narratives about the Maize Mother, the Twin Brothers and their Grandmother, Spider Woman, as well as Quetzalcoatl the benevolent snake. The great human migration within the Americas cannot be stopped; human beings are natural forces of the Earth, just as rivers and winds are natural forces.

Deep down the issue is simple: The so-called "Indian Wars" from the days of Sitting Bull and Red Cloud have never really ended in the Americas. The Indian people of southern Mexico, of Guatemala and those left in El Salvador, too, are still fighting for their lives and for their land against the "cavalry"

---

1. The Treaty of Guadalupe Hidalgo, signed in 1848, recognizes the right of the Tohano O'Odom (Papago) people to move freely across the U.S.–Mexico border without documents. A treaty with Canada guarantees similar rights to those of the Iroquois nation in traversing the U.S.–Canada border.

patrols sent out by the governments of those lands. The Americas are Indian country, and the "Indian problem" is not about to go away.

One evening at sundown, we were stopped in traffic at a railroad crossing in downtown Tucson while a freight train passed us, slowly gaining speed as it headed north to Phoenix. In the twilight I saw the most amazing sight: Dozens of human beings, mostly young men, were riding the train; everywhere, on flat cars, inside open boxcars, perched on top of boxcars, hanging off ladders on tank cars and between boxcars. I couldn't count fast enough, but I saw fifty or sixty people headed north. They were dark young men, Indian and mestizo; they were smiling and a few of them waved at us in our cars. I was reminded of the ancient story of Aztlán, told by the Aztecs but known in other Uto-Aztecan communities as well. Aztlán is the beautiful land to the north, the origin place of the Aztec people. I don't remember how or why the people left Aztlán to journey farther south, but the old story says that one day, they will return.

33

Police Accounts of Normal Force

JENNIFER HUNT

There are several ways to read this article. On the one hand, it instructs us about police behavior and how police officers do their work. Another is to see the way bureaucracies and formal procedures are contradicted by informal norms and group consensus. A third reading, and the one Jennifer Hunt intends, dissects the social construction of the reality in which police officers make sense of their work and their actions. The accounts police provide for their actions "normalize" an unpredictable and complex world. As you read this essay, think how you, too, normalize events in your everyday world and what this means for those with whom you interact.

The police are required to handle a variety of peacekeeping and law enforcement tasks including settling disputes, removing drunks from the street, aiding the sick, controlling crowds, and pursuing criminals. What unifies these diverse activities is the possibility that their resolution might require the use of force. Indeed, the capacity to use force stands at the core of the police mandate.

The bulk of the sociological literature on the use of force by police is concerned with analyzing the objective causes of "excessive" force. Some social scientists, for example, suggest that the incidence of extra-legal force correlates with characteristics of individual officers—in particular, their authoritarianism, age, or length of service. Others emphasize the relevance of the behavior and characteristics of the target population, including demeanor, sex, race, and class. Still others investigate the legal and organizational roots of force. They are concerned with how formal rules and/or subcultural norms may influence the police officer's decision to employ force.

Although representing diverse perspectives, these approaches share a similar underlying orientation to use of force by police. First, they all specify, in advance of study, formal or legal definitions of permissible force, definitions of permissible force, definitions that are then used to identify deviations legally classifiable as brutal or "excessive." This procedure disregards the understandings and standards police officers actively employ in using and evaluating force in the course of their work. Second, these studies are primarily concerned with identifying the objective conditions held to determine "excessive" force defined in this way. As a result, they minimize the active role of consciousness in police decisions to use force, tending to depict such decisions as mere passive responses to external determinants.

In contrast, sociologists working within the symbolic interactionist tradition have displayed particular interest in the police officer's own assessment of what constitutes necessary force. This research has varied in how such assessments are conceptualized. Rubinstein (1973: 302) for example, suggests that police use force instrumentally to control persons whom they perceive as presenting a physical threat. In contrast, Van Maanen (1978) explores how police, in reacting to others, are highly attentive to symbolic violation of their authority, dispensing harsh treatment to categories of persons who commit such violations.

The following research departs from and seeks to extend the symbolic interactionist concern with police officers' own assessments of the use of force. It explores how police themselves classify and evaluate acts of force as either legal, normal, or excessive. Legal force is that coercion necessary to subdue, control, and restrain a suspect in order to take him into custody. Although force not accountable in legal terms is technically labelled excessive by the courts and the public, the police perceive many forms of illegal force as normal. Normal force involves coercive acts that specific "cops" on specific occasions formulate as necessary, appropriate, reasonable, or understandable. Although not always legitimated or admired, normal force is depicted as a necessary or natural response of normal police to particular situational exigencies.

Most officers are expected to use both legal and normal force as a matter of course in policing the streets. In contrast, excessive force or brutality exceeds even working police notions of normal force. These are acts of coercion that cannot be explained by the routine police accounting practices ordinarily used to justify or excuse force. Brutality is viewed as illegal, illegitimate, and often immoral violence, but the police draw the lines in extremely different ways and at different points than do either the court system or the public.

These processes of assessing and accounting for the use of force, with special reference to the critical distinction between normal and excessive force as drawn by the police, will be explored in what follows. The study begins by examining how rookie police learn on the street to use and account for force in a manner that contradicts what they were taught at the academy. It then considers "normal force" and the accounting processes whereby police discriminatively judge when and how much force is appropriate in specific situations and incidents. It concludes with a discussion of excessive force and peer reactions to those who use it frequently.

The article is based on approximately eighteen months of participant observation in a major urban police department referred to as the Metro City P.D. I attended the police academy with male and female recruits and later rode with individual officers in one-person cars on evening and night shifts in high crime districts.[1] The female officers described in this research were among the first 100 women assigned to the ranks of uniformed patrol as a result of a discrimination suit filed by the Justice Department and a police-woman plaintiff.

LEARNING TO USE NORMAL FORCE

The police phrase "it's not done on the street the way that it's taught at the academy" underscores the perceived contradiction between the formal world of the police academy and the informal world of the street. This contradiction permeates the police officer's construction of his world, particularly his view of the rational and moral use of force.

In the formal world of the police academy, the recruit learns to account for force by reference to legality. He or she is issued the regulation instruments and trained to use them to subdue, control, and restrain a suspect. If threatened with great bodily harm, the officer learns that he can justifiably use deadly force and fire his revolver. Yet the recruit is taught that he cannot use his baton, jack, or gun, unnecessarily to torture, maim, or kill a suspect.

When recruits leave the formal world of the academy and are assigned to patrol a district, they are introduced to an informal world in which police recognize normal as well as legal and brutal force. Through observation and instruction, rookies gradually learn to apply force and account for its use in terms familiar to the street cop. First, rookies learn to adjust their arsenals to conform to street standards. They are encouraged to buy the more powerful weapons worn by veteran colleagues as these colleagues point out the inadequacy of a wooden baton or compare their convoy jacks to vibrators. They quickly discover that their department-issued equipment marks them as new recruits. At any rate, within a few weeks, most rookies have dispensed with the wooden baton and convoy jack and substituted them with the more powerful plastic nightstick and flat headed slapjack.[2]

Through experience and informal instruction, the rookie also learns the street use of these weapons. In school, for example, recruits are taught to avoid hitting a person on the head or neck because it could cause lethal damage. On the street, in contrast, police conclude that they must hit wherever it causes the most damage in order to incapacitate the suspect before they themselves are harmed. New officers also learn that they will earn the respect of their veteran coworkers not by observing legal niceties in using force, but by being "aggressive" and using whatever force is necessary in a given situation.

---

1. Nonetheless masculine pronouns are generally used to refer to the police in this article, because the Metro P.D. remained dominated by men numerically, in style and in tone.

2. Some officers also substitute a large heavy duty flashlight for the nightstick. If used correctly, the flashlight can inflict more damage than the baton and is less likely to break when applied to the head or other parts of the body.

Peer approval helps neutralize the guilt and confusion that rookies often experience when they begin to use force to assert their authority. One female officer, for example, learned she was the object of a brutality suit while listening to the news on television. At first, she felt so mortified that she hesitated to go to work and face her peers. In fact, male colleagues greeted her with a standing ovation and commented, "You can use our urinal now." In their view, any aggressive police officer regularly using normal force might eventually face a brutality suit or civilian complaint. Such accusations confirm the officer's status as a "street cop" rather than an "inside man" who doesn't engage in "real police work."

Whereas male rookies are assumed to be competent dispensers of force unless proven otherwise, women are believed to be physically weak, naturally passive, and emotionally vulnerable. Women officers are assumed to be reluctant to use physical force and are viewed as incompetent "street cops" until they prove otherwise. As a result, women rookies encounter special problems in learning to use normal force in the process of becoming recognized as "real street cops." It becomes crucial for women officers to create or exploit opportunities to display their physical abilities in order to overcome sexual bias and obtain full acceptance from coworkers. As a result, women rookies are encouraged informally to act more aggressively and to display more machismo than male rookies. Consider the following incident where a young female officer reflects upon her use of force during a domestic disturbance:

And when I get there, if goddamn, there isn't a disturbance going on. So Tom comes, the guy that I went to back up. The male talks to him. I take the female and talk to her. And the drunk (cop) comes and the sergeant comes and another guy comes. So while we think we have everything settled, and we have the guy calmed down, he turns around and says to his sister, no less, that's who it is, "Give me the keys to my car!" And with that, she rips them out of her pocket and throws them at him. Now, he goes nuts. He goes into a Kung fu stance and says he's gonna kill her. The drunk cop says, "Yo, knock it off!" and goes to grab him and the guy punches him. So Mike (the drunk cop) goes down. Tommy goes to grab him and is wrestling with him. And all the cops are trying to get in there. So I ran in with my stick and I stick the guy in the head. But I just missed Tommy's face and opened him (the suspect) up. So all of a sudden everybody's grabbin' him and I'm realizing that if we get him down, he won't hurt anybody. So I pushed the sergeant out of the way and I got my stick under the guy's legs and I pulled his legs out from under him and I yelled, "Tommy, take him down." I pulled his legs and he went down and I sat on him. So Tommy says, "Well, cuff him." And I says, "I can't find my goddamned cuffs." I molested my body trying to get my cuffs. . . .

So, when I [finally] get my cuffs, we cuff him. And we're sitting there talking. And Tommy, he has no regard for me whatsoever. . . . The guy's opened up and he bled all over Tommy's shirt. And I turned around and said, "Tommy, look at your shirt. There's blood all over your shirt." He said, "Who the hell almost clobbered me?" I said, "I'm sorry Tom, that was me." He said, "You're the one that opened him up? And I said, "Yeh. I'm sorry, I didn't mean to get so close to you." . . .

So when the sergeant came out he said, "And you, what do you mean telling me to get outta the way." He said, "Do you know you pushed me outta your way." . . . And I said, "I didn't want you to get hurt . . . and I was afraid he was gonna kick one of you." And he says, "I still can't believe you pushed me outta your way. You were like a little dynamo." And I found after that I got respect from the sergeant. He doesn't realize it but he treated me differently after that.

Her colleagues' reactions provided informal instruction in the use of normal force, confirming that her actions under these circumstances were reasonable and even praiseworthy.

For a street cop, it is often a graver error to use too little force and develop a "shaky" reputation than it is to use too much force and be told to calm down. Thus officers, particularly rookies, who do not back up their partners in appropriate ways or who hesitate to use force in circumstances where it is deemed necessary are informally instructed regarding their aberrant ways. If the problematic incident is relatively insignificant and his general reputation is good, a rookie who "freezes" one time is given a second chance before becoming generally known as an untrustworthy partner. However, such incidents become the subject of degrading gossip, gossip that pressures the officer either to use force as expected or risk isolation. Such talk also informs rookies about the general boundaries of legal and normal force.

For example, a female rookie was accused of "freezing" in an incident that came to be referred to as a "Mexican standoff." A pedestrian had complained that "something funny is going on in the drugstore." The officer walked into the pharmacy where she found an armed man committing a robbery. Although he turned his weapon on her when she entered the premises, she still pulled out her gun and pointed it at him. When he ordered her to drop it, claiming that his partner was behind her with a revolver at her head, she refused and told him to drop his. He refused, and the stalemate continued until a sergeant entered the drugstore and ordered the suspect to drop his gun.

Initially, the female officer thought she had acted appropriately and even heroically. She soon discovered, however, that her hesitation to shoot had brought into question her competence with some of her fellow officers. Although many veterans claimed that "she had a lot a balls" to take her gun out at all when the suspect already had a gun on her, most contended "she shoulda shot him." Other policemen confirmed that she committed a "rookie mistake"; she had failed to notice a "lookout" standing outside the store and hence had been unprepared for an armed confrontation. Her sergeant and lieutenant, moreover, even insisted that she had acted in a cowardly manner, despite her reputation as a "gung-ho cop," and cited the incident as evidence of the general inadequacy of policewomen.

In the weeks that followed, this officer became increasingly depressed and angry. She was particularly outraged when she learned that she would not receive a commendation, although such awards were commonly made for "gun pinches" of this nature. Several months later, the officer vehemently expressed the wish that she had killed the suspect and vowed that next time she would "shoot first and ask questions later." The negative sanctions of supervisors and colleagues clearly encouraged her to adopt an attitude favorable to using force with less restraint in future situations.

Reprimand, gossip, and avoidance constitute the primary means by which police try to change or control the behavior of coworkers perceived as unreliable or cowardly. Formal accusations, however, are discouraged regardless of the seriousness of the misconduct. One male rookie, for example, earned a reputation for cowardice after he allegedly had to be "dragged" out of the car during an "assist officer." Even then, he apparently refused to help the officers in trouble. Although no formal charges were filed, everyone in the district was warned to avoid working with this officer.

Indeed, to initiate formal charges against a coworker may discredit the accuser. In one incident a male rookie, although discouraged by veteran officers and even his district captain, filed charges of cowardice against a female rookie. The rookie gained the support of two supervisors and succeeded in having the case heard before the Board of Inquiry. During the trial he claimed the woman officer failed to aid him in arresting a man who presented physical resistance and had a knife on his person. In rebuttal, the woman testified that she perceived no need to participate in a physical confrontation because she saw no knife and the policeman was hitting the suspect. In spite of conflicting testimony, she was found guilty of "Neglect of Duty." Although most veterans thought the woman was "flaky" and doubted her competence, they also felt the male rookie had exaggerated his story. Moreover, they were outraged that he filed formal charges and he quickly found himself ostracized.

At the same time that male and female rookies are commended for using force under appropriate circumstances, they are reprimanded if their participation in force is viewed as excessive or inappropriate. In this way, rookies are instructed that although many acts of coercion are accepted and even demanded, not everything goes. They thereby learn to distinguish between normal and brutal force. In the following incident, for example, a policewoman describes how she instructed a less experienced officer that her behavior was unreasonable and should be checked. Here, the new officer is chastised for misreading interactional cues and overreacting to minor affronts when treating a crazy person involved in a minor dispute as if he were a serious felon.

> But like I said, when I first heard about it (another fight) I'd wondered if Mary had provoked it any because we'd gone on a disturbance and it was a drunk black guy who called to complain that the kid who lived upstairs keeps walking

through his apartment. The kid to me looks wacky. He's talking crazy. He's saying they shoulda sent men. What are you women going to do. Going on and on. And to me it was a bullshit job. But Mary turns around and says, "We don't have to take that from him. Let's lock him up." I said, "Mary forget it." And the kid has numchuck sticks on him and when he turned his back . . . he had them in his back pocket. So, as he's pulling away saying you're scared, like a little kid, I turned around and said, "I've got your sticks." And I go away. Mary . . . so Mary was . . . I looked at her and she was so disappointed in me . . . like I'd turned chicken on her. So I tried to explain to her, I said, "Mary, all we have is disorderly conduct. That's a summary offense. That's bullshit." I said, "Did you want to get hurt for a summary offense?" I said, "The guy was drunk who called to complain. It wasn't even a legit complaint." I said, "It's just . . . You've got to use discretion. If you think I'm chicken think of the times when a 'man with a gun' comes over the air and I'm the first car there." I said, "When it's worth it, I'll do anything. When it's not worth it, I'll back off." And I think she tries to temper herself some because Collette and her, they finally had a talk about why they hated each other. And Collette said to her, "I think you're too physical. I think you look for fights." And I think maybe Mary hearing it twice, once from me and once from Collette, might start to think that maybe she does provoke. Instead of going up . . . I always go up to them friendly and then if they act shitty I get shitty.

In summary, when rookies leave the academy, they begin to familiarize themselves with street weapons and to gain some sense of what kinds of behavior constitute too little or too much force. They also begin to develop an understanding of street standards for using and judging appropriate and necessary force. By listening to and observing colleagues at work and by experiencing a variety of problematic interactions with the public, newcomers become cognizant of the occasions and circumstances in which to use various degrees and kinds of force. But at the same time, they are learning not only when and how to use force, but also a series of accounting practices to justify and to legitimate as "normal" (and sometimes to condemn) these acts of coercion. Normal force is thus the product of the police officers' accounting practices for describing what happened in ways that prefigure or anticipate the conclusion that it was in some sense justified or excusable and hence "normal." It is to a consideration of the ways in which officers learn to provide such accounts for normal force that I now turn.

ACCOUNTING FOR NORMAL FORCE

Police routinely normalize the use of force by two types of accounts: excuses and justifications. Excuses deny full responsibility for an act of force but acknowledge its inappropriateness. Acts of force become excusable when they are depicted as the natural outcome of strong, even uncontrollable emotions normally arising in certain routine sorts of police activities. Through such accounts, officers excuse force by asserting that it is a "natural," "human" reaction to certain extreme, emotionally trying situations. Justifications accept responsibility for the coercive act in question but deny that the act was wrongful or blameworthy.

Police justify force through two analytically distinct kinds of accounts: situational and abstract. In the former, the officer represents force as a response in some specific situation needed to restore immediate control or to reestablish the local order of power in the face of a threat to police authority. In contrast, abstract accounts justify force as a morally appropriate response to certain categories of crime and criminals who symbolize a threat to the moral order. As an account, abstract justification does not highlight processes of interactional provocation and threats to immediate control, but rather legitimates force as a means of obtaining some higher moral purpose, particularly the punishment of heinous offenders.

None of these accounts are mutually exclusive, and are often combined in justifying and excusing the use of force in any specific instance. For example, police consider it justifiable to use force to regain control of someone who has challenged an officer's authority. However, an officer may also excuse his behavior as an "overreaction," claiming he "snapped out" and lost control, and hence used more force or different kinds of force than were required to regain control. Mixed accounts involving situational and abstract justifications of force are also frequent: force may be depicted as necessary to regain control when an officer is physically assaulted; but at the same time it may also be justified as punishment appropriate to the kind of morally unworthy person who would challenge an officer's authority.

EXCUSES AND NORMAL FORCE

Excuses are accounts in which police deny full responsibility for an act but recognize its inappropriateness. Excuses therefore constitute socially approved vocabularies for relieving responsibility when conduct is questionable. Police most often excuse morally problematic force by referring to emotional or physiological states that are precipitated by some circumstances of routine patrol work. These circumstances include shootouts, violent fights, pursuits, and instances in which a police officer mistakenly comes close to killing an unarmed person.

Policework in these circumstances can generate intense excitement in which the officer experiences the "combat high" and "adrenaline rush" familiar to the combat soldier. Foot and car pursuits not only bring on feelings of danger and excitement from the chase, but also a challenge to official authority. As one patrolman commented about a suspect: "Yeh, he got tuned up (beaten) . . . you always tune them up after a car chase." Another officer normalized the use of force after a pursuit in these terms:

> It's my feeling that violence inevitably occurs after a pursuit. . . . The adrenaline
> . . . and the insult involved when someone flees increases with every foot of the
> pursuit. I know the two or three times that I felt I lost control of myself . . . was
> when someone would run on me. The further I had to chase the guy the madder
> I got. . . . The funny thing is the reason for the pursuit could have been for some-
> thing as minor as a traffic violation or a kid you're chasing who just turned on a
> fire hydrant. It always ends in violence. You feel obligated to hit or kick the guy
> just for running.

Police officers also excuse force when it follows an experience of helplessness and confusion that has culminated in a temporary loss of emotional control. This emotional combination occurs most frequently when an officer comes to the brink of using lethal force, drawing a gun and perhaps firing, only to learn there were no "real" grounds for this action. The officer may then "snap out" and hit the suspect. In one such incident, for example, two policemen picked up a complainant who positively identified a suspect as a man who just tried to shoot him. Just as the officers approached the suspect, he suddenly reached for his back pocket for what the officers assumed to be a gun. One officer was close enough to jump the suspect before he pulled his hand from his pocket. As it turned out, the suspect had no weapon, having dropped it several feet away. Although he was unarmed and under control, the suspect was punched and kicked out of anger and frustration by the officer who had almost shot him.

Note that in both these circumstances—pursuit and near-miss mistaken shootings—officers would concede that the ensuing force is inappropriate and unjustifiable when considered abstractly. But although abstractly wrong, the use of force on such occasions is presented as a normal, human reaction to an extreme situation. Although not every officer might react violently in such circumstances, it is understandable and expected that some will.

SITUATIONAL JUSTIFICATIONS

Officers also justify force as normal by reference to interactional situations in which an officer's authority is physically or symbolically threatened. In such accounts, the use of force is justified instrumentally—as a means of regaining immediate control in a situation where that control has become tenuous. Here, the officer depicts his primary intent for using force as a need to reestablish immediate control in a problematic encounter, and only incidentally as hurting or punishing the offender.

Few officers will hesitate to assault a suspect who physically threatens or attacks them. In one case, an officer was punched in the face by a prisoner he had just apprehended for allegedly attempting to shoot a friend. The incident occurred in the stationhouse and several policemen observed the exchange. Immediately, one officer hit the prisoner in the jaw and the rest immediately joined the brawl.

Violations of an officer's property such as his car or hat may signify a more symbolic assault on the officer's authority and self, thus justifying a forceful response to maintain control. Indeed, in the police view, almost any person who verbally challenges a police officer is appropriately subject to force. In the following extract, a female officer accounts in these ways for a colleague's use of force against an escaping prisoner:

> And so Susan gets on the scene (of the fight). They cuff one of the girls, and she throws her in the back seat of the car. She climbs over the back seat, jumps out of the car with cuffs on and starts running up the stairs. Susan and Jane are trying to cuff the other girl and all of a sudden Susan looks up and sees her cuffs running away. She (Jane) said Susan turned into an animal. Susan runs up the steps grabs the girl by the legs. Drags her down the five steps. Puts her in the car. Kicks her in the car. Jane goes in the car and calls her every name she can think of and waves her stick in her face.[3]

On rare occasions, women officers encounter special problems in these regards. Although most suspects view women in the same way as policemen, some seem less inclined to accord female officers de facto and symbolic control in street encounters, and on a few occasions seem determined to provoke direct confrontations with such officers, explicitly denying their formal authority and attempting none too subtly to sexualize the encounter. Women officers, then, might use force as a resource for rectifying such insults and for establishing control over such partially sexualized interactions.

* * *

ABSTRACT JUSTIFICATIONS

Police also justify the use of extreme force against certain categories of morally reprehensible persons. In this case, force is not presented as an instrumental means to regain control that has been symbolically or physically threatened. Instead, it is justified as an appropriate response to particularly heinous offenders. Categories of such offenders include: cop haters who have gained notoriety as persistent police antagonizers; cop killers or any person who has attempted seriously to harm a police officer; sexual deviants who prey on children and "moral women"; child abusers; and junkies and other "scum" who inhabit the

---

3. Note that this account employs both the justifications of reestablishing real and symbolic control, and the excuse of emotionally snapping out in response to this symbolic challenge and to the resulting pursuit.

street. The more morally reprehensible the act is judged, the more likely the police are to depict any violence directed toward its perpetrator as justifiable. Thus a man who exposes himself to children in a playground is less likely to experience police assault than one who rapes or sexually molests a child.

"Clean" criminals, such as high level mafiosi, white-collar criminals, and professional burglars, are rarely subject to abstract force. Nor are perpetrators of violent and nonviolent street crimes who prey on adult males, prostitutes, and other categories of persons who belong on the street.[4] Similarly, the "psycho" or demented person is perceived as so mentally deranged that he is not responsible for his acts and hence does not merit abstract, punitive force.

Police justify abstract force by invoking a higher moral purpose that legitimates the violation of commonly recognized standards. In one case, for example, a nun was raped by a 17-year-old male adolescent. When the police apprehended the suspect, he was severely beaten and his penis put in an electrical outlet to teach him a lesson. The story of the event was told to me by a police officer who, despite the fact that he rarely supported the use of extralegal force, depicted this treatment as legitimate. Indeed, when I asked if he would have participated had he been present, he responded, "I'm Catholic. I would have participated."

EXCESSIVE FORCE AND PEER RESPONSES

Although police routinely excuse and justify many incidents where they or their coworkers have used extreme force against a citizen or suspect, this does not mean that on any and every occasion the officer using such force is exonerated. Indeed, the concept of normal force is useful because it suggests that there are specific circumstances under which police officers will not condone the use of force by themselves or colleagues as reasonable and acceptable. Thus, officer-recognized conceptions of normal force are subject to restrictions of the following kinds:

(1) Police recognize and honor some rough equation between the behavior of the suspect and the harmfulness of the force to which it is subject. There are limits, therefore, to the degree of force that is acceptable in particular circumstances. In the following incident, for example, an officer reflects on a situation in which a "symbolic assailant" (Skolnick, 1975: 45) was mistakenly subject to more force than he "deserved" and almost killed:

> One time Bill Johnson and I, I have more respect for him than any other policeman. . . . He and I, we weren't particularly brutal. If the guy deserved it, he got it. It's generally the attitude that does it. We had a particularly rude drunk one day. He was really rude and spit on you and he did all this stuff and we even had

---

4. The categories of persons who merit violence are not unique to the police. Prisoners, criminals, and hospital personnel appear to draw similar distinctions between morally unworthy persons; on the latter, see Sudnow (1967: 105).

to cuff him lying down on the hard stretcher, like you would do an epileptic. . . . We were really mad at this guy. So, what you normally do with drunks is you take them to the district cell. . . . So we were really mad. We said let's just give him one or two shots. . . . slamming on the brakes and having him roll. But we didn't use our heads. He's screaming and hollering "You lousy cops" and we slammed on the brakes and we didn't use our heads and we heard the stretcher go nnnnnnBam and then nothing. We heard nothing and we realized we had put this man in with his head to the front so when we slammed on the brakes this stretcher. . . . I guess it can roll four foot. Well, it was his head that had hit the front of it and we heard no sounds and my God, I've never been so scared. Me and Bill we thought we killed him. So I'm saying "Bill, what are we gonna do? How are we gonna explain this one." The guy's still saying nothing. So, we went to Madison Street and parked. It's a really lonely area. And we unlocked the wagon and peeked in. We know he's in there. We were so scared and we look in and there's not a sound and we see blood coming in front of the wagon and think "Oh my God we killed this man. What am I gonna do? What am I gonna tell my family?" And to make a long story short, he was just knocked out. But boy was I scared. From then on we learned, feet first.

(2) Although it is considered normal and natural to become emotional and angry in highly charged, taut encounters, officers nonetheless prefer to minimize the harmful consequences of the use of force. As a result, officers usually acknowledge that emotional reactions that might lead to extreme force should be controlled and limited by coworkers if at all possible. In the following account, for example, an officer justified the use of force as a legitimate means to regain situational control when physically challenged. Nonetheless, he expressed gratitude to his partner for stopping him from doing serious harm when he "snapped out" and lost control:

Well, I wasn't sure if she was a girl until I put my hand on her shoulder and realized it was a woman's shoulder. I was trying to stop her. But it happened when she suddenly kicked me in the balls. Then everything inside of me exploded and I grabbed her and pushed her against the car and started pressing her backwards and kept pressing her backwards. All of a sudden something clicked inside of me because I noticed her eyes changed and her body caved in and she looked frightened because she knew that I was gonna kill her. And I stopped. I think I stopped because Susan was on the scene. She must have said something. But anyway she (Susan) told me later that I should calm down. And I snapped at her and told her to mind her own business because she didn't know what happened. The girl kicked me in the balls. But she was right about it. I mean it was getting to me. I'd never hit a woman before.

(3) Similarly, even in cases where suspects are seen as deserving some violent punishment, this force should not be used randomly and without control.

Thus, in the following incident, an officer who "snapped out" and began to beat a child abuser clearly regarded his partner's attempt to stop the beating as reasonable.

> We get a call "meet complainant" and I drive up and there's a lady standing out in front of the house and she's saying, "Listen officer, I don't know what the story is but the neighbors in there. They're screaming and hollering and there's kicking going on in there and I can't take it. I can't sleep. There's too much noise." Nothing unusual about that. Just a typical day in the district. So the next thing you do is knock on the door and tell them to please keep the noise down or whatever you do. You say to yourself it's probably a boy friend-girl friend fight. So I knock on the door and a lady answers just completely hysterical. And I say, "Listen, I don't know what's going on in here," but then I hear this, just this screeching. You know. And I figure well I'm just going to find out what's going on so I just go past the lady and what's happening is that the husband had. . . . The kid was being potty trained and the way they were potty training this kid, this two-year-old boy, was that the boyfriend of this girl would pick up this kid and he would sit him down on top of the stove. It was their method of potty training. Well, first of all you think of your own kids. I mean afterwards you do. I mean I've never been this mad in my whole life. You see this little two-year-old boy seated on top of the stove with rings around it being absolutely scalding hot. And he's saying "I'll teach you to go." . . . It just triggered something. An uncontrollable. . . . It's just probably the most violent I ever got. Well you just grab that guy. You hit him ten, fifteen times . . . you don't know how many. You just get so mad. And I remember my partner eventually came in and grabbed me and said, "Don't worry about it. We got him. We got him." And we cuffed him and we took him down. Yeah that was bad.

Learning these sorts of restrictions on the use of normal force and these informal practices of peer control are important processes in the socialization of newcomers. This socialization proceeds both through ongoing observation and experience and, on occasion, through explicit instruction. For example, one veteran officer advised a rookie, "The only reason to go in on a pursuit is not to get the perpetrator but to pull the cop who gets there first offa the guy before he kills him."

It is against this background that patrol officers identify excessive force and the existence of violence-prone peers. Some officers become known for recurrently committing acts of coercion that exceed working notions of normal force and that cannot be excused or justified with routine accounting practices. In contrast to the officer who makes a "rookie mistake" and uses excessive force from inexperience, the brutal cop does not honor the practices of normal force. Such an officer is also not effectively held in check by routine means of peer control. As a result, more drastic measures must be taken to prevent him from endangering the public and his colleagues.

One rookie gained a reputation for brutality from frequent involvement in "unnecessary" fights. One such incident was particularly noteworthy: Answering a call on a demented male with a weapon, he came upon a large man pacing the sidewalk carrying a lead pipe. The officer got out of the patrol car and yelled in a belligerent tone of voice, "What the fuck are you doing creep?" At this point "the creep" attacked the officer and tried to take away his gun. A policewoman arrived on the scene, joined the fight, called an assist, and rescued the patrolman. Although no one was hurt, colleagues felt the incident was provoked by the officer who aggressively approached a known crazy person who should have been assumed to be unpredictable and nonresponsible.

When colleagues first began to doubt this officer's competence, he was informally instructed to moderate his behavior by veteran and even rookie partners. When his behavior persisted, confrontations with fellow officers became explosive. When peers were unable to check his behavior, complaints were made to superiors. Officially, colleagues indicated they did not want to work with him because of "personality problems." Informally, however, supervisors were informed of the nature of his provocative and dangerous behavior. The sergeant responded by putting the rookie in a wagon with a responsible partner whom he thought might succeed in controlling him. When this strategy proved unsuccessful, he was eventually transferred to the subway unit. Such transfers to "punishment districts," isolated posts, "inside units," or the subway are typical means of handling police officers deemed dangerous and out of control.

As this discussion indicates, the internal control of an exceptionally or inappropriately violent police officer is largely informal. With the exception of civilian complaints and brutality suits, the behavior of such officers rarely becomes the subject of formal police documents. However, their reputations are often well known throughout the department and the rumors about their indiscretions educate rookies about how the line between normal force and brutality is drawn among working police officers.

It takes more than one incident of excessively violent behavior for a police officer to attain a brutal reputation. The violent officer is usually involved in numerous acts of aggressive behavior that are not accountable as normal force either because of their frequency or because of their substance. However, once identified as "brutal," a "head beater," and so on, an officer's use of force will be condemned by peers in circumstances in which competent officers would be given the benefit of the doubt. For example, one officer gained national notoriety during a federal investigation into a suspicious shooting. Allegedly, a local resident had thrown an axe at the patrol wagon. According to available accounts, the police pursued the suspect inside a house and the officer in question shot him in the head. Although witnesses claimed the victim was unarmed, the officer stated that he fired in self defense. The suspect reportedly attacked him with a metal pipe. This policeman had an established reputation for being "good with his hands," and many colleagues assumed he had brutally shot an unarmed man in the aftermath of a pursuit.

CONCLUSION

The organization of policework reflects a poignant moral dilemma: for a variety of reasons, society mandates to the police the right to use force but provides little direction as to its proper use in specific, "real life" situations. Thus, the police, as officers of the law, must be prepared to use force under circumstances in which its rationale is often morally, legally, and practically ambiguous. This fact explains some otherwise puzzling aspects of police training and socialization.

The police academy provides a semblance of socialization for its recruits by teaching formal rules for using force. It is a semblance of socialization because it treats the use of force as capable of rationalization within the moral and legal conventions of the civilian world. The academy also, paradoxically, trains recruits in the use of tools of violence with potential for going far beyond the limitations of action imposed by those conventions. Consequently, the full socialization of a police officer takes place outside the academy as the officer moves from its idealizations to the practicalities of the street. This movement involves several phases: (1) a decisive, practical separation from the formal world established within the academy; (2) the cultivation of a working distinction between what is formally permissible and what is practically and informally required of the "street cop"; and (3) the demonstration of competence in using and accounting for routine street practices that are morally and legally problematic for those not working the street.

The original dilemma surrounding the use of force persists throughout the socialization process, but is increasingly dealt with by employing accounts provided by the police community that reduce and neutralize the moral tension. The experienced "street cop" becomes an expert at using techniques of neutralization to characterize the use of force on the streets, at judging its use by others, and at evaluating the necessity for using force by standards those techniques provide. Use of these techniques also reinforces the radical separation of the formal and informal worlds of policework, duplicating within the context of the organization itself the distinction between members and outsiders. This guarantees that members will be able to distinguish between those who can and cannot be trusted to use force and to understand the conditions under which its use is reasonable.

As accounts neutralizing the use of force, justifications and excuses both serve—though each in a different way—to manage the tension inherent in situations fraught with moral insecurity. They conventionalize but do not reform situations that are inherently charged and morally ambiguous. In this way they simultaneously preserve the self-image of police as agents of the conventional order, provide ways in which individual officers can resolve their personal doubts as to the moral status of their action and those of their colleagues, and reinforce the solidarity of the police community.

REFERENCES

Emerson, R. M. (1969). *Judging Delinquents: Context and Process in Juvenile Court.* Chicago: Aldine.

Rubinstein, J. (1973). *City Police.* New York: Ballantine.

Skolnick, J. (1975). *Justice Without Trial.* New York: John Wiley.

Sudnow, D. (1967). *Passing On: The Social Organization of Dying.* Englewood Cliffs, NJ: Prentice-Hall.

Van Maanen, J. (1978). "The asshole," in P. K. Manning and J. Van Maanen (eds.) *Policing: A View From the Street.* Santa Monica, CA: Goodyear.

34

The Foundations of Third World Poverty

FROM *Promises Not Kept: The Betrayal of
Social Change in the Third World*

JOHN ISBISTER

*Prospects for positive change in the poorest countries of the world are not bright,
at least in the immediate future. Much of the reason lies in the past relationship
between poor and wealthy countries and the chain of events this relationship set in
motion. Isbister's discussion encourages us to recognize that we are all tied into the
global community, and that the benefit to each of us is dependent on a strategy of
global change that benefits us all.*

In the economic sphere, the legacy of imperialism is central. The dependency
theorists are correct in insisting that imperialism formed the economic
structures of the Third World, which even today leave the vast majority of
the human race in desperately poor conditions.

* * *

When we turn to * * * the effects of imperialism upon the economies and
societies of Asia, the Middle East, Africa and Latin America, then the fact
that the imperialists were capitalist is centrally important. The essence of capitalism is alienation. The factors of production—land, labor and capital—are
treated in a capitalist system as commodities, to be bought or sold. They are
not part of a person's birthright. In many peasant societies, in contrast, the
factors of production are inherently connected as part of an integrated system. A person is born to a village society and automatically cultivates land
passed down from one generation to the next, using the product to sustain
the family. These peasants, although usually exploited by a landowning or ruling class, are nonetheless secure in knowing their place in the world. The
advent of imperialism broke this world apart, creating labor forces that
worked for wages on other people's projects, and land that could be bought
and sold. Imperialism converted the peasants of the Third World into separate
components of the capitalist system, components whose survival depended
upon the vagaries of global markets over which they had no control.

Before the arrival of the imperialists, the majority of the people of the Third
World were involved in producing food for their own use—as hunters and
gatherers in some regions, but for the most part as cultivators of the soil. They
typically produced some surplus food, over and above their own needs, which
was used to support a ruling group, but this was usually a small portion of their

production. For the most part, they produced what they needed to survive. Imperialism changed this picture. It did not totally displace subsistence production, of course, because people still had to eat; on top of subsistence production, however, the imperialists imposed the production of primary export commodities—agricultural goods and minerals from the colonies that were intended for use in the metropolitan centers. The colonies were turned into a vast production system for sugar, cacao, tobacco, wheat, cotton, meat, fish, jute, coffee, coconuts, rubber, wool, palm oil, rice, bananas, ground nuts, indigo, tin, gold, silver, bauxite, copper and many more products.

As Europe developed its manufacturing industries in the nineteenth century, and as its own peasants were drawn off the land and into its unspeakable cities, it required new sources of primary agricultural commodities—both to feed the urban labor force and to provide raw materials for the factories. It was no coincidence, then, that colonial export production intensified at the same time that capitalist industrial production was growing in Europe; the colonial exports were required for the growth of industry at the imperial centers.

Imperialism produced a world of economic specialization: manufacturing in the core of Europe and agricultural and mining production in the periphery of the Third World. The doctrines of free trade and comparative advantage * * * provided an intellectual justification for this specialization.

* * *

The case against comparative advantage, and against the world division of production brought about by the imperialists, is not entirely easy to make, because there are obvious counterexamples. Canada is the best of the counterexamples. From the sixteenth century through to the twentieth, Canada fit precisely into the imperialist economic mode: it produced primary products for export to Europe, and it imported European manufactured goods. On the basis of those primary exports it was successful; it developed into one of the richest countries in the world, with a standard of living higher than most European countries. Canada developed its economy to a high level by exploiting a series of primary exports, or "staples." In the sixteenth century the French discovered the rich fisheries off the coast of Newfoundland. Their successors ventured inland, eventually across the entire continent, in search of beaver furs, which were processed into felt hats for European consumers. The fur trade was succeeded by timber, and then by the greatest staple export of all, wheat. In the twentieth century, wheat was supplemented by minerals. Immigrants flocked to the new land to develop each staple export as it came along. The income they generated was used both to raise their standard of living and to reinvest in productive activities designed for local use. In Canada, primary exports became the engine of sustained economic growth. A national manufacturing sector grew up behind the staples to meet the needs of the local settlers, and in this way Canada developed a technologically advanced, productive modern economy.

To cite the Canadian example is to show, however, how exceptional it was, for the export industries established in most of the rest of the colonial world did not lead automatically to self-sustaining economic growth for the local population. Far more often they led to poverty, to destitution on the land and to urbanization without hope. Even in Argentina, which for many decades resembled Canada, and by as late as the 1920's had a higher standard of living based upon its beef export industry, stagnation eventually set in.

The best answer to the question of why the concentration on colonial agricultural export production led to stagnation in the Third World instead of to prosperity as in Canada lies in the fact that the exports transformed the social structures of the Third World (but not of Canada) in such a way as to render genuine economic development less likely. The heart of social transformation in the Third World was the fact that the local labor force, or the land, or both, had to be wrested, often forcibly, from their existing uses. The problem of forcibly changing the use of local labor and land did not arise in Canada, because in that colony the native population was either exterminated or shunted off to reservations, leaving behind them lands that for the most part had never been tilled. But in the Third World, the local populations generally stayed and were in possession of the land.

The colonialists in the Third World often confronted intensive labor shortages. Frequently the local people did not constitute the sort of labor force that capitalist enterprises required; they were not willing to give up their subsistence pursuits and work for wages—at least not for the low wages normally offered by the white man. In some cases forced labor of the local people resulted in many deaths—for example, in the mines and plantations of the Spanish empire in Latin America. The slave trade was the first answer to this problem—millions of Africans were shipped to the western hemisphere—until it was effectively shut down towards the beginning of the nineteenth century. As the nineteenth century progressed, however, the need for colonial labor only increased, so other expedients were developed. Indentured service, or the labor contract, became common; it was a system by which a person made the commitment to work in a foreign land for a period of years in return for a guaranteed wage and a return passage home. Indentured Indians, Chinese and other Asians were shipped long distances to work in semifree conditions in the imperialist plantations. Many did not return to their homelands, and their descendants today create ethnic heterogeneity in many areas of the Third World.

In addition to importing labor, the Europeans devised ways of forcing the local people to work for them. In Indonesia the Dutch established the "culture system," a kind of throwback to European medieval feudalism, by which native people were required to devote a certain portion of their land and labor to the production of export products, these to take the place of taxes. A common technique in Africa and elsewhere was to impose a hut tax or a head tax. These were taxes that had to be paid in the imperialist's currency by each person. But the peasants did not earn or use this currency in their villages. So in order to pay the tax they had to earn the currency, and in order to earn the currency they had to work as laborers for the white man. The head tax led to the pernicious colonial theory of the "backward-bending supply curve of labor": the lower the wage rate the longer the natives would work, since their goal was to earn a certain fixed amount in order to be able to pay the hut tax. It was a system of forced labor, pure and simple. Frequently taxes did not induce sufficient work, however, and they were supplemented by more direct means: the compulsion of labor by military force. The use of armed force by King Leopold of Belgium in the Congo to create a labor force was particularly notorious.

* * *

If the accumulation of a labor force was a problem, the amassing of land to be used by capitalist enterprises for export crops was often even more difficult. Most of the land was, of course, already occupied. The Europeans were faced with the need either to expel the local people from the most fertile land, or to persuade them to grow export crops in their villages. Expulsion was often the order of the day. * * * The land distribution in southern and East Africa became unbelievably skewed, with the Europeans, a small proportion of the population, owning the great majority of the land and the Africans crowded into small areas with inferior soil.

Far more common were the large plantations, in Africa and Asia owned and overseen by Europeans and worked exclusively by natives. * * * Landholding patterns became incredibly unequal; it was common in many areas of the Third World for a scant 1 or 2 percent of the landowners to control at least half of the arable land. The land available for peasant use was reduced proportionately and, of course, many of the peasants, having lost their land, had to work as wage laborers, usually for very low wages, on the great plantations.

* * *

The imperialist world economy, and the insatiable demand of European industrialization for food and raw materials, therefore transformed the agricultural sectors of the Third World, where the great majority of the populations were located. Imperialism forced millions of people to migrate, it separated masses of people from the land and recreated them as wage laborers and it brought village-based, peasant agriculture into world markets.

In assessing this tremendous impact, it is helpful to return to the comparison of the Third World with Canada, since Canada parlayed a succession of primary exports into steady economic growth and one of the world's highest standards of living. Why did the concentration on primary exports not pay similar dividends in the Third World? It is a puzzle. Some of the answers that have been given to it over the years seem not very satisfying. Raul Prebisch and some other Latin American economists argued that the problem was declining terms of trade—essentially that the prices of primary products were falling in world markets to such an extent that, even though Third World countries were selling more and more, they were earning less and less and could afford fewer imports of manufactured goods. The argument is valid for some primary exports and for some countries, over some time periods, but recent scholarship has shown conclusively that as a general explanation for the continuing poverty of the Third World it collapses. Certainly it cannot be a general explanation for the poverty of primary exporters, for if it were, Canada would be poverty stricken as well.

Another line of argument has been that the imperialists and their successors sent the profits that they earned back to their homelands, rather than reinvesting those profits in local enterprises. Modern imperialism and neo-colonialism are seen through these lenses as a way of looting the Third World, just as surely as the sixteenth-century Spaniards looted the gold and silver of the Americas. This argument has more to it, since there certainly were enormous transfers of funds from the colonial areas back to Britain and the other colonial powers. It is not really satisfactory, though, as an explanation of continuing poverty, since profits were repatriated from Canada, too, and since even after subtracting the repatriated profits, considerable new wealth stayed in the colonies as a consequence of the export activities.

A more promising explanation is F. S. Weaver's, who argues that the export industries created new wealth and that the wealth reinforced whatever social structure was already existing in the colony. In Canada, the British settlers who populated most of the country outside the province of Quebec were entrepreneurial capitalists to begin with. There was no question of transforming them from feudal or subsistence peasants—they were capitalists from the day they entered the country, in the sense that they were committed to the market, to buying and selling, to producing for export and not for their own use. The income they earned was reinvested in the expansion of their small-scale enterprises, including family farms.

But in the colonies of what is now the Third World, conditions were very different. The relationship that the imperialists had to the natives, and that the *hacendados* had to the peons, was one of oppression. So, when the ruling classes in the Third World accumulated wealth through the export of primary products, they used that wealth and the power that went along with it to intensify the oppression of the local people and thereby to reinforce their own status. Imperialism reinforced the conditions that were already there. Profits were used to expand plantations, but for the local people this simply meant being part of a larger labor force, separate from their ancestral homes and working for minimal wages. Peasant-based export agriculture in theory might have been more beneficial to the local people, but in practice there were severe limits to the expansion of peasant agriculture, because the people stuck to their subsistence farming techniques; consequently, sufficient wealth seldom flowed to the villages to allow them really to escape from their poverty.

One could imagine conditions, therefore, under which agricultural and mineral exports could have led to the prosperity of the Third World—if the local people had not been oppressed, if they had been able to benefit from their own work, if they had been allowed the freedom to be creative and inventive. But these were not the conditions of the European empires.

An enormous system of worldwide trade in primary commodities grew up; it was a system that depended upon impoverished labor forces, in many cases pulled unceremoniously away from their villages and cultures. Income was earned in the colonies from these export industries, but it was not earned by the working people who might have been able to use it creatively to improve their lives. It was earned by upper and middle classes, who used it to increase their consumption and to secure their control over the poor.

By contrast, the primary export producers in Canada—the fur traders, the lumberjacks, the small farmers and the miners—slowly accumulated wealth and increased their demands for manufactured goods that could be produced locally. Over time an integrated economy was developed, with primary exports and manufacturing both growing and supporting each other. In the Third World, since most of the new income was kept from the workers, people could not afford manufactured products. The Latin American "structuralist" school has been particularly successful in showing how the local income generated by imperialist trade went into the hands of an increasingly well-off minority of the population, who turned to European imports to satisfy their demands for sophisticated consumer goods. No mass market for simple manufactured goods ever arose, and so local manufacturing could not get a start.

* * *

If imperialism harmed the self-sufficiency of Third World agriculture, it absolutely devastated its manufacturing. Before the age of imperialism, the Third World had not enjoyed industrial production such as exists currently in the developed countries. Factory production is a result of the European industrial revolution. But most Third World areas did have thriving craft sectors, producing textiles, pottery, household utensils and the like. These were systematically destroyed by the imperialists, not at the muzzle of a gun but as a consequence of marketplace competition. The European industrial revolution spewed out manufactured goods that were much cheaper, and often of higher quality, than the colonies' crafts. The imperialists had no motive to protect the local crafts; on the contrary, they had every incentive to open up local markets to European exports. Imperialism led therefore to the collapse of manufacturing and craft production in the Third World.

* * *

[A]n entire class of independent craftspeople disappeared. They were for the most part people with highly developed skills who were used to making business decisions on their own, and many of them were to some extent entrepreneurial.

They might very well have been able to adapt the new European technologies to their own needs, and as a consequence have led the way to the economic development of their societies. But they were wiped out. Almost the entire Indian textile industry was eliminated because of the import of cheap cotton goods from Britain.

The economic effects of European imperialism were therefore massive. Millions of people were pulled away from their accustomed pursuits to work in capitalist and export enterprises. Almost all were kept at low, subsistence incomes, without opportunity to share the benefits obtained from export production. Land that had been tilled for centuries for subsistence food crops was expropriated for the growth of export crops. In the countryside, single-crop agriculture brought with it ecological deterioration. Manufacturing and crafts disappeared, and as a consequence the economies of many Third World areas became much more specialized and concentrated.

PART FOUR

SOCIAL INSTITUTIONS

35

FROM *The Protestant Ethic and the Spirit of Capitalism*

MAX WEBER

Why did capitalism (and industrialization) emerge in Western Europe rather than in ancient China, Egypt, or India? All had sufficient knowledge and resources. What made the difference? In this classic study, Max Weber (1864–1920) presents his famous thesis about the connection between early Protestant beliefs and the emergence of industrial capitalism. His view of the fate of the Protestant ethic is, to many people, prophetic for the twentieth and twenty-first centuries. A contemporary of Émile Durkheim, Weber began writing soon after the death of Karl Marx. Weber is one of sociology's founders.

In the title of this study is used the somewhat pretentious phrase, the *spirit* of capitalism. What is to be understood by it? The attempt to give anything like a definition of it brings out certain difficulties which are in the very nature of this type of investigation.

If any object can be found to which this term can be applied with any understandable meaning, it can only be an historical individual, i.e. a complex of elements associated in historical reality which we unite into a conceptual whole from the standpoint of their cultural significance.*

* * *

"Remember, that *time* is money. He that can earn ten shillings a day by his labour, and goes abroad, or sits idle, one half of that day, though he spends but sixpence during his diversion or idleness, ought not to reckon *that* the only expense; he has really spent, or rather thrown away, five shillings besides.

* * *

"Remember, that money is of the prolific, generating nature. Money can beget money, and its offspring can beget more, and so on. Five shillings turned is six, turned again it is seven and threepence, and so on, till it becomes a hundred pounds. The more there is of it, the more it produces every turning, so that the profits rise quicker and quicker. He that kills a breeding-sow, destroys

---

*[This is what Weber calls an "ideal type" concept that has become a commonly used feature of twentieth-century sociology.]

all her offspring to the thousandth generation. He that murders a crown, destroys all that it might have produced, even scores of pounds.

* * *

"For six pounds a year you may have the use of one hundred pounds, provided you are a man of known prudence and honesty.

"He that spends a groat a day idly, spends idly above six pounds a year, which is the price for the use of one hundred pounds.

"He that wastes idly a groat's worth of his time per day, one day with another, wastes the privilege of using one hundred pounds each day.

"He that idly loses five shillings' worth of time, loses five shillings, and might as prudently throw five shillings into the sea.

"He that loses five shillings, not only loses that sum, but all the advantage that might be made by turning it in dealing, which by the time that a young man becomes old, will amount to a considerable sum of money."

It is Benjamin Franklin who preaches to us in these [preceding paragraphs].

* * *

That it is the spirit of capitalism which here speaks in characteristic fashion, no one will doubt, however little we may wish to claim that everything which could be understood as pertaining to that spirit is contained in it. Let us pause a moment to consider this passage, the philosophy of which Kürnberger sums up in the words, "They make tallow out of cattle and money out of men." The peculiarity of this philosophy of avarice appears to be the ideal of the honest man of recognized credit, and above all the idea of a duty of the individual toward the increase of his capital, which is assumed as an end in itself. Truly what is here preached is not simply a means of making one's way in the world, but a peculiar ethic. The infraction of its rules is treated not as foolishness but as forgetfulness of duty. That is the essence of the matter. It is not mere business astuteness, that sort of thing is common enough, it is an ethos. *This* is the quality which interests us.

* * *

And in truth this peculiar idea, so familiar to us to-day, but in reality so little a matter of course, of one's duty in a calling, is what is most characteristic of the social ethic of capitalistic culture, and is in a sense the fundamental basis of it. It is an obligation which the individual is supposed to feel and does feel towards the content of his professional activity, no matter in what it consists, in particular no matter whether it appears on the surface as a utilization of his personal powers, or only of his material possessions (as capital).

* * *

Thus the capitalism of to-day, which has come to dominate economic life, educates and selects the economic subjects which it needs through a process of economic survival of the fittest. But here one can easily see the limits of the concept of selection as a means of historical explanation. In order that a manner of life so well adapted to the peculiarities of capitalism could be selected at all, i.e. should come to dominate others, it had to originate somewhere, and not in isolated individuals alone, but as a way of life common to whole groups of men. This origin is what really needs explanation. Concerning the doctrine of the more naïve historical materialism, that such ideas originate as a reflection or superstructure of economic situations.[†] * * * At this point it will suffice for our purpose to call attention to the fact that without doubt, in the country of Benjamin Franklin's birth (Massachusetts), the spirit of capitalism (in the sense we have attached to it) was present before the capitalistic order. There were complaints of a peculiarly calculating sort of profit-seeking in New England, as distinguished from other parts of America, as early as 1632. It is further undoubted that capitalism remained far less developed in some of the neighbouring colonies, the later Southern States of the United States of America, in spite of the fact that these latter were founded by large capitalists for business motives.

* * *

To be sure the capitalistic form of an enterprise and the spirit in which it is run generally stand in some sort of adequate relationship to each other, but not in one of necessary interdependence. Nevertheless, we provisionally use the expression spirit of (modern) capitalism to describe that attitude which seeks profit rationally and systematically in the manner which we have illustrated by the example of Benjamin Franklin. This, however, is justified by the historical fact that that attitude of mind has on the one hand found its most suitable expression in capitalistic enterprise, while on the other the enterprise has derived its most suitable motive force from the spirit of capitalism.

* * *

It will be our task to find out whose intellectual child the particular concrete form of rational thought was, from which the idea of a calling and the devotion to labour in the calling has grown, which is, as we have seen, so irrational from the standpoint of pure * * * self-interest, but which has been and still is one of the most characteristic elements of our capitalistic culture. We are here particularly interested in the origin of precisely the irrational element which lies in this, as in every conception of a calling.

LUTHER'S CONCEPTION OF THE CALLING

* * *

Now it is unmistakable that even in the German word *Beruf,* and perhaps still more clearly in the English *calling,* a religious conception, that of a task set

---

[†][Weber is critiquing Marx's idea of historical materialism.]

by God, is at least suggested. * * * And if we trace the history of the word through the civilized languages, it appears that neither the predominantly Catholic peoples nor those of classical antiquity have possessed any expression of similar connotation for what we know as a calling (in the sense of a life-task, a definite field in which to work), while one has existed for all predominantly Protestant peoples.

* * *

Like the meaning of the word, the idea is new, a product of the Reformation. * * * It is true that certain suggestions of the positive valuation of routine activity in the world, which is contained in this conception of the calling, had already existed in the Middle Ages, and even in late Hellenistic antiquity. We shall speak of that later. But at least one thing was unquestionably new: the valuation of the fulfilment of duty in worldly affairs as the highest form which the moral activity of the individual could assume. This it was which inevitably gave every-day worldly activity a religious significance, and which first created the conception of a calling in this sense. The conception of the calling thus brings out that central dogma of all Protestant denominations. * * * The only way of living acceptably to God was not to surpass worldly morality in monastic asceticism, but solely through the fulfilment of the obligations imposed upon the individual by his position in the world. That was his calling.

Luther developed the conception in the course of the first decade of his activity as a reformer.

* * *

[L]abour in a calling appears to him as the outward expression of brotherly love. This he proves by the observation that the division of labour forces every individual to work for others. * * * [T]he fulfilment of worldly duties is under all circumstances the only way to live acceptably to God. It and it alone is the will of God, and hence every legitimate calling has exactly the same worth in the sight of God.

* * *

ASCETICISM AND THE SPIRIT OF CAPITALISM

[I]f that God, whose hand the Puritan sees in all the occurrences of life, shows one of His elect a chance of profit, he must do it with a purpose. Hence the faithful Christian must follow the call by taking advantage of the opportunity. "If God show you a way in which you may lawfully get more than in another way (without wrong to your soul or to any other), if you refuse this, and choose the less gainful way, you cross one of the ends of your calling, and you refuse to be God's steward, and to accept His gifts and use them for Him when He requireth it: you may labour to be rich for God, though not for the flesh and sin."‡ * * *

Wealth is thus bad ethically only in so far as it is a temptation to idleness and sinful enjoyment of life, and its acquisition is bad only when it is with the purpose of later living merrily and without care. But as a performance of duty in a calling it is not only morally permissible, but actually enjoined. The parable of the servant who was rejected because he did not increase the talent which was entrusted to him seemed to say so directly. To wish to be poor was, it was often argued, the same as wishing to be unhealthy; it is objectionable as a glorification of works and derogatory to the glory of God. Especially begging, on the part of one able to work, is not only the sin of slothfulness, but a violation of the duty of brotherly love according to the Apostle's own word.

The emphasis on the ascetic importance of a fixed calling provided an ethical justification of the modern specialized division of labour. In a similar way the providential interpretation of profit-making justified the activities of the business man. * * * But, on the other hand, it has the highest ethical appreciation of the sober, middle-class, self-made man. "God blesseth His trade" is a stock remark about those good men who had successfully followed the divine hints.

* * *

Let us now try to clarify the points in which the Puritan idea of the calling and the premium it placed upon ascetic conduct was bound directly to influence the development of a capitalistic way of life. As we have seen, this asceticism turned with all its force against one thing: the spontaneous enjoyment of life and all it had to offer.

* * *

As against this the Puritans upheld their decisive characteristic, the principle of ascetic conduct. For otherwise the Puritan aversion to sport, even for the Quakers, was by no means simply one of principle. Sport was accepted if it served a rational purpose, that of recreation necessary for physical efficiency. But as a means for the spontaneous expression of undisciplined impulses, it was under suspicion; and in so far as it became purely a means of enjoyment, or awakened pride, raw instincts or the irrational gambling instinct, it was of course strictly condemned. Impulsive enjoyment of life, which leads away both from work in a calling and from religion, was as such the enemy.

* * *

Man is only a trustee of the goods which have come to him through God's grace. He must, like the servant in the parable, give an account of every penny

---

‡[Richard Baxter, Nonconformist (Puritan) scholar, 1615–1691.]

entrusted to him, and it is at least hazardous to spend any of it for a purpose which does not serve the glory of God but only one's own enjoyment. What person, who keeps his eyes open, has not met representatives of this viewpoint even in the present? The idea of a man's duty to his possessions, to which he subordinates himself as an obedient steward, or even as an acquisitive machine, bears with chilling weight on his life. The greater the possessions the heavier, if the ascetic attitude toward life stands the test, the feeling of responsibility for them, for holding them undiminished for the glory of God and increasing them by restless effort. The origin of this type of life also extends in certain roots, like so many aspects of the spirit of capitalism, back into the Middle Ages. But it was in the ethic of ascetic Protestantism that it first found a consistent ethical foundation. Its significance for the development of capitalism is obvious.

This worldly Protestant asceticism, as we may recapitulate up to this point, acted powerfully against the spontaneous enjoyment of possessions; it restricted consumption, especially of luxuries. On the other hand, it had the psychological effect of freeing the acquisition of goods from the inhibitions of traditionalistic ethics. It broke the bonds of the impulse of acquisition in that it not only legalized it, but (in the sense discussed) looked upon it as directly willed by God. The campaign against the temptations of the flesh, and the dependence on external things, was, as besides the Puritans the great Quaker apologist Barclay expressly says, not a struggle against the rational acquisition, but against the irrational use of wealth.

* * *

On the side of the production of private wealth, asceticism condemned both dishonesty and impulsive avarice. What was condemned as covetousness, Mammonism, etc., was the pursuit of riches for their own sake. For wealth in itself was a temptation. But here asceticism was the power "which ever seeks the good but ever creates evil"; what was evil in its sense was possession and its temptations. For, in conformity with the Old Testament and in analogy to the ethical valuation of good works, asceticism looked upon the pursuit of wealth as an end in itself as highly reprehensible; but the attainment of it as a fruit of labour in a calling was a sign of God's blessing. And even more important: the religious valuation of restless, continuous, systematic work in a worldly calling, as the highest means to asceticism, and at the same time the surest and most evident proof of rebirth and genuine faith, must have been the most powerful conceivable lever for the expansion of that attitude toward life which we have here called the spirit of capitalism.

When the limitation of consumption is combined with this release of acquisitive activity, the inevitable practical result is obvious: accumulation of capital through ascetic compulsion to save. The restraints which were imposed upon the consumption of wealth naturally served to increase it by making possible the productive investment of capital.

* * *

As far as the influence of the Puritan outlook extended, under all circumstances—and this is, of course, much more important than the mere encouragement of capital accumulation—it favoured the development of a rational bourgeois economic life; it was the most important, and above all the only consistent influence in the development of that life. It stood at the cradle of the modern economic man.

* * *

THE SPIRIT OF CAPITALISM TODAY

At present under our individualistic political, legal, and economic institutions, with the forms of organization and general structure which are peculiar to our economic order, this spirit of capitalism might be understandable, as has been said, purely as a result of adaptation. The capitalistic system so needs this devotion to the calling of making money, it is an attitude toward material goods which is so well suited to that system, so intimately bound up with the conditions of survival in the economic struggle for existence, that there can to-day no longer be any question of a necessary connection of that acquisitive manner of life with any single *Weltanschauung*. In fact, it no longer needs the support of any religious forces, and feels the attempts of religion to influence economic life, in so far as they can still be felt at all, to be as much an unjustified interference as its regulation by the State. In such circumstances men's commercial and social interests do tend to determine their opinions and attitudes. Whoever does not adapt his manner of life to the conditions of capitalistic success must go under, or at least cannot rise. But these are phenomena of a time in which modern capitalism has become dominant and has become emancipated from its old supports.

* * *

The Puritan wanted to work in a calling; we are forced to do so. For when asceticism was carried out of monastic cells into everyday life, and began to dominate worldly morality, it did its part in building the tremendous cosmos of the modern economic order. This order is now bound to the technical and economic conditions of machine production which to-day determine the lives of all the individuals who are born into this mechanism, not only those directly concerned with economic acquisition, with irresistible force. Perhaps it will so determine them until the last ton of fossilized coal is burnt. In Baxter's view the care for external goods should only lie on the shoulders of the "saint like a light cloak, which can be thrown aside at any moment." But fate decreed that the cloak should become an iron cage.

Since asceticism undertook to remodel the world and to work out its ideals in the world, material goods have gained an increasing and finally an inexorable power over the lives of men as at no previous period in history. To-day the spirit of religious asceticism—whether finally, who knows?—has escaped from the cage. But victorious capitalism, since it rests on mechanical foundations, needs its [asceticism's] support no longer. The rosy blush of its laughing heir, the Enlightenment, seems also to be irretrievably fading, and the idea of duty in one's calling prowls about in our lives like the ghost of dead religious beliefs. Where the fulfilment of the calling cannot directly be related to the highest spiritual and cultural values, or when, on the other hand, it need not be felt simply as economic compulsion, the individual generally abandons the attempt to justify it at all. In the field of its highest development, in the United States, the pursuit of wealth, stripped of its religious and ethical meaning, tends to become associated with purely mundane passions, which often actually give it the character of sport.

No one knows who will live in this cage in the future, or whether at the end of this tremendous development entirely new prophets will arise, or there will be a great rebirth of old ideas and ideals, or, if neither, mechanized petrification, embellished with a sort of convulsive self-importance. For of the last stage of this cultural development, it might well be truly said: "Specialists without spirit, sensualists without heart; this nullity imagines that it has attained a level of civilization never before achieved."

36

Love, Arranged Marriage, and the Indian Social Structure

GIRI RAJ GUPTA

For most of you, the idea of marrying someone you do not love borders on the absurd or abusive. In many societies, however, arranged marriages are common and result in lasting and satisfying bonds between husband and wife. Marital success is dependent not only on how partners feel toward one another. The social supports for their partnership and family are critical. In India's Hindu society, the family not only plays a major role in arranging a marriage but in making the marriage a success.

Marriage is an immemorial institution which, in some form, is found everywhere. Mating patterns are closely associated with marriage, more so with the social structure. It's not the institution of marriage itself, but the institutionalization of mating patterns which determine the nature of family relationships in a society. Primitive societies present a wide array of practices ranging from marriage by capture to mutual love and elopement. Yet, the people who marry through customary practice are those who are eligibles, who consciously followed the established norms, and who did the kind of things they were supposed to do. The main purpose of marriage is to establish a family, to produce children, and to further the family's economic and social position. Perhaps, there are some transcendental goals too. Generally, women hope for kind and vigorous providers and protectors and men for faithful mothers and good housekeepers; both undoubtedly hope for mutual devotion and affection too. Irrespective of the various ways of instituting marriage, most marriages seem to have these common goals.

There are few works commenting on mating patterns in India. Though some monographs on tribal and rural India have treated the subject, nevertheless, serious sociological attention has only infrequently been given. The present paper attempts to explain the variables as a part of the cultural system which help in promotion and sustenance of the arranged marriage, particularly in the Hindu society in India. In addition, the paper also critically analyzes the present-day mating patterns which relate to precautionary controls working against the potentially disintegrative forces of change; especially those endangering family unity, religious structure, and the stratification system.

ROMANTIC LOVE VERSUS CONJUGAL LOVE

One is intrigued by the cultural pattern in India where the family is characterized by arranged marriage. Infatuation as well as romantic love, though, is reported quite in abundance in the literature, sacred books, and scriptures, yet is not thought to be an element in prospective marital alliance (see Meyer 1953: 322–39).

Sanskrit or Hindi terms like *sneh* (affection) and *prem* or *muhbbat* carry two different meanings. *Sneh* is nonsensual love, while *prem* is a generic term connoting love with god, people, nation, family, [neighbor], and, of course, lover or beloved. In fact, there is a hierarchy of relationships. In Urdu literature, concepts like *ishque ruhani* (love with the spirit), *ishque majazi* (love with the supreme being), and *ishque haqiqi* (love with the lover or beloved) are commonly referred to love relationships. Interestingly, the humans supposedly reach the highest goal of being in love with god through the love they cherish among humans. Great love stories in mythology and history illustrate the emotion, as opposed to reason, which characterize the thoughts and acts of persons in love. The quality of the emotions may be characterized best by the altruistic expressions of a person for the person in love. Most people in India do not go around singing of their love as one might imagine after watching Indian movies and dramatic performances. Even the proximity, intimacy, freedom, and permissiveness characterized in such media are rarely commonplace in the reality of the day-to-day life. In general, to verbalize and manifest romantic expressions of love is looked upon as a product of poets' or novelists' fantasies. Yet, at least theoretically, to be in love with someone is a highly cherished ideal.

In one of the most ancient scriptures, Rgveda, it was wished that a person's life be of a hundred-year duration. The Hindu sages in their theory of *purusharthas* suggested four aims of life: *dharma,* righteousness, which provides a link between animal and god in man; *artha,* acquisitive instinct in man, enjoyment of wealth and its manifestations; *kama,* instinctive and emotional life of man and the satisfaction of sex drives and aesthetic urges; and *moksha,* the end of life and the realization of an inner spirituality in man (see Kapadia 1966: 25).

The Hindu scriptures written during 200 B.C. to 900 A.D. mention eight modes of acquiring a wife known as Brahma, Daiva, Arsha, Prajapatya, Asura, Gandharva, Rakshasa, and Paisacha. Only the first four are known as *dharmya,* that is, according to religion. An exchange of gifts between the subjects' families marks the wedding ceremony, but no dowry is paid. In the Asura form payment of the bride price is the main element, while Rakshasa and Paisacha, respectively, pertain to the abduction and seduction of a girl when she is unconscious. The Gandharva marriage refers to a marriage by mutual choice. The Hindu lawgivers differ in their opinions and interpretations of this kind of marriage; some called it the best mode of marriage, while others viewed it stigmatic on religious and moral grounds. However, there is no reliable data to support or justify the popularity of any one of these modes of marriage. The first four kinds pertain to arranged marriages in which the parental couple ritually gives away the daughter to a suitable person, and this ideal continues to be maintained in the Hindu society. Opposed to these are four others, three of which were objected to by the scriptwriters in the past and viewed as illegal today, though nevertheless, they happen. The Gandharva mode, though opposed to the accepted norm, is nearest to what may be variously termed as "free-choice," "romantic," or "love" marriage. Yet through the ages Hindu revivalism and other socioreligious and economic factors discredited the importance of Gandharva marriage.

Diversified sects of Muslims and Christians view marriage as a civil contract as opposed to a sacrament. However, marriages are arranged most often with the consent of the subjects. The Muslims, at least theoretically, permit polygamy according to Islamic law; however, they prefer monogamy. As opposed to Hindu and Christian communities it is customary that the boy's party initiates a marriage proposal (see Kapadia 1966: 209–14; Kurian 1974: 357–58, 1975).

Most Indian marriages are arranged, although sometimes opinions of the partners are consulted, and in cases of adults, their opinions are seriously considered. Another aspect of this pattern is that individuals come to believe that their life mate is predestined, their fate is preordained, they are "right for each other," they are helpless as far as choice is concerned and therefore must succumb to the celestial forces of the universe. That the entire syndrome, typical for the society, represents a complex set of forces working around and upon the individual to get married to a person whom one is destined to love. It is also believed to be good and desirable that critical issues like the choosing of a life partner should be handled by responsible persons of family and kin group. However, it is generally possible that persons in love could marry if related prohibitions have been effectively observed.

Generally, love is considered a weak basis for marriage because its presence may overshadow suitable qualities in spouses. Therefore, arranged marriages result from more or less intense care given to the selection of suitable partners so that the family ideals, companionship, and co-parenthood can grow, leading to love. Ernest Van Den Haag writes about the United States:

> A hundred years ago, there was every reason to marry young—though middle-class people seldom did. The unmarried state had heavy disadvantages for both sexes. Custom did not permit girls to be educated, to work, or to have social, let alone sexual, freedom. . . . And, though, less restricted than girls shackled to their families, single men often led a grim and uncomfortable life. A wife was nearly indispensable, if only to darn socks, sew, cook, clean, take care of her man. (1973: 181)

Goode views romantic love paradoxically, and calls it the antithesis of "conjugal love," because marriage is not based upon it, actually a couple strives to seek it within the marital bond (1959: 40). The latter, presumably, protect the couple against the harmful effects of individualism, freedom, and untoward personality growth. It may be worthwhile here to analyze the structural conditions under which mating relationships occur and to see how they relate to various values and goals in Indian society.

A study conducted in 1968, on 240 families in Kerala, a state which has the highest literacy rate in India, reveals that practical consideration in the selection of mates rather than free-choice or romantic love becomes the basis of marriage. In order of importance, the study reports that the major qualities among the girls considered important are: good character, obedience, ability to manage home, good cook, should take active part in social and political affairs, educated, religious, depending entirely on husband for major decisions, fair complexion, good companion with similar intellectual interests, and beauty (Kurian 1974: 335). Among the boy's qualities, his appearance, charm, and romantic manifestation do not count much, while the social and economic status of his family, education, and earning potential overshadow his personal qualities (Kurian 1974: 355; see also Ross 1961: 259).

The Kerala study further illustrates some interesting trends, such as: that only 59 percent of the respondents thought that meeting the prospective wife before marriage contributes to marital happiness. The parental preferences about the nature of choice of spouse of their children showed that 5.8 percent wanted to arrange the marriage without consulting sons and daughters, while 75.6 percent wanted to arrange the marriage with the consent of sons and daughters, 17.3 percent were willing to allow free choice to their children with their approval, and only 1.3 percent will allow freedom of choice without parental interference (Kurian 1974: 358). In fact, what Srinivas observed over three decades ago in Mysore was that "romantic love as a basis of marriage is still not very deep or widely spread in the family mores of India today," has not yet changed much (see Srinivas 1942: 60).

The dilemma of a boy who had fallen in love with a girl from a lower caste is reported from a study of Bangalore, a city of about a million people:

> My love affair has caused me great trouble, for my intense love of the girl and the devotion to my parents cannot be reconciled. My parents don't like our engagement, and I cannot displease them, but on the other hand I cannot give up my girl who has done so much for me. She is responsible for progress and the bright future which everyone says is ahead of me. The problem is my greatest headache at the present time. (Ross 1961: 269)

During my own fieldwork during 1963–67, in Awan, a community of about three thousand people in Rajasthan state, having extensive and frequent urban contacts, it took me no time to figure out that a question inquiring about "romantic" or "love" marriage would be futile, because people simply laughed it away. Parental opinion was reinforced by several other considerations. One man, a community elite, remarked:

> Young people do not know what love is; they are, if at all, infatuated which is very transitory and does not entail considerations of good marital life. If my son marries, I wish to see that the girl is well-raised, obedient, preserves the family traditions, ready to bear the hardships with us, and to nurse us in our old age.

Love, a premarital manifestation, is thus thought to be a disruptive element in upsetting the firmly established close ties in the family, a transference of loyalty from the family of orientation to a person, and a loss of allegiance of a person, leaving the family and kin group in disdain for personal goals.

Continued loyalty of the individual to the family of orientation and kin group is the most cherished ideal in the Indian family system. To preserve this ideal, certainly the simplest recourse is child marriage or adolescent marriage. The child is betrothed, married, and most often placed in a job and generally provides the deference demanded by the elders. Though this pattern does not give much opportunity to the individual to act freely in matrimonial affairs, it maintains a close link of the couple with the father's household which requires much physical, social, and emotional care throughout the family cycle and particularly in old age. The relationships in the extended joint family are all-important.

The Hindu scriptural texts prescribe that a person should go through *grahstashrama* (a stage of householder's life) which includes procreation of children. The status system gives high prestige to the parents of large families. Kinship and religious values stress the need for a male heir. Large families provide security, both in economic and social terms, for the old and the destitute and the ill in a country where old-age pensions, disability, sickness benefits, and unemployment as well as medical insurance are either nonexistent or inadequate. When a family has several children, their marriages have to be spaced for economic as well as social reasons, which in turn necessitates early marriages.

Similar to other indigenous civilizations, a high value is placed upon chastity, especially female virginity in its ideal form. Love as play or premarital activity is not encouraged. Rather, elders consider it as their most important duty to supervise nubile girls. Marriage is an ideal, a duty, and a social responsibility usually preceded by highly ritualized ceremonial and festive events illustrating gradual involvement, especially of the female preparatory to the initiation of her marital role. Interestingly, all these ritual activities are role oriented (such as contributing to the long and prosperous life of the prospective husband) rather than person oriented (such as taking vows for the success of a person who is in love). This is one of those most pertinent factors which infuses longevity to the marital bond. The upper caste ideal that a girl could be ritually married only once in her lifetime and destined to marry the same person in lives to come continues to determine explicit and categorical aversion among girls to premarital interactions with strangers. Paradoxically, though, there is an implicit assumption that a person's marriage to a person of the opposite sex is governed by supreme celestial forces; in actual practice, mundane realities usually settle a marriage.

The early marriage of the person does not permit much personal independence and is further linked with another structural pattern in which the kinship rules define a class (caste, subcaste, regional group) of eligible future spouses. In other words, in the interest of homogamy and sanctity of the kin group, marriage should occur early. Thus, this would eliminate the chances of an unmarried adult to disregard a link with his or her kin group and caste. Problems arise at times when a person goes across the narrow limits of a group, often losing his chances of obtaining the usual support from the family, the kin group, and the caste. However, transgressions of basic family norms by an individual which may cause loss of identity, rejection, and an aggravated departure from the value system are rare. Often it is circumventing rather than contradicting the system which provides clues to change. Under such a pattern, elders negotiate and arrange marriages of their children and dependents with a likelihood of minimum generational conflict reinforcing greater chances of family unity. Adolescent physical and social segregation is marked by a greater emphasis on the learning of discrete sex roles idealizing, at least theoretically, parental roles.

As found in Western cultures, the youth culture frees the individual from family attachments thus permitting the individual to fall in love; and love becomes a substitute for the interlocking of kinship roles. The structural isolation of the Western family also frees the married partners' affective inclinations, that they are able to love one another (Parsons 1949: 187–89). Such a pattern is absent in the Indian family system.

Contrary to this, in India, marriage of a boy indirectly strengthens his bonds with the family of orientation. It is one of the major crises which marks his adulthood and defines his responsibilities towards his parents and the kin group. His faith and sentimental involvement in the family of orientation is an acknowledgment of the usual obligations incurred in his raising and training. A pervasive philosophy of individualism appears to be spreading and suggests a trend toward free mate choices, equality for women, equal divorce rights, and taking up of traditionally known ritually inferior but lucrative occupations; this militantly asserts the importance of the welfare of the person over any considerations of the continuity of the group. The trend toward conjugal family systems, widespread as it is, is generally confined to the urbanized regions (Gore 1958; Kapur 1970). Moreover, these changes where they appear on one hand, are viewed as social problems and as symptoms of the breakdown of time-honored ways; on the other, they are looked at as indicators of personal achievement, individual fulfilment, and family prestige.

SOCIALIZATION

The cultural pattern demands that a child in India cannot isolate himself from his parents, siblings, and other members of the extended family.

The maturation process is rarely fraught with problems or turmoil associated with parent and adolescent children as they all learn to play new roles and feel new feelings. A child's expanding world gradually gives a mature sense of responsibilities to share in most of the important decisions in his life cycle. Covert parent-child conflict is shadowed by affection and sentimental ties helping the adolescents to achieve desirable balance between rebellion and conformity, individual wishes and feelings of the parents. Occasionally, this causes some problems. Since parents make decisions about most significant aspects of the family, including the marriage of their children, passive, indifferent, and sometimes negative feelings develop in the children as they seek to be dependent on other members of the family.

The family in India is known for its cohesive function, especially providing for the emotional needs of its members. Most often, this function is effectively performed by the extended kin group which, in fact, is a segment of the caste or subcaste. Adults, as well as children, must have love and security in order to maintain emotional stability under the stresses of life and in order to meet the emotional demands made upon them by the crises. In addition to providing the positive emotional needs of its members by personal sacrifices done by the members on a regular basis throughout the life cycle of the family, it also provides a safe outlet for negative feelings. Conflicts arising from interpersonal relations are generally handled by the older members, and care is taken by them to ensure that roles and responsibilities are clearly defined. Conflicts are resolved and mitigated by a general concern in the group favoring the emotional satisfaction of the individual. A person throughout his adolescence is never isolated from the family. Thus, not only generations, but extended and local units of kin groups are forced into a more intensive relationship. The affectional ties are solidified by mutual care, help in crisis situations, and assistance provided. This often destroys negative feelings. Several rituals, rites, and ceremonial occasions reinforce the unity of the family (Dube 1955: 131–58; Gupta 1974: 104–16). In general, a person substantially invests his emotions and feelings in his family and kin group, denial of which may be hazardous to his psyche. Such a deep involvement of the individual causes his emotional dependence on the family and acceptance to its wishes in most of the crucial decisions and events in his life, including marriage.

PREMARITAL INTERACTION AND MATE SELECTION

India is perhaps the only subcontinent which provides a wide variety of mate selection processes from an open to a very closed system, from marriage by capture in the primitives to the arranged marriage among Hindus and

Muslims. Moreover, rules prohibiting certain classes of persons from marrying one another also vary, such as three to four clan avoidance rules in central and northern parts to preferential cross-cousin or maternal uncle and niece marriages in the south. In other words, rules regarding the definition of incest or areas of potential mates vary substantially. Most people in the Northern states, for example, prohibit marriage between persons of similarly named clans and extend this rule to several other related clans, such as of mother's clan, mother's mother clan, and father's mother clan. The people bearing these clan names may be living several hundred miles away * * * but are usually thought to be related. From this point of view, then, the ideal mate for any person could also be a stranger, an outsider, but an individual related to him in distant terms. * * * A person living across a state belonging to one's caste has a greater chance of being an eligible for a prospective mate than a person belonging to some other caste living next door. Caste is thus an extended kin group and, at least theoretically, membership in which is related through various kinds of kinship ties. Marriage alliances within the *jati* (caste or subcaste) reinforce kinship and family ties and cause a sort of evolution of the class system. Class generally determines future marital alliances within the caste. The resources assessed by a family in seeking a marital alliance from another family play a crucial role in determining the decision about the alliance. The voices of the significant members of the family are crucial in making a marriage since newlywed couples are barely into adulthood and have neither the material nor psychological resources to start a household of their own. Later in their married life when they have resources, they may still consider the opinions of the significant members because the disadvantages of not adhering to such opinions are greater than the annoyances of living together.

A SOCIOLOGICAL PARADIGM OF ARRANGED MARRIAGES

Recent research on the changing aspects of the family in India (Collver 1963; Conklin 1974; Desai 1964; Gore 1965; Gould 1968; Gupta 1974; Hooja 1968; Kapur 1970; Kurian 1961, 1974; Orenstein 1959, 1961, 1966; Ross 1961; Shah 1974; Singer 1968) suggests that there has been little change in the joint family system in India, which is a vanguard of the arranged marriage.

The above discussion gives us to understand that what is needed in our approach to arranged marriage is a frame of reference which is more fully on the sociological level. As a step toward this goal, a general theoretical approach to the arranged marriage or "conjugal love" relationship has been formulated which, it is believed, takes account of the historical, cultural, and psychological levels, and brings into central focus the sociological level. The following tentative theoretical formulation is proposed only as a first attempt to outline what sociological factors are generally responsible to the growth of "conjugal love" as opposed to "romantic love." By any conservative estimate, love marriages occur in only less than 1 percent of the population.

1. It is important to note that arranged marriages are closely associated with "closed systems" wherein the hierarchies are very intricate and more than one factor such as historical origins, ritual positions, occupational affiliations, and social distance determinants play significant roles in defining the in-group and the out-group, particularly in marital alliances. In such systems, group identity is marked by strong senses of esoteric values, and such values are preserved and reinforced by attributes which distinguish a group in rank and its interaction with others. That is, most proximate ties of the individuals ought to be within their own group.

2. Continuity and unity of the extended family is well-preserved since all the significant members of the family share the mate-selection decision make-up which involves several persons who are supposedly known to have experience and qualifications to find a better choice as against the free choice of the subject. Obviously, this leads to lower age at marriage and, in turn, strengthens the predominance of the family over the individual choice.

3. Any possible problems emerging from a couple's functioning in marital life become problems for the whole family. Advice and counseling from the members of the extended family to improve the couple's relationship, weathering life's storms, or even sharing in crises are reinforced by the shared responsibilities. This is also partly responsible for denouncing the idea of divorce and forces working against it. This is not to say that this, in fact, resolves all the conflicts in marriage.

4. As long as the social system is unable to develop a value system to promote individualism, economic security outside the family system, and a value system which advances the ideals of nuclear family, the individuals in such a system continue to demand support from the family which, in turn, would lead to reemphasizing the importance of arranged marriage. Forces of modernization supporting the "romantic ideal" would continue to find partial support in such a system as long as the sources of moral and material support for the individual are based in the extended/joint family system.

5. It is difficult to assume that arranged marriage is related to the low status of a woman since man is also a party to it. If the concept of "free choice" is applicable to either sex, perhaps it will not support the ideal of arranged marriage. Apparently, an individual who opts for free choice or a "love marriage" is likely to dissociate from his/her family, kin group, caste, and possibly community, which he/she cannot afford unless he/she has been ensured tremendous support from sources other than these conventional institutions.

6. Arranged marriages, in general, irrespective of caste or class categories, help in maintaining closer ties with several generations. Families in such a system are an insurance for the old and the orthodox,

a recluse for the devout and the defiant, a haven for the invalid and the insipid.

7. The demographic situation in India, as in most developing societies, is also a contributing factor, among others, to the early arranged marriages. After independence, India has made many advancements in science, technology, and medicine. * * * life expectancy, which was 29 years in 1947, is now 54 years. However, the vicious circle of early child marriage, early pregnancy, high mortality rate, and replacement of the population are closely interwoven to ensure society from extinction. While the value system notoriously maintains this chainwork, the declining mortality rate further accentuates early marriages to shelve off the economic burden of the family by spacing weddings. The family protects and insulates from ruining itself by arranging marriages as early as possible and for using its resources for status aggrandizement.

Since the changes in Indian society often present a welter of traditional and modern, conventional as well as prestige and [glamor]-oriented marital role models with significant changes in the value system, it is quite probable that in the long run, "romantic ideal" will pervade the system. Whether such changes will be a part of a continuum, that is, revitalization of the mythological past or acceptance of the ideals of the modern West, preserving tenacity and positive elements of its own against the swaggering forces of change, has yet to be seen.

REFERENCES

Chekki, D. A. (1968). Mate selection, age at marriage and propinquity among the Lingayats of India. *Journal of Marriage and the Family,* 30 (November): 707–11.

Collver, A. (1963). The family cycle in India and the United States. *American Sociological Review,* 28: 86–96.

Conklin, G. H. (1974). The extended family as an independent factor in social change: A case from India. *Journal of Marriage and Family,* 36 (November): 798–804.

Cormack, M. (1953). *The Hindu woman.* New York: Bureau of Publications, Columbia University.

Desai, I. P. (1964). *Some aspects of family in Mahuva.* Bombay: Asia Publishing House.

Dube, S. C. (1955). *Indian village.* New York: Cornell University Press.

Goode, W. J. (1959). The theoretical importance of love. *American Sociological Review,* 24: 38–47.

———. (1963). *World revolution and family patterns.* New York: Free Press.

Gore, M. S. (1968). *Urbanization and family change.* Bombay: Popular Prakashan.

Gupta, G. R. (1974). *Marriage, religion and society: Pattern of change in an Indian village.* New York: Halsted Press.

Hate, C. A. (1970). Raising the age at marriage. *The Indian Journal of Social Work,* 30: 303–09.

Hooja, S. (1968). Dowry system among the Hindus in North India: A case study. *The Indian Journal of Social Work,* 38: 411–26.

Kapadia, K. M. (1966). *Marriage and family in India,* 3rd ed. London: Oxford University Press.

Kapur, P. (1970). *Marriage and the working woman in India.* Delhi: Vikas Publications.

Karve, I. (1965). *Kinship organization in India.* Bombay: Asia Publishing House.

Klass, M. (1966). Marriage rules in Bengal. *American Anthropologist,* 68: 951–70.

Kurian, G. (1961). *The Indian family in transition.* The Hague: Mouton.

———. (1974). Modern trends in mate selection and marriage with special reference to Kerala. In G. Kurian, Ed., *The Family in India—A Regional View* (pp. 351–67). The Hague: Mouton.

———. (1975). Structural changes in the family in Kerala, India. In T. R. Williams, Ed., *Psychological Anthropology.* The Hague: Mouton.

Madan, T. N. (1965). *Family and kinship: A study of the Pandits of rural Kashmir.* New York: Asia Publishing House.

Mandelbaum, D. G. (1970). *Society in India,* vol. I & II. Berkeley: University of California Press.

Meyer, J. J. (1953). *Sexual life in ancient India.* New York: Barnes & Noble.

Orenstein, H. (1959). The recent history of the extended family in India. *Social Problems,* 8: 341–50.

———. (1961). The recent history of family in India. *Social Problems,* 8 (Spring): 341–50.

———. (1966). The Hindu joint family: The norms and the numbers. *Pacific Affairs,* 39 (Fall-Winter): 314–25.

Parsons, T. (1949). *Essays in sociological theory.* Glencoe, Illinois: Free Press.

Ross, A. D. (1961). *The Hindu family in its urban setting.* Toronto: University of Toronto Press.

Shah, A. M. (1974). *The household dimension of family in India.* Berkeley: University of California Press.

Singer, M. (1968). The Indian joint family in modern industry. In M. Singer & B. S. Cohn, Eds., *Structure and change in Indian society.* Chicago: Aldine Publishing Co.

Srinivas, M. N. (1942). *Marriage and family in Mysore.* Bombay: New Book Co.

Van Den Haag, E. (1973). Love or marriage. In M. E. Lasswell & Thomas E. Lasswell, Eds., *Love, marriage and family: A developmental approach* (pp. 181–86). Glenview, Illinois: Scott, Foresman and Co.

Vatuk, S. (1972). *Kinship and urbanization.* Berkeley: University of California Press.

37

Shared Paternity

KIM A. McDONALD

Conventional evolutionary wisdom has it that males of all species prefer to kill the offspring of other males in order to promote the survival of only their own genes. Humans rarely do this. Instead, men use their power to restrict women's sexual activity to only themselves. Then they use various measures that give their own children an advantage over others, thus improving the chance their own genes will survive. Behind this is the notion that males are in control of reproductive strategies. A great deal of new research shifts the locus of control to females. Some of this research is discussed in this provocative essay that challenges our most deeply held beliefs about gender, monogamy, and "the best interests of the child."

Recent studies of multiple fatherhood in indigenous societies in South America are forcing scientists to rethink their notions about the evolutionary roles of female fidelity and male provisioning.

Many biologists and anthropologists had assumed that those behaviors arose as a result of an evolutionary compact between men and women—one in which fathers provided resources for their mates and children in exchange for knowing that their children are genetically their own.

Reinforced by the belief in Western societies since biblical times that a child can have only one biological father, those gender-specific behaviors—which presumably enhanced the survival of offspring—also underpinned many scientists' explanations about the evolution of human sexuality and the division of labor among men and women.

According to that view, the African hominid ancestors of modern humans had a reproductive strategy in which females were only periodically capable of conception and mated with multiple males. Like chimpanzees, the hominids engaged in relatively little food sharing, and the males had minimal roles in providing food for their children.

THE KEY ADAPTATION

That reproductive strategy was replaced in modern humans by an arrangement in which men provided for their mates and young in exchange—according to the theory—for paternity certainty from women, who are capable of conceiving throughout the year.

"This popular scenario of human evolution makes men providing things for their wives and children the key adaptation that separates us from the other primates," said Kristen Hawkes, head of the anthropology department at the University of Utah. "The thing that's distinctive about our lineage is that men work. Women and children, as a consequence, can consume things that they wouldn't otherwise."

"Concern for paternity certainty is presumed to dominate relations between husbands and wives," said Stephen J. Beckerman, a professor of anthropology at the Pennsylvania State University. "Women are supposed to be naturally inclined to be faithful to a single man. Men are supposed to be inherently jealous and possessive about women."

However, studies that he, Ms. Hawkes, and other researchers have conducted on some of the more than a dozen societies in South America whose members believe that biological fatherhood can be "partible," or shared, are forcing the scientists to rethink that Darwinian view of fatherhood. Many of those scholars met here at the annual meeting of the American Association for the Advancement of Science to discuss the implications of their findings.

"Throughout lowland South America, there is a belief in the partibility of paternity," said Mr. Beckerman at the gathering. "The belief, in essence, is that all of the men who have sex with a woman around the beginning of her pregnancy and all through her pregnancy share the biological paternity of her child. In this view, the fetus is considered to grow by repeated contributions of semen."

The pervasiveness of those beliefs among at least 18 widely separated and distinct cultures in South America, said Mr. Beckerman, suggests that social views about fatherhood are not universal and do not follow the standard picture of the evolution of human sexuality. In fact, he noted, examples of a belief in partible paternity are being discovered outside South America, in indigenous societies in New Guinea, Polynesia, and India.

"All of this calls into question this presumed evolutionary bargain between men and women in which, in effect, female fidelity and guaranteed paternity are the coin with which women pay for resources provided by their mates," he said.

MINIMIZING SEXUAL JEALOUSY

Far from being simply an aberrant challenge to traditional evolutionary thinking, notions of partible paternity may actually be a strategy with real benefits to those societies that recognize multiple fathers.

Mr. Beckerman said his team's studies on the Bari of Venezuela and work by others on the Aché of eastern Paraguay showed that, in both societies, children with multiple fathers were more than twice as likely to survive to their adolescent years as children born to a single father.

"Ethnographic fieldwork suggests that the secondary fathers may have important roles in contributing food to the children and goods to the woman or protection to the children or the woman," said Mr. Beckerman.

What's more, the concept of multiple fatherhood may minimize sexual jealousy, a source of potentially lethal conflict between men. Mr. Beckerman said that one of the more fascinating findings in his work with the Bari, a lowland horticultural society, was that "we never got a man expressing jealousy over his wife taking a lover.

"Presumably, it's because, when that happens, the husband, in effect, has purchased a life-insurance policy. If he dies, then there is some other male who has at least a residual obligation to those children, most of whom probably belong to the husband. So, it's to his benefit to have his wife take a lover or two."

Not all indigenous South America cultures share the same view of multiple fatherhood.

The Canela of Amazonia, in Brazil, for example, actively encourage many sexual partners for pregnant women because they believe that numerous contributions of semen are required to produce a viable fetus.

William H. Crocker, emeritus curator for South American ethnology at the Smithsonian Institution's National Museum of Natural History, in Washington, who has studied the Canela, said this society also believed offspring would grow to resemble the men who contribute the most semen. As a result, he said, "a pregnant woman seeks affairs with men besides her husband, with whom she wants her fetus to be like."

In contrast, the Curripaco Indians, who live in Amazonia on the border of Venezuela and Colombia, believe premarital sex is wrong, but accept the concept of multiple fathers if a mother identifies her lover and that man accepts his role as a father. Often, such women will identify lovers of high social status from desirable villages.

"From their perspective, biological paternity is something that is negotiated," said Paul Valentine, an anthropologist at the University of East London who has been studying the Curripaco since 1981. "This notion of partible paternity can be used in all different kinds of social arrangements such that people can actually choose the strategy that's beneficial to them."

THE EVOLUTIONARY PARADIGM

Ms. Hawkes of Utah said that what was clear about all of those societies was that they do not fit the evolutionary paradigm—that, as humans evolved, males shifted their efforts away from competition with one another for mates to parental nurturing.

Her own studies of the Aché of eastern Paraguay and the Hadza of northern Tanzania, she said, "don't support the notion that men's work is about providing for their kids."

"The products of a man's labors in hunting and collecting honey do not provide more for a man's own wife and children than they do for anybody else. And if a man were really concerned about providing for her, the patterns of his work would be quite different from the ones we see. Male mating competition provides a much more interesting, powerful, more potentially useful set of hypotheses for explaining the evolution of our lineage and, perhaps, for explaining some of the variability we see ethnographically in the modern world."

Robert L. Trivers, a professor of anthropology at Rutgers University who did some of the most influential theoretical work on paternal investment in the 1970s, said in an interview that Ms. Hawkes "makes a compelling initial case for the possibility that, where big game is the usual prey, competition may be for access to women and not parental investment *per se.*" But he suspected that males in such societies were probably making some effort to see that their own children get disproportionately more than other children.

As to why modern Western societies have far-more-rigid rules for mating and fatherhood than do the Bari or Aché, Ms. Hawkes thinks it may be related to the need to minimize the lethal consequences of mating competition in modern society.

"The cost of a fight is much greater among armed humans as a result of their technology," she said. "One of the ways to reduce the cost of that fight is to develop conventions about immediate claims on male mating rights."

SIMILAR BEHAVIOR IN WESTERN SOCIETY

Nevertheless, the concept of multiple fathers may be more common in Western society than is believed—even though it isn't sanctioned or recognized as such.

"You don't have to delve far beneath the surface of the average British woman to find behavior that looks very similar to the sort of behavior of the lowland. South American cultures," said R. Robin Baker, a former zoology professor at the University of Manchester, who is now a lecturer and author.

His studies of British women suggest that Western women subconsciously bias conception to their clandestine lovers, rather than their long-term partners, by having sex with their lovers more often during their fertile periods and more often without contraception.

In the responses he received to a survey of 4,000 women, many of whom reported affairs, he said, "the implication is always that, now I've met somebody who can offer me something more genetically than my long-term partner." He added that confidential attempts to check paternity in Europe and North America bear out the fact that fidelity among women is not as common in Western society as one would believe.

"One in 10 children don't belong to their mother's long-term partners, they don't belong to their putative fathers," he said. "The take-home message is that if you compare a British woman with a Bari woman, the difference is one of degree rather than kind. We're dealing with a genetic legacy that is the result of 60 million years of primate evolution."

To Helen E. Fisher, an anthropologist at Rutgers who has spent most of her career studying the evolutionary aspects of mating and pair bonding in humans, partible paternity in South American societies and adultery among Western women come as no surprise.

"Fidelity never was a female reproductive strategy," she said in an interview. "Women have always * * * had clandestine relationships on the side." * * * Ms. Fisher said that women as well as men had "evolved a dual reproductive strategy"—a need to form pair bonds combined with a wandering eye that allows them to take advantage of reproductive opportunities. "In some societies," she added, "the rules are lifted, and it's just more out in the open."

38

Domestic Networks

FROM *All Our Kin: Strategies for Survival in a Black Community*

CAROL B. STACK

How far do family ties and responsibilities extend? For many African-American families they extend beyond parents and children to cousins, aunts, uncles, and even fictive kin. Decades of discrimination and institutional racism have left many people with few resources of their own to draw on in times of need, and so helping relationships have remained a critical feature of the extended family. Linking ethnicity, class, and gender, Carol Stack reminds us of the strength and resilience of the human community.

In The Flats the responsibility for providing food, care, clothing, and shelter and for socializing children within domestic networks may be spread over several households. Which household a given individual belongs to is not a particularly meaningful question, as we have seen that daily domestic organization depends on several things: where people sleep, where they eat, and where they offer their time and money. Although those who eat together and contribute toward the rent are generally considered by Flat's residents to form minimal domestic units, household changes rarely affect the exchanges and daily dependencies of those who take part in common activity.

The residence patterns and cooperative organization of people linked in domestic networks demonstrate the stability and collective power of family life in The Flats. Michael Lee grew up in The Flats and now has a job in Chicago. On a visit to The Flats, Michael described the residence and domestic organization of his kin. "Most of my kin in The Flats lived right here on Cricket Street, numbers sixteen, eighteen, and twenty-two, in these three apartment buildings joined together. My mama decided it would be best for me and my three brothers and sister to be on Cricket Street too. My daddy's mother had a small apartment in this building, her sister had one in the basement, and another brother and his family took a larger apartment upstairs. My uncle was really good to us. He got us things we wanted and he controlled us. All the women kept the younger kids together during the day. They cooked together too. It was good living."

Yvonne Diamond, a forty-year-old Chicago woman, moved to The Flats from Chicago with her four children. Soon afterwards they were evicted. "The landlord said he was going to build a parking lot there, but he never did. The old place is still standing and has folks in it today. My husband's mother and father took me and the kids in and watched over them while I had my baby. We stayed on after my husband's mother died, and my husband joined us when he got a job in The Flats."

When families or individuals in The Flats are evicted, other kinsmen usually take them in. Households in The Flats expand or contract with the loss of a job, a death in the family, the beginning or end of a sexual partnership, or the end of a friendship. Welfare workers, researchers, and landlords have long known that the poor must move frequently. What is much less understood is the relationship between residence and domestic organization in the black community.

The spectrum of economic and legal pressures that act upon ghetto residents, requiring them to move—unemployment, welfare requirements, housing shortages, high rents, eviction—are clear-cut examples of external pressures affecting the daily lives of the poor. Flats' residents are evicted from their dwellings by landlords who want to raise rents, tear the building down, or rid themselves of tenants who complain about rats, roaches, and the plumbing. Houses get condemned by the city on landlords' requests so that they can force tenants to move. After an eviction, a landlord can rent to a family in such great need of housing that they will not complain for a while.

Poor housing conditions and unenforced housing standards coupled with overcrowding, unemployment, and poverty produce hazardous living conditions and residence changes. "Our whole family had to move when the gas lines sprung a leak in our apartment and my son set the place on fire by accident," Sam Summer told me. "The place belonged to my sister-in-law's grandfather. We had been living there with my mother, my brother's eight children, and our eight children. My father lived in the basement apartment 'cause he and my mother were separated. After the fire burned the whole place down, we all moved to two places down the street near my cousin's house."

When people are unable to pay their rent because they have been temporarily "cut off aid," because the welfare office is suspicious of their eligibility, because they gave their rent money to a kinsman to help him through a crisis or illness, or because they were laid off from their job, they receive eviction notices almost immediately. Lydia Watson describes a chain of events starting with the welfare office stopping her sister's welfare checks, leading to an eviction, co-residence, overcrowding, and eventually murder. Lydia sadly related the story to me. "My oldest sister was cut off aid the day her husband got out of jail. She and her husband and their three children were evicted from their apartment and they came to live with us. We were in crowded conditions already. I had my son, my other sister was there with her two kids, and my mother was about going crazy. My mother put my sister's husband out 'cause she found out he was a dope addict. He came back one night soon after that and murdered my sister. After my sister's death my mother couldn't face living in Chicago any longer. One of my other sisters who had been adopted and raised by my mother's paternal grandmother visited us and persuaded us to move to The Flats, where she was staying. All of us moved there—my mother, my two sisters and their children, my two baby sisters, and my dead sister's children. My sister who had been staying in The Flats found us a house across the street from her own."

Overcrowded dwellings and the impossibility of finding adequate housing in The Flats have many long-term consequences regarding where and with whom children live. Terence Platt described where and with whom his kin lived when he was a child. "My brother stayed with my aunt, my mother's sister, and her husband until he was ten, 'cause he was the oldest in our family and we didn't have enough room—but he stayed with us most every weekend. Finally my aunt moved into the house behind ours with her husband, her brother, and my brother; my sisters and brothers and I lived up front with my mother and her old man."

KIN-STRUCTURED LOCAL NETWORKS

The material and cultural support needed to absorb, sustain, and socialize community members in The Flats is provided by networks of cooperating kinsmen. Local coalitions formed from these networks of kin and friends are mobilized within domestic networks; domestic organization is diffused over many kin-based households which themselves have elastic boundaries.

People in The Flats are immersed in a domestic web of a large number of kin and friends whom they can count on. From a social viewpoint, relationships within the community are "organized on the model of kin relationships." * * * Kin-constructs such as the perception of parenthood, the culturally determined criteria which affect the shape of personal kindreds, and the idiom of kinship, prescribe kin who can be recruited into domestic networks.

There are similarities in function between domestic networks and domestic groups which [one scholar] characterizes as "workshops of social reproduction." Both domains include three generations of members linked collaterally or otherwise. Kinship, jural and affectional bonds, and economic factors affect the composition of both domains and residential alignments within them. There are two striking differences between domestic networks and domestic groups. Domestic networks are not visible groups, because they do not have an obvious nucleus or defined boundary. But since a primary focus of domestic networks is child-care arrangements, the cooperation of a cluster of adult females is apparent. Participants in domestic networks are recruited from personal kindreds and friendships, but the personnel changes with fluctuating economic needs, changing life styles, and vacillating personal relationships.

In some loosely and complexly structured cognatic systems, kin-structured local networks (not groups) emerge. Localized coalitions of persons drawn from personal kindreds can be organized as networks of kinsmen. Goodenough * * * correctly points out that anthropologists frequently describe "localized kin groups," but rarely describe kin-structured local groups. * * *

The localized, kin-based, cooperative coalitions of people described in this chapter are organized as kin-structured domestic networks. For brevity, I refer to them as domestic networks.

* * *

GENEROSITY AND POVERTY

The combination of arbitrary and repressive economic forces and social behavior, modified by successive generations of poverty, make it almost impossible for people to break out of poverty. There is no way for those families poor enough to receive welfare to acquire any surplus cash which can be saved for emergencies or for acquiring adequate appliances or a home or a car. In contrast to the middle class, who are pressured to spend and save, the poor are not even permitted to establish an equity.

The following examples from Magnolia and Calvin Waters' life illustrates the ways in which the poor are prohibited from acquiring any surplus which might enable them to change their economic condition or life style.

In 1971 Magnolia's uncle died in Mississippi and left an unexpected inheritance of $1,500 to Magnolia and Calvin Waters. The cash came from a small run-down farm which Magnolia's uncle sold shortly before he died. It was the first time in their lives that Magnolia or Calvin ever had a cash reserve. Their first hope was to buy a home and use the money as a down payment.

Calvin had retired from his job as a seasonal laborer the year before and the family was on welfare. AFDC alloted the family $100 per month for rent. The housing that the family had been able to obtain over the years for their nine children at $100 or less was always small, roach infested, with poor plumbing and heating. The family was frequently evicted. Landlords complained about the noise and often observed an average of ten to fifteen children playing in the household. Magnolia and Calvin never even anticipated that they would be able to buy a home.

Three days after they received the check, news of its arrival spread throughout their domestic network. One niece borrowed $25 from Magnolia so that her phone would not be turned off. Within a week the welfare office knew about the money. Magnolia's children were immediately cut off welfare, including medical coverage and food stamps. Magnolia was told that she would not receive a welfare grant for her children until the money was used up, and she was given a minimum of four months in which to spend the money. The first surplus the family ever acquired was effectively taken from them.

During the weeks following the arrival of the money, Magnolia and Calvin's obligations to the needs of kin remained the same, but their ability to meet these needs had temporarily increased. When another uncle became very ill in the South, Magnolia and her older sister, Augusta, were called to sit by his side. Magnolia bought round-trip train tickets for both of them and for her three youngest children. When the uncle died, Magnolia bought round-trip train tickets so that she and Augusta could attend the funeral. Soon after his death, Augusta's first "old man" died in The Flats and he had no kin to pay for the burial. Augusta asked Magnolia to help pay for digging the grave. Magnolia was unable to refuse. Another sister's rent was two months overdue and Magnolia feared that she would get evicted. This sister was seriously ill and had no source of income. Magnolia paid her rent.

Winter was cold and Magnolia's children and grandchildren began staying home from school because they did not have warm winter coats and adequate shoes or boots. Magnolia and Calvin decided to buy coats, hats, and shoes for all of the children (at least fifteen). Magnolia also bought a winter coat for herself and Calvin bought himself a pair of sturdy shoes.

Within a month and a half, all of the money was gone. The money was channeled into the hands of the same individuals who ordinarily participate in daily domestic exchanges, but the premiums were temporarily higher. All of the money was quickly spent for necessary, compelling reasons.

Thus random fluctuations in the meager flow of available cash and goods tend to be of considerable importance to the poor. A late welfare check, sudden sickness, robbery, and other unexpected losses cannot be overcome with a cash reserve like more well-to-do families hold for emergencies. Increases in cash are either taken quickly from the poor by the welfare agencies or dissipated through the kin network.

Those living in poverty have little or no chance to escape from the economic situation into which they were born. Nor do they have the power to control the expansion or contraction of welfare benefits * * * or of employment opportunities, both of which have a momentous effect on their daily lives. In times of need, the only predictable resources that can be drawn upon are their own children and parents, and the fund of kin and friends obligated to them.

39

The Emotional Geography of Work and Family Life
FROM *The Time Bind: When Work Becomes Home and Home Becomes Work*
ARLIE RUSSELL HOCHSCHILD

In the past two decades Americans who are employed full-time are working more and more hours, despite their support for "family values" and a belief that parents need to spend more time with their children. The apparent contradiction is addressed by Arlie Hochschild in this essay that preceded her book, The Time Bind. *On the basis of fieldwork with many working parents, she provides an analysis of how people manage both their time and emotions. This leads to some interesting insights about the possible future of work and family.*

Over the last two decades, American workers have increasingly divided into a majority who work too many hours and a minority with no work at all. This split hurts families at both extremes, but I focus here on the growing scarcity of time among the long-hours majority. For many of them, a speed-up at the office and factory has marginalized life at home, so that the very term "work-family balance" seems to them a bland slogan with little bearing on real life. In this chapter, I describe the speed-up and review a range of cultural responses to it, including "family-friendly reforms" such as flextime, job sharing, part time work and parental leave. Why, I ask, do people not resist the speed-up more than they do? When offered these reforms, why don't more take advantage of them? Drawing upon my ongoing research in an American Fortune 500 company, I argue that a company's "family-friendly" policy goes only as deep as the "emotional geography" of the workplace and home, the drawn and redrawn boundaries between the sacred and the profane. I show how ways of talking about time (for example, separating "quality" from "quantity" time) become code words to describe that emotional geography. * * *

A WORK-FAMILY SPEED-UP

Three factors are creating the current speedup in work and family life in the United States. (By the term "family", I refer to committed unmarried couples, same-sex couples, single mothers, two-job couples and wage-earner-housewife couples. My focus is on all families who raise children.) First of all, increasing numbers of mothers now work outside the home. In 1950, 22 per cent of American mothers of children eighteen and under worked for pay; in 1991, 67 per cent did. Half of the mothers of children age one year and younger work for pay.

Second, they work in jobs which generally lack flexibility. The very model of "a job" and "career" has been based, for the most part, on the model of a traditional man whose wife cared for the children at home. Third, over the last 20 years, both women and men have increased their hours of work. In her book, *The Overworked American* the economist, Juliet Schor, argues that over the last two decades American workers have added an extra 164 hours to their year's work—an extra month of work a year. Compared to 20 years ago, workers take fewer unpaid absences, and even fewer *paid* ones. Over the last decade, vacations have shortened by 14 per cent. The number of families eating evening meals together has dropped by 10 per cent. Counting overtime and commuting time, a 1992 national sample of men averaged 48.8 hours of work, and women, 41.7. Among young parents, close to half now work more than 8 hours a day. Compared to the 1970s, mothers take less time off for the birth of a child and are more likely to work through the summer. They are more likely to work continuously until they retire at age 65. Thus, whether they have children or not, women increasingly fit the profile of year-round, life-long paid workers, a profile that has long characterized men. Meanwhile, male workers have not reduced their hours but, instead, expanded them.

Not all working parents with more free time will spend it at home tending children or elderly relatives. Nor, needless to say, if parents do spend time at home, will all their children find them kind, helpful and fun. But without a chance for more time at home, the issue of using it well does not arise at all.

COOL MODERN, TRADITIONAL, WARM MODERN STANCES TOWARD THE SPEED-UP

Do the speed-up people think the speed-up is a problem? Does anybody else? If so, what cultural stances toward gender equity, family life and capitalism underlie the practical solutions they favor? If we explore recent writing on the hurried life of a working parent, we can discern three stances toward it.

One is a *cool modern* stance, according to which the speed-up has become "normal," even fashionable. Decline in time at home does not "marginalize" family life, proponents say, it makes it different, even better. Like many other popular self-help books addressed to the busy working mother, *The Superwoman Syndrome,* by Marjorie Schaevitz offers busy mothers tips on how to fend off appeals for help from neighbors, relatives, friends, how to stop feeling guilty about their mothering. It instructs the mother how to frugally measure out minutes of "quality time" for her children and abandons as hopeless the project of getting men more involved at home. Such books call for no changes in the workplace, no changes in the culture and no change in men. The solution to rationalization at work is rationalization at home. Tacitly such books accept the corrosive effects of global capitalism on family life and on the very notion of what people need to be happy and fulfilled.

A second stance toward the work-family speed-up is traditional in that it calls for women's return to the home, or quasi-traditional in that it acquiesces to a secondary role, a lower rank "mommy track," for women at work. Those who take this sort of stance acknowledge the speed-up as a problem but deny the fact that most women now have to work, want to work, and embrace the concept of gender equity. They essentialize different male and female "natures," and notions of time, for men and women—"industrial" time for men, and "family" time for women.

A third warm modern stance is both humane (the speed-up is a problem) and egalitarian (equity at home and work is a goal). Those who take this approach question the terms of employment—both through a nationwide program of worksharing, (as in Germany), a shorter working week, and through company-based family friendly reforms. What are these family-friendly reforms?

- flextime; a workday with flexible starting and quitting times, but usually 40 hours of work and the opportunity to "bank" hours at one time and reclaim them later;
- flexplace; home-based work, such as telecommuting.
- regular or permanent part-time; less than full-time work with full- or pro-rated benefits and promotional opportunities in proportion to one's skill and contribution;
- job sharing; two people voluntarily sharing one job with benefits and salary pro-rated;
- compressed working week; four 10-hour days with 3 days off, or three 12-hour days with 4 days off;
- paid parental leave;
- family obligations as a consideration in the allocation of shift work and required overtime.

Together, worksharing and this range of family-friendly reforms could spread work, increase worker control over hours, and create a "warm modern" world for women to be equal within. As political goals in America over the last 50 years, worksharing and a shorter working week have "died and gone to heaven" where they live on as Utopian ideals. In the 1990s, family-friendly reforms are the lesser offering on the capitalist bargaining table. But are companies in fact offering these reforms? Are working parents pressing for them?

The news is good and bad. Recent nationwide studies suggest that more and more American companies offer their workers family-friendly alternative work schedules. According to one recent study, 88 per cent of 188 companies surveyed offer part-time work, 77 per cent offer flex-time of some sort, 48 per cent offer job-sharing, 35 per cent offer some form of flexplace, and 20 per cent offer a compressed working week. (But in most companies, the interested worker must seek and receive the approval of a supervisor or department head. Moreover, most policies do not apply to lower-level workers whose conditions of work are covered by union contracts.)

But even if offered, regardless of need, few workers actually take advantage of the reforms. One study of 384 companies noted that only nine companies reported even one father who took an official unpaid leave at the birth of his child. Few are on temporary or permanent part-time. Still fewer share a job.

* * *

INSIDE A FORTUNE 500 COMPANY

Why, when the opportunity presents itself, do so few working parents take it? To find out, I set about interviewing managers, and clerical and factory workers in a large manufacturing company in the northeastern United States—which I shall call, simply, the Company. I chose to study this Company because of its reputation as an especially progressive company. Over the last 15 years, for example, the Company devoted millions of dollars to informing workers of its family-friendly policies, hiring staff to train managers to implement them, making showcase promotions of workers who take extended maternity leaves or who work part-time. If change is to occur anywhere, I reasoned, it was likely to be within this Company.

But the first thing I discovered was that even in this enlightened Company, few young parents or workers tending elderly relatives took advantage of the chance to work more flexible or shorter hours. Among the 26,000 employees, the average working week ranged from 45 to 55 hours. Managers and factory workers often worked 50 or 60 hours a week while clerical workers tended to work a more normal, 40-hour, week. Everyone agreed the Company was a "pretty workaholic place." Moreover, for the last 5 years, hours of work had increased.

EXPLANATIONS THAT DON'T WORK

Perhaps workers shy away from applying for leaves or shortening their hours because they can't afford to earn less. This certainly explains why many young parents continue to work long hours. But it doesn't explain why the wealthiest workers, the managers and professionals, are among the least interested in additional time off. Even among the Company's factory workers, who in 1993 averaged between eleven and twelve dollars an hour, and who routinely competed for optional overtime, two 40-hour-a-week paychecks with no overtime work were quite enough to support the family. A substantial number said they could get by on one paycheck if they sold one of their cars, put in a vegetable garden and cut down on "extras." Yet, the overwhelming majority did not want to.

Perhaps, then, employees shied away from using flexible or shorter hour schedules because they were afraid of having their names higher on the list of workers who might be laid off in a period of economic downturn. Through the 1980s, a third of America's largest companies experienced some layoffs, though this did not happen to managers or clerical workers at this company.

By union contract, production workers were assured that layoffs, should they occur, would be made according to seniority and not according to any other criteria—such as how many hours an employee had worked. Yet, the workaholism went on. Employees in the most profitable sectors of the Company showed no greater tendency to ask for shorter or more flexible hours for family reasons than employees in the least profitable sectors.

Is it, then, that workers who could afford shorter hours didn't *know* about the Company's family-friendly policies? No. All of the 130 working parents I spoke with had heard about alternative schedules and knew where they could find out more.

Perhaps the explanation lies not with the workers but with their managers. Managers responsible for implementing family-friendly policies may be openly or covertly undermining them. Even though Company policy allowed flexibility, the head of a division could, for reasons of production, openly refuse a worker permission to go part-time or to job-share, which some did. For example when asked about his views on flextime, the head of the engineering division of the Company replied flatly, "My policy on flextime is that there is no flextime." Other apparently permissive division heads had supervisors who were tough on this issue "for them." Thus, there seemed to be some truth to this explanation for why so few workers stepped forward.

But even managers known to be cooperative had few employees asking for alternative schedules. Perhaps, then, workers ask for time off, but do so "off the books". To some extent, this "off the books" hypothesis did hold, especially for new fathers who may take a few days to a week of sick leave for the birth of a baby instead of filing for "parental leave," which they feared would mark them as unserious workers.

Even counting informal leaves, most women managers returned to full-time 40- to 55-hour work schedules fairly soon after their 6 weeks of paid maternity leave. Across ranks, most women secretaries returned after 6 months; most women production workers returned after 6 weeks. Most new fathers took a few days off at most. Thus, even "off the books," working parents used very little of the opportunity to spend more time at home.

Far more important than all these factors seemed to be a company "speed-up" in response to global competition. In the early years of the 1990s, workers each year spoke of working longer hours than they had the year before, a trend seen nationwide. When asked why, they explained that the Company was trying to "reduce costs," in part by asking employees to do more than they were doing before.

But the sheer existence of a company speed-up doesn't explain why employees weren't trying to actively resist it, why there wasn't much backtalk. Parents were eager to tell me how their families came first, how they were clear about that. (National polls show that next to a belief in God, Americans most strongly believe in "the family.") But, practices that might express this belief—such as sharing breakfast and dinner—were shifting in the opposite direction. In the minds of many parents of young children, warm modern intentions seemed curiously, casually, fused with cool modern ideas and practices. In some ways, those within the work-family speed-up don't seem to want to slow down. . . .

WORK AND FAMILY AS EMOTIONAL CULTURES

Through its family-friendly reforms, the Company had earned a national reputation as a desirable family-friendly employer. But at the same time, it wasn't inconvenienced by having to arrange alternate schedules for very many employees. One can understand how this might benefit a company. But how about the working parents?

For the answer, we may need a better grasp of the emotional cultures, and the relative "draw" of work and family. Instead of thinking of the workplace or the family as unyielding thing-like structures, Giddens suggests that we see structures as fluid and changeable. "Structuration," Anthony Giddens, [author of *New Rules of Sociological Method*] tells us, is the "dynamic process whereby structures come into being." For structures to change, there must be changes in what people do. But in doing what they do, people unconsciously draw on resources, and depend on larger conditions to develop the skills they use to change what they do.

With this starting point, then, let us note that structures come with—and also "are"—emotional cultures. A change in structure requires a change in emotional culture. What we lack, so far, is a vocabulary for describing this culture, and what follows is a crude attempt to create one. An emotional culture is a set of rituals, beliefs about feelings and rules governing feeling which induce emotional focus, and even a sense of the "sacred." This sense of the sacred selects and favors some social bonds over others. It selects and reselects relationships into a core or periphery of family life.

Thus, families have a more or less *sacred core* of private rituals and shared meanings. In some families what is most sacred is sexuality and marital communication (back rubs, pillow talk, sex), and in other families the "sacred" is reserved for parental bonds (bedtime cuddles with children, bathtime, meals, parental talk about children). In addition, families have secondary zones of less important daily, weekly, seasonal rituals which back up the core rituals. They also have a profane outer layer, in which members might describe themselves as "doing nothing in particular"—doing chores, watching television, sleeping. The character and boundaries of the sacred and profane aspects of family life are in the eye of the beholder. "Strong families" with "thick ties" can base their sense of the sacred on very different animating ideas and practices. Families also differ widely on how much one member's sense of the sacred matches another's and on how much it is the occasion for expressing harmony or conflict. Furthermore, families creatively adapt to new circumstances by ritualizing new activities—for example, couples in commuter marriages may "ritualize" the phone call or the daily e-mail exchange. Couples with "too much time together" may de-ritualize meals, sex, or family events. Furthermore, families have different structures of sacredness. Some have thick actual cores and thin peripheries, others have a porous core and extensive peripheral time in which people just "hang out." But in each case, emotional culture shapes the experience of family life.

Emotional cultures stand back-to-back with ideas about time. In the context of the work—family speed-up, many people speak of actively "managing time, finding time, making time, guarding time, or fighting for time." Less do they speak of simply "having" or "not having" time. In their attempt to take a more active grip on their schedules, many working parents turn a telephone answering machine on at dinner, turn down work assignments and social engagements, and actively fight to defend "family time."

One's talk about time is itself a verbal practice that does or doesn't reaffirm the ritual core of family life. In the core of family life, we may speak more of living in the moment. Because a sacred activity is an end in itself, and not a means to an end, the topic of time is less likely to arise. If it does, one speaks of "enjoying time," or "devoting time." With the work-family speed-up, the term "quality time" has arisen, as in "I need more quality time with my daughter," a term referring to freedom from distraction, time spent in an attitude of intense focus. In general, we try to "make" time for core family life because we feel it matters more.

In the intermediate and peripheral zones of family life, we may speak of "having time on our hands, wasting or killing time." In the new lexicon, we speak of "quantity time." In general, we feel we can give up peripheral time, because it matters less. More hotly contested is the time to participate in a child's school events, help at the school auction, buy a birthday gift for a babysitter, or call an elderly neighbor.

With a decline in this periphery, the threads of reciprocity in the community and neighborhood grow weaker. By forcing families to cut out what is "least important," the speed-up thins out and weakens ties that bind it to society. Thus, under the press of the "speed-up," families are forced to give up their periphery ties with neighbors, distant relatives, bonds sustained by "extra time." The speed-up privatizes the family. The "neighborhood goes to work," where it serves the emotional interests of the workplace. Where are one's friends? At work.

Although the family in modern society is separated from the workplace, its emotional culture is ecologically linked to and drawn from it. Both the family and workplace are also linked to supportive realms. For the family, this often includes the neighborhood, the church, the school. For the workplace, this includes the pub, the golf club, the commuter van friendship network. A loss of supportive structure around the family may result in a gain for the workplace, and vice versa. Insofar as the "periphery" of family life protected its ritual core, to a certain degree for working parents these ties are not so peripheral at all.

A gender pattern is clear. Because most women now must and for the most part want to work outside the home, they are performing family rituals less. At the same time, men are not doing them very much more. Together, these two facts result in a net loss in ritual life at home.

At the same time, at some workplaces, an alternative cultural magnet is drawing on the human need for a center, a ritual core. As family life becomes de-ritualized, in certain sectors of the economy, the engineers of corporate cultures are re-ritualizing the workplace. Thus, the contraction of emotional culture at home is linked to a socially engineered expansion of emotional culture at work.

WORK LIKE A FAMILY, AND FAMILY, FOR SOME, LIKE WORK

At a certain point, change in enough personal stories can be described as a change in culture, and I believe many families at the Company are coming to this turning-point now. Pulled toward work by one set of forces and propelled from the family by another set of forces, a growing number of workers are unwittingly altering the twin cultures of work and family. As the cultural shield surrounding work has grown stronger, the supportive cultural shield surrounding the family has weakened. Fewer neighborhood "consultants" talk to one when trouble arises at home, and for some, they are more to help out with problems at work.

* * *

THE MODEL OF FAMILY AS A HAVEN IN A HEARTLESS WORLD[1]

When I entered the field, I assumed that working parents would *want* more time at home. I imagined that they experienced home as a place where they could relax, feel emotionally sheltered and appreciated for who they "really are." I imagined home to feel to the weary worker like the place where he or she could take off a uniform, put on a bathrobe, have a beer, exhale—a picture summed up in the image of the worker coming in the door saying, "Hi honey, I'm home!." To be sure, home life has its emergencies and strains but I imagined that home was the place people thought about when they thought about rest, safety and appreciation. Given this, they would want to maximize

---

1. [This refers to Christopher Lasch's examination of the American family in his book, *Haven in a Heartless World.*]

time at home, especially time with their children. I also assumed that these working parents would not feel particularly relaxed, safe or appreciated at work, at least not more so than at home, and especially not factory workers.

When I interviewed workers at the Company, however, a picture emerged which partly belied this model of family life. For example, one 30-year-old factory shift supervisor, a remarried mother of two, described her return home after work in this way:

> I walk in the door and the minute I turn the key in the lock my oldest daughter is there. Granted she needs somebody to talk to about her day. The baby is still up . . . she should have been in bed two hours ago and that upsets me. The oldest comes right up to the door and complains about anything her father said or did during the evening. She talks about her job. My husband is in the other room hollering to my daughter, "Tracy, I don't ever get no time to talk to your mother because you're always monopolizing her time first before I even get a chance!" They all come at me at once.

The un-arbitrated quarrels, the dirty dishes, and the urgency of other people's demands she finds at home contrast with her account of going to work:

> I usually come to work early just to get away from the house. I go to be there at a quarter after the hour and people are there waiting. We sit. We talk. We joke. I let them know what is going on, who has to be where, what changes I have made for the shift that day. We sit there and chitchat for five or ten minutes. There is laughing. There is joking. There is fun. They aren't putting me down for any reason. Everything is done in humour and fun from beginning to end. It can get stressful, though, when a machine malfunctions and you can't get the production out.

Another 38-year-old working mother of two, also a factory worker, had this to say:

> My husband is a great help (with caring for their son). But as far as doing housework, or even taking the baby when I'm at home, no. When I'm home, our son becomes my job. He figures he works five days a week, he's not going to come home and clean. But he doesn't stop to think that I work seven days a week. . . . Why should I have to come home and do the housework without help from anybody else? My husband and I have been through this over and over again. Even if he would pack up the kitchen table and stack the dishes for me when I'm at work, that would make a big difference. He does nothing. On his weekends off, I have to provide a sitter for the baby so he can go fishing. When I have my day off, I have the baby all day long. He'll help out if I'm not here . . . the minute I'm here he lets me do the work.

To this working mother, her family was not a haven, a zone of relief and relaxation. It was a workplace. More than that, she could only get relief from this domestic workplace by going to the factory. As she continued:

> I take a lot of overtime. The more I get out of the house, the better I am. It's a terrible thing to say, but that's the way I feel!

I assumed that work would feel to workers like a place in which one could be fired at the whim of a profit-hungry employer, while in the family, for all its hassles, one was safe. Based as it is on the impersonal mechanism of supply and demand, profit and loss, work would feel insecure, like being in "a jungle." In fact, many workers I interviewed had worked for the Company for 20 years or more. But they were on their second or third marriages. To these employed, *work* was their rock, their major source of security, while they were receiving their "pink slips" at home.

To be sure, most workers *wanted* to base their sense of stability at home, and many did. But I was also struck by the loyalty many felt toward the Company and a loyalty *they felt* coming from it, despite what might seem like evidence to the contrary—the speed-up, the restructing. When problems arose at work, many workers felt they could go to their supervisors or to a human resources worker and resolve it. If one division of the Company was doing poorly, the Company might "de-hire" workers within that division and rehire in a more prosperous division. This happened to one female engineer, very much upsetting her, but her response to it was telling:

> I have done very well in the Company for twelve years, and I thought my boss thought very highly of me. He'd said as much. So when our division went down and several of us were de-hired, we were told to look for another position within the Company *or* outside. I thought, "Oh my God, *outside*!" I was stunned! Later, in the new division it was like a remarriage. . . . I wondered if I could love again.

Work was not always "there for you," but increasingly "home," as they had known it, wasn't either. As one woman recounted, "One day my husband came home and told me, 'I've fallen in love with a woman at work. . . . I want a divorce.'"

Finally, the model of family-as-haven led me to assume that the individual would feel most known and appreciated at home and least so at work. Work might be where they felt unappreciated, "a cog in the machine"— an image brought to mind by the Charlie Chaplin classic film on factory life, *Modern Times*. But the factory is no longer the archetypical workplace and, sadly, many workers felt more appreciated for what they were doing at work than for what they were doing at home. For example, when I asked one 40-year-old technician whether he felt more appreciated at home or at work, he said:

> I love my family. I put my family first . . . but I'm not sure I feel more appreci-ated by them (laughs). My 14-year-old son doesn't talk too much to anyone when he gets home from school. He's a brooder. I don't know how good I've been as a father . . . we fix cars together on Saturday. My wife works opposite shifts to what I work, so we don't see each other except on weekends. We need more time together—need to get out to the lake more. I don't know. . . .

This worker seemed to feel better about his skill repairing machines in the factory than his way of relating to his son. This is not as unusual as it might seem. In a large-scale study, Arthur Emlen found that 59 per cent of employees rated their family performance "good or unusually good" while 86 per cent gave a similar rating to their performance on the job.

This overall cultural shift may account for why many workers are going along with the work–family speed-up and not joining the resistance against it. A 1993 nationally representative study of 3400 workers conducted by The Families and Work Institute reflects two quite contradictory findings. On one hand, the study reports that 80 per cent of workers feel their jobs require "working very hard" and 42 per cent "often feel used up by the end of the work day." On the other hand, when workers are asked to compare how much time and energy they *actually* devoted to their family, their job or career and themselves, with how much time they would *like* to devote to each, there was little difference. Workers estimate that they actually spend 43 per cent of their time and energy on family and friends, 37 per cent on job or career, and 20 per cent on themselves. But they *want* to spend just about what they *are* spending—47 per cent on family and friends, 30 per cent on the job, and 23 per cent on themselves. Thus, the workers I spoke to who were "giving" in to the work-family speed-up may be typical of a wider trend.

CAUSAL MECHANISMS

Three sets of factors may exacerbate this reversal of family and work cultures; trends in the family, trends at work, and a cultural consumerism which reinforces trends in the family and work.

First, half of marriages in America end in divorce—the highest divorce rate in the world. Because of the greater complexity of family life, the emotional skills of parenting, woefully underestimated to begin with, are more important than ever before. Many workers spoke with feeling about strained relationships with step-children and ex-wives or husbands. New in scope, too, are the numbers of working wives who work "two shifts," one at home and one at work, and face their husband's resistance to helping fully with the load at home—a strain that often leaves both spouses feeling unappreciated.

Second, another set of factors apply at work. Many corporations have emotionally engineered for top and upper middle managers a world of friendly ritual and positive reinforcement. New corporate cultures call for "valuing the individual" and honoring the "internal customer" (so that requests made by employees within the Company are honored as highly as those by customers outside the Company). Human relations employees give seminars on human problems at work. High-performance teams, based on co-operation between relative equals who "manage themselves", tend to foster intense relations at work. The Company frequently gives out awards for outstanding work at award ceremonies. Compliments run freely. The halls are hung with new plaques praising one or another worker on recent accomplishments. Recognition luncheons, department gatherings and informal birthday remembrances are common. Career planning sessions with one's supervisor, team meetings to talk over "modeling, work relations, and mentoring" with co-workers all verge on, even as they borrow from, psychotherapy. For all its aggravation and tensions, the workplace is where quite a few workers feel appreciated, honored, and where they have real friends. By contrast, at home there are fewer "award ceremonies" and little helpful feedback about mistakes.

In addition, courtship and mate selection, earlier more or less confined to the home-based community, may be moving into the sphere of work. The later age for marriage, the higher proportion of unmarried people, and the high divorce rate all create an ever-replenishing courtship pool at work. The gender desegregation of the workplace, and the lengthened working day also provide opportunity for people to meet and develop romantic or quasi-romantic ties. At the factory, romance may develop in the lunchroom, pub, or parking lot; and for upper management levels, at conferences, in "fantasy settings" in hotels and dimly lit restaurants.

In a previous era, an undetermined number of men escaped the house for the pub, the fishing hole, and often the office. A common pattern, to quote from the title of an article by Jean Duncombe and Dennis Marsden, was that of "workaholic men" and "whining women." Now that women compose 45 per cent of the American labor force and come home to a "second shift" of work at home, some women are escaping into work too—and as they do so, altering the cultures of work and home.

Forces pulling workers out of family life and into the workplace are set into perpetual motion by consumerism. Consumerism acts as a mechanism which maintains the emotional reversal of work and family. Exposed to advertisements, workers expand their material "needs." To buy what they now "need," they need money. To earn money, they work longer hours. Being away from home so many hours, they make up for their absence at home with gifts which cost money. They "materialize" love. And so the cycle continues.

Once work begins to become a more compelling arena of appreciation than home, a self-fulfilling prophecy takes hold. For, if workers flee into work from the tensions at home, tensions at home often grow worse. The worse the tensions at home, the firmer the grip of the workplace on the worker's human needs, and hence the escalation of the entire syndrome.

If more workers conceive of work as a haven, it is overwhelmingly in some sense *against their wishes*. Most workers in this and other studies say they value family life above all. Work is what they do. Family is why they live. So, I believe the logic I have described proceeds despite, not because of, the powerful intentions and deepest wishes of those in its grip.

MODELS OF FAMILY AND WORK IN THE FLIGHT PLAN OF CAPITALISM

To sum up, for some people work may be becoming more like family, and family life more like work. Instead of the model of the *family* as haven from work, more of us fit the model of *work* as haven from home. In this model, the tired parent leaves a world of unresolved quarrels, unwashed laundry and dirty dishes for the atmosphere of engineered cheer, appreciation and harmony at work. It is at work that one drops the job of *working* on relating to a brooding adolescent, an obstreperous toddler, rivaling siblings or a retreating spouse. At last, beyond the emotional shield of work, one says not, "Hi honey, I'm home," but "Hi fellas, I'm here!" For those who fit this model, the ritual core of family life is not simply smaller, it is less of a ritual core.

How extensive is this trend? I suspect it is a slight tendency in the lives of many working parents, and the basic reality for a small but growing minority. This trend holds for some people more than others and in some parts of society more than in others. Certain trends—such as the growth of the contingency labor force[2]—may increase the importance of the family, and tend toward reinstalling the model of family as haven, and work as "heartless world." A growing rate of unemployment might be associated with yet a third "double-negative" model according to which neither home nor work are emotional bases, but rather the gang at the pub, or on the street.

But the sense of sacred that we presume to be reliably attached to home may be more vulnerable than we might wish.

Most working parents more deeply want, or want to want, a fourth, "double-positive" model of work-family balance. In the end, these four patterns are unevenly spread over the class structure—the "haven in a heartless world" more at the top, the "double-negative" more at the bottom, the "reverse-haven" emerging in the middle.

---

2. [The contingency labor force is those employees who work on a short-term contractural basis or are hired as temporary workers.]

Each pattern of work and family life is to be seen somewhere in the flight plan of late capitalism. For, capitalist competition is not simply a matter of market expansion around the globe, but of local geographies of emotion at home. The challenge, as I see it, is to understand the close links between economic trends, emotional geographies, and pockets of cultural resistance. For it is in those pockets that we can look for "warm modern" answers.

40

Hanging Tongues: A Sociological Encounter with the Assembly Line

WILLIAM E. THOMPSON

This story may sound familiar to many of you: what looks like a well-paying job and an avenue to the good life turns out to be a mirage, a treadmill, and a trap. By the time we recognize the mirage for what it is, the alternative paths have become blocked by consumer debt and family commitments, creating obstacles that can prove nearly insurmountable.

This qualitative sociological study analyzes the experience of working on a modern assembly line in a large beef plant. It explores and examines a special type of assembly line work which involves the slaughtering and processing of cattle into a variety of products intended for human consumption and other uses.

Working in the beef plant is "dirty work," not only in the literal sense of being drenched with perspiration and beef blood, but also in the figurative sense of performing a low-status, routine, and demeaning job. Although the work is honest and necessary in a society which consumes beef, slaughtering and butchering cattle is generally viewed as an undesirable and repugnant job. In that sense, workers at the beef plant share some of the same experiences as other workers in similarly regarded occupations (for example, ditchdiggers, garbage collectors, and other types of assembly line workers).

* * *

THE SETTING

The setting for the field work was a major beef processing plant in the Midwest. At the time of the study, the plant was the third largest branch of a corporation which operated ten such plants in the United States.

* * *

The beef plant was organizationally separated into two divisions: Slaughter and Processing. This study focused on the Slaughter division in the area of the plant known as the *kill floor*. A dominant feature of the kill floor was the machinery of the assembly line itself. The line was composed of an overhead stainless steel rail which began at the slaughter chute and curved its way around every work station in the plant. Every work station contained specialized machinery for the job performed at that place on the line. Dangling from the rail were hundreds of stainless steel hooks pulled by a motorized chain. Virtually every part of the line and all of the implements (tubs, racks, knives, etc.) were made of stainless steel. The walls were covered with a ceramic tile and the floor was made of sealed cement. There were floor drains located at every work station, so that at the end of each work segment (at breaks, lunch, and shift's end) the entire kill floor could be hosed down and cleaned for the next work period.

Another dominant feature of the kill floor was the smell. Extremely difficult to describe, yet impossible to forget, this smell combined the smells of live cattle, manure, fresh beef blood, and internal organs and their contents. This smell not only permeated the interior of the plant, but was combined on the outside with the smell of smoke from various waste products being burned and could be smelled throughout much of the community. This smell contributed greatly to the general negative feelings about work at the beef plant, as it served as the most distinguishable symbol of the beef plant to the rest of the community. The single most often asked question of me during the research by those outside the beef plant was, "How do you stand the smell?" In typical line workers' fashion, I always responded, "What smell? All I smell at the beef plant is money."

* * *

METHOD

The method of this study was nine weeks of full-time participant observation as outlined by Schatzman and Strauss (1973) and Spradley (1979; 1980). To enter the setting, the researcher went through the standard application process for a summer job. No mention of the research intent was made, though it was made clear that I was a university sociology professor. After initial screening, a thorough physical examination, and a helpful reference from a former student and part-time employee of the plant, the author was hired to work on the *Offal* crew in the Slaughter division of the plant.

* * *

THE WORK

* * * The line speed on the kill floor was 187. That means that 187 head of cattle were slaughtered per hour. At any particular work station, each worker was required to work at that speed. Thus, at my work station, in the period of one hour, 187 beef tongues were mechanically pulled from their hooks; dropped into a large tub filled with water; had to be taken from the tub and hung on a large stainless steel rack full of hooks; branded with a "hot brand" indicating they had been inspected by a USDA inspector; and then covered with a small plastic bag. The rack was taken to the cooler, replaced with an empty one, and the process began again.

It would be logical to assume that if a person worked at a steady, continuous pace of handling 187 tongues per hour, everything would go smoothly; not so. In addition to hanging, branding, and bagging tongues, the worker at that particular station also cleaned the racks and cleaned out a variety of empty stainless steel tubs used to hold hearts, kidneys, and other beef organs. Thus, in order to be free to clean the tubs when necessary, the "tongue-hanger" had to work at a slightly faster pace than the line moved. Then, upon returning from cleaning the tubs, the worker would be behind the line (*in a hole*) and had to work much faster to catch up with the line. Further, one fifteen-minute break and a thirty-minute lunch break were scheduled for an eight-hour shift. Before the "tongue-hanger" could leave his post for one of these, all tongues were required to be properly disposed of, all tubs washed and stored, and the work area cleaned.

My first two nights on the job, I discovered the consequences of working at the line speed (hanging, branding, and bagging each tongue as it fell in the tub). At the end of the work period when everybody else was leaving the work floor for break or lunch, I was furiously trying to wash all the tubs and clean the work area. Consequently, I missed the entire fifteen minute break and had only about ten minutes for lunch. By observing other workers, I soon caught on to the system. Rather than attempting to work at a steady pace consistent with the line speed, the norm was to work sporadically at a very frenzied pace, actually running ahead of the line and plucking tongues from the hooks before they got to the station. With practice, I learned to hang two or three tongues at a time, perform all the required tasks, and then take an unscheduled two or three minute break until the line caught up with me. Near break and lunch everybody worked at a frantic pace, got ahead of the line, cleaned the work areas, and even managed to add a couple of minutes to the scheduled break or lunch.

Working ahead of the line seems to have served as more than merely a way of gaining a few minutes of extra break time. It also seemed to take on a symbolic meaning. The company controlled the speed of the line. Seemingly, that took all element of control over the work process away from the workers. * * * However, when the workers refused to work at line speed and actually worked faster than the line, they not only added a few minutes of relaxation from the work while the line caught up, but they symbolically regained an element of control over the pace of their own work.

* * *

COPING

One of the difficulties of work at the beef plant was coping with three aspects of the work: monotony, danger, and dehumanization. While individual workers undoubtedly coped in a variety of ways, some distinguishable patterns emerged.

Monotony

The monotony of the line was almost unbearable. At my work station, a worker would hang, brand, and bag between 1,350 and 1,500 beef tongues in an eight-hour shift. With the exception of the scheduled fifteen-minute break and a thirty-minute lunch period (and sporadic brief gaps in the line), the work was mundane, routine, and continuous. As in most assembly line work, one inevitably drifted into daydreams (e.g., Garson, 1975; King, 1978; Linhart, 1981). It was not unusual to look up or down the line and see workers at various stations singing to themselves, tapping their feet to imaginary music, or carrying on conversations with themselves. I found that I could work with virtually no attention paid to the job, with my hands and arms almost automatically performing their tasks. In the meantime, my mind was free to wander over a variety of topics, including taking mental notes. In visiting with other workers, I found that daydreaming was the norm. Some would think about their families, while others fantasized about sexual escapades, fishing, or anything unrelated to the job. One individual who was rebuilding an antique car at home in his spare time would meticulously mentally rehearse the procedures he was going to perform on the car the next day.

Daydreaming was not inconsequential, however. During these periods, items were most likely to be dropped, jobs improperly performed, and accidents incurred. Inattention to detail around moving equipment, stainless steel hooks, and sharp knives invariably leads to dangerous consequences. Although I heard rumors of drug use to help fight the monotony, I never saw any workers take any drugs nor saw any drugs in any workers' possession. It is certainly conceivable that some workers might have taken something to help them escape the reality of the line, but the nature of the work demanded enough attention that such a practice could be ominous.

Danger

The danger of working in the beef plant was well known. Safety was top priority (at least in theory) and management took pride in the fact that only three employee on-the-job deaths had occurred in twelve years. Although deaths were uncommon, serious injuries were not. The beef plant employed over 1,800 people. Approximately three-fourths of those employed had jobs which demanded the use of a knife honed to razor-sharpness. Despite the use of wire-mesh aprons and gloves, serious cuts were almost a daily occurrence. Since workers constantly handled beef blood, danger of infection was ever present. As one walked along the assembly line, a wide assortment of bandages on fingers, hands, arms, necks, and faces could always be seen.

In addition to the problem of cuts, workers who cut meat continuously sometimes suffered muscle and ligament damage to their fingers and hands.

In one severe case, I was told of a woman who worked in processing for several years who had to wear splints on her fingers while away from the job to hold them straight. Otherwise, the muscles in her hand would constrict her fingers into the grip position, as if holding a knife.

* * *

When I spoke with fellow workers about the dangers of working in the plant, I noticed interesting defense mechanisms. * * * After a serious accident, or when telling about an accident or death which occurred in years past, the workers would almost immediately dissociate themselves from the event and its victim. Workers tended to view those who suffered major accidents or death on the job in much the same way that nonvictims of crime often view crime victims as either partially responsible for the event, or at least as very different from themselves (Barlow, 1981). "Only a part-timer," "stupid," "careless" or something similar was used, seemingly to reassure the worker describing the accident that it could not happen to him. The reality of the situation was that virtually all the jobs on the kill floor were dangerous, and any worker could have experienced a serious injury at any time.

* * *

Dehumanization

Perhaps the most devastating aspect of working at the beef plant (worse than the monotony and the danger) was the dehumanizing and demeaning elements of the job. In a sense, the assembly line worker became a part of the assembly line. The assembly line is not a tool used by the worker, but a machine which controls him/her. A tool can only be productive in the hands of somebody skilled in its use, and hence becomes an extension of the person using it. A machine, on the other hand, performs specific tasks, thus its operator becomes an extension of it in the production process. * * * When workers are viewed as mere extensions of the machines with which they work, their human needs become secondary in importance to the smooth mechanical functioning of the production process. In a bureaucratic structure, when "human needs collide with systems needs the individual suffers" (Hummel, 1977: 65).

Workers on the assembly line are seen as interchangeable as the parts of the product on the line itself. An example of one worker's perception of this phenomenon at the beef plant was demonstrated the day after a fatal accident occurred. I asked the men in our crew what the company did in the case of an employee death (I wondered if there was a fund for flowers, or if the shift was given time off to go to the funeral, etc.). One worker's response was: "They drag off the body, take the hard hat and boots and check 'em out to some other poor sucker, and throw him in the guy's place." While employee death on the job was not viewed quite that coldly by the company, the statement fairly accurately summarized the overall result of a fatal accident, and importance of any individual worker to the overall operation of the production process. If accurately summarized the workers' perceptions about management's attitudes toward them.

* * *

Sabotage

It is fairly common knowledge that assemblyline work situations often led to employee sabotage or destruction of the product or equipment used in the production process (Garson, 1975; Balzer, 1976; Shostak, 1980). This is the classic experience of alienation as described by Marx (1964a,b). * * * At the beef plant I quickly learned that there was an art to effective sabotage. Subtlety appeared to be the key. "The art lies in sabotaging in a way that is not immediately discovered," as a Ford worker put it (King, 1978:202). This seemed to hold true at the beef plant as well.

* * *

The greatest factor influencing the handling of beef plant products was its status as a food product intended for human consumption. * * * Though not an explicitly altruistic group, the workers realized that the product would be consumed by people (even family, relatives, and friends), so consequently, they rarely did anything to actually contaminate the product.

Despite formal norms against sabotage, some did occur. It was not uncommon for workers to deliberately cut chunks out of pieces of meat for no reason (or for throwing at other employees). While regulations required that anything that touched the floor had to be put in tubs marked "inedible," the informal procedural norms were otherwise. When something was dropped, one usually looked around to see if an inspector or foreman noticed. If not, the item was quickly picked up and put back on the line.

Several explanations might be offered for this type of occurrence. First, since the company utilized a profit-sharing plan, when workers damaged the product, or had to throw edible pieces into inedible tubs (which sold for pet food at much lower prices), profits were decreased. A decrease in profits to the company ultimately led to decreased dividend checks to employees. Consequently, workers were fairly careful not to actually ruin anything. Second, when something was dropped or mishandled and had to be rerouted to "inedible," it was more time-consuming than if the product had been handled properly and kept on the regular line. In other words, if no inspector noticed, it was easier to let it go through on the line. There was a third, and seemingly more meaningful, explanation for this behavior, however. It was against the rules to do it, it was a challenge to do it, and thus it was fun to do it.

The workers practically made a game out of doing forbidden things simply to see if they could get away with it. * * * New workers were routinely socialized into the subtle art of rulebreaking as approved by the line workers. At

my particular work station, it was a fairly common practice for other workers who were covered with beef blood to come over to the tub of swirling water
designed to clean the tongues, and as soon as the inspector looked away, wash
their hands, arms, and knives in the tub. This procedure was strictly forbidden
by the rules. If witnessed by a foreman or inspector, the tub had to be emptied,
cleaned, and refilled, and all the tongues in the tub at the time had to be put
in the "inedible" tub. All of that would be a time-consuming and costly procedure, yet the workers seemed to absolutely delight in successfully pulling off
the act. As Balzer (1976:90) indicates:

> Since a worker often feels that much if not all of what he does is done in places
> designated by the company, under company control, finding ways to express
> personal freedom from this institutional regimentation is important.

Thus, artful sabotage served as a symbolic way in which the workers could
express a sense of individuality, and hence, self-worth.

THE FINANCIAL TRAP

Given the preceding description and analysis for work at the beef plant, why did
people work at such jobs? Obviously, there are a multitude of plausible answers
to that question. Without doubt, however, the key is money. The current economic situation, the lack of steady employment opportunities (especially for the
untrained and poorly educated), combined with the fact that the beef plant's
starting wage exceeded the minimum wage by approximately $5.50 per hour
emerge as the most important reasons people went to work there.

Despite the high hourly wage and fringe benefits, however, the monotony,
danger, and hard physical work drove many workers away in less than a week.
During my study, I observed much worker turnover. Those who stayed displayed an interesting pattern which helps explain why they did not leave. Every
member of my work crew answered similarly my questions about why they
stayed at the beef plant. Each of them took the job directly after high school,
because it was the highest-paying job available. Each of them had intended to
work through the summer and then look for a better job in the fall. During that
first summer on the job they fell victim to what I label the "financial trap."

The "financial trap" was a spending pattern which demanded the constant
weekly income provided by the beef plant job. This scenario was first told to me
by an employee who had worked at the plant for over nine years. He began the
week after his high school graduation, intending only to work that summer in
order to earn enough money to attend college in the fall. After about four
weeks' work he purchased a new car. He figured he could pay off the car that
summer and still save enough money for tuition. Shortly after the car purchase,
he added a new stereo sound system to his debt; next came a motorcycle; then
the decision to postpone school for one year in order to continue working at the

beef plant and pay off his debts. A few months later he married; within a year purchased a house; had a child; and bought another new car. Nine years later, he was still working at the beef plant, hated every minute of it, but in his own words "could not afford to quit." His case was not unique. Over and over again, I heard stories about the same process of falling into the "financial trap." The youngest and newest of our crew had just graduated high school and took the job for the summer in order to earn enough money to attend welding school the following fall. During my brief tenure at the beef plant, he purchased a new motorcycle, a new stereo, and a house trailer. When I left, he told me he had decided to postpone welding school for one year in order "to get everything paid for." I saw the financial trap closing in on him fast; he did too.

* * *

SUMMARY AND CONCLUSIONS

There are at least three interwoven phenomena in this study which deserve further comment and research.

First is the subtle sense of unity which existed among the line workers. * * * The line both symbolically and literally linked every job, and consequently every worker, to each other. * * * A system of "uncooperative teamwork" seemed to combine simultaneously a feeling of "one-for-all, all-for-one, and every man for himself." Once a line worker made it past the first three or four days on the job which "weeded out" many new workers, his status as a *beefer* was assured and the sense of unity was felt as much by the worker of nine weeks as it was by the veteran of nine years. Because the workers maintained largely secondary relationships, this feeling of unification is not the same as the unity typically found on athletic teams, in fraternities, or among various primary groups. Yet it was a significant social force which bound the workers together and provided a sense of meaning and worth. Although their occupation might not be highly respected by outsiders, they derived mutual self-respect from their sense of belonging.

A second important phenomenon was the various coping methods * * * the beef plant line workers developed and practiced * * * for retaining their humanness. Daydreaming, horseplay and occasional sabotage protected their sense of self. Further, the prevailing attitude among workers that it was "us" against "them" served as a reminder that, while the nature of the job might demand subjugation to bosses, machines, and even beef parts, they were still human beings.

* * *

A third significant finding was that consumer spending patterns among the beefers seemed to "seal their fate" and make leaving the beef plant almost impossible. A reasonable interpretation of the spending patterns of the beefers is that having a high-income/low-status job encourages a person to consume conspicuously. The prevailing attitude seemed to be "I may not have a nice job, but I have a nice home, a nice car, etc." This conspicuous consumption enabled workers to take indirect pride in their occupations. One of the ways of overcoming drudgery and humiliation on the job was to surround oneself with as many desirable material things as possible off the job. These items (cars, boats, motorcycles, etc.) became tangible rewards for the sacrifices endured at work.

The problem, of course, is that the possession of these expensive items required the continual income of a substantial paycheck which most of these men could only obtain by staying at the beef plant. These spending patterns were further complicated by the fact that they were seemingly "contagious." Workers talked to each other on breaks about recent purchases, thus reinforcing the norm of immediate gratification. A common activity of a group of workers on break or lunch was to run to the parking lot to see a fellow worker's new truck, van, car or motorcycle. Even the seemingly more financially conservative were usually caught up in this activity and often could not wait to display their own latest acquisitions. Ironically, as the workers cursed their jobs, these expensive possessions virtually destroyed any chance of leaving them.

Working at the beef plant was indeed "dirty work." It was monotonous, difficult, dangerous, and demeaning. Despite this, the workers at the beef plant worked hard to fulfill employer expectations in order to obtain financial rewards. Through a variety of symbolic techniques, they managed to overcome the many negative aspects of their work and maintain a sense of self-respect about how they earned their living.

REFERENCES

Balzer, Richard (1976). *Clockwork: Life In and Outside an American Factory.* Garden City, NY: Doubleday.

Barlow, Hugh (1981). *Introduction to Criminology.* 2d ed. Boston: Little, Brown.

Garson, Barbara (1975). *All the Livelong Day: The Meaning and Demeaning of Routine Work.* Garden City, NY: Doubleday.

Hummel, Ralph P. (1977). *The Bureaucratic Experience.* New York: St. Martin's Press.

King, Rick (1978). "In the sanding booth at Ford." Pp. 199-205 in John and Erna Perry (eds.), *Social Problems in Today's World.* Boston: Little, Brown.

Linhart, Robert (translated by Margaret Crosland) (1981). *The Assembly Line.* Amherst: University of Massachusetts Press.

Marx, Karl (1964a). *Economic and Philosophical Manuscripts of 1844.* New York: International Publishing (1844).

——— (1964b). *The Communist Manifesto.* New York: Washington Square Press (1848).

Schatzman, Leonard, and Anselm L. Strauss (1973). *Field Research.* Englewood Cliffs, NJ: Prentice-Hall.

Shostak, Arthur (1980). *Blue Collar Stress.* Reading, MA: Addison-Wesley.

Spradley, James P. (1979). *The Ethnographic Interview.* New York: Holt, Rinehart & Winston.

——— (1980). *Participant Observation.* New York: Holt, Rinehart & Winston.

41

The McDonald's System

<small>FROM</small> *The McDonaldization of Society*

GEORGE RITZER

McDonald's has become a buzzword not only for fast food but for a way of organizing activities, calculated to maximize efficiency by minimizing opportunities for error. For some this is wonderful, but for others this is lifeless and without joy, despite the images that appear in McDonald's commercials. Ultimately, it may not be as efficient as it seems.

THE DIMENSIONS OF McDONALDIZATION: FROM DRIVE-THROUGHS TO UNCOMFORTABLE SEATS

Even if some domains are able to resist McDonaldization, this book intends to demonstrate that many other aspects of society are being, or will be, McDonaldized. This raises the issue of why the McDonald's model has proven so irresistible. Four basic and alluring dimensions lie at the heart of the success of the McDonald's model and, more generally, of the process of McDonaldization.

First, McDonald's offers *efficiency*. That is, the McDonald's system offers us the optimum method for getting from one point to another. Most generally, this means that McDonald's proffers the best available means of getting us from a state of being hungry to a state of being full. * * * Other institutions, fashioned on the McDonald's model, offer us similar efficiency in losing weight, lubricating our cars, filling eyeglass prescriptions, or completing income tax forms. In a fast-paced society in which both parents are likely to work, or where there may be only a single parent, efficiently satisfying the hunger and many other needs of people is very attractive. In a highly mobile society in which people are rushing, usually by car, from one spot to another, the efficiency of a fast-food meal, perhaps without leaving one's car while passing by the drive-through window, often proves impossible to resist. The fast-food model offers us, or at least appears to offer us, an efficient method for satisfying many of our needs.

Second, McDonald's offers us food and service that can be easily *quantified* and *calculated*. In effect, McDonald's seems to offer us "more bang for the buck." (One of its recent innovations, in response to the growth of other fast-food franchises, is to proffer "value meals" at discounted prices.) We often feel that we are getting a *lot* of food for a modest amount of money. Quantity has become equivalent to quality; a lot of something means it must be good. As two observers of contemporary American culture put it, "As a culture, we tend to believe—deeply—that in general 'bigger is better.'" Thus, we order the *Quarter Pounder,* the *Big* Mac, the *large* fries. We can quantify all of these things and feel that we are getting a lot of food, and, in return, we appear to be shelling out only a nominal sum of money. This calculus, of course, ignores an important point: the mushrooming of fast-food outlets, and the spread of the model to many other businesses, indicates that our calculation is illusory and it is the owners who are getting the best of the deal.

There is another kind of calculation involved in the success of McDonald's— a calculation involving time. People often, at least implicitly, calculate how much time it will take them to drive to McDonald's, eat their food, and return home and then compare that interval to the amount of time required to prepare the food at home. They often conclude, rightly or wrongly, that it will take less time to go and eat at the fast-food restaurant than to eat at home. This time calculation is a key factor in the success of Domino's and other home-delivery franchises, because to patronize them people do not even need to leave their homes. To take another notable example, Lens Crafters promises us "Glasses fast, glasses in one hour." Some McDonaldized institutions have come to combine the emphases on time and money. Domino's promises pizza delivery in one-half hour, or the pizza is free. Pizza Hut will serve us a personal pan pizza in five minutes, or it, too, will be free.

Third, McDonald's offers us *predictability.* We know that the Egg McMuffin we eat in New York will be, for all intents and purposes, identical to those we have eaten in Chicago and Los Angeles. We also know that the one we order next week or next year will be identical to the one we eat today. There is great comfort in knowing that McDonald's offers no surprises, that the food we eat at one time or in one place will be identical to the food we eat at another time or in another place. We know that the next Egg McMuffin we eat will not be awful, but we also know that it will not be exceptionally delicious. The success of the McDonald's model indicates that many people have come to prefer a world in which there are no surprises.

Fourth and finally, *control,* especially through the *substitution of non-human for human technology,* is exerted over the human beings who enter the world of McDonald's. The humans who work in fast-food restaurants are trained to do a very limited number of things in precisely the way they are told to do them. Managers and inspectors make sure that workers toe the line. The human beings who eat in fast-food restaurants are also controlled, albeit (usually) more subtly and indirectly. Lines, limited menus, few options, and uncomfortable seats all lead diners to do what the management wishes them to do— eat quickly and leave. Further, the drive-through (and in some cases walk-through) window leads diners to first leave and then eat rapidly. This attribute has most recently been extended by the Domino's model, according to which customers are expected to *never* come, yet still eat speedily.

McDonald's also controls people by using nonhuman technology to replace human workers. Human workers, no matter how well they are programmed and controlled, can foul up the operation of the system. A slow or indolent worker can make the preparation and delivery of a Big Mac inefficient. A worker who refuses to follow the rules can leave the pickles or special sauce off a hamburger, thereby making for unpredictability. And a distracted worker can put too few fries in the box, making an order of large fries seem awfully skimpy. For these and other reasons, McDonald's is compelled to steadily replace human beings with non-human technologies, such as the soft-drink dispenser that shuts itself off when the glass is full, the french-fry machine that rings when the fries are crisp, the preprogrammed cash register that eliminates the need for the cashier to calculate prices and amounts, and, perhaps at some future time, the robot capable of making hamburgers. (Experimental robots of this type already exist.) All of these technologies permit greater control over the human beings involved in the fast-food restaurant. The result is that McDonald's is able to reassure customers about the nature of the employee to be encountered and the nature of the service to be obtained.

In sum, McDonald's (and the McDonald's model) has succeeded because it offers the consumer efficiency and predictability, and because it seems to offer the diner a lot of food for little money and a slight expenditure of effort. It has also flourished because it has been able to exert greater control through non-human technologies over both employees and customers, leading them to behave the way the organization wishes them to. The substitution of non-human for human technologies has also allowed the fast-food restaurant to deliver its fare increasingly more efficiently and predictably. Thus, there are good, solid reasons why McDonald's has succeeded so phenomenally and why the process of McDonaldization continues unabated.

A CRITIQUE OF McDONALDIZATION: THE IRRATIONALITY OF RATIONALITY

There is a downside to all of this. We can think of efficiency, predictability, calculability, and control through nonhuman technology as the basic components of a *rational* system. However, as we shall see in later chapters, rational systems often spawn irrationalities. The downside of McDonaldization will be dealt with most systematically under the heading of the *irrationality of rationality*. Another way of saying this is that rational systems serve to deny human reason; rational systems can be unreasonable.

For example, the fast-food restaurant is often a dehumanizing setting in which to eat or work. People lining up for a burger, or waiting in the drive-through line, often feel as if they are dining on an assembly line, and those who prepare the burgers often appear to be working on a burger assembly line. Assembly lines are hardly human settings in which to eat, and they have been shown to be inhuman settings in which to work. As we will see, dehumanization is only one of many ways in which the highly rationalized fast-food restaurant is extremely irrational.

Of course, the criticisms of the irrationality of the fast-food restaurant will be extended to all facets of our McDonaldizing world. This extension has recently been underscored and legitimated at the opening of Euro DisneyLand outside Paris. A French socialist politician acknowledged the link between Disney and McDonald's as well as their common negative effects when he said that Euro Disney will "bombard France with uprooted creations that are to culture what fast food is to gastronomy."

Such critiques lead to a question: Is the headlong rush toward McDonaldization around the world advantageous or not? There are great gains to be made from McDonaldization, some of which will be discussed below. But there are also great costs and enormous risks, which this book will focus on. Ultimately, we must ask whether the creation of these rationalized systems creates an even greater number of irrationalities. At the minimum, we need to be aware of the costs associated with McDonaldization. McDonald's and other purveyors of the fast-food model spend billions of dollars each year outlining the benefits to be derived from their system. However, the critics of the system have few outlets for their ideas. There are no commercials on Saturday morning between cartoons warning children of the dangers associated with fast-food restaurants. Although few children are likely to read this book, it is aimed, at least in part, at their parents (or parents-to-be) in the hope that it will serve as a caution that might be passed on to their children.

A legitimate question may be raised about this analysis: Is this critique of McDonaldization animated by a romanticization of the past and an impossible desire to return to a world that no longer exists? For some critics, this is certainly the case. They remember the time when life was slower, less efficient, had more surprises, when people were freer, and when one was more likely to deal with a human being than a robot or a computer. Although they have a point, these critics have undoubtedly exaggerated the positive aspects of a world before McDonald's, and they have certainly tended to forget the liabilities associated with such a world. More importantly, they do not seem to realize that we are *not* returning to such a world. The increase in the number of people, the acceleration in technological change, the increasing pace of life—all this and more make it impossible to go back to a nonrationalized world, if it ever existed, of home-cooked meals, traditional restaurant dinners, high-quality foods, meals loaded with surprises, and restaurants populated only by workers free to fully express their creativity.

While one basis for a critique of McDonaldization is the past, another is the future. The future in this sense is what people have the potential to be if they are unfettered by the constraints of rational systems. This critique holds that people have the potential to be far more thoughtful, skillful, creative, and well-rounded than they now are, yet they are unable to express this potential because of the constraints of a rationalized world. If the world were less rationalized, or even derationalized, people would be better able to live up to their human potential. This critique is based not on what people were like in the past, but on what they could be like in the future, if only the constraints of McDonaldized systems were eliminated, or at least eased substantially. The criticisms to be put forth in this book are animated by the latter, future-oriented perspective rather than by a romanticization of the past and a desire to return to it.

THE ADVANTAGES OF McDONALDIZATION: FROM THE CAJUN BAYOU TO SUBURBIA

Much of this book will focus on the negative side of McDonald's and McDonaldization. At this point it is important, however, to balance this view by mentioning some of the benefits of these systems and processes. The economic columnist, Robert Samuelson, for example, is a strong supporter of McDonald's and confesses to "openly worship McDonald's." He thinks of it as "the greatest restaurant chain in history." (However, Samuelson does recognize that there are those who "can't stand the food and regard McDonald's as the embodiment of all that is vulgar in American mass culture.")

Let me enumerate some of the advantages of the fast-food restaurant as well as other elements of our McDonaldized society:

■ The fast-food restaurant has expanded the alternatives available to consumers. For example, more people now have ready access to Italian, Mexican, Chinese, and Cajun foods. A McDonaldized society is, in this sense, more egalitarian.

■ The salad bar, which many fast-food restaurants and supermarkets now offer, enables people to make salads the way they want them.

■ Microwave ovens and microwavable foods enable us to have dinner in minutes or even seconds.

■ For those with a wide range of shopping needs, supermarkets and shopping malls are very efficient sites. Home shopping networks allow us to shop even more efficiently without ever leaving home.

■ Today's high-tech, for-profit hospitals are likely to provide higher quality medical care than their predecessors.

■ We can receive almost instantaneous medical attention at our local, drive-in "McDoctors."

■ Computerized phone systems (and "voice mail") allow people to do things that were impossible before, such as obtain a bank balance in the middle of the night or hear a report on what went on in their child's class during the day and what home-work assignments were made. Similarly, automated bank teller machines allow people to obtain money any time of the day or night.

■ Package tours permit large numbers of people to visit countries that they would otherwise not visit.

- Diet centers like Nutri/System allow people to lose weight in a carefully regulated and controlled system.
- The 24-second clock in professional basketball has enabled outstanding athletes such as Michael Jordan to more fully demonstrate their extraordinary talents.
- Recreational vehicles let the modern camper avoid excessive heat, rain, insects, and the like.
- Suburban tract houses have permitted large numbers of people to afford single-family homes.

CONCLUSION

The previous list gives the reader a sense not only of the advantages of McDonaldization but also of the range of phenomena that will be discussed under that heading throughout this book. In fact, such a wide range of phenomena will be discussed under the heading of McDonaldization that one is led to wonder: What isn't McDonaldized? Is McDonaldization the equivalent of modernity? Is everything contemporary McDonaldized?

While much of the world has been McDonaldized, it is possible to identify at least three aspects of contemporary society that have largely escaped McDonaldization. First, there are phenomena traceable to an earlier, "premodern" age that continue to exist within the modern world. A good example is the Mom and Pop grocery store. Second, there are recent creations that have come into existence, at least in part, as a reaction against McDonaldization. A good example is the boom in bed and breakfasts (B&Bs), which offer rooms in private homes with personalized attention and a homemade breakfast from the proprietor. People who are fed up with McDonaldized motel rooms in Holiday Inn or Motel 6 can instead stay in so-called B&Bs. Finally, some analysts believe that we have moved into a new, "postmodern" society and that aspects of that society are less rational than their predecessors. Thus, for example, in a postmodern society we witness the destruction of "modern" high-rise housing projects and their replacement with smaller, more livable communities. Thus, although it is ubiquitous, McDonaldization is *not* simply another term for contemporary society. There *is* more to the contemporary world than McDonaldization.

In discussing McDonaldization, we are *not* dealing with an all-or-nothing process. Things are not either McDonaldized or not McDonaldized. There are degrees of McDonaldization; it is a continuum. Some phenomena have been heavily McDonaldized, others moderately McDonaldized, and some only slightly McDonaldized. There are some phenomena that may have escaped McDonaldization completely. Fast-food restaurants, for example, have been heavily McDonaldized, universities moderately McDonaldized, and the Mom and Pop grocers mentioned earlier only slightly McDonaldized. It is difficult to think of social phenomena that have escaped McDonaldization totally, but I suppose there is local enterprise in Fiji that has been untouched by this process. In this context, McDonaldization thus represents a process—a process by which more and more social phenomena are being McDonaldized to an increasing degree.

Overall, the central thesis is that McDonald's represents a monumentally important development and the process that it has helped spawn, McDonaldization, is engulfing more and more sectors of society and areas of the world. It has yielded a number of benefits to society, but it also entails a considerable number of costs and risks.

Although the focus is on McDonald's and McDonaldization, it is important to realize that this system has important precursors in our recent history. * * * That is, McDonaldization is not something completely new, but rather its success has been based on its ability to bring together a series of earlier innovations. Among the most important precursors to McDonaldization are bureaucracy, scientific management, the assembly line, and the original McDonald brothers' hamburger stand.

42

Job on the Line

WILLIAM M. ADLER

Two women share the same job. For decades Molly James performs the work in Patterson, New Jersey; then Balbina Duque Granados does it in Matamoros, Mexico. Molly James is laid off; Balbina Duque Granados struggles to make ends meet. The global transformation of work benefits consumers with lower prices and a wider range of products. It brings industry to formerly agrarian countries and changes them forever. But the unrecorded costs are considerable. In this highly personal account we are able to see many of the negative features of globalization. The challenge of globalization in the years ahead will be to address these hidden costs.

At 3 o'clock on a warm June afternoon, the second of two wash-up bells rings for the final time. Mollie James stands hunched over the sink as she rinses her hands with industrial soap alongside her co-workers. She first came to work here, on the assembly line at Universal Manufacturing Company in Paterson, New Jersey, a few years after the factory opened in 1951. She was the first woman at the factory to run a stamping machine, the first to laminate steel. She was among the first female union stewards and among the first African American stewards; hers was a self-assured presence any grievant would want on their side. And now, after 34 years on the line—nearly two-thirds of her life—she is the last to go.

At the end of every other shift for more than three decades, Mollie and her fellow employees beat a quick path to the plant parking lot. On this day there is less sense of hurry. There are still children to feed, clothes to wash, bills to pay, errands to run, other jobs to race to. But as she and the others leave the washroom, no one seems pressed to leave. All about the plant entrance, and out in the lot, people stand in small clusters, like mourners at their own wake, talking, laughing, hugging, crying. Almost always Mollie James is outgoing and outspoken, her voice loud and assertive, her smile nicely lighted. At 59 she is a strong woman, her strength forged from a life of hard work and sacrifice, and faith in God. She is not one to betray her emotions, but this day is different. Her bearing has turned to reserve, her normally quick eyes dull and watery. Her working life is over, and that is the only life she has ever known.

Universal had always turned a tidy profit. Its signature product, ballasts that regulate the current in fluorescent lights, attracted attention only when the ballast failed—causing the light fixture to hum or flicker. In the mid-1980s, however, the locally owned company was twice swept up in the gale winds of Wall Street's merger mania. Twice within eight months Universal was sold, both times to firms headed by disciples of Michael Milken, the Street's reigning evil genius. Not long after the second sale, to a Los Angeles-based electrical components conglomerate called MagneTek, Inc., movers began pulling up the plant's massive machinery, much of which had been bolted to the floor when the factory opened.

Mollie had sensed what was happening in January 1989, the morning she came to work and noticed the hole in the floor. It wasn't a hole, really, in the sense of an opening; it was more of a void: a great yawning space of discolored concrete where just the afternoon before had sat a steel-stamping machine, a hulking piece of American industrial might. Before long, more holes appeared, each tracing the outline of the base of another machine, like chalk around a sidewalk corpse.

Now, on the last day, when there is no one left to say goodbye to, Mollie slumps behind the wheel of her rusting 1977 Dodge Charger and follows the procession out of the lot. It is not far, three miles or so, from the plant in Paterson's industrial Bunker Hill neighborhood to the three-story, three-family house she owns on the near East Side. Upon pulling into her customary space in the driveway, Mollie sits in the car a good long while, letting the heat of the summer afternoon settle her. By the time she fits the key into the back-door lock and begins climbing the three flights of stairs to her bedroom, she has stopped crying.

The machine that Mollie used to stamp steel for three decades makes its way south, past factories that Universal opened in Mississippi and Arkansas during the 1960s and 1970s to take advantage of cheaper labor and taxes, before arriving in Matamoros, Mexico, a booming border city just across the Rio Grande from Brownsville, Texas. On a blindingly blue morning, MagneTek executives from "corporate" in L.A. arrive for the gala ribbon cutting of the first MagneTek plant here. Plant manager Chuck Peeples, an affable Arkansas expatriate, leads the officials on a tour of the gleaming factory. Outfitted in natty going-native panama hats emblazoned with the company's royal-blue capital-M "power" logo, the MagneTek honchos parade past equipment ripped from the shopworn floor in Paterson, machinery now operated by a young, almost entirely female workforce. These women, primarily in their teens and 20s, have come north to Matamoros in search of work and a better future than the bleakness promised in the jobless farming towns of the interior.

Balbina Duque Granados found a job at MagneTek in 1993, after leaving her family's home in a picturesque but poor mountain village of central Mexico. Just out of her teens, she has an easy, dimpled smile and long black hair worn in a ponytail. With its comparatively low wages, endless supply of labor, lack of regulation, and proximity to the United States, Matamoros is a magnet for *maquiladoras,* the foreign-owned assembly plants that wed First World engineering with Third World working conditions. Balbina's probationary pay is slightly less than $26 a week, or about 65 cents an hour. It is difficult work, winding coils, repetitive and tiring and mind numbing, but it is a job she is thrilled to have—her "answered prayer." And although Balbina doesn't know it, it is not just any job. It is Mollie's job.

The job in which Mollie James once took great pride, the job that both fostered and repaid her loyalty by enabling her to rise above humble beginnings and provide for her family—that job does not now pay Balbina Duque a wage sufficient to live on. Embedded in that central fact, and in the intersecting lives and fates of the two women who held that single job, is a broader story about the fundamental changes currently remaking the economy—the ways in which "free trade" harms democracy, undermines stable businesses and communities, and exploits workers on both sides of the border, both ends of the global assembly line.

At a few minutes before 2 o'clock on a cold, pitch-black morning in November 1950, Mollie and her father, Lorenzo Brown, waited anxiously on the platform of the ornate World War I-era train station in Richmond, Virginia. The Browns were from Cartersville, 45 miles west, in the rolling farmland of central Virginia. Mollie was headed to Penn Station in Newark, New Jersey, to meet her fiance, Sam James, who would take her home, to Paterson, to her new life. She was dressed in her finest: a new navy-blue suit, new shoes, new hairdo. She carried nearly everything she owned in a half-dozen sky-blue suitcases her father had given her for the trip.

Mollie was traveling alone, but the "colored" train cars of the Silver Meteor, and indeed those of the other great northbound coaches—the Champion, the Florida Sunbeam, the Silver Comet—were full of Mollie Browns: black southerners crossing the Mason-Dixon Line, heading for the promised land. Mollie's intended was waiting at the station in his new, yellow, two-door Ford to take her to Paterson, a city of 140,000 residents some 15 miles west of New York City. Sam drove her home to the one-room apartment he rented for $20 a week above the flat where his sister and brother-in-law lived. Although the accommodations were far from luxurious—Mollie and Sam shared a kitchen and bath with other upstairs tenants—her new life seemed as bright as Sam's shiny car.

Paterson at precisely the middle of the 20th century was absolutely humming, filled with vibrant neighborhoods, a bustling downtown retail and cultural district, and above all, factories small and large, producing everything from textiles to machine tools to electrical components. "There were so many places to work, I could have five jobs in the same day," Mollie recalled years later. "And if I didn't like one, I could leave and get another, sure."

Mollie's new hometown was born of entrepreneurial dreamers and schemers. The city had been founded on the 16th anniversary of the Declaration of Independence, July 4, 1792, not as a municipality but as a business: the home of the country's first industrial corporation, the Society for Useful Manufactures. The grand plans of the society and its guiding light, Alexander Hamilton, ultimately failed, but Paterson established itself as a cradle of American industry. The city became renowned for its textile mills—silk, especially—and later for the union-busting tactics of its mill owners. During the 19th century, textile manufacturers in Paterson were responsible for what were probably the nation's first runaway shops, opening "annexes" in rural Pennsylvania to take advantage of workers who could be subjected to longer hours for half the wages paid in New Jersey. In 1913, the Industrial Workers of the World mobilized Paterson's 25,000 employees to walk away from their looms, effectively nailing shut the nation's silk-manufacturing center. Able to rely on their nonunion factories, mill owners refused to negotiate; starved into submission, the strikers were forced to return to work with neither gains in wages nor improved working conditions.

By the time the 19-year-old Mollie Brown arrived in Paterson, the economy was booming. Unemployment was low, wages high. In her first few years in town, Mollie ran through several jobs. "You'd just catch the bus and go from factory to factory and see who was hiring." Among her stops was a low-slung cement building in northeast Paterson. The sign out front said UNIVERSAL MANUFACTURING CO. The owner himself, a gregarious man named Archie Sergy, showed her through the plant, explaining that the company made a part for fluorescent lights called a ballast. "They showed me how it was made, the whole assembly line. I learned there's a lot to it, a *very* lot." The starting salary was 90 cents an hour, but the company was about to implement a second shift, from 3 P.M. to midnight, that would pay an extra dime an hour. Those hours were ideal for Mollie. She and Sam had three children under the age of five and another on the way, and if she were to work nights and he days, the couple could care for the children without hiring a sitter. She accepted the job. "I hope you'll be here a long time," Sergy told her. "I hope we'll all be here a long time!"

By the early 1960s, Universal employed a workforce of some 1,200. Archie Sergy and his top managers continued to demonstrate a sincere interest in the welfare of their employees. "They never treated you as inferior, regardless of whether you cleaned the toilets or whatever your job was," Mollie says. "They'd walk up and down the line and talk to us, joke with us, sometimes have their sandwiches with us right there on the line. * * * If you needed a home loan, they'd give it to you, and you could make arrangements to pay it back."

Sergy saw the world as an industrialist, not a financier, and he maintained a steely eyed focus on quality and customer service to the degree that it probably hurt profit margins. But his company was no social service agency; it venerated the bottom line as much as any self-respecting capitalist enterprise. Mollie and her co-workers enjoyed good wages and job security in large part because they belonged to Teamsters Local 945, which bargained for higher pay and better benefits. In 1963, determined to insulate Universal from threats of work stoppage, Sergy followed the tradition established by the early Paterson silk makers: He opened an annex, a Universal factory in the Deep South. The new plant was located in rural Mississippi, providing Sergy with a low-wage workforce as well as an ever-present threat of plant closing to quiet employees in Paterson.

That same year, strapped for operating capital and lacking a successor, Sergy also succumbed to the lure of Wall Street: He sold Universal to a New York-based conglomerate. Sergy remained as titular head of Universal, but outsiders controlled the economic destiny of the women and men who toiled there. This was most evidently revealed when Sergy announced to the employees in April 1968, seven months before his death, that the parent company itself had been swallowed whole by *another* conglomerate. "We're all working for a company out of Chicago," he said. "Who they are I have no idea."

Whether those who held the purse strings were faceless financiers from New York or Chicago or Los Angeles didn't matter much to Mollie James. Owners came and went, and the principal visible sign of each transition was a new company name on the payroll checks. So when word spread in early 1986 that an outfit called MagneTek was the new owner, Mollie took the news calmly. Surely some things would change—managers in, managers out, maybe—but she had no reason to question her job security. Although the company had added a second Southern plant, in Arkansas, Paterson was still the flagship. Mollie came to work for Universal—and stayed—because of the peace of mind that came from a secure job: a job she could raise a family on, buy a house, a car, borrow money against, count on for the future.

But right away Mollie could tell the future was darkening. Like the earlier owners, MagneTek was a faraway, far-flung holding company, but the previous management's hands-off, don't fix-it-if-it-ain't-broke page was missing from its corporate manual. "It started the day our name disappeared from the building," she says. "Poof, no more Universal."

By the end of 1988, not only had Universal's name vanished from the plant; its machines, too, were disappearing, torn from the floor like trees from their roots. "The movers came at night, like thieves, sometimes just taking one piece at a time," Mollie recalls. "We'd come in in the mornings and there'd be another hole in the floor."

The machinery had been used to make a large specialty ballast known as the HID, or High Intensity Discharge, the kind used in thousand-watt fixtures installed in outdoor stadiums. Paterson was the lone Universal plant manufacturing the HID; making its precision-wound coils required different training and equipment than the garden-variety 40-watt fluorescent ballast the two Southern plants pumped out by the tens of thousands daily.

If Paterson's workers were more sophisticated, they were also more costly. Mollie earned $7.91 an hour, 75 cents more than she would have earned in Mississippi and almost a dollar more than in Arkansas. But if the wages down South were low, they were not low enough. They were not the cheapest possible wages. They weren't as low as workers earned in Mexico, where the prevailing pay at the maquiladoras was less than $8 a day. And so, in the early months of 1988, the machines began disappearing, bound ultimately for Matamoros. "All we kept hearing was how good a job we were doing," Mollie says, "that we had nothing to worry about, that we'd always have work in Paterson."

The nightly bus to Matamoros would not roll through the depot nearest Balbina Duque's village until 9:15. It was only mid-morning, just a couple of hours since she'd said her goodbyes to the family, since she'd pressed her lips for the last time to her baby son's cheek and handed him to her mother. It was only mid-morning, and already Balbina could feel the tropical sun on her face, could feel her funds dwindling fast. She had started with 200 pesos, the equivalent of about $65, and now that she'd paid a man nearly $20 to taxi her the hour from Monte Bello, her mountain village—a place of clean and clear air, brilliant high-desert flowers, and almost surrealistically bright light—to the bus station in town, and now that she'd bought a couple of tamales from a sidewalk vendor and a one-way ticket to the border for $30, Balbina was down to less than $15.

Balbina had turned 20 only weeks earlier. She was leaving for Matamoros, 400 miles north, to look for work in the maquiladoras. She was torn about going, especially about having to leave behind her 18-month-old son, Iban. "If there were work here," Balbina said in Spanish during a visit home some years later, "everyone would stay."

There was nothing to keep them at home. Balbina's village comprised maybe 1,000 people living in a couple of hundred pastel-colored homes with thatched roofs. There was neither running water nor electricity. Much of Balbina's day was spent filling and refilling a water bucket from a central well down a hill and carrying it back on her head to use for bathing, laundry, washing dishes, cooking, and drinking. A typical day might require 24 trips to the well, a chore that claimed three to four hours beginning at first light.

The interminable, grueling days were not for Balbina. Monte Bello felt like a sentence from which she needed to escape. It was a place for "people too old to work or too young to work," she said. "For me there was nothing. If you do not work in the fields there is nothing else to do." She decided she would celebrate her 20th birthday with her family, and then, as soon as she had saved enough for the bus fare, would take off for the border, where the maquiladoras favor young women for their nimble fingers and compliant minds, and where a job in a *maquila* trumps any other employment options.

It was dark when Balbina finally boarded the bus. Heading north, through a vast valley of corn, Highway 85 was flat as a tortilla. With two seats to herself, Balbina was able to curl into a comfortable enough position, and sleep came at once. When the bus pulled into Matamoros at dawn, she had to rouse herself from a dream about her son. Meeting her at the central station on Canales Avenue was a distant aunt, who escorted her to a small dwelling in the liltingly named *Colonia Vista Hermosa*—Beautiful View. But there was little beauty in the *colonia;* it was wedged between a pungent, milky-white irrigation canal and the Finsa park, the massive industrial park where MagneTek and other foreign-owned maquiladoras employed most of the working-age residents of Vista Hermosa.

One morning, the second Friday of 1993, Balbina and her younger sister, Elsa, caught a ride downtown to the headquarters of the big maquiladora workers' union, the SJOI—the Spanish acronym for the Union of Industrial Workers and Day Laborers. Four times weekly, waves of several thousand applicants washed up at dawn at the SJOI offices, the de facto employment agency for the maquilas. All nonsalaried workers applied through its central hiring hall, women on Mondays and Fridays, men on Tuesdays and Thursdays.

It was not yet 7 o'clock, and Balbina and Elsa had already been in line for an hour, a line that snaked through the three-story building, past the armed guard at the door, and stretched outside for more than a block. By eight, they had squeezed and elbowed and prodded their way inside the assembly hall, a room roughly the size and ambience of a drafty old high-school gymnasium. Mounted fans whirred overhead, efficiently distributing the rank air and grime into all corners.

At 8:30, with no conspicuous signal that the cattle call was on the verge of starting, there was a near stampede toward the makeshift elevated stage at the front quadrant of the room. The entire room seemed like an aquarium, one rear corner of which had suddenly been tipped, causing its entire contents to flow into its diagonal. For the next few hours, Balbina, Elsa, and 1,600 other hopefuls would be crammed nose to shoulder, as close to the stage as possible, like groupies at a rock concert.

At 8:40, three union officials emerged from the anteroom beside the stage. Through a two-way mirror, they had been keeping an eye on the surging crowd while their clerks matched the day's maquila employment needs with the application forms on file. All morning long, the fax machines and phones in the union headquarters had been ringing with the day's specifications from the companies. One maquila, for instance, asked for 91 applicants, all of whom should be 16 (the legal minimum age) or older, with a secondary-school education and without "scheduling problems"—code for childless. All the maquilas favor youth, and some, MagneTek for one, insist on it. "*No mayores de 27 años*"—None older than 27—the company's director of industrial relations instructed in a faxed letter to the union. Women in their late teens and early 20s are considered in the prime of their working lives; a 31-year-old is unlikely to be hired, and a 35-year-old is considered a relic.

When the tally of the day's employment needs was deemed complete, the officials stepped onto the stage, and into the bedlam. Between them and the spirited throng were three steps cordoned by a thin chain, a flimsy plywood railing, and a bouncer the size of an offensive lineman, whose sartorial taste ran to late Elvis: a white shirt unbuttoned nearly the length of his heroic torso, a gold medallion dangling to his midsection, and a formidable, gleaming pompadour crowning a Frigidaire face and muttonchop sideburns.

Following a call to order on a tinny public-address system, a woman unceremoniously announced the day's available jobs. "We're calling workers for Deltronicos," she said, referring to the GM car-radio subsidiary, and then read a list of 50 names. The "lucky ones," as one disappointed applicant called them, made their way through a pair of swinging doors, where a fleet of old Loadstar school buses waited to transport them to the Finsa park for a job interview and medical screening with their prospective employer. If their luck held, they would then be hired for a 30-day probationary period at lower, "training" wages before attaining full-employee status.

The drill was repeated for each maquila until the day's hiring needs were met. Neither Balbina nor Elsa were among the lucky ones, but they knew that few are chosen on the first go-round; some they met had endured several months of twice-weekly trips to the hall. Each Monday and Friday over the next few weeks the Duques returned faithfully. In March, Balbina's prayers were finally answered. She was assigned to a third-shift coil-winding job at MagneTek. All she knew about the job was that her sister-in-law once worked in the same plant, a low-lying white building no more than 75 yards from her tiny house. What she did not know was that Mollie James once held that very job.

Balbina started work at MagneTek the same year President Clinton signed the North American Free Trade Agreement, designed in large part to hasten the spread of maquiladoras. The trade deal enables companies to take advantage of 700,000 workers at 1,800 plants all along the border in ways that would not be tolerated in the United States. When MagneTek first set up shop in Matamoros, employees worked six-day weeks in a stifling, poorly ventilated plant; speaking on the line or going to the bathroom was grounds for suspension.

Although the company has improved working conditions in the last few years, sexual harassment and discrimination remain a constant of factory life. Many female employees at MagneTek have firsthand stories to tell about sexism on the job. "When new girls come in," says a 31-year-old MagneTek retiree who asked not to be identified, "a supervisor gives them the eye and asks them to go for a walk." Balbina says she received similar propositions when she started work at Plant 1. "My supervisor asked if I wanted to work more overtime. I told him I did, but that I wouldn't go to a hotel with him to get it."

The other constant of factory life is low wages. Even when she works an eight-hour overtime shift, as she usually does two or three times a week, Balbina finds it impossible to make ends meet on a MagneTek salary. "*No alcance,*" she says. It doesn't reach. For years she surmounted her weekly shortfall by pooling her income and expenses with Elsa. The sisters lived, like nearly all of their co-workers, "*en montón*"—in a heap: two adults and five children in two small rooms, the kitchen in front, the bedroom in the rear. Their shared three-family flat was a cement structure 45 feet by 15 feet by 10 feet high. Its corrugated metal roof doubled as the ceiling. Their were cinder-block walls between the three units that stopped about a foot short of the ceiling, making for a pungent stew of sound and aroma when all three families were home.

The shadeless yard—of mud or dust, depending on the season—was fenced by chicken wire and a rickety gate, and served as an extension of the kitchen. The residents shared a clothesline, an outhouse, and a single spigot—the lone source of water. Balbina believes the water flowed from an open canal running near plants in the industrial park that manufacture pesticides or use toxic solvents. The water had to be boiled, of course; sometimes there was propane to do so, sometimes not.

The neighborhood, Vista Hermosa, exists in a commercial and municipal twilight zone. It sprang up to serve the maquiladoras, not the residents. There are several high-priced convenience stores in the colonia, but no full-fledged grocers, no place to buy meat. Nor is there a pharmacy or medical clinic. There is no police presence, and vandalism and petty theft are rampant. There is one school, an overcrowded kindergarten. Older students catch the same bus to school that drops off first-shift workers at the industrial park. "You have to adapt to the maquilas' routine," says a neighbor with school-age children, "because they're not going to adapt to ours."

The city mostly shuns residents because of the high cost and low return of providing them with services. "They have no money," says Andres Cuellar, the city historian of Matamoros, "so no city official accepts responsibility." But a former mayor offers a different explanation: Federal policy prevents the city from taxing the maquilas to improve the colonias. "We insisted before the federal government that we don't have the financial means to support the maquilas' growth," says Fernando Montemayor Lozano, mayor from 1987 until 1989. "Besides the salaries paid to Mexican workers, the maquiladora contribution is practically zero here." It was not until 1991 that running water was piped into the neighborhood (but not as yet into houses), and only in 1993 were the first houses wired for electricity. The roads remain unpaved and deeply rutted. Nor does the city provide trash pickup; Balbina and her neighbors burn their garbage in a nearby ditch.

Vista Hermosa breeds disease like it does mosquitoes. The lack of septic and sewage lines, potable water, and sanitation services puts the neighborhood at great risk for all manner of illnesses, from intestinal parasites to tuberculosis. But the gravest, most frightening threat comes not from the neighborhood, but from beyond the chain-link fence around the Finsa park. The fence, less than a football field away from Balbina's house, may divide the First and Third worlds, but it also unites them under a single toxic cloud. When the maquilas illegally dump toxic waste into irrigation canals, when a hot north wind blows the acrid smell of *chapapote*—pitch—from the MagneTek plant over its workers' homes, when runoff from a pesticide plant spills into a ditch, when chemical spills or leaks or explosions or fires erupt in the air, it doesn't take a Sierra Club member to understand the environmental wasteland the maquilas have created.

Nor does it take an epidemiologist to question the cause of an outbreak of anencephaly—babies born with either incomplete or missing brains and skulls. In one 36-hour period in the spring of 1991, three babies were born without brains at a single hospital across the river in Brownsville. Doctors soon learned of dozens of other anencephalic births in Brownsville and Matamoros. From 1989 to 1991, the rate of such defects for Brownsville was 10 times the U.S. average, or about 30 anencephalic births per 10,000 births. During the same years, there were 68 cases in Matamoros and 81 in Reynosa, a maquila site upriver.

Many who have studied the outbreak suspect it was due to industrial pollution unchecked by regulatory agencies in both countries. "These were atrocities committed by two uncaring governments," says Dr. Margaret Diaz, the occupational health specialist in Brownsville who detected the anencephaly cluster. "They are the product of years of neglect."

In a lawsuit filed in 1993, families of 28 children born with anencephaly or spina bifida—an incomplete closure of the spinal cord—blamed the outbreak on contamination from the Matamoros maquilas. The families sued 40 maquilas, including MagneTek, charging that the companies negligently handled "toxic compounds" and that the birth defects occurred after "exposure to toxins present in the local environment." The companies steadfastly denied wrongdoing, but internal memoranda documented that some plants released toxic emissions into the air in quantities impermissible in the United States. And trash sifted from the Matamoros city dump established that the maquilas were burning their industrial waste there, rather than disposing of it in the United States, as required by law. One videotape made by an investigator for the families portrays the charred but clearly visible remains of a MagneTek rapid-start ballast. The companies eventually paid a total of $17 million to the stricken families and cleaned up their worst excesses.

Although MagneTek and other companies insist they are improving conditions both inside and outside their plants, wages remain at poverty levels. Rolando Gonzalez Barron, a maquila owner and former president of the Matamoros Maquila Association, points to an advertising supplement in the *Brownsville Herald* lauding companies for their financial contributions to Matamoros schools. "Take 'Adopt-a-School,'" he says. "We put sewerage and bathrooms in schools where little girls had to do their necessities outside."

What about paying a living wage so that the parents of those little girls could afford indoor plumbing themselves? "Yes," Gonzalez replies, "housing needs to be developed, but our main goal is to create value for our customers."

What about your employees? What is your obligation to them? "If a worker is not eating," Gonzalez says, sounding every bit the farmer discussing a plow horse, "he's not going to work for you. We need to meet at least the basic needs."

But the basic needs—"eating, housing, clothing," as Gonzalez puts it—are unmet, and the evidence is as obvious and irrefutable as the colonia in MagneTek's backyard, where Balbina and her neighbors wrestle every single day with ferociously difficult decisions: Should I work overtime or huddle with my children to keep them warm? Buy meat or medicine? Pay the light bill or the gas bill? She makes those decisions based on a daily salary of 58 pesos, the equivalent of $7.43. That's an hourly wage of 92 cents—roughly the same starting wage Mollie James earned nearly half a century before. And Balbina often makes those decisions after working a grueling double shift—from 3:30 in the afternoon until six the following morning, after which she arrives home in time to fix breakfast for her children, accompany her oldest to school, and squeeze in a few hours of sleep before heading back to the plant in the afternoon.

No alcance. It doesn't reach. Over and over one hears this. *No alcance,* but we make it reach. They make it reach by taking odd jobs, or by scavenging for recyclables at the Matamoros city dump—an otherworldly metropolis of its own covering 50 acres—or peddling wares in the plant during breaks and shift changes. "It's prohibited," Balbina says, "but the company looks the other way and almost everybody does it." There are the ubiquitous Avon ladies, as well as sellers of homemade candy, tamales and gorditas, clothes, marijuana. And some sell their bodies, living *la doble vida*—the double life of coil-winder by day and prostitute by night.

Balbina has yet to resort to a second job. Instead, she works overtime as often as possible and recently moved into a government-subsized house; it is more comfortable than the one she shared with her sister, but it is hers only as long as she keeps her job. She is 29, an advanced age for a maquiladora worker. She lives with her boyfriend, a fellow MagneTek employee, and they stagger their shifts so that one provides child care while the other is working. Still, even the small necessities remain out of reach. "I need a lock for the door," Balbina says one afternoon. "I don't need it now, but soon I will."

Why not now?

"There is nothing worth locking now," she replies.

Mollie James never again found full-time work. She received a severance payment, after taxes, of $3,171.66—about $93 for each of the 34 years she worked. She collected unemployment benefits for six months and then enrolled in a computer-repair school, receiving a certificate of completion and numerous don't-call-us responses to job inquiries. Late last year, at the age of 68, she took a part-time job as an attendant at a nursing home. For the remainder of her income, she depends on Social Security and the rent she collects from the three-family house she owns, as well as a monthly pension of $71.23 from her

Teamsters local. "That's nothing," she says. "That doesn't even pay your tele-phone bill. It's gone before you know it."

Although Paterson is a tenacious city, it seems defined by what is gone. Its last heyday was during and after World War II, when entrepreneurs like Archie Sergy and migrants like Mollie James helped sustain the city as a proud symbol of industrial might. But the old factory district near the Great Falls has been in ruins for decades, and although a number of the ancient brick mills have been splendidly restored—as a museum, a hospital clinic, and housing for artists—Paterson today is thought of as one of those discarded American places, a city so squalid, so defeated, that few people who do not live or work in Paterson venture there.

Mollie James has spent a half-century in Paterson. She married and divorced there, raised four children, bought a house. She sunk deep roots, and would like nothing better than to see the seeds of renewal take sprout, but she is fed up with high taxes, crime, the unstable economy. Like many "up-South" blacks of retirement age, she thinks often about going home, to rural central Virginia, to the land she left as a teenager. She still owns her childhood home amid three wooded acres.

During a trip back home not long ago, Mollie visited the cemetery where her parents are buried. It is where she wishes to be buried as well. "They better not put me in no dirt up there in New Jersey," she says. "Bring me back home, brother."

Balbina, too, dreams of returning to her ancestral home, to the quiet and clear air of Monte Bello, where she could raise her children in a calm, safe place. But there is no work around Monte Bello for her, no future there for her children. She is more concerned with the immediate future of her job. In the last cou-ple of years, MagneTek closed the two old Universal plants in Arkansas and Mississippi and transferred the bulk of those operations not to Matamoros, but 60 miles upriver to Reynosa, where the union is even weaker, the wages lower still. Now the talk in Matamoros is that the company will once again use the threat of a move, as it did first in Paterson and then in the Southern plants, as a lever for lower wages.

Balbina scoffs at the notion of transferring to Reynosa if the company relo-cates her job there. "What if they were to move again?" she asks. "Maybe to Juárez or Tijuana? What then? Do I chase my job all over the world?"

43

Religious Community and American Individualism

FROM *Habits of the Heart: Individualism and Commitment in American Life*

ROBERT N. BELLAH, RICHARD MADSEN, WILLIAM M. SULLIVAN, ANN SWIDLER, AND STEVEN M. TIPTON

Belief in God and regular church attendance are higher in the United States than in any other industrialized country. Americans are also very independent-minded and pride themselves on this. In this selection from one of sociology's most widely read studies, the authors explore the apparent contradiction between participating in a community of believers and deciding for oneself what to believe.

Religion is one of the most important of the many ways in which Americans "get involved" in the life of their community and society. Americans give more money and donate more time to religious bodies and religiously associated organizations than to all other voluntary associations put together. Some 40 percent of Americans attend religious services at least once a week (a much greater number than would be found in Western Europe or even Canada) and religious membership is around 60 percent of the total population.

In our research, we were interested in religion not in isolation but as part of the texture of private and public life in the United States. Although we seldom asked specifically about religion, time and again in our conversations, religion emerged as important to the people we were interviewing, as the national statistics just quoted would lead one to expect.

For some, religion is primarily a private matter having to do with family and local congregation. For others, it is private in one sense but also a primary vehicle for the expression of national and even global concerns. Though Americans overwhelmingly accept the doctrine of the separation of church and state, most of them believe, as they always have, that religion has an important role to play in the public realm.

* * *

THE LOCAL CONGREGATION [—INVOLVEMENT AND INDEPENDENCE]

We may begin a closer examination of how religion operates in the lives of those to whom we talked by looking at the local congregation, which traditionally has a certain priority. The local church is a community of worship that contains within itself, in small, so to speak, the features of the larger church, and in some

Protestant traditions can exist autonomously. The church as a community of worship is an adaptation of the Jewish synagogue. Both Jews and Christians view their communities as existing in a covenant relationship with God, and the Sabbath worship around which religious life centers is a celebration of that covenant. Worship calls to mind the story of the relationship of the community with God: how God brought his chosen people out of Egypt or gave his only begotten son for the salvation of mankind. Worship also reiterates the obligations that the community has undertaken, including the biblical insistence on justice and righteousness, and on love of God and neighbor, as well as the promises God has made that make it possible for the community to hope for the future. Though worship has its special times and places, especially on the Sabbath in the house of the Lord, it functions as a model or pattern for the whole of life. Through reminding the people of their relationship to God, it establishes patterns of character and virtue that should operate in economic and political life as well as in the context of worship. The community maintains itself as a community of memory, and the various religious traditions have somewhat different memories.

The very freedom, openness, and pluralism of American religious life makes this traditional pattern hard for Americans to understand. For one thing, the traditional pattern assumes a certain priority of the religious community over the individual. The community exists before the individual is born and will continue after his or her death. The relationship of the individual to God is ultimately personal, but it is mediated by the whole pattern of community life. There is a givenness about the community and the tradition. They are not normally a matter of individual choice.

For Americans, the traditional relationship between the individual and the religious community is to some degree reversed. On the basis of our interviews, we are not surprised to learn that a 1978 Gallup poll found that 80 percent of Americans agreed that "an individual should arrive at his or her own religious beliefs independent of any churches or synagogues." From the traditional point of view, this is a strange statement—it is precisely within church or synagogue that one comes to one's religious beliefs—but to many Americans it is the Gallup finding that is normal.

Nan Pfautz, raised in a strict Baptist church, is now an active member of a Presbyterian congregation near San Jose. Her church membership gives her a sense of community involvement, of engagement with issues at once social and moral. She speaks of her "commitment" to the church, so that being a member means being willing to give time, money, and care to the community it embodies and to its wider purposes. Yet, like many Americans, she feels that her personal relationship to God transcends her involvement in any particular church. Indeed, she speaks with humorous disdain of "churchy people" such as those who condemn others for violations of external norms. She says, "I believe I have a commitment to God which is beyond church. I felt my relationship with God was O.K. when I wasn't with the church."

For Nan, the church's value is primarily an ethical one. "Church to me is a community, and it's an organization that I belong to. They do an awful lot of good." Her obligations to the church come from the fact that she has chosen to join it, and "just like any organization that you belong to, it shouldn't be just to have another piece of paper in your wallet." As with the Kiwanis or any other organization, "you have a responsibility to do something or don't be there," to devote time and money, and especially to "care about the people." It is this caring community, above all, that the church represents. "I really love my church and what they have done for me, and what they do for other people, and the community that's there." Conceived as an association of loving individuals, the church acquires its value from "the caring about people. What I like about my church is its community."

* * *

In talking to Art Townsend, the pastor of Nan's church, we found views quite consonant with hers. Art is not unaware of the church as a community of memory, though he is as apt to tell a story from the Maharishi or a Zen Buddhist text as from the New Testament. But what excites him are the individuals themselves: "The church is really a part of me and I am a part of the church, and my shift professionally has gone from 'how can I please them and make them like me so that I can keep my job and get a promotion' to 'how can I love them, how can I help these beautiful, special people to experience how absolutely wonderful they are.'" It is the self—both his and those of others—that must be the source of all religious meaning. In Art's optimistic vision, human beings need to learn to "lighten up" as "one of the steps to enlightenment." His job in turn is to "help them take the scales from their eyes and experience and see their magnificence." Difficulties between people are misunderstandings among selves who are ultimately in harmony. If a couple who are angry or disappointed or bored with each other really share their feelings, "you get into a deeper level, and what happens is that feelings draw together, and you actually, literally feel the feeling the same way the other person feels it. And when you do, there is a shift, there is a zing, and it is like the two become one."

For Art Townsend, God becomes the guarantee of what he has "experienced in my life, that there is nothing that happens to me that is not for the fulfillment of my higher self." His cheery mysticism eliminates any real possibility of sin, evil, or damnation, since "if I thought God were such a being that he would waste a human soul on the basis of its mistakes, that would be a little limiting." In consonance with this primarily expressive individualist ethos, Art's philosophy is remarkably upbeat. Tragedy and sacrifice are not what they seem. "Problems become the playground of consciousness" and are to be welcomed as opportunities for growth.

Such a view can justify high levels of social activism, and Art Townsend's church engages in a wide variety of activities, volunteering as a congregation to care for Vietnamese refugee families, supporting broader understanding of the homosexual minority, and visiting the sick or distressed in the congregation. A member such as Nan Pfautz carries her sense of responsibility further, participating through the church in a range of activities from environmental protection to fighting multinational corporations marketing infant formula in the Third World. But it is clear for her, as for Art Townsend, that the ultimate meaning of the church is an expressive-individualist one. Its value is as a loving community in which individuals can experience the joy of belonging. As the church secretary says, "Certainly all the things that we do involve caring about people in a loving manner, at least I hope that we do." She puts it succinctly when she says, "For the most part, I think this community is a safe place for a lot of people."

Art Townsend's Presbyterian church would be viewed as theologically liberal. A look at a nearby conservative church brings out many differences but also many similarities. Pastor Larry Beckett describes his church as independent, conservative, and evangelical, and as neither liberal nor fundamentalist. At first glance, this conservative evangelical church is more clearly a community of memory than Art Townsend's. Larry Beckett indicates that its central beliefs are the divinity of Christ and the authority of scripture. A great deal of time is given to the study and exposition of scripture. Larry even gave a brief course on New Testament Greek so that the original text would be to some degree available to the congregation. While Larry insists that the great commandment to love God and one's neighbor is the essence of biblical teaching, his church tries to follow the specific commandments as much as possible. It is, for example, strongly against divorce because of Jesus' injunction (Matt. 19:6) against putting asunder what God has joined together. The firm insistence on belief in God and in the divinity of Christ, the importance of Christ as a model for how to act, and the attempt to apply specific biblical injunctions as far as possible provide the members of this church with a structure of external authority that might make the members of Art Townsend's congregation uneasy. Not so different socially and occupationally from the nearby Presbyterian church, and subject to many of the same insecurities and tensions, the members of this evangelical church have found a faith that is secure and unchanging. As Larry Beckett says, "God doesn't change. The values don't change. Jesus Christ doesn't change. In fact, the Bible says He is the same yesterday, today and forever. Everything in life is always changing, but God doesn't change."

* * *

For Larry Beckett and the members of his congregation, biblical Christianity provides an alternative to the utilitarian individualist values of this world. But that alternative, appealing precisely because it is "real clear," does not go very far in helping them understand their connection to the world or the society in which they live. The Bible provides unambiguous moral answers about "the essential issues—love, obedience, faith, hope," so that "killing or, say, murdering is never right. Or adultery. A relationship outside of your marriage is never right. The Bible says that real simple." To "follow the Scriptures and the words of Jesus" provides a clear, but narrow, morality centered on family and personal life. One must personally, as an individual, resist temptation and put the good of others ahead of one's own. Christian love applies to one-to-one relationships—I may not cheat my neighbor, or exploit him, or sell him something I know he can't afford. But outside this sphere of personal morality, the evangelical church has little to say about wider social commitments. Indeed, the sect draws together those who have found a personal relationship to Christ into a special loving community, and while it urgently seeks to have everyone make the same commitment, it separates its members off from attachment to the wider society. Morality becomes personal, not social; private, not public.

Both Larry Beckett's conservative church and Art Townsend's liberal one stress stable, loving relationships, in which the intention to care outweighs the flux of momentary feelings, as the ideal pattern in marriage, family, and work relationships. Thus both attempt to counter the more exploitative tendencies of utilitarian individualism. But in both cases, their sense of religious community has trouble moving beyond an individualistic morality. In Art Townsend's faith, a distinctively religious vision has been absorbed into the categories of contemporary psychology. No autonomous standard of good and evil survives outside the needs of individual psyches for growth. Community and attachment come not from the demands of a tradition, but from the empathetic sharing of feelings among therapeutically attuned selves.

Larry Beckett's evangelical church, in contrast, maintains a vision of the concrete moral commitments that bind church members. But the bonds of loyalty, help, and responsibility remain oriented to the exclusive sect of those who are "real" Christians. Direct reliance on the Bible provides a second language with which to resist the temptations of the "world," but the almost exclusive concentration on the Bible, especially the New Testament, with no larger memory of how Christians have coped with the world historically, diminishes the capacity of their second language to deal adequately with current social reality. There is even a tendency visible in many evangelical circles to thin the biblical language of sin and redemption to an idea of Jesus as the friend who helps us find happiness and self-fulfillment. The emphasis on love, so evident within the community, is not shared with the world, except through missionary outreach.

There are thousands of local churches in the United States, representing an enormous range of variation in doctrine and worship. Yet most define themselves as communities of personal support. A recent study suggests that what Catholics look for does not differ from the concerns of the various types of Protestants we have been discussing. When asked the direction the church should take in future years, the two things that a national sample of Catholics most asked for were "personal and accessible priests" and "warmer, more personal parishes." The salience of these needs for personal intimacy in American religious life suggests why the local church, like other voluntary communities, indeed like the contemporary family, is so fragile, requires so much energy to keep it going, and has so faint a hold on commitment when such needs are not met.

RELIGIOUS INDIVIDUALISM

Religious individualism, evident in these examples of church religion, goes very deep in the United States. Even in seventeenth-century Massachusetts, a personal experience of salvation was a prerequisite for acceptance as a church member. It is true that when Anne Hutchinson began to draw her own theological conclusions from her religious experiences and teach them to others, conclusions that differed from those of the established ministry, she was tried and banished from Massachusetts. But through the peculiarly American phenomenon of revivalism, the emphasis on personal experience would eventually override all efforts at church discipline. Already in the eighteenth century, it was possible for individuals to find the form of religion that best suited their inclinations. By the nineteenth century, religious bodies had to compete in a consumers' market and grew or declined in terms of changing patterns of individual religious taste. But religious individualism in the United States could not be contained within the churches, however diverse they were. We have noted the presence of individuals who found their own way in religion even in the eighteenth century. Thomas Jefferson said, "I am a sect myself," and Thomas Paine, "My mind is my church." Many of the most influential figures in nineteenth-century American culture could find a home in none of the existing religious bodies, though they were attracted to the religious teachings of several traditions. One thinks of Ralph Waldo Emerson, Henry David Thoreau, and Walt Whitman.

Many of these nineteenth-century figures were attracted to a vague pantheistic mysticism that tended to identify the divine with a higher self. In recent times, what had been a pattern confined to the cultural elite has spread to significant sections of the educated middle class. Tim Eichelberger, a young Campaign for Economic Democracy activist in Southern California, is typical of many religious individualists when he says, "I feel religious in a way. I have no denomination or anything like that." In 1971, when he was seventeen, he became interested in Buddhism. What attracted him was the capacity of Buddhism to allow him to "transcend" his situation: "I was always into change and growth and changing what you were sort of born into and I was always interested in not having that control me. I wanted to define my own self." His religious interest involved the practice of yoga and a serious interest in leading a nonviolent life. "I was into this religious purity and I wanted the earth around me to be pure, nonviolence, nonconflict. Harmony. Harmony with the earth. Man living in harmony with the earth; men living in harmony with each other." His certainty about nonviolence eventually broke down when he had to acknowledge his rage after being rejected in a love relationship. Coming to terms with his anger made him see that struggle is a part of life. Eventually, he found that involvement in CED gave an expression to his ideals as well as his understanding of life as a struggle. His political concern with helping people attain "self-respect, self-determination, self-realization" continues his older religious concern to define his own self. But neither his religion nor his politics transcend an individualism in which "self-realization" is the highest aspiration.

That radical religious individualism can find its own institutional form is suggested by the story of Cassie Cromwell, a suburban San Diego volunteer a generation older than Eichelberger, who came to her own religious views in adolescence when she joined the Unitarian church. She sums up her beliefs succinctly: "I am a pantheist. I believe in the 'holiness' of the earth and all other living things. We are a product of this life system and are inextricably linked to all parts of it. By treating other living things disrespectfully, we are disrespectful of ourselves. Our very survival depends on the air 'god,' the water, sun, etc." Not surprisingly, she has been especially concerned with working for ecological causes. Like Eichelberger, she began with a benign view of life and then had to modify it. "I used to believe that man was basically good," her statement of her philosophy continues. "I didn't believe in evil. I still don't know what evil is but see greed, ignorance, insensitivity to other people and other living things, and irresponsibility." Unlike most of those to whom we talked, Cassie is willing to make value judgments about religion and is openly critical of Christianity. She believes that "the Christian idea of the superiority of man makes it so difficult to have a proper concern for the environment. Because only man has a soul, everything on the earth can be killed and transformed for the benefit of man. That's not right."

Commoner among religious individualists than criticism of religious beliefs is criticism of institutional religion, or the church as such. "Hypocrisy" is one of the most frequent charges against organized religion. Churchgoers do not practice what they preach. Either they are not loving enough or they do not practice the moral injunctions they espouse. As one person said, "It's not religion or the church you go to that's going to save you." Rather it is your "personal relationship" with God. Christ will" come into your heart" if you ask, without any church at all.

In the cases of Tim Eichelberger and Cassie Cromwell, we can see how mystical beliefs can provide an opening for involvement in the world. Nonetheless, the links are tenuous and to some extent fortuitous. Both had to modify their more cosmic flights in order to take account of evil and aggression and work for the causes they believe in. The CED provides a focus for Eichelberger's activities, as the ecology movement does for Cassie. But their fundamental views were formed outside those contexts and their relation to the respective groups, even Cassie's longstanding connection with the Unitarians, remains one of convenience. As social ideals, neither "self-realization" nor the "life system" provide practical guidance. Indeed, although both Tim and Cassie value "harmony with the earth," they lack a notion of nature from which any clear social norms could be derived. Rather, the tendency in American nature pantheism is to construct the world somehow out of the self. * * * If the mystical quest is pursued far enough, it may take on new forms of self-discipline, committed practice, and community, as in the case of serious practitioners of Zen Buddhism. But more usually the languages of Eastern spirituality and American naturalistic pantheism are employed by people not connected with any particular religious practice or community.

INTERNAL AND EXTERNAL RELIGION

Radically individualistic religion, particularly when it takes the form of a belief in cosmic selfhood, may seem to be in a different world from conservative or fundamentalist religion. Yet these are the two poles that organize much of American religious life. To the first, God is simply the self magnified; to the second, God confronts man from outside the universe. One seeks a self that is finally identical with the world; the other seeks an external God who will provide order in the world. Both value personal religious experience as the basis of their belief. Shifts from one pole to the other are not as rare as one might think.

Sheila Larson is, in part, trying to find a center in herself after liberating herself from an oppressively conformist early family life. * * * The two experiences that define her faith took a similar form. One occurred just before she was about to undergo major surgery. God spoke to her to reassure her that all would be well, but the voice was her own. The other experience occurred when, as a nurse, she was caring for a dying woman whose husband was not able to handle the situation. Taking over care in the final hours, Sheila had the experience that "if she looked in the mirror" she "would see Jesus Christ." Tim Eichelberger's mystical beliefs and the "nonrestrictive" nature of his yoga practices allowed him to "transcend" his family and ethnic culture and define a self free of external constraint.

Conversely, cosmic mysticism may seem too threatening and undefined, and in reaction a religion of external authority may be chosen. Larry Beckett was attracted to Hinduism and Buddhism in his counter-cultural stage, but found them just too amorphous. The clarity and authority that he found in the New Testament provided him with the structure that till then had been lacking in his life.

Howard Crossland, a scientist and a member of Larry Beckett's congregation * * *, finds a similar security in his religion. He tends to view his Christianity as a matter of facts rather than emotion: "Because I have the Bible to study, it's not really relying on your emotions. There are certain facts presented and you accept the facts." Not surprisingly, Crossland is concerned about his own self-control and respects self-control in others. He never went through a countercultural phase, but he does have memories of a father who drank too much—an example of what can happen when control gets lost. In his marriage, in relation to his children, and with the several people who work under him, Crossland tries to be considerate and put the good of others ahead of his own. As he sees it, he is able to do that because of the help of God and His church: "From the help of other members of the congregation and with the help of the Holy Spirit, well, first of all you accept God, and then He gives you help to do good to your fellowman, to refrain from immorality, to refrain from illegal things."

Ruth Levy, [an] Atlanta therapist * * * comments on what she calls "born-again Jews," who are in many ways similar to born-again Christians. They come from assimilated families who haven't kept kosher in three generations, yet "incredibly, they do stuff that my grandparents may not even have done." What these born-again Jews are doing is "instilling structure, discipline, and meaning." They have found that "to be free to do anything you want isn't enough. There isn't anything you want to do."

Since these two types of religion, or two ways of being religious, are deeply interrelated, if our analysis is correct, some of the obvious contrasts between them turn out to be not quite what they seem. It is true that the first style emphasizes inner freedom and the second outer control, but we cannot say that the first is therefore liberating and the second authoritarian, or that the first is individualistic and the second collectivist. It is true that the first involves a kind of radical individualism that tends to elevate the self to a cosmic principle, whereas the second emphasizes external authorities and injunctions. But the first sees the true self as benevolent and harmonious with nature and other humans and so as incompatible with narrow self-seeking. And the second finds in external authority and regulation something profoundly freeing: a protection against the chaos of internal and external demands, and the basis for a genuine personal autonomy. Thus, though they mean somewhat different things by freedom and individuality, both hold these as central values. And while the first is clearly more focussed on expressive freedom, the second in its own way also allows important opportunities for expressive freedom in intensely participatory religious services and through emphasis on love and caring. Finally, though conservative religion does indeed have a potential for authoritarianism, particularly where a magnetic preacher gathers inordinate power in his own hands, so does extreme religious individualism. Where a guru or other religious teacher is thought to have the secret of perfect personal liberation, he or she may gain excessive power over adherents.

44

Faith at Work

RUSSELL SHORTO

The number of Americans identifying themselves as evangelical and fundamentalist Christians has grown rapidly in recent decades. In addition to challenging legal barriers separating church and state, a movement has emerged that seeks to bring religion into areas of social life that are usually free of religious practices. Though perplexing to many Europeans and others in advanced industrial societies, politicians and the U.S. president publicly profess their faith and urge others to accept their religious values as part of the social landscape. This essay describes one part of that landscape, a bank in a small town, where people identify themselves as "marketplace Christians" and operate their business as they think Jesus would want them to.

Chuck Ripka is a moneylender—that is to say, a mortgage banker—and his institution, the Riverview Community Bank in Otsego, Minn., is a way station for Christ. When he's not approving mortgages, or rather especially when he is, Ripka lays his hands on customers and colleagues, bows his head and prays: "Lord, I pray that you will bring Matt and Jaimie the best buyer for their house so that they have the money to purchase the new home they feel called to. And I pray, Lord, that you grant me the wisdom to give them the best advice to meet their financial needs."

The bank is F.D.I.C. approved. It has a drop ceiling and fluorescent lighting. Current yield on a 30-year mortgage is 5.75 percent. The view out Ripka's office window is of an Embers chain restaurant. Yet for all the modern normalcy, the sensibility that permeates the place comes straight out of the first century A.D., when Christianity was not a churchbound institution but an ecstatic Jewish cult traveling humanity's byways.

The bank opened 18 months ago as a "Christian financial institution," with a Bible buried in the foundation and the words "In God We Trust" engraved in the cornerstone. In that time, deposits have jumped from $5 million to more than $75 million. The phone rings; it's a woman from Minneapolis who has $1.5 million in savings and wants to transfer it here. "I heard about the Christian bank," she tells Ripka, "and I said, 'That's where I want my money.'" Because of people like her, Riverview is one of the fastest growing start-up banks in the state, and if you ask Ripka, who is a vice president, or his boss, the bank president, Duane Kropuenske, whose office wall features a large color print of two businessmen with Christ, or Gloria Oshima, a teller who prays with customers at the drive-up window, all will explain the bank's success in the same way. Jesus Christ has blessed them because they are obedient to his will. Jesus told them to take his word out of the church and bring it to where people interact: the marketplace.

Chuck Ripka says he sometimes slips and says to people, "Come on over to the church—I mean the bank." He's not literally a man of the cloth, but in the parlance of the initiated, he is a marketplace pastor, one node of a sprawling, vigorous faith-at-work movement. An auto-parts manufacturer in downtown Philadelphia. An advertising agency in Fort Lauderdale. An Ohio prison. A Colorado Springs dental office. A career-counseling firm in Portland, Ore. The Curves chain of fitness centers. American Express, Intel. The Centers for Disease Control and Prevention. The I.R.S. The Pentagon. The White House. Thousands of businesses and other entities, from one-man operations to global corporations to divisions of the federal government, have made room for Christianity on the job, and in some cases have oriented themselves completely around Christian precepts. Well-established Christian groups, including the Billy Graham Evangelistic Association and the Promise Keepers, are putting money and support behind the movement. There are faith-at-work newsletters and blogs and books with titles like "God@Work," "Believers in Business" and "Loving Monday."

The idea is that Christians have for too long practiced their faith on Sundays and left it behind during the workweek, that there is a moral vacuum in the modern workplace, which leads to backstabbing careerism, empty routines for employees and C.E.O.'s who push for profits at the expense of society, the environment and their fellow human beings. No less a figure than the Rev. Billy Graham has predicted that "one of the next great moves of God is going to be through believers in the workplace." To listen to marketplace pastors, you would think churches were almost passé; for them work is the place, and Jesus is the antidote to both cubicle boredom and Enron-style malfeasance.

Os Hillman, a former golf professional and advertising executive in Georgia, is an unofficial leader of the movement. "We teach men and women to see their work as not just where they collect a check, but actually as their calling in life," he says. "We teach them to see what the Bible says about work, to see the spiritual value of their work." Through two organizations, the International Coalition of Workplace Ministries and Marketplace Leaders, Hillman and his wife, Angie, offer workshops, publish books and organize conferences. More than 900 "workplace ministries" are listed in I.C.W.M.'s member directory, and Hillman's faith-at-work e-mail devotional—which features stories noting that Jesus and the apostles all had jobs and that most of the parables in the New Testament have workplace settings—goes out to 80,000 subscribers daily.

Of course, Christianity isn't the only spiritual force in the workplace. There is an overarching faith-at-work movement afoot. Some companies are paying for, or at least allowing, workplace meditation sessions and Talmudic-study groups and shamanistic-healing retreats for employees. But this remains an over-whelmingly Christian nation. According to the Gallup polling organization (which itself fits into the subject of this article, as George Gallup Jr. is an evangelical Christian who has called his work "a kind of ministry"), 42 percent of Americans consider themselves evangelical or born again, and the aggressiveness with which some evangelicals are asserting their faith on the job suggests that the movement's impact, for better or worse, is going to come from them.

Most mainline Christian denominations have been slow to embrace the movement. Church leaders either haven't recognized it as significant or have determined that since it takes place outside the walls of their institutions, it is by definition not of concern to them. But some pastors are out in front of their leaders: they have left their churches to become workplace-ministry consultants or have landed jobs as "corporate chaplains," spiritual counselors hired by companies as a perk for employees. Rich Marshall, who is now a consultant, was a pastor in San Jose, Calif., for 25 years. "I realized what I was preaching in my pulpit wasn't helping people in their work lives," he says. "Now I'm on the road, speaking to businesspeople about integrating faith and work."

Looked at in light of some recent trends, there is a certain logic in all of this. First came the withering of the mainline Christian denominations and the proliferation of new, breakaway churches. Then consumerism took hold: today, many serious Christians are transient, switching churches and theologies again and again to suit their changing needs. With traditional institutions fragmenting and many people both hungry for spiritual guidance and spending more time at work than ever, it was perhaps inevitable that the job site would become a kind of new church.

When it comes to writing about religion, objectivity is a false god. In the interest of full disclosure, I would like to state here that my own orientation is secular but that I also believe that all religions have more or less equal dollops of spiritual truth in them, which become corrupted by personal and cultural dross. This puts me at a certain distance from most of the people in this article. For one thing, all the marketplace Christians I encountered were firmly of the belief that Christian truth is the only truth and that part of their duty as Christians is to save the unsaved.

My task, then, was to try to understand a phenomenon that has, from my perspective, an inherent conflict in it. One of the movement's objectives is to give Christians an opportunity to "out" themselves on the job, to let them express who they are, freely and without feeling persecuted. Few would argue with such a goal: it suits an open society. And if it increases productivity and keeps C.E.O.'s from turning into reptiles, all the better.

Then again, the idea of corporations dominated by a particular religious faith has a hint of oppressiveness, a "Taliban Inc." aspect. As it is, Christian holidays are the only official religious holidays in 99 percent of American workplaces surveyed by the Tanenbaum Center for Interreligious Understanding.

Religious-discrimination complaints to the Equal Employment Opportunity Commission have increased 84 percent since 1992 and 30 percent since 2000. Georgette Bennett, the director of the Tanenbaum Center, attributes the rise in part to the influx of workers from Asian and African countries and an overall aging of the largely Christian homegrown workforce, leading to a clash of traditions. "Added to that is the way in which religion has entered the public square and been politicized," she says.

Some friction may come from the insistence of marketplace Christians on seeing offices and factories as arenas for evangelism. Converting others, after all, is what being an evangelical Christian is all about. One tenet listed in the Riverview Community Bank's first annual report is to "use the bank's Christian principles to expand Christianity." If that wasn't clear enough, Ripka put it in even starker terms for me: "We use the bank as a front to do full-time ministry." Ken Beaudry, a marketplace pastor whose heating-oil company is just down the road from the Riverview bank, takes the same view. "It's all about understanding that your business has a cause," he says. "It's about recognizing that we exist as a company not just to make profits, but to change society. And our employees are on board with that."

On-the-job evangelism extends far beyond Ripka's community. In 2001, Angie Tracey, an employee at the Centers for Disease Control, organized what she calls a "comprehensive workplace ministry," among the first officially sanctioned employee religious groups within the federal government. She says that many colleagues have been "saved" at her group's Bible studies and other gatherings on government property, and she describes the federal agency's not-yet-saved employees as "fertile ground." Her program has spread rapidly within the C.D.C., and employees at other divisions of the federal government—the Census Bureau, the General Services Administration, the Office of Personnel Management— have contacted her about bringing the Word into their workplaces, too.

To explore this movement, I felt I needed a guide. Of all the marketplace pastors I spoke with, Ripka stood out at once in the intensity of his faith, his commitment to using his workplace as a vehicle for spreading it and his openness— his purity, if you will. There was also a modest personal connection between us; we are the same age and both grew up Catholic. After several telephone conversations, we made a kind of pact. He would welcome me into his bank and his home and would open up to me his world so that I might better understand why he and others think the faith-at-work movement is part of the next phase of Christianity.

And what would Ripka get in return? "The Lord told me you would call, Russell," he said in our first conversation. Through me, he would get a chance to spread the Word.

So, the first thing to know about Chuck Ripka is that he says Jesus talks to him—actually speaks to him, calling him "Chuck." Ripka is 45, a father of five and grandfather of two who has been married to his high-school sweetheart for 25 years. He has a compact build and pinprick eyes; he talks in a soft, rapid monotone. He once fasted for 40 days and 40 nights, just as Jesus did in the wilderness. He says he has performed more than 60 faith healings in the bank and has "saved" another 60 people on bank premises. Knowing him at first only via telephone, and listening to his talk of visions and voices and Satan and ecstatic healings, I began to think of him as potentially unbalanced. Yet on meeting him, I quickly discovered that he is a pillar of his community. The mayor stopped by his office for a chat while I was there. The chief of police and the superintendent of schools see him for prayer. He occasionally gives spiritual counseling to Carl Pohlad, the owner of the Minnesota Twins. Ripka runs a quarterly faith-in-the-workplace lunch, which attracts up to 260 area businesspeople. Many Christian business owners and residents say they consider him to be not only a community leader and an expert in small-business loans but also a conduit of the divine, a genuine holy man.

* * *

He worked odd jobs after high school and was born again when he was 21, during an Amway meeting. Shortly after, Jesus began talking to him. "I used to assume that all Christians heard God the way I do," he said. "But I realized over time that a lot of people don't hear, or they don't recognize, his voice. They think, Are these my thoughts or God's?"

Like many marketplace Christians, the Ripkas have an individualistic theology. Though they currently belong to a Christian and Missionary Alliance church—an evangelical subdivision that holds, among other things, that the second coming of Jesus Christ is imminent—they have changed churches often, and for periods of time have belonged to no church. One of Chuck's refrains is that he's no theologian: he can't rattle off scriptural citations to suit every situation. So while quite a few people look to him as a spiritual leader, his own faith is based not on a denomination's core doctrine so much as on inner voices and convictions.

An individual reliance on the voice of God is part of the increasingly free-form nature of charismatic and evangelical Christianity in America. It jibes with the tradition's ultimate goal—a personal relationship with Jesus Christ—but many evangelical leaders worry that it's dangerously subjective. "Pat Robertson is the one who uses it most: 'God told it to me,'" says Michael Cromartie, the director of the Evangelicals in Civic Life program of the Ethics and Public Policy Center, a conservative research center. "I think theologically that's unfounded." Nonetheless, it seems fairly common among marketplace pastors. Don Couchman, a dentist in Colorado who has made his dental practice a workplace ministry, related a story not long ago about how in the middle of performing a root canal, the Lord spoke to him and told him to go on a pilgrimage to Argentina. I interrupted to ask how he knew it was the Lord. "The sheep know the shepherd's voice," he said. (Some workplace Bible-study groups, including those at the Riverview bank, feature training in how to distinguish between God's voice and random thoughts.)

Ripka had his marketplace epiphany 20 years ago when he was a salesman at Levitz furniture in downtown St. Paul. "From out of the blue the Lord said to me, 'Chuck, one day you're going to pray with a customer,'" Ripka said. "Then several months later, I saw a man standing in the store looking at beds, and the Lord said, 'This is the one.' The man started to walk toward me, and I felt nervous and I said, 'Lord, I need your help.' The gentleman started to talk to me, and soon he was telling me he was divorced and his wife had custody of their children. Then he said: 'Why am I telling you this? I came in to buy a mattress.' I told him that three months before, the Lord told me someone would come in and we would pray together. So we did. And then something really important happened. The man bought a mattress. The Lord said, 'Chuck, I wanted to show you how to talk to people about me at work, and I wanted to prove to you that you would be able to do that and prosper.'"

It took some time, but when the Lord spoke next on the topic, he was very specific. "The Lord told me in 2000 that Duane Kropuenske and I were supposed to begin a new bank," Ripka said. Ripka worked for Kropuenske and his wife, Patsy, at a bank in the 90's. When the couple were considering opening a new one, they wanted to found it on Christian principles. "One day Duane came to me and said, 'The Lord told me I should talk to Chuck Ripka,'" Patsy Kropuenske says. When her husband got in touch with Ripka, Ripka was already expecting the call. Plans for Christianizing the bank expanded as they developed the project, with the three principals believing more every day that they were doing God's work.

As with all bankers, Ripka and the Kropuenskes care a lot about money, but they see it as a token of God's favor rather than a thing in itself. "The Lord spoke to me again on the day we opened," Ripka said. "He told me: 'Chuck, if you do all the things I want you to do, I promise I'll take care of the bottom line. I'm going to cause such a rate of growth, the secular world is going to take notice.' And that is happening."

One of the most striking things about the Riverview Community Bank is its location. This isn't exactly the Bible Belt. We are 30 miles northwest of Minneapolis, that bastion of Minnesota's secular-liberal tradition. The adjoining communities of Otsego and Elk River lie on either shore of a lazy bend in the Mississippi, a smaller mirror image of the Twin Cities to the south. This is big-sky country, a landscape of wide prairies and cornfield sunsets, but change is all around. Much that was farmland just a few years ago is now bustling exurbia, where brand-new Targets and OfficeMaxs and Applebees sit like boxy packages on the horizon. Few residents commute to Minneapolis or St. Paul; few seem even to venture there. They have their own culture, which is fast evolving, and religion is part of the change. The Minnesota stereotype of Garrison Keillor's Lake Wobegon—the pinched, resourceful, left-leaning Lutheran who eschews emotion—is becoming less common. There is more charismatic and evangelical expression in the state than ever before.

"I was born and raised here, and of course we were Lutherans," Patsy Krop-uenske says. "Confessing your faith vocally—that wasn't our style. There's been a cultural change, and I feel it's something that's needed, with the way the world is going today. With all the terrorism and fear, people need guidance." She and her husband had long been serious about their faith: Duane sends $50 a month to support the televangelist Robert Schuller's "Hour of Power" program and has a shelf of American eagle statuettes in his office to show for it. But when Chuck and Kathi Ripka healed Patsy's debilitating back pain in the bank, the day before it opened—laying their hands on her and praying—the healing demonstrated to her the kind of power Christ would bring to the bank, and she became more open in her faith.

As you drive along Route 101, heading here from Minneapolis, the bank is visible from three-quarters of a mile away: a massive temple-like structure of red stone blocks. Step inside, and you are softly assaulted by muted tones, wall-to-wall carpeting and curvilinear faux-wood desks—standard-issue bank décor. Spend some time, and you begin to soak up an atmosphere of, well, peace. It is a very calm, orderly place, governed by Christian principles from the ground up. Many marketplace pastors say they try to be fair and above-board with customers and competitors alike and will even refer business to a competitor they know can do a better job of meeting a client's needs. At the Riverview bank, Ripka says, they make a special point of arranging loans for "ethnic" churches in the Twin Cities, which typically have a hard time getting banks to approve them. And when customers are behind on payments, he says, Riverview will "give more grace" than the typical bank.

The atmosphere of calm extends to the bank's 42 employees, who seem strikingly contented. Most are Christians, meaning not merely that they were raised in a Christian household but that their faith is overt. "I've been in the banking business for 15 years, but this is my first Christian bank," says Shelly Nemerov, the operations officer, and laughs. "I was a Christian before, but I didn't have a relationship with God. Here, I've gone from saying I'm a Christian to actually being a Christian." She handles returned checks and overdrafts, and at some point, under the Riverview influence, she had a Christian epiphany about her work: "You hear constant problems—'I'm out of work,' 'My husband left me'—and I used to think. Yeah, I've heard it all before. Then it hit me: these people need help. So now I say: 'What can I help you do? Can I teach you how to balance an account or how to manage your money?' And I'll say, 'I think we should pray over this.'"

Praying with customers is one thing Riverview has become known for. Gloria Oshima, a teller, was hired because of her previous experience at the nearby First National Bank of Elk River, but her faith, which she describes as "bold," was also apparent in the job interview: "When Gloria came applying for a job, I had a vision of her praying with customers," Ripka says. Referring to the bank's drive-up window, Oshima says: "The Holy Spirit speaks to me when certain people drive up. A young lady pulled up one day. I looked at her, and she had tears in her eyes. I said: 'Are you O.K.? Would you mind if I prayed for you?' She said O.K. I said, 'Inside the bank, or right here?' She said, 'This is fine here.' So we prayed. I asked the Lord to remove the hurts within her and bless her day. She came again later, into the lobby this time, and she said, 'I'm doing so good, and I just wanted to thank you for your prayers.'"

Considering that many bank customers—those seeking loans, say, or involved in bankruptcy—are at a vulnerable moment in their lives, some may see this as preying on the weak. But the people at Riverview say they are only doing their jobs—their *real* jobs. They seem to have realized that they are in a unique position not only to offer comfort to people who are going through difficult times but also to zoom in on lost souls. Nemerov says that none of the bankrupt or overdrawn customers she has offered to pray with have ever said no, and she is confident she knows why: "Their hearts are already broken down and ready for it."

Well, all right, this is strange-sounding stuff. To someone unfamiliar with marketplace Christianity, the questions pile up. Is this legal? Aren't there separation-of-church-and-state issues here somewhere? What about discrimination?

As it happens, thanks to the value American law places on religious expression, proselytizing on the job is perfectly legal, even in a government workplace, even when it's the boss who is doing the pushing. If the legal aspects of the Christian-workplace phenomenon seem bewildering, it may be because, while the United States has always been a deeply religious nation, until recently it has also been fairly resolute about keeping faith out of the public sphere. Thomas Jefferson's famous metaphor of a wall of separation between church and state has long been a part of the national psyche. The historical reasons for erecting that wall are worth restating. The European experience of the 16th and 17th centuries, the effects of which carried over into the 18th, was of state-sponsored religious warfare, of populations decimated and minorities oppressed in the name of one branch of Christianity or another. Part of the genius and daring of the framers of the American system was in their decision to break with the European tradition of establishing a national church, in their conviction that religion was too combustible a material to be fused with political power.

You might think that recent religion-inspired violence would result in a renewed conviction to keep religion out of the public sphere, yet just the opposite has been happening. A major response in this country to Islamic terrorism has been a rippling of Christian muscle. In the post-9/11 universe, Christians have become more aggressive in pushing a religious agenda on social issues ranging from gay marriage to stem-cell research. "The whole war on terror has made evangelicals more politically engaged," says Michael Cromartie of the Ethics and Public Policy Center.

The workplace-ministry phenomenon, too, seems to have gained momentum since 9/11, but it is also part of the broad trend that began in the 80's with the rise of the Moral Majority and continued at the national political level with the emergence of the Christian Coalition. Many workplace ministries have received legal advice from the public-interest law firm the American Center for Law and Justice, which was founded in 1990 by Pat Robertson "to undo the damage done by almost a century of liberal thinking and activism." In 1990, there were about 50 coalitions of workplace ministries, according to Os Hillman's research; today there are thousands of businesses that, in the words of yet another consortium of workplace ministries, the American Chamber of Christians in Business, have "Jesus Christ as our chairman of the board." And as with the Riverview Community Bank, they aren't restricted to the Bible Belt. Rich Marshall, a marketplace-ministry consultant and the author of "God @ Work," crisscrosses the country giving seminars on the topic. The week I spoke to him he was going to be in Los Angeles, El Paso and Rutland, Vt. Two years ago, Don Thomas, a Christian business executive in San Francisco, started looking for like-minded businesses in his famously liberal area with whom his company might ally and says he received "an overwhelming response." There are now 43 organizations in the Bay Area Coalition of Workplace Ministries.

The laws governing religion in the workplace are technically fairly clear, but in practice they can be nearly impossible to enforce. While proselytizing is legal, what is forbidden is religious harassment, the creation of a hostile work environment or using religion as a basis for hiring, raises or promotions. Businesses like the Riverview Community Bank are acutely aware of this. Ask Duane Kropuenske about a Christian litmus test for employees and he practically recites chapter and verse from the Civil Rights Act of 1964, which laid down the law on a wide variety of discrimination. "I have stressed when I hire people that it's based on their qualifications, and we have no intent to pressure them into any kind of religious experience," he says. They might choose to join one of the bank's Bible-study groups or pray with Chuck Ripka, but "it's not going to have any involvement with their next raise or promotion or that type of thing."

When I asked Ripka if a Jew or Muslim had ever applied for a job at the bank, his choice of language was a bit odd: "We don't really have that in our community at this point." But his response highlights some of the realities that govern many marketplace ministries. The population of the Otsego–Elk River area is well over 90 percent white and Christian, according to Stephanie Klinzing, the mayor of Elk River (who is herself a charismatic Catholic and an enthusiastic supporter of the bank and other Christian businesses in the community). Besides that, why would a Jew or Muslim or Hindu apply for a job at a business that is known throughout the area to the flamboyantly Christian? So there is a certain self-selecting aspect to a business that wears its faith on its sleeve.

Then, too, Ripka added that in its hiring the bank pays no mind to employees' religious backgrounds, and for a reason quite beyond mere legality. "It doesn't matter where they are in their walk," he said. "In the job interview, I sit down and explain to them that we're doing God's work at our bank. We don't say, 'You have to do this'"—meaning become as devout as some in the bank are—"but we say it's something that will probably happen." What you are isn't important, because they hope to make you into something new.

It doesn't always work. I spoke with one employee of the bank, who asked that her name not be used, and she told me that while she had been raised Catholic, she did not consider herself part of the bank's Christian culture. "You will never find me going into Chuck's office to pray," she said. On the other hand, she said that the bank was a "wonderful" place to work because "here the people are all nice—it's a healthy environment." Another employee, a young man who until recently worked at a competing bank, also said that while he hasn't given his soul to Jesus, he liked the wholesome atmosphere of Riverview, and that the only downside was having to put up with his former colleagues teasing him about his bosses making him say his prayers before bed.

There's a matter of competing rights in all of this. When you apply for a loan, or walk into a grocery store, or take your seat on an airplane, do you have a right to expect a secular atmosphere, uncontaminated by religiosity? Or is the greater right that of the company's owners to express their faith? For a long time, Alaska Airlines has included a prayer card with in-flight meals, a practice that was instituted by a former executive. "It has received mixed reviews, some people liking it and others writing to tell us they don't appreciate it," a spokesman for the airline says. No one has taken the airline to court over it, and in a case of the bottom line trumping all, the prayer cards have largely vanished as in-flight meals have. But the salient point is that under United States law, freedom of religious expression trumps many other rights.

A related factor is the surprisingly vague status of the workplace in the eyes of the law. You might think that the establishment clause of the First Amendment forbids religious expression in a federal workplace, but in 1997, President Clinton issued guidelines creating a broad area of religious freedom for federal employees, including the right to evangelize, while forbidding government endorsement of a religion. Curiously, the situation regarding corporations is less clear. Is a bank—or a restaurant or a factory or a corporate headquarters—in the public or the private realm? "The separation of church and state is as firmly established as any doctrine can be, but the separation of corporation and state is not nearly as well defined," says Alan Wolfe, director of the Boisi Center for Religion and American Public Life at Boston College. "An issue like the role of religion in the workplace is fuzzy because we've never defined the public nature of a corporation. And I think many corporations themselves have been confused about how to deal with it."

Beginning in the 90's, many large corporations were sued by employees who claimed discrimination in hiring and promotions because of race, gender or sexual orientation. In the aftermath, as a vehicle for handling diversity issues, some corporations formed or formalized employee "affinity groups"—complete with by-laws and objectives—that could meet on company property, often during the lunch hour, and would be given a small budget from the corporation. Some companies included religious groups in their roster of affinity groups; others balked—apparently confused about how to deal with religion.

"Employers thought if they allowed religious expression in the workplace, they would get in trouble legally," says Jay Sekulow, the chief counsel for the American Center for Law and Justice. "It was a knee-jerk response. But the tide has turned, and it's a much more receptive environment today." Not everyone is on board, though. General Motors is involved in a lawsuit right now brought by an employee who has demanded the right to form a Christian group under G.M.'s affinity-group program. Coca-Cola, as part of the settlement of a $192 million racial-discrimination suit brought by employees, agreed to establish affinity groups, but religious groups are not among them. There is a Christian group operating within the company, which the workplace-ministry leader Os Hillman points out as an example of the acceptance the movement has won at big corporations, but Coca-Cola begs to differ. "The Christian group here is almost an underground group, and they're certainly not company sanctioned," says Racquel White, a Coca-Cola spokeswoman. "We don't sanction political or religious groups. What happened was, a number of employee groups popped up after our discrimination suit. They're not supposed to be doing it. Our preference is to stay out of these types of stories. Frankly, we'd rather not even talk to you about it."

That kind of corporate thinking seems to be on the way out, however. "The large corporations tend to be agnostic, not only with respect to religion but everything," Alan Wolfe says. "They don't want to offend anybody who is a potential market. They tend to think of themselves as in the public sphere and to institute policies according to their perception of political correctness."

Which brings us to the Pacific Northwest. We are in a gray conference room at one of the Oregon campuses of Intel, the world's biggest maker of computer chips. Sixteen engineers and programmers sit around a table during lunch hour, eating pizza and sandwiches from the company cafeteria and discussing the Book of Ruth. William McSpadden, a 43-year-old design engineer, father of five and hardcore weekend soccer coach, leads the Bible study. He describes the 200 or so local participants in the Intel Bible-Based Christian Network as "about half conservative Christians, even fundamentalists, with the rest being Presbyterians, Methodists, Catholics and the like."

Intel was in the forefront of public corporations that brought religion into the mix of their employee groups, thanks in part to the fact that one of its corporate heads, Patrick Gelsinger, its chief technology officer, is an evangelical Christian who has written a book on faith and work. The Bible network became an authorized company affinity group in 1997. There are four Bible-study sessions per week here at the Jones Farm campus, where 4,700 of the company's 15,000 employees work, plus special events and a monthly faith-at-work community-outreach gathering at a local Borders. "When I started at Intel in 1983, we had an informal Bible-study group." McSpadden says after the Bible-study meeting as he erases the whiteboard and his colleagues head back to work. "The company probably didn't even know it was going on. Its being formalized basically makes life easier. It means I can book a conference room without feeling I'm going against company wishes."

An hour later, in a smaller conference room in which a prayer rug lies angled toward Mecca, 12 men—members of the Intel Muslim Employee Group—stream in in ones and twos, go through the ritual motions of prayer, chat with one another for a few minutes, then head back to work. Like the company's 17 other diversity groups, the Muslims get a budget of about $2,300 a year from Intel and a designated space. Mostafa Arifin, a 29-year-old computer engineer from Bangladesh wearing a scruffy beard and an Eddie Bauer T-shirt, says there are about 100 participants in the Muslim group at the Jones Farm campus, nearly all of them men from overseas. Mostly they meet to pray, but occasionally they hold events. After 9/11, they discovered they had a public-education role to play, and they held sessions on Islam in the cafeteria.

So this is sort of a best-case scenario of how religion in the workplace is playing out at large companies. Religious groups at Intel are on equal footing with the Parents Group, the Recent College Graduates Group, the Latino Network and the Gay, Lesbian, Bisexual and Transgender Group. Yet there remains a slight difference between the Christians and the other religious groups. David Nash, of the Jewish employee group, says his members wouldn't dream of trying to attract other Intel employees to Judaism, and the Muslims say much the same thing.

McSpadden says he worried at first that the company would disallow proselytizing: "We were a little concerned. One of the key tenets of Christianity is evangelism, and if they said Bible study couldn't involve evangelism, that would be difficult for us." This is the sort of thing that gives diversity-training professionals headaches. "There are traps all around this issue," says Mauricio Velásquez, C.E.O. of the Diversity Training Group, a consulting agency in Virginia. "A boss says, 'I was only proselytizing.' And the employee says, 'No, you're excluding me from opportunities because I'm not a Christian.' How do you prove it?"

According to McSpadden, this isn't a problem at Intel. The company allows the Christian group to proselytize, provided it's within the confines of their meetings. And that seems to keep it tidy—and marginalized. Bernie Dehler, another participant in the Intel Bible-Based Christian Network, notes that the results of their evangelizing efforts are puny. When I was at Intel, bulletin boards in the hallways featured designs advertising an ice cream social sponsored by the Bible network. "Thousands of people see those signs, and we'll get maybe 30 at the ice cream social," Dehler said. And he added cheerfully, "We're weird, and we know it."

Back in Minnesota, as Chuck Ripka and I were leaving the bank to go to a meeting of local business leaders, a small encounter took place that was treated as so commonplace by everyone involved that I failed to see its significance at first. A couple—a man in a track suit and a very pregnant woman—showed up at the bank asking to see Ripka. He greeted them warmly. They looked distressed but hopeful.

They were having all sorts of problems. She was about to have her fifth child, and they were short of money: they needed $80,000 right away. The man was in the ministry—he works with children whose parents are incarcerated—and the couple's church, which caters to recent immigrants, was on the brink of financial collapse. They weren't coming to Ripka for a loan, however, but for spiritual guidance. They were feeling lost and overwhelmed by all their problems. "The Lord put it in my mind to come and pray with Chuck today," the woman told me, so on the spot they drove the 40 miles to the bank. Ripka prayed with them, asking Christ to give them peace and strength, and the couple were visibly overjoyed by the experience.

So there you have a sort of representative, topsy-turvy vignette for this story: a minister and his wife seeking out a mortgage banker for spiritual guidance and gratefully receiving his prayers in the bank parking lot.

Ripka then asked the couple to come with us to the meeting we were going to attend. The four of us drove a mile down the road, crossing the Mississippi into the city of Elk River. At a room in the public library, we found 25 men—they were all men, as it happened—sitting in a circle on metal chairs and taking turns praying. When Ripka introduced the couple, they were given chairs in the center of the circle, and the men prayed for them and their ministry and family. Then began a series of prayers for the well-being of the community, prayers so intense that some of the men had tears in their eyes.

Later I met several of the men for lunch at the Olde Main Eatery downtown. One owns the local fitness center; another runs a heating-oil business. As they talked, their ideas and objectives expanded. It turned out that their group—Pray Elk River—is part of a network of municipal officials, ministers and small-business owners across the country that has the goal of winning whole towns over to Christ. One component of that is organizing "intercessory prayer" teams. It is the belief of many Christians that targeted, concentrated prayer aimed at a problem can work like a laser to destroy it. Stephanie Klinzing, the mayor, who is part of the group, told me that the purpose of Pray Elk River is to bring together church, government and marketplace leaders to help the community. "We have a group of intercessors who pray for the town council, for the city, for me as mayor," she said. Ripka is part of this. "When she has difficulties as mayor," he said, "she'll call me and some others and ask us to pray over it." It turns out that even before the Riverview Community Bank was built, intercessors were praying over the bare ground where the building would be erected.

Rick Heeren—a businessman and the author of "Thank God It's Monday!"—is the Midwest representative for the national umbrella organization, which is called Harvest Evangelism. He told me that Harvest Evangelism had chosen Elk River as a "detonator city" through which, ultimately, the nation will be turned to Jesus Christ. (Other detonator cities include Honolulu and San Jose.) The Pray Elk River group has organized prayer sessions at businesses, in the schools, over the local radio station and at a public "prayer fair." * * *

* * *

But as Christianity moves into a broader arena, directly confronting some of the social mores that an open, secular society is built on, it presents a new challenge. A question that will probably be asked as the movement grows is, This is legal, but is it right? Protecting religion and religious expression is one hallmark of American society. Another is protecting minorities. And there is probably no more insidious form of bullying than religion.

It's possible, though, that the point will become moot. While marketplace Christianity has the law on its side—as well as America's deep and historic regard for religious faith—other forces may work against it. Alan Wolfe says he thinks the phenomenon has a natural limit. Evangelicals and other Christians who are charged to spread the Word in secular society, he argues, face becoming contaminated by that society. Unlike fundamentalists, who withdraw from the secular culture, they engage it, using pop music, books, television and now the workplace to spread their message. But as you do that, the message becomes swamped by the might of the broader culture. Wolfe points to the Coors beer company as an example. "They used to be known as an evangelical company—never mind the fact that they were selling beer in the first place, a product that used to be considered a sin—but as they grew, that spiritual purity changed. Today their television advertisements are almost pornographic." The challenge, Wolfe says, is for the workplace ministries to keep their faith pure as they expand. As if on cue, the same day I spoke to Wolfe, Chuck Ripka called to tell me that the Riverview bank was expanding, adding its first branch in the town of Anoka, 10 miles away.

* * *

45

From *Amish Society*

JOHN A. HOSTETLER

One of the most basic sociological truths is that people seek to organize their lives, families, and communities in order to become the kind of people they most admire. This is especially true for the Amish, who see their own beliefs as tied to the maintenance of their communities. In this study you can see how beliefs dictate a way of living, while at the same time a pattern of social structure upholds and reinforces the beliefs that dominate the society.

Small communities, with their distinctive character—where life is stable and intensely human—are disappearing. Some have vanished from the face of the earth, others are dying slowly, but all have undergone change as they have come into contact with an expanding machine civilization. The merging of diverse peoples into a common mass has produced tension among members of the minorities and the majority alike.

The Old Order Amish, who arrived on American shores in colonial times, have survived in the modern world in distinctive, viable, small communities. They have resisted the homogenization process more successfully than others. In planting and harvest time one can see their bearded men working the fields with horses and their women hanging out the laundry in neat rows to dry. Many American people have seen Amish families, with the men wearing broad-brimmed black hats and the women in bonnets and long dresses, in railway depots or bus terminals. Although the Amish have lived with industrialized America for over two and a half centuries, they have moderated its influence on their personal lives, their families, communities, and their values.

The Amish are often perceived by other Americans to be relics of the past who live an austere, inflexible life dedicated to inconvenient and archaic customs. They are seen as renouncing both modern conveniences and the American dream of success and progress. But most people have no quarrel with the Amish for doing things the old-fashioned way. Their conscientious objection was tolerated in wartime, for after all, they are meticulous farmers who practice the virtues of work and thrift.

In recent years the status of the Amish in the minds of most Americans has shifted toward a more favorable position. This change can scarcely be attributed to anything the Amish have done; rather, it is the result of changes in the way Americans perceive their minority groups. A century ago, hardly anyone knew the Amish existed. A half-century ago they were viewed as an obscure sect living by ridiculous customs, as stubborn people who resisted education and exploited the labor of their children. Today the Amish are the unwilling objects of a thriving tourist industry on the eastern seaboard. They are revered as hard-working, thrifty people with enormous agrarian stamina, and by some, as islands of sanity in a culture gripped by commercialism and technology run wild.

In the academic community several models have been advanced for understanding Amish society. Social scientists, like other Americans, have been influenced by the upward push of an advancing civilization and changes in the social discourse between the dominant society and its minorities. University teachers have traditionally taught their students to think of the Amish people as one of many old-world cultural islands left over in the modern world.

* * *

The Amish are a church, a community, a spiritual union, a conservative branch of Christianity, a religion, a community whose members practice simple and austere living, a familistic entrepreneuring system, and an adaptive human community. In this chapter several models will be discussed in terms of their usefulness and limitations as avenues for understanding Amish society as a whole. By models I mean structured concepts currently used by anthropologists to characterize whole societies. The serious reader will want to transcend the scientific orientation and ask, What is the meaning of the Amish system? What, if anything, is it trying to say to us?

A COMMONWEALTH

The Amish are in some ways a little commonwealth, for their members claim to be ruled by the law of love and redemption. The bonds that unite them are many. Their beliefs, however, do not permit them solely to occupy and defend a particular territory. They are highly sensitive in caring for their own. They will move to other lands when circumstances force them to do so.

Commonwealth implies a place, a province, which means any part of a national domain that geographically and socially is sufficiently unified to have a true consciousness of its unity. Its inhabitants feel comfortable with their own ideas and customs, and the "place" possesses a sense of distinction from other parts of the country. Members of a commonwealth are not foot-loose. They have a sense of productivity and accountability in a province where "the general welfare" is accepted as a day-to-day reality. Commonwealth has come to have an archaic meaning in today's world, because when groups and institutions become too large, the sense of commonwealth or the common good is lost. Thus it is little wonder that the most recent dictionaries of the American English language render the meaning of commonwealth as "obsolescent." In reality, the Amish are in part a commonwealth. There is, however, no provision for outcasts.

It may be argued that the Amish have retained elements of wholesome provincialism, a saving power to which the world in the future will need more and more to appeal. Provincialism need not turn to ancient narrowness and ignorance, confines from which many have sought to escape. A sense of province or commonwealth, with its cherished love of people and self-conscious dignity, is a necessary basis for relating to the wider world community. Respect for locality, place, custom, and local idealism can go a long way toward checking the monstrous growth of consolidation in the nation and thus help to save human freedom and individual dignity.

A SECTARIAN SOCIETY

Sociologists tend to classify the Amish as a sectarian society. Several European scholars have compared the social structure of "sect" and "church" types of religious institutions. The established church was viewed as hierarchic and conservative. It appealed to the ruling classes, administered grace to all people in a territorial domain, and served as an agency of social control. The sect was egalitarian. Essentially a voluntary religious protest movement, its members separated themselves from others on the basis of beliefs, practices, and institutions. The sects rejected the authority of the established religious organizations and their leaders. The strains between sect and church were viewed as a dialectic principle at work within Christianity. The use of an ideal type helped to clarify particular characteristics of the sectarian groups. The Anabaptists, for example, were described as small, voluntary groupings attempting to model their lives after the spirit of the Sermon on the Mount (Matt. 5, 6, 7) while also exercising the power to exclude and discipline members. Absolute separation from all other religious loyalties was required. All members were considered equal, and none were to take oaths, participate in war, or take part in worldly government.

Sects have employed various techniques of isolation for maintaining separateness. Today the extreme mobility of modern life brings people together in multiple contexts. The spatial metaphors of separation (i.e., valley, region, sector, etc.) are fast becoming obsolete. Nevertheless, modern sectarians turn to psychic insularity and contexts that protect them from mainstream values and competing systems. Members of the sect remain segregated in various degrees, chiefly by finding a group whose philosophy of history contradicts the existing values so drastically that the group sustains itself for a generation or more. To the onlooker, sectarianism, like monasticism, may appear to serve as a shelter from the complications of an overly complex society. For its participants, it provides authentic ways of realizing new forms of service and humility as well as protection from mainstream culture.

Sectarians, it is claimed, put their faith first by ordering their lives in keeping with it. The established churches compromise their faith with other interests and with the demands of the surrounding environment. Sectarians are pervasively religious in that they practice their beliefs in everyday life. Sects are often considered marginal or odd groups of alienated people with fanatic ideas. Yet the sects have had an immense influence in shaping the course of history. The British sociologist Bryan Wilson has observed that sects are "self-conscious attempts by men to construct their own societies, not merely as political entities with constitutions, but as groups with a firm set of values and mores, of which they are conscious." The growth of religious toleration in America has resulted in the development of religious pluralism in a manner that has not been realized in Europe. Wilson, who has characterized modern Christian sects into several types, classes the Amish as *introversionist* rather than *conversionist* or *reformist*. "Salvation is to be found in the community of those who withdraw from involvement in the affairs of mankind." The Amish recognize the evil circumstance of man, attempt to moderate its influence upon them, and retreat into a community to experience, cultivate, and preserve the attributes of God in ethical relationships.

The sectarian model lends itself to a historical, religious context. As a model, it offers some insight into the proliferation of groups with a negative orientation during a specific time period. Today there are many types of movements that did not exist in the early stages of industrialization. Sects may lose their spontaneity in a variety of ways. While the model may teach us something of how sects originate and grow from a protest movement to a separate religious entity, it does not provide us with a knowledge of the dynamics of the group. The Amish, for example, are not sectarians in the sense that they demand that others conform to their practices. Nor do they claim to base all actions on holy writ. They are not in conflict with the dominant culture in the same way, or with the same intensity, as are a number of sects such as the "apocalyptic" or "manipulationist" types.

Many sectarian societies, including the Amish, make little or no attempt to communicate their message. They recognize instinctively that authentic communication would mean greater literacy, education, and sophistication, and this would mean the beginning of the end. "The contribution of the sect to the larger society is," according to Martin Marty, "made best through the sympathetic observer who carries with him a picture of the advantages or particularity and assertiveness back to the world of dialogical complexity." In the Amish case, the message of the sectarian society is exemplary. A way of living is more important than communicating it in words. The ultimate message is the life. An Amish person will have no doubt about his basic convictions, his view of the meaning and purpose of life, but he cannot explain it except through the conduct of his life.

A FOLK SOCIETY

Anthropologists, who have compared societies all over the world, have tended to call semiisolated peoples "folk societies," "primitives," or merely "simple societies." These societies constitute an altogether different type in contrast to the industrialized, or so-called civilized, societies. The "folk society," as conceptualized by Robert Redfield, is a small, isolated, traditional, simple, homogeneous society in which oral communication and conventionalized ways are important factors in integrating the whole of life. In such an ideal-type society, shared practical knowledge is more important than science, custom is valued more than critical knowledge, and associations are personal and emotional rather than abstract and categoric.

Folk societies are uncomfortable with the idea of change. Young people do what the old people did when they were young. Members communicate intimately with one another, not only by word of mouth but also through custom and symbols that reflect a strong sense of belonging to one another. A folk society is *Gemeinschaft*-like,[1] there is a strong sense of "we-ness." Leadership is personal rather than institutionalized. There are no gross economic inequalities. Mutual aid is characteristic of the society's members. The goals of life are never stated as matters of doctrine, but neither are they questioned. They are implied by the acts that constitute living in a small society. Custom tends to become sacred. Behavior is strongly patterned, and acts as well as cultural objects are given symbolic meaning that is often pervasively religious. Religion is diffuse and all-pervasive. In the typical folk society, planting and harvesting are as sacred in their own ways as singing and praying.

The significance of the Amish as an intimate, face-to-face primary group has long been recognized. Charles P. Loomis was the first to conceptualize the character of the Amish. In his construction of a scale he contrasted the Amish as a familistic *Gemeinschaft*-type system with highly rational social systems of the *Gesellschaft*-type in contemporary civilization.

The folk model lends itself well to understanding the tradition-directed character of Amish society. The heavy weight of tradition can scarcely be explained in any other way. The Amish, for example, have retained many of the customs and small-scale technologies that were common in rural society in the nineteenth century. Through a process of syncretism, Amish religious values have been fused with an earlier period of simple country living when everyone farmed with horses and on a scale where family members could work together. The Amish exist as a folk or "little" community in a rural subculture within the modern state, as distinguished from the primitive or peasant types described in anthropological literature. Several aspects of Redfield's folk-society model and features of the Toennies-Loomis *Gemeinschaft* aid us in understanding the parameters of Amish society. They are *distinctiveness, smallness of scale, homogeneous culture patterns,* and the *strain toward self-sufficiency.*

---

1. The German term, *Gemeinschaft,* is often translated as "community." Ferdenand Toennies's classic work, *Gemeinschaft und Gesellschaft* provided sociology with this concept which is contrasted to urban, modern and industrialized society *(Gesellschaft).*

Distinctiveness. The Amish people are highly visible. The outsider who drives through an Amish settlement cannot help but recognize them by their clothing, farm homes, furnishings, fields, and other material traits of culture. Although they speak perfect English with outsiders, they speak a dialect of German among themselves.

Amish life is distinctive in that religion and custom blend into a way of life. The two are inseparable. The core values of the community are religious beliefs. Not only do the members worship a deity they understand through the revelation of Jesus Christ and the Bible, but their patterned behavior has a religious dimension. A distinctive way of life permeates daily life, agriculture, and the application of energy to economic ends. Their beliefs determine their conceptions of the self, the universe, and man's place in it. The Amish world view recognizes a certain spiritual worth and dignity in the universe in its natural form. Religious considerations determine hours of work and the daily, weekly, seasonal, and yearly rituals associated with life experience. Occupation, the means and destinations of travel, and choice of friends and mate are determined by religious considerations. Religious and work attitudes are not far distant from each other. The universe includes the divine, and Amish society itself is considered divine insofar as the Amish recognize themselves as "a chosen people of God." The Amish do not seek to master nature or to work against the elements, but try to work with them. The affinity between Amish society and nature in the form of land, terrain, and vegetation is expressed in various degrees of intensity.

Religion is highly patterned, so one may properly speak of the Amish as a tradition-directed group. Though allusions to the Bible play an important role in determining their outlook on the world, and on life after death, these beliefs have been fused with several centuries of struggling to survive in community. Out of intense religious experience, societal conflict, and intimate agrarian experience, a mentality has developed that prefers the old rather than the new. While the principle seems to apply especially to religion, it has also become a charter for social behavior. "The old is the best, and the new is of the devil," has become a prevalent mode of thought. By living in closed communities where custom and a strong sense of togetherness prevail, the Amish have formed an integrated way of life and a folklike culture. Continuity of conformity and custom is assured and the needs of the individual from birth to death are met within an integrated and shared system of meanings. Oral tradition, custom, and conventionality play an important part in maintaining the group as a functioning whole. To the participant, religion and custom are inseparable. Commitment and culture are combined to produce a stable human existence.

These are some of the qualities of the little Amish community that make it distinctive. "Where the community begins and where it ends is apparent. The distinctiveness is apparent to the outside observer and is expressed in the group consciousness of the people of the community." The Amish community is in some aspects a functional part of modern society but is a distinctive subculture within it.

PART FIVE

SOCIAL CHANGE IN THE MODERN WORLD

46

Jihad vs. McWorld

BENJAMIN R. BARBER

The globalizing forces creating a more interconnected world are breaking down barriers of geography, politics, culture, and economics and opening up possibilities for sharing and mutual support. But the richer and more powerful of the world—dominant over the poorer and less powerful—are often viewed with suspicion. In response, people in many parts of the world are trying to erect protective barriers against the forces that would draw them into a global marketplace of goods, services, ideas, and popular culture. Bernard Barber believes the prospect for democracy is not good with either the global or the local scenario, but neither is it hopeless.

Just beyond the horizon of current events lie two possible political futures—both bleak, neither democratic. The first is a retribalization of large swaths of humankind by war and bloodshed: a threatened Lebanonization of national states in which culture is pitted against culture, people against people, tribe against tribe—a Jihad in the name of a hundred narrowly conceived faiths against every kind of interdependence, every kind of artificial social cooperation and civic mutuality. The second is being borne in on us by the onrush of economic and ecological forces that demand integration and uniformity and that mesmerize the world with fast music, fast computers, and fast food—with MTV, Macintosh, and McDonald's, pressing nations into one commercially homogenous global network: one McWorld tied together by technology, ecology, communications, and commerce. The planet is falling precipitantly apart *and* coming reluctantly together at the very same moment.

These two tendencies are sometimes visible in the same countries at the same instant: thus Yugoslavia, clamoring just recently to join the New Europe, [has exploded] into fragments; India is trying to live up to its reputation as the world's largest integral democracy while powerful new fundamentalist parties like the Hindu nationalist Bharatiya Janata Party, along with nationalist assassins, are imperiling its hard-won unity. States are breaking up or joining up: the Soviet Union has disappeared almost overnight, its parts forming new unions with one another or with like-minded nationalities in neighboring states. The old interwar national state based on territory and political sovereignty looks to be a mere transitional development.

The tendencies of what I am here calling the forces of Jihad and the forces of McWorld operate with equal strength in opposite directions, the one driven by parochial hatreds, the other by universalizing markets, the one re-creating ancient subnational and ethnic borders from within, the other making national borders porous from without. They have one thing in common: neither offers much hope to citizens looking for practical ways to govern themselves democratically. If the global future is to pit Jihad's centrifugal whirlwind against McWorld's centripetal black hole, the outcome is unlikely to be democratic—or so I will argue.

McWORLD, OR THE GLOBALIZATION OF POLITICS

Four imperatives make up the dynamic of McWorld: a market imperative, a resource imperative, an information-technology imperative, and an ecological imperative. By shrinking the world and diminishing the salience of national borders, these imperatives have in combination achieved a considerable victory over factiousness and particularism, and not least of all over their most virulent traditional form—nationalism. It is the realists who are now Europeans, the Utopians who dream nostalgically of a resurgent England or Germany, perhaps even a resurgent Wales or Saxony. Yesterday's wishful cry for one world has yielded to the reality of McWorld.

The market imperative. Marxist and Leninist theories of imperialism assumed that the quest for ever-expanding markets would in time compel nation-based capitalist economies to push against national boundaries in search of an international economic imperium. Whatever else has happened to the scientistic predictions of Marxism, in this domain they have proved farsighted. All national economies are now vulnerable to the inroads of larger, transnational markets within which trade is free, currencies are convertible, access to banking is open, and contracts are enforceable under law. In Europe, Asia, Africa, the South Pacific, and the Americas such markets are eroding national sovereignty and giving rise to entities—international banks, trade associations, transnational lobbies like OPEC and Greenpeace, world news services like CNN and the BBC, and multinational corporations that increasingly lack a meaningful national identity—that neither reflect nor respect nationhood as an organizing or regulative principle.

The market imperative has also reinforced the quest for international peace and stability, requisites of an efficient international economy. Markets are enemies of parochialism, isolation, fractiousness, war. Market psychology attenuates the psychology of ideological and religious cleavages and assumes a concord among producers and consumers—categories that ill fit narrowly conceived national or religious cultures. Shopping has little tolerance for blue laws, whether dictated by pub-closing British paternalism, Sabbath-observing Jewish Orthodox fundamentalism, or no-Sunday-liquor-sales Massachusetts puritanism. In the context of common markets, international law ceases to be a vision of justice and becomes a workaday framework for getting things done—enforcing contracts, ensuring that governments abide by deals, regulating trade and currency relations, and so forth.

Common markets demand a common language, as well as a common currency, and they produce common behaviors of the kind bred by cosmopolitan city life everywhere. Commercial pilots, computer programmers, international bankers, media specialists, oil riggers, entertainment celebrities, ecology experts, demographers, accountants, professors, athletes—these compose a new breed of men and women for whom religion, culture, and nationality can seem only marginal elements in a working identity. Although sociologists of everyday life will no doubt continue to distinguish a Japanese from an American mode, shopping has a common signature throughout the world. Cynics might even say that some of the recent revolutions in Eastern Europe have had as their true goal not liberty and the right to vote but well-paying jobs and the right to shop (although the vote is proving easier to acquire than consumer goods). The market imperative is, then, plenty powerful; but, notwithstanding some of the claims made for "democratic capitalism," it is not identical with the democratic imperative.

The resource imperative. Democrats once dreamed of societies whose political autonomy rested firmly on economic independence. The Athenians idealized what they called autarky, and tried for a while to create a way of life simple and austere enough to make the polis genuinely self-sufficient. To be free meant to be independent of any other community or polis. Not even the Athenians were able to achieve autarky, however: human nature, it turns out, is dependency. By the time of Pericles, Athenian politics was inextricably bound up with a flowering empire held together by naval power and commerce—an empire that, even as it appeared to enhance Athenian might, ate away at Athenian independence and autarky. Master and slave, it turned out, were bound together by mutual insufficiency.

The dream of autarky briefly engrossed nineteenth-century America as well, for the underpopulated, endlessly bountiful land, the cornucopia of natural resources, and the natural barriers of a continent walled in by two great seas led many to believe that America could be a world unto itself. Given this past, it has been harder for Americans than for most to accept the inevitability of interdependence. But the rapid depletion of resources even in a country like ours, where they once seemed inexhaustible, and the maldistribution of arable soil and mineral resources on the planet, leave even the wealthiest societies ever more resource-dependent and many other nations in permanently desperate straits.

Every nation, it turns out, needs something another nation has; some nations have almost nothing they need.

The information-technology imperative. Enlightenment science and the technologies derived from it are inherently universalizing. They entail a quest for descriptive principles of general application, a search for universal solutions to particular problems, and an unswerving embrace of objectivity and impartiality.

Scientific progress embodies and depends on open communication, a common discourse rooted in rationality, collaboration, and an easy and regular flow and exchange of information. Such ideals can be hypocritical covers for power-mongering by elites, and they may be shown to be wanting in many other ways, but they are entailed by the very idea of science and they make science and globalization practical allies.

Business, banking, and commerce all depend on information flow and are facilitated by new communication technologies. The hardware of these technologies tends to be systemic and integrated—computer, television, cable, satellite, laser, fiber-optic, and microchip technologies combining to create a vast interactive communications and information network that can potentially give every person on earth access to every other person, and make every datum, every byte, available to every set of eyes. If the automobile was, as George Ball once said (when he gave his blessing to a Fiat factory in the Soviet Union during the Cold War), "an ideology on four wheels," then electronic telecommunication and information systems are an ideology at 186,000 miles per second—which makes for a very small planet in a very big hurry. Individual cultures speak particular languages; commerce and science increasingly speak English; the whole world speaks logarithms and binary mathematics.

Moreover, the pursuit of science and technology asks for, even compels, open societies. Satellite footprints do not respect national borders; telephone wires penetrate the most closed societies. With photocopying and then fax machines having infiltrated Soviet universities and *samizdat* literary circles in the eighties, and computer modems having multiplied like rabbits in communism's bureaucratic warrens thereafter, *glasnost* could not be far behind. In their social requisites, secrecy and science are enemies.

The new technology's software is perhaps even more globalizing than its hardware. The information arm of international commerce's sprawling body reaches out and touches distinct nations and parochial cultures, and gives them a common face chiseled in Hollywood, on Madison Avenue, and in Silicon Valley. Throughout the 1980s one of the most-watched television programs in South Africa was *The Cosby Show*. The demise of apartheid was already in production. Exhibitors at the 1991 Cannes film festival expressed growing anxiety over the "homogenization" and "Americanization" of the global film industry when, for the third year running, American films dominated the awards ceremonies. America has dominated the world's popular culture for much longer, and much more decisively. In November of 1991 Switzerland's once insular culture boasted best-seller lists featuring *Terminator 2* as the No. 1 movie, *Scarlett* as the No. 1 book, and Prince's *Diamonds and Pearls* as the No. 1 record album. No wonder the Japanese are buying Hollywood film studios even faster than Americans are buying Japanese television sets. This kind of software supremacy may in the long term be far more important than hardware superiority, because culture has become more potent than armaments. What is the power of the Pentagon compared with Disneyland? Can the Sixth Fleet keep up with CNN? McDonald's in Moscow and Coke in China will do more to create a global culture than military colonization ever could. It is less the goods than the brand names that do the work, for they convey life-style images that alter perception and challenge behavior. They make up the seductive software of McWorld's common (at times much too common) soul.

Yet in all this high-tech commercial world there is nothing that looks particularly democratic. It lends itself to surveillance as well as liberty, to new forms of manipulation and covert control as well as new kinds of participation, to skewed, unjust market outcomes as well as greater productivity. The consumer society and the open society are not quite synonymous. Capitalism and democracy have a relationship, but it is something less than a marriage. An efficient free market after all requires that consumers be free to vote their dollars on competing goods, not that citizens be free to vote their values and beliefs on competing political candidates and programs. The free market flourished in junta-run Chile, in military-governed Taiwan and Korea, and, earlier, in a variety of autocratic European empires as well as their colonial possessions.

The ecological imperative. The impact of globalization on ecology is a cliché even to world leaders who ignore it. We know well enough that the German forests can be destroyed by Swiss and Italians driving gas-guzzlers fueled by leaded gas. We also know that the planet can be asphyxiated by greenhouse gases because Brazilian farmers want to be part of the twentieth century and are burning down tropical rain forests to clear a little land to plough, and because Indonesians make a living out of converting their lush jungle into toothpicks for fastidious Japanese diners, upsetting the delicate oxygen balance and in effect puncturing our global lungs. Yet this ecological consciousness has meant not only greater awareness but also greater inequality, as modernized nations try to slam the door behind them, saying to developing nations, "The world cannot afford *your* modernization; ours has wrung it dry!"

Each of the four imperatives just cited is transnational, transideological, and transcultural. Each applies impartially to Catholics, Jews, Muslims, Hindus, and Buddhists; to democrats and totalitarians; to capitalists and socialists. The Enlightenment dream of a universal rational society has to a remarkable degree been realized—but in a form that is commercialized, homogenized, depoliticized, bureaucratized, and, of course, radically incomplete, for the movement toward McWorld is in competition with forces of global breakdown, national dissolution, and centrifugal corruption. These forces, working in the opposite direction, are the essence of what I call Jihad.

JIHAD, OR THE LEBANONIZATION OF THE WORLD

OPEC, the World Bank, the United Nations, the International Red Cross, the multinational corporation . . . there are scores of institutions that reflect globalization. But they often appear as ineffective reactors to the world's real actors: national states and, to an ever greater degree, subnational factions in permanent rebellion against uniformity and integration—even the kind represented by universal law and justice. The headlines feature these players regularly: they are cultures, not countries; parts, not wholes; sects, not religions; rebellious factions and dissenting minorities at war not just with globalism but with the traditional nation-state. Kurds, Basques, Puerto Ricans, Ossetians, East Timoreans, Quebecois, the Catholics of Northern Ireland, Abkhasians, Kurile Islander Japanese, the Zulus of Inkatha, Catalonians, Tamils, and, of course, Palestinians—people without countries, inhabiting nations not their own, seeking smaller worlds within borders that will seal them off from modernity.

A powerful irony is at work here. Nationalism was once a force of integration and unification, a movement aimed at bringing together disparate clans, tribes, and cultural fragments under new, assimilationist flags. But as Ortega y Gasset noted more than sixty years ago, having won its victories, nationalism changed its strategy. In the 1920s, and again today, it is more often a reactionary and divisive force, pulverizing the very nations it once helped cement together. The force that creates nations is "inclusive," Ortega wrote in *The Revolt of the Masses*. "In periods of consolidation, nationalism has a positive value, and is a lofty standard. But in Europe everything is more than consolidated, and nationalism is nothing but a mania. . . ."

This mania has left the post-Cold War world smoldering with hot wars; the international scene is little more unified than it was at the end of the Great War, in Ortega's own time. There were more than thirty wars in progress last year, most of them ethnic, racial, tribal, or religious in character, and the list of unsafe regions doesn't seem to be getting any shorter. Some new world order!

The aim of many of these small-scale wars is to redraw boundaries, to implode states and resecure parochial identities: to escape McWorld's dully insistent imperatives. The mood is that of Jihad: war not as an instrument of policy but as an emblem of identity, an expression of community, an end in itself. Even where there is no shooting war, there is fractiousness, secession, and the quest for ever smaller communities. Add to the list of dangerous countries those at risk: In Switzerland and Spain, Jurassian and Basque separatists still argue the virtues of ancient identities, sometimes in the language of bombs. Hyperdisintegration in the former Soviet Union may well continue unabated—not just a Ukraine independent from the Soviet Union but a Bessarabian Ukraine independent from the Ukrainian republic; not just Russia severed from the defunct union but Tatarstan severed from Russia. Yugoslavia makes even the disunited, ex-Soviet, nonsocialist republics that were once the Soviet Union look integrated, its sectarian fatherlands springing up within factional motherlands like weeds within weeds within weeds. Kurdish independence would threaten the territorial integrity of four Middle Eastern nations. Well before the current cataclysm Soviet Georgia made a claim for autonomy from the Soviet Union, only to be faced with its Ossetians (164,000 in a republic of 5.5 million) demanding their own self-determination within Georgia. The Abkhasian minority in Georgia has followed suit. Even the good will established by Canada's once promising Meech Lake protocols is in danger, with Francophone Quebec again threatening the dissolution of the federation. In South Africa the emergence from apartheid was hardly achieved when friction between Inkatha's Zulus and the African National Congress's tribally identified members threatened to replace Europeans' racism with an indigenous tribal war. After thirty years of attempted integration using the colonial language (English) as a unifier, Nigeria is now playing with the idea of linguistic multiculturalism—which could mean the cultural breakup of the nation into hundreds of tribal fragments. Even Saddam Hussein has benefited from the threat of internal Jihad, having used renewed tribal and religious warfare to turn last season's mortal enemies into reluctant allies of an Iraqi nationhood that he nearly destroyed.

The passing of communism has torn away the thin veneer of internationalism (workers of the world unite!) to reveal ethnic prejudices that are not only ugly and deep-seated but increasingly murderous. Europe's old scourge, anti-Semitism, is back with a vengeance, but it is only one of many antagonisms. It appears all too easy to throw the historical gears into reverse and pass from a Communist dictatorship back into a tribal state.

Among the tribes, religion is also a battlefield. ("Jihad" is a rich word whose generic meaning is "struggle"—usually the struggle of the soul to avert evil. Strictly applied to religious war, it is used only in reference to battles where the faith is under assault, or battles against a government that denies the practice of Islam. My use here is rhetorical, but does follow both journalistic practice and history.) Remember the Thirty Years War? Whatever forms of Enlightenment universalism might once have come to grace such historically related forms of monotheism as Judaism, Christianity, and Islam, in many of their modern incarnations they are parochial rather than cosmopolitan, angry rather than loving, proselytizing rather than ecumenical, zealous rather than rationalist, sectarian rather than deistic, ethnocentric rather than universalizing. As a result, like the new forms of hypernationalism, the new expressions of religious fundamentalism are fractious and pulverizing, never integrating. This is religion as the Crusaders knew it: a battle to the death for souls that if not saved will be forever lost.

The atmospherics of Jihad have resulted in a breakdown of civility in the name of identity, of comity in the name of community. International relations have sometimes taken on the aspect of gang war—cultural turf battles featuring tribal factions that were supposed to be sublimated as integral parts of large national, economic, postcolonial, and constitutional entities.

THE DARKENING FUTURE OF DEMOCRACY

These rather melodramatic tableaux vivants do not tell the whole story, however. For all their defects, Jihad and McWorld have their attractions. Yet, to repeat and insist, the attractions are unrelated to democracy. Neither McWorld nor Jihad is remotely democratic in impulse. Neither needs democracy; neither promotes democracy.

McWorld does manage to look pretty seductive in a world obsessed with Jihad. It delivers peace, prosperity, and relative unity—if at the cost of independence, community, and identity (which is generally based on difference). The primary political values required by the global market are order and tranquillity, and freedom—as in the phrases "free trade," "free press," and "free love." Human rights are needed to a degree, but not citizenship or participation—and no more social justice and equality than are necessary to promote efficient economic production and consumption. Multinational corporations sometimes seem to prefer doing business with local oligarchs, inasmuch as they can take confidence from dealing with the boss on all crucial matters. Despots who slaughter their own populations are no problem, so long as they leave markets in place and refrain from making war on their neighbors (Saddam Hussein's fatal mistake). In trading partners, predictability is of more value than justice.

The Eastern European revolutions that seemed to arise out of concern for global democratic values quickly deteriorated into a stampede in the general direction of free markets and their ubiquitous, television-promoted shopping malls. East Germany's Neues Forum, that courageous gathering of intellectuals, students, and workers which overturned the Stalinist regime in Berlin in 1989, lasted only six months in Germany's mini-version of McWorld. Then it gave way to money and markets and monopolies from the West. By the time of the first all-German elections, it could scarcely manage to secure three percent of the vote. Elsewhere there is growing evidence that *glasnost* will go and *perestroika*—defined as privatization and an opening of markets to Western bidders—will stay. So understandably anxious are the new rulers of Eastern Europe and whatever entities are forged from the residues of the Soviet Union to gain access to credit and markets and technology—McWorld's flourishing new currencies—that they have shown themselves willing to trade away democratic prospects in pursuit of them: not just old totalitarian ideologies and command-economy production models but some possible indigenous experiments with a third way between capitalism and socialism, such as economic cooperatives and employee stock-ownership plans, both of which have their ardent supporters in the East.

Jihad delivers a different set of virtues: a vibrant local identity, a sense of community, solidarity among kinsmen, neighbors, and countrymen, narrowly conceived. But it also guarantees parochialism and is grounded in exclusion. Solidarity is secured through war against outsiders. And solidarity often means obedience to a hierarchy in governance, fanaticism in beliefs, and the obliteration of individual selves in the name of the group. Deference to leaders and intolerance toward outsiders (and toward "enemies within") are hallmarks of tribalism—hardly the attitudes required for the cultivation of new democratic women and men capable of governing themselves. Where new democratic experiments have been conducted in retribalizing societies, in both Europe and the Third World, the result has often been anarchy, repression, persecution, and the coming of new, noncommunist forms of very old kinds of despotism. During the past year, Havel's velvet revolution in Czechoslovakia was imperiled by partisans of "Czechland" and of Slovakia as independent entities. India seemed little less rent by Sikh, Hindu, Muslim, and Tamil infighting than it was immediately after the British pulled out, more than forty years ago.

To the extent that either McWorld or Jihad has a *natural* politics, it has turned out to be more of an antipolitics. For McWorld, it is the antipolitics of globalism: bureaucratic, technocratic, and meritocratic, focused (as Marx predicted it would be) on the administration of things—with people, however, among the chief things to be administered. In its politico-economic imperatives McWorld has been guided by laissez-faire market principles that privilege efficiency, productivity, and beneficence at the expense of civic liberty and self-government.

For Jihad, the antipolitics of tribalization has been explicitly antidemocratic: one-party dictatorship, government by military junta, theocratic fundamentalism—often associated with a version of the *Führerprinzip* that empowers an individual to rule on behalf of a people. Even the government of India, struggling for decades to model democracy for a people who will soon number a billion, longs for great leaders; and for every Mahatma Gandhi, Indira Gandhi, or Rajiv Gandhi taken from them by zealous assassins, the Indians appear to seek a replacement who will deliver them from the lengthy travail of their freedom.

THE CONFEDERAL OPTION

How can democracy be secured and spread in a world whose primary tendencies are at best indifferent to it (McWorld) and at worst deeply antithetical to it (Jihad)? My guess is that globalization will eventually vanquish retribalization. The ethos of material "civilization" has not yet encountered an obstacle it has been unable to thrust aside. Ortega may have grasped in the 1920s a clue to our own future in the coming millennium.

> Everyone sees the need of a new principle of life. But as always happens in similar crises—some people attempt to save the situation by an artificial intensification of the very principle which has led to decay. This is the meaning of the "nationalist" outburst of recent years. . . . things have always gone that way. The last flare, the longest; the last sigh, the deepest. On the very eve of their disappearance there is an intensification of frontiers—military and economic.

Jihad may be a last deep sigh before the eternal yawn of McWorld. On the other hand, Ortega was not exactly prescient; his prophecy of peace and internationalism came just before blitzkrieg, world war, and the Holocaust tore the old order to bits. Yet democracy is how we remonstrate with reality, the rebuke our aspirations offer to history. And if retribalization is inhospitable to democracy, there is nonetheless a form of democratic government that can accommodate parochialism and communitarianism, one that can even save them from their defects and make them more tolerant and participatory: decentralized participatory democracy. And if McWorld is indifferent to democracy, there is nonetheless a form of democratic government that suits global markets passably well—representative government in its federal or, better still, confederal variation.

With its concern for accountability, the protection of minorities, and the universal rule of law, a confederalized representative system would serve the political needs of McWorld as well as oligarchic bureaucratism or meritocratic elitism is currently doing. As we are already beginning to see, many nations may survive in the long term only as confederations that afford local regions smaller than "nations" extensive jurisdiction. Recommended reading for democrats of the twenty-first century is not the U.S. Constitution or the French Declaration of Rights of Man and Citizen but the Articles of Confederation, that suddenly pertinent document that stitched together the thirteen American colonies into what then seemed a too loose confederation of independent states but now appears a new form of political realism, as veterans of Yeltsin's new Russia and the new Europe created at Maastricht will attest.

By the same token, the participatory and direct form of democracy that engages citizens in civic activity and civic judgment and goes well beyond just voting and accountability—the system I have called "strong democracy"— suits the political needs of decentralized communities as well as theocratic and nationalist party dictatorships have done. Local neighborhoods need not be democratic, but they can be. Real democracy has flourished in diminutive settings: the spirit of liberty, Tocqueville said, is local. Participatory democracy, if not naturally apposite to tribalism, has an undeniable attractiveness under conditions of parochialism.

Democracy in any of these variations will, however, continue to be obstructed by the undemocratic and antidemocratic trends toward uniformitarian globalism and intolerant retribalization which I have portrayed here. For democracy to persist in our brave new McWorld, we will have to commit acts of conscious political will—a possibility, but hardly a probability, under these conditions. Political will requires much more than the quick fix of the transfer of institutions. Like technology transfer, institution transfer rests on foolish assumptions about a uniform world of the kind that once fired the imagination of colonial administrators. Spread English justice to the colonies by exporting wigs. Let an East Indian trading company act as the vanguard to Britain's free parliamentary institutions. Today's well-intentioned quick-fixers in the National Endowment for Democracy and the Kennedy School of Government, in the unions and foundations and universities zealously nurturing contacts in Eastern Europe and the Third World, are hoping to democratize by long distance. Post Bulgaria a parliament by first-class mail. Fed Ex the Bill of Rights to Sri Lanka. Cable Cambodia some common law.

Yet Eastern Europe has already demonstrated that importing free political parties, parliaments, and presses cannot establish a democratic civil society; imposing a free market may even have the opposite effect. Democracy grows from the bottom up and cannot be imposed from the top down. Civil society has to be built from the inside out. The institutional superstructure comes last. Poland may become democratic, but then again it may heed the Pope, and prefer to found its politics on its Catholicism, with uncertain consequences for democracy. Bulgaria may become democratic, but it may prefer tribal war. The former Soviet Union may become a democratic confederation, or it may just grow into an anarchic and weak conglomeration of markets for other nations' goods and services.

Democrats need to seek out indigenous democratic impulses. There is always a desire for self-government, always some expression of participation, accountability, consent, and representation, even in traditional hierarchical societies. These need to be identified, tapped, modified, and incorporated into new democratic practices with an indigenous flavor. The tortoises among the democratizers may ultimately outlive or outpace the hares, for they will have the time and patience to explore conditions along the way, and to adapt their gait to changing circumstances. Tragically, democracy in a hurry often looks something like France in 1794 or China in 1989.

It certainly seems possible that the most attractive democratic ideal in the face of the brutal realities of Jihad and the dull realities of McWorld will be a confederal union of semi-autonomous communities smaller than nation-states, tied together into regional economic associations and markets larger than nation-states—participatory and self-determining in local matters at the bottom, representative and accountable at the top. The nation-state would play a diminished role, and sovereignty would lose some of its political potency. The Green movement adage "Think globally, act locally" would actually come to describe the conduct of politics.

This vision reflects only an ideal, however—one that is not terribly likely to be realized. Freedom, Jean-Jacques Rousseau once wrote, is a food easy to eat but hard to digest. Still, democracy has always played itself out against the odds. And democracy remains both a form of coherence as binding as McWorld and a secular faith potentially as inspiriting as Jihad.

47

Modernization's Challenge to Traditional Values: Who's Afraid of Ronald McDonald?

RONALD INGLEHART AND WAYNE E. BAKER

Even before Max Weber wrote his famous thesis about the relationship between the emergence of capitalism and its religious underpinnings in Calvinism (Reading 35), social thinkers were examining the relationship between economic growth and traditional values. The colonial experience Isbister describes (Reading 34) has been followed by an expansion of the global economy that challenges the lifestyle, social relationships and most deeply held cultural beliefs and practices of non-Western peoples. In this examination of data from the World Values Survey, the authors assess this impact and find a more complex and varied outcome. In some ways, as you have seen earlier (Reading 44) the United States remains a most unusual exception to the predictions of modernization.

The World Values Survey—a two-decade-long examination of the values of 65 societies coordinated by the University of Michigan's Institute for Social Research—is the largest investigation ever conducted of attitudes, values, and beliefs around the world. This study has carried out three waves of representative national surveys: the first in 1981–1982, the second in 1990–1991, and the third in 1995–1998. The fourth wave is being completed in 1999–2001. The study now represents some 80% of the world's population. These societies have per capita GNPs ranging from $300 to more than $30,000. Their political systems range from long-established stable democracies to authoritarian states.

The World Values Survey data have been used by researchers around the world for hundreds of publications in more than a dozen languages. Studies that have been based on the data cover a wide range of topics, including volunteerism in Europe, political partisanship and social class in Ireland, democratization in Korea, liberalization in Mexico, future values in Japan, and the religious vote in Western Europe.

This article examines the relationship between cultural values and economic globalization and modernization: What impact does economic development have on the values of a culture, and vice versa? Is a future "McWorld" inevitable?

RICH VALUES, POOR VALUES

The World Values Survey data show us that the world views of the people of rich societies differ systematically from those of low-income societies across a wide range of political, social, and religious norms and beliefs. The two most significant dimensions that emerged reflected, first, a polarization between *traditional* and *secular-rational* orientations toward authority and, second, a polarization between *survival* and *self-expression* values. By *traditional* we mean those societies that are relatively authoritarian, place strong emphasis on religion, and exhibit a mainstream version of preindustrial values such as an emphasis on male dominance in economic and political life, respect for authority, and relatively low levels of tolerance for abortion and divorce. Advanced societies, or *secular-rational,* tend to have the opposite characteristics.

A central component of the survival vs. self-expression dimension involves the polarization between materialist and postmaterialist values. Massive evidence indicates that a cultural shift throughout advanced industrial society is emerging among generations who have grown up taking survival for granted. Values among this group emphasize environmental protection, the women's movement, and rising demand for participation in decision making in economic and political life. During the past 25 years, these values have become increasingly widespread in almost all advanced industrial societies for which extensive time-series evidence is available.

Economic development brings with it sweeping cultural change, some modernization theorists tell us. Others argue that cultural values are enduring and exert more influence on society than does economic change. Who's right?

One goal of the World Values Survey is to study links between economic development and changes in values. A key question that we ask is whether the globalization of the economy will necessarily produce a homogenization (or, more specifically, an Americanization) of culture—a so-called "McWorld."

In the nineteenth century, modernization theorists such as Karl Marx and Friedrich Nietzsche made bold predictions about the future of industrial society, such as the rise of labor and the decline of religion. In the twentieth century, non-Western societies were expected to abandon their traditional cultures and assimilate the technologically and morally "superior" ways of the West.

Clearly now, at the start of the twenty-first century, we need to rethink "modernization." Few people today anticipate a proletarian revolution, and non-Western societies such as East Asia have surpassed their Western role models in key aspects of modernization, such as rates of economic growth. And few observers today attribute moral superiority to the West.

On the other hand, one core concept of modernization theory still seems valid: Industrialization produces pervasive social and cultural consequences, such as rising educational levels, shifting attitudes toward authority, broader political participation, declining fertility rates, and changing gender roles. On the basis of the World Values Surveys, we believe that economic development has systematic and, to some extent, predictable cultural and political consequences. Once a society has embarked on industrialization—the central element of the modernization process—certain changes are highly likely to occur. But economic development is not the *only* force at work.

In the past few decades, modernization has become associated with *post-industrialization*: the rise of the knowledge and service-oriented economy. These changes in the nature of work had major political and cultural consequences, too. Rather than growing more materialistic with increased prosperity, postindustrial societies are experiencing an increasing emphasis on quality-of-life issues, environmental protection, and self-expression.

While industrialization increased human dominance over the environment—and consequently created a dwindling role for religious belief—the emergence of postindustrial society is stimulating further evolution of prevailing world views in a different direction. Life in postindustrial societies centers on services rather than material objects, and more effort is focused on communicating and processing information. Most people spend their productive hours dealing with other people and symbols.

Thus, the rise of postindustrial society leads to a growing emphasis on self-expression. Today's unprecedented wealth in advanced societies means an increasing share of the population grows up taking survival for granted. Their value priorities shift from an overwhelming emphasis on economic and physical security toward an increasing emphasis on subjective well-being and quality of life. "Modernization," thus, is not linear—it moves in new directions.

HOW VALUES SHAPE CULTURE

Different societies follow different trajectories even when they are subjected to the same forces of economic development, in part because situation-specific factors, such as a society's cultural heritage, also shape how a particular society develops. Recently, Samuel Huntington, author of *The Clash of Civilizations* (Simon & Schuster, 1996), has focused on the role of religion in shaping the world's eight major civilizations or "cultural zones": Western Christianity, Orthodox, Islam, Confucian, Japanese, Hindu, African, and Latin American. These zones were shaped by religious traditions that are still powerful today, despite the forces of modernization.

Other scholars observe other distinctive cultural traits that endure over long periods of time and continue to shape a society's political and economic performance. For example, the regions of Italy in which democratic institutions function most successfully today are those in which civil society was relatively well developed in the nineteenth century and even earlier, as Robert Putnam notes in *Making Democracy Work* (Princeton University Press, 1993). And a cultural heritage of "low trust" puts a society at a competitive disadvantage in global markets because it is less able to develop large and complex social institutions, Francis Fukuyama argues in *Trust: The Social Virtues and the Creation of Prosperity* (Free Press, 1995).

The impression that we are moving toward a uniform "McWorld" is partly an illusion. The seemingly identical McDonald's restaurants that have spread throughout the world actually have different social meanings and fulfill different social functions in different cultural zones. Eating in a McDonald's restaurant in Japan is a different social experience from eating in one in the United States, Europe, or China.

Likewise, the globalization of communication is unmistakable, but its effects may be overestimated. It is certainly apparent that young people around the world are wearing jeans and listening to U.S. pop music; what is less apparent is the persistence of underlying value differences.

MAPPING AND PREDICTING VALUES

Using the 1995–1998 wave of the World Values Survey, we produced a map of the world's values, showing the locations of 65 societies on the two cross-cultural dimensions—traditional vs. secular-rational values and survival vs. self-expression values.

What the map shows us is that cross-cultural variation is highly constrained. That is, if the people of a given society place a strong emphasis on religion, that society's relative position on many other variables can be predicted—such as attitudes toward abortion, national pride, respect for authority, and child-rearing. Similarly, survival vs. self-expression values reflect wide-ranging but tightly correlated clusters of values: Materialistic (survival-oriented) societies can be predicted to value maintaining order and fighting inflation, while post-materialistic (self-expression-oriented) societies can be predicted to value freedom, interpersonal trust, and tolerance of outgroups.

Economic development seems to have a powerful impact on cultural values: The value systems of rich countries differ systematically from those of poor countries. If we super-impose an income "map" over the values map, we see that all 19 societies with an annual per capita GNP of over $15,000 rank relatively high on both dimensions, placing them in the upper right-hand corner. This economic zone cuts across the boundaries of the Protestant, ex-Communist, Confucian, Catholic, and English-speaking cultural zones.

On the other hand, all societies with per capita GNPs below $2,000 fall into a cluster at the lower left of the map, in an economic zone that cuts across the African, South Asian, ex-Communist, and Orthodox cultural zones. The remaining societies fall into two intermediate cultural-economic zones. Economic development seems to move societies in a common direction, regardless of their cultural heritage. Nevertheless, distinctive cultural zones persist two centuries after the industrial revolution began.

Of course, per capita GNP is only one indicator of a society's level of economic development. Another might be the percentage of the labor force engaged in the agricultural sector, the industrial sector, or the service sector. The shift from an agrarian mode of production to industrial production seems to bring with it a shift from traditional values toward increasing rationalization and secularization.

But a society's cultural heritage also plays a role: All four of the Confucian-influenced societies (China, Taiwan, South Korea, and Japan) have relatively secular values, regardless of the proportion of their labor forces in the industrial sector. Conversely, the historically Roman Catholic societies (e.g., Italy, Portugal, and Spain) display relatively traditional values when compared with Confucian or ex-Communist societies with the same proportion of industrial workers. And virtually all of the historically Protestant societies (e.g., West Germany, Denmark, Norway, and Sweden) rank higher on the survival/self-expression dimension than do all of the historically Roman Catholic societies, regardless of the extent to which their labor forces are engaged in the service sector.

We can conclude from this that changes in GNP and occupational structure have important influences on prevailing world views, but traditional cultural influences persist.

Religious traditions appear to have had an enduring impact on the contemporary value systems of the 65 societies. But a society's culture reflects its entire historical heritage. A central historical event of the twentieth century was the rise and fall of a Communist empire that once ruled one-third of the world's population. Communism left a clear imprint on the value systems of those who lived under it. East Germany remains culturally close to West Germany despite four decades of Communist rule, but its value system has been drawn toward the Communist zone. And although China is a member of the Confucian zone, it also falls within a broad Communist-influenced zone. Similarly, Azerbaijan, though part of the Islamic cluster, also falls within the Communist superzone that dominated it for decades.

THE DEVIANT U.S.

The World Value Map clearly shows that the United States is a deviant case. We do not believe it is a prototype of cultural modernization for other societies to follow, as some postwar modernization theorists have naively assumed. The United States has a much more traditional value system than any other advanced industrial society.

On the traditional/secular-rational dimension, the United States ranks far below other rich societies, with levels of religiosity and national pride comparable to those found in developing societies. The United States does rank among the most advanced societies along the survival/self-expression dimension, but even here it does not lead the world. The Swedes and the Dutch seem closer to the cutting edge of cultural change than do the Americans.

Modernization theory implies that as societies develop economically their cultures tend to shift in a predictable direction. Our data supports this prediction. Economic differences are linked with large and pervasive cultural differences. But we find clear evidence of the influence of long-established cultural zones.

Do these cultural clusters simply reflect economic differences? For example, do the societies of Protestant Europe have similar values simply because they are rich? No. The impact of a society's historical-cultural heritage persists when we control for GDP per capita and the structure of the labor force. On a value such as *interpersonal trust* (a variable on the surival/self-expression dimension), even rich Catholic societies rank lower than rich Protestant ones.

Within a given society, however, Catholics rank about as high on interpersonal trust as do Protestants. The shared historical experience of given nations, not individual personality, is crucial. Once established, the cross-cultural differences linked with religion have become part of a national culture that is transmitted by the educational institutions and mass media of given societies to the people of that nation. Despite globalization, the nation remains a key unit of shared experience, and its educational and cultural institutions shape the values of almost everyone in that society.

THE PERSISTENCE OF RELIGIOUS AND SPIRITUAL BELIEFS

As a society shifts from an agrarian to an industrial economy and survival comes to be taken for granted, traditional religious beliefs tend to decline. Nevertheless, as the twenty-first century opens, cleavages along religious lines remain strong. Why has religion been so slow to disappear?

History has taken an ironic turn: Communist-style industrialization was especially favorable to secularization, but the collapse of Communism has given rise to pervasive insecurity—and a return to religious beliefs. Five of the seven ex-Communist societies for which we have time-series data show rising church attendance.

Throughout advanced industrial societies we see two contrasting trends: the decline of attendance at religious services on the one hand, and on the other the persistence of religious beliefs and the rise of spirituality. The need for answers to spiritual questions such as why we are here and where we are going does not die out in postindustrial society. Spiritual concerns will probably always be part of the human outlook. In fact, in the three successive waves of the World Values Survey, concern for the meaning and purpose of life became *stronger* in most advanced industrial societies.

CONCLUSION: WHITHER MODERNIZATION?

Economic development is associated with pervasive, and to an extent predictable, cultural changes. Industrialization promotes a shift from traditional to secular-rational values; postindustrialization promotes a shift toward more trust, tolerance, and emphasis on well-being. Economic collapse propels societies in the opposite direction.

Economic development tends to push societies in a common direction, but rather than converging they seem to move along paths shaped by their cultural heritages. Therefore, we doubt that the forces of modernization will produce a homogenized world culture in the foreseeable future.

Certainly it is misleading to view cultural change as "Americanization." Industrializing societies in general are *not* becoming like the United States. In fact, the United States seems to be a deviant case: Its people hold much more traditional values and beliefs than do those in any other equally prosperous society. If any societies exemplify the cutting edge of cultural change, it would be the Nordic countries.

Finally, modernization is probabilistic, not deterministic. Economic development tends to transform a given society in a predictable direction, but the process and path are not inevitable. Many factors are involved, so any prediction must be contingent on the historical and cultural context of the society in question.

Nevertheless, the central prediction of modernization theory finds broad support: Economic development is associated with major changes in prevailing values and beliefs. The world views of rich societies differ markedly from those of poor societies. This does not necessarily imply cultural convergence, but it does predict the general direction of cultural change and (insofar as the process is based on intergenerational population replacement) even gives some idea of the rate at which such change is likely to occur.

In short, economic development will cause shifts in the values of people in developing nations, but it will not produce a uniform global culture. The future may *look* like McWorld, but it won't feel like one.

48

Grassroots Activism: Mothers of East Los Angeles

MARY PARDO

This retrospective on community activism in East Los Angeles shows how places and individuals are changed when people make their voices heard. Mary Pardo's life-history approach allows us to hear the voice of the women who worked on behalf of their families and communities. Despite obstacles of gender, class, ethnicity, and personal inexperience, they organized and confronted the powerful forces of the city and state. This is democracy in action.

THE COMMUNITY CONTEXT: EAST LOS ANGELES RESISTING SIEGE

In 1984, the state of California commissioned a public relations firm to assess the political difficulties facing the construction of energy-producing waste incinerators. The report provided a "personality profile" of those residents most likely to organize effective opposition to projects:

> middle and upper socioeconomic strata possess better resources to effectuate their opposition. Middle and higher socioeconomic strata neighborhoods should not fall within the one-mile and five-mile radii of the proposed site. Conversely, older people, people with a high school education or less are least likely to oppose a facility.[1]

The state accordingly placed the [toxic waste incinerator] plant in Commerce, a predominantly Mexican American, low-income community. This pattern holds throughout the state and the country: three out of five Afro-Americans and Latinos live near toxic waste sites, and three of the five largest hazardous waste landfills are in communities with at least 80 percent minority populations.

Similarly, in March 1985, when the state sought a site for the first state prison in Los Angeles County, Governor Deukmejian resolved to place the

---

1. Cerrell Associates, Inc., "Political Difficulties Facing Waste-to-Energy Conversion Plant Siting," Report Prepared for California Waste Management Board, State of California (Los Angeles, 1984): 43.

1,700-inmate institution in East Los Angeles, within a mile of the long-established Boyle Heights neighborhood and within two miles of thirty-four schools.
Furthermore, violating convention, the state bid on the expensive parcel of
industrially zoned land without compiling an environmental impact report or
providing a public community hearing. * * *

In spring 1986, after much pressure from the 56th assembly district office
and the community, the Department of Corrections agreed to hold a public
information meeting, which was attended by over 700 Boyle Heights residents. From this moment on, Vigil observed, "the tables turned, the community mobilized, and the residents began calling the political representatives
and requesting their presence at hearings and meetings."[2] By summer 1986,
the community was well aware of the prison site proposal. Over two thousand
people, carrying placards proclaiming "No Prison in ELA," marched from Resurrection Church in Boyle Heights to the 3rd Street bridge linking East Los
Angeles with the rapidly expanding downtown Los Angeles. This march
marked the beginning of one of the largest grassroots coalitions to emerge
from the Latino community in the last decade.

Prominent among the coalition's groups is "Mothers of East Los Angeles,"
a loosely knit group of over 400 Mexican American women. MELA initially
coalesced to oppose the state prison construction but has since organized
opposition to several other projects detrimental to the quality of life in the central city. Its second large target is a toxic waste incinerator proposed for Ver-
non, a small city adjacent to East Los Angeles. This incinerator would worsen
the already debilitating air quality of the entire county and set a precedent
dangerous for other communities throughout California. When MELA took up
the fight against the toxic waste incinerator, it became more than a single-
issue group and began working with environmental groups around the state.
As a result of the community struggle, AB58 (Roybal-Allard), which provides
all Californians with the minimum protection of an environmental impact
report before the construction of hazardous waste incinerators, was signed
into law. But the law's effectiveness relies on a watchful community network.
Since its emergence, "Mothers of East Los Angeles" has become centrally
important to just such a network of grassroots activists including a select
number of Catholic priests and two Mexican American political representatives. Furthermore, the group's very formation, and its continued spirit and
activism, fly in the face of the conventional political science beliefs regarding
political participation.

Predictions by the "experts" attribute the low formal political participation
(i.e., voting) of Mexican American people in the U.S. to a set of cultural "retar-
dants" including primary kinship systems, fatalism, religious traditionalism
traditional cultural values, and mother country attachment. The core activists

---

2. James Vigil, Jr., field representative for Assemblywoman Gloria Molina, 1984–1986,
Personal Interview, Whittier, Calif., 27 September 1989.

in MELA may appear to fit this description, as well as the state-commissioned profile of residents least likely to oppose toxic waste incinerator projects. All the women live in a low-income community. Furthermore, they identify themselves as active and committed participants in the Catholic Church; they claim an ethnic identity—Mexican American; their ages range from forty to sixty; and they have attained at most high school educations. However, these women fail to conform to the predicted political apathy. Instead, they have transformed social identity—ethnic identity, class identity, and gender identity—into an impetus as well [as] a basis for activism. And, in transforming their existing social networks into grassroots political networks, they have also transformed themselves.

TRANSFORMATION AS A DOMINANT THEME

From the life histories of the group's core activists and from my own field notes, I have selected excerpts that tell two representative stories. One is a narrative of the events that led to community mobilization in East Los Angeles. The other is a story of transformation, the process of creating new and better relationships that empower people to unite and achieve common goals.

First, women have transformed organizing experiences and social networks arising from gender-related responsibilities into political resources. When I asked the women about the first community, not necessarily "political," involvement they could recall, they discussed experiences that predated the formation of MELA. Juana Gutiérrez explained:

> Well, it didn't start with the prison, you know. It started when my kids went to school. I started by joining the Parents Club and we worked on different problems here in the area. Like the people who come to the parks to sell drugs to the kids. I got the neighbors to have meetings. I would go knock at the doors, house to house. And I told them that we should stick together with the Neighborhood Watch for the community and for the kids.

Erlinda Robles similarly recalled:

> I wanted my kids to go to Catholic school and from the time my oldest one went there, I was there every day. I used to take my two little ones with me and I helped one way or another. I used to question things they did. And the other mothers would just watch me. Later, they would ask me, "Why do you do that? They are going to take it out on your kids." I'd say, "They better not." And before you knew it, we had a big group of mothers that were very involved.

Part of a mother's "traditional" responsibility includes over seeing her child's progress in school, interacting with school staff, and supporting school activities. In these processes, women meet other mothers and begin developing a network of acquaintanceships and friendships based on mutual concern for the welfare of their children.

Although the women in MELA carried the greatest burden of participating in school activities, Erlinda Robles also spoke of strategies they used to draw men into the enterprise and into the networks:

> At the beginning, the priests used to say who the president of the mothers guild would be; they used to pick 'um. But, we wanted elections, so we got elections. Then we wanted the fathers to be involved, and the nuns suggested that a father should be president and a mother would be secretary or be involved there [at the school site].

Of course, this comment piqued my curiosity, so I asked how the mothers agreed on the nuns' suggestion. The answer was simple and instructive:

> At the time we thought it was a "natural" way to get the fathers involved because they weren't involved; it was just the mothers. Everybody [the women] agreed on them [the fathers] being president because they worked all day and they couldn't be involved in a lot of daily activities like food sales and whatever. During the week, a steering committee of mothers planned the group's activities. But now that I think about it, a woman could have done the job just as well!

So women got men into the group by giving them a position they could manage. The men may have held the title of "president," but they were not making day-to-day decisions about work, nor were they dictating the direction of the group. Erlinda Robles laughed as she recalled an occasion when the president insisted, against the wishes of the women, on scheduling a parents' group fundraiser— a breakfast—on Mother's Day. On that morning, only the president and his wife were present to prepare breakfast. This should alert researchers against measuring power and influence by looking solely at who holds titles.

Each of the cofounders had a history of working with groups arising out of the responsibilities usually assumed by "mothers"—the education of children and the safety of the surrounding community. From these groups, they gained valuable experiences and networks that facilitated the formation of "Mothers of East Los Angeles." Juana Gutiérrez explained how preexisting networks progressively expanded community support:

> You know nobody knew about the plan to build a prison in this community until Assemblywoman Gloria Molina told me. Martha Molina called me and said, "You know what is happening in your area? The governor wants to put a prison in Boyle Heights!" So, I called a Neighborhood Watch meeting at my house and we got fifteen people together. Then, Father John started informing his people at the Church and that is when the group of two to three hundred started showing up for every march on the bridge.

MELA effectively linked up preexisting networks into a viable grassroots coalition.

Second, the process of activism also transformed previously "invisible" women, making them not only visible but the center of public attention. From a conventional perspective, political activism assumes a kind of gender neutrality. This means that anyone can participate, but men are the expected key actors. In accordance with this pattern, in winter 1986 an informal group of concerned businessmen in the community began lobbying and testifying against the prison at hearings in Sacramento. Working in conjunction with Assemblywoman Molina, they made many trips to Sacramento at their own expense. Residents who did not have the income to travel were unable to join them. Finally, Molina, commonly recognized as a forceful advocate for Latinas and the community, asked Frank Villalobos, an urban planner in the group, why there were no women coming up to speak in Sacramento against the prison. As he phrased it, "I was getting some heat from her because no women were going up there."

In response to this comment, Veronica Gutiérrez, a law student who lived in the community, agreed to accompany him on the next trip to Sacramento. He also mentioned the comment to Father John Moretta at Resurrection Catholic Parish. Meanwhile, representatives of the business sector of the community and of the 56th assembly district office were continuing to compile arguments and supportive data against the East Los Angeles prison site. Frank Villalobos stated one of the pressing problems:

> We felt that the Senators whom we prepared all this for didn't even acknowledge that we existed. They kept calling it the "downtown" site, and they argued that there was no opposition in the community. So, I told Father Moretta, what we have to do is demonstrate that there is a link (proximity) between the Boyle Heights community and the prison.

The next juncture illustrates how perceptions of gender-specific behavior set in motion a sequence of events that brought women into the political limelight. Father Moretta decided to ask all the women to meet after mass. He told them about the prison site and called for their support. When I asked him about his rationale for selecting the women, he replied:

> I felt so strongly about the issue, and I knew in my heart what a terrible offense this was to the people. So, I was afraid that once we got into a demonstration situation we had to be very careful. I thought the women would be cooler and calmer than the men. The bottom line is that the men came anyway. The first times out the majority were women. Then they began to invite their husbands and their children, but originally it was just women.

Father Moretta also named the group. Quite moved by a film, *The Official Story,* about the courageous Argentine women who demonstrated for the return of their children who disappeared during a repressive right-wing military dictatorship, he transformed the name "Las Madres de la Plaza de Mayo" into "Mothers of East Los Angeles."

However, Aurora Castillo, one of the cofounders of the group, modified my emphasis on the predominance of women:

> Of course the fathers work. We also have many, many grandmothers. And all this IS with the support of the fathers. They make the placards and the posters; they do the security and carry the signs; and they come to the marches when they can.

Although women played a key role in the mobilization, they emphasized the group's broad base of active supporters as well as the other organizations in the "Coalition Against the Prison." Their intent was to counter any notion that MELA was composed exclusively of women or mothers and to stress the "inclusiveness" of the group. All the women who assumed lead roles in the group had long histories of volunteer work in the Boyle Heights community; but formation of the group brought them out of the "private" margins and into "public" light.

Third, the women in "Mothers of East L.A." have transformed the definition of "mother" to include militant political opposition to state-proposed projects they see as adverse to the quality of life in the community. Explaining how she discovered the issue, Aurora Castillo said,

> You know if one of your children's safety is jeopardized, the mother turns into a lioness. That's why Father John got the mothers. We have to have a well-organized, strong group of mothers to protect the community and oppose things that are detrimental to us. You know the governor is in the wrong and the mothers are in the right. After all, the mothers have to be right. Mothers are for the children's interest, not for self-interest; the governor is for his own political interest.

The women also have expanded the boundaries of "motherhood" to include social and political community activism and redefined the word to include women who are not biological "mothers." At one meeting a young Latina expressed her solidarity with the group and, almost apologetically, qualified herself as a "resident," not a "mother," of East Los Angeles. Erlinda Robles replied:

> When you are fighting for a better life for children and "doing" for them, isn't that what mothers do? So we're all mothers. You don't have to have children to be a "mother."

* * *

Fourth, the story of MELA also shows the transformation of class and ethnic identity. Aurora Castillo told of an incident that illustrated her growing knowledge of the relationship of East Los Angeles to other communities and the basis necessary for coalition building:

> And do you know we have been approached by other groups? [She lowers her voice in emphasis.] You know that Pacific Palisades group asked for our backing. But what they did, they sent their powerful lobbyist that they pay thousands of dollars to get our support against the drilling in Pacific Palisades. So what we did was tell them to send their grassroots people, not their lobbyist. We're suspicious. We don't want to talk to a high-salaried lobbyist; we are humble people. We did our own lobbying. In one week we went to Sacramento twice.

The contrast between the often tedious and labor-intensive work of mobilizing people at the "grassroots" level and the paid work of a "high salaried lobbyist" represents a point of pride and integrity, not a deficiency or a source of shame. If the two groups were to construct a coalition, they must communicate on equal terms.

The women of MELA combine a willingness to assert opposition with a critical assessment of their own weaknesses. At one community meeting, for example, representatives of several oil companies attempted to gain support for placement of an oil pipeline through the center of East Los Angeles. The exchange between the women in the audience and the oil representative was heated, as women alternated asking questions about the chosen route for the pipeline:

> "Is it going through Cielito Lindo [Reagan's ranch]?" The oil representative answered, "No." Another woman stood up and asked, "Why not place it along the coastline?" Without thinking of the implications, the representative responded, "Oh, no! If it burst, it would endanger the marine life." The woman retorted, "You value the marine life more than human beings?" His face reddened with anger and the hearing disintegrated into angry chanting.

The proposal was quickly defeated. But Aurora Castillo acknowledged that it was not solely their opposition that brought about the defeat:

> We won because the westside was opposed to it, so we united with them. You know there are a lot of attorneys who live there and they also questioned the representative. Believe me, no way is justice blind. . . . We just don't want all this garbage thrown at us because we are low-income and Mexican American. We are lucky now that we have good representatives, which we didn't have before.

Throughout their life histories, the women refer to the disruptive effects of land use decisions made in the 1950s. As longtime residents, all but one share the experience of losing a home and relocating to make way for a freeway.

* * *

The freeways that cut through communities and disrupted neighborhoods are now a concrete reminder of shared injustice, of the vulnerability of the community in the 1950s. The community's social and political history thus informs perceptions of its current predicament; however, today's activists emphasize not the powerlessness of the community but the change in status and progression toward political empowerment.

Fifth, the core activists typically tell stories illustrating personal change and a new sense of entitlement to speak for the community. They have transformed the unspoken sentiments of individuals into a collective community voice. Lucy Ramos related her initial apprehensions:

> I was afraid to get involved. I didn't know what was going to come out of this and I hesitated at first. Right after we started, Father John came up to me and told me, "I want you to be a spokesperson." I said, "Oh no, I don't know what I am going to say." I was nervous. I am surprised I didn't have a nervous breakdown then. Every time we used to get in front of the TV cameras and even interviews like this, I used to sit there and I could feel myself shaking. But as time went on, I started getting used to it.
>
> And this is what I have noticed with a lot of them. They were afraid to speak up and say anything. Now, with this prison issue, a lot of them have come out and come forward and given their opinions. Everybody used to be real "quietlike."

She also related a situation that brought all her fears to a climax, which she confronted and resolved as follows:

> When I first started working with the coalition, Channel 13 called me up and said they wanted to interview me and I said OK. Then I started getting nervous. So I called Father John and told him, "You better get over here right away." He said, "Don't worry, don't worry, you can handle it by yourself." Then Channel 13 called me back and said they were going to interview another person, someone I had never heard of, and asked if it was OK if he came to my house. And I said OK again. Then I began thinking, what if this guy is for the prison? What am I going to do? And I was so nervous and I thought, I know what I am going to do!

Since the meeting was taking place in her home, she reasoned that she was entitled to order any troublemakers out of her domain:

> If this man tells me anything, I am just going to chase him out of my house. That is what I am going to do! All these thoughts were going through my head. Then

Channel 13 walk into my house followed by six men I had never met. And I thought, Oh, my God, what did I get myself into? I kept saying to myself, if they get smart with me I am throwing them ALL out.

At this point her tone expressed a sense of resolve. In fact, the situation turned out to be neither confrontational nor threatening, as the "other men" were also members of the coalition. This woman confronted an anxiety-laden situation by relying on her sense of control within her home and family—a quite "traditional" source of authority for women—and transforming that control into the courage to express a political position before a potential audience all over one of the largest metropolitan areas in the nation.

People living in Third World countries as well as in minority communities in the United States face an increasingly degraded environment. Recognizing the threat to the well-being of their families, residents have mobilized at the neighborhood level to fight for "quality of life" issues. The common notion that environmental well-being is of concern solely to white middle-class and upper-class residents ignores the specific way working-class neighborhoods suffer from the fallout of the city "growth machine" geared for profit.

In Los Angeles, the culmination of postwar urban renewal policies, the growing Pacific Rim trade surplus and investment, and low-wage international labor migration from Third World countries are creating potentially volatile conditions. Literally palatial financial buildings swallow up the space previously occupied by modest, low-cost housing. Increasing density and development not matched by investment in social programs, services, and infrastructure erode the quality of life, beginning in the core of the city. Latinos, the majority of whom live close to the center of the city, must confront the distilled social consequences of development focused solely on profit. The Mexican American community in East Los Angeles, much like other minority working-class communities, has been a repository for prisons instead of new schools, hazardous industries instead of safe work sites, and one of the largest concentrations of freeway interchanges in the country, which transports much wealth past the community. And the concerns of residents in East Los Angeles may provide lessons for other minority as well as middle-class communities. Increasing environmental pollution resulting from inadequate waste disposal plans and an out-of-control "need" for penal institutions to contain the casualties created by the growing bipolar distribution of wages may not be limited to the Southwest. These conditions set the stage for new conflicts and new opportunities, to transform old relationships into coalitions that can challenge state agendas and create new community visions.

Mexican American women living east of downtown Los Angeles exemplify the tendency of women to enter into environmental struggles in defense of their community. Women have a rich historical legacy of community activism, partly reconstructed over the last two decades in social histories of women who contested other "quality of life issues," from the price of bread to "Demon Rum" (often representing domestic violence).

But something new is also happening. The issues "traditionally" addressed by women—health, housing, sanitation, and the urban environment—have moved to center stage as capitalist urbanization progresses. Environmental issues now fuel the fires of many political campaigns and drive citizens beyond the rather restricted, perfunctory political act of voting. Instances of political mobilization at the grassroots level, where women often play a central role, allow us to "see" abstract concepts like participatory democracy and social change as dynamic processes.

* * *

The work "Mothers of East Los Angeles" do to mobilize the community demonstrates that people's political involvement cannot be predicted by their cultural characteristics. These women have defied stereotypes of apathy and used ethnic, gender, and class identity as an impetus, a strength, a vehicle for political activism. They have expanded their—and our—understanding of the complexities of a political system, and they have reaffirmed the possibility of "doing something."

They also generously share the lessons they have learned. One of the women in "Mothers of East Los Angeles" told me, as I hesitated to set up an interview with another woman I hadn't yet met in person,

> You know, nothing ventured nothing lost. You should have seen how timid we were the first time we went to a public hearing. Now, forget it, I walk right up and make myself heard and that's what you have to do.

49

Greenpeace and Political Globalism

PAUL WAPNER

The last half century has seen the growth of worldwide concern about the environment. With a global population of more than 6 billion people and concerns about global warming, the depletion of nonrenewable resources, prophecies of future water wars, loss of biodiversity, and pollution of the seas it is not surprising that thousands of organizations have been created to protest, address, and reverse what many people see as the folly of human action. No environmental group is more widely recognized than Greenpeace, an international direct-action organization that seeks to foster in people an "environmental sensibility" and spur them to action. This article looks at the social organization, ideology, and tactics of Greenpeace, as well as the basic assumptions of the group about the process of social change.

Nonstate-oriented politics is nothing new. Since the dawn of social life, human beings have worked to shape and direct collective affairs independent of formal government. In recent years, however, scholars have begun thinking theoretically about this type of activity and, in so doing, have provided a degree of conceptual clarity to it. In particular, the contributions of social movement theory, poststructuralism, feminism, and critical thought have broadened understandings of power and thus have heightened our sensitivity to how politics takes place in the home, office, and marketplace, as well as in the halls of congresses and parliaments. Politics, in this sense, is much more subtle to notice than the conduct of governments but, according to proponents of these orientations, no less significant for political affairs.

It is with a more comprehensive notion of power that I wish to begin investigating the ways in which transnational environmental groups engage in world civic politics. By suspending judgment about what constitutes real politics, one can focus on diverse forms of agency that actually shape world environmental affairs. In this chapter, I describe the ways in which activists work outside of, around, or at the margins of governmental activity in their efforts to alleviate global environmental problems. This descriptive element will sensitize readers to genuinely alternative forms of political activism.

In addition to describing forms of nonstate environmental politics, one must still ask the political question about them: namely, do they make a difference? Does all the time, money, and human energy involved actually contribute to addressing and partly alleviating environmental problems? Specifically, in what ways does a non-state-oriented type of political action actually affect world environmental affairs? That activists employ such a politics is, as I will demonstrate, true; but does it really matter in terms of world politics? In this chapter, in addition to describing the work of transnational activists, I furnish evidence to suggest that their efforts actually do matter in world political events. They create conditions that direct the actions of others within a world context.

To begin, I want to draw attention to a level of analysis that has a long history in the study of world politics but which is, at present, still underdeveloped and underappreciated. This is the level at which norms, values, and discourse operate in the global arena outside the domain of states. It is that dimension of world experience where widespread, shared understandings among people throughout the globe act as determinants for present conditions on the planet. It is part of, for want of a better phrase, the *cultural* school of thought which believes that ideas within societies at large structure human collective life. Working within this tradition, the key argument of this chapter is that transnational environmental groups contribute to addressing global environmental problems by heightening worldwide concern for the environment. They persuade vast numbers of people to care about and take actions to protect the earth's ecosystem. In short, they disseminate what I call an *ecological sensibility.* This serves an important political function in coming to terms with the environmental threat.

A sensibility operates as a political force insofar as it constrains and directs widespread behavior. It works at the ideational level to animate practices and is considered a form of *soft law* in contrast to the *hard law* of government directives, policies, and so forth. Scholars make it a habit of differentiating between hard and soft law insofar as they distinguish legal and cultural factors in their understanding of social change. On the one hand, there are those who claim that governmental action is the key to social change. Laws, policies, and directives drive social norms, and thus as they change, the entire configuration of social life will shift. Those who share this perspective see governmental action as the "base" with cultural and social life being the "superstructure." On the other hand, there are those who claim that social norms are central to social change. Governmental decrees, from this perspective, are not the source of change but merely reflections of it. Laws and policies arise out of, or give authoritative expression to, norms that already enjoy widespread acceptance. Scholars sharing this view see social norms as the "base" and governmental directives as the "superstructure."

Differentiating legal and cultural factors, while analytically helpful, is misguided when it forces a thinker to choose between them. When it comes to such large categories of social analysis, it is a mistake to assume that one dimension of social change is definitively more significant than the other. The obvious response to such differentiation is that both factors are important. Indeed, some argue that they are in dialectical relation to each other. As Christopher Stone writes, "in general, laws and cultural norms are mutually reinforcing. Formal laws arise from cultures, and command obedience in proportion to their coherence with the fundamental beliefs of the culture. Cultures, however, are not static. Law, and especially the activities of law making and legal reform, are among the forces that contribute to cultural evolution."

In this chapter, I do not weigh in on the ideational side and argue for its primacy nor celebrate the dialectical relationship. Rather, I simply emphasize the degree to which widely held conceptualizations animate large-scale practices and use this to show how efforts to disseminate an ecological sensibility have world political significance. What makes such efforts political, it should be clear, is not that they are ultimately codified into law or governmental decree but that they represent the use of power to influence and guide widespread behavior. An ecological sensibility, then, is not itself an answer to global environmental threats nor *the* agent for shifting one state of affairs to another. It is, however, an important part of any genuine response to environmental harm. Put simplistically for the moment, it creates an ideational context which inspires and motivates people to act in the service of environmental well-being and thus constitutes the milieu within which environmentally sound actions can arise and be undertaken. While not solely responsible for the *existence* of this sensibility, transnational environmental groups deserve substantial credit for *spreading* it throughout the world. [. . .]

Since 1972, Greenpeace has grown from having a single office in Vancouver to staffing offices in over thirty countries and, until recently, a base in Antarctica. Greenpeace has offices in the developed as well as the developing world, including Russia and Eastern Europe. Its eco-navy consists of eight ships, and it owns a helicopter and a hot-air balloon. It employs over 1,000 full-time staff members, plus hundreds of part-timers and thousands of volunteers. As of July 1994, it had over 6 million members worldwide and an estimated income of over $100 million. All money comes from voluntary donations, 90 percent of which is in the form of small contributions from individual members. Additionally, Greenpeace sends hundreds of canvassers out each night to raise funds and educate the general public about current environmental issues. Finally, it has expanded its area of concern. While originally focused on nuclear weapons testing, it is now concerned with all threats to the planetary ecosystem. In short, from 1972 to the present Greenpeace has grown into a full-scale, transnational environmental organization.

TRANSNATIONAL ORGANIZATIONAL STRUCTURE

Greenpeace sees the bulk of global environmental problems falling into four categories: toxic substances, energy and atmosphere, nuclear issues, and ocean and terrestrial ecology. Greenpeace works for environmental protection by dividing its attention among these four issue areas, also called campaigns. Within each of these, Greenpeace works on numerous subissues. For example, under the rubric of its nuclear campaign, Greenpeace focuses on reprocessing and dumping of nuclear material, sea-based nuclear weapons and nuclear testing. Under the rubric of ocean ecology, Greenpeace concentrates on whales, sea turtles, fisheries, and dolphins.

As a transnational environmental group concerned with threats to the entire planet, Greenpeace undertakes its campaigns and projects worldwide. The problems associated with toxic substances, energy, and atmosphere and so forth are not limited to individual countries. Almost all parts of the world are vulnerable to the environmental consequences involved. Greenpeace is organized to allow it to address these dilemmas on a global scale.

The top tiers of the organization are made up of the Greenpeace Council, an executive board, and regional trustees. The council is made up of representatives from all the countries where Greenpeace has offices and meets once a year to decide on organizational policy. The council is one of the ways Greenpeace coordinates its diverse activities. The council sets guidelines for the general operation of Greenpeace, approves the international budget, and develops long-term goals. Because council members come from around the world, decisions can reflect a sensitivity to differing regional and local aspects of environmental problems. To provide greater efficiency in day-to-day operations, and to emphasize coordination among campaigns and projects, there is an executive board that ratifies all council resolutions and makes significant decisions for Greenpeace throughout the year when the council is not in session. The board consists of both voting and nonvoting members and is elected by the Greenpeace Council.

In addition to the council and the executive board, there are regional trustees that provide the final stamp of approval for Greenpeace's overall operations. Trustees are representatives of the areas of the world where Greenpeace has offices. These include Latin America, the Pacific, North America, and Europe. While the trustees generally approve all decisions put forward by the council and the executive board, it serves as the final arbiter of Greenpeace policies. Because individual trustees represent diverse regions of the world, as a whole the trustees advance a global rather than a national or even regional orientation within Greenpeace.

Aside from the council and executive board, Greenpeace organizes itself worldwide along the lines of its four campaign areas. Heading each campaign is an international coordinator. He or she designs the way specific campaigns play themselves out in different regional and national contexts. For example, the campaign coordinator of toxic substances orchestrates all Greenpeace projects that contribute to achieving the aims of the toxics campaign. She or he provides the global perspective to different projects.

Underneath international campaign coordinators are project directors. Project directors are scattered across the globe and work on subissues of the larger campaigns. For example, there are nine projects currently being under-taken by the toxics campaign. One of these focuses on the pulp and paper industry. The pulp and paper industry is responsible for 50 percent of all organchlorine discharges into the earth's waterways. Organchlorine is dan-gerous to both humans and the natural environment; it is known to cause sterility and cancer in mammals. The project's aim is to change the production process of the industry away from bleaching procedures that use chlorine. The bulk of the pulp and paper industry is located in a number of countries, and Greenpeace pursues the project in each of them. The project director oversees all these efforts. Project directors, like campaign coordinators, take a global perspective on their respective projects. They make sure that separate Green-peace activities throughout the world support each other and fit together to advance the cause of their specific project.

Working under the project coordinators are regional and national cam-paigners. Campaigners devise specific Greenpeace activities. They identify what they take to be the most effective ways to communicate with people and change environmentally destructive practices. For purposes of this chapter, one should think of campaigners as organizers of concrete activities that aim to alter people's perceptions of particular environmental threats. To use the pulp and paper example, there are campaigners in a number of countries including the United States, Canada, Sweden, and Germany. Campaigners focus on the pulp and paper industries in their respective countries, taking into account the governmental, cultural, and industrial attributes of each country to address the problem. Regional and national campaigners are key to Greenpeace's global efforts because they understand the particular contexts within which environ-mental damage is being caused and fashion appropriate responses. They take the general intentions of projects and overall campaigns and translate them into concrete actions that are tailored for specific geographical and political contexts.

Working with campaigners are a host of assistants and volunteers who help carry out specific activities. There are literally thousands of these people throughout the world. They paint banners, circulate petitions, research issues, organize protests, and take part in direct, nonviolent actions. All levels of activ-ity are designed, at least in theory, to advance the goals of specific campaigns.

GREENPEACE'S POLITICS

Key to all Greenpeace's efforts is the insight that people do not damage the ecosystem as a matter of course. Rather, they operate in an ideational context that motivates them to do so. People are not machines; they do not respond directly to situations. In the words of Harry Eckstein, people are moved by "predispositions which pattern behavior." In the language of social science, human behavior is a matter of "oriented action." People process experience into action through general conceptions or interpretations of the world. At the most general level, but also the most important, then, an important step toward protecting the earth is to change the way vast numbers of people understand the world. It involves persuading them to abandon their anti-ecological or non-ecological attitudes and practices, and to be concerned about the environmental well-being of the planet. In short, it requires disseminating an ecological sensibility.

People respond to situations through interpretive categories that reflect a particular understanding of everyday circumstances. Such mediating orientations are cultural in character. They reflect customary, socially transmitted understandings that are embedded in the prevailing values, norms, and modes of discourse. Greenpeace targets and tries to alter these dispositions. It literally attempts to manipulate values, norms, and modes of discourse; it seeks to alter people's conceptions of reality. Greenpeace hopes that in so doing, people will undertake actions that are more respectful of the ecological integrity of the planet.

Central to Greenpeace's efforts is the practice of "bearing witness." This is a type of political action, originating with the Quakers, which links moral sensitivities with political responsibility. Having observed a morally objectionable act, one cannot turn away in avoidance. One must either take action to prevent further injustice or stand by and attest to its occurrence. While bearing witness often works to stop specific instances of environmental destruction, in general, it aims simply to present ecological injustice to the world. This offers as many people as possible an alternative understanding of contemporary affairs and sets them in motion against such practices. One way Greenpeace does this is by engaging in direct, nonviolent action and advertising it through the media worldwide.

Direct, nonviolent action is a form of political practice that shares much with the passive resistance of Mahatma Gandhi and Martin Luther King. It is a vehicle for confrontation and an outreach to other citizens. For Greenpeace, such action includes climbing aboard whaling ships, parachuting from the top of smokestacks, plugging up industrial discharge pipes, and floating a hot-air balloon into a nuclear test site. Such actions create images that can be broadcasted through the media to spark interest and concern of the largest audience.

Greenpeace is able to capture media attention because its actions are visually spectacular. According to political theorist J. Glenn Gray, human beings have what the New Testament calls "the lust of the eye." This is a primitive urge for visual stimulation; it describes the aesthetic impulse. The urge is lustful because it requires the novel, the unusual, the spectacular. The eye cannot satiate itself on the familiar, the everyday, the normal. Greenpeace actions excite the eye. They portray people taking dangerous risks. These grab attention and thus receive media coverage. By offering spectacular images to the media, Greenpeace invites the public to bear witness; it enables people throughout the world to know about environmental dangers and tries to pique their sense of outrage.

A number of years ago it was difficult to use direct, nonviolent action to change political conditions around the globe. While direct action has always been a political tool for those seeking change, the technology did not exist to publicize specific actions to a global audience. Recent innovations in communication technologies have allowed information to whip around the globe within seconds, linking distant corners of the world. Greenpeace plugs into this planetwide communication system to advertise its direct actions.

For example, in the 1970s Greenpeace ships used Morse code to communicate with their offices on land. Information from sailing expeditions would be translated in a central office and then sent out to other offices and onto the media via the telephone. This was cumbersome and expensive and compromised much of the information that could prove persuasive to public audiences. After weeks at sea, ships would return with still photographs, and these would be the most convincing images Greenpeace could use to communicate about environmental destruction taking place on the high seas.

With the advent of affordable innovations in the field of communications, Greenpeace has been able to update its ability to reach diverse and numerous audiences. Instead of Morse code, Greenpeace ships now use telephones, fax machines, and satellite uplinks to communicate with home offices. This allows for instantaneous information to be communicated and verified. Moreover, Greenpeace uses video cameras to capture its actions. Footage can be taken of whaling expeditions, ocean dumping of nuclear wastes, and discharging of toxic substances into streams and waterways. This documents more accurately actual instances of environmental destruction and the risks that Greenpeace members undertake to protect the environment. Once Greenpeace has footage and photographs of such abuse, it sends them into peoples' homes across the world through the planetwide mass communication system. Greenpeace has its own media facilities and uses these to get its information out to the public. Aside from attracting journalists and television crews to their actions, Greenpeace provides its own photographs to picture editors and has facilities to distribute edited, scripted, and narrated video news spots to television stations in eighty-eight countries within hours.

To see how Greenpeace uses direct, nonviolent action to make the world bear witness, consider its whale campaign. For years, Greenpeace has been trying to preserve whale populations and guard them from extinction. This is part of a larger campaign to generate more awareness and concern for the mass depletion of species currently taking place throughout the world. One technique Greenpeace uses to do this is direct action on the high seas. In one of its early expeditions, for instance, Greenpeace sent a ship to pursue a Russian whaling fleet. One of Greenpeace's first actions was to document the fleet's activities. Greenpeace found that the Russians were killing whales that were smaller than the official allowable size, as designated by the International Whaling Commission. To record this, Greenpeace filmed the killing of an undersized whale and took still photographs of a human being perched over it to demonstrate that it was merely a whale calf. Greenpeace noticed, moreover, that the sheer size and capability of the fleet enabled it to take large catches and thus threaten the sperm whale population in the area. To dramatize this, Greenpeace members boarded inflatable dinghies and positioned themselves between harpoon ships and pods of whales. In essence, they tried to discourage harpooners from firing by threatening to die for the cause. This proved effective as numerous times Russian whalers did not shoot their harpoons for fear of killing Greenpeace members. What turned out to be crucial was that Greenpeace captured this on film. Footage was broadcasted on television stations and still photographs were reproduced in newspapers and magazines worldwide. Greenpeace has engaged in numerous similar actions since then and continues to use such strategies.

A second example of direct action is Greenpeace's campaign to stop ozone depletion. In 1989, Greenpeace members infiltrated a DuPont manufacturing plant in Deepwater, New Jersey. Activists climbed the plant's 180-foot water tower and hung a huge, blue-ribbon banner awarding DuPont a prize for being the world's number-one ozone destroyer. (At the time, DuPont produced half of the chlorofluorocarbons [CFCs] used in the US and 25 percent of world annual production.) The following day, Greenpeace bolted a steel box—with two people inside—onto the plant's railroad tracks and blocked the export of CFCs from the plant. Greenpeace draped the box with a banner that read, "Stop Ozone Destruction Now," with a picture of the earth in the background and used it to stage an 8-hour blockade holding up rail cars carrying 44,000 gallons of CFCs.

What is curious is that, according to Greenpeace, within minutes of removing the blockade, business proceeded as usual. The plant continued to function, producing and sending out substances that are proven to erode the stratospheric ozone layer. Nonetheless, something had happened in those brief 8 hours; something had changed. While DuPont workers continued to manufacture CFCs, they now did so knowing that others knew about and were concerned with the environmental effects. Moreover, because Greenpeace captured its actions on film and distributed video news spots to television stations throughout the world, vast numbers of people were now able to understand the connection between the production of CFCs and ozone depletion. In short, the utility of Greenpeace's activity in this case had less to do with the blocking action and more to do with the message that was conveyed. Greenpeace gave the ozone issue form and used the image of disrupting DuPont's operations to send out a message of concern. As Paul Watson, an early member of Greenpeace put it, "When you do an action it goes through the camera and into the minds of people. The things that were previously out of sight and out of mind now become commonplace. Therefore you use the media as a weapon."

POLITICAL STRATEGIES

Greenpeace obviously does more than perform direct actions. It also lobbies government officials, gathers information, organizes protests and boycotts, produces record albums and other educational merchandise, and carries out scientific research. While many of these endeavors, especially lobbying, are directed specifically at states, a large percentage of Greenpeace's work is not meant to change states' policies per se but is aimed at changing the attitudes and behavior of the more general public. It seeks to change prevailing, and at times internationally shared, values, norms, and modes of discourse. It strives to "sting people with an ecological sensibility regardless of occupation, geographical location, or access to government officials. [. . .]

50

Old Age as a Time of New Opportunities

FROM *The Fountain of Age*

BETTY FRIEDAN

For many people, to approach old age is to take a step toward death. From a medical standpoint, aging has often been seen as a pathology, a process of decline and debilitation. But old age, like childhood, youth, and middle age, is a social construction that changes over time and varies from one society to another. In this reading, the author takes on personal challenges that put into question the typical view of aging and reject the idea of aging as a limitation. To age is not to be diminished, but to become something new, and possibly something better.

I knew the minute I heard about it that I wanted to go. Not necessarily for the reason that I gave myself or my friends, though I was too embarrassed to talk about it much. What was a sophisticated urban woman of my age doing, setting off on an Outward Bound wilderness-survival expedition in the North Carolina mountains with nine strangers? Of course, I had always had a secret yen for wilderness exploration, adventure; loved to read books about men sailing across the Pacific in a raft, or climbing Annapurna or Mount Everest, even though I personally was afraid of heights, and never could quite get the hang of sailing.

* * *

I had made a decade resolution, on my sixtieth birthday, that I was going to give myself some travel just for adventure, trekking in the Himalayas, or a boat ride down the Amazon, before it was too late. But that sort of thing didn't seem to appeal to my friends, and I hated traveling alone. Besides, I was always too busy: deadlines, social calendar, the women's movement, and this endless research on age.

Suffering, still, myself that denial and dread of age that made it so hard truly to celebrate my milestone sixtieth birthday, I had started seeking out individuals, environments, experiences that seemed to promise the different kind of breakthrough that I was calling the fountain of age. In a health spa in Mexico, I had come across a zesty woman whom I had thought to be around thirty-three until she came in to Christmas dinner with her children, grandchildren, and the "younger man" she was living with, a gray-haired architect. She mentioned that she had just signed up for an experiment in wilderness survival that Outward Bound was trying out in September, for the first time, for people over fifty-five. Would you send me their literature, I heard myself asking . . .

She had to be kidding! I read the list: "Standard Mountain Wilderness Age 16½+," "Managers-Executive Mountain Wilderness Age 22+," "Everglades Expedition Age 18+." And then, near the bottom, "Going Beyond—Intensive for Adults 55+." But was this for me? Besides an intimidating four-page medical exam form for my doctor to fill out, including an EKG, there were another four pages of instructions on "Physical Conditioning": ". . . work yourself up to 3 or 4 miles of continuous jogging for at least one month before your course begins. Do as many sit-ups, pushups as you can in one set on a daily basis, then add one every other day . . . pull-ups to build upper body strength. . . ."

I had never been able to do sit-ups, much less pull-ups. An athlete I'm not. I used to get all A's in school, except for D in gym. How I hated volleyball, tennis. Upper body strength? God knows I have enough to lug two or three too-heavy suitcases through crowded airports; my husband, every man I've ever traveled with, always complained about how much too much I packed; but, given feminist morality, I wouldn't let a man carry my bags for me anyhow. "You're more likely to get a hernia than I am," I would say.

* * *

I figured I would manage the whole thing by jogging three and a half miles every morning for a week, with my new mountaineering boots on. Twice around the Central Park bicycle track across from my apartment, which was three and a half miles, usually took me an hour; my friends called my seventeen-minute miles a "schlog." Even my doctor said I should try to make it more "aerobic." But when it came to filling out the Outward Bound medical exam, he said: "Are you out of your mind? This is for people who are physically tough. I can just see you halfway up some mountain cliff they'll order you to climb—it's an authoritative outfit—having an asthma attack."

Well, if he wouldn't sign it, I didn't have to go—honorably reprieved! "Come off it, Charlie," I protested. "It's a program designed for people my age. They're not going to have us climb rocks or anything dangerous like that." He called the doctor on the Outward Bound staff and they agreed I was not to do anything I didn't "feel up to." "You can go," my doctor said, "but I still think you're crazy."

* * *

Suppressing second thoughts, I spent the plane ride to Asheville and the two-hour wait in the airport proofreading an overdue manuscript, which I dropped in the airport mailbox, with a scribbled note of instructions in case I didn't come back alive, and then dashed into the airport john to change into sweatsuit and boots—ready for the trail as instructed, with a last goodbye to modern plumbing. Among a crowd of blue-jeaned teenagers getting into vans, I saw a couple of sturdy Sunday School teacher types, a mustached man who

looked like a spaghetti commercial, a hearty balding giant in suspender over-
alls (plumber, undertaker, small-town grocer?), and my friend Cecelia
Hurwich! "You actually came!" she said incredulously. "Why not!" I growled.

SATURDAY: On the Outward Bound van, heading for our first campsite, we eye
each other suspiciously. We were told to introduce ourselves first names only,
and no "what do you do, where do you come from?" As we ride across the state
line, into South Carolina, then Georgia, we are told that the Outward Bound
experience requires leaving behind your professional role and past identity
along with your city clothes, and dealing with each other on a "here-and-now"
basis. As part of that immediacy, we will not be told where we are going and
what we are going to do much before it happens. The three "leaders" giving out
all this are lean, muscular, marathon-runner types: Dave, Judy, Keg. The seven
of us victims introduce ourselves with hearty bluffness, nervous laughs, or (me)
noncommittal blankness: Ruth, Letha, Jerry, Earl, Bob, Cecelia, an unglam-
orous-looking lot, long in the tooth middle-American, except for Cecelia, unbelievably chic in Army surplus jungle camouflage from head to toe.

At the first campsite, a grassy little hill off the road, our gear is handed out:
backpack, poncho, sleeping bag, groundcloth, tin cup (which is to serve as
eating plate, drinking glass, and washing bowl), spoon, water bottle, and iodine
to purify it. We are to pack all this, plus our clothes, in the backpack, and our
city stuff will be taken away in the truck and stored until we head back home.

* * *

And now a little sunset jog, three miles down the road and back. We are
assured that Outward Bound is not competitive, each at his own pace. But
everyone's pace is clearly a lot faster than mine. That mousy-looking Letha
lags way behind the others but, to my horror, I can't even keep up with her!

* * *

Around the campfire, we share why each of us is here, "going beyond."
Ruth, a sturdy, sensible-looking woman, says with a perky gleam in her eye:
"I've had the feeling lately my horizons are closing in. I've done my best for my
kids. There aren't that many movies, plays, museums, restaurants, I want to
go to. I want some new things to do with my life. I'd like to climb a few peaks
before I settle for a rocking chair. I don't want the circle to close."

Earl, the huge southern hulk with the slightly pompous manner of a judge or
minister or Rotary Club toastmaster, was attracted, quite simply, by "the risk
of it. To come here for ten days, completely removed from anything we're used
to, not knowing what will happen, who the others will be."

This is the first and only Outward Bound group where women outnumber
men. In fact, women have only been admitted to such expeditions, which
started as all-male, in the last few years. Even now, many more *young* men venture on these wilderness trips than young women. Do women become more

adventurous with age? After they've lived through or grown beyond the feminine mystique, are women more likely to risk, or relish, new ways to test themselves than men? Could that be one reason women live longer? All the men admit they've had a yearning to do something like this for years—mountain trekking, river rafting—but wouldn't have dared come before for fear of being shown up by a lot of twenty-five-year-olds.

I smooth my sleeping bag over a flat, fragrant bed of pine needles. Since that little bottle of water we each carry is all we have to wash with, and drink (no stream near this camp), I congratulate myself on having brought along a big tube of Noxzema—I can "wash" my face, hands, underarms in the dark, without water, and wipe it off with Kleenex (or even leaves?). Lying there, looking at the stars from my sleeping bag, I feel surprisingly comfortable, free of the vague fears and guilts that keep me brooding, awake, at home. On this hard ground, alone, I don't feel dreary, gray, bitter, heavy, lonely as in those grim hotel-motel rooms. I give, and get, too much of my energy now in that impersonal public life, where strangely I sometimes have a hint of that old nameless feeling women used to complain of, "trapped" inside their role as housewives and mothers (or men in their breadwinner role). *I'm somebody's wife, somebody's mother; I'm a lawyer bucking for partner; I'm a spokesperson for women's liberation—but who am I myself?*

It feels good, to be stripped down to one's self, away from the role. It's a long time since I've had this feeling of trying something really new . . . not knowing what to expect.

SUNDAY: I wake up suddenly, in the black night. My psychological alarm clock works—it's 5:00 A.M. Jerry, who has volunteered to do breakfast, is lighting the stove. I'm glad of the chance to go to the john, "wash," and get "dressed" before the others wake up. Does one get more or less inhibited, prize the dignity of privacy more as one gets older? Or does one lose the vanity, modesty, or sexual inhibition of youth? Each one of us here seems to map out her/his own space in this open place. At first, I go quite far away to change, behind a screen of trees or brush. After a day or so, I don't stray so far; I "change" inside my sleeping bag, and, like the others, merely avert my eyes, washing my teeth in the same water that will also clean my cup after breakfast.

The Chatooga River, where we head now for two days of shooting rapids, is where they made the movie *Deliverance.* We are handed out life jackets and hard-hat helmets. We pick up three guides, who show us how to paddle the rubber rafts, "drawing" right or left, and "ferrying" across the current by heading beyond where you really have to go, then letting the current swing you back. After lunch (sardines, bread, and cheese eaten sitting on a rock), all the guides and instructors get in one raft and our "crew" is on its own, in the other two. The rapids begin to get scary. We take turns in different positions. I do not volunteer to be captain. I'm glad no one here knows that I am supposed to be a leader of women. Sitting up in the bow, paired with that big guy, Earl,

I begin to get the hang of it: the rhythmic swing of the paddle, the flick of the wrist, and when and how to set the blade against the current, or "draw" or "sweep" in longer circles. They have put Earl on the left and me on the right, because "draw left" is the crucial stroke to get into, then out of, most of these rapids. After we miss a few, it becomes clear that Earl, despite his brawn, does not have the extra upper body strength for a strong left draw. But if I sweep out to the right, and, Cece behind me backpaddles, Earl's left draw works okay. "Have you done this before?" asks Judy, surprised at my sudden competence. "In summer camp," I remember. "In college. And on my honeymoon. The Songo River." About fifty, forty years ago.

We head into Stage III of the river—not the most dangerous, but getting there. To prepare for tomorrow, when we'll be shooting rapids with drops of twelve feet and more—Corkscrew Rapid, Sock 'Em Dog, Screaming Left Turn, Five Falls, Jawbone—we are given a drill on what to do if you fall overboard. I lie on my back, stiff, with my feet up so they don't get stuck under a rock, and let myself be carried by the rushing current down the rapids like a log. At the bottom the entire waterfall roars over my head and up my nose. For a minute, I panic—I can't get my breath. But it's not asthma, just water. I finally catch the rope, get pulled into shore.

Now we go over Bull Sluice, a tortuous tunnel rapid that seems to drop twenty feet at least. You have to lean into the raft, keeping yourself anchored under its rim so you don't get swept out as the raft slams from one rock wall to the other, is turned around, and then hurled forward and down by the roaring water. The guide gets in our raft for this one. "Drift forward. Draw left." Earl draws, I sweep right, we plunge over, there's nothing to hang on to, the raft is hurtling down, slamming into the wall, I lean in, lean in, dig my feet under the tube and lean in, we hit bottom, and paddle like crazy. Nobody falls in—but coming out of the turn we get stuck on a rock, have to get out in the water and push-pull the raft off.

Coming across a calm stretch to a small beach where we'll camp, I take in the cliffs and the trees and the tired soaking amazed exhilaration that I'm still alive—what a beautiful river! Deliverance indeed.

* * *

MONDAY: For Stage IV of this Chatooga River, a guide takes charge of each raft again. These next rapids are too tricky for novice amateurs to navigate—so maybe it wasn't just cowardice, my not wanting to play captain here. Starting out, I feel scared a bit still, but after that terrified moment, poised at the brink, I'm excited but calm underneath, paddling forward, then feverishly into, across the current, being twirled around, leaning in, bracing my feet, as we go over the falls, backwards—Jawbone, Shoulder Bone, Corkscrew, Rapid, Sock 'Em Dog, Screaming Left Turn—and then coming out of it, paddling frantically into that calm stretch at the bottom, soaking wet but not so cold today because of the socks Earl told me to wear under my sneakers. In the calm stretch below Five Falls, I take my turn as captain, and manage to steer the clumsy raft from the stern.

The young guides, who've spent years mastering each rock and rapid of this tricky beautiful river, tell us how they dreaded taking on people as "old" as we were purported to be. They figured we would hardly have the strength to paddle the rafts ourselves; they'd have to drag us through. They'd practiced CPR and emergency rescue drills and splints for our brittle, breakable bones. But, as it turns out, they didn't have to exert any extra effort and we are the first group in years where no one has fallen overboard!

At the "circle" before we take leave of the guides, they try to figure out what made the difference. "You weren't trying to show off and outdo each other, like the kids do." Maybe we've outgrown macho, even the men? "You have better balance and survival instincts." "We had to in order to have survived this long," Earl cracks. The guides had been sure we wouldn't have enough "power" for those tricky turns, and at first we didn't seem to. But in the end, we somehow acquired as much "power" as was needed. "You listened more intently," Dave ventured. "You cooperated more with each other, you weren't trying to show off, paddling in six different directions. I guess you made up for whatever actual differences in muscular strength by cooperation." Or, maybe, wisdom? "And will," Judy said; "you really wanted to do it."

* * *

TUESDAY: We squat on the ground, learning to take our bearings with map and compass. The troika leaves us to make our own way over the ridge, to our next destination, across Steele's Creek. It's clear from the map that we will have to leave the trail and bushwhack our way down the mountainside to the creek. Bob and Cece take the lead positions, trailblazers; Earl volunteers for the rear. He has been so effortlessly the leader, I figure he's holding back to give the others a chance. But I get very touchy when he keeps coming up behind me and offering me a hand, when there's a rock to climb or a steep slide to negotiate. I find a big stick to sort of lean on, climbing—it makes me feel more balanced. At least hand me that stick, he says, as I wriggle under a fallen branch, with that pack on my back. Oh well . . . once we leave the trail, it's rough, scratchy, dense. Going down, you have to lean backward or it feels like the pack will overbalance you and fall on top. It's hard to climb under things with that pack. The stick doesn't really help. I go down from tree to tree, using branches as brakes. My pack begins to feel heavy again. I try sliding down on my behind— it works. The seat of my pants is now caked with mud, but who's looking!

It's getting dark already, surely it's not that late. It's been sunny and warm up until now; a storm is coming. The ridge we've been climbing down suddenly ends in a kind of precipice, no way down to the creek which we can now hear. We have to retrace our way back up that steep hill I just slid down and go over the next ridge. It starts to rain. The creek is wide, and not all that shallow. Those rocks look slippery. The three guys make a human bridge on the rocks, passing our backpacks across hand to hand. Earl falls in. I decide not even to try jumping from rock to rock. I'll go across in the creek itself; surely jungle boots, sweat pants won't take long to dry.

As we get out our boring bread, cheese, tuna for wet lunch, a "circle" is called. The troika, which has rejoined us, orders all food and common camp gear into the middle. What now? What's *now* is twenty-four hours of "solitary"—each one of us is to be deposited in our own little spot of wilderness along the creek, to survive alone for the next twenty-four hours. With four pieces of rope (to make a shelter out of our ponchos) and a ration of crackers, cheese, trail mix (raisins, sunflower seeds, granola), and an apple or orange. I've read about those solitary wilderness vigils but never thought they'd ask our age group to do it!

My spot is a dense jungle of black-green vines, wild giant rhododendrons choking tall trees (pine, spruce, whatever), rotting branches, stumps, rocks, and dank masses of vegetation rising rather steeply from the creek bed. Only one place, six or eight feet square, seems level enough between some trees to set up camp in. Some big fallen branches are clotting it up. I drag them out of the way, clear the rocks off my floor of decaying leaves. It's going to rain again, soon. I string up the poncho between four trees.

* * *

It's very noisy in these woods, crashing sounds. Did I hear Judy say something about bears? Should I sing to scare any animals away? At least, no rapists or other human beings will be prowling around on a night like this. The funny thing is, all my life I've been terrified of being alone. And now, I'm not even scared! Being alone is not my problem—it's how to keep my sleeping bag from getting wetter. I remember the warnings about hypothermia: if you get too cold and wet, your body temperature falls, and you could die even if you don't feel freezing cold.

After endless hours, too wet to sleep, I see a light approaching. It's Dave, checking, "solitary" or no. That's nice and flexible, in the face of such a storm. Am I cold? Oh no, I say cheerily, just a bit wet. From underneath, for some strange reason. He says it's because my groundcloth is sticking out beyond the edges of my shelter; it draws the water in. I should have tucked it under, all around. After he leaves, I kick myself for being so macho—and take an asthma pill, just in case.

* * *

WEDNESDAY: I don't think I slept at all. But suddenly the rain has stopped. I can see the creek again; it's getting light.

* * *

Back at the campsite, the troika has made a huge fire and cooked a hot chowder. Judy has even baked gingerbread. I toast my wool-wet body by that fire until stream pours out around me. It starts to rain again; we make a circle under the tarp to share our solitary adventures.

* * *

Earl invented a plastic-container portable toilet ("at my age I have to pee a lot, I didn't want to get out of my sleeping bag in the middle of the night") and spent two hours "counting all my blessings," after which he slept through that roaring storm. Ruth and Jerry both thought they'd heard, or felt, the paws of bears on their backs. Far from giving us an easier solo than the younger groups, Dave says it was the worst storm in all his years of Outward Bound solos. Bob and Earl both insist they didn't experience the "spiritual inner change" such solitary vigils are supposed to bring about. They "didn't have time to meditate."

* * *

I tell them about my lifelong terror of being alone, which I must have gotten over last night. I tell them about a dream I had before I came here—about a marvelous adventurous man I was secretly drawn to, but kept picking a fight with. Was that man my adventurous independent self, which keeps me "going beyond" even though I dread following it, in my fear of being alone?

Cece tells us how all her life she'd been "a terribly dependent person, leaning on my parents, my husband, even my children. I was a good hostess, dressed beautifully, did a little tennis, modern dance, interior decorating, but I never did anything really hard. Then, one day, I fell asleep driving; my car crashed and turned over; I nearly died. When I survived, I knew I had to start living my life." She went back to school, was divorced, started backpacking. "Now I'm so independent, I don't need anybody. All the things I used to need a man for I can do myself now—taxes, money, changing a tire. It scares me sometimes how independent I've gotten." Then she adds: "I like being back with you guys better than being alone, but being by myself isn't necessarily lonely."

* * *

THURSDAY: By morning, between the shared body heat and the wind, my bag and clothes and even my jungle boots are dry. We set off again, with compass and map, taking bearings off various mountain peaks, heading for a poetic-sounding campsite called Starry Night. Trails keep petering out in precipices; we have to bushwhack again, slow, tough going, much signaling from front to rear, calling "circles" to consult. It no longer bothers me, bringing up the rear, though some remnant of pride makes me try to get a little ahead whenever we're on level ground. * * * Cece, who boasts she trekked over Kilimanjaro in Africa last year, finds a trail that isn't on our map at all, which leads us to a paved road. We get to a dirty campsite—which turns out unpoetically to be Starry Night—by the middle of the afternoon.

* * *

As we sit around the campfire, groaning at Earl's increasingly bawdy jokes told with that parsonlike pomposity, two strange figures crash out of the darkness. Two blond girls (I do mean girls; they don't look fifteen) are introduced as Ann and Kitty, our "climbing instructors" for tomorrow. They don't look much like Hillary and Tenzing. "What are your-um-qualifications?" Bob asks, a bit gracelessly. It seems they are professional mountain climbers, who have been scaling rock and ice peaks all over America and the world for some years now.

FRIDAY: We are given hard-hat helmets again, and heavier ropes, to knot around our legs like diapers and secure with belaying pins. We simulate flat dry runs "on belay"—climbing a cliff with a rope around your waist, attached to the waist of a person at the top, secured in turn by a rope around a tree, as she belays your slack, or holds or hauls you up if you fall—and "on rappel," where you go down a sheer perpendicular cliff by bracing your feet against the rock, butt out, harnessed like an elevator to a rope which she plays out from above as you descend.

* * *

Now, one by one, we each have to belay up a sixty-foot practice cliff, and rappel down thirty feet or so on the other side. Cece is my belay partner. She looks like she's climbing up the walls of a four- or five-story building, as I belay the rope from on top, but she doesn't have any trouble. I can't even seem to get started myself.

* * *

I keep losing my footing and swing on the ropes out of control, but thirty feet is nothing after that spreadeagle. I more or less kick-fall myself down that rock, *fast,* so I never really do get the hang of rappel or feel in control, as I finally did on the river raft; I just want to get it over with. It's not as if I ever intend to rappel down a cliff in my life again.

* * * [L]ate afternoon, we pick up our backpacks to climb Table Rock—a mountain with a flat rock on top like the one where the spaceship landed in *Close Encounters of the Third Kind.* Climbing that mountain, even with a pack on my back again, is practically a pleasure—it's a *human* trail, with ground to put your feet on. At least I can redeem my ignominy by concocting a gourmet dinner. Bob is lugging new cans of chicken and tomato sauce—curry again or chicken cacciatore? The trail climbs like a corkscrew to the base of Table Rock, up through a crevice, and around and around.

Finally, we come out on the top of Table Rock. The whole mountain range sweeps below us. The sun is setting. It's windy. No trees on top of this mountain, no soft pine needles, just hard rock. "Let's not bother with dinner," someone says. "Too late, too cold." Bob explodes: "I've carried these two heavy cans all the way up here, we're damn well getting dinner out of it!" I dump my pack by Cece and get to work on chicken cacciatore—I don't think Bob really likes curry. "Easy on the spices," he begs.

* * *

Letha says: "It makes me wonder, all these things I've done this week I would never have thought I could do—it makes me wonder what other things I've never done that I could do now." I have a strange stunned feeling of really "going beyond" today—of risking something I was truly afraid of, and surviving. But it wasn't just the height, the falling, I was afraid of. I risked doing something I really was no good at—and survived. There's a headiness to doing something at this age you've never done before, when you don't have to prove anything anymore.

* * *

[SATURDAY:] We're to end with a marathon run back to Outward Bound headquarters, where we're spending the last night. We change to shorts, running shoes, right there on the road, no one bothers with modesty now. "Go all out, this last time," Dave says. I schlog along as usual, but what the hell—I step up my speed on the home stretch and finally manage to pass someone (Ruthie, Letha?), and there on top of the little hill waits a crowd of young people. They've completed their own training, I guess, and are cheering us ancients. I sprint up that hill in real all-out style—and then stop at the top and put my hands on my knees to catch my breath. No real point to pass the finish line ahead of Ruth or Letha.

The seven of us go to the cabin where we'll spend the night, on bunk beds that look drearier than pine needles. The bonds between us jar against these room walls. * * *

Each group was to perform a skit after dinner. On the trail Bob and I had concocted a three-act drama called *Going Way Beyond,* trusting the others to improvise their parts. In our plot it turns out that offering Outward Bound to geriatric cases over fifty-five was a sinister scheme to collect the insurance they take out on all our lives, because the river rafting and rock climbing which only test the young are sure to kill us. So instead of toilet paper, the instructors say look for shiny three-petal leaves, etc. We survive, unkillable despite our years, until they direct us to take a "trust fall" off Table Rock. As one by one we back over the edge, the leaders weep: "What commitment!"

The kids howl. Enormous applause. A young girl says to me later in the washhouse, "That wasn't fair, you know how to do it better." She keeps staring at my white-streaked hair: "You people actually *climbed* Table Rock?" To my amazement, Cece seemed as nervous about improvising her own lines as I was on the cliff. To each! Later, in a quiet back room, we old ones share finally our real-life identities—and the differences we will take away.

"After this, you feel you can do anything," says Jerry, who owns a computer business in Iowa. "But how do we keep on 'going beyond' back home?" He's fifty-six, and for the first time he and his wife are going to be alone together, with their last kid off to school.

"The people I know back home think I'm crazy for doing such things at my age," says Earl, who is seventy-two. He sold his prosperous insurance agency after nursing his wife for seven years before she died. Now, he goes all over the world, consulting on pension plans, taking jobs that will get him to new places where he wants to go. Getting a bit bored with travel, he's now thinking of volunteering at his local community college to teach illiterates to read. He also seems to have a number of lady friends he likes to take dancing. "I lead a double life," he says.

Bob, heading for sixty, let his partners buy him out of the Madison Avenue advertising agency he ran, and now runs his own one-man shop out of his home in New Jersey. He got tired of the commuting rat race. "I began asking myself what kind of life do I want to *live*?" he says. He's been trying his hand at a lot of things he'd never done before—sailing, gliding. "But this is a different kind of going beyond: to have been with a group of strangers—who became closer than family—for eight days, and to have seen nothing but noble manifestations of the human spirit. With all we went through, there was no jealousy, spite, meanness, cruelty, selfishness, artificiality; we were all completely open with each other, without boasting about or even knowing the jobs that define each of us at home."

"I learned here that I can be much more than I ever thought I could," says Cece, who amazes everybody by revealing she is sixty-four. She looks thirty-five—until you get close enough to take in the lines and wisdom of her face. "I was always a woman people looked at. Now suddenly I'm the oldest woman in the room. Now, instead of trying so hard to look younger, I want to explore my own aging process. I've been limiting myself. Now, I'm less interested in the outside, in being beautiful. I want to find new, harder things to do."

* * *

Letha is a social worker in Kansas, a widow who got her master's degree after she nursed her own daughter through a serious illness, then started a Halfway House to help young psychiatric patients get back into the community. Now, she wants to go beyond that and run a hospice for the dying.

I am last in the circle. I say who I am. The women, it seems, have known all along, but had not broken my cover. "I never had much use for women's lib," Bob says in confusion. Earl is incredulous. "Then, you must be a celebrity," he says. "I just liked you for your gutsy spirit." I could have kissed him (and later did).

* * *

And then I had this glimmer about the fountain of age, which I shared with the others—that going beyond youth, we each might finally be able to celebrate being who we really are. "To be who you really are is to be celebrated," I suggest now to the others. The strength we found on the expedition into the wilderness to risk *being ourselves,* to go beyond those roles we've leaned on and hidden behind—and the wisdom, the compassion, the sensitivity and flexibility we've all seen, in ourselves and each other, on this expedition into the wilderness—are these perhaps unique strengths that can emerge in age, which we don't expect, or recognize, or value enough in ourselves or others if we only measure ourselves against the standards of youth?

"I forgot my age," Cece said. "I giggled again, which I stopped doing back home." Judy, our respected instructor, who is in her thirties (I had thought her older), says: "I'm confronting my own aging. People see me as old because I'm over thirty now." She's left teaching, where she could have "stayed thirty years and retired with a good pension, but I wouldn't have lived." This winter she'll work as a cashier at a ski resort and her husband as an instructor, to learn the ropes so they can branch out with a new life for themselves, in the mountains.

* * *

During the next few years, after this first adventure in "going beyond," I began—more or less consciously, with a shifting mixture of exhilaration and fear, spurts of ease, bogs of dreary doubt—to move onto new trails in my own life. I certainly didn't "retire." I didn't actually even say to myself: *Face it, after sixty, after sixty-five, it's a no-win proposition, to keep on playing the old games, trying to beat the odds, to stay on top, in the old way, in work or women's movement politics—or in search of love partners, or dinner party invitations.*

I still got caught up in those games—maybe it was not possible to be completely free of them—and, I must admit, they got more and more depressing with age. Maybe because they didn't seem worth the effort anymore? But the sense that it was possible now to *go beyond* those games, in work and love, became more and more clear to me as I listened to men and women who were doing just that, and tried some new directions of my own. I had moments of panic when they didn't seem to be succeeding, or I couldn't see where they were leading. But I was surprisingly undismayed even when they failed, and I became more and more lighthearted at following serendipitous openings, at risking new ways.

It was a liberating revelation, "going beyond" on the Chatooga River, that we ancients, pooling our energies and the skills of our life experience, were able to surmount those dangerous rapids with fewer casualties and less need of outside care or rescue than any younger group. Evidently even in a task that demands the muscular strength easier to come by in youth, qualities that may emerge with age—wisdom born of experience, freedom from youthful competitive compulsion, cooperation, empathy—can more than compensate for whatever losses of muscle power or memory also come with age. I stopped worrying that I could no longer count on total recall of an interview if I didn't take notes; the significance was clearer, deeper, and not forgotten, months later—and I do take notes. To discover that even unathletic I, with some new training, could manipulate a boat around those rapids and bring back skills unused for forty years, convinced me more than any of my research that I might try new, completely different ways of working—in my writing, lecturing, teaching—or even, for a change, something I had never tried before, that I might not be very good at (the cello?). Of course, that is the real liberation of age: the amazing lightness and solidity of no longer feeling the need to prove oneself, to be the best, to outdo the others, to compete—and of being able to fail. What does it really matter?

* * *

On my expedition, it became clear on those mountain trails that Earl Arthurs, who turned out to be the oldest of us all, well into his seventies, was the strongest, and most effective, and sensitive in his leadership, of all our group. But his stroke alone was not really all that strong, we discovered in the rapids. And how gracefully he held back, climbing, to give the younger men and us women a chance to lead, and how unobtrusively and gently he helped me over those rough spots. I was becoming convinced now that such skills as emerged in Earl, and all of us, on that mountain trail "going beyond," could be discovered, named, nourished, and used in our day-to-day lives. I was almost certain they could be of value to the professions, corporations, government, or community service from which we are now expected to retire. I was sure there could be a liberation, with age, to use such abilities to meet real needs, and for real rewards, in our communities outside the bureaucracies of professional career. Somehow we have to "go beyond" that division between "love" and "work" that defined us in our youth.

As for love, in those ten days "going beyond," the bonds that developed among previous strangers, women and men, of disparate background and temperament—but with a common yearning and willingness to risk new adventure—were so solid and comfortable that no one felt lonely, unsupported; we became a kind of family. (Marlene's group meets every year now, for some new adventure. Ours is contemplating a canoe trip in the Everglades.) But these bonds were not based on the sexual coupling or the social competition or the rearing of children or even the shared memories that created and sustained the bonds of our youth.

After my expedition, I became more and more conscious of the need and possibility of nourishing such families of friends, for myself and other women my age, widowed, divorced, whose children were rightfully now absorbed in their own childrearing families and who were not likely to remarry. Surely, men had such needs too, that might or might not be met as couple, in the old way.

After, finally, coming to terms with the parameters of my own age, I became more and more convinced that it *was* possible—though it will not necessarily happen unless we make it happen—to "go beyond" one's previous limitations and pitfalls, the self-defeating, paralyzing traps and plateaus, in both work and love, responding to and using serendipity as it might emerge, or even painful tragedy, in the most surprising ways. But I didn't yet have a clear map. All I could do was try to make sense of my own and other people's experiences of "going beyond" the dreams, expectations, limitations, dilemmas, and problems that defined our youth to that new place that can expand, rather than restrict, the parameters of our age.

51

An Alternative to Globalization

BILL McKIBBEN

Poverty, lack of technology, poor health, and illiteracy throughout the world have been the focus of international development efforts of industrial nations for the past five decades. With the rise of globalization these efforts became synonymous with the incorporation of the poorest areas of the world into the global economic system. Now some countries, locales, and groups are raising questions about globalization and looking for ways to improve their way of life without participating in a system which they believe favors those who are already rich, strong, and technologically advanced. As Bill McKibben recognizes, this may only be a dream, or it may be a sign of the future.

The eastern end of the village of Gorasin, on the edge of the Louhajang River in the district of Tangail, in the nation of Bangladesh, has no store that we would recognize, no car, no electric lines, no television. No telephone. There are just small fields, a cow, some chickens, barefoot children, banana palms swaying in the breeze. The call to prayer from a nearby muezzin drifts over the cropland. It is about as far from the center of the world as you can possibly get. And that may be the point.

Hovering over all the issues about the World Bank and the World Trade Organization and the spread of genetically modified crops, hovering over everything that's happened since the 1999 Battle of Seattle is a big question: Is there really any alternative to the General Course of things? Is there some imaginable future that does not lead through the eternal Westernization, the endless economic expansion, that is the gospel of our time? Is there some alternative to Progress?

Gorasin is one of those places that suggests there might be. "Suggests" is about as strong as I'd like to get. Alternatives get quickly overwhelmed in the modern world, co-opted or submerged beneath the staggering flow of business as usual. But, at least right now, life in Gorasin is worth a look.

If we think about Bangladesh at all, it is as a basket case. A hundred and thirty million people crowded into an area the size of Wisconsin. Constant flooding, with the regular scattering of killer cyclones. A 10-letter word for woe.

If you ask the World Bank what needs to happen in Bangladesh, their answer—detailed in a report called "Bangladesh 2020"—is to turn it into another Thailand or, better yet, another Singapore: to ramp up its growth rate, produce crops like cut flowers for export, "manage" a "transition to urbanization, and exploit its huge supply of cheap labor to allow a leap up the development ladder. "There is no alternative to accelerated growth." If you ask Monsanto,[1] the key is high-yielding varieties of rice including new genetically engineered strains: "golden rice," say, designed to eliminate vitamin A deficiency. If you ask international donor agencies, the secret is more microcredit, like the pioneering Grameen Bank projects that have captured worldwide attention in recent years. "If you want to work on misery, Bangladesh is the ultimate misery you can have," says Atiq Rahman, of the Bangladesh Center for Advanced Studies, a local NGO.[2]

Those are the standard views: that Bangladesh lives in a state of back wardness that can be "fixed" through an application of technology, capital, exposure to the discipline of the markets. To quote from the World Bank report, "Backwardness in the form of cheap labor gives Bangladesh a strong competitive potential edge." In other words, an inexhaustible supply of poor people willing to work at low wages is its greatest asset. In the words of Rahman, who co-authored the Bank report, Bangladeshis are now at a "survival" stage and need to make a "quantum leap" to some higher level of development, a leap that inevitably leads to urbanization, an export-oriented economy, more fertilizer, big electric power plants. And when you look at the country's sad statistics for nutrition, for life expectancy, for literacy, then it's easy to defend the conventional wisdom: The average person dies at 60, and the infant mortality rate is 10 times that of the United States.

But there is another way of looking at things, a Gorasin way, one developed closer to home, less despairing and less grandiose at the same time. "People say that it's a miracle Bangladesh can survive its food and energy crises, that it somehow perseveres," Sajed Kamal, a solar energy educator, told me as we walked the town's fields. "The real miracle, though, is that you could contrive a way to have a food crisis. If you stick something in the ground here, it grows." So Bangladesh, it's worth noting, is able to feed itself.

Our guides that day were the people who lived in Gorasin, who lived in small huts, smaller than trailer homes. They were showing us sesame seed plants, loofah sponge gourds, eggplants, sugarcane, bamboo. Onions, pulses, all manner of local leafy greens. All grown without pesticides, without fertilizer, and without seed imported from the laboratories of the West. Gorasin sits in a large self-declared pesticide-free zone, one of several organic oases established

---

1. Monsanto is a leading biotechnology corporation specializing in genetically modified agricultural products (ed.).

2. NGO is the acronym for Non-Governmental Organization. Thousands of privately funded (many through small contributions) organizations work worldwide to reduce poverty, increase literacy and health, address environmental problems, improve human rights, build low-cost housing, and promote small-scale technology (ed.).

around the country by adherents of the *Nayakrishi,* or "New Agriculture" movement. The movement arose in response to numerous environmental hazards that the villagers believe were traceable to pesticides.

"When we women went to collect water, we would be affected," one villager was saying. She was twentysomething, beautiful, gregarious. "Our skin would absorb the poisons. We would get itchiness, get gastric trouble. Now we've adopted our own solution. The water is pure again."

"The cows used to eat the grass and drop dead," one man added. "And then the villagers would fight each other."

"We grew up with a saying: 'We Bengalis are made of rice and fish,'" said another man. "Then the fish started catching diseases. We are not scientists, but we made the connection between pesticide and fish death. Since we've started organic farming, the fish are now healthier and more plentiful."

"A fertilized plant jumps up fast and falls right over," said a third. "Our plants are strong and healthy. Theirs, you eat it and you get sick. The minute you say 'Nayakrishi' in the market, though, people will pay more, because they know they're saving on health care."

A few miles away, at the Nayakrishi training school for the Tangail district, 25 varieties of papaya are growing. A hundred and twelve varieties of jackfruit, all cataloged by the farmers by taste, size, color, season, habitat. Wicker baskets and clay pots in a darkened shed contain 300 varieties of local rice, 20 kinds of bitter gourd, 84 varieties of local beans.

"Do you know how much it costs to build a gene bank like the ones where botanists store plant varieties?" asks Farhad Mazhar, a founder of the Center for Development Alternatives, known by its Bengali acronym, UBINIG, the Dhaka-based NGO that helped launch the Nayakrishi movement. "No scientist can afford to catalog hundreds of varieties of rice. But farmers are doing it as part of household activity. Our little seed station has more vegetables than the national gene bank, which spends millions. But we can do it for free."

For free, and in the process, they insist, they can rejuvenate village life. Farida Akhter, Mazhar's partner running UBINIG, is one of Bangladesh's leading feminists. She set up the nation's only women's bookstore and led a long fight against contraceptive abuses by international agencies. But if you ask her what single step would do the most to improve the lot of Bengali women, she does not hesitate: "I'd want rural women to have control over seeds again. That's women's power, or was before the multinationals started selling their new varieties in the last few decades. Traditionally, the woman is the one who knows what a good seed is, what will germinate, how to store it. Maybe they like the sound of the seed when they flick it, the weight of it on the winnowers, how it looks. They'll cut a seed with their teeth and listen to the sound it makes. They know how to dry it, how many times to put it under the sun, and whether to use the morning sun or the afternoon sun. Men used to discuss with their wives what kind of crop to raise for next year. But now they listen to the seed seller. The woman has become redundant, a burden."

Farhad Mazhar was in Seattle for the WTO protests. "I strongly believe in globalization," he says. "I'm not a national chauvinist. We need more interaction at the international level. We need cultural exchanges, all that sort of thing. But that's not happening here in Bangladesh, and it's not happening in all the other countries like us. We're just a source of raw materials." Certainly not a source of ideas. Ideas flow the other way.

Bangladesh became a country in 1971, following a brief civil war. "Civil war" is actually a misnomer: Pakistan, backed rhetorically by the United States, carried out what may have been the most efficient genocide of the 20th century, killing as many as 3 million Bengalis in nine months before a resistance army aided by Indian troops drove them out. That carnage was followed in short order by famine and cyclones. Then a military coup shut off the new nation's political life. Since then, Bangladesh has made the world news only sporadically, usually when the waters of the Ganges and the Brahmaputra overflow their banks. (Two or three thousand need to drown before it makes the back pages of American newspapers.) As a relatively calm Muslim country, without geopolitical significance and with a minuscule economy, it would be hard to imagine a less newsworthy place. But 1 human in 50 now lives there, and its grand history stretches back into the mists far enough to qualify it as a cradle of civilization. Still, for the rest of the planet, its only outstanding feature today is poverty.

"Poverty is the most salable commodity we have here," says Khushi Kabir, a longtime grassroots organizer. Experts jet in, stay at the Sheraton in Dhaka, issue reports, and leave. Local academics vie for "consultancies," making bids that sometimes require kickbacks to government officials. And the expert advice has often gone spectacularly wrong. A huge Flood Action Plan, for instance, called for ever-higher embankments to keep the rivers at bay. But Bangladesh is not Holland: The huge silt deposits kept raising riverbeds, and the floodwater that eventually topped the dikes had nowhere to drain. "One area in the southwest was underwater for 10 years," says Kabir.

Later, in an effort to curb diarrheal disease, UNICEF helped drill thousands of deep tube wells around the country and ran advertisements urging people to stop drinking surface water. But they neglected to sample the subsurface geology, and so tens of millions began drinking water contaminated with naturally occurring arsenic. The water has killed some already; others, disfigured by the melanoma lesions that arsenic causes, can no longer be given in marriage. UNICEF's new ads tell people not to drink from the tube wells.

Other international aid has worked better: The country's fertility rate has fallen quickly and the International Center for Diarrheal Disease Research has cut the incidence of cholera, which is endemic in the region. But local activists say the benefits aren't worth the costs: "Absolutely we would be better off if everyone trying to 'help' us just went home," says Mazhar. "If they did, then the people in the country would be able to come up with their own ideas."

Those ideas would, necessarily, center on village life. Though Dhaka, a chaotic megacity with a population uncountably north of 10 million, dominates the political life of the nation, 80 percent of Bengalis still live in rural areas. Which is not to say that they live in Iowa, or the Punjab, or any of the other places that the word *rural* conjures in our minds. In the first place, Bangladesh is almost as much liquid as solid. There is water everywhere you look, and much of the year many villages are accessible mostly by canoe. Land holdings tend to be tiny, many under an acre. And the place feels, to a Westerner, almost unbelievably crowded. The population density dwarfs that of India or China; it approaches the density of Hong Kong. Even in rural farming districts, there is simply no such thing as a lonely road. Rickshaws, bicycles, buses, draft animals, and pedestrians jam every vista. One Bengali said the reason his country did not excel at most international sports was simple: "Where is the room for a soccer pitch?"

That picture of a standing-room-only floodplain sounds pretty desperate to our ears, as if the population of our Eastern seaboard were ordered to somehow make a living in Chesapeake Bay. But at least for the moment this huge population of Bengalis manages to feed itself. Partly that's a result of the "Green Revolution," the rice strains that, whatever their toll in pesticides and fertilizers, have boosted grain yields. But mostly that's a function of the simple biology of a hot delta. Floods regularly renew the soil, the sun shines most of the year, and so fruit trees grow in two years to a girth that would require five decades on a New England hillside. Plants jump from the ground. There's an almost obscene lushness everywhere. And the large population means that there are plenty of people to manage that lushness, to help make the most of it.

Here's what I mean. We were sitting one day on the front porch of a one-acre organic farm about an hour from Dhaka. It was a hobby farm, whose owner was mostly concerned with his rosebushes. Still, without getting up, we could see guava, lemon, pomegranate, coconut, betel nut, mango, jackfruit, apple, lichee, chestnut, date, fig, and bamboo trees, as well as squash, okra, eggplant, zucchini, blackberry, bay leaf, cardamom, cinnamon, and sugarcane plants, not to mention dozens of herbs, far more flowers, and a flock of ducklings. A chicken coop produced not just eggs and meat, but waste that fed a fishpond, which in turn produced thousands of pounds of protein annually, and a healthy crop of water hyacinths that were harvested to feed a small herd of cows, whose dung in turn fired a biogas cooking system. "Food is everywhere, and in 12 hours it will double," Kamal said.

So what do you do with that kind of fertility? The World Bank report recommends that you figure out ways to grow "higher-value" crops for export; they cite the Colombian cut-flower industry as an example. It could supply vegetables to other parts of Asia, "graduating from a minor supplier at present to a major player in the long term." That would probably generate the most money, cash that would be plowed into expanding the industries that could take advantage of the country's cheap labor pool.

Or you could follow UBINIG'S advice and focus on farms like those of Gorasin. "Any 'development' policy here must give agriculture priority," says Farhad Mazhar. "Don't destroy it any further, because you've got no way to take care of those people." The choice you make will depend on your sense of the future. The sheer growth in human numbers * * * could mean that you have no choice but to make a mad dash for modernization, figuring out every possible way to convert your country's resources to cash. But it will also depend on how you see the people living in Bengali villages. Are they desperately poor? Or is, in Mazhar's words, "the whole Western construction of poverty" suspect? "The real question," he insists, "is, What are the livelihood strategies of the bulk of people, and what kind of development enhances or destroys those strategies?"

That is, do you want a few lightbulbs run off rooftop solar generators, or do you want to run electric lines to the three-quarters of the country that currently lacks them? Do you want more people moving to the cities, or do you want to develop an organic agriculture that can absorb more labor? Those are questions, not answers. Rahman, the development expert, says that rooftop solar is only a beginning: "Once people have the 'little power,' they want 'big power' from electric lines," he says. Even though big power in a poor country can imply expense, pollution, dependence.

Here's another way of asking the same thing: How do you address the problem of vitamin A deficiency? Large numbers of poor people around South Asia suffer from a variety of micronutrient deficiencies—their diets lack sufficient iron or zinc or vitamin A, also known as beta-carotene. If you don't get enough, you can go blind. In 1999, European researchers announced they had managed to genetically modify rice so that it would express vitamin A to anyone who ate a bowlful, as surely as if they had popped a vitamin pill. Within a year the major biotech companies had announced agreements to license the technology free of charge to poor nations. As *Time* magazine put it last year, "The biotech industry sees golden rice as a powerful ally in its struggle to win public acceptance." An industry group ran a massive ad campaign touting the new technology with a rapid-fire montage of children and farms against a backdrop of swelling music.

But the advertisements look a little different from the organic farms of the Bengali floodplain, where farmers insist they have a different solution to the problem. The Nayakrishi movement held a small seminar for peasant farmers on the new technology at an open-air meeting hall in the Tangail district one day while I was there. A Filipino agriculture expert discussed the plans— that by 2003 the International Rice Research Institute would be producing genetically modified seeds for them to plant. The farmers—illiterate, most of them—kept interrupting with questions and sermonettes. They weren't concerned about frankenfoods. Instead, they instantly realized that the new rice would require fertilizer and pesticide. More to the point, they kept saying, they had no need of golden rice because the leafy vegetables they could grow in their organic fields provided all the nutrition they needed. "When we cook the green vegetables, we are aware not to throw out the water," said one woman. "Yes," said another. "And we don't like to eat rice only. It tastes better with green vegetables."

This is neither simplistic nor sentimental. In fact, there's plenty of evidence to show that as the Green Revolution spread in the last four decades, nutrient deficiency followed close behind. A plant like bathua, a leafy vegetable that provided beta-carotene to Indians for an eternity, becomes such a competitor of wheat once you start using chemical fertilizers that it requires herbicides to destroy it. A steady decline in the consumption per capita of vegetables, fruits, beans, and spices took place in Bangladesh even as the consumption of rice increased. Plants growing wild around the margins of Gorasin's fields provide massive quantities of vitamins A and C, or folic acid, iron, and calcium. But the spread of any high-yielding variety like golden rice tends to reduce that crop diversity. "There may or may not be issues of biosafety," said the Filipino expert. "The real question is, Do we really need this?"

Again, the answer depends on how you see the world. Maybe it's too late for Bangladesh to go back to a balanced diet, particularly in urban areas where bathua and amaranth are hard to come by. There's a kind of inevitability to the argument for a technological, capital-intensive future that comes from a scarcity of successful counter examples. There aren't many places that have chosen an alternative path. Kerala, perhaps, the state of 30 million people in the south of India that has achieved Western levels of life expectancy, literacy, infant mortality, and fertility on an average income per capita of $300 per year. But the World Bank and Monsanto don't talk about Kerala; they talk about Thailand and Singapore.

"The Nayakrishi fields can be twice as productive as 'modern' agriculture," says Mazhar. "But I can't get anyone from the World Bank to come out and test my claims. We don't fit with the model." The Nayakrishi movement is small, with only tens of thousands of farmers in a nation with tens of millions. And although it is growing, it remains insubstantial against the sheer scale of Bangladesh. But Nayakrishi hints at other ways of addressing other issues, like energy: The Bangladesh Rural Advancement Committee has begun using microcredit[3] programs to help peasants finance solar systems for their rooftops, and biogas generators for their cookstoves. The dung from three cows lets you cook all your meals for a day and frees you from crouching by the fireside to feed rice straw to the flame. That's a kind of progress that doesn't show up easily in anyone's statistics, but you can feel it in the strain on your back at the end of the day. It's a kind of progress that could conceivably mix with newer technologies.

---

3. Microcredit refers to banking policies that loan small amounts of money to poor people who lack collateral to guarantee loans. The Grameen Bank which originated in Bangladesh is best known for this (ed.).

* * *

The night we left Gorasin, we sat in the courtyard by everyone's small huts. The whole village of 35 or 40 people was on hand. Two babies were using a grapefruit as a ball, which every person in the village would roll back to them with great smiles. It takes a village to raise a child, indeed, and to raise a crop. And to raise a song, as well: One of the men, Akkas Ali, mentioned that he had written a hundred songs praising organic agriculture, tunes he and the other men had sung at local markets in an effort to convert other farmers. We ate fat bananas, and rosy grapefruit, and listened as the sun set.

"Nayakrishi has corrected my mistakes," he sang in a reedy Bengali, as the rest of the village clapped rhythmically.

"Food from Nayakrishi is so much better. No longer do I eat the poisons.

Why should I eat that life-destroying stuff?

Bangladesh will come to an end,

Unless you turn to Nayakrishi.

If you use organic fertilizer, the Almighty will be behind you,

And you'll be having no more gastric problems."

As I say, the sun was setting over Gorasin. I have no idea if this represents a vision of the future, or a fragment of a fleeting past.

It depends on how you look at it.

ACKNOWLEDGMENTS

William Adler, "Job on the Line." Copyright © 2000. Foundation for National Progress. Reprinted with permission.

Elijah Anderson, "The Code of the Street" from *The Atlantic Monthly* (May 1994), pp. 81–94. Reprinted by permission of the author.

Heidi Ardizzone and Earl Lewis, "Love and Race Caught in the Public Eye" from *Chronicle of Higher Education*, June 8, 2001, pp. B7–9. Reprinted by permission of the authors.

Benjamin R. Barber, published originally in *The Atlantic Monthly* (March 1992) as an introduction to *Jihad vs. McWorld* (Ballantine paperback, 1996), a volume that discusses and extend the themes of the original article. Benjamin R. Barber is Kekst Professor of Civil Society at the University of Maryland, Director, New York office, The Democracy Collaborative and the author of many books, including *Fear's Empire, Strong Democracy* (1984), *Jihad vs. McWorld* (Times Books, 1995), *A Place for Us* (Farrar, Strauss & Giroux, 1998), *A Passion for Democracy: American Essays* (Princeton University Press, 1998), *The Truth of Power: Intellectual Affairs In the Clinton White House* (W.W. Norton & Company, 2001).

Robert Bellah, et al., from *Habits of the Heart: Individualism and Commitment in American Life,* pp. 225–37. Copyright © 1985, 1996 Regents of the University of California. Reprinted by permission.

Peter Berger, from *An Invitation to Sociology*. Copyright © 1963 by Peter L. Berger. Used by permission of Doubleday, a division of Random House, Inc.

Joel Best, from Damned Lies and Statistics: Untangling Numbers from the Media, Politicians, and Activists, pp. 1–7, 161–71. Copyright © 2001. The Regents of the University of California. Reprinted by permission.

Allan Brandt, "Racism and Research: The Case of the Tuskegee Syphilis Study" from *The Hasting Center Report* (December 1978), pp. 21–29. Reprinted by permission of the publisher.

Michael Burawoy, from *Social Forces*, vol 82. Copyright © 2004 by the University of North Carolina Press. Used by permission of the publisher.

William Chambliss, "The Saints and the Roghnecks" by Chambliss, in *Society* (vol. 11), pp. 24–31, 1973. Reprinted by permission of the publisher, Transaction Publishers.

Emile Durkheim, reprinted with the permission of The Free Press, a division of Simon & Schuster Adult Publishing Group, from *The Rules of Sociological Method* by Emile Durkheim, pp. 50–59 edited with an Introduction by Steven Lukes. Translated by W.D. Halls. Copyright © 1982 by Steven Lukes. Translation, Copyright © 1982 by The Macmillan Press. Ltd. All rights reserved.

Barbara Ehrenreich, *Nickel and Dimed: On (Not) Getting By in America*. Reprinted by permission of International Creative Management, Inc. Copyright © 1999 by Barbara Ehrenreich. First appeared in *Harper's Magazine*.

D. Stanley Eitzen, "Upward Mobility through Sport?" from *Z Magazine* (March 1999), pp. 14–19. Reprinted by permission of the author.

Joe R. Feagin and Robert Parker, "The Rise and Fall of Mass Rail Transit" from *Building American Cities: The Urban Real Estate Game*, pp. 154–59. Reprinted by permission of the authors.

E. & R. Fernea, "A Look Behind the Veil," from *Human Nature* Magazine (Volume 2, No. 1, 1979) pp. 68–77. © 1979 by *Human Nature* Magazine Fernea/Fernea. Reprinted with permission of Wadsworth, a division of Thomson Learning: www.thomsonrights.com. Fax 800-730-2215.

Betty Friedan, reprinted and edited with the permission of Simon and Schuster Adult Publishing Group, from *The Fountain of Age* by Betty Friedan. Copyright © 1993 by Betty Friedan. All rights reserved.

Herbert J. Gans, "The Positive Functions of the Undeserving Poor" from *American Journal of Sociology* 78, no. 2 (1972), pp. 275–88. Used by permission of Herbert J. Gans.

Robert Glennon, from *Water Follies* by Robert Glennon. Copyright © 2002 by the author. Reproduced by permission of Island Press, Washington D.C.

Erving Goffman, "On Face-Work: An Analysis of Ritual Elements in Social Interaction" from *Psychiatry: Journal for the Study of Interpersonal Processes* (vol. 18, no. 3, August 1955), pp. 213–31. Reprinted by permission of Guilford Publications, Inc.

Giri Raj Gupta, "Love, Arranged Marriage, and the Indian Social Structure" from *Cross-Cultural Perspectives of Mate-Selection and Marriage*. (Westport, Conn.: Greenwood Publishing Group, 1979). Copyright © 1979. Reprinted by permission of the author.

Arlie Russell Hochschild, *The Time Bind: When Work Becomes Home and Home Becomes Work* by Arlie Russell Hochschild. Copyright © 1997 by Arlie Russell Horchschild. Reprinted by permission of Georges Borchard, Inc., for the author.

John Hostetler, *Amish Society*, pp. 3–12. © 1993 John Hopkins University Press. Reprinted with permission of The John Hopkins University Press.

Jennifer Hunt, "Police Accounts of Normal Force" from *Journal of Contemporary Ethnography*. Reprinted by permission of the Publisher, Sage Publications, Inc.

Ronald Ingelhart and Wayne E. Baker, "Modernization's Challenge to Traditional Values" from *The Futurist*. Reprinted by permission of World Future Society.

John Isbister, *Promises Not Kept: The Betrayal of Social Change in the Third World*. (Bloomfield, Conn.: Kumarian Press, 2001), 86–96. Reprinted by permission.

Herbert C. Kelman and V. Lee Hamilton, "The My Lai Massacre" from *Crimes of Obedience*, pp. 1–21. Copyright © 1989 by Yale University Press. Reprinted by permission of Yale University Press.

Clyde Kluckholm, "Queer Customs" from *Mirror for Man* (University of Arizona Press, 1968), pp. 24–33. Reprinted by permission of Bruce Kluckholm.

Karl Marx and Friedrich Engels, "Manifesto of the Communist Party" from *The Marx-Engels Reader*, 2nd edition, trans. Robert C. Tucker, pp. 473–78. Copyright © 1978, 1972 by W. W. Norton & Company, Inc. Used by permission of W. W. Norton & Company, Inc.

Kim A. McDonald, "Shared Paternity in South American Tribes Confounds Biologists and Anthropologists" from *The Chronicle of Higher Education* (April 9, 1999). Reprinted by permission of *The Chronicle of Higher Education*.